The Fall and Rise of Jerusalem

The Fall and Rise of Jerusalem

Judah under Babylonian Rule

Oded Lipschits

Winona Lake, Indiana
Eisenbrauns
2005

Library of Congress Cataloging-in-Publication Data

Lipschitz, Oded.
  [Yerushalayim ben ḥurban le-hitḥadashut. English]
  The fall and rise of Jerusalem : Judah under Babylonian rule / by Oded
    Lipschits.
      p.   cm.
  Rev. ed. of author's dissertation.
  Includes bibliographical references and indexes.
  ISBN 1-57506-095-7 (hardback : alk. paper)
    1. Judaea (Region)—History.   2. Jews—History—Babylonian captivity,
  598–515 B.C.   3. Bible. O.T.—Criticism, interpretation, etc.
  4. Palestine—Antiquities.   I. Title.
  DS110.J78L57   2005
  933—dc22
                                                              2005027037

This book is dedicated to the memory of my father

David (Alex) Lipschits

I am filled with strong longings for that boy of two who was left alone during the Second World War yet found within himself the strength to rise up from the ruins of his family and nation; to build a family; and to be a father, teacher, and educator.

His life is a genuine saga of Falling and Rising.

> *So then, yours is truly a journey through memory! . . . It was to slough off a burden of nostalgia that you went so far away!*
>
> — Italo Calvino, *Invisible Cities* (translated by William Weaver; Orlando: Harcourt, 1974; Italian original: *Le città invisibili*, 1972) 98

Contents

Acknowledgments

This book began as a study conducted during my M.A. and doctoral studies in the Department of Jewish History at Tel Aviv University. The first form of the study was a doctoral dissertation submitted to the Senate of Tel Aviv University in January 1997. In the time that has elapsed between then and the completion of the manuscript of this book in early 2002, I expanded the research and supplemented the dissertation. Various sections of the manuscript have also been published in other forums in Israel and abroad. The Hebrew version of this book was published in March 2004, resulting in changes and bibliographical updates to the English manuscript in 2003–4.

While writing my dissertation, I was fortunate to have the advice of my teacher, Prof. Nadav Naʾaman. His support was a source of inspiration throughout the process. His door was always open, and the opportunity to clarify research topics helped me greatly to elucidate various issues and focus the discussion. His warm attitude and extensive help continued even after I completed the doctoral dissertation, and for all of this I wish to thank him from the depths of my heart.

I received much advice and help from teachers, colleagues, and friends, among whom were Prof. Yaʾirah Amit, Prof. Itzhak Beit-Arieh, Prof. Israel Finkelstein, Prof. Yair Hoffman, Prof. Gary Knoppers, Prof. Manfred Oeming, Prof. Zippora Talshir, Prof. David Vanderhooft, and Prof. Ran Zadok.

I also wish to thank the university authorities and the Buchman Foundation for the stipend that I received during my doctoral studies (1993–95). I also received scholarships from the Wolff Foundation (1991, 1992), from the Center for Research of the Land of Israel and Its Settlement at Yad Ben Zvi (1995), and from the Yaniv Foundation of the Chaim Rosenburg School of Jewish Studies (2000, 2002, 2004). I am grateful to all of them.

I received assistance in the last stages of the research, in organizing the bibliography, and in editing the material, from students and research assistants who worked with me during 1998–2000, thanks to scholarships that they were awarded due to the initiative and generosity of Isaac Gattegno and with the assistance of Doron Ofer and Michael Gee.

The maps were drawn by Ms. Yehudit Dekel of the Sonia and Marco Nadler Institute of Archaeology in Tel Aviv University.

My gratitude extends also to my mother, Yehudit Lipschits, as well as to Naʾavah and Joseph Moreno, for pitching in to clear pockets of space and time for research and writing.

Above all, special thanks go to my wife, Yael. There is no one like you.

Finally, my four beloved children: Or, Tal, Na'amah, and Iddo—your cheerful and heartwarming presence made it possible to take the breaks needed to stretch my limbs and recharge my batteries.

Oded Lipschits
Alon Ha-Galil and Tel-Aviv University

Introduction

The years of the Babylonian Empire constituted the most important turning point in the history of Judah and the Judeans in the first millennium B.C.E. Babylon's first 15 years of rule in Ḫatti-land (604–589 B.C.E.) were fraught with more turbulence than any other period in the history of the kingdom of Judah. The small kingdom was passed from hand to hand between Egypt and Babylon in a battle of Titans, and the entire period was characterized by governmental instability and steadily increasing religious agitation. For the first time, the king was sent into exile and, with him, many of the nation's elite. The conflict between the exiles and those who remained in the land along with the rifts between the political-religious leadership in Jerusalem and many of those living in peripheral areas all reflect the strong inner turbulence that developed in Judah, at least partly in response to the external pressure. The inner tumult, combined with the external instability, hastened the end of the kingdom.

Babylon's expedition against Judah in 588–586 B.C.E. sealed Judah's fate and for generations afterward shaped the national consciousness, the people's perception of religion and ritual, and the nation's historical memory. Jerusalem—"the city that the Lord had chosen out of all the tribes of Israel, to put His name there" (1 Kgs 14:21)—the ancient capital of Judah, ceased to exist, leaving a huge hole in the heart of the nation and dealing a severe blow to its social, economic, and political life. The destruction of the Temple—"the habitation of Your house and the place where Your glory dwells" (Ps. 26:8)—the ancient spiritual, cultic, and religious center of the nation, left an enormous hole and led to a major crisis that was attended by the need to reshape the account of the nation's history and to give the history new meaning. The royal house that had ruled the kingdom since its establishment and that many believed would "be established before the Lord for ever" (1 Kgs 2:45) fared no better. Zedekiah's sons were put to death, his eyes were put out, and he was brought to Babylon, where he died. Meanwhile, Jehoiachin, who was imprisoned in Babylon, was the last remnant of the Davidic royal line. Compounding the leadership vacuum and the severe religious crisis was the exiling of Jerusalem's residents, including many of the nation's elite from among the priestly families, the aristocracy, and the royal family, who had controlled the kingdom's economy, led the nation, and shaped its consciousness, culture, and religion.

Jerusalem was not the only city that was destroyed. The urban and military centers in the Shephelah were also laid waste, and all of the governmental apparatus and the army of Judah ceased to exist. In the wake of these events came the collapse of the outlying settlements in the Jordan Valley and along the western shore of the Dead Sea, the Negev, the southern hills of Judah, and the southern Shephelah. Many of the residents abandoned these areas, and the Judahites who had inhabited these areas for centuries quickly became a small minority within an Arabian-Idumean majority that steadily grew in strength.

Thus, at the time of Babylonian rule, an unprecedented demographic shift took place in Judah that resulted in the dwindling of the local population, leaving it less than half its previous size.

However, the destruction, exile, and national crisis were the beginning of a new stage in the history of the people and the land. The exiled elite in Babylon were forced to adjust to life without a land, without a nation, and without the Temple. They were exposed to the influence of the wealthy, powerful, ancient Babylonian culture and religion (and, in the course of time, to the cultures and religions of the Persian Empire) and developed new patterns of community life and a new system of faith, ideas, and ways of looking at history that were suited to exiles living as a small minority in a foreign country. The need to understand the past and to reshape spiritual life and religion led to the creation of an extensive body of literature, unparalleled in size and importance. This was the beginning of a new Judaism—the Judaism of the Second Temple period.

The people who remained in their houses in the land, on the other hand, without a royal house, Temple, or ancient capital were forced to develop alternatives that, until then, could not have evolved. Because of the religious and ritual supremacy of Jerusalem at the end of seventh century B.C.E., along with its social and political centrality, the development of alternate centers was prohibited, particularly after the reform of Josiah. The power and sanctity of the royal house and the immense power of the old elite also prevented change, as long as both existed. However, after the royal house and the old elite had disappeared, there was room for a new elite, an alternate local leadership under the aegis of the Babylonians, and other government and religious centers as well to emerge.

A large Judean population remained in two areas left intact by the Babylonians: in the region of Benjamin, north of Jerusalem, and in the northern Judean hills, south of the city. It was in these two areas that many of those who remained in Judah settled after the destruction of Jerusalem, and here the process of rebuilding under the protection of the Babylonian Empire began. In place of the devastated city of Jerusalem, the Babylonians established Mizpah in the region of Benjamin as the capital of the province. In place of the House of David, they appointed Gedaliah, son of Ahiqam, son of Shaphan, from one of the most respected and renowned families in the land. In place of the Temple in Jerusalem, and at a time when its ruins were a pilgrimage destination for small groups and individuals, alternative centers of worship arose in the country (Mizpah, Gibeon, Bethel, and perhaps even Shechem), and these sites competed with one another for the place of honor and promoted their religious traditions from earlier periods in national history.

All of these changes had unprecedented social, ideological, and religious significance, and this is attested by the various debates embedded in the biblical literature: Who was "Judah"—the people exiled to Babylon or those who remained in the land? Were those who were exiled the ones who had sinned and therefore been punished? Or were those who were left behind (proof that they had not sinned) entitled to inherit the lands and property of those in exile? If Jerusalem was not the eternal capital of the Lord, what was its status now and what was the status of the capital that replaced it? If the Temple in Jerusalem was not the only site where worship of the God of Israel might be carried on, what was the alternative? What was the status of the House of David, exiled in Babylon? What should one's attitude be toward the new leaders appointed by the Babylonians?

However, the time of Babylonian rule was relatively brief, as were the changes in society, religion, and religious ritual instituted by the people remaining in Judah. After two generations of Babylonian exile, the time for redemption arrived. Cyrus, who inherited the rule of the entire area occupied by the Babylonian Empire (539 B.C.E.), conquered the city of Babylon. With the support of the Persian regime, the exiled elite in Babylon through their representatives, the returnees to Zion, initiated the long process by which Jerusalem was again established as the nation's uncontested political, social, and religious capital. Success was finally achieved by the exiles, after long years of struggle against economic hardship, the neighboring provinces, and the large number of residents who had remained in Judah—residents who were less than delighted to reassume the yoke of the new-old elite leadership.

Both the dwindling population of the Benjamin region during the Persian Period and the abandonment of the important centers that had developed there during the Babylonian years are evidence of the shifts that took place in Judah during the "Return to Zion." The polemics embedded in the Bible against alternate religious and political centers such as Mizpah, Bethel, Gibeon, and Shechem display evidence of attempts to obliterate the enhancement of these sites' status during the period between the destruction of Jerusalem and its return to center stage. The "myth of the empty land" was granted credence by means of a historical "blackout." The exiled elite who participated in the Return to Zion, along with their representatives in Judah, attempted to expunge the history of those who remained in the land during the Babylonian exile. The historiographical literature opened with the period of return being a direct continuation of the period of destruction.

Despite the acknowledged importance of the period of Babylonian rule as a time when the religious, social, and cultural character of the Judahites was consolidated, despite the centrality of this era in the crystallization and shaping of biblical literature, and despite the decisive geopolitical events of this time, the era is one of the least investigated and least known in the history of the Jewish people and in the history of Palestine. In much of past historical and archaeo- logical literature, this period has been viewed as transitional between the First Temple Period, which ended with the destruction of Jerusalem and the Temple (586 B.C.E.), and the Second Temple Period, which began in the days of the Re- turn to Zion (538 B.C.E.). Even in modern scholarship, this period continues to be perceived as the "dark ages" in terms of history and an era that has no inde- pendent raison d'être in terms of archaeology.

The paucity of historical sources from this era, either biblical or extrabiblical, could explain the historical blackout. The brevity of the period of Babylonian rule (less than 70 years) could explain the difficulty of identifying and charac- terizing the material culture of this period. However, it seems to me that the ma- jor factor affecting research on the period has been the core attitudes and prior historical perceptions that researchers have brought to the material. Of course, these perspectives were influenced by the historiographical literature itself in its accounts of the "destruction of Judah" and "the exile period"; by the lamenta- tions and prophecies attributed to this time; and, primarily, by perspectives pre- sented in the literature of the Return to Zion, which gave shape to "the myth of the empty land."

In this book I will present an extensive, comprehensive profile of the period of Babylonian rule over Judah and will establish the importance of this time as shaping the demographic and geopolitical processes that would eventuate in Pal- estine between the end of the First Temple Period and the Persian, Hellenistic, and Roman periods. This background will provide a basis for reexamining the perceptions and biases embedded in biblical historiography and for identifying the time, place, and goals of these compositions, as well as their target audiences.

Chapter 1

The End of the Kingdom of Judah:
The Geopolitical Background

1.1. *The Geopolitical Situation and the Geographic Region*

The Fertile Crescent is the cradle of ancient Near Eastern civilization. As early as the end of the fourth millennium B.C.E., centers of political, economic, and cultural power had emerged on both sides of the Crescent. These cultures were the dominant empires in the Near East until the final third of the first millennium B.C.E., when the region was conquered by Alexander the Great.

The land "between the rivers" ("Mesopotamia" in Greek) is located at the eastern edge of the Fertile Crescent, between the Tigris and the Euphrates. It is here that the civilizations of Sumer, Akkad, Babylonia, and Assyria flourished. The Euphrates delineates the western boundary of Mesopotamia, but even in the earliest periods the cultural impact of Mesopotamia was felt much farther westward—throughout Anatolia, Syria, and even into northern Palestine. Nevertheless, only in the mid-eighth century B.C.E. did Assyria succeed in conquering the entire region of Syria–Palestine. Assyria established its control over the entire region down to the border of Egypt and, for a short period, ruled Egypt as well.

The southwestern edge of the Fertile Crescent gave rise to the development of Egyptian civilization. For long periods, Egyptian economic and cultural influence was felt in Syria, Phoenicia, and Israel. While Egypt was developing as a political and military power, it also succeeded in achieving control over parts of this expanse, and for a short period in the second half of the second millennium B.C.E., even ruled most of the Levant. Egypt inherited Assyrian control of Syria, the Phoenician coast, and Israel when Assyria weakened and withdrew from its foothold in the west. In the last quarter of the seventh century B.C.E., Egypt established a veritable empire that, at its peak, reached the banks of the Euphrates.[1]

Between these two major centers of power, wealth, and culture on both sides of the Fertile Crescent lay a vast region that included Syria, Phoenicia, and Israel. This region had immense importance for the empires surrounding it. In

---

1. For a summary of the process of the retreat of Assyria and the establishment of Egypt as a sort of "Successor State," see Na'aman 1991a: 33–41; Redford 2000: 183–95.

addition to the potential for exploitation of its natural resources and maintenance of maritime and overland commerce, the empires used the region as a
defense zone or starting point for future attacks against the opposing empire.

As far as the empires were concerned, this region was a single geographical
and political unit. The Euphrates was its northeastern border, the area between
the Upper Euphrates and the Taurus and Amanus Mountains was the northern
border, and Naḥal Besor (Wadi Shelaleh)² served as the southern boundary.
The Mediterranean seaboard defined this area on the west, and the Arabian
Desert was the eastern frontier, enclosing the inhabited regions of Bashan,
Gilead, Moab, Ammon, and Edom. Nonetheless, during no period before the
Assyrian conquest in the eighth century B.C.E. did the kingdoms of Syria and
Israel belong to a single geopolitical unit. Apart from one fleeting episode in the
fourteenth century B.C.E., these areas were not governed by a single ruler and
were never part of one administrative framework. In documents from the second
millennium and the beginning of the first millennium B.C.E., there is not even a
general designation for this combined region.

It was only after the Assyrian conquest that the entire region between the
Euphrates and the border of Egypt was united into one political and territorial
unit, known as *eber nāri* ('Beyond the River'). This was when the Assyrians put
an end to the independence of the ethnic and political entities that had previously existed and annexed most of them to Assyria, turning them into Assyrian
provinces. The Assyrians brought about far-ranging changes in the cultural,
economic, and demographic characteristics of the region; established Assyrian
control; and determined the region's fate for generations to come. This situation continued with only minor modifications during the following centuries,
under the rule of Egypt, Babylon, and Persia, when all of the area west of the
Euphrates was included in the fifth satrapy, which was also known as *eber nāri*.
It is against this background that one must understand the appearance of the
Hebrew term עבר הנהר (*ʿēber hannāhār*) (in Aramaic עבר נהרה [*ʿăbar nahărāh*];
עבר נהרא [*ʿăbar nahărāʾ*]) in various biblical sources, particularly in the historiographical sources from the Persian Period³ but also once in a reference to the
days of Solomon (1 Kgs 5:1, 4[4:21, 24]).⁴ This geopolitical reality, created in
the eighth century B.C.E., is also what lies at the basis of the descriptions of
boundaries in the stories of the patriarchs—that is, in the divine promise to

---

2. For identification of the southern boundary, see Naʾaman 1979: 74–80; 1986a: 244–51;
1995a: 111; 2001: 263–65, with further literature and references to previous discussions. For a
different opinion, see Ephʿal 1982a: 91, 104; Rainey 1982a: 131–32; Aḥituv 1984: 203 n. 631.
On this subject, see also Hooker 1993: 203–14.

3. This term is used 15 times in Ezra (chaps. 4–8) and three more times in Nehemiah
(chap. 3).

4. The term *ʿēber hannāhār* is mentioned twice in v. 4 as the jurisdiction of Solomon's rule:
"For he ruled over all the land Beyond the River, from Tiphsah as far as Gaza, over all the kings
Beyond the River."

Abraham, "To your offspring I assign this land, from the river of Egypt to the great river, the river Euphrates" (Gen 15:18 NJPSV; see Na'aman 1986a: 244–45, with further literature).

In contrast to this vast area, there was a more limited area that included southern Syria–Palestine, referred to in various documents from the second millennium B.C.E. as Canaan. This area corresponds to the land of Canaan whose borders are described in Num 34:1–12 and, with minor changes, also in Ezek 47:13–20. It is also parallel to the name Retenu, which appears in Egyptian sources from the early part of the second millennium B.C.E. In later periods in Egyptian history, additional names are used for this region, among them Djahi and Ḫurru.[5]

> The kingdom of Judah was then a small part of the large region lying between the two main powers at the two ends of the Fertile Crescent. It is clear, therefore, that the history of Judah cannot be understood without a knowledge of the overall layout of the region in which it was located and without understanding the balance of power between the empires and their interests in the region.
>
> That is the purpose of this chapter. First, I will briefly discuss the geopolitical organization of the area of Beyond the River, as it was shaped for generations by Assyria and as it continued, with slight modifications, during the rule of the Egyptians, Babylonians, and Persians (§1.2). Next, I will present the historical background of the end of Assyrian rule in this region and explain the conclusion of the *Pax Assyriaca* (§1.3). Thus, we will learn about the two empires that struggled over succession to the Assyrian Empire and understand their interests in the area (§§1.4–5). At the end of the chapter, I will reconstruct the history of the Babylonian-Egyptian struggle to inherit the territory formerly occupied by the Assyrian Empire (§1.6). This battle of titans from the two empires for control of the Levant also shook up the little kingdom of Judah. The battle had an important role in the revolt of and the destruction of the kingdom.

1.2. *The Region "Beyond the River" under Assyrian Rule*

In the hundred years of Assyrian rule, the geopolitical character of the Levant was determined for generations to come, starting with the establishment of the Assyrian Empire in the region in the days of Tiglath-pileser III (745–727 B.C.E.) until Assyria's retreat at the beginning of the last third of the seventh century B.C.E.[6] During this era, the political and national scheme changed totally: it was

---

5. This subject will not be discussed here; see Na'aman's discussion (1999a: 31–37, with further literature).

6. The area of northern Syria, which included Arpaddu and Kullani, was captured by Tiglath-pileser III in 740 and 738 B.C.E. In that year, all of the kings of southern Syria and Israel acknowledged Assyria's superiority and paid it tribute. Apart from the most southern and

refashioned according to Assyrian economic, military, and strategic interests. Some kingdoms, mainly the strongest and largest, were obliterated, their territory was annexed to Assyria, and they became Assyrian provinces. In the territory once occupied by those kingdoms, there was heavy destruction and the deportation of large populations, who were replaced by exiles from remote regions. Several of the kingdoms, particularly the southern part of Israel and Transjordan, became Assyrian vassal kingdoms who were under constant surveillance. These vassal kingdoms were compelled to pay high tributes, and the states' economies were subsumed into the economic system of the Assyrian Empire (for a summary of the subject, see Grayson 1995b: 959–68).

The following pages describe the geopolitical and administrative organization that was fashioned by the Assyrians and that apparently continued to be in force when the Egyptians, Babylonians, and Persians ruled the area.[7]

Northern Syria and the Syrian Coast

There is no information available on the new administrative organization imposed on northern Syria after Tiglath-pileser III conquered it in the early years of his reign (740–738 B.C.E.) or after Sargon II (721–705 B.C.E.) suppressed the revolt against him (720 B.C.E.). Nevertheless, in light of the region's importance as a northern portal to Syria–Palestine and because it was the quickest route to the Syrian and Phoenician coasts, we may assume that the Assyrian organization was basically maintained under Babylonian and Persian rule.

The province of Arpad (Arpadda) was established in the territory of the sacked kingdom of Arpaddu, which had extended from the Euphrates to the Amanus Mountains. The area was annexed to Assyria in 740 B.C.E., and, after suppression of the revolt that broke out against Sargon II, Assyrian rule in the region was firmly established (Grayson 1991: 75; Dion 1997: 132–36). *The province of Kullanīa-Kalnē/Kinalūa* was established in the land of Unqi/Patina, around Kunulua, the capital of the kingdom. This territory was annexed to Assyria in 738 B.C.E. and extended between the Orontes River and the Syrian coast, south of Cilicia.[8]

---

eastern parts, this region was conquered by Tiglath-pileser between 732 and 730 B.C.E. and was under Assyrian rule for a century. As discussed below (§1.3, pp. 11ff.), the date of Ashurbanipal's death (627 B.C.E.) may be used as the point in time when Assyrian influence on the region finally disappeared.

7. Against the opinion of Vanderhooft 1999: 82–83; 90–104. I will discuss any deviation from Assyrian administrative organization that came about in the time of Egyptian or Babylonian rule.

8. On this subject, see Kessler 1975: 52; Grayson 1991: 76; Elat 1991: 25 and nn. 32–34; Hawkins 1995: 94–95, with further literature; Dion 1997: 167–68. On the history of the kingdom of Unqi/Patina and on the archaeological finds at Tell Ta'yinat (ancient Kunulua), see Harrison 2001: 115–32, with further literature. Cilicia was annexed to Assyria during the time of Tiglath-pileser III or of Shalmaneser V.

The province of Ḫatarikka/Ḥadrāk[9] was also established in 738 B.C.E. and stretched over the northern part of the kingdom of Hamath, east of the Lower Orontes,[10] apparently in the territory of the kingdom of Luʿash, which was the kingdom of Nuḫašše during the Bronze Age, called Luḫuti in the Assyrian texts.[11] *The province of Ṣimirra* (*Ṣumur*) was established at the same time, extending over the westernmost sections of the kingdom of Hamath, on the Mediterranean Coast, mainly between the cities of Arwāda (Arwād) and Ṣimirra (Simyra/Ṣumra) (Kessler 1975: 49–63; Elat 1991: 27 and n. 32; Hawkins 1995: 97; Dion 1997: 164–65, 168). The location of *the province of Manṣuāti* is unclear. There are some who place it in the south of the Beqaʿ Valley in Lebanon (Weippert 1992: 50–53, and 51, fig. 1; Naʾaman 1995a: 104, and 105, fig. 1; Dion 1997: 153), but it is preferable to place it in the western sections of the kingdom of Hamath, between the city of Ḥamāt and the cities of Arwāda and Ṣimirra on the Mediterranean Coast, northwest of the province of Ṣubat/Ṣubite (Lipiński 1971: 393–99; Hawkins 1995: 97; and see also Parpola and Porter 2001: 13).

Central and Southern Syria

Three provinces were established in the territories of Aram Damascus, which was the largest and most important of the kingdoms in the region when it was conquered by Tiglath-pileser III (732 B.C.E.):[12] *the province of Qarnīna* (*Qarnaim*) included the Bashan and the Hauran;[13] *the province of Dimašqa* included the area east of the Anti-Lebanon ridge (Naʾaman 1995a: 104, and 105, fig. 1); and *the province of Ṣūbat/Ṣūbite* (*Ṣôbā*)[14] extended over the northern Beqaʿ of Lebanon and the Anti-Lebanon Mountains (Kessler 1975: 52–55; Naʾaman 1995a: 104; 1999b: 421–25; Parpola and Porter 2001: 15). Twelve years after the conquests of Tiglath-pileser III, parallel to the annexation of the territories of the kingdom of Israel, Sargon II also annexed the rest of the territories of the kingdom of Hamath and established an Assyrian province there (*the province of Ḥamāt* [*Amattu*]). The administrative organization that Sargon imposed on this region is not known (Hawkins 1995: 97), but it seems that the province's territory included the eastern zones of the devastated kingdom of

---

9. On the name, see Dion 1997: 142. For a summary of the archaeological finds at Tell Afis and the identification of this site with the Aramaean city of Ḥadrāk (Assyrian Ḫatarikka), see Mazzoni 2001: 99–114, with further literature.

10. On the location of this province, see the map in Parpola and Porter 2001: 24.

11. See Hawkins 1995: 96 and pl. 1, p. 101; Dion 1997: 168–67; for the geographical problem, see Dion 1997: 139–43, and for discussion of the name of the province, see pp. 73, 142–43. On the history of the kingdom of Luʿash/Luḫuti, see Mazzoni 2001: 99–106, who includes a discussion of the geographical setting (pp. 106–9).

12. Tadmor 1994: 279–82; on this topic, see also the opinion of Garelli 1991: 50.

13. See Tadmor 1994: 210; Naʾaman 1995: 104, and 105, fig. 1; for additional literature, see Bienkowski 2000: 47 n. 10.

14. On the name, see Dion 1997: 174 n. 15, with further literature.

Hamath.[15] In any case, these provinces created a territorial link between the provinces established in the former kingdom of Hamath in northern Syria and in Aram Damascus in southern Syria.

The silence of the sources regarding what was happening in inland Syria during the subsequent years of Assyrian rule and throughout the time of Egyptian and Babylonian rule gives rise to the conjecture that there were no significant changes in the array of provinces in the region.[16] This is evidence of the Assyrians' success in annihilating the power of the kingdoms in the region and abolishing the national distinctions of their populations. Similarly, during the rule of the Egyptians and Babylonians in the Syrian region, political entities did not develop, nor was there any military threat to their rule.

Northern and Central Palestine

The system of provinces established by Tiglath-pileser III in the former kingdom of Israel remained until the coming of the Babylonians and Persians. This administrative division of the territory included the establishment of two provinces in the lands wrested from the kingdom of Israel as early as 732 B.C.E. *The province of Dū'ru (Dôr)* covered the narrow expanse of the Carmel coast and reached the Yarkon River in the south.[17] *The province of Magidû* encompassed Upper and Lower Galilee, the Beth Shean Valley, and the Jezreel Plain (Na'aman 1995a: 107; Stern 2001: 46–49). After the destruction of the kingdom of Israel, Sargon II annexed the rest of the territory to Assyria in 720 B.C.E. and established a third province, *the province of Sāmerīna*.[18] The lands of this province consisted of all of the Samarian hills, as well as the eastern part of the Sharon and the northern coastal plain, including Apqu (Tel Aphēk) and Gazru (Gezer/Gazra).[19] Following E. Forrer and A. Alt, most scholars assumed that in addition to these provinces another province existed in the northern part of Transjordan during the time of Tiglath-pileser III: *the province of Gal'ad (Gil'ad/Gilead)*.[20]

---

15. On the presumption that Manṣuate lay west and the province of Ṣūbat/Ṣūbite lay south of it; on this subject, see also Na'aman 1995b: 107.

16. As will be discussed below, after Assyria retreated from the region, great changes took place in the status of Tyre and Sidon on the Phoenician coast. However, there is no account of what happened in northern Phoenicia and on the Syrian coast as far as Cilicia, and there is no way of knowing if there was any change in the status of the provinces that Assyria established. On the Assyrian system in Syria, see Weippert 1982: 395–409; Hawkins 1995: 95–97; Na'aman 1995a: 105; Fales 2002.

17. See Stern 1990a: 147–55; 1990b: 12–30; 2001: 12, 385–407; Na'aman 1995a: 106; Gilboa 1996: 122–35. On this province during the Persian Period, see Lemaire 1990: 56–59.

18. On this subject, see Tadmor 1973: 69–72. For additional literature, see Na'aman 1993b: 107 n. 3.

19. See Na'aman 1995a: 106–7, and fig. 1, p. 105; Stern 2001: 49–51; Zertal 2003: 384. The theory of some scholars that Josiah annexed Samaria after the Assyrian retreat from the region should be dismissed. On this subject, see, e.g., Redford 1992: 445. Arguments against this theory are presented below.

20. See Forrer 1920: 61; Alt 1929: 203–5; and further literature in Na'aman 1995a: 107 n. 11.

However, Oded (1970: 177–86) and Naʾaman (1995a: 107) doubt that there is textual support for this assumption, and there is no concrete evidence for a system of Assyrian provinces in the northern part of Transjordan.

The success of the Assyrian organization in northern and central Palestine, as well as in Syria, is reflected by the fact that, after the Assyrian retreat, no independent political entity developed and the population did not demonstrate any sense of national identity. This state of affairs enabled Assyria and, later on, Egypt, Babylon, and Persia, to control this region and to exploit its economic, commercial, and strategic potential.

The Phoenician Coast and Northern Coast of Palestine

South of the two Assyrian provinces that had been firmly established along the Syrian coast and north of Phoenicia at the beginning of Tiglath-pileser III's reign (the province of Kullania/Kalnē and the province of Ṣimirra/Ṣumur), *Gubla* (*Byblos*) continued to be a vassal kingdom, apparently throughout Assyrian rule. Its southern border was at Nahr al-Kalb (Parpola 1970: 135; Oded 1982a: 166–70; Elat 1991: 26; Naʾaman 1994c: 7). During this period, two Assyrian provinces were established south of Gubla and along the coastal region above the Sharon Plain (where the province of Dūʾru/Dôr was located). One province was established in 677/6 B.C.E. by Esarhaddon (680–669 B.C.E.). Its territory included the area of the kingdom of Ṣidon in the region between Beirut in the north (Nahr al-Kalb?) and the Zaharani, or Litani, River in the south. Its capital was *Kār-Esarhaddon*, which had been built by the Assyrians close to Ṣidūnu (Ṣidôn) (Tadmor 1966: 98; Grayson 1991: 125; Redford 1992: 358; Naʾaman 1995c: 17–19 and 108, fig. 3). *The province of Ṣurru/Ṣūr (Tyre)* was established in the last days of Esarhaddon or in the early days of Ashurbanipal (669–627 B.C.E.). Its area consisted of the region south of the Litani (Zaharani) River, north of Mount Carmel (Grayson 1991: 126, 144–45; Naʾaman 1994c: 7–8; 1995a: 107–9 and fig. 3, p. 108). Neither the island of Tyre nor Samsimurūna or Arwāda, which extended to the north, was annexed.

It is possible that, after the Assyrian withdrawal from the region (in the last third of the seventh century B.C.E.) and certainly at the beginning of Babylonian rule (605/4 B.C.E.), some of the provinces in this region reverted and became vassal kingdoms again.[21] The economic importance of the Phoenician coast was undoubtedly not lost on the Babylonians when they conquered the entire area,

---

21. One of the main pieces of evidence for reconstructing the history of Phoenicia in the first years of Nebuchadrezzar's rule is the Istanbul prism fragment. The text was published by Unger (1931: 282–94), and Landsberger (1933: 298) corrected the reading in col. ii 25, dating it correctly to Nebuchadrezzar's 7th year. The king of Tyre is mentioned together with the kings of Gaza, Sidon, Arwad, and Ashdod, testimony to a major change in the first years of Babylonian rule in the area and perhaps even earlier, in the days of Egyptian rule after the Assyrian retreat. On this subject, see Berger 1973: 313; Elat 1991: 29–30; Vanderhooft 1999: 34, 92–98; and Naʾaman 2000: 41.

and they fully understood the great advantage in granting independence to the inhabitants in all matters pertaining to maritime trade.[22] One can assume that the Egyptians had a different policy in this region, and it is probable that Psammetichus I had a royal estate in the Lebanon Mountains. Corroboration for this can be found in the Wadi Brisa Inscription, in which there is a description of a military campaign conducted by Nebuchadrezzar into Phoenicia and the capture of the area from the hands of "a foreign enemy [that] was ruling and robbing it of its riches."[23]

Philistia

Assyrian rule in Philistia[24] had been established in the late eighth century B.C.E., during the reign of Sargon II and Sennacherib.[25] *Asdūdu* (Ashdod) was an isolated Assyrian province among the vassal city-states in the region. Heading the province was a local vassal king and, alongside, an official Assyrian governor.[26] The place apparently became a production center for pottery, which was marketed in the nearby agricultural and industrial centers (Gitin 1997: 84). North and south of Ashdod, the vassal city-states of Isqalūna (Ashkelon), Anqarrūna (Ekron), and Ḫazzat (Gaza) continued as they had in the past. These

---

22. The Assyrians and the Babylonians did not engage in maritime trade at all, and the Persians were totally dependent on the Phoenicians, at least in the Mediterranean Sea. On this subject, see Elat 1991: 23–29.

23. The inscription was published by Weissbach (1906). Katzenstein (1973: 298–304) associated the "foreign enemy" with Egypt and assumed that the Egyptians only had commercial relations with the region but that they did not really govern it. This view is hard to accept; see on the subject: Otzen 1964: 78–95; Malamat 1983: 253–54, and n. 22.

24. The term 'Philistia' (^{kur}*Pilištu/Pelištî*) is used in Assyrian inscriptions to denote a well-defined geographical zone, and the term 'Philistines' in these inscriptions refers to population groups in Assyria who apparently were conscious of a common origin (Eph'al 1997: 32–33). It is not known whether there was any political or military cooperation between the kingdoms in Philistia under Assyrian rule, and (following Eph'al) it appears that each of them tried in every way to take advantage of political and military situations to improve their status.

25. These arrangements were in effect until the death of Ashurbanipal and the outbreak of the revolt in Babylonia in 627 B.C.E. Other historical reconstructions, according to which there had been earlier changes in the region, should be dismissed; according to these reconstructions, changes occurred because of the Scythian invasion or following Egypt's earlier invasion of Israel. On this subject, see the discussion in §1.3 (pp. 11ff. below).

26. From an inscription of Sargon II, it emerges that an Assyrian governor was stationed in Asdūdu (apparently in 712 B.C.E.), and a governor of the city is mentioned as the eponym of the year 669 B.C.E. The province of Asdūdu continued to exist in the Persian Period and apparently even before that, under Babylonian rule. Thus, it would seem that the Assyrian organizational structure remained in place throughout the years of Assyrian rule and were the territorial and administrative basis for Babylonian and Persian rule. In contrast, we know that in the days of Sennacherib a king governed the city. For an explanation of this special and extraordinary duality, see Tadmor 1964: 272–76. For a critique of Tadmor's proposal, see Na'aman 1979: 72; 1994a: 9–11, with further literature. On the province of Ashdod during the Persian Period, see Lemaire 1990: 54–56.

city-states were strengthened territorially and economically under the reign of the Assyrian kings,[27] apparently because the kings recognized Philistia's strategic importance as the gateway to Egypt, as well as its economic importance (Elat 1978: 30–34; 1990: 67–88; Oded 1982a: 168). *Isqalūna* (Ašqelôn/Ashkelon) was an important port and central commercial hub, and a vast wine production industry thrived there as well (Stager 1996b: *61–*74; Gitin 1997: 84). At the end of the eighth century B.C.E., even before the campaign of Sennacherib, the territory of this kingdom included the enclave near Iappû (Yafo/Jaffa) (Na'aman 1998: 222–23). There is no evidence that the territorial situation in this region changed under any stage of Assyrian rule (Elat 1991: 26 n. 29), although it is likely that the enclave was transferred to the administration of neighboring *Anqarrūna* (Ekron) at some stage (Na'aman 1998: 223–25). Ekron, an important center for the production of oil, and apparently of textiles as well (Gitin 1997: 87–93), was the main party to profit from the harsh blow dealt to Judah by Sennacherib's campaign (701 B.C.E.). Its growth during the seventh century B.C.E., under Assyrian rule, is connected directly to the weakening of the kingdom of Judah and the major damage done to the territories of the kingdom in the coastal plain.[28] *Ḥazzat* (Gaza) was the southernmost of the Philistine kingdoms and served as the major outlet port for merchandise that arrived as a result of Arabian trade. During the reign of Tiglath-pileser III and the early days of Sargon II, major Assyrian effort was focused on Gaza and its surroundings because of its importance. Accordingly, it is not surprising that Gaza remained a loyal Assyrian vassal kingdom from the time of Sargon II until the collapse of the Assyrian rule in this region (Tadmor 1964: 271; Katzenstein 1994: 37–38; Na'aman 2004: 55–64).

Transjordan

The small kingdoms of Transjordan maintained their fealty to Assyria during the reigns of Sennacherib, Esarhaddon, and Ashurbanipal.[29] The Assyrians had a primary economic and military interest in protecting the eastern frontier of their empire against nomadic onslaughts and in stabilizing the political system

---

27. In the days of Sennacherib, territory was wrested from Judah and given to three Philistine kingdoms to solidify Assyrian influence. The Assyrian gain was twofold: (1) it strengthened its control of the southwestern border of its empire near the Egyptian border and (2) it gained economically because of the prosperity of these kingdoms and the integration of their ports into Arabian trade. For further literature on this subject, see Gitin 1997: 99–100.

28. On this subject, see Dothan and Gitin 1994: 18–25; Gitin 1997: 77–104; 1998: 274–78; A. Mazar 1994: 260–63. It is hard to accept, though one cannot totally rule out, the suggestion by Stager (1996b: *70–*71) and Vanderhooft (1999: 75) that the growth of Ekron should be linked with the Egyptian period of rule, after the withdrawal of Assyria from the region.

29. See M. Weippert 1987: 99–100; Millard 1992: 35–39; Bienkowski 2000: 48–52. In contrast to the thesis presented by Oded 1970: 180–86, see Kletter 1991: 43 and Bienkowski 2000: 48–52.

there.[30] Assyria provided protection to the inhabitants of the region and encouraged the production of the area's distinctive raw materials. In addition, Assyria's protection helped develop the trade routes that transformed the Transjordan into an important junction in Assyrian commerce with the Arabian tribes in the east and south. For the first time, the region's inhabitants were able to integrate into the imperial economic system, and this is evidenced by enormous development of the kingdoms in this area. The phenomenon of development was most evident in *Udūmu* (*Edom*), where the archaeological finds show that there was a wave of settlement in the seventh century B.C.E. The natural features of the region did not allow for the growth of a kingdom prior to this era; however, its location on the roads leading to the Gulf of Elath and to Arabia, and from there to Gaza, brought about the great prosperity on which the kingdom was subsequently established.[31] In *Bīt-Ammān* (Ammon), the archaeological data attest to extensive settlement and cultural prosperity under Assyrian rule (Stern 2001: 258). The patterns of settlement and characteristics of the material culture of *Māʾab* (Moab) in the seventh century B.C.E. are not clear, and one cannot observe in Moab the cultural and settlement prosperity that appears in the other two small Transjordanian kingdoms (Kletter 1991: 33–50; Hübner 1992: 137–46; Stern 2001: 259–67).

Judah (Iaʾudu)

Judah was a small, peripheral, mountainous kingdom within the political, economic, and military structure that existed in the region in the seventh century B.C.E. The intense trauma inflicted on the kingdom by Sennacherib's campaign of 701 B.C.E. had calamitous consequences for the Shephelah and led to a grave weakening of its military might and diminishing of its human resources (A. Mazar 1994: 260–63; Naʾaman 1995a: 113). At the same time, Judah enjoyed the economic prosperity that was shared by the entire region under Assyrian rule in the first two-thirds of the seventh century B.C.E.[32] The eastern and southern border areas, particularly the Negev and the Jordan Valley,[33] were integrated into the Assyrian and international commercial system and flourished both demographically and economically. In the Judean highland and the Benja-

---

30. See Bennet 1978: 165–71; 1982: 181–87; Ephʿal 1982a: 147–55; M. Weippert 1987: 99–100; Naʾaman 1995a: 113–14. But see the minimalist view presented by Bienkowski 2000: 48–53.

31. On this subject, see Bienkowski 1990: 91–109; 1992: 99–112; 1994: 258; 1995: 41–92; 2000: 44–58; 2001: 257–69; Millard 1992: 35–37; Knauf 1992: 50; 1995: 93–94, 97–99; Naʾaman 1993b: 118; 1995a: 114; Gitin 1997: 81–82; Stern 2001: 268–94.

32. For a summary of the archaeological finds of this time period and reconstruction of the historical picture, see Finkelstein 1994: 169–87, with further literature.

33. On the Negev, see Naʾaman 1987: 4–15; Finkelstein 1992: 161; Beit-Arieh 1999a: 1–3. On the Jordan Valley, see Naʾaman 1991a: 42; Stern 1993: 192–97; Lipschits 2000: 31–42, with further literature.

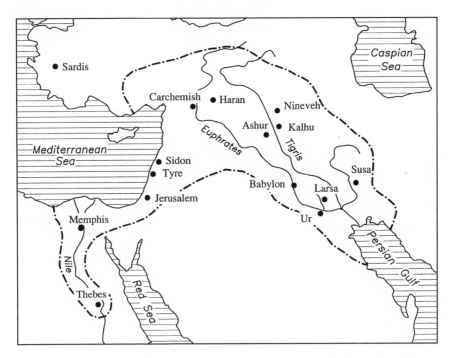

Map 1. *The Assyrian Empire after the Second Campaign of Ashurbanipal to Egypt (664/663 B.C.E.).*

min region, a gradual process of rehabilitation took place, and Jerusalem was established as the central city.[34]

1.3. *The End of the Pax Assyriaca Era*

In the first half of the seventh century B.C.E., the Assyrian Empire was at the height of its power. The Empire controlled the entire Fertile Crescent and had established a faithful royal dynasty in Egypt; it appeared that there was no power in the world that could withstand the Assyrian Empire's military might. The *Pax Assyriaca* was the major reason for the flourishing of the economy and commerce in the Levant; strong intercultural connections were forged.

However, within several years, the Assyrian Empire collapsed and fell, never to rise again. In all of ancient history, the fall of the Assyrian Empire is one of the most impressive and renowned; the military process was rapid, and a great power was toppled from the height of its influence, might, and wealth within a

---

34. See Broshi 1974: 21–26; Finkelstein 1994: 169–87, with further literature.

Map 2. Major cities in Mesopotamia.

short time, after which it disappeared totally from the stage of history.[35] A single
Babylonian document explains the destruction of the Assyrian Empire as the re-
venge of the gods for the previous subjugation of Babylon and the destruction
wrought by the Assyrians on Babylonian urban centers and temples.[36] A similar

35. For different explanations of this process and for further literature, see Zawadzki 1988:
14–22; Naʾaman 1991a: 33–41; 1991b: 243–67; Grayson 1992: 746–47, and see also below.
36. On the Babylonian document BM 55467, see Gerardi 1986: 30–38. For a summation
and further literature, see Machinist (1997: 186–87), and see also the evaluation of this document by Vanderhooft (1999: 26). Nabopolassar, king of Babylon, in his inscriptions also explains the subjugation to Assyria as the anger of the Babylonian gods against their country.
See Langdon 1912: 68, lines 17–21; Al-Rawi 1985: 3, lines i 28–ii 5, with English translation
on p. 5.

biblical explanation is well known.[37] From the perspective of the historian, the Assyrian Empire fell in the wake of its failure to solve the "Babylonian problem"[38]—to put an end to the repeated revolts that broke out in Babylonia, which had intensified during the reign of Sin-šar-iškun (627–612 B.C.E.) (Oates 1986: 114, 123; Naʾaman 1991b: 266).

A starting point for the historical process that ended in the fall of the Assyrian Empire is the death of Aššur-etel-ilāni (627 B.C.E.), the son and successor of Ashurbanipal (669–631 B.C.E.).[39] His son and heir, Sin-šar-iškun (627–612 B.C.E.), succeeded to the throne, but a short time later Sin-šum-lišir revolted against him.[40] Sin-šum-lišir succeeded in taking control of the cities in northern Babylonia, among them Babylon and Nippur, and he apparently ruled in Babylon for three months before being routed by the army of Sin-šar-iškun (Borger 1969: 237–39; Naʾaman 1991b: 255–56; Tadmor 1999: 188). We may assume that Nabopolassar used these events to strengthen his power in southern Babylonia, and

37. A view similar to the Babylonian perspective, though from a different religious, cultural, and historiographic approach, is also found in several biblical passages (Isa 10:5–27; Ezek 32:22–23; Jonah; Nahum; Zeph 2:13–15). According to this view, Assyria is the great conqueror, who at God's command also conquered Israel as punishment for Israel's sins. The same Assyria was itself conquered as punishment by God for its haughtiness and overconfidence. On this subject, see Machinist 1997: 181–86.

38. On Assyrian-Babylonian relations during the more than one hundred years of Assyrian rule over Babylonia, see Brinkman 1984.

39. On the traditional chronology of the last Assyrian kings, see Borger 1965: 59–78; Oates 1965: 135–59; von Soden 1967: 241–55. Naʾaman (1991b: 243–67) has established the chronology that I use here for the last Assyrian kings and on which I base my reconstruction of the collapse of the empire. According to this chronology, Ashurbanipal ruled from 669 to 631 B.C.E., Aššur-etel-ilāni ruled from 631 to 627 B.C.E., Sin-šar-iškun ruled from 627 to 612 B.C.E., and Aššur-uballiṭ II ruled from 612 to 609 B.C.E. The months that Sin-šum-lišir ruled were, then, during the year 626 B.C.E. Naʾaman (1991b) discusses the rationale for these dates and provides a discussion of the literature supporting alternative chronologies. The great innovation of this method is the back-dating of Ashurbanipal's death by about four years from the accepted date of the traditional chronology (from 627 to 631 B.C.E.), and an implication of this change is that the year of Aššur-etel-ilāni's death is the same as the date of Kandalanu's death (627 B.C.E.). A chronological approach similar to the method used by Naʾaman, which did not take the Ḫarran inscription of Nabonidus's mother into consideration, is used by Falkner (1952–53: 305–10, esp. p. 310)—who wrote before the publication of the inscription; and van Dijk (1962: 39–62, esp. p. 57), who ignored the inscription. On this subject, see also Frame 1995: 261. Recently, Beaulieu (1997: 367–93) has supported Naʾaman's chronology, with minor revisions, on the basis of his discussion of the Uruk documents. Reade (1998: 255–65) also arrived at similar conclusions on the basis of a reconstruction of the Assyrian Eponym List (however, compare this with the views he expressed in 1970: 1–9, particularly p. 5). For a critique of the chronology proposed by Naʾaman, see Zawadzki 1995: 67–73; Gerber 1998: 72–93; Vanderhooft 1999: 63–68.

40. Sin-šum-lišir was still the chief eunuch in the days of Ashurbanipal and Aššur-etel-ilāni, even winning deep appreciation from Ashurbanipal for his loyalty. On this subject, see Tadmor 1999: 188, with further literature. On dating the revolt to 627 B.C.E., see Beaulieu 1997: 374–80, 387.

only after the fall of Sin-šum-lišir did he initiate a revolt of his own.[41] Parallel to the assault on the city of Nippur, the armies of Nabopolassar took Babylon from Sin-šar-iškun's garrison, which was encamped there after suppressing the revolt of Sin-šum-lišir, which had ended several months earlier.[42] The Assyrian response was not long in coming. A few weeks later, during the month of Tašritu (October 626 B.C.E.), the Assyrian army managed to recapture Nippur and to pursue Nabopolassar to Uruk without succeeding in conquering the city.[43] At the same time, another Assyrian force was sent out to reconquer Babylon. However, this force was defeated by Nabopolassar's army.[44] This was the last Assyrian attempt to capture the city of Babylon and the end of a prolonged period during which the city's residents fought for their independence.

As a result of these battles and his success in establishing his power in Babylon and Uruk, Nabopolassar officially ascended the throne on the 26th of the month of Araḫsamnu (November 22/23, 626 B.C.E.),[45] even though his rule had been recognized previously by most of the cities in Babylonia.[46] This was the end of an era when, according to the Babylonian Chronicle, "there was no king in the land" (BM 25127, lines 14–15).

During the next two years (625–624 B.C.E.), the Assyrians attempted to suppress Nabopolassar's revolt, concentrating their efforts particularly in northern Babylonia. In the chronicle from the 1st year of Nabopolassar's reign (625/624

---

41. On the questions of whether there was a treaty between Nabopolassar and Sin-šum-lišir and whether they collaborated in the revolt against Assyria (each from the territory where his rule was based), or whether Nabopolassar only exploited the revolt by Sin-šum-lišir to strengthen his power, see Naʾaman 1991b: 256. Tadmor (1998: 353–57; 1999: 188) proposed that it was Nabopolassar who killed Sin-šum-lišir; however, this view is difficult to accept. On the rise of Nabopolassar and the evolution of the "Chaldean" dynasty, see §1.5 (pp. 29ff.) below.

42. See the Babylonian Chronicle BM 25127, lines 1–3; Wiseman 1956: 5, 50–51; Grayson 1975a: 17, 87–88. See the reconstruction by Naʾaman 1991b: 256–57, 259–60 and see also Sack 1991: 16–17.

43. See the Babylonian Chronicle BM 25127, lines 9–14; Wiseman 1956: 7, 50–51; Grayson 1975a: 17, 88. See the reconstruction by Brinkman (1984: 109–10) and by Naʾaman (1991b: 260).

44. See the Babylonian Chronicle BM 25127, lines 10–13; Wiseman 1956: 7, 50–51; Grayson 1975a: 17, 88. See the reconstruction by Oates 1965: 143–45 and by Naʾaman 1991b: 258–60. For a different reconstruction of this period, as part of the view that Chronicle BM 25127, lines 1–17, describes the events of two years (627–626 B.C.E.), see Brinkman 1984: 110; Zawadzki 1988: 48–54. For a critique of this overall view, see Naʾaman 1991b: 257–59.

45. Because, according to Mesopotamian practice, the day started after the sun set and ended with its setting on the following day, when the date is converted into the Gregorian calendar (where the date changes at midnight) one must include the date of the evening (between sunset and midnight) as well as the date of the following day (until sunset). On this date, see Parker and Dubberstein 1956: 11; Hayes and Hooker 1988: 85. For the historical reconstruction, see Naʾaman 1991b: 257–59, with further literature and a critique of the reconstruction according to the "two-year theory."

46. See the Babylonian Chronicle BM 25127, lines 14–15; Wiseman 1956: 7, 50–51, 93–94; Grayson 1975a: 17–18, 88.

B.C.E.), there is a description of the campaign conducted by the Assyrians against Sippar.[47] Apparently, the city had been conquered by the Assyrians, despite the fact that this is not mentioned in the chronicle, nor is the fact that Nabopolassar's army failed to conquer Nippur in the summer of 625 B.C.E.[48]

The events of the year 624/623 B.C.E., followed by the withdrawal of Assyria from Babylonia, proclaimed the beginning of the end of the Empire. At the beginning of the month Ululu (August 624 B.C.E.), an additional Assyrian offensive was thwarted, one that apparently had been designed to seize control of the main route to Nippur and to relieve the Assyrian garrison stationed there.[49] The Assyrian weakness paved the way for a revolt by the city of Dēr, located close to the border of Babylonia and Elam (summer 623 B.C.E.).[50] Apparently, Elam also threw off the Assyrian yoke at this time.[51] The Assyrians could not sit idly by while the revolt spread, and in the fall of that year (September 623 B.C.E.), Sin-šar-iškun concentrated enormous effort on the defeat of Nabopolassar and suppression of the revolts that had begun in the other cities of Babylonia. The Assyrian offensive initially enjoyed rousing success; a Babylonian attempt to capture Nippur failed, and, in a counteroffensive, the Assyrians succeeded in taking Uruk.[52]

However, an internal revolt, probably by the Assyrian commander in the west,[53] completely transformed the situation. The Assyrian offensive in Babylonia was contained, and Sin-šar-iškun left Babylonia with his entire army to combat the serious internal threat. Apparently, the Assyrian king was successful in

---

47. See the Babylonian Chronicle BM 25127, lines 18–21; Wiseman 1956: 52–53; Grayson 1975a: 18, 88–89, and the note to line 21. Grayson assumed that the name of the month (he believed it was Simanu or Duzu) was omitted. But one may accept Wiseman's view that the description in line 21 reverts one day backward, and the events described actually happened on the 20th of the month of Aiaru, after the previous line described the events of the 21st of the same month. On this subject, see also Zawadzki 1988: 57–64; Naʾaman 1991b: 260–61 and n. 55.

48. See the Babylonian Chronicle BM 25127, lines 22–24; Wiseman 1956: 9, 52–53; Grayson 1975a: 18, 89; Beaulieu 1997: 386. On the pro-Babylonian tendencies of the chronicle, see Zawadzki 1988: 114–43; and Naʾaman 1991b: 261, who dates the Babylonian loss to 624 B.C.E.

49. See the Babylonian Chronicle BM 25127, lines 25–26; Wiseman 1956: 9–10, 52–53; Grayson 1975a: 18, 89.

50. On the location of the city, see Parpola and Porter 2001: 8.

51. See the Babylonian Chronicle BM 25127, line 29; Wiseman 1956: 10, 52–53; Grayson 1975a: 18, 89.

52. See the Babylonian Chronicle BM 25127, lines 29–32; Wiseman 1956: 52–53; Grayson 1975a: 18, 89–90. Evidence for this emerges from the documents found at Uruk; see Beaulieu 1997: 367–94. These documents show that the city was conquered by the Assyrians between August and October 623 B.C.E., and this accords with the description in the Babylonian Chronicle (see especially pp. 382–83).

53. On the reconstruction of the text in the segment from Chronicle BM 25127, lines 33–38, see Cavaignac 1957: 28–29. For a different reconstruction of the text, see Wiseman 1956: 10–11, 52–53, 79; Grayson 1975a: 90; but see the response to Wiseman by Cavaignac 1960: 141–43, and see also Zawadzki 1988: 84–86.

suppressing the revolt after 100 days,[54] and he continued to rule until 612 B.C.E. However, this revolt had a serious effect on the power and status of the Assyrians in the region Across the River,[55] as it did in Babylonia, because it enabled Nabopolassar to capture the last Assyrian strongholds in central Babylonia and to establish his control throughout the land. At the beginning of Araḫsamnu (end of October 622 B.C.E.), the Babylonian siege of Uruk had begun (Zawadzki 1979: 175–84; 1988: 37), and after several setbacks, when control of the city passed back and forth,[56] it ultimately fell to Nabopolassar (between February and October 620 B.C.E.). Nippur was apparently also conquered that same year.[57] Thus, Assyria was driven back from its last outposts in Babylonia, and Nabopolassar was able to establish his sovereignty firmly over the entire country (Naʾaman 1991b: 264–65; Beaulieu 1997: 373, 380–81, 383; Reade 1998: 263; Vanderhooft 1999: 27–28). From that moment on, the Babylonian kingdom developed rapidly and in several years was able to take part in Assyria's final annihilation.

According to the Babylonian Chronicle (the so-called "Gadd Chronicle"), which describes events between the 10th and 17th years of Nabopolassar's rule (616–609 B.C.E.),[58] the Babylonians were successful (in the late spring and over the summer of 616 B.C.E.) in pushing the Assyrians back toward the Middle Euphrates and reaching the Baliḫ River.[59] At this stage, the Egyptian army rallied to the aid of Assyria.[60] Psammetichus I (664–610 B.C.E.) was in the middle of the process of establishing his sovereignty over the coastal regions of Syria, Lebanon, and Israel. He was aware of the advantage of the continued existence of Assyria, which had lost its power. A weakened Assyria did not pose a threat to his reign in the areas under his control; Assyria served as a kind of buffer be-

---

54. See the Babylonian Chronicle BM 25127, line 39; Wiseman 1956: 10–11, 54–55; Grayson 1975a: 90.

55. It was not for nothing that Josiah enacted his reform in 622 B.C.E. (2 Kgs 22:3, 23:23), and it seems that during these years Assyria withdrew from all of its footholds in the region Across the River, where Egypt had now advanced and established itself as a sort of "Successor State." On this subject, see the discussion below, and see Naʾaman 1991a: 33–41.

56. For this reconstruction, see Beaulieu 1997: 382–83.

57. According to Grayson's reconstruction (1975b: 30), the importance of the conquest of Nippur by Nabopolassar is marked in the same segment of the chronicle that alludes to Nippur joining Babylon in the early days of the king's reign. On this subject, see also the opinion of Cole 1996: 79–80.

58. The chronicle was published by Gadd in 1923 and also two years later by Lewy (1925). Wiseman (1956: 54–65, 79–84, and pls. 9–12) included it in the publication of the Babylonian Chronicles, as did Grayson 1975a: 90–96, Chronicle no. 3.

59. See the Babylonian Chronicle BM 21901, lines 1–9; Wiseman 1956: 11–12, 54–55; Grayson 1975a: 18, 91. On this subject, see also Vanderhooft 1999: 28, with further literature.

60. On the connection between the 26th Dynasty in Egypt and Assyria, and on the history of the relations between the two empires, see §1.4, pp. 20ff. below. There is no evidence of the presence of the Egyptians in northern Syria before 616 B.C.E. Apparently, they gained control of the entire region between Riblah and Carchemish only after the final weakening of Assyria, when the Babylonian forces had already reached the Middle Euphrates. On this subject, see James 1991: 715; Redford 1992: 446.

tween Egypt and the Medes and Babylonians, who were becoming powerful in the east at that time. It appears that the Egyptian ruler understood the danger posed to his rule if Assyria were to disappear from the map, and, consequently, he tried to support it (on this issue, see §1.4 below).

According to the Babylonian Chronicle, in the month of Tašritu (October 616 B.C.E.), Egyptian and Assyrian forces headed down the Euphrates and attacked the city of Gablinu, but after failing to capture it, they withdrew.[61] The Babylonian Chronicle contains no evidence of a continued Egyptian presence in the region, and the next time that Egypt assisted Assyria was six years later. It appears that during this period Egypt continued to make an effort to establish its rule over regions west of the Euphrates, without sending forces beyond the river (Redford 1992: 447, with further literature).

The collapse of Assyria in the following years was rapid. In the month of Addaru of the 10th year of Nabopolassar's rule (March 615 B.C.E.), Babylonian forces managed to rebuff the Assyrian army at the Tigris, pushing them beyond the province of Arrapha to the Lower Zab, causing many casualties and taking much plunder.[62] At this stage, a genuine threat had already been leveled against the city of Aššur, and it is no wonder that only two months after the first campaign, in the month of Aiaru of the 11th year of Nabopolassar's rule (May 615 B.C.E.), the king gathered his army and set out against the ancient Assyrian capital.[63]

Approximately one month later, during the month of Simanu (June 615 B.C.E.), when it became clear that the city of Aššur would be able to hold out and that the forces of Sin-šar-iškun were due to arrive, the Babylonian army retreated down the Tigris toward the city of Takrit. The Assyrians pursued the retreating Babylonian army and for 10 days laid siege to the city of Takrit. The Babylonian Chronicle claims victory for the besieged Babylonian force, and it appears that, after the failure of the Assyrians, they returned to Aššur.[64] Approximately half a year later, in the month of Arahsamnu (October–November 615 B.C.E.), the army of the Medes entered the province of Arrapha. However, the Babylonian Chronicle is fragmentary at this point, and the relationship between the Medes' presence in this region and the Babylonian presence there at the beginning of the same year is not clear. In any event, it is reasonable to assume that the Medes conquered the region in preparation for the campaign against Nīnuwa (Nineveh) in the summer of the following year.[65]

---

61. See the Babylonian Chronicle BM 21901, lines 10–11; Wiseman 1956: 12–13, 54–55; Grayson 1975a: 18, 91.

62. See the Babylonian Chronicle BM 21901, lines 11–15; Wiseman 1956: 54–57; Grayson 1975a: 18, 91–92; Parker and Dubberstein 1956: 27.

63. See the Babylonian Chronicle BM 21901, line 16; Wiseman 1956: 13, 56–57; Grayson 1975a: 18, 92; Parker and Dubberstein 1956: 27.

64. See the Babylonian Chronicle BM 21901, line 17–22; Wiseman 1956: 13, 56–57; Grayson 1975a: 18, 92.

65. See the Babylonian Chronicle BM 21901, line 31; Wiseman 1956: 13, 56–57; Grayson 1975a: 18, 92.

In the month of Abu of the 12th year of Nabopolassar (July–August 614 B.C.E.), the Medes left Arrapḫa, attacked Kalḫu (Nimrūd) and Nīnuwa (Nineveh), and continued rapidly northward to capture the nearby city of Tarbiṣu. Afterward, they went back down the Tigris and laid siege to the city of Aššur. The Babylonian army came to the aid of the Medes only after the Medes had begun the decisive offensive against the city, capturing it, killing many of its residents, and taking many others captive.[66] Nabopolassar, the king of Babylon, and Umakištar (Kyaxares), king of the Medes, met near the ruins of the devastated city and signed an anti-Assyrian pact, which was to deal the final death blow to Assyria within a few years.[67]

Nonetheless, the Assyrians did not concede defeat, and their last attempt to resist Babylon took place in the 13th year of Nabopolassar's reign. In the region of Suḫu on the Middle Euphrates, which Babylon captured in 616 B.C.E., a revolt began in the month of Aiaru (May–June 613 B.C.E.). Nabopolassar hastened to suppress the revolt, captured the city of Raḫilu, and laid siege to the city of ʿAna (Anatu). At the height of the siege, the Assyrian army (headed by Sin-šar-iškun) drew near, which led to the hasty retreat of the Babylonian army.[68] A battle was no longer required, because at the beginning of the 14th year of his reign (April–May 612 B.C.E.), Nabopolassar and his army headed toward the Tigris. There he met Umakištar and his army, and together the two kings proceeded toward Nineveh. They laid siege to the city in the month of Simanu (June 612 B.C.E.), continuing through the month of Abu (August 612 B.C.E.), when the walls of the Assyrian city were breached and it was conquered and brutally razed.[69] The Chronicle contains references to the fate of Sin-šar-iškun (line 44), but this segment of the chronicle is broken and unclear.[70] The battle ended on the 20th of Ululu (September 14/15, 612 B.C.E.),[71] when Umakištar returned to his country. Nabopolassar sent his army to the northwest, toward the city of Naṣibina (Nisibin) and the land of Ruṣapu, where they seized

---

66. See the Babylonian Chronicle BM 21901, lines 24–28; Wiseman 1956: 13–14, 56–57; Grayson 1975a: 18, 93. It is possible that the intention of this description was to stress that the Babylonians had no part in the cruel conquest of the city. On this subject, see Wiseman 1956: 14.

67. See the Babylonian Chronicle BM 21901, line 29; Wiseman 1956: 14, 58–59; Grayson 1975a: 18, 93; Oates 1965: 152. On various other accounts of the events of this year, particularly those described by Diodorus, see Wiseman 1956: 14–15.

68. One can assume that the Babylonian army was not prepared for face-to-face combat against the Assyrians. See the Babylonian Chronicle BM 21901, lines 31–37; Wiseman 1956: 15, 58–59; Grayson 1975a: 18, 93–94; Oates 1965: 152–53.

69. See the Babylonian Chronicle BM 21901, lines 38–46; Wiseman 1956: 16–17, 56–61; Parker and Dubberstein 1956: 27; Oates 1965: 153; Grayson 1975a: 18, 94. On the archaeological accounts of destruction and the historical reconstruction, see Stronach and Lumsden 1992: 227–33; Stronach 1997: 307–24, with further literature.

70. For a reconstruction of the fate of the Assyrian king, see Gadd 1923: 18–19; Saggs 1962: 120; Grayson 1975a: 92–94.

71. Line 47 in the Chronicle. Date calculation follows Parker and Dubberstein 1956: 27.

plunder and captives.[72] Meanwhile, the last Assyrian king, Aššur-uballiṭ II, ascended the throne in Ḫarrānu (Haran),[73] and although he surely demanded possession of all the territories of the kingdom, at this stage Assyria had in fact ceased to exist.[74]

In the month of Duʾuzi of the 15th year of Nabopolassar's reign (June–July 611 B.C.E.), the king of Babylon and his army headed for the Upper Euphrates and the Baliḫ River, where he established his rule as far as the border of Ḫarran.[75] Thus, the Babylonians completed their assumption of control of the territories to the west of Naṣibina, which had been conquered one year previously, and prepared the ground for a campaign against Ḫarran itself. This campaign, joined by the Medes, took place in the month of Araḫsamnu (November 610 B.C.E.), after a five-month period during which Nabopolassar traversed Assyria in order to ensure the stability of his rule there. The Median-Babylonian army intimidated Aššur-uballiṭ II and the Egyptian army that came to its assistance.[76] The Babylonians laid siege to Ḫarran and, during the winter of 610 and the beginning of 609 B.C.E., the last Assyrian center capitulated. In the month of Addaru (March 609 B.C.E.), Nabopolassar was able to return to Babylon, leaving a garrison in Ḫarran and in other cities along the Baliḫ and the Euphrates.[77]

The Egyptian presence in Ḫarran in 609 is worthy of some attention because, after Aššur-uballiṭ II established his alternative capital there, Egypt found it easier to help him withstand the attacks of the Median-Babylonian army. Furthermore, Assyria's end must have already appeared imminent; if Egypt wished to avoid direct engagement with the forces rising in the east, it had to attempt to provide Assyria with assistance. At the same time, it seems that the main reason

---

72. See the Babylonian Chronicle BM 21901, lines 47–49; Wiseman 1956: 17, 60–61; Grayson 1975a: 18, 94.

73. See the Babylonian Chronicle BM 21901, lines 47–49; Wiseman 1956: 17, 60–61; Grayson 1975a: 18, 94.

74. According to Oates (1991: 181–82, 189–90), apart from a few scant remains of the destroyed city of Kalḫu (Nimrūd), apparently immediately following the years of the destruction (614–612 B.C.E.), there are no traces of renewed settlement in either Nineveh or Aššur until the Hellenistic Period. In contrast, Dalley (1993: 134–47) believes that, at Nineveh as at Kalḫu and Aššur, rehabilitation and rebuilding took place a short time after the destruction of 612 B.C.E., which is evidence that most of the population continued to live in these cities. On this subject, see also Machinist 1997: 179 n. 4, and also pp. 179–80 n. 5 on the continued settlement (including written documents) in sites west of the core of the kingdom, as at Dūr-Katlimmu (T. Šēḫ Ḥamad) and Til-Barsib/Tarbusībi (T. Aḥmar).

75. See the Babylonian Chronicle BM 21901, lines 53–57; Wiseman 1956: 18, 60–61; Grayson 1975a: 19, 95.

76. Redford (1992: 447) hypothesized that the Egyptian army in Ḫarran was composed of Egyptian garrison forces that were stationed in Syria. Psammetichus himself accompanied part of the Egyptian forces in the first part of the campaign, and he died outside the Egyptian borders. On this subject, see also M. J. Smith 1991.

77. See the Babylonian Chronicle BM 21901, lines 58–65; Wiseman 1956: 18–19, 60–63; Grayson 1975a: 19, 95–96.

for the Egyptian presence across the Euphrates, on the banks of the Baliḫ, was the rise to power of Necho II after the death of his father, Psammetichus I, in late July or August of 610 B.C.E.[78] The fact that Necho II embarked on a campaign to aid Assyria only several months after taking the throne is strong evidence of the cardinal importance that he assigned to the last remaining chance to preserve Assyria's power base east of the Euphrates. This may also help explain the battle that took place only three months after the establishment of Babylonian rule in Ḫarran (March 609 B.C.E.). According to the account in the Babylonian Chronicle, Aššur-uballiṭ II, supported by a large Egyptian army, attacked Ḫarran in the month of Du'uzi in the 16th year of Nabopolassar's rule (June/July 609 B.C.E.).[79] This was a desperate attempt by the Assyrian king and his Egyptian allies to regain a foothold on the banks of the Baliḫ, during which he laid siege to the Babylonian garrison stationed in the city. The siege lasted two months (until the month of Ululu, August/September 609 B.C.E.), and the Assyrian-Egyptian army retreated when Nabopolassar and his army came to the rescue of the city, or perhaps even earlier.[80]

This is the last time that Assyria is mentioned in the Babylonian Chronicles, and it disappears from the stage of history. After Assyria's disappearance, Babylon and Egypt came into direct contact with each other, and an era began during which the two empires struggled for control of the entire Fertile Crescent. Before reconstructing the main events of this period and considering the consequences and significance of the struggle, we must understand the two powers: the Egyptian Empire during the 26th Dynasty and the Babylonian Empire of the Neo-Babylonian Period (the age of the Chaldean dynasty).[81]

1.4. *The Egyptian Empire of the 26th (Saite) Dynasty*[82]

The 26th (Saite) Egyptian Dynasty was established by the Assyrian kings Esarhaddon (680–669 B.C.E.) and Ashurbanipal (669–627 B.C.E.) as a counter-

---

78. From the Babylonian Chronicle it is not clear whether the campaign of 610 B.C.E. was conducted at the end of Psammetichus I's rule or the beginning of Necho II's rule, but the latter possibility seems more logical. The first year of Necho II's rule was partial, comprising only five months, and ended on January 13, 609 B.C.E. On this subject, see Hornung 1966: 38–39; Freedy and Redford 1970: 474. On the chronology of the reign of Necho II, see the discussion by Redford (2000: 190–93), with further literature. On the character of Necho II and the nature of his reign, see Redford 1992: 447–48, with further literature on p. 447 n. 68. On this subject, see also pp. 20ff. below.

79. See the Babylonian Chronicle BM 21901, lines 66–68; Wiseman 1956: 19, 62–63; Grayson 1975a: 19, 96.

80. See the Babylonian Chronicle BM 21901, lines 68–70; Gadd 1923: 36; Wiseman 1956: 19, 62–63; Grayson 1975a: 19, 96. In this context, see the proposed reconstruction by Gadd (1923: 23–24) of the events of those years. One cannot accept the proposal by Rowton (1951: 128–29), who suggests that Necho remained in Riblah and never set out for the Euphrates after he arrived late for the battle.

81. See the discussion of these terms below.

82. In this section, I will expand a bit on the background of the campaigns of the kings of Assyria, Esarhaddon and Ashurbanipal, to Egypt and the establishment of the 26th Egyptian

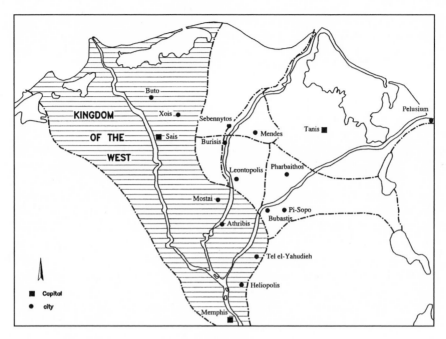

Map 3. The Delta area during the seventh century B.C.E.

weight to the 25th (Cushite) Dynasty that controlled all of Egypt at that time.[83] During Esarhaddon's first successful campaign into Egypt (671 B.C.E.),[84] he succeeded in surprising Taharqa the Cushite (690–664 B.C.E.). Although Taharqa and his army managed to take up positions against him, Esarhaddon dealt him a resounding defeat (or perhaps several defeats). The Egyptian ruler was forced to retreat to Memphis, which he had no time to fortify and which fell after a short battle. Taharqa fled southward to Thebes (No-Amun), leaving behind his family and wealth (Redford 1992: 360–61). Esarhaddon tried to establish his rule in

Dynasty in order to clarify the nature of the connection between Assyrian and Egypt in the second half of the seventh century B.C.E. For discussions of the 26th Egyptian Dynasty, with special emphasis on the beginning of the Dynasty, see Kienitz 1953: 11–47; 1968: 256–82; Spalinger 1976: 133–47; 1978b: 49–57; Redford 1992: 430–35. For a general overview of the relations between Assyria and Egypt in the days of Esarhaddon and Ashurbanipal, see Gyles 1959: 13–25; Drioton and Vandier 1962: 574–92; Otzen 1964: 35–62; Kitchen 1973b: 399–406; Spalinger 1974a: 295–326; 1974b: 316–28; 1978a: 22–47.

83. For an up-to-date review of the 25th (Cushite) Egyptian Dynasty, see Morkot 2000, with further literature.

84. On the abortive effort by Esarhaddon to invade Egypt in 674 B.C.E., see Tadmor 1966: 99; Kitchen 1973b: 391; James 1991: 699; Redford 1992: 359, with further literature. In contrast, see Brinkman 1990: 92–94.

Lower Egypt, installing Assyrian officials and garrisons that worked in concert with the local rulers, some of whom were replaced; others were reappointed.[85] Among those whose official status was confirmed was Necho I (671–664 B.C.E.), ruler of the kingdom of the west. His capital was the city of Sais.[86]

A short time after the Assyrian army left Egypt, Taharqa returned and took Memphis, making an attempt to reestablish his rule in the Delta region (Tadmor 1966: 100; Spalinger 1974a: 319; Redford 1992: 364). The Assyrian campaign against Taharqa was halted in Palestine, due to the illness and death of Esarhaddon (669 B.C.E.; see Olmstead 1923: 384–85; Tadmor 1966: 99). However, his son Ashurbanipal ascended the throne in 668 B.C.E. and quickly set out for Egypt (667/666 B.C.E.).[87] This time, too, the Assyrian army had a resounding victory over the Cushites. Taharqa was again forced to flee from Memphis southward, apparently to Thebes, and perhaps even farther south, to Napatah. The Assyrian sources show that Ashurbanipal restored to office the local rulers who had been appointed by his father, and among these was Necho I, who functioned as an Assyrian vassal (Luckenbill 1927: §§770–83).[88] Nonetheless, even after this campaign, the Assyrians were unsuccessful in establishing their rule in Egypt, and a short time after their armies departed, many of the local rulers joined Taharqa and prepared to revolt.[89] The plot was discovered and cruelly suppressed when, for reasons unknown, Ashurbanipal decided to release Necho I and to return him to Sais as his appointed sovereign. Psammetichus, his son, was given an Assyrian name (Nabû-šezi-banni), and he was appointed as the prince of Athribis.[90] Without any intention of doing so, by this act Ashurbanipal established the 26th Egyptian (Saite) Dynasty. This dynasty was destined to reunite Egypt after a long period of decline and was to have an important impact on the history of Assyria and the kingdoms and provinces in the Levant (James 1991: 701, 710).

---

85. For a summary of the general practice of the Assyrian rulers toward the local rulers in Egypt, see Spalinger 1976: 133; Morkot 2000: 273–80.

86. On Assyria's takeover of Egypt and the reign of Necho I, see Kitchen 1973b: 391–98; Spalinger 1974b: 316–28; James 1991: 699–708, 710–11; Redford 1992: 360–64. For more literature on Necho I, see Redford 1992: 364 nn. 203, 204, and for more literature on Egypt during this period, see p. 430 nn. 1, 2. On the chronology of this period, see the designated literature in Spalinger 1976: 143 n. 1.

87. For a detailed discussion of the sources and reconstruction of this campaign, see Spalinger 1974b: 316–28, with further literature.

88. For an evaluation of the reliability of the Assyrian documentation and a historical reconstruction, see Tadmor 1966: 100; James 1991: 700, 704; Onasch 1994: 116–23; Morkot 2000: 277–80, with further literature.

89. For a reconstruction of the events of this journey, see James 1991: 700, 704. It should be noted that Spalinger's reconstruction (1974a: 321–23) is different.

90. See Spalinger 1974a: 319–21, with further literature; Morkot 2000: 280. Spalinger (1974a: 323) dates this agreement to the time of Ashurbanipal's second journey and links it with the continued cordial relations between the Saite Dynasty and Assyria.

Even after these arrangements, Assyrian rule of Egypt did not achieve stability and, again after a brief period, Memphis was retaken by Tanwetamun (664–656 B.C.E.), cousin and heir to Taharqa and the last king of the 25th (Cushite) Dynasty.[91] Necho I honored the pact he had made with Ashurbanipal; he took the lead in opposing the Cushite conquest and was apparently killed for that reason (664 B.C.E.). It is possible that his son Psammetichus fled north and returned to Egypt with the Assyrian army, which hastened to reestablish Assyrian rule in Egypt for the third time (Spalinger 1974b: 323; 1976: 136; Morkot 2000: 295). On the second campaign of Ashurbanipal to Egypt (664/663 B.C.E.), his army pursued Tanwetamun to Thebes, and after the latter fled south to Nubia, the Assyrians conquered the city and carried off its treasures to Assyria (Redford 1992: 364; Morkot 2000: 296–97; cf. Nah 3:8–10). This campaign led to the end of the 25th Dynasty in Egypt, and Tanwetamun never left Nubia again.[92]

After the conclusion of the Assyrian campaign, Psammetichus I (664–610 B.C.E.) succeeded his father.[93] There were few political changes at this time in Lower Egypt (which remained politically divided); other rulers in the Delta also retained control of their own territories (Redford 1992: 364, 430, with further literature). There is a paucity of information about the activities of Psammetichus at the beginning of his rule, but, within a few years (apparently by 658 B.C.E.), he succeeded in firmly establishing his rule throughout the Delta region (Kitchen 1973b: 401–4; Spalinger 1976: 138–39; James 1991: 711–12). He was aided by mercenaries from Asia Minor and western Anatolia, perhaps supported by Gyges, king of Lydia, and apparently also by Assyria.[94] There is no information available on the battles that Psammetichus waged against the rest of the Delta rulers. It is likely that continued political and military pressure, perhaps

---

91. On this subject, see Kitchen 1973b: 393–94, 400; Spalinger 1974b: 316–28; Redford 1992: 364, 432, with further literature; Morkot 2000: 293–99. The attitude of the other Delta princes is unclear, and there is a difference of opinion about it among the various scholars. Kitchen (p. 393) argued that the Delta rulers recognized the rule of Tanwetamun. Spalinger (pp. 323–24) argued that the Delta rulers did not join Tanwetamun and even fought his attempt to base the renewed rule of his dynasty in the region, and that only some of them finally signed an agreement with the Cushite potentate.

92. See Spalinger 1974b: 324–25; Burstein 1984: 31–34; James 1991: 702; Redford 1992: 364. In this context, see the reservations of Morkot 2000: 297, 302, who thinks that Tanwetamun was still considered king in Upper Egypt until the 8th year of his reign. See also Morkot 2000: 297–98 for his appraisal of the information preserved in later Greek sources, according to which Tanwetamun tried again to take control of Lower Egypt.

93. On the chronology of the reign of Psammetichus I, see Parker 1957: 208–12; Hornung 1966: 38–39; Kitchen 1973b: 399–407; Spalinger 1976: 133, with further literature in n. 1, p. 143.

94. See Spalinger 1976: 136–39, 142; Cogan and Tadmor 1977: 79–80, 84; Burstein 1984: 31; James 1991: 711–12; Redford 1992: 433. According to Jeremiah (46:9), Lydians served in the Egyptian army, and Herodotus (2.152) says that Psammetichus I used Ionian and Carian mercenaries.

together with focused military action, is what succeeded in establishing his sovereignty and afforded him recognition by the other rulers.

Two years later (656 B.C.E.), Psammetichus also established his aegis over
Upper Egypt. Through diplomatic action (in which he was aided by the rulers of
Herakleopolis, with whom he had family ties), the "Fourth Prophet of Amūn"
and mayor of Thebes, Montuemhat, allowed Amenirdis II, Divine Worshiper of
Amūn, to adopt Nitocris (Neitiqert), daughter of Psammetichus, as her protégé
and junior partner.[95] This act reflected the Theban rulers' recognition of Psammetichus's sovereignty. At this point, Upper and Lower Egypt were united under
his rule, opening a new chapter in Egyptian history.[96] During this time, Psammetichus was powerful and confident enough to cease paying tribute to Assyria
and to transform himself from a protected subject to an independent king. Despite this, he apparently remained a loyal ally of Assyria, and there is no evidence of any hostility between the two kingdoms.[97]

When Assyria withdrew from the Levant 20 years later, in the beginning of
the third decade of the seventh century B.C.E., Egypt easily established its rule
there.[98] Within several years, Egypt stabilized its border on the Euphrates and,
in 616 B.C.E., set out from there to help Assyria in the war against Babylon and
the Medes. Psammetichus I had a real interest in helping Sin-šar-iškun withstand the unending onslaught of Assyria's rivals from the east and south. As

---

95. This adoption was a political move, since Amenirdis II adopted Nitocris even though
Shepwenwepet II was still alive and in office as the Divine Worshiper of Amūn. See Kitchen
1973b: 236–39; Spalinger 1976: 139, 142; James 1991: 706, 709, 712; Redford 1992: 432; Morkot 2000: 299–301.

96. On this subject, see Kitchen 1973b: 391–406; Spalinger 1974a: 316–26; 1974b: 322–25;
1976: 139–40; Burstein 1984: 31; Naʾaman 1991a: 38–39; James 1991: 709; Redford 1992:
432–35, with further literature.

97. See Tadmor 1966: 101; Kitchen 1973b: 406–7; Spalinger 1974a: 323; 1976: 135–36,
142; 1978b: 51; Naʾaman 1991a: 38–41. Malamat 1968: 137–56; 1983: 231; 1988: 118–21;
2000: 85–86, Zawadzki 1988: 20; Vanderhooft 1999: 69–70; Morkot 2000: 298–99 and others
argue that during this time period Egypt threw off the Assyrian yoke; however, see in contrast
the view of Naʾaman (1991a). For a different reconstruction of events, with an emphasis on
the early disappearance of Assyria and Egypt's entry into the vacuum left behind after the
Scythian withdrawal from the region, see Redford 1992: 438–45. For a summary of the arguments for Assyria's early withdrawal, see Vanderhooft 1999: 64–68, with further literature. In
contrast, for a thesis regarding Assyria's later withdrawal from the Levant, see Naʾaman 1991a:
33–41. For arguments against the reconstruction of a large-scale Scythian invasion to the region, see Naʾaman 1991a: 48–49, with further literature.

98. Note the scarab with the name of Psammetichus I, found in Stratum VIIIb at Yabneh-
Yam, which is dated to the second half of the seventh century B.C.E. (Fantalkin 2000: 64; 2001:
74). The site was apparently laid waste before the destruction of Meṣad Ḥashavyahu, Ashkelon, Ekron, and Timna; see Fantalkin 2000: 63–64; 2001: 72–73. On the circumstances of
Egypt's penetration of the Levant, see Zawadzki 1988: 21; Naʾaman 1991a: 38–41, with further
literature. On this subject, see also the survey by James (1991: 708–14) and the different reconstruction by Redford (1992: 441); Redford argues that the Egyptian penetration of the Levant
and the establishment of its rule were perceived by Assyria as hostile actions, but at this stage
the Assyrians no longer had the power to stop Egypt.

long as Assyria continued to exist, even as a kingdom gradually losing its territorial holdings (among them its major cities), Egypt could strengthen its rule in the area west of the Euphrates without exposing itself to direct confrontation with the powerful Median-Babylonian army. Nonetheless, there is only one known instance of Egypt's helping Assyria during the time of Psammetichus I (616 B.C.E.), and even this aid was limited in scope and insignificant in its consequences (see §1.3 above). It was only when Necho II ascended the throne (610 B.C.E.) that Egyptian policy changed. In addition to the campaigns conducted by the young king in an effort to assist Assyria in its fight for survival (610–609 B.C.E.),[99] he intensified his effort to establish his reign and status in northern Syria and on the western banks of the Euphrates. The Egyptian action also included attempts to establish a foothold east of the Euphrates, apparently as a first step toward an offensive into Mesopotamia. However, at this stage, the Egyptians encountered a Babylonian opponent superior in strength that, under Nebuchadrezzar's leadership, was prepared to take over the Levant within a few years (see §1.6, pp. 32ff.).

Thus, it seems that, from the Egyptian perspective, the year 609 B.C.E. was a starting point in a frontal struggle against Babylon. Egypt had established itself as an empire throughout the Levant as far as the Euphrates, although its presence was particularly felt in the regions lying along the Mediterranean coast. The border between the two empires was temporary: If Egypt were to emerge victorious, it would be able to expand its rule beyond the Euphrates and even pose a threat to Babylonia itself. If Egypt lost, the Babylonians would break through to the Levant, and from there they could constitute a threat to Egypt itself (Redford 2000: 190).

*   *   *

The Egyptians ruled the Levant for a quarter of a century, from the time of the Assyrian retreat at the beginning of the last third of the seventh century B.C.E. until the decisive Babylonian victories, after which Egypt was pushed out of its footholds in Asia (605/604 B.C.E.). There are few accounts left from this period, but from them we learn that the Egyptians aspired to establish a stable government in the entire region and acted to accomplish this in a variety of ways—both politically and militarily.

Egypt had two major reasons for establishing its rule in the region of Syria–Palestine: *From the economic point of view,* Egypt's major interest in the Levant was in Phoenicia.[100] The economic importance of the ports and cedar lumber

99. From the Babylonian Chronicle it is not clear whether the campaign of 610 B.C.E. was conducted at the end of Psammetichus's reign or at the beginning of Necho II's, but the second possibility seems more likely. On this, see the discussion above, §1.3 (p. 19).

100. On the Egyptian finds from this period on the Phoenician coast and their significance, see Katzenstein 1973: 298–304. Katzenstein sees this material as evidence of the commercial

was great, and, considering this, it is clear why Egypt established its sovereignty first and foremost on the Phoenician coast, between Tyre and Arwad (Katzenstein 1973: 299 n. 24; 313 n. 100; Redford 1992: 442). Psammetichus I owned land in the Lebanon Mountains, perhaps a royal estate, where his officials supervised the cutting of cedar trees and their transportation to Egypt.[101] The Egyptians also assigned great importance to the Via Maris, which made land trade possible between Egypt and the Levant (Redford 1992: 435; Vanderhooft 1999: 70–71). It also seems that wine and oil from Israel were of great importance to Egypt's economy.[102]

From the strategic point of view, after the disappearance of Assyria, Egypt was left with no choice: its border now was on the Euphrates River, and that was where direct conflict with the Babylonians began. At this stage, it was clear to both sides that the Euphrates was a provisional border. They both tried to establish footholds on the other side of the river as a base for a future offensive. At this time, Egypt had two spheres of strategic interest.

The immediate sphere of interest included primarily Philistia, which was perceived as Egypt's immediate "security zone." This area was the only overland gateway to Egypt from the north and served as a crucial foothold for anyone interested in crossing the desert and invading the hinterland. This fact required the Egyptians to entrench themselves in the region, maintaining tight control all along the Via Maris leading northward. This was the major and, in fact, only artery of traffic for anyone who wished to move troops in the direction of Egypt, and it is clear that it also had great importance (as did the ports that lined it) for transferring Egyptian troops to the other side of the Euphrates (Redford 1992: 444 and further literature in n. 57). It is with this in mind that we can understand why the Egyptians sited a fortress at Meṣad Ḥashavyahu and why we find evidence for the presence of mercenary soldiers in Stratum VIIIb at Yabneh-Yam, as well as at Ashkelon, Ekron and Timna.[103]

---

ties between Egypt and Syria. In contrast, Otzen (1964: 90–96) and Redford (1992: 435) interpret this evidence as indicating direct Egyptian rule of the region. On this subject, see also Malamat 1983: 253, and n. 22. For a general summary of trade during the 26th Dynasty, see Drioton and Vandier 1962: 583–84.

101. Two Egyptian inscriptions give evidence for this: one was published by Porter and Moss 1931: 211, and the second by Breasted 1962: §970. See also Freedy and Redford 1970: 477; Redford 1992: 442; Katzenstein 1973: 299, 313; 1993: 184, and see the critique by Malamat 1983: 232 n. 20.

102. In contrast to the view held by Stager (1996b: 70*–71*) and Vanderhooft (1999: 71–77), who claim that a flowering took place in Philistia and adjacent territories precisely under Egyptian rule in the region, Gitin (1997: 99–100 and n. 65, with further literature) argues that a decline may be detected in the status and output of the great manufacturing centers for wine and oil at Ashkelon and Ekron, cities that had flourished previously under Assyrian rule.

103. Naveh (1962: 99) was the first to propose that the establishment of Meṣad Ḥashavyahu be assigned to mercenaries posted there by Psammetichus I, before it was conquered by Josiah. However, he later retracted this proposal (NEAEHL 557) and now supports the

The remote sphere of interest included northern Syria, as far as the west bank of the Euphrates. As stated previously, the importance of this region was not great as long as Assyria continued to exist, even as a diminished kingdom. However, with its disappearance, the Euphrates became Egypt's first line of defense against Babylonian invasion attempts. It was of strategic importance in preventing the establishment of Babylonian outposts on the western side of the Euphrates that might serve as a springboard for a large overland offensive into Syria. This area also could serve as a springboard for attacks launched by Egypt beyond the Euphrates, depending on the ability of the Egyptian army to establish bridgeheads east of the Euphrates that would allow them to pour in massive forces across the river (James 1991: 716).

These economic and strategic interests help us to understand the military steps taken by Egypt and the nature of its rule in the region. When Assyria withdrew from the region, in the last third of the seventh century B.C.E., Egypt .succeeded it as a "Successor State" (Naʾaman 1991a: 40; see also §1.3, p. 16). Along the Mediterranean coast, the Egyptians inherited a line of provinces that extended from the Syrian coast (Kullani/Kinalua and Ṣimirra/Ṣumur) throughout the Phoenician coast (Kār-Esarhaddon and Tyre) down to the Plain of Sharon (Duʾru). In Philistia, there were one province (Ashdod) and three vassal city-states (Gaza, Ashkelon, and Ekron). In the hilly region of Israel, there were one small kingdom (Judah) and two provinces (Sāmerīna and Magidû). East of the Jordan, there were three small independent kingdoms (Ammon, Moab, and Edom). All of Syria was divided into six provinces (from Arpad/Arpaddu and Ḥatarikka in the north to Hamath/Hamattu, Ṣubat/Ṣubite, Manṣuate and Dimašqu in the south).

Egypt governed this area for more than 20 years, until Babylonia took control in 605/604 B.C.E., and for most of this time (up to 610 B.C.E.), Psammetichus I

---

proposal of Tadmor (1966: 102 n. 59) and of Strange (1966: 138) that Greek mercenaries under Josiah founded the site (compare also with the earlier proposal by Cross 1962a: 42). This proposal has been accepted by many scholars, except those who prefer Naveh's original proposal and support the thesis of two separate stages in the history of the site (I. Eshel 1986–87: 236). The tendency among modern researchers to return to Naveh's original proposal seems to be based primarily on the historical discussion (following) and an analysis of the archaeological finds. For a comprehensive discussion of the material finds at the site, the characteristics of the site, and a comparison with finds from other coastal sites, see Fantalkin 2000; 2001. On the importance of mercenaries in Egypt under Psammetichus and the fortress at Meṣad Ḥashavyahu in this context, see Redford 1992: 443–44. On this subject, see also Miller and Hayes 1986: 389; Naʾaman 1991a: 44–51; Finkelstein 1995: 148; Kletter 1999: 42; Vanderhooft 1999: 78–80. On the parallel between the population at Meṣad Ḥashavyahu and the situation in the Egyptian fortresses on the Egyptian border at this time (Migdol and Daphnae/Tahpanhes), see Naʾaman 1991a: 44–46, with further literature. In light of these findings, one must reject Wenning's exceptional proposal that the site be dated to Jehoiakim's rule (1989: 169–96). It appears clear that by the 5th year of Jehoiakim's rule (604 B.C.E.), Meṣad Ḥashavyahu was already destroyed (Naʾaman 1991a: 45–48; Fantalkin 2000: 25–26; 66–70; 2001: 75–81).

was the ruler. In this short period, for which there is scant historical documentation, Egypt was interested primarily in the coastal region (from Philistia to Phoenicia), where the important ports were situated, where the international route
lay, and where its economic interests were concentrated (Otzen 1964: 90–92;
Katzenstein 1973: 298–316; Malamat 1983: 253–54, and n. 22; Redford 1992:
435; Vanderhooft 1999: 70–71). It is possible that, having learned their lesson
from their struggle with Assyria in the first half of the seventh century b.c.e., the
Egyptians established their foothold in Philistia immediately upon the Assyrian
armies' retreat. According to accounts preserved in Herodotus's *History* (2.157),
the Egyptians laid siege to Ashdod for 29 years[104] until they captured the city.[105]
There is no information about the other Philistine coastal cities.[106] However,
one may conjecture that during the long years of the *Pax Assyriaca* they maintained close ties with Egypt and that they were the first to recognize its status as
a successor state. In any event, the establishment of Egyptian rule in Philistia
was rapid, and the Philistine city-states continued to pledge fealty to Egypt even
during the early years of Babylonian rule in the region (see §§1.6, 2.1).

At a fairly early stage of Egyptian rule of the region, Egypt established control
as far as Phoenicia, subjugating Tyre and apparently Arwad as well (Katzenstein
1973: 299 n. 24; 313 n. 100; Redford 1992: 442). Tyre was restored to its status
as a vassal city-state at this time.[107] It is not clear to what extent Egypt was in-

---

104. One may assume that the many years that Ashdod was under tight Assyrian control
caused it to be less connected to Egypt, and with the Assyrian withdrawal, Ashdod attempted
to establish independence.

105. Tadmor (1966: 102; and see also Cogan and Tadmor 1988: 300) proposed understanding the number 29 as referring to the 29th year of Psammetichus I, i.e., 635 b.c.e., and deduced
from this the date of Assyria's withdrawal from the region. However, see Na'aman's argument
(1991a: 39–40) in support of the common explanation that the number represents a chronological speculation by Herodotus, based on 28 years of Scythian rule in Asia. On this subject,
see also Malamat 1983: 231–32; James 1991: 714; Redford 1992: 441–42, with further literature in n. 44. On the archaeological evidence of the Egyptian conquest, see the opinion of the
excavators: Dothan and Freedman 1967: 11 n. 46; 141; Dothan et al. 1971: 115; Dothan and
Porat 1982: 57–58; *NEAEHL* 1.93; and see the critique by Vanderhooft 1999: 71–72.

106. See Redford 1992: 442. All that is known about Ekron is that at the end of the seventh century b.c.e. there was some decline in the city from the prosperity it had enjoyed under
Assyrian rule (Dothan and Gitin 1994: 23–25). Nonetheless, we cannot know whether this decline took place before the Egyptian takeover of the area or during the days of Egyptian rule.

107. In Jer 25:22 and 27:3, there are references to the kings of Tyre and Sidon as being
among those who conspired against the king of Babylon. In the Istanbul prism fragment of Nebuchadrezzar (no. 7834; Unger 1931: 282–94), which Landsberger (1933: 298) correctly assigned to Nebuchadrezzar's seventh year (and see also Vanderhooft 1999: 34 n. 119), there are
references to the kings of Tyre, Sidon, Arwad, Gaza, and Ashdod—apparently a list of Nebuchadrezzar II's vassal kings (Berger 1973: 313; Wiseman 1985: 74–75; Elat 1991: 29–30; Vanderhooft 1999: 92–99). To this must be added the brief accounts of Nebuchadrezzar's conquest
of Tyre and Sidon; and see below. Two Egyptian inscriptions support the idea that Psammetichus owned land in the mountains of Lebanon, perhaps a royal estate where his officials oversaw the production and export of cedar (and see above, p. 26 n. 105). Additional support for
this may be found in the inscription from Wadi Brisa, where there is a description of a military
campaign conducted by Nebuchadrezzar in Lebanon and the conquest of the area by "a foreign

terested in the hinterland or what effort it invested in extending its rule there. Nevertheless, Necho's presence at Megiddo and the killing of Josiah (2 Kgs 23:29), the later deposing of Jehoahaz from the throne (v. 33), and the appointment of Eliakim-Jehoiakim (v. 34) attest to Egypt's desire to establish its control of the entire area. In light of this analysis of the international events and the biblical accounts, it appears that at this stage Judah was overshadowed by Egypt and could not conduct an independent foreign policy, certainly not in the lowland, the coastal region, or the Jezreʿel Valley.[108]

There is no information available about other aspects of Egyptian organization, but it is reasonable to assume that at this time it was important for them firmly to establish their control of Syria in preparation for engagement with the Babylonians in the area of the Euphrates. From the Egyptian center in Riblah (compare 2 Kgs 23:33), they established the structure that enabled them to control central Syria and southward. There is no information about similar Egyptian activity in northern Syria. However, the military ventures they initiated there in 608–605 B.C.E. are evidence of the great importance that they attributed to this region as their base for campaigns against the Babylonians from both sides of the Euphrates.[109]

1.5. The Rise of the Neo-Babylonian[110] Dynasty and Its Interests "Across the River"

In the first quarter of the first millennium B.C.E., just before the Assyrian conquest, the ancient centers in Ur (Uru), Uruk (Erech), Nippur, Dilbat, Barsip (Borsippa), Kiš (Ḫursagkalama), Kutê (Kûtâ/Kutha), Sippar, and Bābili (Babylon) had a well-established administrative system, a flourishing economy, a well-organized ritual in the temples, a strong priestly class, and a well-developed material and spiritual culture. Nonetheless, these Babylonian cities did not have any tradition of military and political cohesiveness, and their natural inclination

---

enemy who ruled there and plundered its wealth." On this inscription, see further literature above, n. 23 (p. 8).

108. See also the discussion in §1.6 below and the reconstruction by Naʾaman 1991a: 33–60, with further literature.

109. Katzenstein (1973: 298, 302) maintained that throughout this period (at least until 610 B.C.E.) "there was no real Egyptian overlordship over greater Syria and Phoenicia," but in contrast see the opinions expressed by Kienitz 1953: 20; Spalinger 1976: 133–47; and Redford 1992: 444–48; and see also §1.6 below.

110. By the term *Neo-Babylonian* (= NB) I refer to the accepted chronological definition, which is used in modern research literature to denote the period of time between the establishment of the Chaldean dynasty by Nabopolassar (626 B.C.E.) and the conquest of Babylon by the Persians (539 B.C.E.). It is important to distinguish between the chronological-historical term and the linguistic term, which is used to refer to the Akkadian dialect characteristic of the Babylonian region between the end of the second millennium B.C.E. and the mid-sixth century B.C.E. (CAD Ḫ vi). Von Soden (GAG §2, g–h), for example, included the historical Neo-Babylonian period in the linguistic "Late Babylonian (*Spätbabylonisch*) Period," which began ca. 625 B.C.E.

was toward independent existence. Nippur was the center of Assyrian rule; in Babylon, a Babylonian king sat enthroned, and some cities (Babylon, Ur, Uruk, Kutha, Nippur, Borsippa, and Sippar) were ancient and important centers of ritual, which also played a key political and economic function. Alongside these, various tribes (primarily Chaldeans and Arameans) controlled extensive parts of the country, and they contributed to overall destabilization and, in particular, to the destabilization of the relationships among the various cities.[111]

Assyrian control over Babylonia (747–626 B.C.E.) accelerated the unification of the diverse factions in the area and led to a gradual revival of nationalism and the building of a strong, cohesive kingdom.[112] The population of the ancient urban centers melded with the tribal groups—Arameans and Chaldeans—who lived in and around the cities. This assemblage constituted the basis of the new Babylonian kingdom that, with the help of the Medes, succeeded in freeing itself from Assyrian domination.[113]

The "Chaldean" king, Nabopolassar,[114] was gradually acknowledged king of all of the cities in Babylonia and officially ascended the throne on the 26th of Araḫsamnu (November 22/23, 626 B.C.E.).[115] The Neo-Babylonian kingdom grew rapidly under his rule. In less than 20 years, it progressed from the status of a subject kingdom fighting for its independence to an empire that had established control over Mesopotamia and had begun to fight Egypt for control of the Levant.

Direct conflict between Babylon and Egypt first erupted in 609 B.C.E. The failure of the Assyrians and Egyptians to restore control over Ḫarran symbolized the final disappearance of Assyria from the arena. The Euphrates was now the boundary between Babylon and Egypt, and the result was direct conflict between the two powers that had inherited the territories of the Assyrian Empire.

The Babylonians had two major reasons to contend with Egypt for control of the Levant.

From the economic point of view, the Babylonians had a deep interest in taking control of the area west of the Euphrates because their land had been hard hit during the decades of struggle against Assyria. In addition to destruction of some of the urban centers, the economy was damaged during the long years of war, commercial life was stagnant, and the agricultural infrastructure was destroyed. After freeing itself from Assyrian domination, Babylonia required a process of

---

111. On this subject, see the summary by Brinkman 1984: 1–2, 123 and the extended review on pp. 3–38.

112. On this subject, see the summary by Brinkman 1984: 2, 125 and the extended review on pp. 39–111.

113. On the process of driving Assyria out of Babylonia and the consolidation of the Neo-Babylonian kingdom, see §1.3 above.

114. On the problem with the Chaldean origin of the dynasty, see Olmstead 1925: 29–30; Hallo and Simpson 1971: 145; Brinkman 1984: 110 n. 551; Wiseman 1985: 5–6.

115. See the Babylonian Chronicle BM 25127, lines 14–15; Wiseman 1956: 7, 50–51; Grayson 1975a: 17–18, 88. See also the discussion above, §1.3.

rebuilding in all areas of the economy. This ranged from the physical rehabilitation of the urban centers, commerce, agriculture, and craft industries through the location of sources of raw materials and the training of skilled workers. The Medes had taken control of the major roads in northern Mesopotamia as well as the important sources of raw materials in southeast Anatolia, making it difficult for this rehabilitation to proceed. As a result, Babylonian revenues had shrunk dramatically just at a time when the rehabilitation and rebuilding of Babylon together with all of the cities in Babylonia required a steady supply of goods and raw materials.

In light of these factors, it is easy to understand the tremendous potential envisioned by the Babylonians with regard to Ḫatti-land (as they called the area west of the Euphrates). They were much taken with the possibility of plundering all of the territories conquered, receiving generous tribute from the kingdoms of the region, collecting annual taxes, and obtaining goods and raw materials. It is also reasonable to assume that they were aware of the economic potential of trade with the Arabs, maritime trade, and the natural resources that the region offered, including both lumber and stone that were so lacking in Mesopotamia. One may also conjecture that the economic factor was an additional incentive fuelling Babylonian aspiration to control Egypt (as Assyria had done not many years previously) and to harness the economic potential of this region to the benefit of the Babylonian economy.

From the strategic-military point of view, the Babylonians were unable to permit the Egyptian presence on the Euphrates River, because it represented a constant threat to their control of Mesopotamia. Apart from the tangible danger of an Egyptian invasion beyond the Euphrates, an added danger was that their presence tended to encourage anti-Babylonian pacts. At this stage, the Babylonians had two different spheres of interest: *the immediate sphere of interest* was the need to repel the Egyptians as far as possible from the banks of the Euphrates and to establish Babylonian outposts on the other side of the river that would serve as a bridgehead for pouring troops into the region of "Across the River." *The remote sphere of interest* was the direct consequence of driving the Egyptians westward from the Euphrates. It is doubtful that the Babylonians planned in advance how far to the west and south they would force the Egyptians. It is similarly doubtful that they understood the significance of the Levant as a "security zone" and that controlling it was crucial to keeping the Egyptians at bay and ensuring Babylonian control of Mesopotamia. It seems that, for the Babylonians, Egypt was the primary target. They understood that in order to guarantee their hold on Ḫatti-land they must conquer Egypt and establish their dominion there, just as the Assyrians had in the seventh century B.C.E. With this in mind, we can understand why, from the very outset of their interest in this region, the Babylonians concentrated their attention on the coastal region along the Via Maris, leading to Egypt.[116]

---

116. See the discussion below, §2.1.

1.6. *The Babylonian–Egyptian Struggle (609–605 B.C.E.)* [117]

The importance of the events that took place in 610–609 B.C.E., which led to the disappearance of Assyria, was as clear to Egypt as to the Babylonians. This is evidenced by the effort that both parties invested in seizing control of Ḫarran. Nabopolassar staged two consecutive campaigns with the objective of rebuffing Assyria and establishing his rule over the city and its environs. At the same time, the Egyptians, headed by Necho II, mounted two consecutive campaigns with the objective of offering aid to Assyria and preventing the Babylonian takeover of the city. We also have information about Necho's efforts to establish Egyptian mastery over the Levant: Riblah became a major Egyptian center, and from there Necho probably organized the Egyptian governance of central and northern Syria. [118] One must assume that, at the same time, he made similar arrangements in the other areas under his control. This helps us to understand the political structure established in Judah after the killing of Josiah at Megiddo, when the Egyptians rallied to the aid of Assyria only a few weeks before the battle at Ḫarran (probably at the end of May or early June 609 B.C.E.). [119] After the battle, as part of his effort to control the area west of the Euphrates, Necho deported Jehoahaz, son of Josiah, who had been enthroned in Judah without Necho's approval (2 Kgs 23:34). Necho then appointed Jehoahaz's older brother Jehoiakim and exacted a heavy tribute (vv. 35–36).

During the same time that Egypt was establishing itself in the Levant, the Babylonians were establishing their control along the southern border of the kingdom of Urarṭu in a series of three campaigns. By the autumn of the 17th year of his reign (September 609 B.C.E.), immediately after the withdrawal of Assyrian-Egyptian forces from Ḫarran, Nabopolassar continued northward toward the border of Urarṭu, apparently with the aim of subjugating the mountain inhabitants and preventing them from invading the areas near the Euphrates that Assyria had previously ruled. [120] An additional campaign to the same area was conducted in the following year. Between the months of Ululu and Tebeth of Nabopolassar's 18th year (from August/September to December 608 B.C.E.), the king set out at the head of an army along the banks of the Tigris and conquered the easternmost sections of the hilly regions. [121] The third campaign in

---

117. A reconstruction of the historical movements during this period is derived primarily from the Babylonian Chronicles and the information in the biblical books of Kings and Jeremiah. For the scant extant Egyptian sources relevant to this period, see Redford 2000: 183–85, with further literature.

118. See the note in 2 Kgs 23:33 and the discussion by James 1991: 716 and Redford 1992: 449.

119. See the discussion in §2.1 below, where a more-detailed reconstruction of the events that transpired in Judah at that time is presented.

120. See the Babylonian Chronicle BM 21901, lines 70–75; Wiseman 1956: 19–20, 62–63; Grayson 1975a: 19, 96.

121. See the Babylonian Chronicle BM 22047, lines 1–4; Wiseman 1956: 20, 64–65; Grayson 1975a: 19, 97.

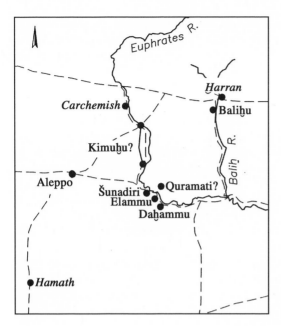

Map 4. The Middle
Euphrates during the
Babylonian-Egyptian struggle.

this series took place between the months of Simanu and Ululu in the king's
19th year (from May to August 607 B.C.E.). He and his army set out again, along
with his heir, Nebuchadrezzar, at the head of his own army. Nabopolassar returned to Babylon a month later and temporarily left the campaign to his son.[122]
Nebuchadrezzar's return to Babylon in the month of Ululu enabled Nabopolassar to muster his troops in the month of Tašritu (October 607 B.C.E.)[123] and to
set out for the Middle Euphrates, as part of the beginning of the direct struggle
against Egypt. According to the description in the Babylonian Chronicle, the
Babylonian army crossed the Euphrates and laid siege to the city of Kimuḫu. The
siege continued until the month of Kislimu (December 607 B.C.E.), when the
city was conquered and a garrison was stationed there.[124] The Babylonian objective apparently was to establish a foothold west of the Euphrates as the basis of
future activity beyond the river and to threaten the Egyptian garrison that was at
Carchemish at the time (Grayson 1975a: 21).

---

122. See the Babylonian Chronicle BM 22047, lines 5–11; Wiseman 1956: 20, 64–65; Grayson 1975a: 19, 97.

123. The 19th year of Nabopolassar's rule was an intercalation year and there were two
months of Ululu, so, between the return of Nebuchadrezzar in the month of Ululu and the
departure of Nabopolassar in Tašritu, at least one full month had elapsed. On this subject, see
Parker and Dubberstein 1956: 27.

124. See the Babylonian Chronicle BM 22047, lines 12–15; Wiseman 1956: 20–21, 64–65,
83; Grayson 1975a: 19, 97–98.

The Babylonian threat was clear, and the Egyptian reaction was not long in coming. During the spring or early summer of 606 B.C.E., an Egyptian force set out for Kimuḫu and laid siege to it for four months. According to the Babylonian Chronicle, the city fell to the Egyptians, and the Babylonian garrison that had been there was defeated.[125] Nabopolassar did not come to the aid of his troops, perhaps because of the great danger involved both in crossing the Euphrates with a large army and in fighting a battle with the Egyptians, who were located on the western bank of the river. It was only in the month of Tašritu (September/October 606 B.C.E.) that the Babylonians set out again toward the Middle Euphrates and encamped at the city of Quramati, which is south of Kimuḫu and east of the Euphrates.[126] From there, the Babylonian forces set out to conquer the cities of Šunadiri, Elammu, and Daḫammu, which are west of the Euphrates, apparently with the plan of creating an alternate bridgehead to cross the river.[127] The conquest of these cities was completed in the month of Ṣabaṭu (January/February 605 B.C.E.), and Nabopolassar returned to Babylon. But a short time later (between mid-February and mid-April), the Egyptian army left Carchemish, crossed the river, and conquered the city of Quramati. The Babylonian army was forced to retreat, and the Egyptians established an outpost east of the Euphrates that could serve as a launching point for future offensives against the territories controlled by Babylon in that region.[128]

The events of summer 605 B.C.E. decided the outcome of the battle. The Egyptian threat forced the Babylonians to concentrate all of their power for the decisive battle with the Egyptians, which occurred under the leadership of the heir apparent, Nebuchadrezzar, who set out at the head of the Babylonian army.[129] His target was Carchemish, the chief Egyptian stronghold on the banks of the Euphrates. On his route, Nebuchadrezzar must certainly have passed Quramati and east of Kimuḫu. Although there is no information about the conquest of these cities, it is reasonable to assume that there were no longer any Egyptians left in them, because it is doubtful that the Babylonians would have dared to leave Egyptian troops behind their lines while continuing to move toward Carchemish (Grayson 1956: 23).

Nebuchadrezzar and his army crossed the Euphrates and moved to the west bank of the river at an unknown location, apparently close to Carchemish. In

---

125. See the Babylonian Chronicle BM 22047, lines 16–18; Wiseman 1956: 21, 66–67; Grayson 1975a: 19, 98.

126. On the difficulties in identifying the city, see Wiseman 1956: 83.

127. See the Babylonian Chronicle BM 22047, lines 19–22; Wiseman 1956: 21–23, 66–67; Grayson 1975a: 19, 98.

128. See the Babylonian Chronicle BM 22047, lines 23–26; Wiseman 1956: 23, 66–67; Grayson 1975a: 19, 98.

129. See the Babylonian Chronicles BM 22047, lines 27–28; BM 21946, lines 1–2; Wiseman 1956: 23, 66–67; Grayson 1975a: 19, 98–99.

the battle against the Egyptian army, they won a decisive victory.[130] The city was captured and the remnants of the Egyptian army withdrew to the province of Hamath, where they were overtaken by the Babylonians, who dealt the Egyptians a mortal blow.[131] According to the Babylonian Chronicle, Nebuchadrezzar's army captured the province of Hamath on the same day, thus completing the victory.[132] Within a short time, the die had been cast. From then on, it was clear that the Babylonians were destined to rule throughout the Levant. The Egyptians had to make haste to defend the borders of their own kingdom.

The death of King Nabopolassar on the 8th of the month of Abu of that year (August 15/16, 605 B.C.E.),[133] after more than 20 years of rule, symbolized the end of the era of the establishment of the Babylonian Empire. Nebuchadrezzar's rise to power on the 1st of Ululu (September 6/7, 605)[134] and his first 2 years of reign were marked by the Babylonian takeover of all of the area of Ḥatti-land. The struggle of the titans for control of the lands of the Assyrian Empire had been decided: Babylon won a resounding victory, and Egypt was driven back from all of its holdings in Asia. However, the struggle did not end, and just as Babylonia and Egypt understood this, the kingdoms in the region, including Judah, understood it as well. This was the beginning of a period of great uncertainty, which affected the fate of the region and shaped the events that continued to take place there.

---

130. It is not clear whether Necho II was in Carchemish at this time; there is no mention of him in the Babylonian Chronicle (see Wiseman 1956: 24, and note on p. 84). The prophecy in Jer 46:2 does not provide a clearer picture: "For Egypt; concerning the army of Pharaoh Necho, king of Egypt, who was on the river Euphrates at Carchemish, whom Nebuchadrezzar, king of Babylon, defeated in the fourth year of Jehoiakim, son of Josiah, king of Judah."

131. See the Babylonian Chronicle BM 21946, lines 2–7; Wiseman 1956: 23–24, 66–69; Grayson 1975a: 19, 99.

132. See the Babylonian Chronicle BM 21946, line 8; Wiseman 1956: 25, 66–69; Grayson 1975a: 19, 99. The ease with which Syria fell into the hands of the Babylonians is evidence that the Egyptians had not succeeded in truly establishing their dominion there, and they held the region largely by filling the vacuum left when the Assyrians withdrew. The Assyrian provinces that remained were testimony to Assyria's success in breaking the strength of the large territorial kingdoms that had previously existed in the region and that constituted the main obstacle in the process of Assyria's takeover of the region at the end of the eighth century B.C.E.

133. See the Babylonian Chronicle BM 21946, line 10; Wiseman 1956: 25–26, 68–69; Grayson 1975a: 19–20, 99; Parker and Dubberstein 1956: 27.

134. According to the description of line 11 in the chronicle; and see also Wiseman 1985: 17–19.

Chapter 2

Judah under Babylonian Rule

2.1. The Babylonian Domination of Ḫatti-Land and the Characteristics of Nebuchadrezzar II's Policy

> And these nations will serve the king of Babylon for seventy years. (Jer 25:11)

During the first two years of Nebuchadrezzar II's reign (605–604 B.C.E.), Babylon seized control of Ḫatti-land. The Babylonian kingdom, which had grown into a colossal empire in only a few years, was inexperienced in maintaining control of extensive territories that were a great distance from Babylon. It is reasonable to assume that the Babylonian rulers' knowledge of the system of provinces and kingdoms in Ḫatti-land was limited, and there is no evidence that Nebuchadrezzar tried to develop or defend this region. It appears that his policy was to maintain the lowest possible level of involvement, to invest minimal effort in establishing his control there, and to continue to maintain the geopolitical and administrative structures that had been established during Egyptian and Assyrian rule. The major importance of Ḫatti-land at this time was a result of its function as a land bridge to Egypt. Nebuchadrezzar knew that Egypt was the only power that could threaten the existence of the young empire and that he could not establish his rule firmly in the region as long as there was a threat of Egyptian invasion.

The Babylonian policy in Ḫatti-land did not change even after the failure of their attempted invasion of Egypt at the end of 601 B.C.E., which led to the weakening of their control over the entire region. After rebuilding their army, the Babylonians reestablished control of the inland and Mediterranean coast vassal states and continued to depend on their allegiance. In keeping with this policy, the Babylonians allowed the House of David to remain in power, despite the revolt by Jehoiakim, contenting themselves with exiling Jehoiachin and part of the nation's elite.

However, in the days of Psammetichus II (595–589 B.C.E.) and even more so during the early days of Ḫophra (589–570 B.C.E.), Egypt began to threaten Babylonian rule directly, instigating instability among the kingdoms of the region. These actions forced Nebuchadrezzar to reconsider his regional policy. It was at this time, apparently, that he decided to introduce changes in policy,

36

shifting from indirect rule that depended on the loyalty of the vassal kingdoms to direct rule over provinces that were immediately subject to him. This was the beginning of a new era during which the Babylonians gradually but steadily captured all of the kingdoms in the region, annexed them, and transformed them into provinces subject to direct rule. The fate of Judah was sealed when it became the first kingdom to be conquered as part of the revised Babylonian policy.

To understand the historical picture, we will survey the process by which the Babylonians rapidly gained control over Ḫatti-land (605–604 B.C.E.; §2.1.1) and describe what was happening in Judah during that period (§2.1.2). We will study the abortive efforts by Babylon to invade Egypt (601 B.C.E.) and the significance of this failure for the kingdoms in Palestine (including Judah). Against this background, we will reconstruct the circumstances that led to Jehoiakim's revolt (§2.1.3). The deportation of Jehoiachin and the appointment of Zedekiah will be described as part of the renewed consolidation of the Babylonians in the region (§2.1.4). Nebuchadrezzar's policy change in the first decade of the sixth century B.C.E. and his decision to move from indirect rule over vassal kingdoms to direct rule over provinces will be described in §2.1.5. All of this will serve as background to a reconstruction of the events of the destruction of Jerusalem, which will be discussed in the next chapter.

2.1.1. Babylonian Domination of Ḫatti-Land (605–604 B.C.E.)

For the king of Babylon seized all that had belonged to the king of Egypt. (2 Kgs 24:7)

Only five years had elapsed since the beginning of the direct confrontation between Babylon and Egypt, from the final disappearance of Assyria as a power in 609 B.C.E. to the conquest of all of the Levant by the armies of Nebuchadrezzar in 604 B.C.E. The decisive battle that paved the way for the Babylonian army's conquest of all of Ḫatti-land took place at Carchemish in the early summer of the last year of Nabopolassar's reign (between May and July 605 B.C.E.).[1] The army of Nebuchadrezzar, Babylonian successor to the throne, crossed the Euphrates, routed the Egyptian army camped at Carchemish, and broke through into Syria.[2] This was described by the prophet Jeremiah: "Concerning the army

---

1. See the Babylonian Chronicles BM 22047, lines 27–28; BM 21946, lines 1–2; Wiseman 1956: 25, 66–67; Grayson 1975a: 19, 98–99.
2. See the Babylonian Chronicle BM 21946, lines 2–5; Wiseman 1956: 23–25, 66–67; Grayson 1975a: 19, 99. In the destruction stratum at Carchemish that is assigned to this period, rich Egyptian objects were uncovered, including a bronze ring with the name of Psammetichus I and four seal impressions with the name of Necho II (Woolley 1921: 123–29). For a summation of this subject, see James 1991: 716–17.

of Pharaoh Necho, king of Egypt, which was at Carchemish on the river Euphrates when Nebuchadrezzar king of Babylon defeated (it) . . ." (Jer 46:2), and "In
the north, by the river Euphrates, they stumble and fall" (v. 6). The lyrical description in Jer 46:2–12 expresses the strong impression left by the Egyptian defeat, and this accords with the description in the Babylonian Chronicle.[3] The
Egyptian army that survived the battle of Carchemish retreated southward, and,
according to the description in the Babylonian Chronicle, Nebuchadrezzar's
army pursued them to the region of Hamath, where the Egyptians were overtaken and dealt a resounding blow.[4] During the same campaign, the Babylonians
took control of the entire region of Hamath,[5] testimony to the fact that the
Egyptians had failed to establish genuine control over Syria and had not established a strong line of defense other than a single outpost on the bank of the
Euphrates.[6]

Nebuchadrezzar did not wait long to see if Egypt would recover, and he
continued to strike quickly. In the second half of August 605 B.C.E., after the
death of his father, he was compelled to return to Babylon to establish his rule.[7]

---

3. The prophecy of Jeremiah in 46:1–12 refers to these events of early summer 605 B.C.E.
and is dated by the prophet to the fourth year of Jehoiakim's rule (v. 2; Hoffman 2001: 15–16,
760–62). For a general discussion and various opinions about the originality of the prophecy
and its date, see Holladay 1989: 312–13. For a discussion of the date and historical background
of the prophecy, see pp. 316–18, with further literature. The fact that Nebuchadrezzar was
called "king of Babylon" in v. 2 may suggest that the prophecy was written later that same summer, when the heir to the throne became king. Jeremiah's description (46:9) of the mercenary
soldiers who were an important element in the Egyptian army, "Men of Cush and Put carrying
shields, Lydians grasping their bows," corresponds with our information about the army of the
Saite Dynasty; see the previous discussion, in chap. 1 (§1.4, pp. 20–29). On the different versions of Jer 46:9 and on the linguistic problems with this verse, see Thompson 1980: 686, 689;
Holladay 1989: 316, 321.

4. See the Babylonian Chronicle BM 21946, lines 6–7; Wiseman 1956: 25–26, 68–69;
Grayson 1975a: 19, 99.

5. See the Babylonian Chronicle BM 21946, line 8; Wiseman 1956: 25, 66–69; Grayson
1975a: 19, 99. For a reconstruction of the reading KUR Ḫa[-ma-a]-tú, see the comment by Oded
1966: 104, with furthur literature on p. 107; Grayson 1975a: 99.

6. On this subject, see also the evaluation by James 1991: 716–71. Additional support for
this may be found in the description of the route of the Babylonians to Carchemish, when pass-
ing through places previously occupied by the Egyptians. There is no evidence of any conflict
or any Egyptian forces of any kind in the strongholds along the Euphrates, and Necho may
have made do with the major garrison force stationed in Carchemish. On this subject, see also
Wiseman 1956: 24–25. Redford (1992: 454) argues that Nebuchadrezzar's direct assault on the
Egyptian center at Carchemish took the Egyptians totally by surprise and was the decisive factor in the outcome. One may also accept his evaluation that the Babylonian victory was made
possible only because the major Egyptian force had not yet reached Carchemish (and perhaps
had been destroyed at Hamath) or did arrive but not in time to deploy for combat.

7. According to the description in the Babylonian Chronicle (BM 21946, lines 9–11),
Nabopolassar died in the month of Abu (August 15/16, 605 B.C.E.) and Nebuchadrezzar ascended the throne on the first of Ululu (September 6/7, 605 B.C.E.; Wiseman 1956: 25, 66–
69; Grayson 1975a: 19, 99; Parker and Dubberstein 1956: 27). Apparently Nebuchadrezzar's
authority was immediately recognized by the tribal heads, palace officials, and the potentates
of the Babylonian cities (Wiseman 1956: 85; 1991: 231).

As soon as he felt sufficiently confident to leave Babylon, he returned to Ḫatti-land.[8] It seems that his main objective was to put Babylon's control of Syria on a firm footing all the way to the center of the region. Therefore, he ranged this region for an indefinite period of time during the autumn and early winter of his "accession year,"[9] collected heavy tribute, and returned to Babylon in the month of Šabaṭu (February 604 B.C.E.). It would be difficult to assume that the Babylonians made any changes, at this stage, in the political organization that was in place in northern Syria. The structure was already well rooted, and there were no other political systems in that region or population with a national identity on which to base any other structure.[10]

Apparently, as of early 604 B.C.E., the Babylonians had established their control as far as the Orontes and had transformed Riblah into their major administrative and military center in Ḫatti-land, after the city had previously been used as the regional Egyptian center (compare 2 Kgs 23:33–25:6; Jer 39:5–6; 52:26–27; see Wiseman 1956: 26). Nonetheless, the Babylonian Chronicle does not mention the presence of any Egyptian army outside of Egypt. It appears that Egyptian rule throughout southern Syria, the Phoenician coast, and Palestine crumbled after the battle at Carchemish. Necho's army withdrew to Egypt, leaving the entire region like a fruit ripe for the Babylonians to pluck.[11]

---

8. The fact that Nebuchadrezzar had already returned from his campaign to Ḫatti-land during the month of Šabaṭu (February 604 B.C.E.) indicates that he had embarked on this campaign a short time after he ascended the throne, proof of the fact that he felt secure enough to leave his country. On the campaign to Ḫatti-land in late 605 and early 604 B.C.E., see the Babylonian Chronicle BM 21946, lines 12–13; Wiseman 1956: 27, 68–69; Grayson 1975a: 20, 100; Hyatt 1956a: 280. I accept Wiseman's proposal (1956: 27) that Nebuchadrezzar, upon his father's death, made haste to return to Babylon with part of his army, and as soon as it became possible, returned to the rest of his army, which had been left in Syria.

9. The term *rēs-šarūti* ('the accession year') refers to the period of time between Nebuchadrezzar's ascent to the throne and the 1st of Nissan, when the king participated in the New Year celebration and the years of his reign began to be counted.

10. In disagreement with Vanderhooft (1999: 90–104), it seems that there is no evidence whatsoever of such changes in the Babylonian sources. A suggestion of this may be found in two documents discovered in the Ebabbar temple at Sippar, which mention the governor of Arpad as someone who brought an offering (Joannès 1994: 21–22). However, there is grave doubt whether any historical reconstruction can be based on this evidence.

11. See Redford 1992: 454–55. It may that Jeremiah's prophecy (25:1–14), "in the fourth year of Jehoiakim, the son of Josiah, king of Judah, that was the first year of Nebuchadrezzar, king of Babylon" (v. 1), refers to this period. The expression הַשָּׁנָה הָרִאשֹׁנִית ('the first year') is mentioned in the Bible in this place only (in the MT, lacking in the LXX; and see Thompson 1980: 509; Holladay 1986: 662, with further literature) and is the only example in the Bible that can be compared with the term *reš-šarūti* (accession year) mentioned in the Babylonian Chronicles, which counted the nine months between the death of Nabopolassar on the 8th of Abu 605 B.C.E. and the 1st of Nissan 604 B.C.E. (Holladay: 1986: 668, with further literature). For a different opinion, according to which there are different usages of this term, see Malamat 1983: 244 and n. 5. For extensive literature on this subject, see Galil 1991: 14 n. 40. The central theme of the prophecy is the prophet's warning that an invasion by Babylon "against this land and its citizens and against all these peoples round about" (v. 9) is imminent. On the date of this

According to the Babylonian Chronicle, the Babylonians mounted a campaign in Ḫatti-land in the second half of 604 B.C.E. (between Simanu and Šabaṭu, June 604–January/February 603 B.C.E.). During this campaign, "[Nebuchadrezzar] marched about victoriously. . . . All the kings of Ḫatti-land came before him and he received their vast tribute."[12] This is probably the period when the Babylonians subjugated the territories of southern Syria and Palestine, down to Gaza.[13] Against this background, one can understand why, according to the Babylonian Chronicle, none of the local kings dared stand up to Nebuchadrezzar, except for the king of Ashkelon.[14] The proximity of Ashkelon to the Egyptian border and the long years of Egyptian rule were apparently the factors that led the king of this small kingdom to continue to rely on Egyptian assistance. Not understanding the change that had taken place in the international balance of power, he refused to capitulate to Babylon. The Babylonian response was decisive, and the fate of that city served as an example to the other kingdoms of the region: Ashkelon was conquered in the month of Kislev (November/December 604 B.C.E.),[15] its king was taken into captivity, many prisoners

---

prophecy, see the discussion by Thompson 1980: 510–11; Holladay 1986: 664–69; Hoffman 2001: 490–91, and see also the discussion following.

12. See the Babylonian Chronicle BM 21946, lines 15–20; Wiseman 1956: 28, 68–69; Grayson 1975a: 20, 100–1. Wiseman (1956: 68–69) translated the word *šalṭāniš* in line 16 'unopposed' ("he [Nebuchadrezzar] marched about unopposed"); however, Albright (1956a: 31 n. 14) criticized this translation and interpreted the word as meaning 'victoriously' ("he [Nebuchadrezzar] marched about victoriously"); compare AHw 1159; CAD Š/1 269. This interpretation was adopted by Grayson 1975a: 100.

13. The event described in the title of the prophecy in Jer 47:1 ("What came as the word of the LORD to Jeremiah the prophet concerning the Philistines, before Pharaoh attacked Gaza") could only have taken place when Babylonian power was at an ebb (after the events of 601 B.C.E.), and this means that the Babylonians had occupied Gaza until that time, apparently in 604 B.C.E. On this editorial comment, the purpose of which was to explain the background of the prophecy in vv. 2–6, see Bright 1965: 311–12; Thompson 1980: 695–97; Katzenstein 1983: 249–51; Holladay 1989: 336–37. The fate of Gaza after being conquered by the Egyptians (in 600 or 599 B.C.E.?) is not known. Why the Egyptians captured Gaza is not clear. Was it to establish a permanent direct Egyptian rule in the southern coastal region, on the main road leading to Egypt? On this subject, see Katzenstein 1994: 42–43.

14. It is hard to accept Albright's view (1956a: 31) that Nebuchadrezzar encountered resistance from the local population and the local potentates, who were allies with Egypt, and was therefore compelled to carry out repeated campaigns to the region in the following years. The Babylonian Chronicles provide no evidence of stubborn resistance nor is it indicated by the historical reconstruction of the region in the years when Babylonian rule was being established there. It is more likely that the first campaigns (605–604 B.C.E.) were intended to establish Babylonian rule in Ḫatti-land. The next campaigns (602–601 B.C.E.) were intended to prepare the ground for an invasion of Egypt. It was only the failure of the invasion of Egypt that aroused a temporary wave of anti-Babylonian unrest among the kingdoms in the southern Levant—unrest that was based on hope in the imminent return of Egypt.

15. I accept the opinion of the scholars who link the date of the occupation of Ashkelon in the month of Kislev with the emergency assembly in Jerusalem "in the fifth year of Jehoiakim, son of Josiah, king of Judah, in the ninth month"; see discussion and bibliography below.

and much plunder were seized, and the city itself was razed to the ground.[16] This may have been the time when the territory of Ashkelon was annexed to Ashdod and, thus, there is evidence for the one change that the Babylonians made in the administrative division of the territories that they found in Syria–Palestine.[17] One can assume that the fate of Ashkelon was singular and exceptional[18] and that the Babylonians quickly and easily took control of all Ḫatti-land.[19] That

16. See the Babylonian Chronicle BM 21946, lines 18–20; Wiseman 1956: 28, 68–69; Grayson 1975a: 20, 100. On the debate about the name *Ashkelon* in the Babylonian Chronicles, see Hyatt 1956a: 280; Wiseman 1985:23; and Stager 1996: 72* n. 1. Clear archaeological evidence of the destruction of Ashkelon by the Babylonians has been preserved; see Stager 1996: 61*– 74*. The excavations suggest that there was a direct connection between Ashkelon and Egypt, and the evidence might even indicate an Egyptian presence in the city (pp. 68*–69*). The city remained devastated throughout the sixth century B.C.E. and was rebuilt only during the Persian Period. For bibliography on this subject, see Katzenstein 1994: 41. On the connection between Habakkuk 1–2 and the events of this year, see Cannon 1925: 62–90; Kaufman 1957–60: 360– 68; Miller and Hayes 1986: 406; Ahlström 1993: 782, with further literature. On the words of the Greek poet Alcaeus on the homecoming of his brother Antimenidas, who was a Greek mercenary in the service of the Babylonian army in the war against Ashkelon, see Quinn 1961: 19– 20. The sons of Aga, king of Ashkelon, are mentioned in a Babylonian document from the 13th year of Nebuchadrezzar's reign (592 B.C.E.; Weidner 1939: chart I, line 4; chart III, line 6). A settlement called *Iš-qal-lu-nu* (Ashkelon) existed near Nippur and is mentioned in the Murashu archive. It was apparently the site where exiles from Ashkelon were settled in the days of Nebuchadrezzar II (Tadmor 1966: 102 n. 62; Zadok 1978b: 61; Oded 1979: 25 n. 34).

17. The archaeological evidence portrays a situation in which Ashkelon remained desolate until the beginning of the Persian Period, and it is known that during this period it was part of the province of Ashdod. Although there is no explicit information on this, it is likely that the political situation in the Persian Period is a legacy of the administrative structure instituted by Nebuchadrezzar after the city was captured. Still, one may assume that the historical reality of the Persian Period is the product of slow, prolonged geopolitical processes of which we have no information and which are not based on official Babylonian practice.

18. This is contra the opinion summarized by Vanderhooft 1999: 82–83, who argues that Nebuchadrezzar systematically destroyed Ashkelon, Ekron, Ashdod, Timna, and other cities of Philistia and adjacent areas. There is no historical support for this opinion, and I reject the attempt to assign the destruction of these cities to a single short time-span and to reconstruct the Babylonian policy in this region, as different from the Assyrian policy, on that basis. The disappearance of Greek pottery from the coastal area of Palestine and from the Phoenician coast is a well-known fact in the archaeological record; in contrast to Vanderhooft's opinion (pp. 83–86, with previous literature), it is not connected with increased trade between the Aegean region and Egypt. It would be preferable to interpret the Greek pottery found at Meṣad Ḥashavyahu, as well as at Ekron, Ashkelon, and Timna, as evidence of the presence of Greek mercenaries in the service of the Egyptian army (Fantalkin 2000: 66–70; 2001: 137–47). In this light, it is not surprising that this pottery disappeared from the region after it was conquered by the Babylonians. Some of the Greek mercenaries were deported to Babylon, but it appears that most of them moved to the Nile Delta region, where Greek pottery dating throughout most of the sixth century B.C.E. has been discovered.

19. It is hard to accept Gitin's claim (1998: 276 and n. 2) that connects the destruction of Ekron with this period. Gitin's previous hypothesis (Dothan and Gitin 1994: 4; Gitin 1997: 98–99), that the city was destroyed in 603 B.C.E., has been abandoned in light of Naʾaman's interpretation of the chronicle for 603 (1992: 41–44, Gitin 1998: 276 n. 2, and see below). Note that the destruction of Ekron is not documented in the Babylonian Chronicles, and 603 B.C.E.

the conquest occurred with so little trouble may be explained by the extreme weakness of the small kingdoms that existed in the region and the absence of any counterbalance to Babylonian power after Egypt withdrew. In any event, at the beginning of 603 B.C.E., when Nebuchadrezzar returned to Babylon, his armies were positioned at the gates of Egypt, and he could have begun planning the next stage in the establishment of his Empire—the conquest of Egypt and the elimination of the only enemy who could threaten him.

There are no accounts of Babylonian activity in Judah, Samaria, or Transjordan from the era when Babylon established its rule over Ḥatti-land. It seems that all of the kings of Transjordan, the Phoenician coast, and Philistia capitulated to Nebuchadrezzar during the second half of 604 B.C.E., and it appears that, at this same time, Judah was also subjugated by Babylon (on this subject, see the discussion below). We may assume that the Babylonians believed that they could trust the loyalty of the small kingdoms that existed in Judah and in Transjordan, and they preferred to leave in place the administrative organization that they had found when they arrived on the scene. One of the main expressions of this policy was leaving Jehoiakim, king of Judah, on the throne, even though he had been appointed by Egypt only five years prior.

2.1.2. Judah's Enslavement by Babylon (604 B.C.E.)

> In his days Nebuchadnezzar, king of Babylon, marched forth, and Jehoiakim became his vassal. (2 Kgs 24:1)

The beginning of the Babylonian-Egyptian struggle for control of Syria–Palestine (609 B.C.E.) symbolizes the beginning of the decline of the Judean kingdom as it headed toward destruction. This decline was the result of the small kingdom's location in the struggle between great empires. But it was also the outcome of the reckless and improvident policy of the last kings of Judah and of political and religious turmoil among various sectors of the Jerusalem

---

of all years is the least logical for the city to have been destroyed. According to the historical reconstruction, 601 or 600 B.C.E. are better possibilities (James 1991: 717; Naʾaman 1992: 41–43). Another hypothesis is possible: the city was conquered only in 599/598 B.C.E., when Babylonia reestablished itself firmly in all of the southern part of Palestine (parallel to the Babylonian campaign against Jerusalem). In any case, because Ekron and Ashkelon are not mentioned in the list from the 7th year of Nebuchadrezzar (598–597 B.C.E.), a list that mentions Ashdod and Gaza, this year is the *terminus ad quem* for the destruction of the city (Naʾaman 2000: 40–41). On the letter of Adon, the king of Ekron, to Pharaoh, in which Adon requests Egyptian assistance in resisting the approaching Babylonian army, see Porten 1981: 36–52. For other opinions—that Adon was the king of Aphek, Gaza, Ashdod, Ashkelon, Lachish, or even Tyre and Sidon—see Porten 1981 50–52; Wiseman 1991: 231 and n. 21; Katzenstein 1994: 41 and n. 49. For an extensive bibliography of the first 15 years of research on the papyrus (J.86984 = 3483), see Fitzmyer 1965: 42 n. 1.

elite. The events that took place in Judah immediately after the killing of Josiah at Megiddo,[20] apparently at the time that Necho II went to the assistance of Aššur-uballiṭ II in his attempt to reconquer Ḫarran (June/July 609 B.C.E.), signal the beginning of the decline.[21] There is no information about the circumstances leading up to the anointing of Shalum-Jehoahaz (2 Kgs 23:30b),[22] the younger son of Josiah,[23] or the preference for him over his brother. Despite this lack of information, it is likely that this act reflected a national-activist trend in the circle of those who were not willing to accept Egyptian hegemony.[24] Support for this assumption may be found in the response by Necho II. Upon his return from Ḫarran three months after Josiah's death (August/September 609 B.C.E.),[25]

---

20. The only information on this event provided by the Bible is the death of Josiah at the hands of Pharaoh Necho, king of Egypt, when the latter came to the assistance of the king of Assyria on the Euphrates River (2 Kgs 23:29; Cogan and Tadmor 1988: 291). For a summary of the historical discussion and a consideration of the problems that arise from the nature of the description, see Cogan and Tadmor 1988: 301; Naʾaman 1991a: 53–55; Ahlström 1993: 766–67. In this context, one must consider the uniformity of the closing formulas in the book of Kings: in every case, at the end of a dynasty in Israel when the king was murdered by a contender to the throne, the closing formula is limited to a reference to the rest of the king's deeds and actions and the description of his burial and the accession of his heir is missing (1 Kgs 15:31–32; 16:14, 20; 2 Kgs 15:11–12, 15, 26, 31). In Judah, there are no parallels to this, and in the only case when a king is killed by another king (Ahaziah, who is killed by Jehu), the closing formula is missing and the description is limited to the transportation of his body to Jerusalem, in language similar to that which describes the bearing of Josiah's body (2 Kgs 9:27–28). In my opinion, the author (Dtr²; see the discussion in chap. 5) was familiar with the description of the death of Ahaziah, and he used the closing formula from the description of Ahaziah's death to describe the death of Josiah. On this subject, see the comment by Halpern and Vanderhooft 1991: 195, and see their more extensive discussion on the subject, 1991: 214–15.

21. On the Egyptian-Assyrian battle against the Babylonian foothold in Ḫarran, see the discussion in §1.3 (pp. 19–20). See the description in the Babylonian Chronicle BM 21901, lines 66–68 (Gadd 1923: 36, 41–42; Wiseman 1956: 19, 62–63; Grayson 1975a: 19, 96). On the date of the event at Megiddo based on a computation of the time when the Egyptian army appeared at Harran, see Malamat 1950: 219–20; 1968: 139–40; 1983: 235, and n. 30; Galil 1996: 115–16, with further literature.

22. On the anointing of kings in cases of dispute, compare 1 Sam 10:1; 15:1, 17; 16:3, 12, 13; 2 Sam 2:4, 7; 3:39; 5:3, 17; 12:7; 19:11; 1 Kgs 1:4, 39, 45; 5:15; 19:15, 16; 2 Kgs 9:3, 6, 12. On this subject, see Liver 1959b: 51–53; Malamat 1983: 250 and n. 14; Cogan and Tadmor 1988: 291.

23. Compare 2 Kgs 23:31 with v. 36 and 1 Chr 3:15, and see proposals by Albright 1932a: 92; Liver 1959: 6–7; Rudolph 1955: 28; Malamat 1983: 250–51; Miller and Hayes 1986: 402; Cogan and Tadmor 1988: 305; Seitz 1989: 72–73, 87 and n. 195; Ahlström 1993: 767.

24. Although this trend reflects a continuation of the events preceding the death of Josiah, it is doubtful that this can be regarded as an anti-Egyptian, pro-Babylonian trend, as has been assumed by, e.g., Malamat 1968: 140; 1982: 141; 1983: 251; Cogan and Tadmor 1988: 304; but in contrast see Naʾaman 1991a: 56; Seitz 1989: 68–102; Katzenstein 1993: 184.

25. The brief biblical description of the three months of Jehoahaz's rule and the appointment of Jehoiakim by the Egyptians accords with the information in the Babylonian Chronicle from the 17th year of Nabopolassar (BM 21901, lines 66–75; see the discussion in §1.3, pp. 19–20), which notes that the Egyptian army fought alongside the Assyrians over the city of Ḫarran in the month of Tammuz 609 B.C.E. The battle ended after three months (Ululu 609 B.C.E.),

Necho II deported Jehoahaz to Egypt.[26] In his place, he appointed Jehoahaz's older brother Eliakim, whose name was changed to Jehoiakim,[27] and levied heavy tribute on Judah.[28] Against this backdrop, it is reasonable to assume that Jehoiakim began to count the days of his rule from the time when Josiah died, three months before he ascended the throne.[29]

There is no information about what happened in Judah during the first four years of Jehoiakim's reign. During these years, Egypt established its control over Syria–Palestine in preparation for the decisive battle with the Babylonians over control of the banks of the Euphrates. The proximity of the kingdom of Judah to Egypt and the latter's control over the region did not allow the small kingdom

---

with no decisive result, and when the Babylonians came to the aid of the city, the Assyrians and Egyptians withdrew.

26. See the description in 2 Kgs 23:33a, 34b and see the harsh prophecy of Jeremiah (22:10–12) about Shallum, i.e., Jehoahaz (compare with 1 Chr 3:15). On this subject, see also Avigad 1969: 9; Cogan and Tadmor 1988: 303. It is reasonable to assume that Jehoahaz went to Riblah to obtain Egyptian approval for his reign (Malamat 1968: 140–41; 1983: 252). Necho's response is logical, for by imprisoning Jehoahaz and appointing Jehoiakim king (whose personal loyalty was thereby guaranteed), he made his authority supreme in Judah. On this subject, compare also the allusion in 1 Esd 1:36 to Jehoiakim's part in deporting Jehoahaz (Myers 1974: 30–32). This appears to be a later interpretation of events, and it is doubtful that it can be seen as reliable historical evidence, as claimed, for example, by Scharbert 1967: 128 and Malamat 1982: 141; 1983: 252.

27. On the significance of the change of Eliakim's name, see Bickerman 1979–80: 80–81. See the description in 2 Kgs 23:34a, where the author dismisses Jehoahaz's months of rule and emphasizes: "Then Pharaoh Necho made Eliakim, son of Josiah, king to succeed Josiah, his father." In Jer 1:2–3, too, Jehoahaz is not mentioned among the kings of Judah in whose time Jeremiah prophesied; however, in 22:11, Shallum (Jehoahaz) is mentioned as "king of Judah who succeeded his father, Josiah, on the throne" (and compare also with 1 Chr 3:15). On this subject, see also Montgomery 1951: 550–51; Malamat 1968: 140 and n. 7; 1983: 253; Cogan and Tadmor 1988: 304.

28. On this tribute, see Montgomery 1951: 550–52; Cogan and Tadmor 1988: 304; in contrast, see the evaluation by Malamat 1983: 252 n. 19; Miller and Hayes 1986: 402. On the way in which this episode was described, see the evaluation by Naʾaman 1994b: 67–69, who rightly disclaims the historical significance that Malamat and Miller and Hayes find in the description, attributing it to the author's covert criticism of Jehoiakim. On the features of the writing and tendencies of the author (Dtr²), see the discussion following, in chap. 5.

29. If so, then the time of the beginning of Jehoiakim's reign was during the month of Sivan or early Tammuz (June/July 609 B.C.E.) and not at the end of Elul or during Tishri (August/September 609 B.C.E.), when he officially ascended the throne. This date causes great difficulty for those who regard the 1st of Tishri as the beginning of the new year for kings because, if a king is appointed on the 1st of Tishri 608 B.C.E. as the beginning of his reign, a contradiction with Jer 46:2 results, and if one counts the beginning of his reign as the 1st of Tishri 609 B.C.E., a contradiction with 2 Kgs 23:36 results (and Jehoiakim must be ascribed 12 rather than 11 years of rule). With regard to this difficulty, see the extended discussion by Malamat (1983: 245–47), who despite this, prefers the "Tishri system"; see also the critique by Galil 1991: 14; 1996: 112–13, with further bibliography. In this study, I use the "late dating system," in which the beginning of the year is fixed at the 1st of Nissan, despite the known difficulties in this system. For a summary of these difficulties, see Galil 1991: 7–10; 1996: 108–18, with further bibliography.

any political or military leeway, and it is probable that Jehoiakim had no choice but to remain loyal to Egypt.[30]

The great turning point of 605 B.C.E., when the armies of Nebuchadrezzar defeated the Egyptian army at Carchemish and broke through to Syria, made waves in Judah.[31] It seems that, at this stage, Egypt's rule was also challenged in the other parts of Syria–Palestine. Although we do not have enough information about political activities in Jerusalem and the various approaches advocated by the Judean kingdom's leadership, it is reasonable to assume that there were different opinions about supporting Egypt or supporting Babylon. This makes the words of Jeremiah (25:1–14) all the more striking, words spoken even before the completion of the Babylonian takeover of Ḥatti-land. Jeremiah prophesies that the coming onslaught by Babylon will be "against this land and against its inhabitants and against all these people round about" (v. 9), as well as that the enslavement by Babylon was to last 70 years (v. 11). This he presents as punishment from God: "But you would not listen to me, says the LORD, that you might provoke me to anger with the work of your hands to your own hurt" (v. 7).[32] The prophet elaborates on this by saying that the people and the nation have no free will, and they must submit and accept the Babylonian yoke.[33] It is likely that the prophet did not intend Judah to take *any* activist course, supporting either of the parties, but instead advocated that the people accept whoever God chose to rule over the country and that they reconcile themselves to this fate. These words were directed against other voices that were probably being heard at this stage and that would grow louder over the years; the most distinct of these called for resisting Babylon and supporting Egypt. The only evidence of this is found in Jeremiah's prophecy (2:36): "How very cheaply you regard it to alter your course! But you will be disappointed by Egypt just as you were by Assyria."[34]

---

30. In my opinion, the prophecy/admonition of Jeremiah that contains a description of the building of a new, luxurious palace (22:14–15) should be assigned to this period. The emphasis on the fact that Jehoiakim "panels it [= his palace] with cedar, and paints it with vermilion" might attest to commercial ties with the Phoenician coast, and it is doubtful that this could be attributed to the turbulent period after the Babylonian takeover of Ḥatti-land.

31. The prophecy of Jeremiah (46:1–12), if dated to this year, describes the strong impression made by the Babylonian defeat of the Egyptians. On the date of this prophecy and its historical background, see the discussion in §2.1.1 (pp. 37–38 and n. 3).

32. On this prophecy, see the discussion by Thompson 1980: 509–14; Holladay 1986: 661–69; Hoffman 2001: 490–92, with further bibliography.

33. Jeremiah repeats this viewpoint many times, both in speaking to the nation and its leaders (chap. 21; 37:6–11; 38:2 and more) and in speaking to the king (37:17; 38:17–23, and more).

34. Bright (1965: 18), Thompson (1980: 185–87), and others attributed this prophecy to the days of Josiah, when Egypt supported Assyria against Babylon. However, I am of the opinion that v. 36 should be seen as evidence of a stage after Assyria's final disappearance, when Egypt remained the sole ruler of the entire region. On these matters, see Holladay 1986: 111–12; Hoffman 2001: 128–27; and see also the discussion below.

Thus, we can assume that the subjugation of Judah to Babylon took place during the great Babylonian campaign into Ḫatti-land in the second half of 604 B.C.E. (Wiseman 1956: 28; 1985: 23; Oded 1966: 102–7; Miller and Hayes 1986: 406; Cogan and Tadmor 1988: 308; Ahlström 1993: 781). Neither the attempt by scholars to date this later, in 603 B.C.E.,[35] nor the proposal to date it back to 605 B.C.E.[36] is sufficiently supported by the evidence. Support for the proposition that Judah came under Babylon's domination in 604 B.C.E. may be found in 2 Kgs 24:1, "In his days [= Jehoiakim] Nebuchadnezzar, king of Babylon,

---

35. Pavlovsky and Vogt 1964: 345–46 supported this proposal, as did Malamat 1968: 141–42; 1975b: 131, 144; 1983: 254 n. 24, 257–58, with further literature in n. 34. For a critique of this proposal, see Naʾaman 1992. It must be emphasized that the events of Nebuchadrezzar's 2nd year (603 B.C.E.) are unclear and in dispute, primarily because of damage to the tablet (Wiseman 1956: 28–29, 70). On the basis of the context surrounding the damaged portion of the text (BM 21946, lines 21–23), Wiseman reconstructed the campaign to Ḫatti-land (1956: 29, 70–71), conscious of the problematic nature of his reconstruction. Most scholars have accepted his reading unchallenged; see, for example, the reconstruction proposed by Grayson (1975a: 20, 100). Some have reconstructed the name of the city besieged by the Babylonians on the basis of Wiseman's reconstruction (line 23) and as a result have hypothesized that the date of Judah's subjugation to Babylon was that same year. On the various proposed reconstructions of the cities besieged by Nebuchadrezzar in 603, see Malamat 1983: 258 n. 35; Katzenstein 1994: 42; Wiseman himself has reconsidered his position and has tried to show that the campaign was directed against Phoenicia (1985: 24–29 and n. 166–169). Naʾaman has suggested a different reconstruction of the text, according to which there was a campaign in 603 to the Euphrates River, centered on a siege of the city of Kimuḫu (1992; see there more arguments in favor of my reconstruction).

36. Worschech (1987: 57–63) supported this proposal, and see also the qualified opinion of Hyatt (1956: 280). However, dating Judah's subjugation to 605 does not accord with the description in the Babylonian Chronicles, which say that Nebuchadrezzar did not go beyond Hamath during this year. Jeremiah's prophecy (46:2–12), which contains no allusion to the subjugation of Judah to Babylon in 605 B.C.E., also supports the historical reconstruction that places the Babylonians in central Syria, their armies not yet having penetrated southern Syria–Palestine. The idea that Judah was subjugated to Babylon in 605 is based on slight support from later accounts, whose chronological credibility is dubious. The chief among these accounts is the beginning of the book of Daniel (1:1–2) where, "in the third year of the reign of Jehoiakim, king of Judah, Nebuchadrezzar, king of Babylon, came to Jerusalem and laid siege to it. The LORD gave into his hand Jehoiakim, king of Judah, and some of the vessels of the temple of God." On the difficulties with the date "in the third year," see Montgomery 1927: 113–16; Efron 1974: 466–68. For suggested revisions, see Montgomery 1927; Young 1949: 268; Delcor 1971: 59–60; Clines 1972: 20–21; Efron 1974: 470–77; Malamat 1983: 256; Collins 1993: 130–33, with further literature. The attempt to link this view with the tradition in Josephus (*Ant.* 10.222; *Ag. Ap.* 1.19, 136), who reports that in the battle of Carchemish, the Babylonians took captives from among the Jews, Phoenicians (Canaanites), Syrians (Arameans), and peoples of Egypt (other nations who were under Egyptian rule), seems problematic, for in *Ant.* 10.86 Josephus describes a very unlikely historical situation: by this time, the Babylonians had already "occupied all Syria, with the exception of Judaea, as far as Pelusium" (and see on this subject, Efron 1974: 468). Burstein's (1978: 27) view that, if there is any historical foundation for this tradition, it is an allusion to soldiers from Judah, Syria, and Phoenicia who served in the Egyptian army during the battle of Carchemish, seems acceptable. On this subject, see Oded 1966: 104–5; Worschech 1987: 57–63.

marched forth, and Jehoiakim became his vassal for three years." From information in the Babylonian Chronicles, which notes that Babylon's control over
Ḥatti-land was undermined after the failed invasion of Egypt in Kislev of Nebuchadrezzar's 4th year (November/December 601 B.C.E.), it seems that Judah was
indeed subject to Babylon for a period of exactly three years.[37]

Evidence of the exact timing of Judah's capitulation is found in Jeremiah's
prophecy (36:9–29). According to the description in 36:9 (and compare v. 22),
a general fast day was proclaimed in Jerusalem "in the ninth month of the fifth
year of Jehoiakim, son of Josiah, king of Judah" (November/December 604
B.C.E.).[38] Jeremiah's words, a synopsis of which appears in v. 29 ("The king of
Babylon will surely come and will destroy this land and exterminate from it
both man and beast") aroused great fear among the people's leaders ("when they
heard all the words, they turned to one another in fear," v. 16),[39] and the emphasis is on the fact that "neither the king nor any of his courtiers who heard all
these words showed any fear or rent their clothes" (v. 24). It is probable that at
this stage the news of the razing of Ashkelon had not yet reached Judah and

---

37. It is difficult to accept the attempt by Malamat (1983: 258) and Miller and Hayes
(1986: 406) to interpret the description of three years of subjugation in 2 Kgs 24:1 as evidence
that Jehoiakim paid tribute three times to Babylon (fall or winter of 603 to fall or winter of 601
B.C.E.). See a different reconstruction by Katzenstein (1973: 250) of the payment of tribute
three times in the spring of 603, 602, and 601 B.C.E. The biblical description accords with the
reconstruction that emerges from the Babylonian Chronicles, and it is sufficient to reconstruct
three years of subjugation to Babylon between Kislev or Tevet 604 B.C.E. (the 5th year of Jehoiakim's rule) and Kislev or Tevet 601 B.C.E. (the 8th year of his rule).

38. The LXX reads "in the eighth year of Jehoiakim," and many scholars tend to accept
Lohfink's opinion (1978: 324–28) that the LXX is reliable on this point. See the summary of
the main arguments in: Baumann 1968: 350–73; Holladay 1989: 253, 255–57. Nonetheless,
the linguistic arguments are not clear-cut, and the historical consideration, that the year 601
B.C.E. is better suited to the hopes raised by Jehoiakim for liberation from the Babylonian yoke,
do not accord with the chronological reconstruction of events. From the Babylonian Chronicles we learn that, in Kislev, when the assembly in Jerusalem took place, the Babylonian army
headed by Nebuchadrezzar left for the hinterland of Egypt, and no one in Ḥatti-land had any
reason to believe that this invincible army would be doomed to fail and to return home after
suffering a serious defeat. Even if the Babylonian defeat and retreat took place in the same
month, it is difficult to imagine that the leaders of Judah would have succeeded within such a
short period of time in holding an assembly of "all of the people coming from the cities of Judah to Jerusalem" (v. 9, and see Thompson 1980: 623 on the LXX). In any event, it is not reasonable to think that Jehoiakim would have had the temerity to revolt against Babylon at this
time, before the Egyptians had established themselves in Palestine. In this light, it seems that
Kislev 604 B.C.E. is the more appropriate time when, on the eve of the surrender of Ashkelon,
many people in Judah already understood that there was no choice but to accept the Babylonian yoke. For the view that dates this prophecy to the 5th year of Jehoiakim's rule and the surrender of Jerusalem to between Kislev and Shebat of the same year, see, e.g., Malamat 1983:
257; Wiseman 1985: 23; Miller and Hayes 1986: 405; Hayes and Hooker 1988: 90–91; Redford
1992: 455; Hoffman 2001: 664.

39. On the differences between the MT and LXX, see Thompson 1980: 624, 626; Holladay
1989: 251, 258.

that Jehoiakim quickly surrendered as soon as he heard of the Babylonians' fierce determination—between the month of Kislev and the time that Nebuchadrezzar returned to Babylon, about two months later (Hayes and Hooker 1988: 90–91).

As part of his preservation of the geopolitical structure that he found in place when he conquered the region, Nebuchadrezzar chose to leave Jehoiakim in power, even though he had been crowned by Necho II of Egypt only a few years previously. This step, which for the Babylonians was apparently not unusual, reflected the assumption that a king who was realistic enough to accept the Egyptian yoke would also be realistic enough to submit to Babylonian authority. The Babylonians probably hoped to preserve stability in Judah by this course of action and expected that the local potentates' gratitude would guarantee their fidelity to the new Empire. One must assume that, like all of the kings of the region, Jehoiakim pledged his personal fealty to Nebuchadrezzar, agreeing to fulfill all of the Babylonian demands and to pay heavy tribute.[40]

*   *   *

The total withdrawal of Egypt from all of its holdings in Ḫatti-land and the rapid Babylonian takeover of the entire region, accompanied by a simultaneous message to the kingdoms of the region by their destruction of Ashkelon, left the small kingdoms along the coast and inland no room at all to maneuver. The first three years of Babylonian rule in the region appear to have been peaceful, and although there is no information on Judah during this time, it appears that Jehoiakim remained loyal ("and Jehoiakim was his servant for three years," 2 Kgs 24:1). Nevertheless, there is no doubt that it was as clear to Babylon as to Judah and the other kingdoms of the region that the major test for the Babylonians was yet to come. Until they had subdued the Egyptians, they would never sustain their rule in Ḫatti-land.

At this stage, the major characteristics of Babylonian rule in the region had begun to crystallize. Nebuchadrezzar left in place the administrative structures that had been established during Assyrian and Egyptian rule and conducted a policy of minimal intervention. In contrast to Assyrian custom, he did not practice two-way deportation of populations, nor is there any evidence that action was taken to develop the areas that were annexed (see Vanderhooft 1999: 110–12, with further literature). Even when the Babylonians sacked a major city (e.g., Ashkelon in 604 B.C.E.), they banished the economic, religious, and ruling elite but apparently left behind the rest of the population, while shifting the political and administrative center to an adjacent city (Ashdod?).

---

40. On this subject, see the discussion in Bickerman 1979–80: 69–85, particularly pp. 80–81. For a discussion of the oath of fealty made by the vassal kings to the kings of Assyria and Babylon, see Tsevat 1959: 199–204.

It may be that the Babylonians' need for raw materials and goods dictated their policy of annual campaigns, which were intended to collect the heavy tribute they exacted from subject kingdoms and provinces. In any event, it does not seem that at this stage Babylonian rule was rigid, and the small kingdoms that remained were able to retain internal freedom. Their major burden was the obligation to pay heavy taxes, probably accompanied by other obligations, such as provisioning the Babylonian army during its annual forays, ongoing provisioning of the auxiliary forces, and mustering troops for the Babylonian army as auxiliary forces.

*2.1.3. The Failure of the Babylonian Invasion of Egypt (Winter 601/600 B.C.E.)
and the Weakening of Control over Ḫatti-Land*

> *Then he turned and rebelled against him. (2 Kgs 24:1)*

Nebuchadrezzar's rule over Ḫatti-land was not assured as long as a strong Egypt remained. The chance of an Egyptian invasion was a constant threat to Babylonian rule and a potential catalyst for unrest and the formation of local pacts among the kingdoms that had an anti-Babylonian orientation. Nebuchadrezzar's goal was clear, and an attempt to follow Esarhaddon and Ashurbanipal in their campaigns to conquer Egypt was only a matter of time. Nebuchadrezzar set out on a preparatory expedition into Ḫatti-land at an unknown date during the 3rd year of his reign (between mid-April 602 and late March 601 B.C.E.), at which time he collected heavy tribute, which he may have needed in preparation for the forthcoming campaign.[41]

The campaign to invade Egypt took place in the month of Kislev (November/December 601 B.C.E.), a time that apparently was expressly chosen as the optimal season for crossing northern Sinai and invading the Nile Delta.[42] The

---

41. See the Babylonian Chronicle BM 21946, lines 3–4; Wiseman 1956: 28–29, 70–71; Grayson 1975a: 20, 101. In this section of the Chronicles (line 2), there is a reference to the younger brother of Nebuchadrezzar, Nabû-šumu-lišir, but this section is broken and it is not clear which events are connected with his name. Wiseman (1956: 28–29) originally ruled out the possibility of a revolt in Babylon at this time because immediately afterward there is a description of Nebuchadrezzar leaving for Ḫatti-land. However, Tyborowski (1996: 212) claimed, with justification, that, even after the revolt in the 10th year of his reign, the king set out for a campaign in Ḫatti-land. Wiseman later changed his mind (1985: 7) and posited that there was a conspiracy against Nebuchadrezzar, or that his brother died, but he did not connect these two events. Tyborowski (1996: 213–16) put forward the theory that, from that year onward Nebuchadrezzar had internal problems in Babylon that caused him to cut short his campaigns or to delay them; however, it is doubtful that there is enough support for this theory.

42. We may assume that Jeremiah's words (46:13–26) were spoken against this background: ". . . when Nebuchadrezzar, king of Babylon, was coming to attack the land of Egypt"; according to Jeremiah (vv. 25–26), "Look! I will punish Amon of No and Egypt and its gods, kings, Pharaoh, and those who trust in him; I will deliver them into the power of those who seek their

Babylonian Chronicle states that "the king of Egypt heard (about the Babylonian invasion) and mustered his army" in order to confront the Babylonians; the clash between the warring armies took place "in open battle."[43] Both sides "suffered severe losses" (inflicted major defeat upon each another; see the translation of Grayson 1975a: 101), and apparently it was Nebuchadrezzar's army that suffered the most and was forced to withdraw to Babylon without having achieved its purpose.[44]

The Egyptian success shows that their military might had not been exhausted after the defeat at Carchemish four years prior and that Babylonian superiority was not as remarkable as might have been presumed by their rapid takeover of all the territories of Ḫatti-land.[45] The Babylonian hold on the region was loosened, and Egypt was able to renew its influence on the region that had been under its exclusive control only five years earlier. This reconstruction is congruent with the testimony of Herodotus, who wrote that the Egyptians obtained a new right of entry into Philistia, taking advantage of the opportunity that presented itself and conquering Gaza.[46] This period seems to me to be the most appropriate for the superscription of Jeremiah's prophecy (47:1): "The word of the LORD that came to Jeremiah the prophet concerning the Philistines, before

---

lives, and into the power of Nebuchadrezzar king of Babylon, and his officers" (according to MT; see also Thompson 1980: 694–95; Holladay 1989: 324). See Hayes and Hooker 1988: 91; Redford 1992: 456–57. It is difficult to accept Holladay's dating of this text (1989: 328, 333) to the year 588 B.C.E., and it is also hard to accept the view of Rudolph (1947: 237), who places the prophecy in the year 605 B.C.E., similar to the prophecy in vv. 3–12. The attempt to date the prophecy to 568 B.C.E. also must be rejected (Malamat 1983: 239–40, and further literature in n. 36).

43. See the Babylonian Chronicle BM 21946, rev. line 6; Wiseman 1956: 29, 70–71; Grayson 1975a: 20, 101. Compare with Redford 1992: 458.

44. See the Babylonian Chronicle BM 21946, rev. line 7; Wiseman 1956: 28, 70–71; Grayson 1975a: 20, 101.

45. See Redford's summary (1992: 457–58) on the northeastern border of Egypt during the Saite Dynasty.

46. According to Herodotus (2.159) "[Necho] with his land army met and defeated the Syrians at Magdolus, taking the great Syrian city of Cadytis." The reliability of this tradition is not certain, but it fits well with the historical reconstruction of this period presented here. See Lipiński 1972; Katzenstein 1993: 184; 1994: 42–43; Cogan and Tadmor 1988: 308; Wiseman 1991: 232; Redford 1992: 458–59. On the identification of Cadytis as Gaza, see Albright 1934d: 58, no. 11. On the interpretation of the "Syrians" in Herodotus as referring to Babylonians, see Katzenstein 1983: 249–50. The mistaken identification of Magdolus with Megiddo, which has taken root in the thinking of many scholars, should be rejected. For a more detailed bibliography, see Lipiński 1972: 236 and n. 3. Lipiński (p. 236) and Oren (1984: 7–44) insist that Magdolus is a large city on the Egyptian border, at the terminus of the road that connects Egypt with Palestine. The description of Herodotus accords with the historical reconstruction based on Jer 47:1 (see below) regarding the time when Gaza was defeated by the Egyptian army. According to Lipiński, Herodotus's description can also be used as the basis for reconstructing the site of the battle. This information also attests to Gaza's importance as a central base for the Babylonian army facing the Egyptian border and to the importance of the overland road running through the southern coastal plain.

Pharaoh attacked Gaza,"[47] which seems well anchored in the historical reality of the winter of 601–600 B.C.E. Support for this historical reconstruction may be found in a description of Jehoiakim's revolt against Babylon, only three years after he was subjugated by Nebuchadrezzar (2 Kgs 24:1). It is hard to believe that a revolt of this sort would have been carried out without the support and backing of the Egyptians and, although there is no information about the events that took place at this time, if the Egyptians were able to return to a position of any influence in the region, it is doubtful that Jehoiakim would had any choice other than to cease paying the annual tribute to Babylon.[48]

The aborted invasion of Egypt severely impaired Babylon's military power; Babylon was forced to rejuvenate itself and to rearm the following year (between mid-March 600 and early April 599 B.C.E.).[49] It was only in the winter of the sixth year of Nebuchadrezzar's reign, between Kislev (December 599 B.C.E.) and Addaru (March 598 B.C.E.), that he began to reestablish his control over Hatti-land by means of raids against the desert nomads.[50] This evidence supports the idea that there was a break in the continuity of Babylonian rule over Palestine and a period when the area was subject to Egyptian influence, perhaps even actual Egyptian rule. Additional evidence of this is the fact that the Babylonian Chronicle emphasizes that only Nebuchadrezzar returned to Babylon at the end of his campaign in the month of Addaru; part of his army apparently remained in Syria to continue to strengthen its foothold in the region (Wiseman 1956: 32). We may assume, therefore, that all of these circumstances resulted in a situation in which, during the 7th year of Nebuchadrezzar's reign (between late March 598 B.C.E. and mid-April 597 B.C.E.), the Babylonians were able to

---

47. This verse is a late editor's comment; almost all of it is missing in the LXX, and its purpose was to explain the background to the prophecy in vv. 2–6. See the opinions of Bright 1965: 311–12; Thompson 1980: 696–97; Holladay 1989: 334, 337, with further literature; Hoffman 2001: 775–76. Many scholars reject its historical reliability or assign its historical context to other periods; see the opinions mentioned in Holladay 1989: 336–37. In contrast to these opinions, see the well-founded response of Katzenstein (1983: 249–51; 1994: 42–43), who argues that the most appropriate time for the prophecy was during the Babylonian withdrawal after its aborted invasion of Egypt (apparently at the beginning of 600 B.C.E.). It appears that accurate information was preserved in this editorial comment about the time after the failure of the Babylonian campaign against Egypt. On this subject, see also the opinion of Lipiński 1972: 239.

48. The circumstances of Jehoiakim's revolt were well understood by Josephus (*Ant.* 10.88), who, explaining the text in 2 Kings, wrote: "But in the third year, having heard that the Egyptians were marching against the Babylonian king, he (Jehoiakim) did not pay him tribute." On this subject, see also Katzenstein 1983: 249; 1993: 185.

49. According to the Babylonian Chronicles (BM 21946, rev. line 8), "In the fifth year the king of Akkad stayed in his own land and refitted his numerous horses and chariotry" (Wiseman 1956: 29, 31, 70–71; Grayson 1975a: 20, 101).

50. See the Babylonian Chronicle BM 21946, rev. lines 9–10; Wiseman 1956: 31–32, 70–71; Grayson 1975a: 20, 101. Compare also with Jeremiah's prophecy in 49:28–33. On this subject, see Eph'al 1982a: 170–72; Hayes and Hooker 1988: 91; Redford 1992: 459 n. 138, with further literature.

focus on establishing a stable government as far as the border of Egypt: "The king of Egypt did not leave his country any more, for the king of Babylon seized all that had belonged to the king of Egypt, from the Wadi of Egypt to the river Euphrates" (2 Kgs 24:7).

In the month of Kislev (between mid-December 598 and mid-January 597 B.C.E.), the Babylonian army campaigned into Ḫatti-land.[51] We can assume that Nebuchadrezzar established Babylonian rule over all of the region,[52] but the description in the Babylonian Chronicles focuses on the main target of this campaign—the conquest of the city of Judah (URU *ia-a-ḫu-du*), namely, Jerusalem, on the 2nd of Addaru (March 15/16, 597 B.C.E.).[53] The underpinning of Jehoiakim's revolt was his reliance on Egyptian support for Judah, which led him to expect the Egyptians to do battle with Babylon; but it is likely that Judah was not alone in the fray. The ultimate fate of Gaza (which had been defeated two years previously by the Egyptians) during this campaign is not known.[54] We also do not know if Ekron was defeated and razed at this time.[55]

The campaign in the winter of 598/597 B.C.E. was a continuation of the campaign of the previous year, the Babylonian goal being to consolidate its rule in the southern part of Ḫatti-land. This provides the background for the biblical description in 2 Kgs 24:2 of the invasion of Judah by auxiliary forces, which included bands of Chaldeans,[56] Arameans,[57] Moabites, and Ammonites.[58] Ac-

---

51. See the Babylonian Chronicle BM 21946 rev. line 11; Wiseman 1956: 32–33, 72–73; Grayson 1975a: 20, 102.

52. This is against the view of Wiseman (1956: 33), which has also been adopted by other scholars. The focus of the Babylonian Chronicle on Judah when it describes the campaign of 598/7 B.C.E. may be compared with the focus on Ashkelon in the description of the campaign of 604/3 B.C.E. In both descriptions, the emphasis is on the major objective of the campaign; however, it is doubtful that it was the only objective.

53. See the Babylonian Chronicles BM 21946, rev. line 12; Wiseman 1956: 33–35, 72–73; Grayson 1975a: 20, 102. See also Thiele 1951: 168; 1956: 22; Hayes and Hooker 1988: 92. The reference to the date when Jerusalem fell attests to the importance that this event held in the eyes of the authors of this Chronicle (Wiseman 1991: 232).

54. There were exiles from Gaza in Babylon, but the date of their deportation to Babylon is unknown (Zadok 1978b: 61; Eph'al 1978: 80). One possibility is that the Babylonians deported the residents of Gaza when Babylon conquered all of Philistia in 604 B.C.E., but it is even more reasonable to assume that the deportation took place when the Babylonians were reestablishing their rule in Philistia in the early sixth century B.C.E., after their influence in this region had been weakened following their failed invasion of Egypt (against Redford: 1992: 456).

55. See above (n. 19, pp. 41–42) the reference to the opinions of scholars who date the destruction of Ekron to 604 B.C.E. At the same time, there is much historical reason to date the destruction of Ekron to 598/597, when Babylon reestablished its dominion in the region.

56. On the appearance of Chaldeans in the Bible and in Mesopotamian sources, see Cogan and Tadmor 1988: 306, with further literature.

57. Some scholars prefer to read "Edom" rather than "Aram" here (Stade, Klosterman, Benziger, etc.; and see Burney 1903: 365; Montgomery 1951: 554), basing their opinions on the readings in some of the versions and the assumption that this reading supplements the reference to all of the Transjordanian kingdoms. But the combination of the Chaldean army and

cording to the author of the description (Dtr²), the sending of these bands was to punish Jehoiakim, who was the successor to Manasseh, the "sinner" among the last four kings of Judah.⁵⁹ Nonetheless, in terms of the historical reconstruction, it is likely that the invasion by the auxiliaries preceded the arrival of the Babylonian army and forced some of the residents of Judah to flee outlying areas for Jerusalem.⁶⁰ Only at a later stage did the main Babylonian force arrive in Judah, perhaps with the intention of accepting the king's capitulation. "And Nebuchadrezzar, the king of Babylon, came against the city, while his servants were (still) besieging it" (2 Kgs 24:11).⁶¹

The description in 2 Kings 24 indicates that, from the beginning of the campaign against Jerusalem sometime in the month of Kislev until the capitulation of the city on the 2nd of Addaru, no more than 3 months had elapsed. Thus, we may assume that the Babylonian campaign was intended from the

the Aramean army in Jer 35:11, in a prophecy that is connected to the days of the suppression of Jehoiakim's revolt, supports the MT. Aramean tribes lived close to Babylon, and it is not surprising that Aramean forces fought together with the Babylonian army. A similar reference to the Chaldean and Aramean forces appears in Assyrian texts. On this subject, see also Montgomery (1951: 552; although in my opinion his historical reconstruction should be dismissed); Cogan and Tadmor 1988: 306. For the role of Edom, see Cogan and Tadmor 1988: 306; Wiseman 1991: 232; Ahlström 1993: 779–81, 785 n. 3.

58. We may assume that this was the context for Jeremiah's prophecy in 12:14 (Holladay 1986: 390–91); also compare 35:11 (1986: 31, 246). On the other hand, we cannot accept the LXX version of 2 Chr 36:5, where battalions from Samaria are added to the force, or Malamat's reconstruction (1982: 143; 1983: 260), which is based on this description.

59. This is the reason that, according to the biblical description, the one who sent the battalions against Jehoiakim was God ("And the LORD sent against him . . ."), and they were sent to Judah "to destroy him." Jehoiakim's fate is connected linguistically and conceptually to the sealing of Judah's fate, following the sins of Manasseh (2 Kgs 21:11–16), and has great significance for understanding the author's intentions (Cogan and Tadmor 1988: 307, in contrast to the view of Malamat 1983: 259–60). Nonetheless, we must compare the arrival of the battalions (24:2) with the description of the arrival of the Babylonian army and the beginning of the siege against Jerusalem (v. 10). On the author's ideology and its significance for the nature of the description, see Lipschits 2002: 1–23, with further literature; see also there my comments on the role of Jehoiakim in the description.

60. This is the background for Jeremiah's prophecy in chap. 35, which, according to its superscription, was delivered in the days of Jehoiakim. The speech of the Rechabites (Heb. *bêt hārēkābîm*), "But when Nebuchadrezzar, king of Babylon, invaded our land we said, 'Come, let us go to Jerusalem, out of the way of the armies of the Chaldeans and the Arameans,' so we are living in Jerusalem" (v. 11), corresponds exactly to the historical situation in 2 Kgs 24:2.

61. One could hypothesize that the different ways in which the author describes the coming of the battalions against Jehoiakim (2 Kgs 24:2) and the Babylonian siege of Jerusalem (v. 10), separated by a mere eight verses, was intended to solve a historiographical problem. By the author's reasoning, Jehoiakim was destined for an appropriate punishment. Although he was characterized as the most sinful of the last four kings of Judah, he was also the only one of them who died in Jerusalem (v. 6) and was not punished by being deported by a foreign potentate (compare the fate of Jehoahaz described in 2 Kgs 23:34, the fate of Jehoiachin described in 24:12–16, and the fate of Zedekiah described in 25:6–7). On the author's ideology, see Lipschits 2002b.

very beginning to suppress Jehoiakim's revolt. The king was still alive when the Babylonians planned the campaign, and he died either close to the beginning of it or after the Babylonian force departed for Jerusalem.[62] Research offers several scenarios of Jehoiakim's death, but it appears that his death was not accompanied by any unusual circumstances. He died after a reign of 11 years and was buried in Jerusalem, precisely on the eve of the campaign by Nebuchadrezzar to suppress the revolt and destroy the city.[63] His death saved the city from immediate devastation and gave the small kingdom another 11 years of existence.

Jehoiakim's son Jehoiachin ascended the throne in his father's place.[64] According to the description in 2 Kgs 24:12, his first and only act as king of Judah was to surrender to the Babylonians: "Jehoiachin, king of Judah, surrendered to the king of Babylon."[65] Considering the fact that it was not Jehoiachin who re-

---

62. For a detailed discussion of the subject, see Lipschits 2002b, with further literature. The chronological information indicates that when Nebuchadrezzar planned his campaign Jehoiakim was still alive (Wiseman 1956: 33). His death took place just before the Babylonians' departure for the campaign or immediately after they set out, because, according to the description in 2 Kgs 24:8, his son Jehoiachin ruled for 3 months. The description in 2 Chr 36:9, which states that he ruled for 3 months and 10 days, must be rejected as a textual corruption (Green 1982a: 105; Redford 1992: 459; Lipschits 2002b: 16–18, with further literature). In this light, we must also reject the attempt by Thiele (1951: 167–68; 1956: 22) to fix the date of Jehoiachin's accession to the throne as the 22nd of Ḥeshvan (December 8, 598 b.c.e.). On the premise that Jehoiachin ascended the throne immediately after his father died and ruled for 3 months, this means that Jehoiakim died at the beginning of the month of Kislev. It is doubtful that we can be any more precise. It is hard to accept the view of Green (1982a: 106) that the first 2 days of the month of Addaru, before the fall of Jerusalem, were considered the 3rd month of Jehoiakim's reign. If this were so, Jehoiakim died during the month of Tebeth. Furthermore, we must reject Noth's hypothesis (1958: 138) that Nebuchadrezzar set out on his campaign after Jehoiakim's death, with the aim of crowning a king of his choosing in Judah. The Babylonians could not have organized themselves within a few days for a campaign as complex and extended as this. It is also doubtful that the death of the rebellious king would have been sufficient reason for Nebuchadrezzar and his army to leave Babylon. Consequently, it seems that the Babylonians set out in Kislev for a well-planned campaign that was intended to suppress a revolt in Judah. This was the first time that they could embark on such a campaign, and it was essential for reestablishing their dominion in Ḥatti-land, which had been in a state of turmoil ever since the Babylonian hold over it had been challenged following the failed Egyptian campaign.

63. For a discussion and analysis of the sources and the different versions of the story of Jehoiakim's death, a historical reconstruction of the event, and further literature, see Lipschits 2002b. For a different view, reconstructing Jehoiakim's death according to the prophecies of Jeremiah, see Smit 1994: 46–56.

64. On the various forms of the name in the Bible, see Liver 1959: 7, and n. 15. According to 2 Kgs 24:8 Jehoiachin was 18 years of age when he became king (Albright 1942b: 53; Myers 1965c: 218; Green 1982a: 104–5). The description in 2 Chr 36:9, according to which he was 8 years old when he ascended the throne, is apparently textually corrupt and should be dismissed (Green 1982a: 105). Historically, too, this piece of information does not make sense, because when Jehoiachin went into exile 3 months later (2 Kgs 24:15), his wives were sent into exile together with him, and 5 years later his five sons are mentioned in a Babylonian text (Weidner 1939: 923–35). On this subject, see also the discussion below.

65. Compare with the grim prophecy of Jeremiah (22:24–30) regarding the fate of the deported king and the future of the royal seed. The language of the description of the capitulation

volted, we can understand why the Babylonians did not demolish Jerusalem and allowed Judah to remain as a subject kingdom, with a Davidic dynast on the throne.[66] They did not destroy Jerusalem, but for the first time since gaining control of Ḫatti-land, they actively interfered in the governance of Jerusalem, deported many of its residents, and took much plunder. It is probable that the Babylonians' intent was to stabilize their rule in Judah, and, from their point of view, these actions were the best method to achieve that goal.

2.1.4. The Babylonian Administration in Judah after the Surrender of Jerusalem (597 B.C.E.)

> He deported Jehoiachin to Babylonia. (2 Kgs 24:15)

Nebuchadrezzar left Jehoiakim on the throne after vanquishing Judah in 604 B.C.E.—an action that demonstrated realpolitik and his willingness not to deal harshly with the Judean kingdom and the Davidic line. Even after Jehoiakim's revolt and the disappointment caused by his lack of loyalty, he allowed the Davidic dynasty to remain on the throne. However, this time he intentionally impaired the kingdom's economic strength and deported part of the nation's social, religious, military, and economic elite.

According to 2 Kgs 24:17, Nebuchadrezzar appointed Mattaniah-Zedekiah[67] to be king of Judah instead of his exiled nephew.[68] This description parallels

---

in 2 Kgs 24:12a is problematic, for there is no parallel in the Bible for the use of the term יצא על 'went out on' in the sense of surrendering (compare with Gen 19:23; 41:45; 1 Kgs 8:44; 2 Kgs 12:13; Ps 81:6; Esth 1:17; 2 Chr 6:34). Given this difficulty, we may accept the evidence of some of the versions and hypothesize that there was a confusion of על and אל, as in the case of 23:29 (see Montgomery 1951: 558). The expression לצאת אל in the sense of 'surrender' is known in the Bible in various usages, primarily in the book of Jeremiah in the context of surrender to the king of Babylon (38:2, 17–18). In this regard, compare it with the expression in Jer 21:9: "whoever goes out and surrenders to the Chaldean who are besieging you."

66. See Montgomery 1951: 555. On this subject, see the historical reconstructions by Noth 1954: 136–39; Wiseman 1956: 32; Malamat 1968: 144–47; 1983: 260–62; Cogan and Tadmor 1988: 311.

67. On the names Mattaniah and Zedekiah, on the change of name, on the king's age, and on his familial relationship to Jehoiachin and Jehoiakim, see Montgomery 1951: 557–58; Liver 1959: 7–8; Cogan and Tadmor 1988: 312. On the name in the epigraphic finds from the end of the First Temple Period, see Tur-Sinai 1940: 12; Avigad 1986: 36, 74.

68. The comment in 2 Kgs 24:17 is linguistically and thematically parallel to 23:34, which contains a description of the coronation of Eliakim by the Egyptians and the change of his name to Jehoiakim. This parallelism is not coincidental: the author of the book of Kings wishes to link both events, precisely as he linked the deportation of Jehoahaz to Egypt with the exiling of Jehoiachin to Babylon. In this way, a paradigm is created in which both kings crowned in Judah without the approval of foreign rulers (Jehoahaz and Jehoiachin) are taken into exile after 3 months of rule, while the two kings appointed in their stead by foreign rulers (Jehoiakim and Zedekiah) ruled 11 years, revolted against the sovereign, and brought about terrible catastrophes: Jehoiakim brought about the exile of Jehoiachin, and Zedekiah brought about the destruction of Jerusalem.

what is written in the prophecy of Ezekiel (17:13), "And he [the king of Baby-
lon] took one of the seed royal and made a covenant with him and made him
enter into a treaty,"[69] and it also accords with the description in the Babylonian
Chronicle, which reports that Nebuchadrezzar appointed in Judah "a king of his
own choice (lit., heart)."[70] Behind the appointment were administrative considerations that reflected the Babylonian policy not to cause any unnecessary
trauma to the kingdom, to preserve stability of rule, and not to create a vacuum
that could quickly be filled by elements that the Babylonians would find harder
to control. Furthermore, as a practical matter, we can understand the coronation
of Zedekiah as a Babylonian attempt to put an end to the activity of the pro-
Egyptian (or at least anti-Babylonian) branch of the sons of Josiah. Zedekiah was
the last son of Josiah, full brother (also from the mother's side) of Jehoahaz. Josiah was put to death by Necho (2 Kgs 23:29), and Jehoahaz had been deported
by Necho to Egypt, where he died (2 Kgs 23:31b; 24:18b). Nebuchadrezzar
hoped to secure the loyalty of the recalcitrant kingdom[71] by dealing a not-too-
serious blow to the Judean kingdom and guaranteeing the personal loyalty of the
new ruler,[72] who himself was aware of the constant threat posed to his rule by Jehoiachin, even from exile.[73]

The Babylonian intention of permitting the weakened kingdom to continue
is also reflected in the list of those exiled to Babylon.[74] According to 2 Kgs

---

69. Garscha 1974: 26–34; Hossfeld 1977: 59–62; Lang 1978: 50–53; Zimmerli 1969: 13;
Blenkinsopp 1990: 80; see also Tsevat 1959: 199–204.

70. See the Babylonian Chronicle BM 21946, rev. line 13; Wiseman 1956: 33–35, 72–73;
Grayson 1975a: 20, 102.

71. Josephus (*Ant.* 10.102) understood the events and interpreted them correctly: "[Nebu-
chadrezzar] appointed Jōachimos's [Jehoiachin's] uncle Sacchias [Zedekiah] as king, after receiving his oath that he would surely keep the country for him and attempt no uprising nor
show friendliness to the Egyptians."

72. As stated, clear evidence of the personal pact between Zedekiah and Nebuchadrezzar
has been preserved in Ezek 17:13. On this subject, see Cooke 1936: 187–88; Tsevat 1959: 199–
204; Zimmerli 1969: 384; Malamat 1983: 268–69 and n. 58; Blenkinsopp 1990: 80–81; Duguid
1994: 24, 32–34.

73. On the hopes harbored by various groups in Judah regarding the restoration of the exiled Jehoiachin to the throne, see the words of Hananiah, the son of Azzur, which are quoted
in Jer 28:1–6, and compare Jeremiah's differing opinion (22:24–30). Four administrative documents published by Weidner (1939: 923–35), dated to between 592 and 569 b.c.e., provide information about the status of Jehoiachin in Babylon. There is no doubt that Jehoiachin's
status posed a threat to Zedekiah's status in Judah and made it difficult for him to function.
Nonetheless, contra Albright (1942b: 49–55), it seems to me that Zedekiah's rule was perceived as legitimate by the Babylonians, as well as by large sectors of the people (Weidner
1939: 926). See the allusions to this in Jer 23:5–6; 33:14–16, and see also Lam 4:20. On this
subject, see also Malamat 1983: 270–71.

74. Ever since the study by Stade (1884: 272–74), there has been agreement among most
scholars that, within the original sequence of the description of the deportation of Jehoiachin
(2 Kgs 24:12, 15–16), vv. 13–14 are a later addition. See, e.g., the opinions of Burney 1903:
366; Montgomery 1951: 555–56; Gray 1964: 760–61; Dietrich 1972: 140; Nelson 1981: 88,

24:12aα, Jehoiachin left Jerusalem, surrendered to the Babylonians, and was taken into exile (vv. 12b; 15aα). He was joined by his mother (vv. 12aβ; 15bα)[75] and the eunuchs (12aβ; 15bα).[76] The servants of the king (v. 12aβ)[77] and his officials (vv. 12aβ; 14aα)[78] are also mentioned as those who left Jerusalem with Jehoiachin and surrendered to the Babylonians, but in contrast, they are not listed among those who went into exile (24:15–16; Jer 29:2). The fact that they were allowed to remain in the land may be attributed to the Babylonian desire to

129–30, 145 n. 157; Jones 1984: 637; Würthwein 1984: 473; O'Brien 1989: 268; Seitz 1989: 168–73, 177–89; Brettler 1991: 541–52; and see also the discussion below. For a slightly different view, see Cogan and Tadmor 1988: 312; and in contrast to this view, see the response by Brettler 1991: 543–45. Nelson (1981: 88) has summed up the arguments regarding the secondary nature of these verses and, in particular, has insisted that they make the text cumbersome, difficult to understand, and create problematic redundancies. They also stand out against the parallel in Jer 29:2 (where the exiles are listed in exactly the same order) and the logical sequence in vv. 12, 15–16. Compare the order of exiles in the following texts:

2 Kgs 24:12	2 Kgs 24:15–16	Jer 29:2
Jehoiachin	Jehoiachin	Jeconiah
his mother	mother of the king	the queen mother
	the wives of the king	
his servants		
his officials		
his eunuchs	his eunuchs	the eunuchs
		the officials of Judah and Jerusalem
	the mighty of the land	
	all the men of might	
	the craftsmen and smiths	the craftsmen and smiths

75. The importance of the queen mother is evident from the fact that the mother of each of the kings of Judah is named in the introductory formulas in the description of his rule. It is noticeable in the description of Solomon's relation to his mother, Bathsheba (1 Kgs 2:16), and also appears in the days of Asa (1 Kgs 15:13) and after the death of Jehoahaz (2 Kgs 11:1ff.). See the comments in 1 Kgs 11:19; 2 Kgs 10:13. The (queen) mother of Jehoiakim is also mentioned in Jer 13:18, and, thus, it should come as no surprise that the queen mother was the figure second in importance among those carried into exile. She is also mentioned in the prophecy of Jeremiah in 22:24–30 (see especially v. 26), and Ezekiel (19:2) refers to her as "a lioness . . . among lions." On the queen mother, see de Vaux 1969: 129–31. For an updated review of the research, see Seitz 1989: 52–53.

76. Grayson 1995a: 95–98; Tadmor 1995: 317–25; 1999: 187–88; Deller 1999: 303–11; Fox 2000: 196–203, with further literature.

77. For an extensive discussion on the meaning of the title "servant of the king," see Fox 2000: 53–64, with further literature; Lipschits 2002a.

78. The term שר is used in the Bible 421 times. Many times the term refers in general to a person in a position of authority, a governor, or a commander (Exod 2:14; 2 Sam 3:38; Hos 3:4, etc.). However, even more frequently it refers to a well-defined, specific function in the ruling hierarchy. Some 50 roles are referred to by the title שר, whether the governor of a district, a position of command, an appointment over a specific sector, or a specific position in the king's government. For a summary of this subject, see Duguid 1994; 110; Fox 2000: 158–64, with further literature.

allow the kingdom to continue under Zedekiah.[79] It is also logical that the description of the departure of the wives of the king for exile (v. 15b) does not include a description of their surrender. It is likely that the king's wives remained in the palace and were not taken outside the walls before everything had been arranged with the heads of the Babylonian army.[80] Similarly, the description of "the mighty [notables] of the land" (v. 15bα)[81] going into exile excludes a description of their surrender, probably because, after the conquest of the city, the Babylonians decided who would leave and who would remain in Jerusalem. The exiles were joined by "all the men of might, seven thousand"[82] and "craftsmen and smiths a thousand" (16aα),[83] "all brave men, trained soldiers" (16aβ).[84]

---

79. The assumption is that political-diplomatic realism motivated the Babylonians to leave the ruling apparatus intact in Jerusalem, together with the king from the dynasty of David. This helps to explain the severe suppression of the revolt by Zedekiah and his government some ten years later (see below). Here lie the roots of the accusation that Jeremiah directed against the officials, whom he saw as responsible for taking measures that led to the destruction. On this subject, see the discussion below and the summary by Duguid 1994: 110.

80. On the negotiations between the besiegers and the besieged toward the end of the siege and the terms of surrender and the arrangements to follow, see the discussion in Eph'al 1996: 46–47.

81. The expression אילי הארץ ('the mighty of the land', 'the notables') is used in a similar sense in an identical context in Ezek 17:13. This sense—involving power, leadership, and the context of the social elite—is supported by the reference to "the mighty men of Moab" in Exod 15:15, where the phrase is parallel to the "chiefs of Edom," and by the reference in Ps 88:5 (see also in Isa 60:7; Ezek 32:21). On this subject, see further: Burney 1903: 367; Montgomery 1951: 558. Cogan and Tadmor (1988: 312) have drawn a parallel between this term and the term חורים ('nobles'), which is mainly used in Nehemiah and in 1 Kgs 21:8, 11.

82. The term איש חיל ('man of might') in singular and the term אנשי החיל in plural are used in the Bible 19 times, usually referring to persons of elevated status, wealth, power, and honor. From among this group, princes (Gen 47:6) and judges (Exod 18:21, 25) were appointed, and the term was used as an appellative for the high priest (1 Kgs 1:42). Furthermore, the term also refers to warriors (1 Sam 31:12; 2 Sam 11:16; Jer 48:14, etc.). The term גבורי חיל is used in v. 14 parallel to אנשי החיל. In the entire Bible, גבורי חיל is used 36 times. In the singular, it is used to describe the qualities of a person as a brave warrior or charismatic leader (Judg 11:1; 1 Sam 9:1; 16:18; 1 Kgs 11:28; 2 Kgs 5:1, etc.). In the plural, the term is used primarily in the book of Chronicles (15 times), while in the Deuteronomistic literature it occurs only 6 times, 4 of these in the book of Joshua (1:14; 6:2; 8:3; 10:7) to refer to members of a select army that is at the forefront of the fighting forces. In the book of Kings, it is used twice (2 Kgs 15:20; 24:14): in the first case, it is clear that its meaning is parallel to the meaning of אנשי החיל and has the sense of leadership and elevated status. The conclusion is that, although the Bible, in general, and the Deuteronomistic literature, in particular, tend to differentiate the two terms (איש חיל referring to status and גבור חיל referring to courage and leadership), there is also some overlap between them, perhaps because both civic and military leaders came from the elite families of society.

83. חרש ['craftsman'] is the term for an artist who works with hard materials, such as stone (Exod 28:11; 2 Sam 5:11), wood (2 Sam 5:11; 2 Kgs 12:12; Isa 44:13; 1 Chr 14:1), iron, and copper (2 Chr 24:12). The word occurs in the context of construction (2 Kgs 12:12; 22:6; 1 Chr 14:1); blacksmithery (Isa 54:16); weapons (1 Sam 13:19); idols and molten images (Deut 27:15; Isa 40:19); and with other artisans such as goldsmiths (Isa 41:7; Jer 10:9); quarrymen (Ezek 3:7; 2 Chr 24:12); builders and masons (2 Kgs 22:6; 2 Chr 34:11). The title מסגר ['smith'] occurs

Both the composition and the number of the exiles attest to the propensity of the Babylonians to allow Judah to rebuild itself and to permit the life of the kingdom to continue. The assumption is that, although the deportation of approximately 10,000 people[85] out of a total of 110,000 people in the entire kingdom of Judah[86] was a severe setback, the conquerors nevertheless allowed the continued existence of the smaller, diminished kingdom.[87] The Babylonians, for their part,

---

only 4 times, all of them in the descriptions of the exile (2 Kgs 24:14, 16; Jer 24:1; 29:2) and always in the company of craftsman. Some scholars, because of its use in proximity to the craftsman, believe that it also has the sense of artisan (Burney 1903: 367; Montgomery 1951: 558; Cogan and Tadmor 1988: 312). Support for this viewpoint may also be found in the expression 'pure [= סגור] gold' (1 Kgs 6:20); as a result, we may see smiths as the technicians who aided the craftsmen; they were responsible for the industrial processing of the metals necessary to producing finished products. On the other hand, based on the summary in v. 16b, relying on the parallel in 1 Sam 13:19, and emphasizing the core meaning of the root סגר and linguistic parallels in Ugaritic, Akkadian, and Egyptian, other scholars hypothesize that smiths were technical teams who worked within the military organization and who were responsible for preparing and maintaining the fortifications and the weaponry (Gray 1964: 761; Malamat 1983: 263 and further literature in n. 47). For other proposals, see Cogan and Tadmor 1988: 312.

84. For the expression עושי מלחמה / עושה מלחמה, see 1 Kgs 12:21 (= 2 Chr 11:1); 2 Chr 26:11, 13.

85. The biblical sources on the number of exiles report varying figures (compare 2 Kgs 24:14, 16; Jer 52:28). The attempts to resolve them seem forced and problematic and also ignore the difference in intention of the authors of the book of Kings and the book of Jeremiah, as well as in the sources that were available to each (Cogan and Tadmor 1988: 312). On this subject see, e.g., the suggestion by Janssen (1956: 28–36) and Holladay (1989: 443) that the low number cited in Jer 52:30 is realistic (a total of 4,600 exiles). In contrast, the suggestion by Mowinckel (1946: 93–98) and J. Weinberg (1972: 55–57), who suggest that the numbers reported in Jeremiah 52 (in their opinion, the exiles from Judah) must be added to the numbers in 2 Kings 24 (according to them, the exiles from Jerusalem), for a total of 12,000–14,000 exiles, together with a similar number of emigrants. For more balanced estimates, see Malamat 1968: 152–55; 1983: 264–65; Thompson 1980: 782; D. L. Smith 1989a: 31–32. For a review of the research and bibliography, see Seitz 1989: 181–84. We may suggest that the round number in 2 Kgs 24:14 is part of the trend toward generalization that characterizes this source, which is later and tendentious (see also Albertz 2003: 84). It is possible that the author also was familiar with 2 Kgs 24:16, which records that 7,000 people were deported to Babylon, in addition to the "craftsmen and smiths, a thousand," as well as Jer 52:28, which states that 3,023 Jews were deported to Babylon, resulting in a round number that totaled 10,000, in addition to the "craftsmen and smiths." Many of the Jewish commentators and scholars noticed this numerical agreement and suggested that the number 10,000 should be seen as the actual total number of exiles; see the references and bibliography in Malamat 1983: 265 n. 52. On the source and tendency of vv. 13–14, see the discussion below in §5.1.4 (pp. 299–304).

86. This is a very low estimate, much lower than Albright's estimate (250,000; 1949a: 56) and Janssen's estimate (150,000; 1956: 28); in contrast, see Albertz's estimate (80,000; 2003: 89–90). On the size of the population of Judah at the end of the seventh and the beginning of the sixth centuries B.C.E., in comparison with the population in the middle of the sixth century and that of the mid-fifth century B.C.E., see the discussion below in §4.4 (pp. 258–271).

87. This conclusion contradicts the notion that the entire population of Jerusalem was sent into exile, an idea that is primarily based on 2 Kgs 24:14 (Malamat 1983: 265). This verse is a later addition connected with 25:21b, a verse that very obviously is a generalization. Furthermore, the statement that the entire exiled population numbered "several tens of thousands of people of the inhabitants of Judah" (Malamat 1983: 265) seems exaggerated.

had a clear interest in transferring the exiles to uninhabited territory in Babylon that had been devastated during the wars with the Assyrians and that had been depopulated.[88] The level of danger that Judah represented to Babylonian rule was significantly diminished, because the exiles' importance to the administrative, economic, military, and governance of the kingdom was considerable. This helps explain Jeremiah's definition of the exiles as "figs [that] were very good, like early-ripening figs," which is in contrast to the people remaining, who were like "figs [that] were very bad, so bad that they were not fit to eat" (24:1–10).

That the Babylonian policy toward Judah after the fall of Jerusalem was realistic and well-planned is also evident in terms of the timing of the deportation. According to 2 Kgs 24:12b, Jehoiachin was deported to Babylon in the 8th year of Nebuchadrezzar's rule. His 8th year began on the 1st of Nissan (April 13/14, 597 B.C.E.), about one month after Jerusalem surrendered. This does not correlate with the description in Jer 52:28, according to which 3,023 Judeans were deported in the 7th year of Nebuchadrezzar's reign.[89] It might be that the deportation in Nebuchadrezzar's 7th year took place even before the month of Addaru (Freedy and Redford 1970: 463; Malamat 1983: 263–65; Galil 1991: 15–16; Ahlström 1993: 786), when the capture of Jerusalem was completed, and

---

88. The Babylonian policy of deportation included transferring population groups to Babylon and settling them in separate enclaves. On the logic of this policy in light of Babylonian imperial policy, see Vanderhooft 1999: 110–12. Against the backdrop of this policy, the discovery that there were settlements in the area of Nippur that were named for exiled peoples or the places from which they had been deported is hardly surprising. On this phenomenon, see Eph'al 1978: 80–81, with further literature; Zadok 1978a: 297, 300; 1978b: 60.

89. The hypothesis put forward by Albright (1956a: 28–33), Freedman (1956: 50–60), and others—that the difference between the two accounts is the result of the fact that the author of the book of Jeremiah knew the official method of counting in Babylon, but the author of the book of Kings was not familiar with the system—is untenable. This hypothesis assumes that both 2 Kings and Jeremiah are referring to the same instance of deportation, despite the large numerical discrepancy between them. It is also based on the premise that the author of the description in Kings was not familiar with the Babylonian system of counting, although an analysis of the description shows that he knew Babylonian history well. Furthermore, support for the dating in 2 Kings is found in Ezek 40:1, which notes that 25 years had passed since the deportation "at the beginning of the year, on the tenth day of the month"—a statement that, despite the controversy it stirs (see, e.g., Abramsky 1973: 56–78; Malamat 1983: 263 n. 48, with further literature; Albertz 2003: 85), supports dating the deportation from Judah in the 8th year of Nebuchadrezzar's reign, either at the beginning or the middle of the year (Tadmor 1964: 275–76; Freedy and Redford 1970: 463; Vogt 1975: 225; Cogan and Tadmor 1988: 311; Hayes and Hooker 1988: 92; Galil 1991a: 15–16). In this context, see also the problematic suggestion made by Rudolph (1947: 324), who revises the text in Jeremiah to the "seventeenth year" and assigns the deportation to the time of Zedekiah. Thiele's proposal (1951: 168–73; 1956: 22–27), that there was only one instance of deportation, if the 7th year is numbered according to the Judean calendar (which begins on the 1st of the month of Tishri) and the 8th year is counted according to the Babylonian calendar (which begins with the 1st of the month of Nissan), is also problematic. Thiele is joined in this opinion by Horn (1967: 23) and Green (1982b: 62).

that Nebuchadrezzar hurried home for the New Year celebrations in Babylon.[90] A reference to the deportation of "Judeans" in Jer 52:28 permits us to conjecture that this event refers to those who were captured even before the conquest of Jerusalem, perhaps the socioeconomic elite of the areas around Jerusalem (see Jeremiah's prophecy in 13:18–19).[91] The main deportation, which included the nations' leaders, the king, heads of the army, "the craftsmen and smiths," and some of the priests (and compare with Jer 29:1), occurred only a few weeks or months afterward—in any event, after Nissan 597 B.C.E., when the 8th year of Nebuchadrezzar's rule began. It is to these deportations that the description in 2 Kings 24 refers.[92]

At this point, a few comments regarding the deportation policy of the Babylonian Empire are appropriate. The inhabitants of the Judean kingdom were quite familiar with Assyrian deportation practice. Assyrian deportation consisted of a mass two-way deportation, the objective of which was to break the spirit of the conquered peoples by mixing diverse populations, causing them to assimilate culturally, and transforming them into part of the mosaic of the Assyrian-Aramean nations that the Empire comprised (Oded 1979). In contrast,

---

90. Compare the description in 2 Chr 36:10, which says that Jehoiachin was deported "at the turn of the year." On this expression, which denotes the return of spring after winter, allowing kings to set out on their expeditions, see 2 Sam 11:1 (= 1 Chr 20:1); 1 Kgs 20:22, 26; and see Burney 1903: 236; Hyatt 1956a: 278; Clines 1974: 29–30; Vogt 1975: 227–28; however, against this, see Gray 1964: 378. For additional literature on the subject, see Galil 1991a: 15 n. 44.

91. A combination of the comments in Jer 13:19, 35:1–11, and the information found in the Arad ostraca permits a historical reconstruction that includes the dispatch of auxiliary forces together with the Babylonian advance guard, all of whom arrived before the beginning of the siege on Jerusalem, perhaps as part of Babylon's renewal of its hold on the region. On the basis of these data, a theory that the Negev was cut off from Judah after the deportation of Jehoiachin has developed. On this subject, see Noth 1954: 283; Oded 1977: 470–71; Malamat 1983: 267 and n. 56; Rainey 1987: 23–24; Seitz 1989: 98–99 and n. 232; and see also the discussion below, in chap. 3, pp. 140–146. Compare the opinion of Montgomery (1951: 552), who thinks that there is no significance to the chronological difference and that the variation is between a low number that estimates the number of male exiles and a high number that includes all exiles, including women and children.

92. See Wiseman 1956: 34; Malamat 1983: 259–63; Kutsch 1985: 38–40. On this chronological point, it is of great importance to clarify the precise beginning of Zedekiah's reign. If his 1st year began on the 1st of Nissan in 597 B.C.E., parallel to the beginning of the 8th year of Nebuchadrezzar's reign, a problem of synchronism involving the two kings and the description of the dates of the destruction is created (Galil 1996: 109–10; with further literature). It is much more likely that Zedekiah ascended the throne after the 1st of Nissan 597 B.C.E. and that his 1st year of reign officially began on the 1st of Nissan 596 B.C.E. (Vogt 1975: 227; Hayes and Hooker 1988: 95, and see, in contrast, Galil 1991a: 15; 1996: 111–12, with reference to other opinions). I cannot accept the opinion of Galil (1991a: 11–13, 15; 1996: 113–15) and Edwards (1992: 101–6) that there was no agreement between the Babylonian calendar and the calendar that was in use in Judah, and that there was a discrepancy of one month between the two calendars (the 1st of Nissan according to the Judean calendar falling one month before the 1st of Nissan in the Babylonian calendar); there is no real proof for such a discrepancy. See also Albertz 2003: 80.

the Babylonian method was pragmatic; it was designed to establish Babylonian rule, on the one hand, and, on the other hand, to rebuild and settle the Babylonian regions that had been laid waste in the Assyrian wars. The assumption that this deportation technique was the result of lack of resources is untenable (so Stager 1996b: 71*), as is the supposition that the Babylonians did not intend to establish a well-organized system of provinces (so Vanderhooft 1999: 111). Putting aside for the moment the ideology of ruling an Empire (within the overall ideology of Assyria and Babylon), we must differentiate between the two different starting points from which Assyria and Babylon came to rule Ḫatti-land. The Assyrians conquered an area that was a patchwork of kingdoms, some of them large, powerful, territorial kingdoms. They had to invest much energy in order to establish their rule and to create an array of provinces. In contrast, the Babylonians conquered an area that was already largely organized into provinces and had only small, weak, nonthreatening kingdoms. In any case, the Babylonian deportations were more limited in scope, and they may have established Babylonian rule over the Empire's lands with relatively more speed and facility. The exiles from Judah, as well as other western minorities, were settled as independent communities. This allowed them to preserve their own identity while in exile, even after Judah ceased to exist as a kingdom and throughout the two generations that followed, leading up to the Persian conquest.

2.1.5. Nebuchadrezzar's Change in Policy in Ḫatti-Land (589 B.C.E.): The Conquest and Subjugation of the Vassal Kingdoms

During the 7th year of his reign (598/597 B.C.E.), Nebuchadrezzar extended his Empire to the southern part of Ḫatti-land. It is also likely that he began to organize the administration and garrisons that collected taxes from the local potentates. He was therefore able to embark on a short expedition, going only as far as Carchemish, in the 8th year of his reign (January 596 B.C.E.).[93] During this time, difficulties in other regions began to preoccupy Nebuchadrezzar. At a date sometime in his 9th year (between early April 596 and mid-April 595 B.C.E.), he was forced to campaign along the banks of the Tigris, confronting the king of Elam. According to the Babylonian Chronicle, the king of Elam was intimidated by the might of the Babylonian army and returned to his own land. However, the necessity of mounting a campaign in the region attests to the problems that the Babylonians were having along the eastern border of the

---

93. See the Babylonian Chronicle BM 21946, rev. lines 14–15; Wiseman 1956: 35–36, 72–73; Grayson 1975a: 20, 102. It is difficult to accept the view of Redford (1992: 461) that this short campaign is a reflection of Babylonian weakness, following the failed invasion of Egypt. Nebuchadrezzar reestablished his authority in the campaigns of 599–597 B.C.E. and in the winter of 597/6 B.C.E., and this was long before the appearance of the first signs of weakness that would later challenge the stability of his regime.

Empire.[94] Even more difficult problems awaited Nebuchadrezzar in the 10th year of his reign (595/594 B.C.E.). According to the Babylonian Chronicle, there was a revolt in Babylon that lasted from the month of Kislev to the month of Tebeth (from mid-December 595 to mid-February 594 B.C.E.). This revolt was suppressed only after Nebuchadrezzar ordered the execution of many in his own army and when he had personally trapped the leader of the revolt, whose identity is not known.[95]

It is likely that it was at this time, and perhaps against the background of these signs of weakness, that instability began to appear in Ḥatti-land. In Egypt, Psammetichus II (595–589 B.C.E.) ascended to the throne.[96] His expedition to Nubia in 593 B.C.E. was a resounding military success (Freedy and Redford 1970: 474–75; Spalinger 1978a: 23; Hoffmeier 1981: 166; Redford 1992: 404, 462–63). We may assume that his expedition to the Phoenician coast one year later impressed the kingdoms of the region even more and contributed to the exaggerated belief in the Egyptians' ability to return to a position of power in the region.[97] It is probable that Egypt's demonstrations of growing strength and

94. See the Babylonian Chronicle BM 21946, rev. lines 16–20; Wiseman 1956: 36, 72–73; Grayson 1975a: 20, 102. Compare this description with Jeremiah's prophecy (49:34–38), and see Hyatt 1956: 283; Tadmor 1956: 230 n. 27; Malamat 1983: 273 and n. 71; Miller and Hayes 1986: 410; Wiseman 1991: 233. It is hard to accept the general chronological system and at the same time reject synchronization at this point, as Sarna does (1978: 78).

95. See the Babylonian Chronicle BM 21946, rev. lines 21–22; Wiseman 1956: 36–37, 72–73; Grayson 1975a: 20, 102. For a clue to the identity of the rebels, see Wiseman (p. 37) and compare his later views (1991: 233). The anti-Babylonian ferment that began among the Judean exiles in Babylon and the account in Jeremiah regarding the fate of Ahab, son of Kolaiah, and Zedekiah, the son of Maaseiah, "whom the king of Babylon roasted in the fire" probably should be linked with this time (compare the words that Jeremiah quotes in 27:16; 28:2–4; Holladay 1989: 139–40; 143–44). Rebellion also began to foment in Ḥatti-land at this time (note the anti-Babylonian assembly described in Jeremiah 27, and see the discussion below).

96. It is unlikely that Psammetichus II continued a policy of nonintervention in Asia, following the policy of his father during the last five years of his reign (Gardiner 1961: 451; Katzenstein 1993: 185; 1994: 44). See the different evaluations by Bright 1959: 308; Malamat 1983: 274–75; and see the summary by Redford 1992: 462–65.

97. See Redford 1992: 464–65. There is grave doubt about the reliability of the Rylands Papyrus, where the campaign is described (Griffiths 1909: 92–94; Gardiner 1961: 368; see Greenberg 1957: 304–9; Freedy and Redford 1970: 479–81; Spalinger 1976; 1977; 1978b). It seems that this campaign was of a religious nature, and it is not clear whether Psammetichus even passed through Palestine on his way to the Phoenician coast (Kienitz 1953: 25; Gardiner 1961: 360; Kitchen 1973b: 369; Katzenstein 1994: 44–45). Despite the fact that this was apparently not a military campaign (Malamat 1975b: 142), it might nevertheless have had propaganda value (Freedy and Redford 1970: 479–80), and it is reasonable to assume that hope of liberation from Babylonian subjugation was awakened throughout the region (Miller and Hayes 1986: 412–13). Katzenstein's proposal (1994: 45), that there was prior coordination between Babylon and Egypt, should be dismissed, because there is no allusion to collaboration of any kind, and it is very doubtful that the Babylonians would have been able to limit the Egyptians' maritime activity. It also seems that Spalinger (1978a: 23) is correct when he claims that it is unlikely that the Egyptans were able to establish an empire in Asia or that they were even

Psammetichus's activist foreign policy engendered the anti-Babylonian pact among the kings of Edom, Moab, Ammon, Tyre, Sidon, and Judah reported in the prophecy of Jeremiah (chap. 27).[98] This pact could not have developed without Egyptian support.

Accounts of the pact between Judah and Egypt in the final years of Zedekiah's reign support the assumption that Egypt played a role in undermining the stability of the region. In Ezek 17:15, there is an appeal for cavalry and armed men to be sent from Egypt to help in the revolt against Babylon (Cooke 1936: 188–89; Tsevat 1959: 199–204; Eichrodt 1970: 227; Lang 1978: 138–40; Zimmerli 1969: 365; Blenkinsopp 1990: 80–81). Jer 37:5–11 mentions an Egyptian campaign to Judah at the height of the Babylonian siege against Jerusalem (see below, §§2.2.2, pp. 76–77; 5.2.2b, pp. 316–325). Lachish ostracon no. 3 (lines 14ff.) contains a description of the journey of Coniah, son of Elnathan, the commander of the army, to Egypt, apparently in the 9th year of Zedekiah's rule—the year that the revolt against Babylon was declared.[99]

---

interested in doing so or in directly confronting the Babylonians. It is reasonable to presume that connections were also forged with Zedekiah, king of Judah, during the Egyptian campaign (Miller and Hayes 1986: 412–13). However, the suggestion by Greenberg (1957: 304–9) that it was this campaign that stirred up the revolt in Judah seems farfetched. The mistake of Freedy and Redford (1970: 479) in dating this campaign to 591 B.C.E. instead of 592 B.C.E. (see Malamat 1983: 274, 277, 279 and nn. 73, 78, 83) makes it possible to accept Malamat's proposal (pp. 276–80 nn. 87–88) to connect this event with the assembly described in Ezek 20:1. On this subject, see Miller and Hayes 1986: 412–13; Redford 1992: 464–65. At the same time, Malamat's suggestion that the assembly described in Ezekiel 20 be linked to the prophecy of Hananiah, the son of Azzur, the prophet from Gibeon, must be rejected. To do so is problematic historically and is based on a faulty textual reconstruction and chronological method employed by Malamat.

98. The superscription of this prophecy is a mistake and, apart from the historical illogic in assigning it to the days of Jehoiakim, it also does not accord with the contents of the prophecy (compare v. 3). The background of the arrival of these kings in the royal court of King Zedekiah is not clear, but the words of the prophet imply that the assembly was designed to establish a pact that would lead to rebellion against Babylon. On the scholars' attempts to fix the date of the assembly to 593 B.C.E., especially on the basis of the title of Jeremiah's prophecy in chap. 28, see Bright 1959: 329; 1965: 200; Janzen 1973: 14–19; Malamat 1983: 272–74; Holladay 1989: 32, 114–16; and Hoffman 2001: 530. Sarna's attempt (1978) to date the prophecy earlier in 597 B.C.E. cannot be accepted (see Tadmor, EM 8, col. 313). The absence of the kingdoms of Philistia from this group should not be surprising, because in the years that elapsed from the beginning of the confrontation between Egypt and Babylon over control of Ḫatti-land, Ashkelon and Ekron had been destroyed by the Babylonians, and Ashdod and Gaza by the Egyptians. Apparently, Ashkelon and Gaza continued to exist under Babylonian rule, but the Babylonian control of this area, which was the main corridor to Egypt, was much tighter than its control of the highland and Transjordan.

99. Although referring to this general by the name Coniah, son of Elnathan, has become customary in the research literature, it is not at all certain that this was his name (Tur-Sinai 1940: 77). On the date of the ostracon, see Tur-Sinai 1940: 97, 197–99, and on the historical background and identification of the prophet who went to Egypt with Uriah and who is mentioned in the prophecy of Jeremiah from the period just prior to the deportation of Jehoiachin, see pp. 94–103; and Thomas 1948.

This scenario is the backdrop for understanding why Nebuchadrezzar was so anxious to leave for Ḫatti-land in the winter of 594 B.C.E., immediately after suppressing the revolt in Babylon. According to the Babylonian Chronicle, the kings (and the governors?)[100] of Ḫatti-land expressed their loyalty to him, he received their lavish tribute, and he returned to Babylon.[101] We can assume that this expedition was also connected with the rise of Psammetichus II to the throne in Egypt. An additional reason for the expedition was Nebuchadrezzar's need to demonstrate to his garrison forces as well as to the Babylonian forces in the region that his authority over Ḫatti-land and Babylon was firm and stable and that he was not suffering from any lingering effects of the revolt.

Nebuchadrezzar campaigned again in the month of Kislev in the 11th year of his reign (November 594 B.C.E.),[102] but the Chronicle contains no other information about this campaign.[103] However, the intensive activity of Babylon during this year meshes well with the account in Jer 51:59, in which Zedekiah, king of Judah (or one of his officials), presented himself in Babylon in the 4th year of his reign (594/593 B.C.E.).[104] Although there is no report about the context or consequences of this event, we may assume that this act was required to renew the pledge of fealty or to deliver a report about conditions in the region.[105] The tension and turmoil of these years are also reflected in assemblies devoted to events taking place in Judah held among the exiles in Babylon, as mentioned in Ezekiel.[106]

---

100. Naʾaman (unpublished Hebrew translation of the Babylonian Chronicles) has proposed that the broken text be restored in this way. This reading is supported by the gap in the text of the tablet as well as the historical reconstruction; and see below.

101. See the Babylonian Chronicle, BM 21946, rev. lines 23–24; Wiseman 1956: 37, 72–73; Grayson 1975a: 20, 102.

102. See the Babylonian Chronicle, BM 21946, rev. line 25; Wiseman 1956: 37, 74–75; Grayson 1975a: 20, 102.

103. The Babylonian Chronicles break off in the 11th year of Nebuchadrezzar's reign; the break lasts 37 years, and the next extant segment of the Chronicle describes events that transpired in 557 B.C.E.

104. According to the LXX on this verse, Seraiah, son of Neriah, the son of Mahseiah (the brother of Baruch, the prophet's scribe; see 32:12), who was 'officer of the resting place' (*měnûḥâ*; LXX reads here *měnāḥôt*, i.e., 'officer of the [tribute] gifts'), was sent to Babylon. On the meaning of this title and the interpretations given to it, see Thompson 1980: 770–71; Holladay 1989: 432–34. On the historical context of this event, see Greenberg 1957: 305–6; Freedy and Redford 1970: 475; Redford 1992: 463–64. Most scholars prefer the MT on this point; see the different opinions enumerated by Holladay (1989: 433).

105. It is reasonable to postulate that, when Babylonians received information about the assembly of representatives of the kingdoms in the area of Jerusalem, Zedekiah was called upon to explain his actions. In any event, Zedekiah remained safely on his throne and continued to reign until the eve of the fall of Jerusalem.

106. On the connection between the events of the 4th year of Zedekiah's rule and the first meeting described in Ezekiel (apparently on the 5th of Tammuz, July 593 B.C.E.), see Malamat 1982: 146; 1983: 275–78; Hayes and Hooker 1988: 96. The fact that many of the prophecies were uttered about events that were transpiring in Judah indicates that messages were sent and

A summary of this evidence shows that, under Psammetichus II's reign, Egypt began to establish itself in Judah, Transjordan, and on the Phoenician coast. A regional anti-Babylonian pact began to materialize, and there was a feeling among the kingdoms of the region that Babylonian authority was beginning to falter. Furthermore, neither Nebuchadrezzar's attempt to strengthen his control through campaigns held at the beginning and end of 594 B.C.E. nor the additional campaigns that must have been conducted in subsequent years (for which we have no information) were of any benefit.

The tangible threat to Babylonian control was heightened by the succession of Ḫophra in Egypt (589–570 B.C.E.).[107] Nebuchadrezzar understood that this required a change in Babylonian policy in the region: he could no longer rely on the loyalty of the vassal kingdoms and he needed to be more aggressive in countering instability in the region. This is the background for the change in Babylonian policy, which turned semi-independent vassal kingdoms into provinces whose loyalty to Babylonian authority was guaranteed by direct Babylonian rule and the continuous presence of Babylonian troops and administration. During the next 18 years, the Babylonians put in place a series of policies that stabilized their authority in the region and effectively abolished the existence of vassal kingdoms. As a result, the Babylonians established full dominion as far as the border of Egypt, positioning themselves as a constant threat to invade Egypt.

The absence of Babylonian Chronicles for this period makes it difficult to reconstruct historical events; however, the crisis that took place in Ḫatti-land during this era can also be read in the archaeological evidence (Lehmann 1998: 7–37, with further literature). It seems that securing control of Judah was the first goal of the Babylonians. Later, apparently in 585 B.C.E., they attacked Tyre and Sidon, laying siege to Tyre for 13 years.[108] This siege came to an end in 572

---

messengers and letters were exchanged between the exiles in Babylon and the remnant in Judah. Evidence for this is also found in the description of the letters that Jeremiah sent to the exiles in Babylon (51:59). On this subject, see Ezek 14:1ff.; 16:2; 20:1, as well as the prophecies in chaps. 6–8, 14, 16, 20–21. It appears that the exiles were involved in the disputes among the various groups in Judah and sent a clear message that loyalty to Babylon must be maintained (compare chap. 13; see the discussion below).

107. On the sources for the date of Ḫophra's kingdom and a reconstruction of his reign, see Hoffmeier 1981: 165–70. There is no room for reconstructions such as Katzenstein's (1994: 44–445), who argues that there was a drastic change in Egyptian policy when Ḫophra ascended the throne, while Psammetichus II continued the policy set by Necho II. Ḫophra's policy appears to be a direct continuation and expansion of Psammetichus's policy, which in his brief years of rule weakened Babylonian rule in Asia and began to establish Egypt as a power there (Malamat 1983: 281).

108. Accounts of these activities have been preserved in Josephus (*Ag. Ap.* 1.19, 156; *Ant.* 10.228); compare Ezek 29:18. On this subject, see also Katzenstein 1973: 330; 1994: 186; Wiseman 1991: 235; Redford 1992: 465–66. It is possible that the lamentation over the fall of Sidon in Isaiah 23 was supplemented by several verses (apparently vv. 8–9, 11–12, 15–16) during the Babylonian siege of Tyre. On this subject, see Lipiński 1978. On the appearance of Phoenicians in documents from the Babylonian and Persian periods, see Zadok 1978b: 59–61.

B.C.E., when the king of Tyre, probably Ethbaʿal III, was deported to Babylon.[109] Apparently, during the years of siege against Tyre, the Babylonians also attacked Ammon and Moab[110] and gained control of Gaza, Arwad, and Ashdod.[111]

These facts indicate that the Babylonians exhibited a different attitude toward the kingdoms of Philistia and the Phoenician coast. The former were conquered and turned into Babylonian provinces. Although the fate of the Phoenician kingdoms is unclear, it appears that during most years of Babylonian rule—certainly during the Persian period—these city-states were ruled by kings (Katzenstein 1994: 46–48, and bibliography there). The explanation for this difference in policy is Philistia's strategic importance as the gateway to Egypt and Babylon's need to maintain control over the region. Furthermore, ongoing instability in Philistia, its close ties with and loyalty to Egypt, as well as continuing Egyptian activity in the region throughout this period—all required the Babylonians to strengthen their control by subjugating the region. In contrast, Egypt was less of a threat on the Phoenician coast, and Babylon's economic interests were considerable. A generous measure of political and military autonomy was essential for promoting commerce in the region, including trade with Egypt.[112] The Babylonians profited by this trade, particularly through taxation and control of the centers of commerce.

---

109. Together with Ethbaʿal III, additional personages, apparently from the kingdom's elite, went into exile; see Weidner 1939: 923. At the same time, we must reject the idea put forward by Unger (1926: 315–16; 1931: 35), followed by Katzenstein (1973: 332–33; 1994: 185, and n. 27), and Wiseman (1985: 28) that, after a prolonged siege, Nebuchadrezzar appointed a Šandabakku at Tyre. Landsberger (1933: 298) had already proposed that the reference in question is to the city of Ṣurru near Uruk (Erech), and Joannès (1982: 35–42; 1987: 147–58) soundly established the identity of the site as being between Nippur and Uruk. Against some of the claims by Joannès, see Zadok 1985: 281 and Elat 1991: 32–33, and n. 76. In this context, see the summary of Vanderhooft 1999: 100–102 n. 159.

110. Josephus (*Ant.* 10.181–82) preserves an account that Ammon and Moab were conquered in the 23rd year of Nebuchadrezzar's reign (583/2 B.C.E.), 5 years after the conquest of Jerusalem (cf. Jer 52:30). On the fate of Ammon, also see the vision of Ezekiel (21:23–27) in which the king of Babylon had to choose whether to wage war against Jerusalem or Ammon.

111. Some suburbs were established near Nippur with names such as Ashkelon, Gaza, Qedar, and Bît Arzâ. Apparently these suburbs were built by exiles brought to Babylon during the days of Nebuchadrezzar (Zadok 1978b: 61; Ephʿal 1978: 80, 83, with further literature; and cf. Joannès and Lemaire 1999: 24), shortly after the fall of Jerusalem. The appearance of the Egyptian army in Palestine at the height of the siege on Jerusalem (Jer 37:5–11) could not have occurred unless Egypt had received some sort of cooperation from Gaza (Katzenstein 1994: 46–47). We cannot know whether the Babylonian actions against Gaza took place in 582 B.C.E., as Katzenstein claims, but the actions of the Babylonians against the king and the elite of Gaza were similar to the actions that they had taken against Judah only a short time previously.

112. A fine account regarding trade between Egypt and Babylon during the 5th and 6th years of Nabonidus (551–550 B.C.E.) has been preserved. On this subject, see Oppenheim 1967: 236–54; Brown 1969: 101; Katzenstein 1994: 48.

2.2. The Fall of Jerusalem: A Historical Synthesis

> *Do not put your trust in the words of the lie and keep saying, "The temple of the*
> *LORD , the temple of the LORD , the temple of the LORD are these." (Jer 7:4)*

An analysis of the Babylonian policy in Hatti-land, such as appears in the previous section, shows that continued instability in the southern part of this region together with the increasing threat of Egypt forced Nebuchadrezzar to invest massive resources in maintaining control of the region. My conclusion is that events surrounding the beginning of Hophra's reign (589 B.C.E.) led Nebuchadrezzar to modify his policy: he decided to conquer the remaining small vassal kingdoms close to the border with Egypt, to annex them, and to rule over them directly, as Babylonian provinces.

The consequence of the new Babylonian policy was destructive to the small kingdoms in the region because, in contrast to Assyria, which allowed the vassal kingdoms to continue as a political and economic bridge between it and Egypt, Nebuchadrezzar created a buffer zone that consisted of devastated, impoverished provinces. The Assyrians invested significant effort in regional development, involved the Egyptians in regional trade, and brought about unprecedented prosperity through trade with Arabia. The Babylonians, on the other hand, established a political structure that was designed to guarantee their own control, and there is no evidence that they put any energy toward economic development (see above, §2.1.5). Furthermore, Nebuchadrezzar leveraged the destruction of the region to rebuild parts of Babylonia that had been damaged during the long years of war with Assyria and the destruction and deportation that resulted. Large groups of exiles from the ruling, economic, and religious elite of the Levantine local kingdoms were sent to Babylonia and settled in the devastated areas to develop them.

It is against this backdrop that we must understand the destruction of Jerusalem and the transformation of Judah into a Babylonian province. Despite the unequivocal impression given by the historiographical accounts in the Bible, as well as the prophetic literature and the lamentations over the destruction of Jerusalem, the Babylonian reaction to Zedekiah's revolt should not be viewed as merely an act of vindictiveness against Judah or an impulsive punishment for the revolt. The reaction was a carefully calculated act, with specific political goals, and was the first manifestation of the altered Babylonian policy toward Hatti-land. The intent was to remove the Davidic dynasty from power, because it had proved itself disloyal time and again, and to destroy Jerusalem, which had repeatedly shown itself to be a center of rebellion against Babylonian rule. The Babylonians wanted to establish a province in Judah that would be different in two specific ways: its center would not be Jerusalem and it would not be headed

by a person from the Davidic line. In the biblical description, as in the archaeological evidence, there are no signs that all of the kingdom's territories were destroyed or that the population in its entirety was deported, and it appears that
the Babylonian retaliation focused on the heart of the kingdom—Jerusalem. Total devastation of the entire region would also have been contrary to Babylonian interests, because the Empire needed the population of Judah as the human
nucleus for the new province it had established. The Babylonians also needed
the settlements and their annual agricultural production in order to be able to
collect annual taxes and to provision the Babylonian troops stationed in the
country.

Destruction on the periphery of the kingdom (the Negev, the Jordan Valley,
and the Shephelah) was apparently a side effect of the collapse of the central
system. After the collapse of the economic and political system that these settlements depended on and because there was no army in Judah to protect them,
the border settlements gradually were abandoned. The beginning of this process
can be seen in the early days of the Babylonian siege. It continued when seminomadic groups infiltrated into the area; these groups gradually penetrated from
the south and east during the sixth century, eventually reaching the area of Hebron and Mareshah. This was the situation that the Achaemenids encountered
after they established their control over the territories formerly held by the
Babylonian Empire (see below, chap. 3).

In this section we will survey the history of the fall of Jerusalem and the policies instituted by the Babylonians in Judah afterward. First we will examine the
little that is known about the factors that led to the revolt by Zedekiah against
Babylon (§2.2.1). We will then try to reconstruct the course of the Babylonian
siege of Jerusalem and the unfolding of the days of the destruction (§2.2.2).
Against this background, we will try to describe the political structure instituted
by the Babylonians in Judah after the destruction of Jerusalem. The first act was to
transform Mizpah into the capital of the Babylonian province and to appointment
Gedaliah, son of Ahikam, the son of Shaphan, as the first governor of Judah. After
examining the political orientation of the family of Shaphan, the Scribe, and presenting evidence regarding the status of Gedaliah on the eve of the destruction
(§2.2.3), we will evaluate Gedaliah's status in the Babylonian province (§2.2.4)
and suggest that he had been appointed during the Babylonian siege, even before
the destruction of Jerusalem (§2.2.5). All of this will form the basis for a discussion
of the history of Judah during the era of Babylonian rule (§2.3), from the time of
the destruction (586 B.C.E.) until the beginning of the return to Zion (539/8
B.C.E.), during Persian rule.

2.2.1. The Causes of the Rebellion (589 B.C.E.)

> And Zedekiah rebelled against the king of Babylon. (2 Kgs 24:20)

Zedekiah's decision to rebel against Babylon was based on his evaluation that Babylonian rule in Ḫatti-land was weakening, as well as his belief that Egypt was strong enough to confront the Babylonian army and to assist the rebellious states. Ties between Egypt and Judah grew stronger during the rule of Psammetichus II, and the ascent of Ḫophra to power in Egypt (589 B.C.E.) served as a point of no return, accelerating preparations for rebellion.[113] Egypt's support for the rebellion was a major ingredient without which the rebellion would never have begun.[114] Egypt's retreat in the face of the Babylonian army (perhaps even without confronting it) proved that reliance on Egyptian might was a serious miscalculation, and the fact that Babylonian control of the region continued unchallenged proved that the rebellion itself was also a miscalculation. The decision reached by the nation's leaders in Jerusalem to pursue the revolt even after the retreat by Egypt and the renewal of the Babylonian siege on Jerusalem is proof that additional, stronger factors were at work in their decision to rebel.

There were social, political, and, in particular, ideological-theological factors that led the leaders of Judah to persist in the rebellion against Babylon. The echoes of Sennacherib's campaign more than a century earlier and the remembrance of Jerusalem's rescue from the Assyrians were interpreted generations later as definitive proof of the manifestation of God's power in the world, producing a feeling that God would protect his city. Among the military, political, and religious leadership in Jerusalem, the prevailing belief was that Jerusalem would continue to exist peacefully; it would never fall to an enemy oppressor. This perception led to a relaxation of some of the restraints that had characterized the leadership of the small kingdom throughout most of its life and that enabled the leadership to exercise a greater degree of political, religious, and diplomatic freedom than was prudent at this time.[115] Jeremiah's attempt to combat the leaders' perception and his call, "*Do not put your trust in the words of the lie and keep saying, 'The temple of the LORD , the temple of the LORD , the temple of the LORD are these.'. . . But go, if you will, to my place (of worship), which used to be at Shiloh, where I first established a dwelling place for my name, and see what I did to it because*

---

113. For an extensive discussion on this geopolitical background of the Judean revolt, see above, §2.1.5 (pp. 62–67). Miller and Hayes (1986: 412–13) also have summarized the reasons for Zedekiah's revolt.

114. As stated, there is clear evidence that the ties between Judah and Egypt were tightened on the eve of the fall of Jerusalem. On this subject, see the discussion above, in §2.1.5 (pp. 62–67), and see also below, §2.2.2 (pp. 72–84).

115. We may speculate that the first deliverance of Jerusalem from the Babylonians, after the death of Jehoiakim and following the deportation of Jehoiachin, had a strong influence on this belief (Bright 1959: 177–78).

of the wickedness of my people Israel" (Jer 7:4, 12), is one of the proofs of the power of this idea on the eve of the destruction of Jerusalem.[116]

It is likely that Zedekiah was also influenced by the activists in Jerusalem and the prophets who promoted rebellion against Babylon. A description of the events that took place in the last years of the Judean kingdom resonates with the religious-nationalist fanaticism that was prevalent in Jerusalem. The central role of the prophets (Jeremiah's "false prophets") and the officials, along with the weakness of King Zedekiah, are expressed principally in Jeremiah's prophecies and in the stories about him during the Babylonian siege (chaps. 37–38). Striking confirmation of this is found in Jeremiah's words against "your prophets, your diviners, your dreams [LXX: dreamers], your soothsayers, and your sorcerers who keep telling you not to submit to the king of Babylon" (Jer 27:9) and his condemnation of the prophets, "who keep prophesying to you and saying: 'Look, the vessels of the house of Yahweh will be returned from Babylon very soon now'" (27:16). The situation is also reflected in the clash between Jeremiah and Hananiah, the son of Azzur, the prophet from Gibeon (Jeremiah 28). A short time after Jeremiah had appeared before the representatives of the kings of Edom, Moab, Ammon, Tyre, and Sidon with thongs and a yoke-bar on his neck (27:2–3) and claimed "now it is I who have delivered all these lands into the hands of my servant Nebuchadnezzar, king of Babylon" (27:6), Hananiah took the yoke-bar from Jeremiah's neck and broke it (28:10). He encouraged those present to revolt against Babylon and claimed that "within two years I will bring back to this place all the vessels of Yahweh's house" (28:3).[117]

Prophets were also active among those exiled to Babylon, calling for the breaking of the Babylonian yoke, and Jeremiah acted against them as well, stating, "for it is a falsehood that they are preaching to you in my name. I did not send them—Yahweh's word" (29:9). Jeremiah even notes the names of two prophets (Ahab, son of Kolaiah, and Zedekiah, son of Maaseiah) "whom the king of Babylon roasted in the fire" after they had uttered false words (vv. 21–23). He also comes out against Shemaiah the Nehelamite, who had sent a letter to Jerusalem opposing Jeremiah (vv. 24–32), and he accuses Shemaiah of being a false prophet (v. 31). From all of these accounts, we can see that throughout the period of the decline of Judah leading up to the revolt against Babylon, the

---

116. Many scholars attribute this speech to the Deuteronomistic redactor(s) (see the references in Holladay 1986: 240 n. 7). However, Weippert (1973: 26–48), followed by Thompson (1980: 272–74) and Holladay (1986: 240), have convincingly showed that this section is not Deuteronomistic and is very closely related to the language of Jeremiah's prophecies. Furthermore, as I will discuss in chap. 5 below, there is a vast difference between the ideology that characterizes Deuteronomistic historiography and the ideas expressed in this speech. For a detailed discussion of this subject, see Holt 1986: 73–87.

117. Compare also v. 11, where the words "within two years" are missing from the LXX; this supplement is apparently based on the contents of v. 3. On this subject, see Janzen 1973: 48. See also the note in Malamat 1983: 276.

religious passion of segments of the population played a role: the people's faith in God's protection of his city overcame military and political considerations and fear of Babylonian power.[118]

Apart from scant information about Tyre and Ammon, nothing is known about other kingdoms that may have been part of the anti-Babylonian pact.[119] In one of Ezekiel's visions (21:23–28), there is a description of how difficult it was for the king of Babylon to decide whether to attack Jerusalem or "Rabbah of the Ammonites." The support of Ba'alis, king of Ammon, for Ishmael, son of Nethaniah, in the conspiracy to assassinate Gedaliah, son of Ahikam (Jer 40:14; 41:15), provides a clear indication of his political stance.[120] Tyre probably took its place in the revolt alongside Ammon, because the Babylonians besieged it immediately after they conquered of Jerusalem (Freedy and Redford 1970: 481–82; Zimmerli 1983: 603–4, 718). In any event, neither of these kingdoms possessed any significant military capability that could have threatened the Babylonian army. Ammon was a small, weak kingdom; Tyre's primary strength was at sea. Ammon and Tyre joined forces with Judah, whose military might had been crippled by the deportation of Jehoiachin, and it is doubtful that Judah was truly prepared for the impending Babylonian campaign.

2.2.2. The History of the Days of the Fall of Jerusalem

> On the day that Jerusalem was taken. (Jer 38:28)[120]

Despite the significance and importance of the fall of Jerusalem for the ideology and theology of biblical historiography,[122] and perhaps precisely because of this, the biblical description (2 Kings 25) is characterized by brevity and a dry style, with no theological commentary and no offering of historical lessons. The description is purposeful, focusing on the destiny of the king, the destruction of Jerusalem, and the fate of the people who lived in the city.[123] On the basis of

---

118. Bright (1959: 176), for example, referred to the nationalistic atmosphere on the eve of the revolt against Babylon as "theological madness," and most scholars see the situation this way (see, e.g., Miller and Hayes 1986: 409).

119. This was noted by Ginsberg 1956: 364–65; see also Malamat 1983: 281, and n. 89.

120. On Ba'alis and the role of Ammon in the period of the destruction and afterward, see the following discussion, §2.3.5.

121. The latter part of Jer 38:28 is lacking in the LXX and in the the Syriac (Peshiṭta; Hoffman 2001: 563). On the different versions of this verse, see Holladay 1989: 268.

122. On the nature of the description of the fall of Jerusalem, see the discussion below, in chap. 5, esp. pp. 336–338; cf. pp. 291–295.

123. 2 Kgs 25:1–3 focuses on the days of the Babylonian siege. Verses 4–7 describe the fate of the king and his sons. Verses 8–11 deal with the fate of Jerusalem and its inhabitants. In v. 12, there is a comment on the fate of the rest of the nation. Verses 13–17 focus on the fate of some of the temple tools, and vv. 18–21a describe the killing of 72 of the nation's leaders who were

this brief description, a Babylonian military campaign against Jerusalem may be reconstructed, including the setting of a siege against Jerusalem[124] and the building of a siege wall around it.[125] Apart from a description of the dire circumstances that prevailed in Jerusalem at the end of the siege due to starvation,[126] no additional details are provided.[127] The emphasis is on the date that the siege began, "in the ninth year of his [= Zedekiah's] reign, in the tenth month on the tenth day of the month" (v. 1aα),[128] and its ending "[In the fourth month] on

---

seized in Jerusalem by the Babylonians. Verse 21b is a summary remark: "Thus Judah was carried away captive out of its land." On the features of the description of the fall of Jerusalem, on its message, and the historical information in it, see the discussion below in chap. 5. When we compare the description in Jer 34:7, it becomes apparent how much the description in Kings focuses only on the fate of Jerusalem (compare Bright 1959: 329–30; Thompson 1980: 605–8; Holladay 1989: 234–35). In Jer 37:5, 11 (cf. also 34:21–22; Ezek 17:15–17; 30:20–26; Hab 1:10; Lam 4:17) there is a report of a lull in the Babylonian siege of Jerusalem when the Egyptians came to the assistance of Judah, though there is no allusion to this in 2 Kings 25 (Holladay 1989: 287). For a historical reconstruction of the Babylonian siege of Jerusalem, see below; see also Bright 1959: 330; Oded 1977: 473–74; Malamat 1983: 282–85; Miller and Hayes 1986: 413–15.

124. The meaning of the phrase חנה על ('encamp against') is 'to set up a military camp in order to conquer' a place or to defend it. Cf. Josh 10:5, 31; Judg 7:1; 1 Sam 4:1, 11:1; 2 Sam 11:11; 1 Kgs 16:15; Isa 29:3; Jer 50:29. In the parallel description in Jer 39:1, the text offers an explanation and clearly states: "and they laid siege to it."

125. The word דיק ('siege wall') occurs in the Bible six times. Apart from 2 Kgs 25:1 and the parallel description in Jer 52:4, it occurs only in Ezekiel (4:2; 17:17; 21:27; 26:8). Except for Ezek 26:8, in each case, the verb בנה 'to build' appears in the description of setting up the siege wall; this supports the view, widely held among scholars, that a stone wall encircled the city (Malamat 1983: 289; Cogan and Tadmor 1988: 316–17; Eph'al 1996: 42–43, with further literature). An Akkadian cognate is attested only once: in Esarhaddon's "letter to God," describing the conquest of the city of Shubria, southwest of Lake Van, in 672 B.C.E., there is a description of Assyrian forces climbing over the siege wall "to do battle" (Borger 1956: 104, col. II, line 8; see also Cogan and Tadmor 1988: 316–17; Eph'al 1996: 42–43, with further literature).

126. Cf. Jer 32:24a; 37:21a; 38:9b. See also the grim descriptions in Ezekiel 4 and compare the description in Lam 2:11–12, 20; 4:5. Eph'al (1996: 57) has claimed that the famine was the major and most devastating result of the siege: it was intended to break the spirit of the besieged and weaken their resistance to the point of completely destroying it. For a summary of starvation in times of siege, see Eph'al 1996: 57–63.

127. The absence of detail in this description is striking, particularly in light of additional information reported in the Bible concerning the siege months and the fall of Jerusalem (and see above, n. 123).

128. A parallel date is reported in Ezek 24:1, which states that "the king of Babylon has this very day laid seige to Jerusalem." It is very likely that this date refers to the years of Zedekiah's rule; see Freedy and Redford 1970: 468; Zimmerli 1969: 559–60; Kutsch 1985: 61–63, 70; Galil 1991a: 9; 1996: 110–11. On the assumption that the 1st year of Zedekiah's rule began in Nissan 597 B.C.E., his 9th year began in Nissan 589 B.C.E. If so, the date of the beginning of the siege in that regnal year was the 10th of Tebeth (December 588/January 587 B.C.E.; compare Hayes and Hooker 1988: 97; Galil 1991a: 16). For a different opinion, see Cogan and Tadmor 1988: 317, with further literature. On בשנת התשעית ('in the ninth year'), cf. 2 Kgs 17:6; Jer 28:1; Lachish ostracon no. 20 opens with the same date, btš'␣t byw[m . . .], which, according to Tur-Sinai (1950: 215–16), refers to Zedekiah's 9th year of rule (see also Cogan and Tadmor 1988: 316).

the ninth day of the month" (v. 3aα; compare Jer 39:2; 52:6),[129] in the 11th year of Zedekiah's reign.[130] Based on the data in this description, on the parallel texts in Jeremiah (39:1; 52:4), as well as on Ezek 24:1, the beginning of the siege may be dated to the 10th of Tebeth (= early January 587 B.C.E.) and its ending (when the city surrendered 18 months later) to the 9th of Tammuz (end of July 586 B.C.E.),[131] within the 11th year of Zedekiah's reign (compare 2 Kgs 24:18; Jer 1:3; 39:2; 52:5–6).

Support for these dates is found in Jer 52:29, which mentions the deportation of 832 people from Jerusalem in the 18th year of Nebuchadrezzar's reign. This year ended in Nissan 586 B.C.E., four months before the city capitulated, and we may assume that the people who were deported were those who surrendered before the fall of the city (compare Jer 37:12; 38:19).[132] According to 2 Kgs 25:8 (= Jer 52:12), the major deportation came after the surrender of Jerusalem, in the 19th year of Nebuchadrezzar's reign. Support for this is found in Ezek 33:21, a text that provides the terminus ante quem for the fall of Jerusalem, because, according to the description, "In the twelfth year, in the tenth month, on the fifth (day) of the month after our deportation, a man who had escaped out of Jerusalem came to me with the message: the city has been taken."[133] If the first year of the exile of Jehoiachin was the 8th year of Nebuchadrezzar's reign, which began on the 1st of Nissan 597 B.C.E. (Freedy and Redford 1970: 484), then the twelfth year of the exile was the 19th year of Nebuchadrezzar's reign, which began on the 1st of Nissan 586 B.C.E. If so, then the date when the fugitive from

---

129. Most scholars complete the text according to Jer 39:2 and 52: 6: "in the fourth month" (Burney 1903: 367; Montgomery 1951: 561; Cogan and Tadmor 1988: 315, 317). Support for this may be found in the reference to the "the fast of the fourth month" in Zech 8:19. On this subject, see Mitchell, Smith, and Bewer 1912: 215; Meyers and Meyers 1987: 433–34, 443–44; Redditt 1995: 87.

130. Verse 2; this point has been summarized in Freedy and Redford 1970: 468; see the literature summarized in Galil 1996: 110 n. 12.

131. See Finegan 1950: 64; Freedy and Redford 1970: 467–68; Hayes and Hooker 1988: 97; McFall 1991: 40; Edwards 1992: 101–6, with further literature. On this subject, see also the literature cited by Cazelles 1983: 427–35. In light of these data and texts from Jeremiah and Ezekiel (to be discussed), it is hard to accept the reconstruction proposed by Galil (1991a: 16–17); Galil dates the beginning of the siege to the 10th of Tebeth 587 B.C.E. and argues that it continued for six months (but see a different reconstruction in Galil 1996: 118). It is similarly difficult to accept the reconstruction proposed by Malamat (1983: 282), who dates the end of the siege to 9th of Tammuz 586 B.C.E., after lasting for two and one-half years.

132. Against Holladay 1989: 443; see also Thiele 1956: 25; Horn 1967: 26–27; Malamat 1975b: 133–34; 1983: 288; Vogt 1975: 223–24; Green 1982b: 60–61, 63–67. Despite the chronological disputes among these scholars, they agree regarding the identity of the group of exiles, who were not identical to those who were deported later, from Jerusalem. It is noteworthy that there are no parallels to Jer 52:28–30 in the description in the book of Kings or in LXX Jeremiah, and scholars generally treat these verses as a secondary addition based on data derived from an unknown source: Janzen 1973: 122; Holladay 1989: 438, 443.

133. On the various suggestions for correcting the date in this verse, see Zimmerli 1969: 191–93, with further literature; Blenkinsopp 1990: 149.

Jerusalem reached the exiles in Babylon was the 5th of Tebeth, January 8/9, 585 B.C.E., six months after Jerusalem surrendered and five months after Nebuzaraddan's soldiers began to destroy the city.[134] Assuming that the systematic destruction of the city took several weeks, and that the 1,600-kilometer-long journey to Babylon required at least three months (according to Ezek 7:9 and 8:31, the journey in the opposite direction took four months), then the date cited in Ezekiel seems reasonable and corresponds to the reconstruction given above.

The short description in 2 Kings 25 leaves a gaping hole in our information about what occurred during the siege.[135] At the same time, Jeremiah's "biography"[136] gives reliable and important information that reinforces known facts and even provides additional information. The major addition relates to evidence that an Egyptian army came to assist Judah[137] and arrived when the Babylonian army was besieging Jerusalem.[138] This is also the background to the

---

134. Finegan 1950: 65; and see also Zimmerli 1969: 192–93, with further literature.

135. The missing information regarding events during the Babylonian siege of Jerusalem leaves many questions unanswered. For example, the description of the arrival of Nebuchadrezzar at Jerusalem (25:1a, and cf. Jer 39:1a and 52:1a) does not make it clear whether he arrived at the outset of the campaign and led the army's siege of the city (v. 1a, which is in conflict with the parallel versions in 39:1b; 52:1a), and it is not clear how much time he spent with his army during the siege. Furthermore, Nebuchadrezzar is not mentioned in any of the descriptions of the battle. According to 2 Kgs 25:6, immediately after the siege ended he was in Riblah, the administrative center to which Zedekiah and his sons were brought (Montgomery 1951: 560). According to Jer 38:17 and 22, the officers of the king of Babylon directed the siege, at least at the end, and according to 39:3 they also were in Jerusalem when it surrendered. In light of this, it is probable that Nebuchadrezzar arrived in the region only after the siege had begun, perhaps during the battle against the Egyptian army. There is evidence of this in Jer 37:6–12, as well as in the date of the prophecy in Ezek 29:1–21 (especially in vv. 1, 19). It is reasonable to conclude that, after this battle, Nebuchadrezzar left the management of the siege to his officers and returned to Babylon (Cogan and Tadmor 1988: 323, and n. 13). We may postulate that Nebuchadrezzar returned to the region later, during the summer of the following year. At the time of the capitulation of Jerusalem, he was at Riblah, and Zedekiah was brought to him there after being captured (2 Kgs 25:6). For other reconstructions, see Gray 1964: 764; Freedy and Redford 1970: 470–72, 481; Jones 1984: 641.

136. On the literary genre of the "biography," see Rofé 1988: 106–22, and see also the discussion below, §5.2.2 (pp. 312–347). The information mentioned in the "biography" does not contradict but, instead, supplements information found in other sources. The credibility of this material is bolstered by the fact that it has a clear tendency to focus on the life of Jeremiah, and details of the Babylonian siege are given only incidentally.

137. This information is given in the editorial comments in Jer 37:5, 11, in the prophecy in vv. 6–10, and as background to the description of the prophet's attempt to leave Jerusalem (vv. 12–16).

138. The date of the Egyptian campaign is not specified, and the data for fixing the date are not decisive. For various assessments of this subject, see Freedy and Redford 1970: 424–70; Malamat 1983: 288; Galil 1991a: 16–17. There is no doubt among scholars that the Egyptian king who went to the assistance of Judah was Ḫophra, because Psammetichus II had died from disease in 588 B.C.E. (Hoffmeier 1981: 165). Nonetheless, it is doubtful that the campaign to assist Judah can be linked to the Egyptian campaign to Phoenicia, which is described by Diodorus and Herodotus (Freedy and Redford 1970: 482; and see Hoffmeier 1981: 166–67). On

events described in Jer 34:8–11 and the prophet's words cited in vv. 12–22,[139] though it seems that this passage is a late insertion and its reliability with regard to the historical details mentioned in it is dubious.[140]

The description of the "people" leaving Jerusalem during a lull in the siege (37:12) indicates that many of the besieged took advantage of the opportunity to leave Jerusalem and surrendered to the Babylonians. It is likely that at least some of them were sent by the Babylonians to Mizpah and there joined the Judeans who were beginning to gather in the Benjamin region under the leadership of Gedaliah, the son of Ahikam. It is also possible that this was Jeremiah's intention. The prophet attempted to leave the city "to go to the land of Benjamin," trying to "escape from there among the people" (37:12).[141] He was seized by Irijah, son of Shelemiah, the son of Hananiah (v. 13),[142] whose title בעל פקידות 'Supervisor' shows that he was acting on behalf of the king to monitor those who left through the gate of Benjamin.[143] Irijah accused the prophet of "deserting to the Chaldeans," using the phrase נפל אל.[144] Irijah's major concern was apparently about the negative propaganda that would be spread by the Babylonians over the desertion of a person of Jeremiah's stature.[145] Jeremiah's

---

the description by Josephus (*Ant.* 10.108–10), which is apparently a homiletic interpretation of the text in Jer 37:5, 11, see Hoffmeier 1981: 165–66.

139. Jer 34:21 alludes to the distress caused by the siege of Jerusalem, as background to the covenant made by Zedekiah and the people and the freeing of the slaves (vv. 8–10, 15). The Egyptian campaign and the temporary lull in the siege are described in the prophecy (v. 22) as the cause of the treaty breach and the reenslavement of the people (vv. 11, 16–17). On these verses, see the comprehensive discussion by Thompson 1980: 608–13; and Holladay 1989: 236–44. On the other hand, see Hoffman's view concerning the date of this passage (Hoffman 2001: 648–51, with previous literature).

140. See Hoffman 2001: 648–51. On emancipation of slaves during times of war and siege see Ephʿal 1996: 148–50, with further literature. See also: Sarna 1973; Malamat 1983: 288; Clements 1988: 288.

141. On the meaning of the expression לחלק משם בתוך העם (cognate with the Akk. verb *ḥalāqu*), in the sense of escaping the besieged city and the distress of its inhabitants during the siege, see Ephʿal 1993: 19, with further literature in nn. 22, 23; 1996: 145. See also Ephʿal's critique of one of the proposals common in current research, which takes this expression in the sense of 'to take part of . . .' or 'to obtain his share from . . .' (Thompson 1980: 632–34; Holladay 1989: 265, 287–88); in agreement with Ephʿal, see Hoffman 2001: 687.

142. For the name *Irijah*, the LXX has Zeruiah and the Syriac (Peshiṭta) has Neriah. See Holladay 1989: 265.

143. On the title בעל פקדות, the meaning of which in Akkadian is 'Supervisor' (*bēl piqitti*), see Ephʿal 1993: 22 n. 24; 1996: 145.

144. On the expressions נפל אל and נפל על in the Bible, compare 1 Sam 29:3; 2 Kgs 7:4; 25:11; Jer 21:9; 38:19; 39:9; 52:15; 1 Chr 12:19–20; 2 Chr 15:9. On the meaning of this expression parallel to the expression יצא אל, see Ephʿal 1994: 20 n. 2.

145. Ephʿal (1993: 18–19) draws a parallel between the expression נפל אל and the Akkadian expression *maqātu ana* and postulates that Irijah's main concern was that the Babylonians would derive much benefit from Jeremiah: his being among them would harm the morale of the besieged in Jerusalem, encouraging those who advocated capitulation to Babylon.

attempt to respond to the accusation by saying, "It is a lie; I am not deserting to the Chaldeans" (v. 14aα), may be understood against the background of v. 12. This verse implies that Jeremiah simply wished to escape the besieged city and extricate himself from the misery that prevailed in Jerusalem. Irijah did not accept Jeremiah's explanation (v. 14aβ) because, as far as he was concerned, the major danger was not in what Jeremiah intended but in the way his escape would be interpreted. He arrested Jeremiah and brought him to the officials (v. 14b), who were angry with him. "They flogged him, and threw him into prison in the house of Jonathan, the scribe, which they had converted into a prison" (v. 15).[146] This short description is significant for the historical reconstruction of the period of the siege. It indicates that, after the Babylonian siege on Jerusalem was renewed, after the Egyptian army had retreated before Nebuchadrezzar's army, the number of the besieged had decreased, because those who did not believe that the revolt would succeed had left Jerusalem. Those who remained were people who believed in the cause of the revolt and who were confident that the city could stand firm against the Babylonians. At this moment, for the first time in the history of Judah, two camps with opposing political orientations and apparently also with different ideological roots and social standing were manifested. This fact is very important for understanding the social and political processes that transpired in Judah after the fall of Jerusalem.[147] It also explains the harsh measures taken against anyone suspected of treason, incitement, or lowering the morale of the soldiers.[148]

A two-word description of the fall of the city has been preserved in the book of Kings (2 Kgs 25:4: ותבקע העיר 'Then the city was breached'). It seems that the use of the root בקע ('breach') here is not coincidental.[149] This brief description occurs at the juncture between the description of the Babylonian siege of the city (25:1–3) and a description of what befell Zedekiah (vv. 4aβ–7). It is difficult

---

146. For a literary and conceptual discussion of this text, see below, §5.2.2b (pp. 315–325).

147. See an extensive discussion of this process below, §2.3.2 (pp. 102–109).

148. On maintaining morale during the siege and dealing with hostile elements, see Eph'al 1997: 142–47.

149. The author chose to use an uncommon verb, בקע (cf. Jer 39:2; 52:7), to describe breaking into a city after a siege. Cf., e.g., 2 Sam 23:16 (= 1 Chr 11:18); 2 Kgs 3:26; 2 Chr 21:17, where it is obvious that the act of breaking in does not stand alone but is the opening for a series of additional actions. An unusual use of this root may be found in 2 Chr 32:1, which is quite striking in light of the fact that this verse is based on 2 Kgs 18:13 and Isa 36:1. In most cases, in various literary and linguistic contexts, the root בקע is used of the action of God, a connection that is lacking with roots having similar meanings, such as קרע, גזר, פרץ. Emphasizing the power of God and his share in the activities described by the root בקע is conspicuous in the Pentateuch (Gen 7:11; Exod 14:16, 21; Num 16:31), in poetry (Ps 74:15; 78:13, 15; 141:7); in the Wisdom literature (Prov 3:20; Job 26:8; 28:10; 32:19; Eccl 10:9), and in prophecy (Isa 35:6; 48:21; 58:8; 59:5; Ezek 13:11, 13; 26:10; 29:7; 30:16; Hos 13:8; Mic 1:4; Zech 14:4). On this subject, see also the exhaustive analysis by Brunet 1965: 157–76.

to know if these two words do in fact reflect what happened during the last hours of Jerusalem.[150] The size of the city and the arrangement of its walls permit the hypothesis that the Babylonians succeeded in breaching a segment of the fortifications (in the north or west of the city), leading the king to decide to escape to the south,[151] along with part of his army.[152] His escape route originated at "the gate between the two walls, which was near the king's garden" (25:4aβ).[153] Zedekiah escaped "by the Arabah road" (25:4b),[154] apparently in the direction of one of the Transjordanian kingdoms.[155] However, the Babylonian army pursued him

150. Although there are multiple texts providing evidence that there was famine in the city (2 Kgs 25:3; Jer 37:21a; 38:9b), there are no additional references to war, the Babylonian breakthrough into the city, or the breaching of the walls. When Zedekiah escaped the city, the text uses precise language, stating, "the Chaldeans were all around the city" (2 Kgs 25:4aγ). Jer 39:3 states that, immediately after the Babylonians broke through into the city, the officials of the Babylonian king came and took their seats in the middle gate. For a different reconstruction of events, including a description of the Babylonian breakthrough from the north, see Malamat (1983: 289).

151. The reason for and the timing of the king's flight are unclear. In light of the reference to the famine that raged throughout the city and the emphasis in Jeremiah 37–38 on the king's increasing fear during the siege, we may postulate that, when he understood that hope had run out and that within a short time the Babylonians would conquer the city, he decided to escape. After he was seized, Nebuzaradan was able to enter Jerusalem without a fight and destroy it. On this subject, see Malamat 1968: 154–55; Ahlström 1993: 797.

152. In v. 4 (MT), the text is corrupt, evidence of failure in the process of transmitting the text. (1) The verb in v. 4a and the verbs in 5–6 clearly focus the description on Zedekiah's action. The absence of any reference to the king in v. 4a and the fact that the verse begins with "and all the men of war" requires that a beginning be reconstructed in which Zedekiah is the subject of the sentence. This supplement might be similar to Jer 39:4aα (and the Peshiṭta) but could also be more concise, as in the Lucianic recension: "and the king went out and all the men of war" (Burney 1903: 367–68); or as in the reconstruction by Cogan and Tadmor (1988: 317): "[Zedekiah] and all the soldiers." (2) In v. 4aβ, the verb is missing. In Jer 39:4 (cf. also 52:7) there are two plural verbs ("they fled and they went out of the city"), but there is another option, such as the suggestion of Cogan and Tadmor (1988: 317): "[Zedekiah] and all the soldiers [fled] by night, leaving through the gate between the two walls." Burney (1903: 367–68) discusses the entire verse and relies on the Lucianic recension, which takes the verb at the end of the verse as singular, to reconstruct the text. On this subject, see also Montgomery 1951: 561, 567.

153. On the location of this gate, compare Isa 22:11; Neh 3:15, and see Montgomery 1951: 562; Cogan and Tadmor 1988: 317. It is probable that the king and his army tried to slip away toward Transjordan, and their seizure near Jericho (v. 5aβ) supports this reconstruction. On the king's flight, see Ezek 12:12–14; and on the factual background, see Jones 1984: 643.

154. On the expression "the Arabah road" (v. 4b), cf. 2 Sam 2:29; 4:7. The term *arabah* occurs 60 times in the Bible. In 11 cases, it refers to an area with well-defined geographical features of extensive desert, with sparse water, vegetation, and human life. In most of the other references, it refers to a specific area lying between the southern end of the Dead Sea and the Red Sea (Deut 1:1; 2:8; 3:17; 4:49; Josh 11:2; 2 Sam 2:29; 2 Kgs 14:25, and so on).

155. The possibility of escaping to Transjordan, apparently to Ammon, which was an ally of Zedekiah, is supported by several facts: there were Judean refugees in that region (Jer 40:11–12); there was a connection between Ishmael, the son of Nethaniah, and Baʿalis, king of Ammon (40:14); and Ishmael fled there after the murder of Gedaliah (41:15).

to the steppes of Jericho,[156] where he was seized,[157] "as all his troops dispersed."

The Babylonians now reversed the policy toward the kings of the Davidic line that had been in effect in 604 and 598 B.C.E. This time they were merciless and treated Zedekiah as one who had violated his personal oath of fealty to Nebuchadrezzar. He was brought to Riblah,[158] where Nebuchadrezzar passed judgment on him (v. 6)[159] and harsh punishment was meted out (v. 7): his sons were slaughtered before his eyes (the sons of Zedekiah are mentioned again only in Jer 38:23), and immediately afterward he was blinded.[160] Nebuchadrezzar put him in fetters[161] and had him taken to Babylon.[162] Thus, the Davidic dynasty in Judah was brought to an end as one of the measures that was designed to abolish the kingdom and establish a Babylonian province in its place.

Later, and for the same reason, the Babylonians showed an uncompromising attitude toward Jerusalem as well. Approximately one month after the city capitulated, Nebuzaradan, the chief cook,[163] reached the city and systematically

---

156. Aside from this case and parallels in Jer 39:5; 52:8, the term "the steppes of Jericho" occurs elsewhere only in Josh 4:13; 5:10. We can assume that the reference is to the area west of the Jordan River, just in front of Jericho.

157. For a poetic description of Zedekiah's capture, see Lam 4:19–20.

158. Nebuchadrezzar probably stayed at Riblah during the siege and capture of Jerusalem; see Cogan and Tadmor 1988: 304.

159. There is a problem with the continued use of the 3rd-person pl. in v. 6b in the MT, in contrast to Jer 39:5b and 52:9b, where there is a transition to 3rd-person sing. The expression לדבר משפטים (in 2 Kgs 25:6b: וידבר אתו משפטים) implies that a higher authority has delivered a verdict as consequence for the iniquity of an inferior or subordinate (Montgomery 1954: 562; Cogan and Tadmor 1988: 317–18, where they also discuss the legal significance of the expression in texts from the ancient Near East). In the MT of 2 Kgs 25:7, a plural verb-form occurs ('They slaughtered'), but the other three verbs in this verse are singular. The plural verb seems to ignore Nebuchadrezzar's presence in Riblah, though in all of the various accounts, Zedekiah was brought before him. In this respect it seems that the parallel account in Jer 39:6–7, 10–11 is more complete; here, all of the verbs are 1st-person sing.

160. Zedekiah's punishment is the sort that was dealt out to a vassal who violated his oath of loyalty to his lord; it was the accepted punishment for a slave who betrayed his master (Cogan and Tadmor 1988: 318). A king punished in this manner could not continue to reign (Montgomery 1951: 562). Zedekiah's fate may be compared with that of Samson (Judg 16:21). A parallel account of this event is found in Jer 32:4–5; 34:2–3; Ezek 12:13.

161. Apart from here and parallel accounts in Jer 39:7; 52:11, the expression 'fetters' (Heb. נחשתים) also occurs in Judg 16:21; 2 Sam 3:34; 2 Chr 33:11; 36:6. The word apparently refers to copper fetters that hobbled the feet of prisoners and was one of the punishments inflicted on a vassal king who violated his pact. Cogan and Tadmor (1988: 318) comment that the expression is archaic because, at the end of the Iron Age, fetters were made of iron (cf. Ps 105:18; 149:8).

162. There is additional information in Jer 52:11 describing Zedekiah's incarceration in Babylon: "until the day of his death." On the meaning of the expression בית הפקדות, see Cogan and Tadmor 1988: 318; see there also discussion regarding the source of this information. Compare also to the prophecy of Ezekiel (19:5–9) and see the discussion in Duguid 1994: 35–37.

163. The meaning of the name *Nebuzaradan* (*Nabû-zēr-iddina*) is: 'Nabu has given me offspring'. On the meaning of the title 'the chief cook' (*rab nuḫatimmu*), see Cogan and Tadmor

began to destroy it. There are three different traditions regarding the date of Nebuzaradan's arrival. According to 2 Kgs 25:8, Nebuzaradan arrived "in the fifth month [= Ab], on the seventh day of the month"; the Lucianic recension sets the time as "on the ninth day of the month" (the day set aside as a fast for the destruction of Jerusalem in Jewish tradition); and according to Jer 52:12, it was "on the tenth day of the month." It is doubtful that we can determine which tradition is most likely to be correct or explain the lack of agreement among them.[164] But it is clear that the Lucianic version is secondary and later, and its intent is to show that the destruction took place exactly one month after the capitulation of Jerusalem. The gap between the tradition in 2 Kings and the report in Jeremiah can be explained either by the author's lack of precise information or by the existence of different traditions about the date of the destruction.

In any event, the fact that the systematic destruction of Jerusalem began about a month after the king's flight and the capitulation of the city is evidence that this act was not spontaneous. It was a considered political decision, resolute and unequivocal, the result of a strategic Babylonian decision: to obliterate the center of rebellion and to prevent its future rebuilding, thus eradicating the seeds of ferment and instability in Judah. It seems likely that the Babylonians had allocated one month to those who were responsible for exiling the population from the city and gathering the spoils; when this was complete, they sent forces to raze the city systematically.[165]

Evidence of Nebuchadrezzar's desire to eliminate Jerusalem as a religious and political center may be found in the burning of the centers of government and religious ritual in the city: "the house of the Lord" and "the house of the king (= the palace)" (v. 9).[166] The totality of the devastation is highlighted in the

1988: 318–19, with further literature. Nebuzaradan is referred to by his name and title as the first among Nebuchadrezzar's officers in a prism inscription published by Unger (1931: 282–94, and pls. 52–56).

164. For a discussion of this question and solutions proposed in Jewish tradition, see Naor 1984: 60–66.

165. This conclusion stands in contrast to the conclusion reached by some scholars, namely, that the Babylonian delay in destroying Jerusalem was the result of waiting for instructions from Nebuchadrezzar, who had been delayed in Babylon. On this subject, see, e.g., Malamat 1991: 182.

166. The root שׂרף 'to burn' appears 117 times in the Bible, 35 of these in the immediate context of burning buildings and cities. Almost half of the occurrences (16) refer to Jerusalem, either as part of the threats about the fate of the city (e.g., Jer 21:10; 32:29; 34:2, 22; 37:8, 10; 38:17–18, 23; 39:8; Ezek 5:4; 16:41; 23:47, etc.) or as part of the description of the devastation of the city by the Babylonians (e.g., 2 Kgs 25:9; Jer 39:8; 52:13; 2 Chr 36:19). It is probable that the description of the burning of the major buildings in Jerusalem is based on genuine historical memory. The credibility of that memory can be tested by the results of archaeological excavations in the City of David, particularly in Area G, where a burned stratum dated to the days of the Babylonian destruction has been uncovered (Shiloh 1984a: 16). On this subject, see also the archaeological discussion below. Additional support for the credibility of the description can be found in the strong similarity between the descriptions in the prophetic literature and

description of burning "all of the houses of Jerusalem"[167] and "every large house,"[168] as well as "tore down[169] the walls of Jerusalem all about" (v. 10).[170] This description accords with the archaeological finds that were revealed in the excavations of the City of David and of the Ophel (see the discussion below,

lamentations and the historiographical descriptions discussed here; on this subject, see H.-D. Hoffmann 1980: 345–46; Begg 1989: 50–51.

167. The expression "the houses of Jerusalem" occurs in two other places: it is cited again in Isa 22:10, where there is a reference to the dismantling of the houses to fortify the city wall. On this subject, see Avigad 1980: 147; Geva 1991: 171–75, with further literature on pp. 227–28. Jer 19:13 mentions the houses of Jerusalem as a complement to the houses of the kings and, to a large extent, as a counterbalance. Given these parallel passages, it may be that the author of 2 Kings 25 is referring to the ordinary houses of the inhabitants of Jerusalem. Support for this theory can be found in the parallel account, Jer 39:8, which mentions "the house [singular] of the people." This is a unique expression. It is reasonable to assume that the use of the singular form is the result of its similarity in form to "the house of the king"; reading a plural form ("the houses of the people") would result in a suitable parallel to our interpretation of "the houses of Jerusalem" in 2 Kgs 25:9. Taking all of this into consideration, we may postulate that the purpose of this description was to generalize: all of the residences in Jerusalem were destroyed.

168. On reading *bayit* for MT *bêt*, see Cogan and Tadmor 1984: 316, 319. Given the location of the expression "every large house" within the textual sequence, it is hard to accept the opinion of scholars who see it as a later addition (e.g., Burney 1903: 368; Montgomery 1951: 562; Gray 1964: 706; Jones 1984: 643; Würthwein 1984: 476; Hentschel 1985: 121; García Lopez 1987: 226). On the parallel accounts in the other versions of the OT, see Montgomery 1951: 568; Jones 1984: 643; Begg 1989: 51. The term "large house" is unique, and it may refer to the largest and most munificent houses in the city; by adding this phrase, the author wished to encompass the destruction of all of the houses. For the linguistic problems in this expression, see Cogan and Tadmor 1988: 319.

169. The verb נתץ 'tore down', in the sense of causing ruin and destruction, appears in the Bible 42 times, and most of these occurrences (39) connect the destruction with divine action. The destruction may be of places of idol-worship (see, e.g., Exod 34:13; Lev 14:45; Deut 7:5; 12:3; Judg 2:2; 6:28, 30, 31, 32; 2 Kgs 10:27; 11:18; 23:7, 8, 12, 15; 2 Chr 23:18; 31:1; 33:3; 34:4, 7; 36:19, etc.); of places that God wishes to destroy (see Jer 33:4; Ezek 16:39; 26:9, 12); or of a general destruction that expresses the divine will (see Jer 1:10; 4:26; 18:7; 31:27; Nah 1:6; Ps 58:7; etc.). In only 3 of the 42 occurrences of this verb (Judg 8:17; 9:45; Isa 22:10) does it refer to the destruction of walls, towers, or an entire city, without any direct connection to God's role. These are the only occurrences in which נתץ can be replaced by another similar word, one that is more neutral, such as הרס 'destroyed' or החריב 'ruined'. García Lopez (1987: 222–32; followed by Begg 1989: 49–55) uses the term שרף, alongside the term נתץ, as a central argument in assigning vv. 8–10 (except for 9b) to DtrP. In my opinion, aside from the nice linguistic and conceptual distinction, this hypothesis should not be accepted. Ascribing these verses to a later source leaves the text deficient and appears to be part of a tendency toward a more rigid approach to linguistic distinctions in the text. On the connection between the verb נתץ in the Deuteronomistic history and in the book of Jeremiah, see H.-D. Hoffmann 1980: 342–43.

170. There is very little information about the walls of Jerusalem during the days of the First Temple, and we know very little regarding their course, shape, and gates. The most detailed information comes from a description of the destruction of an extensive section by Jehoash, king of Israel (2 Kgs 14:13); correspondingly, on this occasion, it is specifically noted that Nebuzaradan's troops breached the walls "around" the city. The author apparently thought it important to highlight this fact, which was also of great significance at the time of the Return to Zion (Neh 1:3; 2:17; 4:1). On this subject, see Lipschits 2002c.

§4.3.2, pp. 210–211), as well as the account by Nehemiah (2:13–15) when he surveyed the city walls some 130 years later. The destruction inflicted on the city was exceptionally grievous. The book of Lamentations alludes to the aftermath of this destruction: "The ways to Zion mourn, because no one comes to the solemn assembly; all her gates are desolate" (1:4). "All that pass by clap their hands at you; they hiss and wag their head at the daughter of Jerusalem, saying, 'Is this the city that men call the perfection of beauty, the joy of the whole earth?'" (2:15).

The Babylonian policy toward Jerusalem was also expressed in the exiling of its inhabitants.[171] 2 Kgs 25:11 (compare Jer 39:9; 52:15) describes the deportation of three groups to Babylon; by naming the three groups, the author apparently intended to include everyone who had been living in Jerusalem even before the Babylonian siege. In the first group ("the rest of the people that were left in the city") the author apparently included the military forces that remained in Jerusalem after its surrender.[172] The second group ("those who had deserted to the king of Babylon") consisted of those who surrendered to the Babylonians during the siege.[173] It appears that the third group ("the rest of the

---

171. On the Babylonian policy of deportation, see the discussion above, §2.1.4. Joannès (1994: 21–22) has connected evidence that the governor of Arpad was present at Sippar in the 19th year of Nebuchadrezzar's reign (586 B.C.E.) with the fact that Judeans were deported to Babylon that same year. The governor of Arpad is mentioned as making a ritual offering at the Ebabbar Temple at Sippar in two tablets discovered in Sippar. There are no additional references to a western governor in tablets from Babylonia (see also Vanderhooft 1999: 99–100), but we should remember that there is no evidence to support connecting this event to the deportation of the Judeans, even though they must have passed through Riblah and Arpad on the way to Babylonia.

172. The expression "the rest of the people," which occurs in the Bible 12 times, usually is found in a military context, and it seems to refer to a less-select group of soldiers, in contrast with the other military men mentioned in that context. For example, in the story of Gideon, "the rest of the people" refers to those who did not lap the water (Judg 7:6); in the war against the Ammonites and the Arameans, they are the part of the army that was led by Abishai against the Ammonites (2 Sam 10:10), not the part selected and led by Joab against the Arameans (v. 9). Joab's men ultimately defeated the Arameans (v. 13) and brought about the flight of the Ammonites (v. 14). On this subject, compare 2 Sam 12:28; 1 Kgs 12:23; Zech 14:2; Neh 4:8, 13; 1 Chr 19:11. The interpretation of this expression is also connected to plural forms of שאר, which is used as a technical term for those who were not killed in battle, whether entire nations (Josh 23:4, 7, 12), individuals (1 Sam 11:11; 2 Kgs 10:11, 17; etc.), or even horses (2 Kgs 7:13). The conclusion is that the phrase "the rest of the people that were left in the city" refers to military forces of some kind that did not become casualties in the battle for Jerusalem but were captured after the fall of the city. It is likely that these were not the elite defense forces (or at least, they were not thought to be elite) and that they included the defenders who were not killed, did not escape with Zedekiah and "all the men of war" (2 Kgs 25:4–5; Jer 39:4; 52:7), and were not killed in the first weeks after the fall of the city, when the Babylonian army occupied Jerusalem.

173. On the expression נפל על, see above (p. 76 and nn. 144–45); and see Eph'al's discussion (1984: 18–19). If Eph'al's conclusions are accepted—that this expression refers to those who surrendered to the enemy—we can speculate that the second group exiled by Nebuzaradan included those who escaped from the city during the siege. We may assume that some were

multitude") included the rest of the populace of Jerusalem who were trapped in the city after the siege ended.[174] The deportation was well-planned and well-organized. Inasmuch as the economic, political, and religious elite were already in Babylon, the Babylonians must have carefully sorted the exiles according to instructions that included, in particular, the removal of those who were likely to create problems for the new political structure.[175]

2 Kgs 25:11 implies that the entire population of Jerusalem was deported. This fits the remainder of the context, which deals only with the destruction of the city; there is no reference to other parts of the kingdom. Against this background, the author completed his description with two lists: the list of the tools and vessels from the temple that were dismantled and plundered by the Babylonians (vv. 13–17) and the list of some priests and leaders of the city that were put to death by the Babylonians in Riblah (vv. 18–21a).[176] These lists highlight the completeness and irreversibility of the destruction and lead to the

---

military men and some were civilians who, in light of the situation, decided to flee (and cf. Jer 37:12; 38:19).

174. The word המון appears in the Bible in various declensions 81 times; in most cases, it refers to a large crowd of people. It is difficult to characterize this crowd in terms of its composition (Burney 1903: 369). It is used parallel to military terms (cf. Judg 4:15, parallel to v. 7; 1 Sam 14:15, parallel to vv. 16 and 19; 1 Kgs 20:27, parallel to v. 28) and terms for civilians (cf. 1 Sam 4:13–14). Jer 39:9 and 52:15, which are parallel to our text, provide some additional information that helps us to understand this word. The repetition of ואת יתר העם 'the rest of the people' at the end of Jer 39:9 is taken by most scholars to be a dittography that repeats the beginning of the verse, when compared with 2 Kings (Holladay 1989: 269), but it looks to me like an interpretation of the verse in 2 Kings (and see below). There is no linguistic reason to read האמון here, with Jer 52:15 (contra Thompson 1980: 645; Holladay 1989; and see Cogan and Tadmor 1988: 319, with further literature). The text in chap. 52 seems even more complex, and it is difficult to accept various solutions that derive the meaning of the word from the root אמן (mainly architects/builders and artisans; and see Harrison 1973: 190; Thompson 1980: 645, 773; Holladay 1989: 293; and see the critique by Cogan and Tadmor 1988: 319). On the other hand, the word ויתר 'and the rest of', which precedes המון, usually denotes a portion of a larger group that has already been mentioned or counted (cf. 2 Sam 13:2; 1 Kgs 11:41; 22:47; etc.). In both the immediate context and this specific verse, the military who remained in the city and the general populace (both military and civilian) that surrendered to the Babylonians are mentioned, so we may assume that the author used המון to refer to the rest of the civilian population of Jerusalem—specifically, those who remained in the city and were captured when the city fell (Montgomery 1951: 563; Gray 1964: 766). Thus, the writer of 2 Kings concluded the general description of the deportation of the residents of Jerusalem without mentioning the rest of the inhabitants of the kingdom (Jones 1984: 644). This conclusion is supported by the free interpretation that the author of the book of Jeremiah gave to המון when he wrote, "the rest of the people that were left (in the city?)" (39:6)—although by doing so, he created a redundancy with the first part of the verse.

175. On the description of the deportation as an expression of Deuternomistic ideology, see Janzen 1956: 25–39; Ackroyd 1968: 237–47; Barstad 1996: 25–27. On this subject, see also the discussion below, in chap. 5.

176. On the lists in 2 Kgs 25:13–17 and 18–21a, see Rehm 1982: 233. For the date of the lists, see Eynikel 1996: 191–92, with further literature.

summary statement found in v. 21b: "Thus Judah was carried away captive out of its land."[177]

Despite the intent of the unequivocal message—to communicate the extent of the devastation—the message also seems to reflect a historical reality: the Babylonian campaign did in fact focus on Jerusalem and caused only minimal damage to other parts of the kingdom. Support for this exists in the archaeological evidence that will be presented in chap. 4, as well as in the disappearance of Jerusalem from the historical descriptions of the people left in Judah after the destruction of Jerusalem and the deportation of the nation's elite (see Lipschits 2001: 129–42). This subject, as well as the political, religious, and demographic status of Jerusalem after its destruction, will be discussed in what follows.

2.2.3. Evidence of the Political Orientation of the Family of Shaphan, the Scribe, and the Status of Gedaliah on the Eve of Jerusalem's Fall

The name *Gedaliah/Gedalyahu* occurs in the Bible 32 times, and it appears that it was a common name between the end of the 7th and the 4th centuries B.C.E.[178] His father, *Ahikam*, is mentioned some 20 times, in every case as the father of Gedaliah, and both father and son had a central role in the court of the king from the time of Josiah to the time of Jehoiakim. Ahikam, the son of Shaphan, had an important role in the reforms enacted by Josiah,[179] and Jer 26:24 says that it was he who protected the prophet from the people—evidence of his power and status. This is also the first sign of a "pro-Jeremiah" policy in the family, a policy that is also reflected in other contexts.[180] The name *Shaphan*, the grandfather of Gedaliah, appears in the Bible 30 times. In addition to being mentioned as the father of Ahikam and the grandfather of Gedaliah, he is also referred to as the scribe of King Josiah.[181] Throughout the cult reform of Josiah

---

177. Compare this statement with 2 Kgs 17:23b. The discrepancy between this sweeping statement and the specific contents of the two expanded lists is evidence of how this entire passage is subordinate to transmission of the author's message (Dtr²). For a discussion of the bias of this description and the message it conveys, see below.

178. Aside from the 27 passages in which Gedaliah is mentioned as the son of Ahikam and the grandson of Shaphan, additional personalities by this name are mentioned: the grandfather of the prophet Zephaniah (Zeph 1:1); one of the officials of King Zedekiah (Jer 38:1); the son of Jeduthun, one of those "who prophesied with harps, with psalteries, and with cymbals" (1 Chr 25:3, 9); and a priest in the days of Ezra (Ezra 10:18). The name also occurs in the ostraca from Ḥorvat ʿUza (Beit-Arieh 1999b: 32).

179. 2 Kgs 22:12–14 (= 2 Chr 34:20–22) attests to the central role played by Ahikam, the son of Shaphan, in Josiah's reform as a member of the delegation sent to the prophetess Huldah, along with Hilkiah the priest, Achbor (Abdon in Chronicles) the son of Michaiah, and Shaphan the scribe (who apparently was Ahikam's father).

180. Montgomery 1951: 565; Gray 1964: 771; Cogan and Tadmor 1988: 325; see also the discussion below.

181. Additional genealogical details about Shaphan are known (2 Kgs 22:3, and cf. 2 Chr 34:8), namely, that his father's name was Azaliah and his grandfather's name was Meshullam; however, there is no additional information about these two.

(described in 2 Kings 22 = 2 Chronicles 34), Shaphan had a central role, in organizing the repair of the temple, in reading the book of the law and bringing it to the king, and as part of the delegation sent to the prophetess Huldah.

This family was connected, apparently, to four other personalities who had senior standing in the kingdom of Judah. *Elasah, the son of Shaphan,* is cited in Jer 29:3 as one of Zedekiah's two messengers to Nebuchadrezzar in Babylon; *Gemariah, the son of Shaphan,* is mentioned in Jer 36:10 as possessing a chamber "in the upper court at the entrance of the new gate of Yahweh's house," where Baruch read the words of Jeremiah to all the people. The seal impression "[Belonging] to Gemaryahu, son of Shaphan," found in the excavations at the City of David may be attributed to this same Gemariah.[182] *Micaiah, son of Gemariah, the son of Shaphan,* is mentioned in Jer 36:10–13 as the person who reported to the officials what Baruch had read. *Jaazaniah, the son of Shaphan,* is mentioned in Ezek 8:11 as one of the 70 elders of the house of Israel whom the prophet saw in his vision. Yeivin proposed adding to this family two more names that appear in seal impressions: *Elishama,* who appears on a seal impression as "[Belonging] to Elishama, son of Gedaliah" (Diringer 1934: 256–58, and table 22:13), and *Nehemiah,* who appears on a seal impression as "[Belonging] to Nehemiah(?), son of Micaiah(?)" (Diringer 1934: 190 and table 19:30). However, connecting these men with the family of Shaphan, the scribe, is a speculative enterprise, as is the family lineage proposed by Yeivin.[183]

On the basis of the status of the members of the family of Shaphan, the scribe, the roles they played, and the actions attributed to them, particularly in the book of Jeremiah,[184] we can understand why they were charged with having a pro-Babylonian tendency.[185] However, there is no factual evidence that this family was pro-Babylonian or anti-Egyptian. The actions attributed to them may indicate, at most, their vigorous objection to the activists who hoped to gain Egyptian help in their resistance against the Babylonians. Their policy was

---

182. On this seal impression, see Shiloh 1984a: 18, pl. 35:3; 1985: 78–83. Shiloh suggested that Gemariah was an official and a scribe in the court of King Jehoiakim (1986: 34; Shiloh and Tarler 1986: 204–5), but against this idea, see Avigad 1986: 113–14 n. 149, with further literature. On this subject, see also Shoham 1999: 152–53.

183. On this subject, see Yeivin 1960: 274–79, and the table of families (table A). A more cautious table is presented by Yeivin in *EncMiq* 5, col. 253.

184. Ahikam, the son of Shaphan and father of Gedaliah, was the one who saved Jeremiah from death at the hands of the people (Jer 26:24). Elasah, the son of Shaphan, was one of Zedekiah's two messengers to Babylon (29:3). The words of Jeremiah were read aloud by Baruch in the chamber of Gemariah, the son of Shaphan (36:10); Micaiah, the son of Gemariah, was the one who delivered the substance of the message to the officials of the king (36:10–13).

185. On this subject, see Montgomery 1951: 565; Miller and Hayes 1986: 403–6, 423. The attempt by Yeivin (1960: 272–74) to distinguish between the king's officials, who supported Babylon, and the military men, who supported Egypt, is based on the one-dimensional and hostile description found in "Jeremiah's biography." However, it is highly doubtful that this description reflects historical reality or that the leadership of Judah was divided in this way.

similar to that of Jeremiah, who consistently opposed activism in foreign policy and admonished the leaders of the small kingdom to submit to those whom the LORD had made rulers over the country. In light of this, it seems more accurate to define the ideology of Shaphan's family as politically moderate and cautious, though resolute in terms of domestic affairs. This may help to explain why Gedaliah was appointed to his role by the Babylonians.

These data regarding Shaphan and his family need to be supplemented by hypotheses regarding the status of Gedaliah, who held a prominent position in the Judean administration during the time of Zedekiah. These hypotheses are based on a bulla found in the destruction stratum at Lachish (Tell ed-Duweir), which reads "[Belonging] to Gedaliah, who is over the (royal) house."[186] From the very beginning of the bulla's discovery, the Gedaliah cited on it has been identified as Gedaliah, the son of Ahikam, and his status prior to the destruction as the chief of the king's officials[187] has been emphasized by scholars as one of the major reasons why the Babylonians appointed him to a position of responsibility.[188] Another bulla, with the inscription "[belonging] to Gedaliah, the servant of the king," has also been discovered.[189] Avigad emphasizes the connection between the inscriptions on the two bullas (Avigad 1986: 24–25; Fox 2000: 81–96, with further literature). With this connection in mind, he has argued that the bullas reflect two different periods in Gedaliah's life: at first, he was (only) one of the

---

186. The bulla was published almost simultaneously by Hooke (1935: 195) and Starkey (1935: 206). It was preserved intact, but the specific locus and stratum to which it belongs is unknown and its date is uncertain (Tufnell 1953: 348). It is difficult to accept Mykytiuk's (2004: 235) paleographical argument that the script is to be dated to the mid-seventh century B.C.E. and, hence, the bulla is too early to refer to Gedaliah the son of Ahikam. See, contra this conclusion, the opinion of Vaughn (1999).

187. The title "who is over the (royal) house" appears in the Bible 12 times, 8 times in Kings (1 Kgs 4:6; 16:9; 18:3; 2 Kgs 10:5; 15:5; 18:18, 37; 19:2) and 4 times in Isaiah (22:15; 36:3, 22; 37:2). In 2 Chronicles, analogous titles such as "over the king's house" (2 Chr 26:21) or "the ruler of the house" (2 Chr 28:7) appear, and the meaning is probably identical (Mettinger 1971: 70). It appears that this title existed throughout the years of the Divided Monarchy (1971: 70–71; also see p. 72 on the inscription, ". . . yahu, who is over the [royal] house"). Most of the occurrences imply the lofty status of the position, and this is particularly apparent in the words of Isaiah (22:21–23). He is the one who stood at the head of the king's officials (2 Kgs 18:18, 37; 19:2; and cf. Isa 36:3, 22; 37:2). He was wealthy and powerful (Isa 22:15) and very close to the king (1 Kgs 16:9; 18:5–6). On this subject, see also de Vaux 1936: 97–99; Mettinger 1971: 72–79; Fox 2000: 81–96, with further literature. Given this information, we can dismiss the analysis of May (1939: 146–48), who takes this title also to mean 'regent' and from this draws further conclusions about Gedaliah, who was appointed by Jehoiachin after the latter was deported. For counterarguments, see Liver (1959: 68–69).

188. For a compilation of the evidence on this subject, see Hooke 1935: 195; Starkey 1935: 206; de Vaux 1936: 99–102; Tur-Sinai 1936: 371–88.

189. On this bulla, see Avigad 1986: 24–25. On the title "the servant of the king" in the Bible and in historical reality, see Avigad 1986: 23; Fox 2000: 53–63; Lipschits 2002. Apparently, this title emphasized the close relationship between its bearer and the king; however, the title does not clarify the nature of the office, and some of its bearers could have had, simultaneously, another title that more specifically denoted their role.

king's officials; later he was appointed to the high-ranking position of he "who is over the (royal) house." This hypothesis must be treated with caution (see Becking 1997: 78), because there is no basis for the assumption that we know about all of the persons who held office at that time. Avigad himself notes that another man of the same name, to whom this bulla might have belonged, is known from the Bible (Gedaliah, the son of Pashhur; see Jer 38:1); and there is yet another seal impression that mentions the name Gedaliah ("[belonging] to Gedalyahu/ Hosheʿyahu"; Avigad 1986: 45). On the other hand, there is no contradiction between the titles "who is over the (royal) house" and "the servant of the king," and it is not necessary to assume that the two bullas have significantly different dates, even if they refer to the same official.[190]

Assuming that Gedaliah "who is over the (royal) house" is identical with Gedaliah, the son of Ahikam, we can conclude that the Babylonians appointed one of the senior officeholders in the royal governing apparatus as governor of the land and put him in charge of "the people who were left in the land." This appointment may have combined the interests of both parties. The Babylonians were appointing a person who had served in the highest-ranking position in the royal administration, a man with a history of prudent, moderate policy and with proved governing ability (Harrison 1973: 160; Graham 1984: 57; Lipschits 1999c: 121–23). Such a person could rebuild the country quickly (a clear Babylonian interest), reorganize the governing apparatus under Babylonian supervision, bring stability to the region, and all the while maintain loyalty to the Babylonians (Montgomery 1951: 565; Gray 1964: 771). For Gedaliah, the interest was even clearer: he could rebuild his country and ensure the welfare of the people who remained. By transforming him into the leader of "the people who were left in the land," the Babylonians ensured that the policy that his family had endorsed all along was vindicated.

Against this background, it is difficult to avoid a comparison of the status of Gedaliah and his family and the family of the prophet Jeremiah, who opposed the activist position on the eve of the destruction of the First Temple, with Rabban Yohanan ben-Zakkai and his followers on the eve of the destruction of the Second Temple. Despite the different historical circumstances, we may draw a parallel between Rabban Yohanan ben-Zakkai's departure from Jerusalem and establishment of a center in Yabneh (as a substitute for the devastated city of Jerusalem), on the one hand, and Gedaliah's remaining outside the besieged city of Jerusalem and the establishment of a center at Mizpah, on the other hand.

---

190. As the various archaeological discoveries make clear (e.g., the Eliashib seals from Arad), an official may have had several seals, so we cannot know whether both seals belonged to the same Gedaliah. Furthermore, if it is true that the title "servant of the king" denotes an elevated position and proximity to the king but does not denote a specific position, it is likely that the bullas are contemporary and were used for different purposes. On the possibility that a single person had two or more seals during the First Temple Period, see Barag 1999: 35–38.

Gedaliah's actions are no doubt to be linked with Jeremiah's abortive attempt to leave the city to join the Judeans in the Benjamin region (37:12–16) at the height of the siege; later, he went to the center established in Mizpah as a substitute for the destroyed city of Jerusalem. In both cases, the establishment of an alternate center (Mizpah and Yabneh) was carried out under the aegis of the conquerors (Babylonia and Rome). In both cases, the spiritual leaders held a political orientation opposed to the policies of those who ruled in Jerusalem, and in both cases they understood the futility of staging a revolt. In both cases, their actions were in opposition to the dominant policy in Jerusalem, the center of the revolt; in both cases, their actions were welcomed by the imperial government; and in both cases, the status of the occupied land was altered, and the country became a province.

2.2.4. The Appointment of Gedaliah, the son of Ahikam, as Governor of Judah

Gedaliah's position in Mizpah was officially sanctioned by Babylon (2 Kgs 25:22–26; Jer 40:7–41:18). He was given authority over the territory where "the people who were left in the land" were settled, and he was responsible to serve as an intermediary between the Babylonian government and the local population. This becomes clear from the way that the appointment of Gedaliah as governor is described (2 Kgs 25:22b, 23aα; Jer 40:7aβ, 7bα): it is stated that his appointment was ordered by the king. In every case where the root פקד appears in the Hiphil form in the Bible, it refers to the appointment of a person to an official position of some kind. However, what is absent from both passages is a definition of the position, apart from noting that Gedaliah was appointed over a specific area of responsibility ("appointed over . . .").[191] The conclusion is that the author of this description saw Gedaliah as appointed by the Babylonian authorities to be responsible for Judah (see also Machinist 1992: 79). This parallels Pharaoh's appointment of Joseph over all of Egypt (Gen 39:4–5); his appointment of officials over the entire land (41:34); Jeroboam's being appointed "over all of the labor of the house of Joseph" (1 Kgs 11:28); and Ahasuerus's appointment of officials "in all the provinces of his kingdom" (Esth 2:3).

This conclusion is supported by the accounts that report that the "commanders of the army units" (2 Kgs 25:23b; Jer 40:7) joined Gedaliah and that he gave them his oath (2 Kgs 25:24; Jer 40:9), wanting to pacify their fear of the Babylo-

---

191. For a collection of all of the uses of פקד 'appointed' in the Bible, see André 1980. For the appearance of this root in Assyrian and Babylonian texts, see the summary provided by Ahlström 1993: 799, with further literature. Reservations about this widely accepted interpretation of the text are expressed by Miller and Hayes (1986: 421), who maintain that Gedaliah was appointed by the Babylonians as the first king in Judah who was not of the Davidic line (see also the opinion of Barstad 1988: 29, and n. 17). I will discuss this argument below, but we may refute it on a linguistic basis: הפקיד is nowhere used of the appointment of a king (Cogan and Tadmor 1988: 327).

nians. Gedaliah's ability to soothe the fears of those joining him is evidence of his status and of the authority that he wielded, at least as a liaison between "the people who were left in the land" and the Babylonians.[192] According to Jer 40:10, Gedaliah defined his role this way: "As for me, I will dwell at Mizpah to stand before the Chaldeans when they come to us." The meaning of the expression "to stand before" is equivalent to "reporting in the service of a supreme authority." A parallel to this expression is found in the description of the status and role of Joseph, who was "thirty years old when he entered the service of Pharaoh, king of Egypt" (Gen 41:46); according to vv. 40, 42, 44, he (a) was appointed "over all the land of Egypt," (b) was the most senior of the king's officials, and (c) was the one without whom "no man [would] lift up his hand or foot in all of the land of Egypt." Similarly, Joshua was Moses' senior appointee and "stood before" Moses (Deut 1:38). Likewise, David "stood before" Saul (1 Sam 16:21); the elders "stood before" Solomon, as did the young men with whom Rehoboam consulted (1 Kgs 12:6, 8); in Jeremiah's prophecy, Moses and Samuel "stood before" God (15:1); and so on.[193] Gedaliah's status and position were also supported by a Babylonian bureaucracy and military force of some kind in Mizpah (2 Kgs 25:24aβ, 25bβ; Jer 41:3aβ). This group apparently oversaw Gedaliah's actions and perhaps gave him official support and military backing.[194]

Gedaliah's status is also reflected in the way that the story presents his directions to the "commanders of the army units" (Jer 40:10b), in the imperatives ("gather," "store," "settle"), and in his ability to grant them lands and houses,[195]

---

192. On the literary features of Gedaliah's oath to the "commanders of the army units" and its significance, see Kessler 1965: 293; Harrison 1973: 160; Feinberg 1982: 271; Bullah 1984: 499; Holladay 1989: 295; Hoffman 2000: 103–26.

193. On this subject, see also Thompson 1980: 655; Holladay 1989: 295. Adding to this interpretation is the frequently found expression "to stand to minister" (Num 16:9; Deut 10:8; 18:5; 1 Kgs 8:11; 2 Chr 5:14; 29:11; etc.).

194. Additional evidence comes from the archaeological findings at Tell en-Naṣbeh; see the discussion below, §2.3.3 (pp. 109–112); §4.3.3a (pp. 237–241).

195. Gedaliah's instructions to the "commanders of the army units" (Jer 40:10bβ)—"settle in your cities that you have occupied"—is evidence that he was able to allocate lands and houses to them. It is noteworthy that the LXX says here "in the cities" instead of "in your cities" (Holladay 1989: 271), and this reading seems very reasonable, although it may be a revision of a problematic text. If the phrase reflects the reality of that period, then it attests to the process by which "the people who were left in the land" took over the lands and settlements of those who went into exile. This is of great importance in reconstructing the ideological, political, and economic conflict that arose between the two different parts of the nation. It is sufficient here to note that the expression תפש 'occupied, seized' with regard to towns or settlements always occurs in a military context and is parallel to the verb לכד 'capture' (Josh 8:8; 2 Kgs 14:7; 18:13; Jer 48:41; etc.). It is probable that this instruction reflects the reality of the period when those who remained in Judah, as well as the refugees who returned with the objective of integrating into the life of the province, took over the lands and houses left behind by those who went into exile (Miller and Hayes 1986: 420; Kochman 1980: 102). It also seems to be the case that these actions aroused reactions among the exiles in Babylon. The words of Ezekiel (11:15–16; 33:23–27) reflect anger among the exiles, as well as their feeling of helplessness. On this subject, see

along with a livelihood (2 Kgs 25:24; Jer 40:9–10, 12b).[196] Even his directions
regarding the storage and collection of agricultural produce ("and store them in
your vessels," v. 10bα) imply his authority to collect taxes from the residents of
the provinces. This conclusion accords well with the evidence emerging from
the *mwṣh* seal impressions, which indicate that the province was responsible for
its own provisioning (see below, §3.3.1, pp. 149–152). We may suppose that Gedaliah's decision not to collect taxes reflects the action of a governor conceding
what was owed to him, with the object of helping the residents of the province
establish themselves and rebuild their lives. An apt parallel to this can be seen
in the actions of Nehemiah (5:14–19) who, in a time of duress, waived the right
to collect "the bread of the governor" from the people.[197]

Despite scant and problematic evidence, we may nevertheless conclude that
the Babylonians appointed Gedaliah over Judah. The most fitting title for the
position that he filled is "governor." The opinion of Miller and Hayes that Gedaliah was appointed a vassal king by the Babylonians should be rejected (see
the opinion of Machinist 1992: 79; contra Miller and Hayes 1986: 421–23).
The primary data that Miller and Hayes cite in support of their thesis are the
reference to "the king's daughters" (Jer 41:10) and the description of Ishmael,
the son of Nethaniah: "of the royal seed [= of the royal house], one of the chief
officers of the king" (41:1), whom Miller and Hayes believe to have been connected with the kingship of Gedaliah. They theorize that "the final editors of
Kings material did not wish to reveal his real title" because "it would have required the admission that a non-Davidic person was appointed as king" (Miller
and Hayes 1986: 423). In contrast, I believe that the term "the king's daughters"
as well as the description of Ishmael's origin should be linked to the period
before the destruction: these people were the remnants of the royal house, apparently family members who were not close, or if they were close, were nevertheless not taken into exile. Ishmael is not mentioned in any other text as a
member of the royal family. In contrast to the detailed description of the fate of
the sons of the kings (2 Kgs 25:7; Jer 39:6; 52:10), there is no information about
the exiling of the king's daughters or the Babylonian policy toward them. We
may assume that the Babylonians placed the women under Gedaliah's protec-

---

also Tadmor 1988: 50–53. The opinion of some scholars, that there was a deliberate distribution of agricultural land by the Babylonians, cannot be supported. For a summary, critique, and
bibliography on this subject, see Hoglund 1992: 22–23, and nn. 91, 92.

196. On the economy of Judah during Gedaliah's reign, see the discussion below, §2.3.2
(pp. 102–109).

197. According to these verses, Nehemiah's waiver of "the bread of the governor" was in
contrast to previous practice: "the former governors who had been before me laid burdens upon
the people and had taken from them for bread and wine . . . because the bondage was heavy
upon this people." Support for this may be found in the *mwṣh* seal impressions, which reflect
the fact that the governor had independent sources of provisioning; see more on this below,
pp. 149–152.

tion, just as the prophet Jeremiah had been handed over to him, as well as "men [soldiers], women, children, and eunuchs" (41:16, and compare 43:6; on the text of this verse, see Thompson 1980: 659). Rudolph even connected the presence of the eunuchs with the king's daughters and theorized that the eunuchs were left in Mizpah to protect and serve them (Rudolph 1947: 252). However, against the view of Miller and Hayes, there is no evidence that Gedaliah was appointed king or that Judah continued to hold the status of a kingdom; moreover, the brief duration of his rule would not have given him enough time to establish a royal palace and appoint officials. The theory that the description was omitted by a later editor of the book of Kings has neither textual nor conceptual basis and contravenes the description of Gedaliah's "being appointed" in Mizpah.[198]

There is hardly any information about the ways and means of Babylonian government in the provinces and in the vassal kingdoms inside the borders of the Empire,[199] nor is anything known of the people who were appointed as governors. However, there are accounts of the appointment of local notables to the office of governor during (earlier) Assyrian and (later) Persian rule. We do have accounts from the ninth and eighth centuries B.C.E. of various provincial rulers in the Upper Euphrates; these rulers were active primarily during periods when the central authority was weak (Labat 1968: 37–50). A striking example is found in the bilingual inscription found at Tell-Fakhariya (ancient Sikāni).[200] This inscription reveals that persons bearing Aramaic names were among the local notables and that even members of the royal family served as local potentates under the Assyrians.[201] A similar conclusion can be drawn from the inscriptions found at Suḫu (see Cavigneaux and Ismail 1990; Dion 1995) and accounts of the status of the princes in the Delta region during the time of Esarhaddon and Ashurbanipal.[202]

The analogies from the Persian Period are clearer, and closer in both time and place, because there is a great deal of information about the appointment of

---

198. On the orientation and perspective of the composition and editing of the later parts of the book of Kings, see the discussion in chap. 5, pp. 272–304.

199. See the discussion by Vanderhooft (1999: 99–104) of the scant and insubstantial evidence for Babylonian functionaries in the area "Beyond the River" and his differing opinion about what took place in Judah (pp. 104–10). See also the discussion below.

200. This inscription was published in 1981 by Abou-Assaf and discussed one year later in a comprehensive monograph published by Abou-Assaf, Bordreuil, and Millard (1982). For critiques of the translation of the inscription, its historical significance, and date, as well as additional literature, see Zadok 1982b; Huehnergard 1986; Naveh 1989a: 76–81; 1987: 101–13; Dion 1997: 40–41, with further literature.

201. On Hdys'y's titles and their meaning, on the status of the family, and the time when he was active, see Abou-Assaf, Bordreuil, and Millard 1982: 98–113; Zadok 1982b: 125. For a critique of this view, see Vanderhooft 1999: 105 n. 178. On the name Hdys'y, see Zadok 1982: 123.

202. For the English translation of the document (Rassam Cylinder), which was discovered in 1878, see Luckenbill 1927: 770–83. See also the translation in *ANET*: 294–95; and also see Cogan and Tadmor 1988: 327.

the Jewish governors (among them Sheshbazzar, Zerubbabel, and Nehemiah) in the Persian province of Yehud. On the assumption that the Babylonian administrative structure was perpetuated into this period, we may draw the parallel that the tendency to appoint Jewish governors existed even under Babylonian rule. It makes sense that the Babylonians would have appointed a local person who knew the population, possessed basic knowledge about the region and the existing ruling system, and was able to maintain continuity in government. This suggestion is reinforced by the fact that the Babylonians knew that Gedaliah's family had supported moderate, realistic policies; they may also have been familiar with Gedaliah himself, who may have been the highest-ranking of the king's officials.[203] All of these factors would have enabled Gedaliah to rebuild the region quickly and to repopulate it rapidly, in this way serving both his new masters' interests and also those of his own people who had remained in their land.

The conclusion we may draw is that the Babylonians appointed Gedaliah as governor over Judah; this conclusion is the best way to read the biblical description of events in context of international politics of the sixty century B.C.E.[204]

2.2.5. When Did the Babylonians Appoint Gedaliah Governor over Judah?

The primary historical account of the appointment of Gedaliah and the establishment of a center in Mizpah on the eve of the destruction of Jerusalem is the "biography of Jeremiah."[205] Several traditions were embedded within this "biography," and from these traditions information emerges about the establishment of an alternative center even before the destruction of Jerusalem. The main evidence for the existence of an organized Judahite group outside of the capital city on the eve of the destruction of Jerusalem is found in a description of Jeremiah's last attempts to convince Zedekiah to leave the city and surrender

---

203. Presenting Gedaliah's appointment as an act of Nebuchadrezzar himself is part of the attempt to emphasize the importance of "the people who were left in the land" and does not reflect a credible historical situation. Apparently, Nebuchadrezzar was present in Judah only at the beginning of the siege of Jerusalem and perhaps also for some time afterward (2 Kgs 25:1; Jer 39:1; 52:4); however, when Jerusalem fell, he was in Riblah (2 Kgs 25:6; Jer 39:5; 52:10). Nebuzaradan came to burn the temple and destroy the city (2 Kgs 25:8, 10; Jer 52:12), and it is likely that he carried out the deportation and made the arrangements for the administration of the province of Judah for the subsequent period (2 Kgs 25:11–12; Jer 39:9–10; 52:15–16). This analysis is also consistent with the role of Nebuzaradan in Jer 40:1–6 and the names of the officers mentioned in 39:3, 13. See Hyatt 1956b: 1079; Kessler 1965: 279–80; Rudolph 1947: 224.

204. Contra the opinion of Vanderhooft 1999: 104–10. It is difficult to believe that a conqueror of any kind would have left occupied territories without any political structure and without an administrative/governmental framework, limited and minimal though they were. On this subject, see also Wiseman 1985: 38.

205. On the "biography" within the book of Jeremiah, see the discussion below, §5.2.2 (pp. 312–347, esp. pp. 339–347), and see also Wanke 1971: 151–54; Perdue 1994: 247–59; Hoffman 2001: 57, 679–81, 691–92; Albertz 2003: 302–45, with further literature.

to the Babylonians (Jer 38:14–28a).[206] In response to the prophet's words, "If you will go out to the officials of the king of Babylon, then your life will be saved and this city will not be burned with fire" (38:17), the king says: "I am worried about the Judeans who have deserted to the Chaldeans, that I might be given into their hands and they will mistreat me" (v. 19). Zedekiah is referring to the Judahites who have surrendered to the Babylonians and thus escaped the misery of life in a city under siege.[207] The implication of these words is that this group is in a specific place outside Jerusalem and is being granted some degree of autonomy and freedom of action by the Babylonians. The king's fear is that, if he surrenders to the Babylonians, they will deliver him to this group. This concern attests to the fact that the Babylonians saw this group as the basis for a new scheme that they wished to establish and that Zedekiah, like Jeremiah, knew of it. Zedekiah's words reveal the existence of two groups with differing political orientations: (1) the supporters of the revolt, who were inside Jerusalem, and (2) the supporters of capitulation to Babylon, who were outside of the city. The hostility between the two groups is highlighted by Zedekiah's well-founded fear that he will be handed over to those who support capitulating, and it is also evident in the attitude of the Judean officials toward Jeremiah.

In an attempt to comprehend the process by which the two groups formed, we may point to a remarkable circumstance: the appearance of Egypt, coming to the aid of besieged Jerusalem (Jer 37:5–11; for a historical reconstruction of these events, see above, §2.2.2, pp. 72–84). Against the background of a lull in the siege, when the Babylonians turn to fight the Egyptian army, Jeremiah's attempt to leave the city is described: he tries to "escape from there among the people" (37:12). The account in vv. 12–13aα provides Jeremiah's destination ("to go to the land of Benjamin") and his exit point from the city ("and he was at the gate of Benjamin"), implying that those who left the city set out toward the region of Benjamin. The question is: why did these people leave, and what happened to them? It is difficult to accept the view of some scholars that these people should be identified with the 832 people who were deported in the 18th year of Nebuchadrezzar's reign, as mentioned in Jer 52:29 (see, e.g., the opinion of Malamat 1983: 288; against this view, Albertz 2003: 88). Jeremiah's act is not described as extraordinary or aberrant. He was seized at the gate of Benjamin "among the people" departing for the land of Benjamin only because the officials in Jerusalem feared the propaganda effect of his desertion to the Babylonian side. At the height of the siege, the Judahites who had fled to the region of Benjamin might have been encouraged if Jeremiah had joined them, because he

---

206. On this verse, see Hoffman 2001: 691–92. For a summary of the various opinions on the meaning of these verses, see Holladay 1989: 290.

207. On the significance and meaning of the verb נפל, see p. 76 and nn. 144–45 above, and see also the discussion in Eph'al 1993: 18–19.

would have added religious legitimacy to their choice. On the other hand, the prophet's departure from the city also would have undermined the confidence of the besieged populace and reinforced Jeremiah's statements that their hope in the invulnerability of the city was false.[208]

This context gains additional significance when we consider the fact that the lull in the siege was a decisive time for the crystallization of this group. The impression we have is that the group of "Judeans who deserted to the Chaldeans" (Jer 38:19) were going to assemble at a specific place in the region of Benjamin. Their departure from the besieged city and Jeremiah's attempt to join them are evidence of their political inclination and of their belief that the revolt was hopeless. They clearly already were familiar with the Babylonians; they were not afraid of them, and they were willing to accept their rule. Jeremiah's confident answer to the king, "They will not give you up" (Jer 38:20a), reflects the desire of the writer to demonstrate the relationship between the Babylonians and this Judahite group, as well as the ability of Jeremiah to influence the group and, thus, the fate of the king after he surrendered to the Babylonians.

This is also the context in which the episode described in chap. 32 must be placed, even if this placement reflects a very late perspective (Albertz 2003: 339–45). According to the opening verses (1–5), the prophet had been arrested by the officials and had been placed in "the court of the guard."[209] The emphasis on the location of the field that Jeremiah wished to buy, "in Anathoth in the land of Benjamin" (v. 8), points to the time when a distinction was being created between the fate of the Benjamin region (which was not part of the area destroyed by the Babylonians)[210] and the fate of Jerusalem and the rest of Judah. This contrast is highlighted in vv. 24–25 (Holladay 1989: 209, 216–17), and it reflects the parallel that the author draws between the future of the entire country and the present fate of the Benjaminite region. In light of the possibility of buying fields in the land of Benjamin in his lifetime, Jeremiah prophesies that "houses and fields and vineyards will be bought again in this land" (v. 15). This forms the background against which he summarizes the future anticipated for the entire country: "Fields they shall buy with silver, and they shall sign with a deed and seal and call witnesses in the land of Benjamin and in the region of Jerusalem and in the cities of Judah [and the cities of the hill country and in the

---

208. Inasmuch as religious faith was the impetus for the continuation of the revolt and the refusal to capitulate to Babylon, the insistence on imprisoning the prophet makes perfect sense: it was necessary to silence him.

209. On dating the prophecy to the exilic and postexilic periods, see Hoffman 2001: 612–15, with further literature; Albertz 2003: 339–45. On dating the prophecy to the actual time of the Babylonian siege, see Oded 1977: 473; Holladay 1989: 212–13.

210. The distinctive fate of the Benjamin region has already been noted by Malamat 1950: 226–28, and nn. 31–32, and cf. also his summary 1983: 286–87. On this subject, see Lipschits 1999a, with further literature. See also below, §4.3.3 (pp. 237–249).

cities of the Shephelah and the cities of the Negev]; for I shall restore their fortunes, says the Lord" (v. 44).[211]

Support for this comes from archaeological discoveries, which show almost complete settlement continuity in the region of Benjamin throughout most of the sixth century B.C.E. (Lipschits 1999a; see also §4.3.3, pp. 237–249). Biblical accounts of the history of the region at the beginning of the Persian period are also in harmony with this conclusion (see below; Lipschits 1997b: 7–32). These data help to explain the change that took place in the prophesies of Jeremiah when, on the eve of the destruction that he had foreseen and warned against for years, he embarks on a prophecy of comfort to the people. It is difficult to detach these prophecies from the establishment of the center at Mizpah, from the appointment of Gedaliah, the son of Ahikam as governor, or from Jeremiah's own attempt to move to Mizpah prior to the destruction of Jerusalem. The prophet's behavior afterward, too, as described in the later portions of his "biography" (particularly in 38:14–28), confirms that for him the die had been cast: Jerusalem was to be laid waste. From this point onward, the prophet is looking toward the future, and he knows that the task of rebuilding the nation is the central task that its leaders must assume. This is why the prophet continues to struggle against the officials and works for the capitulation of the city and, thus, to rescue it. According to 38:27, when the officials question him about his conversation with the king, he lies to them, as commanded by the king (vv. 25–26), and does not repeat his actual words. In response, the officials "stopped questioning him, for the matter had not been overheard" (38:27). It is not known how much time passed between this and the final destruction of Jerusalem, but whatever else the prophet did, he "remained in the court of the guard until the day Jerusalem was captured" (v. 28a).

There is additional evidence for the existence of a Judean center at Mizpah even before the destruction of Jerusalem. Jeremiah was transferred to Mizpah immediately after the destruction, when the new center of government, in the early days of Gedaliah's reign, already was functioning. Two parallel versions of this event were incorporated into the "biography";[212] they provide the only information available on the fate of Jeremiah immediately after the destruction. The parallel historical "kernel" in both traditions includes a description of the prophet's being removed from his place of arrest in Jerusalem by senior Babylonian agents (Nebuzaradan or other Babylonian officials) and being sent to the new center in Mizpah. This information accords with the Babylonian practice

---

211. Most parts of this verse are missing in the LXX (44a; 44bβ) and are probably a late addition. On this subject, see the summary of Holladay 1989: 206, 208.

212. See below (§5.2.2, esp. pp. 325–336) a textual discussion of these passages in chaps. 39–40; the discussion argues for the hypothesis that the story of Jeremiah's release by the Babylonians consists of two versions (Hoffman 2001: 712). This hypothesis rejects the theories put forward by Thompson (1980: 651) and Clements (1988: 229); and see below.

of establishing Babylonian provinces on the basis of agents whose loyalty to Babylon was well known, enabling them to rebuild the country quickly. Sending the prophet to Mizpah suited this policy, because Jeremiah was no doubt a well-known person who for many years had struggled for a sane, realistic policy and in pursuit of this had supported capitulation to the Babylonians.[213] In addition, Jeremiah maintained close relations with the various branches of the family of Shaphan, the scribe, and it is probable that Gedaliah himself needed the presence of an influential figure such as Jeremiah. His transfer to Mizpah by the Babylonians was designed to garner support for the new government and to give Gedaliah moral and religious backing at a difficult time, when the rule of the House of David had been abolished, the capital devastated, and the kingdom brought to an end.[214]

For our purposes, the accounts of Jeremiah's transfer to Mizpah immediately after the destruction demonstrate that this center was already functioning. The proximity of events (the destruction of Jerusalem, the deportation to Babylonia, and the transfer of Jeremiah to Mizpah) is noted explicitly in both narratives, and the background for both is the days immediately after the destruction. It is difficult to assume that this chronology of events is the result of narrative reworking or filling in of lacunae, because it is clearly the framework of both versions.[215] The presence of Gedaliah in Mizpah at this time is tacitly understood. He is presented in the text as a person of authority into whose keeping

---

213. On attempts to reconcile the contradicting descriptions or to emend the text in 40:2–6 and to see part of it as Jeremiah's prophecy connected to the prologue in v. 1, see Bright 1965: 244–46; Thompson 1980: 651–52; Holladay 1989: 281, 293–94. Most scholars see these verses as a synthesis of a report of Nebuzaradan's words to Jeremiah and Jeremiah's prophecy (see the survey in Holladay 1989: 281). Holladay, following Bright 1965: 244, proposed that Jeremiah's prophecy begins in v. 2b (changing the language from "your [singular] God" to "your [plural] God)" and continues in v. 3. However, there are difficulties with this perspective, and it is more reasonable to assume that only v. 3b belongs to Jeremiah's prophecy ("for you have sinned against the Lord and have not obeyed His voice; therefore, this thing has come upon you"). This conclusion is supported by the existence of a precisely parallel version of this prophecy in 44:23, which is more complete. This reconstruction is also more logical in terms of the overall sequence, because it turns out that Nebuzaradan's words included a comparison between the fate of the city and the fate of the prophet; the insertion is only included as an explanation for the grim fate of Jerusalem. On this subject, see also the comments by Muilenburg (in McCown 1947: 30–32). On the linguistic problems in Nebauzaradan's speech and its possible connection to the superscription in v. 1, see Janzen 1973: 22, 53; Holladay 1989: 270. On Nebuzaradan's speech, see also Duhm 1901: 313.

214. We may also theorize that sending Jeremiah to Mizpah, and perhaps sending others with him who may have been able to bolster the new rule there, was carried out at the initiative of Gedaliah or at least with the cooperation of the Babylonian authority.

215. In the first version, Jeremiah's transfer is embedded in a narrative of the stationing of the Babylonian king's officers at the gate of Jerusalem and Jeremiah's release from prison (39:3, 14). In the second version, it is mentioned in conjunction with Nebuzaradan and his connection with Jeremiah's release. In this case, emphasis is placed on the removal of Jeremiah from a convoy of exiles to Babylon (40:1), with chains on his hands (v. 4).

Jeremiah can be entrusted,[216] and the center in Mizpah is described as a place to which Jeremiah can be transferred so that he will live "among the people."[217]

Additional support for this understanding is found in an analysis of the excavations at Tell en-Naṣbeh, which is identified as Mizpah (see Zorn 1993a; Lipschits 1999a: 165–70; see also the discussion below, §4.3.3, pp. 237–241). As will be discussed in detail later, Mizpah was transformed from a Judean border city into a Babylonian administrative city without ever being destroyed. As noted above, it is probable that the Babylonians had altered the city into their administrative center during the siege on Jerusalem. These facts explain the presence of the Chaldean officials in Mizpah (2 Kgs 25:24; Jer 41:3; compare 40:9), the fact that in the lists of the Return to Zion (Ezra 2; Nehemiah 7) the city is not even mentioned, and the fact that there is a unique reference to it in Neh 3:7 ("the seat of the governor Beyond the River").

2.3. The Biblical Account of the History of the Province of Judah (586–538 B.C.E.)

In this section, I will examine the historical information in the biblical material regarding the province of Judah from the destruction of Jerusalem (586 B.C.E.) and the first years of Persian rule to the Return to Zion (538 B.C.E.). This is one of the major "dark ages" in the history of Judah, and the paucity of sources makes it difficult to create a historical portrait of the era. Some information may be culled from the prophetic literature (Ezekiel, Isaiah 40–66, Obadiah, Haggai, Zechariah 1–8, and Malachi), from the lamentations on the destruction of Jerusalem and the temple, and from the psalms that were written in Judah after the destruction of Jerusalem, during the Babylonian exile, and during the period of the Return to Zion.[218] However, most of the information currently available for the period is found in two historical sources. The first and most important one, the "biography of Jeremiah," describes events that transpired immediately after the destruction (see below, §5.2.2, pp. 312–347). This appears in abridged form in 2 Kgs 25:22–26 and in its full version in Jer 40:7–41:18. A short period of only a few months is described: the beginning of the rebuilding of Judah after

---

216. See the description of Gedaliah as the one "whom the king of Babylon had made governor over the cities of Judah" (40:5).

217. This subject is common to both versions and is even repeated twice in the second version. See the uniform language in the description of Jeremiah: he is dwelling "among the people" (39:14; 40:5) or "among the people that were left in the land" (40:6).

218. On the information in these texts about Judah during the exilic period, see Janssen's seminal work (1956). This book has not received due credit, despite the fact that Janssen explored many of the historical and conceptual approaches that have flourished in recent years. Nevertheless, by contemporary research standards, it is difficult to accept the methods and approaches Janssen employed; see, e.g., the critique by Barstad (1996: 19 n. 22). The best recent analysis and summary of these books and what is behind them has been done by Albertz (2003; with extensive literature).

the destruction of Jerusalem. The importance of this source lies in its description of life in Judah after Jerusalem was destroyed, as well as its information on the steps taken by the Babylonians to establish a province in Judah under the leadership of Gedaliah, the son of Ahikam. The other source, Ezra 1–6, incorporates several documents from the early days of the Return to Zion, and several events are recounted, the central event being the return from Babylon and the building of the temple. A reconstruction of these events, even from the very late perspective of the time when they were written, provides a picture of the situation that the returnees confronted, which in turn allows us to reconstruct the conditions that prevailed in the Babylonian province of Judah before the return.

A gap of some fifty years separates the events that took place immediately after the destruction of Jerusalem and those at the beginning of the Return to Zion; the historiographical problem is even greater. A majority of scholars today lean toward the notion that Ezra 1–6 is the last unit of the book of Ezra–Nehemiah and that it was not written before the mid-fifth or even the fourth century B.C.E. (some one hundred or more years after the events actually transpired).[219] A theory regarding what actually took place during the main part of the Babylonian Period may be formed by comparing the historical situation at the beginning of the period and at the end, as well as by considering the additional information contained in Cyrus's proclamation and the actions of the first people to return to Zion.

Furthermore, the dearth of historical sources does not necessarily indicate a historical void; the dearth may also be the result of a tendentious desire to hide the existence of the Babylonian province. We will deal below with the ideology of the elite who were deported to Babylon and the process of reestablishing their rule in the early days of the Return to Zion. However, the primary argument in this section (and also in §2.5 below) is that this elite deliberately tried to conceal "the people who remained in the land of Judah" from the historical records and wished to present themselves as coming to an empty land. This is not an unusual inclination, either in world history or in Jewish history, and I believe it was one of the major reasons for the rewriting of the history of this period, the editors' chief aim being to deliver an ideological message to their generation.

2.3.1. *The Tenure of Gedaliah as First Governor of Judah*

Defining the time when Gedaliah served as the Babylonian governor of Judah in Mizpah is important for a reconstruction of events in the province of Judah after the destruction of Jerusalem. There is much dispute on this point, particularly because there are insufficient chronological data to fix the dates of

---

219. Williamson 1983; Eskenazi 1988: 42; Halpern 1990: 85–93; Japhet 1993b; see the detailed discussion by Grabbe (forthcoming); on the other hand, see the conclusions of Schwiderski (2000: 381–82); see also the discussion below.

events.[220] As I argued above (§2.2.5), Gedaliah was appointed to office even before the destruction of Jerusalem, but when the rumor about his appointment began to spread is not clear (2 Kgs 25:23; Jer 40:7). Similarly, it is not known how much time passed between the destruction of Jerusalem and the arrival of the refugees in the Benjamin region (2 Kgs 25:23; Jer 40:7–8, 11–12); how much time elapsed between the beginning of the assembly of the refugees in Mizpah and the assassination of Gedaliah (2 Kgs 25:25; Jer 41:1–3); or the length of time between his murder and the escape of the rest of the people into Egypt (2 Kgs 25:26; Jer 41:16–18).

We may gain insight into Gedaliah's early activity after the destruction of Jerusalem from his first order to the army officers who came to Mizpah (Jer 40:10b): "gather wine and summer fruits and oil and put them in your vessels." The key word is the verb "gather": Gedaliah was granting permission to harvest agricultural produce that the people who came to Mizpah had not labored to produce.[221] The objective of Gedaliah's command was to make clear the immediate opportunities for sustenance and livelihood that the region held for the refugees.[222] The agricultural produce that Gedaliah allowed them to gather included wine,[223] summer fruits,[224] and oil[225]—the three processed products that

---

220. The only sequence of dates appears in the description of Gedaliah's assassination. According to 2 Kgs 25:25a and Jer 41:1a, Ishmael, son of Nethaniah, came to Mizpah "in the seventh month" (Tishri). According to Jer 41:4a, the massacre of 70 of the 80 mourners who came from Shechem to Shiloh and Samaria took place two days later.

221. 'Gathering' (from the root אסף) stresses that the gatherers are not those who worked to produce the crop (cf. Num 11:22, 32; Isa 10:14; Ruth 2:7, etc.). Furthermore, in cases where the order is given to gather a crop that was in fact cultivated by the gatherers, the term emphasizes that the growth of the crop was divinely granted, so that gratitude should be expressed at harvest time (Exod 23:10, 16; Lev 23:39; Deut 11:14, etc.). Gedaliah's instruction here contravenes the biblical law in Deut 23:25. However, we may postulate that the order was a temporary necessity intended to encourage these people to settle there permanently.

222. This also provides a basis for understanding the words of *Yalqut Shim⁽oni*, part II, §328: "You find that for two years the land produced abundant fruits as it had never done before, one year when the children of Israel first entered the land . . . and one year, when they were deported from the land."

223. The Bible does not describe wine as being "gathered," because it is a product that is a result of processing. The usual reference is to gathering תירוש, which is the juice of the grapes before it is fermented (Deut 11:14)—gathering its firstfruits (18:4) and tithe (14:23). Consequently, it may be that the expression is intended to demonstrate how ripe the crop was for harvesting: not only are the grapes ripe and the wine being prepared, but the wine itself has already been fermented, and the settlers can use the finished product.

224. The expression קיץ ('summer fruits') occurs in the Bible ten times in the sense of fruit that ripened in the summer. A nice parallel occurs in Mic 7:1: "I am like the last of the summer fruits, the grape gleanings after the vintage." In light of the phrases in which the term קיץ occurs, it is probable that the fruit is figs; cf. 2 Sam 16:1; Isa 16:9; Jer 48:32; etc. On this subject, see also lines 6–7 in the agricultural calendar from Gezer, as well as *t. Ned.* 4.1. Rashi interpreted the term as dried figs; however, there are other commentators who think that this word refers to all summer fruits (including dates, pomegranates, etc.). On this subject, see also Bullah 1984: 500.

were part of the basic diet in the ancient Near East.[226] He did not mention barley, wheat, and the varieties of legume, because all of these had already been harvested during the summer, before Jerusalem's defeat.[227]

The key to understanding Gedaliah's order is found in the time of year when the order was given, because only during the months of Elul–Tishri (the harvest season for these foodstuffs) would they be mentioned together (see *EncMiq* 2.913–18). If Jerusalem fell to the Babylonians in Tammuz and was razed during the month of Ab, the permission must have been given before the end of Elul. In that season, summer fruits are at their peak, it is harvest season for grapes, and it is just before the beginning of olive-ripening.[228]

The chronology between the murder of Gedaliah and the date of his appointment and early activity is not known. The only chronological datum that the entire story offers is that Ishmael, the son of Nethaniah and murderer of Gedaliah, arrived in Mizpah "in the seventh month" (2 Kgs 25:25; Jer 41:1). The fact that the year is not noted has permitted scholars to posit that Gedaliah governed for an extended time prior to his murder.[229] However, this hypothesis conflicts with the tenor of the description, both in its expanded version and in

---

225. To "gather" oil raises a difficulty similar to "gathering" wine, because oil also is a finished product. Nevertheless, the reference is to the olive harvest, and again the emphasis is on the convenient opportunities for a livelihood that the settlers in Benjamin were offered.

226. There are no parallels to the triple combination of wine, summer fruits, and oil, and the only combinations that occur elsewhere are of oil or summer fruits with wine. Wine and summer fruits are combined in 2 Sam 16:1 and Jer 48:32 (and the combination raisins and summer fruits in 2 Sam 16:1 may be added). The combination of wine and oil appears much more frequently (cf., e.g., Deut 11:14; Hag 2:12; Prov 21:17; 2 Chr 12:40).

227. For the major crops in the land of Israel and their harvest times, see Eph'al (1996: 62). I cannot accept Hoffman's idea (2001: 721) that no one sowed the fields during the Babylonian siege. Agricultural activity in the Benjamin region did not stop during the siege, because it was an important source for the Babylonians' food supply.

228. If it is true that part of the crop was not harvested because of the exigencies of war and because some of the landowners had been deported, then those who remained in the region of Benjamin and those who harvested there after the war would have been able to store the produce as the basis for initiating a rehabilitation and rebuilding process.

229. Some scholars have characterized the rule of Gedaliah as long, and some have even assigned him several years of rule in Mizpah. See, e.g., Harrison 1973: 161; Lindsay 1976: 27 n. 30; Oded 1977: 424–25; Thompson 1980: 657; Cogan and Tadmor 1988: 327; Miller and Hayes 1986: 421–23; Mitchell 1991: 413; Ahlström 1993: 799; Hoffman 2000: 119; 2001: 20; Albertz 2003: 94. These scholars have been influenced by the descriptions in Jeremiah, particularly by the expansion in 40:11–12. However, this expanded version was written with a literary-conceptual objective, namely, to single out Ishmael, the son of Nethaniah, as the guilty party in the assassination and in the flight to Egypt that followed. Therefore, we reject the attempt by Thompson (1980: 657), Seitz (1989: 276), and Albertz (2003: 94) to link the murder of Gedaliah to the third deportation mentioned in Jeremiah (52:30), in the 23rd year of Nebuchadrezzar's reign (582 B.C.E.). This linkage requires that Gedaliah ruled in Mizpah for more than four years, and there is no support for this conclusion. Support for the opinion that Gedaliah ruled in Mizpah only for several weeks may be found in the opinion of Noth (1954: 228), and the clear exposition by Cornill 1905: 414–15; Rudolph 1947: 251; and Holladay 1988: 296.

its abridged form. The narrative focuses on Gedaliah's early days (2 Kgs 25:22–24; Jer 40:7–16) and passes immediately to a description of his assassination (2 Kgs 25:25; Jer 41:1–10) and the escape to Egypt following the assassination (2 Kgs 25:26; Jer 41:11–18). There is no hint of any passage of time or of a gap of several years between Gedaliah's early days and his murder. Noting the month of Ishmael's arrival (2 Kgs 25:25aα; Jer 41:1α) without stating the year is, in my opinion, the author's way of creating a continuum between the destruction of Jerusalem and the murder of Gedaliah, making it clear that the entire episode took only a short time.[230]

Support for this reading of the text may be found in the description of the beginning of the return of the Judean refugees "to the land of Judah, to Gedaliah at Mizpah" (Jer 40:12aβ). According to v. 12b, the returnees began to carry out Gedaliah's instructions "and gathered in an abundant supply of wine and summer fruits." The absence of oil from the description is striking, considering that Gedaliah had commissioned them to "gather in the wine, summer fruits, and oil" (10abα); the omission may be linked to the fact that oil harvesting begins in Jerusalem and the Benjaminite region during the month of Tishri (Harrison 1973: 161; Thompson 1980: 657). The impression we get is that the returnees managed to pick the summer fruits and harvest the grapes but had not yet had time to harvest the olives. The author uses these facts to show us that the murder of Gedaliah took place before the olive harvest. This corresponds to the date accepted by Jewish tradition—Gedaliah was murdered on the 3rd of Tishri (Davidson 1985: 137; Holladay 1989: 296). If this is correct, it is possible to reconstruct the complete chronological sequence between the destruction of Jerusalem and the murder of Gedaliah, approximately two months later, as follows:

> The beginning of the Babylonian siege of Jerusalem was the 10th day of the 10th month (Tebeth) in the 10th year of Zedekiah's reign (2 Kgs 25:1; Jer 39:1; 52:4). According to the narrative, a breach was made in the city wall on the 9th day of the 4th month (Tammuz; 2 Kgs 25:2–3; Jer 39:2; 52:4–6), and on the 7th, 9th, or 10th day of the 5th month (Ab), the Babylonians began to burn the temple, destroy Jerusalem, and deport its inhabitants (2 Kgs 25:8–10; Jer 52:12–15). Thus, Gedaliah managed to rule a bit longer than seven weeks after the destruction, until he was assassinated, apparently on the 3rd of Tishri. This means that the crisis of his assassination came relatively soon after the trauma of the destruction

---

230. It must be remembered that Gedaliah's rule in Mizpah was included in the book of Jeremiah in order to fill in information gaps about Jeremiah. The author/redactor's purpose was to reduce these lacunae as much as possible, resulting in the sequence of dates and proximity of events indicated. Immediately afterward, he described Jeremiah's experiences during the flight to Egypt, only months after the destruction. It is difficult to understand Bright's comment (1965: 253) that "unfortunately the year was not noted." If he means that the year was dropped from the text, there is no evidence of this.

of Jerusalem, when only some of the refugees had returned to Judah and when those who remained in Judah had not yet completed the first stage of stabilization or begun the rebuilding process.

2.3.2. "Those Who Remained in the Land":[231] The Inhabitants of the Babylonian Province of Judah

Within the narrative of the destruction of the kingdom of Judah, there is a report of the deportation of the populace of Jerusalem (2 Kgs 25:11; Jer 39:9; 52:15; see above, pp. 82–84). The narrative does not mention any deportation from other areas of Judah, and this accords with accounts given in 2 Kgs 25:12, Jer 39:10, and 52:16 that "some of the poorest people of the land"[232] were left to be vinedressers[233] and tillers of the soil.[234] However, a textual and conceptual analysis of these accounts, comparison with other biblical texts, and the picture that emerges from the archaeological data show that this report should not be considered as telling the entire story. Instead, this narrative expresses the view-

---

231. On the importance and significance of the root s'r (שאר) in this story, see Hoffman 2000: 103 n. 1.

232. As is demonstrated at length below, the expression דלת הארץ ('the poorest people of the land') is unique to the account of the destruction of Jerusalem and the deportation of the nation's elite, and it implies what the exiles in Babylon and the returnees to Zion wished to convey. The message of this phrase is that the elite of the nation were deported to Babylon and those who remained in the land were a handful of paupers (or as described by the parallel passage in Jer 39:10: "Only some of the poor people who had nothing") whose existence was marginal and of no political importance. The expression appears a total of four times in the Bible, twice in 2 Kings (24:14; 25:12) and twice in Jeremiah (40:7; 52:16; compare the interpretation given to the expression in Jer 39:10). Assuming that Jer 40:7 is a later insertion (it does not appear in the LXX; see below), it becomes clear that the expression is unique to both deportation events. The connection between the two deportations is striking: after the deportation of Jehoiachin, "no one remained, except the poorest people of the land," and then after the destruction of Jerusalem, only "some of the poorest people of the land" were left.

233. Apart from 2 Kgs 25:12 and the parallel verse in Jer 52:16, "vinedresser" appears only in three prophecies (Isa 61:5; Joel 1:11; 2 Chr 26:10). Nonetheless, "vineyard" appears in the Bible numerous times, in a wide range of literary genres, and the word always refers to an orchard of olives or grapes, so there is no doubt about its meaning (Graham 1984: 56; Rosenson 1991: 47).

234. The title יוגב appears only in Jer 52:16; in 2 Kgs 25:12, the letter *yod* was dropped. Jer 39:10 states, "he gave them vineyards and fields" = יגבים, reinforcing the reading in chap. 52 (Burney 1903: 369). The general conclusion among scholars is that this refers to a field of grain (Jones 1984: 644). For a discussion of the subject and a survey of rabbinic interpretation, which is in agreement with this understanding, as well as a survey of modern commentaries, see Rosenson 1991: 47–48. Graham (1984: 56) interpreted the expression as referring to those who worked agricultural terraces, raising mainly grapevines and olives. It is difficult to accept this explanation and even more difficult to understand what, then, is the difference between a vinedresser and a fieldworker. For arguments against this interpretation, see Rosenson 1991: 48–49. It is also difficult to accept the interpretation of the word as "diggers of ditches," deriving it from יקב 'wine cellar' or גב 'water hole' (1991: 48–49). The connection to יקב is linguistically problematic, as is linking it to גב; as a result, many scholars maintain that the meaning is simply obscure (Burney 1903: 369; Montgomery 1951: 568; Cogan and Tadmor 1988: 319).

point of the exiles to Babylon, where it was composed (for extended discussion, see below, §5.1.2, pp. 289–295). It represents the qualitative, economic, and class-oriented judgment of the elite deportees toward those who remained in the land, without any consideration of how many were deported and from where, or how many remained and where. This tendentiousness is more pronounced in the one-sided summary: "So Judah was carried away captive out of its land" (2 Kgs 25:21b; Jer 52:27b), which ends the description of the destruction of Jerusalem,[235] as well as in the double remark about the "poor" who remained in Judah after the deportation of Jehoiachin (the later addition in 2 Kgs 24:14) and after the destruction (25:12).

In contrast, the two versions that stem from the description of the days of Gedaliah (2 Kgs 25:22–26; Jer 40:7–41:18) express a different attitude toward those who remained in Judah:

1. They were not "the poorest people of the land" but rather "the people who remained in the land of Judah" (2 Kgs 25:22a); "men, women [and children and some of the poorest people of the land], from those who were not deported to Babylon" (Jer 40:7),[236] and even "a remnant for Judah" (40:11).

2. Nebuchadrezzar, king of Babylon, was the one who left them (v. 22a), not Nebuzaradan, the commander of the guard (2 Kgs 25:12; Jer 52:16).

3. The Babylonians did not permit "those who remained in Judah" to stay for economic purposes that arose from the Babylonians' own needs (to serve as "vinedressers and tillers of the soil," 2 Kgs 25:12). Instead, they were permitted to remain under the leadership of Gedaliah in order to carry on the national life of the people in their land (2 Kgs 25:22b, 24b; Jer 40:7a, 10b).

---

235. The author wished to draw a parallel between the end of the kingdom of Judah and the end of the kingdom of Israel; compare the language of both verses (2 Kgs 17:23b; 25:21b) that conclude the accounts of the destruction:

2 Kgs 17:23b: ויגל ישראל מעל אדמתו אשורה עד היום הזה
2 Kgs 25:21b: ויגל יהודה מעל אדמתו׃

The last verse (2 Kgs 25:21b) concludes the final statement of the Deuteronomistic history, which was being composed after the destruction (Dtr²). For a detailed discussion of the features of the narrative, the purposes of the author, the ideology expressed in it, and the various stages in the formation of the text, see below, §5.1.2 (pp. 289–295).

236. In the LXX, which at this point seems more reliable, the phrase "children and some of the poorest people of the land" is missing from the text. Thus, the text refers only to "men and women who were not deported from Judah" (Janzen 1973: 53; see also Bullah 1984: 498). The MT probably reflects a later expansion of the text, based on Jer 39:10; 41:16 (where the emphasis is on "and women and children"). The expansion in 43:6 also clearly intends to define more precisely "those who remained in Judah" as an introduction to an account of their fate, which is at the center of the sequel to the story. Some of them were murdered by Ishmael and another group was taken into captivity by him, then released by Johanan, the son of Kareah; the members of this group were among those who went to Egypt.

Regardless of the different point of view regarding "those who remained in Judah," the story about the time of Gedaliah the son of Ahikam in Mizpah does
not contain very much information about their numbers and the places where
they lived.[237] Some information is buried in the narrative and is expressed only
incidentally, which may indicate several basic facts:

1. An unknown number of people remained in the country. Because it was
the Jerusalem elite who were exiled, it is reasonable to assume that most of the
"remnant" were residents of the provincial towns.[238]

2. The population that remained in Judah lost its active urban center but
was able to carry on its previous lifestyle within the new administrative framework.[239] The shift from Judean "citizenship" to Babylonian "citizenship" might
have changed the political framework and the center of government, but the
rural-patriarchal framework remained unchanged. The Babylonians definitely
had an interest in permitting the rural population to continue. The Benjamin
region, which lay north of Jerusalem and near the city, could have served as a
source for essential products during the siege years. Dry-farming crops from the
region, particularly from the orchards and in the wine and oil industries, released the Babylonian government from concern about long supply lines with
regard to these essential commodities.

3. Gedaliah was officially appointed over "those who remained in Judah"
(2 Kgs 25:22b, 23aβ; Jer 40:7).[240] This means that "those who remained" had a

---

237. As presented below, §5.2.2d (pp. 339–347), this is an episodic source, written with
specific ideological goals. It treats the protagonists as representative stereotypes of the ideological circles within the nation. The rest of "those who remained in Judah" are only bystanders in
the events and have almost no active role in the affair. As in many other cases in biblical literature, this source was inserted into Kings and Jeremiah for specific literary and ideological
reasons; the historical information itself was not important.

238. Martin Noth (1954: 296) already had argued that the "authentic nucleus" of Judah remained in the land. On this subject, see also the important work of Janssen (1956, esp. p. 35),
the similar opinion of Ackroyd (1968: 21–30), the development of Barstad's idea of the "myth
of the empty land" (1988: 25–36; 1996: 77–82), and see also Coggins (1975: 1–12) and D. L.
Smith (1989a: 32–34). This hypothesis is supported by the archaeological evidence. On this
subject, see Lipschits 1999a; see also the discussion below, in chap. 4.

239. On these institutions and the changes they underwent after the destruction of Jerusalem and during the days of the exile, see Talmon's survey in Tadmor 1983: 28–34. See also the
discussion below.

240. In Jer 40:7 there is a nice wordplay on the double meaning of the root פקד:

אֶת ...   כִּי הִפְקִיד מֶלֶךְ בָּבֶל
אֹתוֹ ...   וְכִי הִפְקִיד

The meaning of the first verb is 'to nominate officially' (cf. Gen 39:5; Num 1:50; Josh 10:18;
2 Kgs 7:17; Isa 62:6; Esth 2:3; etc.), and the meaning of the second verb is 'to entrust as a deposit' (cf. Lev 5:23; 1 Kgs 14:27; Isa 10:28; Jer 36:20; 37:21; Ps 31:6; 2 Chr 12:10). In this play
on the verb פקד, the author emphasizes the importance of those who remained in Judah, who
were entrusted to Gedaliah by the Babylonians for safekeeping, and he lays the background for
the fate they met after Gedaliah's assassination.

well-defined status and place of habitation, with rights and obligations clearly defined by the Babylonian government.

4. The description of Gedaliah's rule focuses on the region of Benjamin and the environs of Jerusalem.[241] The archaeological data available to us regarding events in the region on the eve of the destruction are relevant to this description (see discussion of this data below, in §4.3.3a (pp. 237–249); see also Lipschits 1997a: 271–310; 1999b). The Benjaminite region was not destroyed, and its residents surrendered to the Babylonians, who began to establish the Babylonian province of Judah even during their siege of Jerusalem. If these assumptions are correct, it is reasonable to assume that most of the residents of the territory of Benjamin became residents of the new province and that Gedaliah was appointed to be their governor. This explanation accords with the political orientation of the residents of Benjamin, as well as the economic interests of the Babylonians during the siege and after the destruction of Jerusalem.

5. According to Jer 39:11–18 and 40:1–6, the Babylonians strictly monitored the pro-Babylonian political orientation of the leadership that remained in Judah, which included people such as Gedaliah and Jeremiah. A similar attitude also appears in Gedaliah's command to the army officers: "Do not be afraid because of the Chaldeans officials; dwell in the land, serve the king of Babylon, and it shall be well with you" (2 Kgs 25:24; compare Jer 40:9–10).[242]

6. The Benjaminites were joined by refugees who apparently had fled from Judah during the Babylonian siege of Jerusalem.[243] Some of them waited in

---

241. The events in both passages are restricted geographically to a specific area at the center of Mizpah. In the version in 2 Kings 25, Mizpah is mentioned twice (vv. 23, 25), and around it "the land of Judah" (v. 22) or "the land" (v. 24) is mentioned. In the version in Jeremiah 40–41, Mizpah is mentioned 13 times (40:8, 10, 12, 13, 15; 41:1 [twice]; 3, 6, 7 ["the city"], 10, 14, 16) and around it are "the cities" (40:10) "in the land of Judah" (40:12). In the middle of these cities is Gibeon (41:12, 16), "the house of the Lord" (41:5, and see below), and there is a reference to the people living "in Geruth Chimham, near Bethlehem" (41:17). For the meaning of the name Geruth Chimham, see Hoffman 2000: 117–18 n. 29; 2001: 724.

242. Apart from the minor difference of וייטב in 2 Kgs 25:24bβ as compared with וייטב in Jer 40:9bβ, the only significant difference between the two versions is the expession 'Fear not the servants of the Chaldeans' אל תראו מעבדי הכשדים (2 Kgs 25:24aβ) compared with 'Do not be afraid to serve the Chaldeans' אל תראו מעבוד הכשדים (Jer 40:9aβ). Many scholars have accepted the version in Jeremiah as primary (Cogan and Tadmor 1988: 326). However, it is my opinion that the version in 2 Kings is better and more original: the LXX supports the text in Kings (Streane 1896: 250; Holladay 1989: 271), and the wording in Jeremiah does not fit well with the continuation of the text and creates an unnecessary redundancy: "Do not be afraid to serve the Chaldeans; dwell in the land and serve the king of Babylon." In contrast, there is great narrative logic in Gedaliah's speech as quoted in 2 Kings, and it fits the goal of the source, which emphasizes the need to overcome the physical fear of "the servants of the Chaldeans" and to accept their rule as a condition for continuing to live in the land (see below). Compare the expression "serve the king of Babylon" to the words of Jeremiah in Jer 27:12, 17.

243. See 2 Kgs 25:25b; Jer 40:7b; 41:3a; 10aα, 13–18. We can assume that some of the refugees who returned to the province of Judah after the destruction were opponents of Zedekiah's rule who had fled Judah even before the beginning of the Babylonian siege. On the basis of the

border areas and in the kingdoms beyond the Jordan River until the end of the war. According to Jer 40:11, these refugees "were in Moab, in Ammon, in Edom, and in all the countries,"[244] and according to the expanded description, they returned "out of all the places where they were scattered" (v. 12a).[245] It is likely that the refugee groups continued to range throughout the border areas,[246] refusing to acknowledge the Babylonian victory and fearful of the Babylonian reaction.[247] With the announcement of Gedaliah's appointment, some of the refugees began to gather at the new center in Mizpah; however, it is doubtful that they came all at once, and it is not likely that they had a "spokesman" or a single "leader" (this was the theory, e.g., of Holladay 1989: 295). Their assembly near Mizpah served the Babylonians' interest because, to take control of these groups and to overcome them, large forces would have been required for a serious effort over a prolonged period of time (Harrison 1973: 160; Davidson 1985: 135). This context provides a basis for understanding Gedaliah's instruction to the army officers to "dwell in your towns that you have taken over" (Jer 40:10bβ). His primary intention was to establish his authority over the entire populace by installing the refugees and the remnants of the army in these settlements, under his rule.

7. Of those who returned to Mizpah, the focus is on the importance of the army officers[248] and the small groups that obeyed the commanders' orders. We

---

parallel behavior in the days of the Second Temple, we may also assume that during the Babylonian siege many residents of Judah fled to the eastern frontier out of fear of the consequences of the siege. Some scholars see an inscription from Khirbet Beit-Lei as proof that refugees also stayed in the Shephelah. For a summary, see Ahlström 1993: 799–800. While it does seem likely that refugees were hiding in this area, according to Naveh (1963), the accepted date of the inscriptions is the end of the eighth century B.C.E., and the refugees had fled Sennacherib's campaign more than a century earlier (701 B.C.E.).

244. See suggestions for revision by Janzen 1973: 149, particularly p. 208 n. 43.

245. Verse 12aα does not appear in the LXX and seems to be a later stereotypical and generalizing expansion (Janzen 1973: 53). See the comments by Feinberg 1982: 271; Holladay 1989: 295–96.

246. On the basis of historical parallels, we may theorize that the major region where these groups traveled was in the eastern littorals of the Judean Hills, in the Judean Desert, and in Transjordan. At least for Transjordan, there are additional accounts of Jewish refugees (Jer 40:11, 13; 41:10, 15; see also below). The word בשדה (Jer 40:7aα), which means 'in the countryside', appears in this story several times to refer to places that were remote from inhabited areas. In this case, use of the term is designed to place those who were "in the countryside" in opposition to Gedaliah, who was appointed "in the land" (v. 7aβ), while in v. 13 the meaning is much more explicit and emphasizes the arrival of the army officers from the countryside "to Gedaliah at Mizpah." Perhaps this is also the intention of 41:8, where "the countryside" is juxtaposed to the pit within the city (41:7; and see below). See also the prophetic language of Jeremiah in 13:27; 14:4–5; cf. also 2 Sam 11:11; 14:18; etc.

247. See Bright 1965: 253; Harrison 1973: 160; Thompson 1980: 654; Feinberg 1982: 271; Davidson 1985: 135; Holladay 1989: 295.

248. It is likely that this refers to the junior officers of several small army units in the Judahite army, whose power, status, and importance are not clear. From the scant information

may assume that the summary list of officers that appears in 2 Kgs 25:23b and Jer 40:8b is drawn from the story itself and based on additional information available to the author; it was designed to introduce those who took part in the story. The names of the main characters are reported: Ishmael, the son of Nethaniah, from the royal family, and Johanan, the son of Kareah, alongside other officers: Seraiah, the son of Tanhumeth; the sons of Ephai, the Netophatite; and Jaazaniah, the son of the Maacathite (see Excursus 1, "The Names in 2 Kings 25:23 and Jeremiah 40:8," pp. 126–131). Despite this, it is important to note that not all of the officers mentioned in the story are listed. We may assume that, for the author of Jeremiah's "biography" and perhaps also for his contemporaries, these army officers symbolized the last of the strength and status of the kingdom of Judah (see Excursus 2, "The Redaction of Jeremiah 40:7, 11," pp. 131–133).

* * * * *

In his words to the army officers (Jer 40:9aβ), Gedaliah took pains to quiet their fears of the Babylonians stationed at Mizpah.[249] The army officers' fear probably stemmed from intimate familiarity with the actions of the Babylonians before and after the destruction; they had seen the imprisonment, deportation, and other punishments that had occurred in the recent past and perhaps were still occurring. Later on, Gedaliah stated to the army officers the condition that was also the main principle in the life of the province after the destruction: "Serve the king of Babylon, and it shall be well with you."[250] It is reasonable to

available on these army officers and their men, the impression is that they belonged to small combat groups that were the last vestiges of the Judahite army. Ishmael, the son of Nethaniah, arrived in Mizpah with ten men (2 Kgs 25:25; Jer 41:1–2); after a battle with the men of Johanan, the son of Kareah "and all the officers of the armies that were with him" (Jer 41:11), he fled to the king of Ammon with eight men (Jer 41:15). Against this backdrop, the reference to המה והאנשים (2 Kgs 25:23aα) is very striking, somewhat less full than the parallel version in Jer (41:7aα), המה ואנשיהם, which is repeated every time that the army officers are mentioned. Compare also 2 Kgs 25:24 with Jer 40:9; 2 Kgs 25:25 with Jer 41:1. See also Jer 40:13; 41:11–16, and compare the MT of Jer 43:2, where the officers are called "all the evil men."

249. At the heart of Gedaliah's words was the call to the new arrivals, אל תראו 'Do not be afraid'. The root ירא appears in the Bible as a verb 293 times, generally meaning 'to fear', and is most often used of fear of God. In most cases the word appears with the object marker את marking the object of fear, God; the preposition מלפני is used similarly in Ecclesiastes (3:14; 8:12, 13; cf. 1 Sam 18:12). The combination of the verb ירא with the preposition מפני appears 19 times and is characteristic primarily of Deuteronomistic literature. This combination usually expresses fear of "earthly" forces, such as foreign armies, powerful people, other nations, etc. Compare Deut 1:29; 5:5; 7:19; Josh 11:6; 1 Sam 18:29; 21:13; 1 Kgs 1:50; 2 Kgs 1:15; 19:6; Jer 1:8; 42:11; Ps 3:7; Neh 4:8. Only in one instance does the expression ירא מפני have God as its object (Exod 9:30). For our purposes, note especially the conclusion of the episode with the highlighted use of this verb in 2 Kgs 25:26; Jer 41:18 (and see the discussion below).

250. The expression עבד את is known both in the sense of observing God-given commandments and ritual ('to serve the Lord') as well as in the sense of ordinary servitude ('to serve the king of Egypt', 'to serve Nebuchadrezzar', etc.). The imperative form of the verb, עבדו את, appears in the Bible 16 times, primarily as a directive to serve God and to observe his rituals

assume that Gedaliah was referring to paying taxes,[251] accepting certain laws regulating daily life in the province; an oath of loyalty by the remnants of the army and their assimilation into economic and political life; and, in particular, their willingness to accept Babylonian authority, as represented by him. In exchange, Gedaliah promised as reward: "and it shall be well with you."[252] This expression apparently promises security and the possibility of a livelihood if the army officers will live in the land. Along with this promise, Gedaliah's words also contain an implicit threat: if the officers do not accept Babylonian protection, it will not go well with them.[253]

The arrival of the army officers in Mizpah and their willingness to accept Gedaliah's oath and, along with it, the Babylonian yoke, is expressed in the text as the desire of "Johanan, the son of Kareah, and all of the army officers" (40:13) to protect Gedaliah. They informed him[254] of the intent of Ishmael, the son of Nethaniah, a member of the royal family (for the purpose of this account, see

---

(9 times as the expression עבדו את ה'). This is the language used in Judg 9:28 and precisely the same language is used in Jeremiah's prophecy when he expresses his desire that Jerusalem surrender to Babylon in order to save itself (27:12, 17).

251. Payment of taxes was surely a basic condition for the existence of Judah as a province, but there is no direct proof of this from the period of Babylonian rule. It is highly unlikely that the words of Lam 1:1 are an allusion to the payment of taxes. Josephus's (*Ant.* 10.163) statement should be taken as an interpretation of the words in Jeremiah, consistent with the circumstances that were known to him from the Roman Period. See also Graham 1984: 57.

252. The root טוב in the *qal* conjugation appears in the Bible 101 times, 18 of these in the book of Jeremiah and 11 in the books of Genesis and Deuteronomy. It is especially common in other Deuteronomistic literature; in contrast, is not common in the prophetic books other than Jeremiah. In most cases, the word appears in speeches after an imperative or after conditional statements; these statements have implied or overt threats about what will happen if the speaker is not obeyed, usually expressed in some form of the word להרע. The use of טוב is widespread in Jeremiah's speeches exhorting a return to observing divine commandments and to accepting Babylonian rule, ending in a threat that is mostly overt (and see 7:5, 23; 13:23; 32:40–41; 38:20; etc.) A parallel use is found in Mic 7:3; Zeph 1:12; Zech 8:15; etc.

253. By putting it this way, the author portrays the extent of Gedaliah's self-confidence: he makes no mention of any anticipated danger, expresses no fear whatsoever of the "officers," and does not qualify the threat implied in his words. It is clear that he is speaking from a position of power, and the concluding words "it shall be well with you" underscore the position of authority from which he is speaking.

254. The army officers begin their speech with the phrase הידע תדע כי ('Did you know that . . . ?'). This expression appears in the Bible 14 times (5 times in Jeremiah, 3 times in 1 Samuel, twice in Genesis and 1 Kings, and once in Joshua and Proverbs), and apart from the exception in Proverbs, in each case it appears with the same meaning and in almost the same form. The expression is part of the speech, generally following ויאמר. After this expression there is always a conjunctive כי 'that', followed by the message that the speaker wishes to deliver. In most cases, the news relates to death or the fear of death or loss, so the introductory expression appears to call attention to the tidings and stresses its importance (cf. Gen 15:13; 43:7; Josh 23:13; 1 Sam 20:3, 9; 28:1; 1 Kgs 2:37, 42; Jer 13:12; 26:15; 40:14; 42:19, 22; Prov 27:23). Aside from this instance, in two additional passages (Gen 43:7; Jer 13:12) this expression is preceded by the interrogative ה to show that the anticipated answer to the question is negative. In the case in question here, interrogative ה emphasizes the fact that Gedaliah does not know what the "officers" are about to tell him or does not ascribe enough importance to the information.

Excursus 2) who was sent by Baꜥalis, the king of Ammon,[255] to murder him. Johanan even said that he was willing to kill Ishmael as a preventive measure, to protect Gedaliah and prolong his rule. By providing these details, the narrator emphasizes the fragile nature of the rehabilitation process and its dependence on Gedaliah. Johanan's words to Gedaliah, "Why should he assassinate you and thus caused all the Judeans who have gathered around you to be scattered, and the remnant of Judah to perish?" (40:15b), reinforce the personal responsibility that Ishmael bore for putting an end to the process and for the migration of the people to Egypt. Ishmael, the son of Nethaniah, is marked as an isolated and deviant figure who is opposed to the rebuilding of the nation and held accountable for the failure of its rejuvenation.

2.3.3. *The Status of Mizpah as the Capital of the Babylonian Province*

Mizpah[256] was the administrative center in which Gedaliah and an unknown number of Chaldeans and Judahites lived. There are references to Mizpah in several narratives from the premonarchic period and the period after the fall of Jerusalem, but in the portions of the Bible that describe the time of the kingdom, Mizpah is hardly mentioned.[257] This is a significant point, especially because in

---

255. This is the only reference in the Bible to Baꜥalis, the king of Ammon. Several suggestions have been made regarding the name, most of them relying on the combination of the god-name Baꜥal with an additional element (*Mazar*-Maisler 1941: 114). This theory receives support from the name בעליסף that was found on a Phoenician bulla (Avigad 1964: 194). Other scholars have proposed seeing the name as בן עליז/בן עליס (*EncMiq* 2.300), while Tur-Sinai (1948: 461) proposed that it was an Akkadian form *bêlišu*, which is not the name of a specific individual but the title of Ishmael's master—that is, the king of Ammon. At the same time, Gordon (1965: 130) suggested identifying this name with בעלס, which appears at Ugarit, or alternatively, *dbaꜥli-ši*, mentioned in a text published by Nougayrol (1955: 16.262: 6). However, in 1984, a bulla bearing this name was discovered at Tell el-Umayri, 13 km southwest of Amman (Herr 1985: 169–72). The inscription on the bulla reads למלכמאור עבד בעלישע ('[belonging to] Milkomʾûr, the servant of Baꜥalyašaꜥ'). The bulla was dated to ca. 600 B.C.E., and בעלישע has been identified with בעלס. Herr has proposed that he should be regarded as the same king of Ammon mentioned in the account of Gedaliah's assassination (Herr 1985: 172; see also Becking 1997: 82). The discovery of the bulla opened up a discussion on the shift of the letter ש > ס in Ammonite (Rendsburg 1988: 73–79). The prevailing theory is that the form בעליס is a distortion of בעל ישע, and the variant spelling is evidence of the different pronunciation of the sibilant letters in Ammonite.

256. For a summary of the historical and archaeological information and for a profile of the site and its environs in the sixth century B.C.E., see Lipschits 1997a: 275–85; 199a: 165–70. A place bearing the name of *Mizpah* is mentioned in the Bible 40 times. In one case, a city by this name is mentioned among the cities of the Shephelah (Josh 15:38). In two cases, the name refers to a place on the northern border of the kingdom of Israel (Josh 11:3, 8; Mazar-Maisler 1930: 75; Naʾaman 1986a: 43, 126). In five other instances, a place bearing this name is mentioned in Gilead (Gen 31:49; Josh 13:26; Judg 10:17; 11:11, 34). In all of the other 32 cases, the name refers to a place in the northern region of Benjamin, on the main road from Jerusalem to Samaria.

257. There is only one clear reference to Mizpah from the period of the monarchy, when it is mentioned as a large city on the border between Judah and Israel (1 Kgs 15:22). It is possible that this is also the city referred to in Hos 5:1 (Andersen and Freedman 1980: 385–86).

the history of the premonarchic era Mizpah is presented as a central assembly place for the people, a site of religious ritual, and the place where the first king of Israel was anointed.[258] These narratives were apparently written after the destruction of Jerusalem, when biases in favor of the region of Benjamin may have gained ascendancy. In other words, traditions regarding Mizpah did not have a chance before this time to enter the historical and prophetic record, which was under the shadow of the status of Jerusalem. It may be assumed that political and religious biases are reflected in these narratives, which have as their background the status of Mizpah as the capital of the Babylonian province. The aim of this redactor (or redactors) was to justify the status of Mizpah in the period after the destruction of Jerusalem by describing its special status in the period before the Davidic dynasty arose in Judah.[259]

All of this raises an interesting question: was there a cult site in Mizpah after the destruction of Jerusalem where the congregation could assemble "before the Lord" (Judg 20:1; 21:5, 8), where one could take an oath ("Now the men of Israel had taken an oath in Mizpah," 21:1), where one could pray (1 Sam 7:5), where one could perform rituals (7:6), and where one could even bring sacrifices (7:9)? Inasmuch as there is no other evidence, it remains only a likely and reasonable possibility that the Babylonians tried to establish Mizpah as both an alternative administrative center to Jerusalem and a religious center.[260]

We have no historical record of the circumstances surrounding the selection of Mizpah as the capital of the Babylonian province of Judah and its transformation from a border city to the capital of the province even before the destruction of Jerusalem.[261] However, from the accounts of the time of Gedaliah, it appears

---

258. In the account of the war against the tribe of Benjamin (Judges 20–21), the place-name Mizpah appears 5 times, both as a place of assembly (20:1, 3) and as a holy place, where all the people are "going up to the Lord" (21:1, 5, 8). In 1 Samuel 7, Mizpah is mentioned 6 times, where again it is singled out as a place of assembly but also as a place of prayer to God and a place where all the people "drew water and poured it out before the Lord." It also apparently had an altar, because Samuel sacrificed a lamb (vv. 5, 6, 7, 9), and it is mentioned as one of the important administrative centers (v. 16), where the first king—Saul—was elected by God and where the people celebrated his coronation (1 Sam 10:17). For the importance of Mizpah as a religious center, see also 1 Sam 7:9–10; on its importance as a gathering point, see 1 Macc 3:46. On this subject, see McCown 1947: 13–22.

259. See also Naʾaman 1994d: 223–24; Blenkinsopp 1998: 28–31, with further literature. This may explain why Saul was anointed king at Mizpah. The text contains evidence of a pro-Benjaminite and anti-Davidic stance and refers to the reign of the only king who was not of the Davidic line (1 Sam 10:17). It may be that these words should be associated with Gedaliah's rule and the opinions current in the region after the destruction of Jerusalem.

260. Blenkinsopp (1998) has argued that, during the time of Babylonian rule, Bethel was the ritual and cultic center, while Mizpah was the administrative center. In my opinion, in spite of the lack of information about Babylonian policy in Judah, we can assume that the Babylonians established a cultic center in Mizpah alongside the administrative center. Bethel was the main rival of Mizpah, together with Gibeon. I will expand on this idea in the next section.

261. See the suggestions by Janssen 1956: 41–42; Graham 1984: 57; Lipschits 1999a: 165–70; 1999b: 476–82. The archaeological material is of decisive importance on this point; see the discussion following, §4.3.3 (pp. 237–241).

that the governmental apparatus was based at least partly on the Judean population who lived in Mizpah. Support for this is found in the archaeological evidence (see below), the description of the murder of the men of Judah who were
with Gedaliah (Jer 41:3), and the reference to "the daughters of the king" who
lived in Mizpah (41:10).[262] Along with Gedaliah and the men of Judah who
were with him, there were also Babylonians. Confirmation of this appears in the
archaeological record (below) and in two comments in the biblical description
of the days of Gedaliah. In the account of Gedaliah's speech to the army officers,
there is a reference to "the Chaldean officials" (lit., 'the servants of the Chaldeans'; 2 Kgs 25:24aβ; Jer 40:9aβ),[263] and in the description of his murder there
is also a reference to the Chaldeans who were with him in Mizpah (2 Kgs 25:25b;
Jer 41:3a). The implication is that there was a garrison force, as well as perhaps
Babylonian administrators whose function was to supervise the activities of the
local administration, to regulate the payment of tribute, and to assure that the
Judahites maintained their loyalty to Babylon.

At the same time, it seems that the number of Chaldeans in Mizpah during
the time of Gedaliah was not very large. According to the narrative of Gedaliah's murder, the garrison army was liquidated by ten of Ishmael's men (2 Kgs
25:25bα; Jer 41:3aα). Those who remained in Mizpah were very afraid of the
Babylonian response to the assassination (2 Kgs 25:26b; Jer 41:18a); thus, we
may conjecture that most of the Babylonian force was stationed elsewhere and
was expected to arrive in the province to restore order after the murder. The fact
that the "army officers" and "the remnant of the people" gathered in the area of
Bethlehem and went down to Egypt (2 Kgs 25:26a; Jer 41:16–17) may show that
Egypt was still perceived as a likely place to seek political asylum for anyone

---

262. The reference to the king's daughters' residence in Mizpah after the destruction naturally implies that the people of the royal house who were not deported to Babylon were entrusted into the care of Gedaliah. Furthermore, there is obvious editorial effort to place these
daughters on the side of Gedaliah, as opposed to Ishmael, the son of Nethaniah, with the object of stressing even more emphatically how aberrant and atypical Ishmael was in his opposition to Gedaliah.

263. The expression "the servants of the Chaldeans" has no parallel in the Bible. The form
of the noun עֶבֶד 'servant' in the plural genitive appears in the Bible 85 times, particularly in the
books of Samuel (37 times) and Kings (15 times), generally together with a specific name or title
("the servants of Abimelech," "the servants of Isaac," "the servants of Pharaoh," "the servants of
David," "the servants of the Lord," etc.). There are no other occurrences of the expression "servants of the . . . ," where the noun governed bears the definite article, and the only parallel appears in the expression "servants of the king" (2 Sam 15:15; 16:6; 1 Kgs 1:9; 2 Kgs 19:5; etc.). In
light of the singular use of עֶבֶד and the evidence that the story contains later on, we may hypothesize that the narrator is referring to the Chaldeans who were with Gedaliah in Mizpah and
perhaps the Judahites who were loyal to them (2 Kgs 25:25; Jer 41:3; Gray 1964: 772). This theory harmonizes well with information about the men of Judah "who deserted to the Chaldeans"
(Jer 38:19), Ishmael's goal in murdering the men of Judah and the Chaldeans "who were with
him in Mizpah," and the great fear of the people after the murder "because of the Chaldeans."
It is noteworthy that the LXX supports the language of the oath in 2 Kings ("Fear not the servants of the Chaldeans"; Streane 1896: 250; Holladay 1989: 271), and this language also seems
logical in terms of the narrative sequence. On this subject, also see n. 243 above.

opposing the Babylonians. This also implies that the Babylonian force was stationed north or west of the province of Judah, leaving the road leading south open to those fleeing. We may also assume that the Babylonians were not very close to Judah, because the refugees did not quickly flee the province. If we accept the superscriptions and narrative segments in Jeremiah 42 as chronologically reliable, then ten days passed before Jeremiah prophesied to the people (v. 7), and only afterward did this group leave for Egypt.

2.3.4. *The Status of Jerusalem and the Temple after the Destruction*[264]

From the time that Babylon established its rule throughout Hatti-land, Judah was a center of instability. This was the result of unending religious ferment that centered around the temple; of the belief that God would defend His city, His temple, and the House of David; and of a combination of these, together with the weakness of the political leadership in Jerusalem. It was apparently against this background that Nebuchadrezzar decided to destroy Jerusalem and the temple in particular and to put an end to the unstable rule of the House of David in Judah. The city was laid waste in a systematic and calculating manner designed to eradicate it as a political and religious center, and it remained desolate and abandoned. Lamentations such as "the roads of Zion mourn, for no one comes to the solemn assembly" (Lam 1:4) and "all who pass by clap their hands at you; they hiss and wag their head at the daughter of Jerusalem, saying: 'Is this the city that men call The Perfection of Beauty, The Joy of the Whole earth?'" (2:15) are apparently a faithful reflection of historical reality. Jerusalem is not mentioned in the account of the days of Gedaliah, son of Ahikam, in Mizpah (2 Kings 22–26; Jer 41:7–41:18).[265] Ignoring Jerusalem is especially significant in light of the fact that the events described in this story surround the city from the north (Mizpah and Gibeon) and from the south (environs of Bethlehem). In view of this and the archaeological picture to be discussed below (see §4.3.2a, pp. 210–214), we may assume that Nebuzaradan's systematic devastation, some four weeks after the city was conquered, was accompanied by political directives that structured this situation and made it permanent.[266] Devastation was the

---

264. For a detailed discussion of the status of Jerusalem and the temple after the destruction, see Lipschits 2001.

265. On the unusual description in Jer 41: 5, see the discussion below.

266. I am referring to the Babylonian policy in principle, which is also reflected in the complex of historical and archaeological evidence. See also Cogan and Tadmor 1988: 319. We should not presume that there was a complete vacuum in the city; urban life, though meager and limited, must have continued. On the basis of the tombs in Ketef Hinnom, Barkay (1985: 94–108; 1993: 107) argued that a significant population continued to live in Jerusalem even after the destruction. Even if we accept the conclusion that people continued to be buried after 586 B.C.E. in family sepulchres, this is not evidence that a significant population continued to live in Jerusalem. The scanty evidence unearthed in some of the excavations in the western hills (Barkay 1993: 107–8) attests to the existence of an indigent population that lived near the City of David and the Temple Mount; however, there is no evidence that this was a large, established population.

spectacle that greeted both those who first began the Return to Zion (compare Zech 1:12; 2:5–9) and those who came last (compare Neh 2:13–17; 7:60). The city recovered and became a large, important urban center again only during the Hellenistic Period.

A more difficult question is that of the fate of the temple and its status after the destruction of the city. The archaeological remains offer no help in evaluating the scale of devastation of the temple; the description in 2 Kgs 25:9a is general and allows for a variety of interpretations and reconstructions (see above, §2.2.2, esp. pp. 80–82). Nonetheless, there can be no doubt that the temple in Jerusalem was destroyed; its vessels were carried off to Babylon; its priests were put to death or deported; and it ceased to exist as national shrine. It was rebuilt only after a hiatus of 70 years (see Hag 2:3; Ezra 3:12) and only then did it begin to reestablish its central importance in Judah and among the Judahite exiles in Babylon and Egypt. I have grave doubts that, after the destruction of Jerusalem, the city and the temple retained as much importance for the various groups who remained in Judah or even for the exiles. In my opinion, there were those who continued to see Jerusalem as the central site for religious ritual and to hope for its speedy rebuilding. However, at the same time, there were also those who sought alternative places of worship and worked to establish them. Bethel, Mizpah, Gibeon, and Shechem were likely candidates, and other places may have also vied for status alongside them. The Babylonian policy after Jerusalem's fall and the prohibition of rebuilding Jerusalem and the temple were decisive factors in the decline in the city's status. However, given the religious and political reality that prevailed in Judah, it is doubtful that Babylon wished to or was able to prevent pilgrimages to the site of the temple ruins. Perhaps pilgrimages even served the Babylonians' purpose by providing visible evidence of the fate of a rebellious city and the punishment suffered by those who relied on the perpetual protection of their God.[267]

Given this scenario, great importance is attached to the fate of the altar in the temple at Jerusalem. Many scholars have conjectured that the absence of any specific reference to the destruction of the altar by the Babylonians implies that it continued to exist.[268] However, it is difficult to accept a hypothesis like this that is based on the silence of the sources and the premise that the altar was a massive structure that required specific action to destroy it. The description in 2 Kgs 25:9 is marked by its concise, all-inclusive language, and the list in vv. 13–17 focuses on the specific vessels of brass, silver, and gold. Nonetheless, an unequivocal impression emerges from these descriptions that agrees with the

---

267. This point is of great importance in reconstructing the state of religion and religious worship in Judah between the destruction of Jerusalem and the period of the Return to Zion; see the discussion following.

268. See Janssen 1956: 46–47, 94–104; Bright 1959: 325; Myers 1965a: xx, 26–27; Miller and Hayes 1986: 426; D. L. Smith 1989: 34–35; Berquist 1995: 17–18; Niehr 1999: 234, with further literature.

absence of any mention of ritual activity in the ruins of the temple in other sources that discuss this period. The general picture obtained is "[we weep] because the mountain of Zion . . . is desolate; foxes prowl over it" (Lam 5:18), and there is even an explicit statement that the altar has been abandoned: "The Lord has abandoned his altar; he has abandoned his sanctuary" (2:7).[269]

The main evidence in the Bible regarding the fate of the altar after the destruction of Jerusalem is the description of the arrival of 80 pilgrims: "from Shechem and Shiloh and Samaria, with their beards shaved and their clothing torn, covered with self-inflicted gashes, and carrying grain offerings and incense to present at the house of the Lord" (Jer 41:5).[270] This large group of pilgrims from the province of Samaria were demonstrating public mourning, apparently over the destruction of Jerusalem and the temple.[271] Although the destination of these pilgrims is not explicitly mentioned in the text, most scholars assume that they were headed for the ruined temple[272] about two months after it had been destroyed.[273] They brought with them offerings and incense, which many scholars interpret as evidence of a sacrifice but there are no references to a live animal.[274] Ishmael, the son of Nethaniah, persuaded the pilgrims to turn aside

---

269. See Hillers 1972: 44. The real-life circumstances that were the basis of the lamentation in Lam 2:7–9 are of great importance. The fate of the altar is the significant addition in this passage, apparently due to its importance and its loss. The reference to the other elements parallels the information in the accounts of the destruction in 2 Kings and Jeremiah. See Jones 1963: 12, but also see the response by Ackroyd 1968: 26 n. 39. With regard to this question, see the important comment by Blenkinsopp (1998: 26), who states that, even if the altar was spared destruction, it had been defiled (cf. Lam 2:20) and could no longer be used for sacrifices.

270. On this text, see Keown, Scalise, and Smothers 1995: 238–39; Holladay 1989: 272; Seitz 1989: 274–79; Lipschits 2001: 137–41, with further literature. On the literary characteristics of this story, see Hoffman 2000: 114–16; 120–21.

271. See Holladay 1989: 297. On the connection of the Northern population to the temple in Jerusalem, see Noth 1966b: 263–64; Janssen 1956: 101–2; Coggins 1975: 28–37.

272. On this subject see, e.g., Welch 1935: 67–68; Rudolph 1947: 160; Noth 1954: 291; Jones 1963: 14–15; Galling 1964: 129; Bright 1965: 25–40; Oded 1977: 478; Ackroyd 1968: 25; 1970: 17; Japhet 1983b: 107; 2000: 369; Holladay 1989: 297; Seitz 1989: 273; Lipschits 2001: 137–41. As exceptions in the scholarship on this subject, we may mention the researchers listed by Ackroyd (1968: 25 n. 33), and add to this Klausner (1949: 1.57–58); Miller and Hayes (1986: 426), who theorized that the intended destination was some site of ritual worship that existed in Mizpah. On this subject, see also Blenkinsopp (1998: 34), who contends that Mizpah served as both the political and the religious center of the province in the early days of Babylonian rule and that, for reasons unknown, Bethel replaced it as a religious center after the murder of Gedaliah.

273. This was the theory of most scholars; see Keown, Scalise, and Smothers 1995: 241; Lipschits 1999c: 118–20; 2001: 129–42, with further literature; Japhet 2000: 369. Reservations regarding this opinion were expressed by Bright 1965: 254 and Thompson 1980: 657. A minority opinion was expressed by Hyatt (1956b: 778, 1087); Lindsay (1976: 27–29); Ahlström (1993: 801); and Hoffman (2000: 120–21; 2001: 20), who postulated that the event took place in 582 b.c.e. As previously stated, it is difficult to accept this view: it has no textual corroboration, and there is insufficient historical evidence to support it.

274. On this subject, see Rendtorff 1967: 25–26, and n. 42; Kochman 1982: 26. For an exhaustive discussion of the incense, see Nielsen 1986: particularly pp. 80, 87, with further

to Mizpah, and when they arrived in the city, he slaughtered them, leaving ten alive in exchange for "hidden stores in the field—wheat, barley, oil, and honey" (41:7–8).

Although many scholars understand the purpose of the story as to blacken the reputation of Ishmael (Keown, Scalise, and Smothers 1995: 241; Hoffman 200: 113–16), almost no one doubts that the story is based on an event that took place after the murder of Gedaliah.[275] Nonetheless, we cannot ignore the notion that the story was connected to the prophecies of Jeremiah 7 (especially vv. 4, 12) and 31:1–13, and it looks as though the event was interpreted in light of them. The connection to chap. 7 was primarily for the purpose of conveying a political-theological message and of completing the cycle of Jeremiah's prophecies about the fate of the temple in Jerusalem. The prophet's call to "all Judah that enter into these gates to worship the Lord" (7:2), not to rely on the temple's enduring forever and to learn from the fate of Shiloh, which had been destroyed (v. 12; cf. 26:6, 9; Ps 78:60), is directly connected to the arrival of the pilgrims from Shiloh at the ruins of the temple in Jerusalem.[276] According to this prophecy, past and present meet: the inhabitants of the devastated Northern Kingdom, whose fate and the fate of whose temple served the prophet as a prototype of the future of Judah and the temple in Jerusalem, arrive to lament the temple in Jerusalem that has been destroyed.

The goal of the connection to chap. 31 was to add another level to the story: to defame Ishmael, this time theologically. We cannot ignore the connection between the description of the arrival of the pilgrims in 41:5 and the words of the prophecy in 31:6, "For there is a day when watchmen have called on Mount Ephraim, 'Arise, let us go up to Zion, to the Lord our God'," which goes on to say in vv. 8–9, "I am going to bring them from the land of the north, and gather them from the ends of the earth. . . . With weeping they shall come, and with consolation I shall lead them; I shall bring them to streams of water, in a straight path, in which they shall not stumble; for to Israel I have been a father, and Ephraim is my firstborn son."[277] The words of this prophecy (cf. 50:4) may explain the places of origin of the pilgrims. They came from three important historical centers within the borders of the kingdom of Israel—centers that had

---

literature. For more on incense and grain offerings, see *TDOT* 7.441–47; 8.407–21. For additional literature, see *NIDOTTE* 2.757, 989–90.

275. An exception is Skinner (1926: 304–5), who maintained that this story is not a description of a historical event but a vision of the future, when people from Israel would see Jerusalem as their capital and make pilgrimages to it. Naʾaman (1993a: 23 n. 52) argued that the aim of this account was to show that, after the destruction, the centrality of Jerusalem in religious ritual was preserved. It is difficult to accept his proposal, because it has no additional confirmation in the "biography" of Jeremiah.

276. I accept Janzen's claim (1973: 36–37) that most parts of the heading in 7:1–2 are secondary; they do not appear in the LXX. For literature on this subject, see Weippert 1973: 27 n. 3; Holladay 1986: 235, 241. On the time and goal of this chapter, see Hoffman 2001: 243–47.

277. Compare also the description of the "hidden stores" in 41:8 to the prophecy in 31:12.

been destroyed. These centers had played an important role in the history of the nation in the days of the patriarchs and the conquest of the land (Shechem); the premonarchic period (Shiloh); and in the kingdom's golden era (Samaria). Nonetheless, the prophet's words, that the pilgrims would come "in a straight path, in which they [would] not stumble," were not fulfilled, and 70 of the pilgrims were murdered by Ishmael. The criticism of Ishmael's act seems stronger than ever in this light, even apart from the fact that it was cruel, senseless, mass murder. Ishmael's deed is perceived as an attempt to bring a halt to ritual activity in Jerusalem and to prevent renewal of the temple's status—all part of his desire to thwart the reconstruction of the land.

Most scholars have assumed, based on the historical reconstruction, that soon after the Babylonian destruction the site of the temple became a center where many pilgrims came to pray, recite lamentations, and bring offerings to God.[278] But there is no evidence that there was official Babylonian permission to perform religious rituals of any kind. It appears that pilgrimages to the site of the ruins were made by small groups and individuals, and the rituals performed were of a spontaneous rather than an official nature. The Babylonian authority did not prohibit or prevent this, apparently because it suited their interest to demonstrate publicly the fate of those who rebelled against them (see also Jones 1963: 12–31; Ackroyd 1970: 17). Support for this reconstruction may be found in the passages that report that Seraiah, the chief priest, Zephaniah, the second priest, and the three doorkeepers were put to death at Riblah by Nebuchadrezzar (2 Kgs 25:18–21; Jer 52:24–27). Just as the elimination of Zedekiah and his sons was intended to put an end to the rule of the House of David in Judah, the killing of the priests was intended to end religious influence in Jerusalem. Nevertheless, nothing is known about appointment of priests from another family, in contrast to the fact that leadership that was not of the Davidic line was appointed.[279] This supports the assumption that no official religious ritual arrangement had been set up in Jerusalem; when the ritual was restored during the days of the Return to Zion, the family of Zadok reestablished itself and its position.

If the description in Jer 41:5 reflects historical reality, then the central motif was bringing the grain offering and incense, both of which emphasize the absence of animal sacrifices. Many scholars have been struck by the parallels in the terminology and historical processes between the cult in Jerusalem after the fall and the situation reflected in the Elephantine papyri, because the temple in Elephantine was also destroyed (410 B.C.E.) and remained in ruins for some time.

278. See, e.g., Welch 1935: 68; Janssen 1956: 46–56; 101–2; Noth 1966: 264; Smith 1989: 33–34; Albertz 1994: 377–82. Hyatt (1956b: 1088) held a minority view on this subject, arguing that the temple in Jerusalem had been sufficiently restored at that time to allow sacrifices to be brought to the site. On this subject, see Ackroyd 1970: 17–18; Ahlström 1971: 114–15.

279. See, e.g. Welch 1935: 68–71; Bright 1959: 325. For an extended discussion on the fate of the priestly houses in Judah under Babylonian and Persian rule, see Blenkinsopp 1998: 25–34.

Regular mourning was observed by the Jewish community for a long time, throughout the time that requests for permission to rebuild the temple were made. Finally, in 407 B.C.E., the instructions sent by Bagohi, governor of Judah, and Delaiah, governor of Samaria, were received, including permission to rebuild the temple and to renew the bringing of grain offerings and incense. This did not include permission to renew animal sacrifice, which was apparently limited to the temple in Jerusalem.[280]

Despite the long difference in time between the two destructions, the differing circumstances, and the different motives behind the imperial authority's prevention of the renewal of animal sacrifice, the parallelism does show that a cult site where only incense and offerings were permitted was inferior to a site where animal sacrifices took place. A later author, apparently from the time of Nehemiah or afterward, also understood the matter this way and was responsible for the addition of the segment in Jer 17:19–27.[281] Beyond the subject of the Sabbath, which lies at the center of this segment, the text emphasizes the prophet's vision of the future, with pilgrims from all over Judah "bringing burnt offerings and sacrifices, grain offerings and incense, bringing also thank offerings to the house of the Lord" (v. 26).

There is no information about events in Jerusalem between the period immediately after the destruction and the beginning of the Return to Zion. The information gap is actually even greater than a mere absence, because there is serious question about who wrote the description of this period that is found in Ezra 1–6.[282] In any case, the theory that the status of religious ritual in Jerusalem was dictated by Babylonian policy necessitates the conclusion that any change in this ritual must have been linked to a change in policy. There is no evidence of such a change, and support for the consistency of policy is found in the contexts reflected in the Psalms that are dated to the period of Babylonian rule.[283]

If we agree that the temple in Jerusalem was not rebuilt during the period of Babylonian rule and that only limited ritual activity continued on the site of the temple's ruins, we can understand why the proclamation of Cyrus was greeted by those who returned to Zion as a major innovation and as having great legal importance. Without getting into the question of the historical reliability of

---

280. On the correspondence between the Jews in Elephantine and the Persian authority, see letters 30–33 in Cowley (1923: 108–16), and compare the translation and discussion by Porten (1996: 139–51: letters B19–B32).

281. See Holladay 1986: 508–11; Hoffman 2001: 402–4. For a different view, see Rudolph 1947: 109, followed by Thompson 1980: 427–28. See also the focused discussion in Greenberg 1972: 27–52.

282. See Williamson 1983: 1–30; Eskenazi 1988: 42; Halpern 1990: 85–93; Japhet 1993b; 2000: 347–48, with further literature.

283. Note how Janssen (1956: 19) bases his arguments on Psalms 44, 74, 89, and 102, and see the discussion in Jones (1963: 24–31) on Psalms 40, 51, 69, and 102. See also Albertz 2003: 140–66.

the proclamation (in either the Hebrew or the Aramaic version) as an original document or as an adaptation of such a document (Williamson 1985: 7, 72–76; Halpern 1990: 85–93; Japhet 1991: 179–80; see below, §2.3.6, pp. 122–126), and without discussing the relationships of those who returned to those who remained in the land, we can say that the change in Persian policy was perceived as the legal basis for building the temple and renewing the practice of bringing sacrifices: "In the first year of his reign, King Cyrus issued a decree: Let the House be rebuilt on the place where they used to offer sacrifices" (Ezra 6:3).[284] According to Ezra 3:1–5, building the altar and renewing the practice of sacrifice on the site were the first acts of those who returned to Zion: "From the first day of the seventh month, they began to sacrifice burnt offerings to the Lord, though the foundation of the temple of the Lord had not yet been laid" (Ezra 3:6; Myers 1965a: 23; cf. Williamson 1985: 40, 47; Blenkinsopp 1988: 94, 98).

2.3.5 The Province of Judah after the Murder of Gedaliah

The attempt by scholars to explain the murder of Gedaliah as an act of madness must be rejected, given the historical reconstruction outlined above.[285] Apparently, Ishmael's immediate motive for murder was his hostility toward Gedaliah, whom he saw as a collaborator with the Babylonians; in addition, he was opposed to the appointment of a person not of the Davidic line to the highest office in the province (Baltzer 1961: 35–36; Miller and Hayes 1986: 424–25; Seitz 1989: 275–76; Ahlström 1993: 800–801; Hoffman 2000: 109). Baalis's cooperation can be seen as an attempt to undermine the Babylonian hold on the conquered kingdom, perhaps as part of the revolt of Ammon against Babylon at that time.[286] In any event, the basic fact that emerges from the narrative is that the murder of Gedaliah was committed by people in circles outside of the province who refused to accept the fact that those who remained in Judah had made peace with the Babylonians. By committing murder,[287] these people wished to

---

284. Compare the translations and interpretation of this verse in Rudolph (1949: 54) and Blenkinsopp (1988: 123).

285. For a survey of the various proposals concerning Ishmael's motivation for murdering Gedaliah, see Holladay 1989: 297–98; Welch 1935: 68; Ahlström 1993: 800. These proposals are largely based on Jer 41:1–10, which emphasizes Ishmael's blood lust, his greed, his jealousy of those who had taken control in Judah, etc. In my opinion, these descriptions are additions intended to blacken his image, and it is doubtful that we can rely on them to reconstruct the circumstances of the murder.

286. According to Ezek 21:28–32, Ammon's rebellion against Babylon took place at the same time as Judah's revolt. We may assume that keeping a refugee in the courtyard of a vassal king was considered a serious offense by the Babylonians.

287. The text in Jer 41:1–3 has been expanded. In terms of the literary form, the expansion was intended to portray the murder negatively and to provide additional details of the act. Some of the expansions in the MT are typical of the entire book (elaboration of names, generalizations, etc.). However, of particular interest, with only a few parallels, is the use of repetition in places where the original text has been noticeably expanded, apparently due to fear that the

prevent the continued rebuilding of Judah and, instead, wished to add Judah to the group opposed to Babylonian rule. The main evidence for this is that, following the murder, great fear gripped those who remained in Mizpah. Their decision to flee Judah is directly linked to fear of Babylonian reaction. The direction of their flight proves that they hoped to receive asylum outside the range of Babylonian control.

Many scholars take the description found in 2 Kgs 25:26 and Jer 41:16–18 literally and conclude that the murder of Gedaliah brought an end to the attempt to recreate Judah as an independent province.[288] Noth, followed by Myers and others, argued that after the murder of Gedaliah Judah completely lost its administrative independence within the Babylonian Empire; it was annexed to the province of Samaria as a mere subprovince (Noth 1954: 286–88; Myers 1965a: xx–xxi).

The historical reconstruction followed by these scholars depends on the historical profile presented by later redactors of the book of Kings and in the "biography" of Jeremiah. However, these two descriptions offer a tendentious and partial picture that does not necessarily reflect the actual events in Judah after the destruction and after the murder of Gedaliah.[289] On the one hand, the goal of the narrative in Kings is to recount for the exiles in Babylon and for those who returned to Zion in the early Persian Period the story of the destruction of Jerusalem and the deportation of the nation's elite. According to this description, the exiles to Babylon are "the true Judah," the country was emptied of its inhabitants, and the only ones who remained were "some of the poorest people of the land." The theological, political, and economic struggle of the exiles against those who remained in Judah and the exiles' desire to establish their right to return and regain positions of power, land, and their previous status are the factors that created "the myth of the empty land." On the other hand, the object of the "biography" of Jeremiah is to demonstrate how the destruction of Jerusalem and the exile were a lost opportunity (Albertz 2003: 4–8) and to explain the circumstances under which the prophet went to Egypt in the company

---

original description would not be understood properly (Tov 1981: 166–67, and see there other examples). The repetition here consists of the verb and subject (ישמעאל היכה), which direct the reader back to the main subject introduced before the text was expanded (p. 166). In this case, Wanke (1971: 95) is right to assume that Jer 41:3a is a secondary addition based on 2 Kgs 25:25.

288. See, e.g., the opinions of Bright 1965: 256; Miller and Hayes 1986: 425. Miller and Hayes have gone further and claim that Gedaliah was appointed as the first king in Judah who was not of the House of David and that his murder led to the transformation of Judah into a province in the Babylonian administration. But there is no support for the theory that Gedaliah was appointed by the Babylonians to be king over Judah in the place of kings from the Davidic line. And there is no textual or other basis for the theory that it was only after the murder of Gedaliah that Judah became a Babylonian province.

289. On the ideological orientation of these narratives and their purposes, see the discussion below in chap. 5.

of those who fled after Gedaliah's murder. The description focuses on the latter group and is not concerned with those who remained in the country; however, later additions to the text created an overall picture according to which the country was emptied of "all the remnant of Judah who had returned [from all the nations to which they had been scattered] to dwell in the land of [Egypt]" (Jer 43:5).[290]

The historiographical tendentiousness of these descriptions is obvious, and the historical picture that they draw does not accord with either the archaeological data or our knowledge of the geopolitical and demographic processes (below, chaps. 3 and 4). An analysis of the passages themselves highlights the tension that exists between the data they contain and the generalizations that were added at a later stage.

According to 2 Kgs 25:25bα and Jer 41:3aα, the Babylonian garrison in Mizpah was eliminated by Ishmael, the son of Nethaniah, and the ten men that came with him. The great apprehension felt by those who remained in Mizpah regarding the Babylonian response to the murder (2 Kgs 25:26b; Jer 41:18a) leads us to conclude that the main Babylonian force was garrisoned nearby and was expected to arrive in the province to restore order after the murder of Gedaliah. The group that fled Mizpah assembled near Bethlehem before going to Egypt (2 Kgs 25:26a; Jer 41:16–17). According to the text, this group was headed by Johanan, the son of Kareah, and there were two small groups of people with him. The first group included "all the army officers that were with him," and it appears that this refers to the "officers" who attacked Gedaliah (2 Kgs 25:23b; Jer 40:8b), who must have been accompanied by some soldiers. The second group consisted of "all the [remnant of the] people whom Ishmael [son of Nethaniah] had taken captive from Mizpah [after he had killed Gedaliah, the son of Ahikam]—men [of war], women, children, and eunuchs whom he brought back from Gibeon" (Jer 41:16).[291] A simple reading of this account would take the group of people as those who were captured by Ishmael and his ten men and who were later released by Johanan, the son of Kareah, and his "army officers" together with their men. The group who remained after the massacre at Mizpah must have been very small, so small that only ten soldiers were needed to capture the group and move it from place to place. It would be safe to assume that this group did not include more than several scores of the elite in Mizpah. Thus, this text provides no basis for a mass departure of Jews to Egypt; the land was not emptied of its inhabitants (Holladay 1989: 298, 301). This conclusion is in harmony with 43:5–6 (Thompson 1980: 669; Albertz 2003:

---

290. On the reconstruction of this verse based on the LXX and 4QJer[b], see Janzen 1973: 182–84; Holladay 1989: 276.

291. On the different versions of this verse, see Janzen 1973: 23–25; Thompson 1980: 659; Holladay 1989: 273, with further literature.

324–25), if we agree that 43:5b is a later addition, because it does not appear in the LXX or in 4QJer[b] (Janzen 1973: 54, 182–83; Holladay 1989: 276).

The description of those "who went down to Egypt" as "all the people both small and great" occurs in 2 Kgs 25:26aα and three times in the "biography" of Jeremiah (42:1, 8; 43:4–5).[292] Apparently, these expansions were intended to enhance the importance of Jeremiah and the size of the audience to whom the prophecies were directed.[293] The expansion occurs again in the context of the appeal in 42:2 (which also includes a paraphrase of Zedekiah's words in 37:3b) and in 43:5b (a verse that was added to make it parallel with 40:12aα).[294]

The conclusion from the above textual discussion is that the group of people who went down to Egypt was relatively small. The group was composed primarily of "the army officers" and those who were rescued from Ishmael—the main people who feared Babylonian reprisals for the murder (Jer 42:14–22; Janssen 1956: 39–42; Ackroyd 1968: 20–31; Oded 1977: 477–79). There is no intimation at all that this group also included additional people from the Benjaminite region or Judah, and it seems clear that the generalizations about the group as "all the people" are part of the later redaction of the story (Wanke 1971: 129; Seitz 1989: 278–79). Many inhabitants remained in the province of Judah, and the Babylonians had to appoint an alternate leadership as replacements for Gedaliah and the elite who had fled to Egypt. Neither this text nor any other biblical account contains any evidence of a change in Judah's status or in the structure of its government.

Despite the importance and centrality of Gedaliah for the initial rebuilding process, we should not assume that establishing the Babylonian province was dependent on one person alone. The archaeological evidence from Benjamin and the northern Judean highlands reveals continuous settlement in these regions until the end of the sixth century B.C.E. Jer 52:30, too, reports that 745

---

292. On the linguistic problems in these verses and the inclusive meaning of "all the people both small and great," see Thompson 1980: 663 and Holladay 1989: 298–301, with further literature. This expression implies that the people behaved as one group (Thompson, p. 663). It is likely that Jeremiah's original words are found in 42:9–12 (Seitz 1989: 277) and that the generalizations are part of a later redaction. For a complete list of the verses that should be considered part of the redaction of this unit, see Wanke 1971: 116–31; Pohlmann 1978: 140–41; Thiel 1981: 62; Seitz 1989: 277–78. There is some disagreement among these scholars, but the differences are insignificant with regard to the verses under discussion here.

293. This tendency is also evident in the open confrontation that developed between Jeremiah and Baruch and the public to whom the prophecies were directed. This confrontation is reflected in the special appeal to אלהיך ('your God', 42:2–3, twice in the second-person singular!) and in Jeremiah's response, which was delivered in second-person plural (42:4). It reached a climax in the general description of the crowd as "all the evil men" (43:2), apparently by Baruch(?), who is accused in 43:3 of inciting the prophet to say things that they did not wish to hear. On the purpose of these verses, see Thompson 1980: 662–64; Holladay 1989: 298–99; Seitz 1989: 275; Hoffman 2001: 725–26.

294. See Janzen 1973: 54, 182–83; Holladay 1989: 276; and cf. the parallel text in 4QJer[b].

Jews were deported in Nebuchadrezzar's 23rd year (582/1 b.c.e.), which implies that Judean settlement in the region continued.[295] No reason is given for the deportation by the Babylonians but, as stated previously, this event should not be linked to the murder of Gedaliah.

Support for this conclusion may be found in the prophet's appeal to the group leaving for Egypt and his attempts to convince them to remain in Judah (42:7–22). Jeremiah mentions the reason for their leaving in the course of en-couraging them to stay, making promises like those that Gedaliah had made: "Do not be afraid of the king of Babylon as you have been; be not afraid of him, says the Lord" (v. 11). He also speaks of rebuilding the country, presents the conditions for living in the land to those who are leaving (42:10aα), and prom-ises them a reward: stability and protection from the Babylonians (vv. 10aβ–11). These words, spoken after the murder of Gedaliah, show that the men of Judah who left for Egypt also knew that the rebuilding process had not yet come to an end. Furthermore, the prophet's predictions of the tragedy that would be-fall those who left for Egypt was addressed only to them and not to those who remained in Judah.

2.3.6. *The Province of Judah in the Babylonian Period according to Sources from the Period of the Return to Zion*

Historical sources on the early days of the Return to Zion are scant and lim-ited. First and foremost among them is the book of Ezra, especially chaps. 1–6.[296] Scholars generally accept that this section of the books of Ezra and Nehe-miah was written last, not before the mid-fifth century b.c.e. It is also generally accepted that its author did not have a full, continuous description of events. To overcome this problem, the author incorporated several documents into the narrative framework that he, for various reasons, attributed to the first days of the Return to Zion and the building of the temple.

The most important, central document with which the author-redactor of Ezra and Nehemiah chose to begin his essay[297] was the edict of Cyrus in its He-brew version (Ezra 1:2–4; for an update on the literature, see Japhet 2000: 356–57 n. 34). Some scholars totally reject the historical credibility of this version of

---

295. See also Miller and Hayes 1986: 425. I cannot accept the view of Hyatt (1956b: 1084); Lindsay (1976: 27–29); Ahlström (1993: 801); Hoffman (2000: 119; 2001: 20); Albertz (2003: 94–95), according to which Gedaliah's murder is placed within this time span, when Nebucha-drezzar was also conducting a campaign toward eastern Transjordan.

296. On the characteristics of this unit, its reliability and originality, see above, p. 98 and the literature in Grabbe (forthcoming).

297. Eskenazi (1988: 42–45) and Japhet (1993b: 119) aptly defined the historiographical proclivity expressed in this choice. For our purposes, what is important is the historiographical perception that was prevalent in the days of the Return to Zion: those "who remained" had no independent existence. Nonetheless, this perception does not imply denial of the actual exist-ence of the "remnant"; see more on this below.

the edict;[298] others think that the precise phrasing, or at least a version close to the original oral or written decree, was embedded in Ezra 1.[299] Support for the latter opinion is the presence of word usage that is not typical of biblical language: the use of the root פקד in the imperative in the sense of giving an order (Williamson 1985: 4), the greeting "May his God be with him,"[300] the description of God as "the God who is in Jerusalem,"[301] and the geographical definition "Jerusalem, which is in Judah."[302] In spite of these data, most scholars see the wording in Ezra 1:2–4 as the work of a Judean author or at least a translation and adaptation of the original version, harmonized with the perceptions prevalent in the days of the Return to Zion.[303] Support for this latter view may be found in the great importance assigned to the edict of Cyrus in Judean historiography, as well as in the biblical idioms scattered throughout, as well as the linguistic and textual problems existing in the decree.[304]

Williamson's suggestion appeals to me. He proposes regarding the proclamation as a document responding to the men of Judah's appeal to Cyrus, using the very language of their request. This source was adapted at a late stage (perhaps even before it was embedded in the beginning of the book of Ezra), so that the Hebrew version of the proclamation does not accurately reflect the original but, rather, the form in which the decree was seen at a more remote time (Williamson 1985: 11–14, with further literature). It appears that the Hebrew version of the decree was reworked in accordance with the Aramaic version, which is embedded as it was originally worded in Ezra 6:3–5.[305]

---

298. For a comprehensive discussion and summary of this approach, see Briend (1996: 33–44), with further literature. This is the common view in German scholarship; see, e.g., Galling (1964: 61–77); Gunneweg (1985: 40–44); Albertz (2003: 121). Similarly, see also Blenkinsopp (1988: 74–76).

299. See, e.g., the opinions of Batten 1913: 23, 60–61; Bickerman 1946: 249–75, esp. p. 266; 1967: 72–108; Kaufman 1956: 162; Liver 1959a: 115; Bright 1959: 362; Myers 1965a: 5; Tadmor 1974: 471; Porten 1979: 174–76; Clines 1984: 36–39; Williamson 1985: 6–8.

300. On the pagan source of this expression, see Bickerman 1976: 81–82. On the parallel to the "cylinder inscription," see Kuhrt (1983: 89–91), and on its being evidence for the authenticity of the decree, see Williamson (1985: 13).

301. Batten (1913: 60–61) argued that this description of God is not consistent with Judahite writing from the days of the Return to Zion but reflects a foreign conception of Jewish divinity at that time. See also Porten 1978: 175; Blenkinsopp 1988: 75.

302. This definition is repeated four times in the wording of the proclamation (twice in v. 3, once in vv. 4 and 5; cf. 2 Chr 36:23) and does not conform to the Judahite world-view or the way Jerusalem is usually referred to in the Bible. For references on this subject, see Williamson 1985: 12 and see also the suggestion by Batten 1913: 59 and the remarks by Porten 1978: 175; Fensham 1982: 43–44; Clines 1984: 37–38; Grabbe 1998: 11; and Davies 1999: 9–10.

303. See Ryle 1907: 5; Schaeder 1930b: 29; de Vaux 1937: 57; Rudolph 1949: 3, 220; Noth 1954: 307; Galling 1964a: 72–73; Tadmor 1983: 14–15; Williamson 1985: 11–14; Blenkinsopp 1988: 74; Grabbe 1999: 21.

304. See, in particular, the contrast between v. 4aα and 4aβ (Williamson 1985: 14).

305. This is the opinion of Japhet (2000: 358–61), and it is precisely the opposite of the opinion held by Batten (1913: 60–61).

Despite the literary character of the Hebrew version of the edict, it may be helpful for understanding the newly changed status of Judah, Jerusalem, and the temple. On the basis of the changes granted by the edict, we may infer their status in the period that preceded the edict. Two main conclusions emerge:

1. The edict of Cyrus relates exclusively to the status of the temple in Jerusalem (Weinberg 2000: 308, with further literature). Furthermore, building a house is mentioned twice in the edict, the house being the "House of the Lord God of Israel" (vv. 2b, 3b), and this is the major change affecting the people and the temple. Getting this permission was the objective of the returnees to Judah, a fact that is reflected in the literary section of Ezra 1–6. This section, which ends with a description of the festivities accompanying the dedication of the temple, highlights this objective and provides a link to the next section (Ezra 7:1ff.). All of this reinforces the reality described above: before the edict, Jerusalem was a site where only meal offerings and incense were permitted—as opposed to animal sacrifices. The status of the temple was not altered for religious reasons; it was a political measure aimed at solidifying Persian rule in Judah. The considerations that led the Persians to allow the construction of the temple were similar to the considerations that guided the Babylonians to destroy it 50 years earlier. Convincing evidence of this may be found in the arguments enumerated in the "letter of accusation," which recounted the reason for the destruction of Jerusalem and cited the rebellious character of the city and its history of disloyalty (Ezra 4:16).

2. The return to Judah and building of Jerusalem have generally been perceived as directly connected with the building of the temple; however, in the edict of Cyrus, no such association is made. Furthermore, according to the wording of the edict in v. 3, the return to Jerusalem was restricted to those who were to build the temple.[306] It is possible that the lack of any reference to returning to the land and rebuilding it is a literary-conceptual issue, but a comparison with the "cylinder inscription"[307] supports the theory that the edict addressed only one subject: the temple (Tadmor 1974). Two major conclusions emerge:

   a. The political status of Judah was already defined, so there was no change in its status (Liver 1958; Kochman 1980: 100–107). The major innovation resulting from the edict was the acknowledgment of the temple's status as the official site of religious ritual in the province (Kochman 1980: 107).

---

306. The absence of references to immigrating to the land or building the temple is the basis of Galling's proposal (1954b: 11–14) that, in addition to Cyrus's proclamation concerning the temple, there was an additional proclamation concerning the return of the Jews to Zion. It is superfluous to note that there is no evidence of a second proclamation. On this subject, see also the treatment by Batten 1913: 58–59; Myers 1965a: 6–7.

307. The inscription was found in Babylon in 1879 and is now in the British museum (B.M. 90920). On this subject, see the discussion in Kuhrt 1983: 83–97, with further literature.

b. The immigrants went to Jerusalem, and their objective was to build the temple (cf., e.g., the description in Ezra 1:5–11). Evidence of this is found in the "letter of accusation," which describes the return of the men of Judah to Jerusalem, rather than to Judah (Ezra 4:12).

One important question concerns the number of immigrants (see more below, §4.4.4, pp. 267–271). In my opinion, it was a small minority of the elite who had been deported to Babylon 50 to 60 years earlier and included the new leadership of the province, the priests and office-holders who were connected with the functioning of the temple. This small immigration could not have changed Jerusalem's physical condition, and proof is found in a description of the condition of the city during the days of Nehemiah (Neh 2:13–15). According to descriptions in Ezra and Haggai, even building the temple was beyond the ability of those who returned, which makes it easier to understand the sparse accounts in Haggai of attempts to convince "those who remained (in Judah)" to help build the temple (Hag 1:2–6). This is perhaps why those engaged in the work at the beginning of construction activities were known as "the remnant of the people" (v. 14).[308] We should, therefore, not be surprised that "the children of Israel who were returned from exile . . . together with all who had joined them by separating themselves from the uncleanliness of the Gentiles" (Ezra 6:21) were the people who took part in the dedication of the temple.[309] The differences in world view between the exiles and those who remained in Judah is, perhaps, why there was tension between the two groups of people, as alluded to in Isa 66:5.

The names of the first governors during the period of the Return to Zion and their titles may help us understand the history of the province of Judah before this era. According to Ezra 5:14, Cyrus appointed Sheshbazzar as governor, and Zerubbabel is also called governor (Hag 1:1, 14; 2:21). It seems that a straight line connects these two governors and Gedaliah, and there is nothing to contravene the idea that Judean governors continued to serve in Judah throughout the sixth century B.C.E. Furthermore, there is no evidence of a change in the province's status at the beginning of the Persian Period. If there was a change during the transition to Persian rule, it was in the appointment of governors from members of the royal family and a restoration of power to the nation's elite, who had been deported to Babylon (see Talmon, in Tadmor 1983: 34). The change in governorship of the province is one of the conspicuous hallmarks of the new era,

---

308. On the significance of the titles "this people" and "this nation" in Haggai's prophecies, see Japhet 1983: 112, and n. 29; she sees these phrases as referring to "the people who remained in the land."

309. Ezra's language later in the narrative takes an even more extreme approach toward those who remained in the land; however, a discussion of this subject would distract us from the purposes of this book.

which was initiated by the Return to Zion and which revived rule by the older elite over the people who had remained in Judah.

Excursus 1:
The Names in 2 Kings 25:23 and Jeremiah 40:8

The preliminary note to the list of names serves as an introduction: this is a list of the army officers who came to Gedaliah "at Mizpah." The list appears to be only a summary, because Ishmael, the son of Nethaniah, comes to Mizpah only at a later stage (2 Kgs 25:25; Jer 41:1), after having spent time in Ammon (Jer 40:14). In Jeremiah, there is a second description of the arrival of Johanan, the son of Kareah, and "all of the army officers who were in the field," at a later date (40:13). This makes it even more difficult to make sense of the arrival of the army officers at an earlier time (2 Kgs 25:23aβ; Jer 40:8aα). Thus, it is reasonable to accept Thompson's hypothesis that the army officers are listed in order of their importance in the narrative (Thompson 1980: 654). At the top of the list are two important figures: Ishmael, the son of Nethaniah (who was the main protagonist), and Johanan, the son of Kareah (who tried to thwart Ishmael's plans, and who is also portrayed in Jeremiah 42–43 as responsible for the flight to Egypt). Next on the list are Seraiah and Jaazaniah, but nothing is known about their actions. They may have been among the army officers who were murdered in Mizpah or, alternatively, among those who collaborated with Johanan, the son of Kareah, until the descent to Egypt. Aside from the fact that the list looks incomplete and lacks the customary beginning, it is also missing at least one officer mentioned in the story: Azariah, the son of Hoshaiah (Jer 42:1; 43:2).

The lists in 2 Kings and Jeremiah had a single source: both begin with the names and the conjunctive *waw* 'and'. The names are identical, and they are cited in the same manner. The main difference is that, in Jeremiah, another son of Kareah and the sons of Ephai are also mentioned. On this subject, see the comparison following (and see below a detailed discussion of these names and the information available about them):

Names of those who came to Gedaliah

according to Jer 40:8		according to 2 Kgs 25:23	
וַיִּשְׁמָעֵאל בֶּן נְתַנְיָהוּ		וַיִּשְׁמָעֵאל בֶּן נְתַנְיָה	
וְיוֹחָנָן וְיוֹנָתָן בְּנֵי קָרֵחַ		וְיוֹחָנָן בְּנֵי קָרֵחַ	
וּשְׂרָיָה בֶּן תַּנְחֻמֶת		וּשְׂרָיָה בֶּן תַּנְחֻמֶת	
וַ בְּנֵי עוֹפַי הַנְּטֹפָתִי		הַנְּטֹפָתִי	
וִיזַנְיָהוּ בֶּן הַמַּעֲכָתִי		וְיַאֲזַנְיָהוּ בֶּן הַמַּעֲכָתִי	

It is difficult to support the idea that there was an organized list of names of the army officers who arrived at Mizpah, because this requires the assumption that the administration (?) of the new center at Mizpah was formally registering everyone who arrived in the city. The description of the later arrival of some of the army officers argues against a registry of this sort and in favor of the hypothesis that the list is a collection of the names of army officers known to the author, some of whom are mentioned in the story itself.

Ishmael: The name *Ishmael* occurs in the Bible 48 times: 21 times in Jeremiah, 18 in Genesis, 7 in Chronicles, twice in 2 Kings, and once in Ezra. This distribution suggests that the name became popular at the end of the Iron Age and during the Persian Period. The name is also popular on seals at the end of the First Temple Period; see, for example, the proliferation of occurrences in Avigad (1986: 54–55) and Diringer (1934: 203–4, 210, etc.). The name Nethaniah/Netanyahu occurs in the Bible 20 times, 16 of which are in 2 Kings and Jeremiah, all referring to the father of Ishmael. It appears also to have been widely used at the end of the First Temple Period. It occurs in the tomb inscriptions from Khirbet el-Qôm (Dever 1969–70: 151), as well as on seals of that era (Diringer 1934: 190–92; and pl. 20:2); on a stamp seal impression found at Tell en-Naṣbeh (McCown 1947: 167–68 n. 2); on a Neo-Assyrian tablet found at Gezer (Pinches 1904; Macalister 1912: 1.23–29); on the ostraca at Arad (Aharoni 1976: nos. 23, 56); and on an ostracon found at Ḥorvat ʿUza (Beit-Arieh 1999a: 32). Attempts to link the name of Elishama, father of Nethaniah (2 Kgs 25:25), to the son of David, who according to the account in 2 Sam 5:16 was born in Jerusalem some 400 years before the destruction (Feinberg 1982: 273) are futile. Feinberg's argument that Nethaniah's father was a descendant who can be traced back to the earlier Elishama's family (p. 273) is also unacceptable. This name occurs in Jer 36:12, 20, and 21 as "Elishama, the scribe," who lived at the time of Jehoiakim, and he can be connected to the seal of "Elishama, the son of the king" (Diringer 1934: 232–33, pl. 21:9; Yeivin 1960: 282–84, with further literature), or to the person mentioned in the stamp impression: "to Elishama, the servant of the king" (Avigad 1986: 23). On the title "the servant of the king," see Lipschits (2002a). The name *Elishama* was common on other seals; see Diringer (1934: 216, 257); Avigad (1986: 54–55, 91).

The designation "of the royal family" (lit., 'of the royal seed', 2 Kgs 25:25) appears in only two other places (Ezek 17:13; Dan 1:3; see also 1 Kgs 11:14). In each of these cases, the phrase refers to the royal family; however, it may refer to the extended family, not necessarily only the sons of the king. Support for the theory that the phrase has a wider meaning is found in the fact that none of the persons referred to here as "of the royal family" appearance in the genealogy of the House of David in 1 Chronicles 3; furthermore, nothing is known about Ishmael and his ancestors. If it be true that these people were not sons of the king, it is likely that the narrative's intent is to claim that Ishmael was part of the extended royal family. The question is why the text bothers to note Ishmael's special status, and here, of all places, because Ishmael has already been mentioned in 2 Kgs 25:23 (= Jer 40:8) as one of the army officers, without further comment. He is also mentioned in Jer 40:14–15, again without further comment, despite the fact that in the context he is going to meet Baʿalis, king of Ammon. Here, precisely in the context of the murder of Gedaliah, there is a comment connecting Ishmael to the House of David, and in Jeremiah there is even an added comment: "and one of the chief officers of the king" (missing in the LXX and in the parallel version in 2 Kings); cf. Jer 39:13 (Harrison 1973: 161; Hoffman 2000: 109; 2001: 722). In my opinion, by making this comment, the narrator wished to insinuate Ishmael's motives for murdering Gedaliah. Ishmael, one of the last remnants of the House of David, who had lost his position to an important official from the days of the kingdom (and who, according to Jeremiah 40–41, was forced to take refuge in Ammon), can neither reconcile himself to Gedaliah's reign nor to the policy Gedaliah charts, and decides to eliminate him (Kessler 1965: 298). The account in 2 Kings suggests all of this as a possible motive for the murder. However, from the tone of the words and the brevity with which they are presented, this rationale may not express the central idea—and the text lays no special emphasis on this idea. The account in Jeremiah has a clear anti-Davidic bias, which is expressed at length in vv. 13–16: with the addition of the title to Ishmael's name ("one of the chief officers of the king"), by smearing his character in the additions in vv. 5–7, 8–10, and 11–15, by mentioning the daughters of the king among the prisoners taken by Ishmael, and by emphasizing the joy with which the rest of the people abandoned him (see also Hoffman 2000: 108–9). On the intentions and purpose of the "biography of Jeremiah," see also the discussion below.

Johanan: The name *Johanan* occurs in the Bible 33 times: 14 times in Jeremiah, 10 times in Chronicles, 5 times in Nehemiah, 3 times in Ezra , and once in Kings. It is striking that the name achieved currency at the end of the First Temple Period, during the exilic period, and during the days of the Return to Zion. Kareah, the father of Johanan is mentioned 15 times, all in this context; there is no one else in the Bible bearing this name. It is difficult to imagine that Kareah is a person's name; it seems more likely that it was a nickname applied to him because he was bald (Noth 1966a: 227; *EncMiq* 7.255). Noth thought that Kareah might be linked to Korah (1966a: 227), but this seems unlikely (*EncMiq* 7.255), as does the connection made by Keil (1989: 842) between "the sons of Kareah" and Korah who, according to 1 Chr 2:43, was the firstborn son of Hebron. Nor can this name be connected to the 5 mighty men of David listed in 1 Chr 12:5. It is more likely that this name refers to the descendants of the family of Korah, to a settlement of this name near Hebron (Wadi al-Qarahi, as Klein suggests) or to one of the quarters within the city (*EncMiq* 7.259, with further literature). The name Johanan also occurs in the Arad Letters (2:29).

Again, however, we cannot know whether the reference is to Korah or to Kareah (Aharoni 1986: 82 translated the name "Koreah"). In the MT of Jer 40:8, another person, named *Jonathan*, appears alongside Johanan, the son of Kareah, and both are called "the sons of Kareah." The LXX of Jeremiah supports the MT of 2 Kings; given this fact, we may conclude that the original text had one name only—Johanan—especially because Jonathan is not mentioned in the narrative at all. Additional support for this conclusion is found in the structure of the list, where only one name at a time is mentioned. All of this leads us to believe that the appearance of Jonathan in the list is the result of an error in the text. The corruption probably resulted from similarity of the spelling and sounds of the two names. It is also possible that one of the copyists of the version in Jeremiah could not decide which form was correct and included both rather than omitting one, resulting in corruption of the text (Janzen 1973: 17).

Seraiah: The name *Seraiah* occurs in the Bible 19 times, and once more as *Seraiahu*. The distribution of the name shows its currency at the end of the First Temple Period and during the period of the exile and the Return to Zion. It appears 6 times in Jeremiah, 5 times in 1 Chronicles, 4 times in Nehemiah, twice in 2 Kings and Ezra, and once in 2 Samuel. This frequency also is reflected in the name's appearance on seals and seal impressions from the end of the kingdom (see, e.g., Avigad 1975: 69; 1978a: 86–87; 1986: 43–44, 93). Among the people who bore this name, we have Seraiah, the son of Neriah, the son of ben Mahseiah (the brother of Baruch, the scribe of Jeremiah), who was שר המנוחה (lit., 'the officer of the resting place', Jer 51:59, 61). This Seraiah may be identified as the owner of the seal that reads "(belonging) to Seraiahu/Neriahu" (Avigad 1978a: 86–87). Seraiah's father, *Tanhumeth*, is only mentioned in the two parallel versions related to the time under study here. This name probably is related to the name *Tanhum*, which appears fairly often in seal impressions; see Grant and Wright 1939: 83–84, and pl. 9:10b; Diringer 1941: 41–42; Thompson 1942: 24–25; Moscati 1951: 73, no. 7; 76, no. 12; Tufnell 1953: 341 and pl. 47a:7; Pritchard 1959a: 27–29; Aharoni 1964: 32; Mazar and Mazar 1989: 131. For a reference to the name in the Arad ostraca, see Aharoni 1976: 72, and for a reference to it on an Ammonite seal, see Avigad 1970: 288. The gender of the word is problematic, because the form appears to be feminine; however, there is no doubt that the name refers here to a man (*EncMiq* 7.617).

The list in 2 Kings refers to Seraiah as "the Netophathite," while in Jeremiah the same term is used for other officers, who are called "the sons of Ephai, the Netophathite." The name *Ephai* does not appear in the Bible in other contexts. Noth (1966: 230) explained the name as a form of עוף ('bird'). Ephai does occur once in a seal impression (Avigad 1986: 63–64) and on the inscription from Khirbet el-Qôm (Room 3 of Tomb no. 1; Dever 1969–70: 151). The name of the place of Seraiah's origin, Netophah, is not mentioned in the list of cities of Judah in Joshua 15. However, it may be that this was a site in Judah close to

Bethlehem and Jerusalem. Netophah is mentioned in the two parallel lists (Ezra 2:22 = Neh 7:26) of the returnees to Zion as a site close to Bethlehem. Its proximity to Bethlehem and to Jerusalem also appears in Neh 12:28, where there is reference to Netophah as a gathering place for the sons of the singers (cf. 2 Sam 23:28–29 [= 1 Chr 11:30]; 1 Chr 9:16; 27:13, 15; and 1 Chr 2:54, where it is used as a surname). From all of this, it seems that the name refers to a broad area that included a central settlement and its environs, including several small satellite settlements. On suggestions for identifying the site, see *EncMiq* 5.829–30; Klein 1939: 16–17; Gray 1964: 771.

Jaazaniah: The last one to arrive in Mizpah was Jaazaniah (יאזניהו), the son of the Maacathite; in Jeremiah, his name is spelled יזניהו. The name and its variations—יזניה, יזניהו, יאזניה, יאזניהו—appear in the Bible 6 times, 3 of these instances in Jeremiah, twice in Ezekiel, and once in 2 Kings. The name was popular only at the end of the First Temple Period and after the destruction of Jerusalem (like the name Azaniah; cf. Neh 10:10 and the papyri from Elephantine). The name *Jaazaniah* also occurs on the ostraca from Arad (59:5) and Lachish (1:3; Aharoni 1976: 90; Tur-Sinai 1938: 23, 26) and on a seal of unknown origin (Diringer 1934: 180–81). No one has been able to identify any of the individuals bearing this name (Avigad 1986: 50). However, it may be possible to identify the owner of a seal found in Tomb 19 in Mizpah, "(Belongs) to Jaazaniahu / the servant of the king" (Badé 1933: 150–51; McCown 1947: 163), as the son of the Maacathite (Badé 1933: 155; McCown 1947: 163; Montgomery 1951: 566). Liver rejected this identification, arguing that Jaazaniah must have been among those who fled with the army officers to Egypt (Jeremiah 42–43) after Gedaliah's murder (1959: 69). However, there is no basis for the theory that Jaazaniah is to be included with the group of army officers after Gedaliah's murder. The main problem concerning Jaazaniah relates to the spelling of his name in Jer 40:8 and 42:1. These are the only two times that the name appears in its defective form—יזניהו, יזניה—while in 40:8, יזניהו בן המעכתי 'Jezaniah, the son of the Maacathite' is mentioned in parallel with 2 Kgs 25:23 as one of the army officers who came to Gedaliah at Mizpah. In 42:1 the name is listed among the army officers: יזניהו בן הושעיה 'Jezaniah, the son of Hoshaiah', together with Johanan, the son of Kareah, who is familiar from the list of the 4 army officers. The LXX reads עזריה 'Azariah' here, the form in which the name is also spelled in 43:2. It is reasonable to read with the LXX and conclude that, in both places, it should be read עזריה בן הושעיה (see also Feinberg 1982: 277). On the one hand, it does not seem reasonable that there were two different people with Johanan, the son of Kareah, in the same place, and thus the narrative must be referring to the same person; on the other hand, there is some logic in assuming that the error occurred because of the proximity of the two names in the list in 40:8. Perhaps it was a deliberate error by the redactor, who did not want to add a 5th name to the names of the 4 officers, which might call into question the credibility of what he had reported. This of course fits the purpose of the story in Jeremiah—to exaggerate details to enhance the reliability of the story. Support for this conclusion comes from an examination of the designation "the Maacathite." The name of Jaazaniah's father was not reported (see the explanation of Gray 1964: 771–72). The personal name Maachah is mentioned in the Bible 18 times (12 times in Chronicles); in most cases, it is a woman's name. As a place-name, it appears 3 times (2 Sam 10:6 [= 1 Chr 19:7]; 2 Sam 10:8), and in each of these occurrences, it refers to a site in the Northern Kingdom and is mentioned in context with Aram Beit-rehob, Aram Zobah, and Ish-Tob. To these three references we can add the reference to the "land that remained" in Josh 13:13, where it is mentioned that the Geshurites and the Maacathites were not displaced from their land, and they "remain among Israel to this day" (Mazar 1961: 16–28; *EncMiq* 5.192–93). The title "the Maacathite" was given to people who came from the kingdom of Maachah (cf. 2 Sam 23:34; 1 Chr 4:19; Gray 1964: 772; Holladay 1989: 295) and also to a Judahite family connected with the concubine of Caleb (1 Chr 2:48; *EncMiq* 5.193; Cogan and Tadmor 1988: 326). There is no reason to connect Jaazaniah, the Maacathite, with Jaazaniah, the son of Hoshaiah, because in the other few parallels the title "Maachathite" appears without the addition of the father's name. This conclusion supports the LXX reading and the reading of Azariah in both places (42:1; 43:2). In sum, then, to the 4 army officers mentioned in the list of 2 Kgs 25:23 and Jer 40:8, we should add one more: Azariah, the son of Hoshaiah. This officer had an important role in all of the events that occurred after the murder of Gedaliah; in fact he and Johanan are the only two officers mentioned in the narrative of the migration to Egypt.

Excursus 2:
The Redaction of Jeremiah 40:7, 11

A textual analysis reveals that the account of the arrival of the army officers (2 Kgs 25:23; Jer 40:8) and the account of the arrival of "all the Judeans" (Jer 40:11) were originally part of one sequence, and Gedaliah took his oath in the presence of both groups. An editor who inserted the source within the "biography of Jeremiah" separated the arrival of the army officers from the arrival of the Judeans. The textual proof of this is that the Judeans who "returned from all the places where they were scattered" (Jer 40:12a) implemented Gedaliah's instructions to the army officers: "What you should do is gather wine and summer fruits and oil" (Jer 40:10b) and, literally: "[they] gathered a great abundance of wine and summer fruits" (40:12b; Kessler 1965: 294). In all likelihood, the original terminology of these two verses was identical. The redactor of MT Jeremiah inserted v. 12a into the text (Janzen 1973: 53) and added the description of the place—"the land of Judah"—which is missing in the LXX. His aim was to accentuate the fact that the men of Judah arrived from places outside the country, in contrast to the army officers, who had been "in the field." In any event, there is a marked attempt here to continue a trend that is already observable in the first redaction, namely, to give precise geographical information and to make the descriptions as accurate as possible. The conclusion is that v. 12 in its original version was shorter, much simpler, and exactly parallel to the verse that describes the arrival of the officers of the army units in Mizpah:

אל גדליהו המצפתה	ויבאו	(v. 8)
ויבאו ארץ יהודה אל גדליהו המצפתה		(v. 12)

Verse 11 also is parallel to v. 7 and continues it. Both verses are parallel thematically and linguistically (Janzen 1973: 149). As the following comparison shows, they are also organized in a parallel manner:

Jer 40:11	Jer 40:7
שמעו כי ...	וישמעו ... כי ...
כל היהודים ... ואשר בכל הארצות ... כל היהודים מכל המקומות ...	כל שרי החילים המה ואנשיהם
כי נתן מלך בבל ... וכי הפקיד ...	כי הפקיד מלך בבל ...
את גדליהו בן אחיקם בן שפן	את גדליהו בן אחיקם ...

The fact that the description of the arrival of the Judeans in Jer 40:11 begins with the conjunction וגם 'likewise', which connects the subject of this verse to the preceding verse (v. 7), reinforces the hypothesis that they originally both were part of one sequence. Thus, we may postulate that the original text read as follows:

40:7: "And when the army officers, they and their men, heard that the king of Babylon had appointed Gedaliah, the son of Ahikam, governor. . . ."

40:11: "Likewise, when all the Judeans who were in Moab, Ammon, and Edom, or who were in other countries, heard that the king of Babylon had left a remnant in Judah and that he had made Gedaliah, son of Ahikam, the son of Shaphan, governor over them. . . ."

40:8a/12a: "Then they came to Gedaliah at Mizpah,"

40:9: "and Gedaliah, the son of Ahikam, the son of Shaphan, pledged an oath to them. . . ."

The conclusion is that the redactor of the "biography of Jeremiah" deliberately separated the army officers from the Judeans, split the account of their arrival in Mizpah into two different chronological stages, and created a new state of affairs in which Gedaliah's oath was only delivered to the army officers. The reason for this is to be found in the role of the officials in the "biography," particularly their attitude toward Jeremiah while he was still inside the besieged city, before the destruction of Jerusalem. The message given in the "biography" is that the principal enemies of Jeremiah turned out to be the ones who accepted his message and began the task of rebuilding the nation after the destruction. To convey this message, the redactor of the "biography" isolated the arrival of the army officers from the arrival of the rest of the people, described Gedaliah's oath as though it had been given only to them. This reconstruction also enabled him to isolate the real opponent of the rebuilding process—Ishmael, the son of Nethaniah— and to place the blame for the opposition on the royal house.

Chapter Three

Changes in the Borders of Judah between the End of the Iron Age and the Persian Period

Demographic and Geopolitical Processes in the Sixth Century B.C.E.

During the period of Babylonian rule in Ḥatti-land, significant demographic and geopolitical processes were affecting Judah. These changes affected the boundaries of Judah and its population for hundreds of years to come. The boundaries of the Babylonian province of Judah shrank (particularly the southern and southwestern border), and a different populace—with an Arabian-Edomite orientation—began to establish itself in the Negev, the southern Judean highland, and the southern Shephelah. This population ultimately brought about the establishment of the province known at the beginning of the Hellenistic period as "Idumea." A certain Judahite population continued to live in these regions, but beginning with the period of Babylonian rule, these regions no longer belonged to the administrative jurisdiction of Judah.

There are very few contemporary historical accounts of the demographic and geopolitical processes that took place in the sixth century B.C.E. To understand these processes, we will examine the demographic and geopolitical picture in the course of time periods that are as long as possible:[1] between the end of the seventh century and the third through second centuries B.C.E. By doing this, we will be able to detect the slow changes that took place and to focus attention on the decisive stages within the process, as well as on its pivot points. It then be-

---

1. On the importance of the *longue durée* in understanding geopolitical processes, see Naʾaman 1991c: 372–73. For bibliography on this subject and a call to balance between the data of the *longue durée* and (the possibility of) rapid, clear-cut changes, see Bunimovitz 1994: 179–81. This method of historical research has been adopted by many scholars who have investigated the boundaries of Judah at the end of the Iron Age and during the Babylonian and Persian Periods. See, for example, Kochman 1980; Ofer 1993: 1.31–39; Naʾaman 1995c: 23. The opposite tack was taken by Alt (1925a: 111), who used the biblical accounts of the Return to Zion to reconstruct the geographic-historical situation at the end of the First Temple Period. Most scholars researching the historical geography of the kingdom of Judah have followed Alt. For a critique of this approach, see Naʾaman 1991a: 49–51.

comes possible to link these changes to central historical events and to evaluate the reciprocal influence between these events and the demographic and geo-political processes.

Methodologically, this research technique is possible because of the conti-nuity that generally existed in regard to the borders of the territories and the sta-bility of their populations and because the changes that characterized them occurred slowly. Indeed, most scholars agree that the transition from Assyrian and Egyptian rule to Babylonian and Persian rule did not witness any significant border changes among the kingdoms and provinces and that most of the admin-istrative structures continued throughout the generations.[2]

> The point of departure for this discussion will be the borders of the kingdom of Judah in its last years (§3.1). The boundaries of Judah during the days of the Sec-ond Temple, from Alexander the Great to the Hasmoneans, will serve as the end-point of the process (§3.2). This discussion will serve as background for an evalu-ation of the biblical and archaeological data from the periods of Babylonian rule (§3.3) and Persian rule (§3.4). The demographic and geopolitical processes in the Babylonian and Persian Periods will be presented as part of a single extended pro-cess, in which the decisive point was the collapse of the kingdom of Judah and the destruction of Jerusalem. The major part of this process took place during the lat-ter sixth century and the first half of the fifth century B.C.E.

3.1. *The Borders of the Kingdom of Judah during the Days of King Josiah*

A discussion of the borders of the kingdom of Judah at the end of the monar-chy relies largely on the information obtained from the town lists of Judah (Josh 15:21–62), Benjamin (18:21–28), Simeon (19:2–8), and Dan (19:40–46). Most scholars have accepted Alt's opinion (1925a: 110–16) concerning the nature[3]

---

2. This was the view of most scholars. On this subject see, for example, the opinions of Foh-rer 1920: 61, 63, 319; Alt 1925a: 108–16; 1934a: 317–21; 1935: 94–97; Avi-Yonah 1949: 17, 20; Noth 1954: 324; Shalit 1960: 102–7; Stern 1982: 238–39; Kochman 1980: 90–91, 101; Na²aman 1994a: 11; 1995c: 22–23, with further literature at n. 51. This is against the view ex-pressed by Hoglund (1992: 16–17) that the Egyptian imperial domination of the Levant was accompanied by a break with the previous Assyrian system of administration and, hence, the Neo-Babylonian and Achaemenid imperial systems in the Levant could not possibly reflect the previous Assyrian patterns.

3. See the seminal article by Alt (1925a: 110–16). For an evaluation of the sources and the history of research on the boundaries of the kingdom of Judah during the time of Josiah, see Na²aman 1991a: 3–33, with further literature. As a point of departure for the discussion of these lists, the usual assumption is that the town lists of Judah and Benjamin were prepared, adapted, and shaped by the author of the book of Joshua. Initially, there was one town list for the entire kingdom of Judah, and the distinction between the towns of the tribe of Judah

and date of the lists,[4] as well as the reality they reflect.[5] Many scholars have regarded the lists as authentic and reliable[6] and have incorporated the information in them into the theory that Josiah was ruling in a political vacuum created by the Assyrian withdrawal from Israel (see Malamat 1983: 228–34). This approach has led to the development of the theory of "the great kingdom of Josiah" and the perception that Josiah took advantage of the political vacuum to expand the borders of his kingdom in all directions.[7]

Na᾿aman, however, has argued against the idea that the kingdom of Judah during Josiah's rule was enlarged and has set forth an opposing theory: that the borders of the kingdom of Judah at the beginning as well as at the end of Josiah's rule reflect a sharp decline in occupation that occurred following Sennacherib's campaign almost a hundred years earlier and, in fact, were more limited than during Hezekiah's time.[8] The claims in the scholarly literature regarding Josiah's eastward expansion[9] as well as the claims regarding his expansion in the Gali-

---

(Josh 15:21–62) and the towns of the tribe of Benjamin (Josh 18:21–28) was made by the author, who attributed it to the tribal administration in Joshua's time (Na᾿aman 1991a: 11–13). On the town list of Simeon, see Na᾿aman (1983: 121–26; 1986a: 62–73), and for the town list of Dan, see Na᾿aman 1991a: 5–7, with further literature.

4. For a discussion of the date of the lists, see Na᾿aman 1991a: 23–33. For a review of the history of the scholarship, see pp. 34–35. For additional bibliography on the various opinions in scholarship regarding the date of the lists, see Garfinkel 1987: 489.

5. The system reflected in the town lists shows a division into five major geographical districts that cover a broad area (the districts of the Negev, Judean hills, the Shephelah, the environs of Jerusalem, and the region of Benjamin). It is possible that in addition to these there was a desert district (Na᾿aman 1991a: 13–16). In contrast to Galil (1984; 1985; 1987), I find it difficult to see these lists as reflecting any evidence of subdivisions that existed within the districts of the kingdom (Na᾿aman 1991a: 13–16). On the other hand, Garfinkel's attempt (1987), based on the epigraphic finds (especially the ostraca) from the end of the First Temple Period, to challenge the basic perception that the town lists give a picture of the districts of the kingdom of Judah, should be dismissed. For a criticism of Garfinkel's opinion, see Eph῾al and Naveh 1988.

6. For a representative statement of this approach, see Galil 1987, with further literature. For a critical appraisal of this view and a summary of the role of the author of the book of Joshua in adapting the lists to the needs of the composition, see Na᾿aman 1991a: 8–13.

7. For a review of the arguments that have been put forward in the research on this subject, see Na᾿aman 1991a: 33–34, 41–51. For additional bibliography on the subject, see Ahlström 1993: 764. The articles listed here demonstrate how deeply rooted this perception is among scholars: Aharoni 1982: 210; Kochman 1980: 99; Bartlett 1989: 147. For a representative exposition of these views in recent scholarship, see Galil 1991: 1–14; Weinfeld 1992: 146; Laato 1992: 76; Suzuki 1992: 32–37; Stern 1993: 192–97; 2001: 134–63.

8. On the circumstances of the Deuteronomist's description of Josiah as someone who was not subject to dictates from outside forces, see Na᾿aman 1991a: 41. The opinion that Josiah's kingdom was quite circumscribed gains credence as the archaeological data is amassed, especially from the Shephelah and the southern part of the Judean hills.

9. Against the opinion of Ginsberg 1956: 347–49; Weinfeld 1992: 164; and others. For additional opinions, see Na᾿aman 1991a: 41–42. On the archaeological evidence from the eastern border of Judah, see Stern 1993; 2001: 134–38; Lipschits 2000.

lee[10] do not hold up under examination (for a collection of arguments against these theories, see Na'aman 1991a: 41–51). There is even less certainty regarding the issue of Josiah's expansion in Samaria.[11] It is reasonable to assume that Josiah had room to maneuver in the central hill country, because Egypt's major interest lay in the coastal area (see §1.4, pp. 25–29), and the population of Samaria had not yet consolidated within any permanent political framework (Na'aman 1991a: 42–43, 57; Ahlström 1993: 764–65). However, even if Josiah's reform had reached the central part of the Samarian mountain region, some major questions remain: Was the reform followed by a change in the kingdom's boundaries? Could Judah have annexed territory from the Assyrian province of Samaria without obtaining permission from the Egyptian imperial ruler?

The description of the reform in 2 Kings 23 is the basis for all of the demographic and historical analysis of Josiah's activity in Samaria.[12] This description, as it was written, indicates that Josiah took action in three geographical regions:[13] the southernmost was Jerusalem and Judah (2 Kgs 23:4–14);[14] north of this area was Bethel (vv. 15–18; cf. v. 4);[15] and still farther north, Samaria

---

10. See Na'aman 1991a: 41–44. For an alternate explanation of accounts of Josiah's "expansion" into the Galilee, see Ahlström 1993: 764–65.

11. It is on the basis of the description of Josiah's death at Megiddo, the short comment in 2 Kgs 23:19, and, particularly, on the basis of the description in 2 Chr 34:6, 7, 33 that Josiah's control of all or at least most of Samaria has been described in the literature. For arguments in support of this perspective, see Mazar 1941: 109–23; Zmirin 1952: 63–64; 88–97; Kallai 1960: 75–79; Malamat 1983: 229–30. The view posited by Nicholson (1963: 380–89; 1967: 1–17) and Moriarty (1965: 399–406)—that Josiah's religious reform, just like Hezekiah's reform, was intended from the outset to unite Israel and Judah and to renew the glorious days of the united kingdom—cannot be supported.

12. On the structure of the literary unit in 2 Kgs 23:4–20, on the textual problems it contains, and on the range of solutions proposed in the scholarly literature, see especially Hollenstein 1977: 321–36; Mayes 1978: 42–43; H.-D. Hoffmann 1980: 218–53; Würthwein 1984: 455; Lohfink 1987. See also the discussion and summary by Long 1991: 273–77.

13. Compare Peres 1946: 1.138 n. 1; and see also Demsky (1991: 101–2), according to whom the word וגם in vv. 9 and 15 highlights the division between the different geographical stages in implementing the reform. See the logical division in the geographical order and the literary structure of vv. 1–14 put forward by Long (1991: 272–75). Cross and Freedman (1953: 56–58) connected these three geographical areas with their "theory of the three phases" of the Josianic reform, and Jepsen (1959: 97–108) proposed another "three phases" theory, but this is not what I am referring to. Against these theories, see Lowery's (1991: 191–93) arguments and the literature he cites. Miller and Hayes (1986: 398–401) defined the three geographical stages differently: Jerusalem, Judah, and beyond the limits of Judah (Bethel?). It is difficult to accept this interpretation, which is based largely on the ideas of Alt (1951: 193–210), regarding the distinction between Jerusalem and its environs and the rest of the limits of Judah, because it requires that Miller and Hayes create an artificial break within the unit in Josh 23:4–14 and posit that the author/editor combined these two chronological/geographical stages.

14. On the literary features of this unit, the textual problems it contains, and the various opinions among scholars regarding it, see Knoppers 1993: 2.175–96.

15. The prevailing view among scholars should be accepted: vv. 16–18 are either a later expansion or a source based on the account in 1 Kings 13. For extensive literature on this subject, see Knoppers 1993: 2.198–99.

(vv. 19–20).[16] However we explain this episode, if we accept the premise that vv. 16–20 (or at least 19–20) are later additions, and if we accept the premise that they are part of the sequence revised by the Deuteronomist,[17] the text reveals clear distinctions among these three geographical areas—they differ in terms of ritual activity; there is evidence of geopolitical differences among the different areas; and the conceptual approaches toward these areas vary.

Geba unquestionably lies within the limits of the first unit—within the borders of Judah before the possible expansion toward Bethel, which took place in Josiah's time. It is clear, therefore, why the author defines the limits of the reform in Judah by using the expression "from Geba to Beer-Sheba," because these dimensions highlight the difference between the boundaries of Judah and the area beyond it, which includes Bethel.[18] Thus, even if there was reform activity in Samaria in Josiah's times, it was of a religious nature and did not result in any changes in the borders of the kingdom. It is doubtful that it was possible to make any substantial change in the boundaries that had been established during Assyrian rule, because the Egyptian Empire, as well as the Babylonian and Persian Empires that followed, surely would not have recognized any such changes.[19] Consequently, the most reasonable assumption is that during Josiah's rule the northern border of Judah was pushed northward from the Geba–Mizpah line and, at most, reached the Bethel–Ophrah line.[20]

---

16. Many scholars have seen vv. 19–20 as part of the later expansion of vv. 16–18; see Na'aman 1991a: 42–43; Knoppers 1993: 2.199, with further literature in n. 57.

17. See Knoppers 1993: 2.200–202. On the problems involved in the interpretation of 2 Chr 34:5–32, see Noth 1943: 178; Williamson 1977: 119–31; Japhet 1977: 282–84, 254–55; Malamat 1983: 230; Na'aman 1991a: 43–44.

18. Galil (1992: 4) has cogently summarized the definition of these boundaries: "there is no doubt that according to the author of the book of Kings the territorial model 'from Geba to Beer-Sheba' did not include the city of Bethel, certainly not the regions north of Bethel." However, his subsequent statement is somewhat unclear: "his [the author-editor's] viewpoint cannot show the exact location of Geba', for the model 'from Geba to Beer-Sheba' was not written by him but rather copied from his sources." Furthermore, the logic of Galil's argument is unclear; he says: (1) the accepted scholarly viewpoint is supportive when it states that Josiah annexed Bethel to Judah; (2) because of this annexation, we cannot identify this Geba as Geba of Benjamin; (3) instead, this Geba should be sought in the Ephraim hills, north of Bethel. Galil himself is aware (p. 5 n. 15) that the expression "from Geba to Beer-Sheba" refers to two imperial centers that controlled the border region. So, if this be the case, there is no need to seek Geba far from the northern border of Judah. Against Galil's identification of Geba, see Lipschits 2004a.

19. Kallai (1960: 76) wrote: "in terms of the consequences, this taking control was of a temporary nature, and was possible only during a period of political turbulence caused by the decline of Assyria. This domination lasted until the rise of the new power which determined governing arrangements in this part of the kingdom." See also Miller and Hayes 1986: 401; Ahlström 1993: 763–65.

20. See Aharoni 1962b: 309; Na'aman 1987: 11–12; 1991a: 25; Ahlström 1993: 765. Demsky's proposal (1991: 101–2)—that this Geba should be identified as Gibeon—should be rejected, primarily because of the unique religious status of Gibeon at the end of the First Temple Period. Confusion of Geba with Gibeon does not occur anywhere else in the Bible and does not appear in any of the versions, especially because the emphasis in the reference to Geba is on its location, and in this respect, Gibeon is too close to Jerusalem.

Just as the precise line of the northern border is difficult to identify, so also is the western border of the kingdom of Judah during the days of Josiah (see Lipschits 1997b: 11–17). The claim that Josiah conquered and annexed the kingdom of Ekron and the entire northern Shephelah as far as Jaffa relies on several fundamental conclusions established by Alt (1925a: 109–11). Scholars have generally not accepted Alt's claim that the town list of Dan (Josh 19:41–46) is part of the original town list document (see Na'aman 1991a: 44 and n. 146). However, Alt's suggestion that the reference to Lod, Hadid, and Ono in the lists of the returnees to Zion (Ezra 2:33; Neh 7:37) is evidence that the exiles from this region were included within the borders of the kingdom of Judah before the destruction (Alt 1925a: 110–11) has been accepted by many and has been used to support the idea that Josiah expanded his rule into the Shephelah. The interpretation of the excavations at Meṣad Ḥashavyahu and the ostraca found there—namely, that they demonstrate Judah's control over the northern Shephelah—has resulted in an almost complete scholarly consensus: most scholars have included this region within the kingdom's borders.[21] However, this view no longer holds up under close inspection; it now seems that the border of the kingdom of Judah did not extend beyond the Tel Erani–Beth-Shemesh–Beth-Horon line.[22] Throughout Josiah's rule, Egypt maintained sovereignty over the entire area. It is not reasonable that the Egyptians would have allowed Judah to control an area that had strategic importance to them as an essential route to Syria (see Na'aman 1991a: 44–49). Thus, it is preferable to see Meṣad Ḥashavyahu as an Egyptian fortress manned by mercenaries of Greek, Judean, and Phoenician origin (this conclusion emerges clearly from the discussion by Fantalkin 2000; 2001). The presence of Judeans in the northern Shephelah, as found in the list of returnees (Ezra 2; Nehemiah 7), should not necessarily be connected with the border of Judah before the destruction of Jerusalem. Instead, their presence in this area can be explained by the circumstances in the border area between Judah and the kingdom of Ekron in the seventh century B.C.E. (see

---

21. Literature on the theory that Meṣad Ḥashavyahu was built by Josiah when he took control of the northern Shephelah and the coastal area south of Jaffa may be found in Na'aman 1991a: 44–45; see pp. 44–51 for a rebuttal of this interpretation of the Meṣad Ḥashavyahu evidence. For the characteristics of the site as a fort manned by Greek mercenaries who were active in the service of the Egyptians, see Fantalkin 2000: 66–70; 2001: 74–75; for the historical background of Egyptian rule in the land of Israel, see above, chap. 1.4, esp. pp. 25–29. For an example of the arguments of those who include the northern Shephelah in the kingdom of Judah, see Aharoni 1962b: 242, 309; Tadmor 1966: 102; Spieckerman 1982: 145; Malamat 1983: 230–31, 240–41; Stern 2001: 140–43.

22. The town-lists in the book of Joshua offer corroboration for this; see Na'aman 1991a: 49, with further literature. On this subject, see also Na'aman 1987: 12–14; 1995c: 18, 23. Both the survey of the Shephelah and excavations carried out in the region reveal the intensity of the devastation caused by Sennacherib's campaign and the extent to which the kingdom of Judah's hold on the region was weakened. This provides the backdrop for the flourishing of the kingdom of Ekron, which had formerly been a small, feeble city-kingdom. On this, see Na'aman 1991a: 49; Dothan and Gitin 1994; Gitin 1997; A. Mazar 1994.

Naʾaman 1991a: 49–51; 1995c: 22, 24, and literature in nn. 40, 43, and 53), as well as the economic prosperity in the coastal region and the settlement activity in the Benjamin region during the Persian Period (see Lipschits 1997b; see also the discussion below).

The Beer-Sheba–Arad Valleys were inside the southern boundary of Judah. However, the boundary did not reach any farther south, and it appears that it did not include the fortresses at Kadesh Barnea and Ein-Hazeva,[23] which apparently were Assyrian strongholds.[24]

There are no unequivocal archaeological or historical data to indicate when the Negev was cut off from the kingdom of Judah (on the archaeological data, see below, §4.3.2c, pp. 224–230). Alt's conclusion that Judah lost the Negev in 598/7 B.C.E. still stands.[25] However, as the discussion that follows shows, it is preferable to see the severing of the southern Hebron hills and the Negev from Judah as a gradual process following the collapse of the kingdom of Judah, after the destruction of the capital.[26] It is difficult—perhaps impossible—to deter-

---

23. This is in contrast to the views of Meshel 1977: 43–50; and Cohen 1983a: 2–14; see Bartlett 1989: 140–43; Naʾaman 1991a: 48–49; 1995c: 22 n. 45; Carter 1991: 62–64; Ussishkin 1994: 5; Finkelstein 1995: 149; Kletter 1995: 318–19.

24. This is in contrast to the views of Cohen 1983b: 16–17; Cohen and Yisrael 1996: 82–83; Stern 2001: 156–58; *NEAEHL* 1335; and Naʾaman 1987: 14–15; 1991a: 47–51; 1997: 60. On the stratigraphy of the site, see Ussishkin 1993.

25. On the basis of Jer 13:18–19, Alt (1925a: 108, 113) concluded that, during the exile of Jehoiachin, the Negev and other areas as far as the north side of Hebron were cut off from Judah. This view has been accepted by other researchers, including Noth 1954: 283; Welten 1969: 166; Meyers 1971: 377–92; Lemaire 1977a: 193–96; Kochman 1980: 95, 101, and n. 16. Lemaire's conclusion seems doubtful, especially when the ostraca from Arad are taken into consideration; see the critique by Malamat 1983: 145, and 250 n. 24. Furthermore, Aharoni's attempt (1976: 160–61; 1978: 312; 1982: 210) to place the destruction of Stratum VI at Arad earlier, to 595/4 B.C.E., on the basis of the word בשלש on a jar found in the Arad excavations (inscription no. 20; Aharoni 1976: 42–43) and to attribute the Judean revolt in 589 B.C.E. to this Babylonian activity should be rejected. For a criticism of this reconstruction, based on the length of the campaign, see Kallai 1960: 73–74; Malamat 1982: 251 n. 38; 1983: 284–85 n. 94; Bartlett 1989: 149; Herzog 1997: 174–79. It is also difficult to accept the conclusions of Beit-Arieh and Beck 1987: 24–25; and Ofer 1993: A, 15; I, 35. Kochman's view (1980: 158–78) of Edomite incursion into the region should similarly be dismissed. For more on this subject, see also the discussion following.

26. The idea of the "collapse of ancient states and civilizations" is based theoretically and historically on the book by Yoffee and Cowgill (1988) and the study by Tainter (1988). For a description of the process of collapse, see Tainter 1988: 4; for the theoretical grounding of the idea, see the article by Yoffee (Yoffee and Cowgill [eds.] 1988: 1–19). Cowgill in his article (pp. 244–76) makes an attempt to link the theoretical models to historical contexts. For the sociological basis, see the articles by Kaufman (pp. 219–35) and Eisenstadt (pp. 236–43) in the same collection. Worthy of special attention for our purposes is Bronson's article (pp. 196–218); his model is particularly applicable to the role of pastoral nomads in the collapse of political systems. For the characteristics of societies organized into ancient states, before and following collapses, see Renfrew 1979: 481–85.

mine whether this process began as early as 597 B.C.E., at the time of the Babylonian campaign against Jehoiakim and the exile of Jehoiachin, but apparently the process was not short or swift and it continued long after the end of the kingdom of Judah.

The main dispute in scholarly circles relates to the presence of Edomites in the area of the Beer-Sheba–Arad Valleys at the end of the seventh and beginning of the sixth centuries B.C.E. and the role of the Edomites in the destruction of the kingdom of Judah. In the seventh century B.C.E., the western border of Edom ran through the Arabah (Glueck 1936: 153–54; Bienkowski and van der Steen 2001: 22).[27] During the Hellenistic Period, the border of the province of Idumea reached Hebron and included the central and southern part of the Shephelah.[28] The spread of Arabian and Edomite elements into the expanse between the Arabah and the Beer-Sheba–Arad Valleys had already taken place in the seventh century B.C.E. However, in the process of Edomite expansion into the territory of Judah, the destruction of Judah's border fortresses in the Beer-Sheba–Arad Valleys was of decisive importance. This was, historically, the point at which all of these groups were able easily to penetrate the empty areas of the destroyed kingdom.[29] The Edomites' role in the destruction and the question of their presence in the area earlier are central to understanding the dynamics of this process.[30]

In recent years, archaeological evidence that attests to the presence of an Edomite population on the southern border of the kingdom of Judah has accumulated.[31] This evidence indicates that south of the small settlements and the border forts maintained by the kingdom of Judah in the valleys of Beer-Sheba

27. The geographical situation, the biblical references (Gen 36:41; Num 34:3–4; Josh 13:2; 15:1, 21; Judg 11:16–18; 1 Kgs 9:26; etc.), and the archaeological evidence all indicate that the *Arabah* was considered part of Edom. The area west of the *Arabah*, toward the Beer-Sheba–Arad Valleys was the natural area for expansion by the Edomites and was even referred to as "the mountain of Seʿir." See Hoffman 1966: 6, and n. 6; Oded 1982b: 175; Ronen 1985: 5 and 15 n. 1; Bartlett 1989: 33–37; Horowitz 1993; Edelman 1995; Beit-Arieh 1996: 30–31; Lindsay 1999: 69–70; however, see the comments by Meshel 1995: 173. The fortress at Ein-Hazeva should be seen in this light (in contrast to the views of Cohen 1995b; Cohen and Yisrael 1996); see the comments by Naʾaman 1997: 60.

28. See the concise summary in Edelman 1995: 1–11, especially pp. 9–11; see Bartlett 1999 on the connection between the late Iron Age II Edomites and the Persian-Hellenistic territory of Idumea.

29. For a summary of the discussion regarding the information in Jer 52:30 and in Josephus, concerning the significance of the year 582 B.C.E., see Beit-Arieh 1995a: 312–15; Hoffman 1972: 86–87; Ronen 1985: 11.

30. For a summary of the research on Edom and the Edomite presence in southern Judah in the Babylonian and Persian Periods, see Ronen 1985: 5–14. For a critique of the thesis put forward by Kochman (1980), see Ronen 1985: 25–31; Kasher 1988a: 12, 67–68.

31. The historical focus of this incursion was in the last third of the seventh century B.C.E., when the Assyrians began to withdraw from the region (Beit-Arieh 1995a: 311; 1996: 28–36). For additional literature on the subject, see Beit-Arieh 1995a: 310–14; 1995b: 33–38.

and Arad[32] lay a large area inhabited by seminomadic groups.[33] Especially prominent among these groups were people whose material culture was similar to the material culture of the kingdom of Edom.[34]

The existence of a temple at Qitmit and the presence of Edomite pottery in Negev sites cannot be taken as evidence of the beginning of a process of an Edomite takeover of southern Judah, even before the fall of Jerusalem (Beit-Arieh 1995a: 314–15; 1996: 34–36; see also Meshel 1995: 172–74; Herzog 1997: 242–44). In my opinion, the archaeological materials from the region may be seen as evidence that nomads and sedentary inhabitants coexisted, at least until the early sixth century B.C.E. and, to some extent, even afterward. This conclusion is based on two major pieces of data:

1. The quantities of "Edomite pottery" in the last strata of the Judean settlements (prior to the destruction) attest to an increasing Edomite presence in this region.[35] It appears that the Edomites and the settlements on the southern border of the kingdom of Judah maintained two-pronged trade relationships: goods were sent from the Arabian Desert or Transjordan to the ports in the southern coastal plain, and there was an economic symbiosis between the grain-growers and the herdsmen.[36]

2. Some of the "Edomite pottery" found in the southern Negev sites shows marked influence from the Judean ceramic tradition. This influence is also noticeable when the shapes and decoration of some of the prototypes in-

---

32. The forts were apparently founded in the late seventh century B.C.E., paralleling the decline in Assyrian dominance (Naʾaman 1991a: 48–49; Beit-Arieh 1995a: 310–15).

33. A sizable share of this population probably did not live in permanent settlements, at least not in the early stages when they were initially settling in the region (at the end of the seventh and beginning of the sixth centuries B.C.E.). For example, see the questions raised by Beit-Arieh (1995a: 310) regarding the population to which the temple at Qitmit belonged. See also Finkelstein 1992: 162.

34. See Bartlett 1972: 26–37; 1982a: 15; 1989: 143; Oded 1982b: 175; Ronen 1985: 9–14; Kasher 1988a: 9–13; Finkelstein 1995: 139–53; Herzog 1997: 242–44; Bienkowski and van der Steen 2001: 26. On the presence of Arabian tribes on the southern border of Judah, see Finkelstein 1992; Beit-Arieh 1995a: 314.

35. On the problems of classifying the pottery as ethnically "Edomite," see Bienkowski 1995: 51; Bienkowski and van der Steen 2001: 26–28. In the southern sites, relatively small quantities of Edomite potsherds have been found, mostly in the various destruction strata. The smallest quantity was found north of Nahal Beer-Sheba (Tel Sheva, Tel Haror, Tell ʿIra, Tel Masos), and a slightly larger quantity was found at ʿAroer (Biran and Cohen 1976: 139, and table 28; Biran 1982: 162 and table 23); Tel Malḥata (about 25% of the total sherds found in the destruction stratum); Ḥorvat Radum, ʿUza, and, of course, Qitmit. For the bibliography on this subject, see previous notes and also E. Mazar 1985: 264; Bartlett 1989: 142–43; Cohen 1995a: 119; Beit-Arieh 1996: 34–36.

36. See Elat 1977: 98–123, 236; 1990: 67–88; Ephʿal 1982a: 75–80; Rainey 1987: 20; Finkelstein 1992: 162; Beit-Arieh 1995a: 314; Cohen 1995a: 119. In this context, see the reservations expressed by Finkelstein (1992: 161–63) and Beit-Arieh (1995a: 314) regarding the course of the chief trade route in the late Iron Age.

cluded in the "Negev-Edomite" pottery assemblage are compared with those that are characteristic of the classic "Edomite" pottery assemblage (Bienkowski and van der Steen 2001: 26–28). Even at the Edomite temple at Qitmit, there is a combination of everyday vessels that were common in sites in Judah at the end of the seventh and beginning of the sixth centuries B.C.E. as well as Edomite vessels that are characteristic of sites in eastern Transjordan.[37]

Two ostraca found at Arad (no. 24, line 20; no. 40, lines 10, 15)[38] and the Edomite ostracon found in the destruction stratum at Ḥorvat ʿUza deserve attention (see Beit-Arieh and Cresson 1985: 96–101; Beit-Arieh 1986a: 38–39; 1995a: 311; 1995b: 36–37; Misgav 1990: 215–17). These objects are generally interpreted as evidence of an Edomite military threat to Judah even before the destruction and of clear military pressure on the eve of the destruction.[39] However, this conclusion relies principally on the background of Jeremiah's words (Jer 13:19) and the expressions of hatred toward the kingdoms of Transjordan, particularly Edom, in the prophetic books (especially in Obadiah) and in portions of the Psalms and Lamentations.[40] Nonetheless, I have grave doubts that we can connect the nomads living on the border of the kingdom of Judah with the references to Edom in the ostraca and the biblical prophecies. These expressions of hostility toward Edom find no support in the actual descriptions of the destruction in 2 Kings and Jeremiah or in the prophecy of Ezekiel (25:12–14) close to the time of the destruction (Hoffman 1966: 58–61; 1972: 76–89; 1973: 105–53; Bartlett 1982a; 1989: 151, 157; 1995: 13–21; Glazier-McDonald 1995: 23–32). In contrast to the accusation in Obad 1:14 ("You should not have stood at the crossway to cut off those of his who escaped, nor should you have handed over his survivors on the day of distress"), Jer 40:11 describes the return of refugees who found asylum in Edom (Hoffman 1966: 108; 1972: 83–89; Bartlett

---

37. See Beit-Arieh 1995a: 304–5. In my opinion, the founding of the Edomite temple at Qitmit can be dated to the period between the two Babylonian campaigns against Jerusalem (597–588 B.C.E.). During this interval, the kingdom of Judah did not have the power to prevent the establishment of the temple only a few kilometers from its southern border while maintaining a normal relationship with the neighboring population before the beginning of the "great struggle."

38. On the ostraca, see Aharoni 1976: 48–51, 72–76; Lemaire 1977a: 188–93, 207–8. For a discussion of the information obtained from the ostraca regarding Edom's involvement in the destruction, see the previous notes, as well as Aharoni 1976: 160–61; Beit-Arieh 1995a: 311, with further literature.

39. See, e.g., Noth 1954: 283–84; Meyers 1971: 380–87; Lindsay 1976: 25; 1999: 61–70; Malamat 1983: 284–85; Naʾaman 1986a: 13; 1987: 15; Rainey 1987: 25; Beit-Arieh 1995a: 311; 1996: 35–36; Ahlström 1993: 787–88, 795. For a different viewpoint, see Bartlett 1982a: 23; 1989: 151–61; Finkelstein 1992: 156–70; Ben-Zvi 1996: 236 n. 22.

40. On the historical estimates, see, e.g., Lindsay 1976: 29–30; Oded 1982b: 189; Beit-Arieh and Beck 1987: 24–25. For a more cautious viewpoint, see Hoffman 1966: 20; 1972: 88; Meyers 1971: 386; Bartlett 1982a: 23; Ronen 1985: 11–13.

1982a; 1989: 154–55; 1995: 20; Edelman 1995: 6–7; Glazier-McDonald 1995;
Ben-Zvi 1996: 236, and see pp. 145–46).

The archaeological and textual evidence for the destruction of southern Judah attests to a long and complex process that is not directly connected to the
kingdom of Edom. Groups of nomads had begun to settle in the area even before
the destruction, and this process was completed somewhat after the destruction.
We may hypothesize that the fortresses built on Judah's southern border were
designed to bring stability to the border and to impose the kingdom's control
over the nomadic groups who lived near the border (see Beit-Arieh 1996: 34–
36). In contrast to the view of Beit-Arieh, these nomadic groups probably were
not part of the kingdom of Edom but, rather, a border population that lived between Edom and Judah (see Herzog 1997: 242–44). An economic symbiosis
gradually emerged between the nomadic elements and the royal fortresses and
settlements in the valleys of Beer-Sheba and Arad. Nonetheless, the predatory
nature of these groups was surely a major factor in the tension that periodically
developed between the two groups. As long as the fortresses remained and the
kingdom was able to impose its authority over the nomads, the situation remained stable. As the kingdom progressively weakened, especially at the beginning of the sixth century B.C.E., after the Babylonian campaign of 598/7 B.C.E.,
its ability to withstand pressure from the south steadily declined. Only a hint of
this can be found in the words of Jeremiah (13:19), but the farfetched interpretation attached to this text cannot be supported: it refers to increasing danger
but cannot be used as evidence that the Edomites had seized the eastern Negev.
The next phase in the growth of Edomite influence took place only after the
Babylonian siege and conquest of Jerusalem.

During the Babylonian siege, the kingdom of Judah was not able to maintain
the garrisons in the fortresses, so the connection between the kingdom and the
fortresses was broken, and the central authority disappeared. There was now no
longer any *raison d'être* for the system of fortresses along the southern border.
Consequently, the system of settlements collapsed as well, and the door was
opened for the seminomadic groups to become a destructive force. When the
border was breached, they began to infiltrate the periphery of the kingdom, destroying some of the settlements that stood in their way and expelling some of
the populace that resisted them: the nomads advanced from the Negev to the
Judean hills and the Shephelah. Because there is no archaeological or historical
evidence to the contrary, it seems clear that not all of the destruction in the area
was the result of a Babylonian military campaign.[41] Some of the destruction may
have resulted from local struggles between the inhabitants of the kingdom of

---

41. The Babylonians concentrated their efforts on Jerusalem and also destroyed the forts on
Judah's western border, but it is doubtful that they had an interest in waging military campaigns
deep into the southern and eastern frontier of the kingdom of Judah. It is possible that some of
the destruction was caused by auxiliary forces drawn from armies from the regions' kingdoms,
but there is no historical information to confirm this.

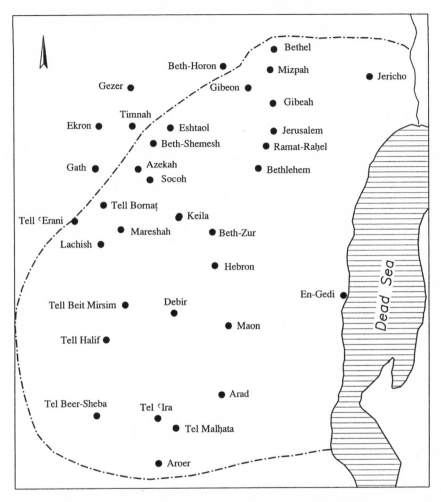

Map 5. The borders of Judah during the reign of King Josiah (after Na'aman 1991a).

Judah and the nomadic groups coming from the south. This population first penetrated the relatively empty areas of the Negev and later the southern hills of Hebron and the south and central Shephelah, which had remained devoid of inhabitants since the Assyrian campaign of Sennacherib (701 B.C.E.). This process of infiltration and migration was prolonged, beginning after the destruction of Jerusalem and continuing throughout the period of Babylonian rule in the sixth century B.C.E.[42] Support for this reconstruction may be found in the reference

---

42. For a review of the opinions of scholars on the reason for this migration, see Bartlett 1989: 143.

to Geshem, the Arabian, as a neighbor of Judah in the Persian Period and the first reference to Idumea as a well-defined geographical and administrative unit in 312 B.C.E.[43] Aramaic ostraca dating to the Persian Period and found in Beer-Sheba (see Naveh 1973; 1979; Lemaire 1996; 2002; forthcoming, with additional literature), Arad (Naveh 1976: 212–13), and additional sites within Idumea (Eph'al and Naveh 1996) contain a few Judean names, evidence that a small Judean population remained in the area.

Because the settlements in the southern Judean hills and in the Shephelah were weakened as a result of the heavy damage caused by the campaign of Sennacherib, incursions by pastoral groups were easier. Even before the collapse of the kingdom of Judah, a clear buffer existed between this region and the region north of Hebron, where the settlement had reverted to its former size by the mid-seventh century B.C.E. (Ofer 1993: 4.51–61; 1998: 52; see the discussion below, §§4.3.2b–c, pp. 218–230). In these relatively uninhabited regions, there was an abundance of space for the infiltration of a new population; there was very little resistance from the local population, which was disorganized and unprotected after the destruction of the kingdom and the collapse of the system of border forts in the Beer-Sheba and Arad Valleys.

In summary, the borders of the kingdom of Judah in its last years expanded slightly northward, reaching the Bethel–Ophrah line. In the west, the border passed through the Eshtaol–Azekah–Lachish line; in the east, it ran through the Jordan–Dead Sea line; and in the south, it ran along the line of Judean forts in the Beer-Sheba and Arad Valleys. The major change took place during the last years of the kingdom, especially during the Babylonian siege. The collapse of all systems left the southern and southwestern border areas of the kingdom vulnerable to the migration and infiltration of nomads who had previously resided south of the border. These people gradually moved northward, settling throughout the entire region, and consolidated into a unit known from the Hellenistic Period onward as Idumea.

3.2. *The Boundaries of Judah during the Hellenistic Period*

The few written sources make it difficult to study the borders of Judah during the Hellenistic Period. This problem leads to two related difficulties: (1) the need to bridge the gap in time for which there are almost no sources and (2) the difficulty in distinguishing between the borders of Judah and the extent of settlement by the Judeans. These problems are particularly striking for the period of Alexander the Great and the Ptolemaic Period.[44] For this reason, most

---

43. Antigonus Monophthalmos attests to this; see the discussion following.

44. For a review of these accounts and bibliography, see Kasher 1988b: 16–30. Note that the first significant accounts come from the middle of the third century B.C.E. and are found in papyri from the archive of Zenon. On the geographical and historical information in this archive, see Klein 1939: 39; also see below. There is agreement among scholars that Judah's borders did

researchers rely on information from the Seleucid Period and the writings of Josephus, projecting the information back onto the Ptolemaic era.

The main historical information that we have from the Hellenistic and Roman Periods relates to the courses of the southern and western boundaries of Judah (Lipschits 1997b: 10–11). The book of Maccabees indicates that *Judah's southern boundary* ran through the Beth-zur line;[45] Hebron was a foreign city,[46] and the Negev was ruled by the Edomites. The first account of *Judah's southwestern boundary* is from the middle of the third century B.C.E.[47] In papyri found in the archive of Zenon, Mareshah is mentioned as a city belonging to Idumea,[48] and in another papyrus Adoraim is mentioned as one of the centers of Idumea (Avi-Yonah 1949: 28). Other information appears in the sources that describe the wars of the Hasmoneans. These sources suggest that Adullam was part of the southwestern Judah, and in contrast, Adoraim, and Mareshah were foreign cities[49] that also controlled their rural surroundings.[50]

In the west, Gezer was included in the province of Ashdod,[51] until it was con-

---

not change under the rule of the Ptolemaic kings (Avi-Yonah 1949: 26; Shalit 1960: 106). On the possibility of temporary border changes in Judah during this period, see the discussion below.

45. See 1 Macc 4:29, 60; 6:7, 26, 31; 11:65; 14:33; 2 Macc 11:5. On this subject, see M. Stern 1972: 55; Kasher 1988b: 101, and n. 155. On the course of the southern boundary, see also Galil's (1992) arguments for the identification of Timnata and Pirʿaton on the list of Bacchides' fortifications.

46. See 1 Macc 5:65. On the possibility that there were Jews in the Hebron region at this time, see Klein 1939: 22, 66. For a description of Judas Maccabeus's campaign, see Kasher 1988b: 83. On the name קוסידע on the ostracon from Khirbet el-Qôm, see Geraty 1975.

47. This statement is correct, with two qualifications: (a) that we remove from the discussion the legendary segments (some quite late) that contain very little geographical and historical information; on this, e.g., see the discussion by Klein 1939: 35–47; and (b) that we disregard the problematic interpretation some scholars have given to the coins inscribed יחזקיה הפחה, particularly to the coin found at Beth-zur (Sellers 1933: 73). Most scholars identified the name יחזקיה with the high priest from the early Ptolemaic Period who is mentioned by Josephus (*Ag. Ap.* 1.22.187, etc.) and on this basis have posited that the high priests were also in charge of the taxation system. For a concise survey of the history of research in this field and references to parallels and bibliography, see Kochman 1980: 8–9, 140; Stern 1982: 225–26. For a critique, see Avigad 1976a: 220; Meyers 1985: 37.

48. On references to Idumea in historical documents from the Hellenistic Period, see Ronen 1985: 54–56 nn. 5–7a; Kochman 1980: 158.

49. Adullam: see 2 Macc 12:38. Adoraim: see 1 Macc 13:20; Josephus, *Ant.* 13.5.6. Mareshah: 1 Macc 5:66; 2 Macc 12:35; Josephus, *Ant.* 12.8.6. For a summary of the available information on Adoraim and Mareshah, see Ronen 1985: 46–47, 56–59, and nn. 10–23. On the conquest of Mareshah and Adoraim by John Maccabeus, see Josephus, *Ant.* 13.9.1; Josephus, *J.W.* 1.3.6 (= 62–63). For the background of this era in the book of *Jubilees* and in rabbinic literature, see Klein 1939: 75–77.

50. See Josephus, *Ant.* 13.9.1 (= 257); 14.5.3 (= 88); Josephus, *J.W.* 1.3.6 (= 63); and see Kasher 1988a: 49–77, with further literature.

51. See 1 Macc 14:34, and compare 4:15; 7:45; 15:28–29, 35. Roll (1996: 511) thought that Gezer of the Bacchides fortifications (1 Macc 9:52) should be identified with Tell Ghaza (Tell Yaʿoz) on the banks of W. Soreq, where impressive remains of the Hellenistic Period have been found. In his opinion, the same city is mentioned in 1 Macc 14:34.

quered by Simon.[52] The accounts of the surrender of the province of Ekron to
Jonathan the Hasmonean in 147 b.c.e. help to define the western boundary of
Judah,[53] especially because this area was apparently not included in the province of Ashdod (1 Macc 14:34). In light of this account, we can conclude that
there was a Judean presence in the Ekron region even before the annexation,
and it was transferred to Judah out of ethnic considerations.[54] It appears that
Lod (Lydda) and its immediate hinterland was also outside the borders of Judah,[55] as were the provinces of Ramathaim and Ephraim, northwest and north
of Lod.[56] Judean presence in these districts must have forced their inhabitants
to join the Hasmoneans (Avi-Yonah 1949: 38; Klein 1939: 38–39; M. Stern
1981: 97, 110; Na'aman 1995c: 23), and the official transference of these districts to Judah came only post factum.[57] Until the transfer of these districts, the
border of Judah ran through Beth-Horon,[58] and despite the fact that there was a
noticeable Judean presence in the area of Lod and Modi'in, this region had not
been previously included within Judah's boundaries.[59] The information available on Ḥadid reveals a similar picture: apart from its being mentioned in the

---

52. See 1 Macc 13:43–44, 53; 14:34; 16:1, 19–22. Support for this hypothesis may be found
in Josephus, *Ant.* 13.9.2 on the refusal of the Roman Senate to recognize Judah's rights over
Gezer, as well as over Jaffa. For an opposing view, see the discussion in Kallai 1960: 97–99. See
also the account in *Ant.* 14.10.5, and see M. Stern 1972: 120–99; Kasher 1988b: 104–5, 113–
14, and n. 4; Schwartz 1991: 51.

53. See 1 Macc 10:89; Josephus, *Ant.* 13.4.4.

54. On the possibility of a Judean presence in the Ekron area during this period, see Kasher
1988b: 92, with further literature.

55. Accounts of the Lydda (Lod) district are scant and later than the beginning of the
Hasmonean revolt (Schwartz 1991: 49). This has stirred many disputes regarding its status at
the end of the First Temple Period and during the Persian and Hellenistic Periods until it officially became part of Judah (see below). In any event, we may include the entire area between
Ḥadid and Modi'in and the western section of the "historical" region of Benjamin in this district (in the Beth-Horon area). See M. Stern 1972: 53–54, 109–10; 1981: 97. There is no evidence of the district's being divided into two distinct areas; it appears that Schwartz (1991:
49–50) is simply repeating earlier attempts to project the demographic character of the region
onto its political status and national affiliation, using the sources (p. 50) that he, himself, admits come from a later time (p. 49). Despite the fine distinctions regarding the nature of the
grant, the intentions behind it, and its date, the conclusions Schwartz draws regarding the par-
tition of the Lydda district oblige him to make other assumptions that are geopolitically problematic (pp. 50–51).

56. Against Kallai 1960: 99–105; see below. For a comprehensive discussion and survey of
the literature on this subject, see M. Stern 1972: 106–10; Schwartz 1991: 49–60 and 56–57
nn. 9–12.

57. See 1 Macc 10:30; 11:28; 34:57; Josephus, *Ant.* 13.5.4. See Schwartz 1991: 57–58, with
further literature in n. 16.

58. See 1 Macc 3:16ff. See Kallai 1960: 96. Scholars who try to prove that the Lydda region
belonged to Judah typically only discuss the sources from the Persian Period (the double list of
the returnees in Ezra 2 and Nehemiah 7, Sanballat's invitation in Neh 6:2, etc.); see, e.g., Kallai 1960: 101–2. This view is also related to the idea that the Hasmonean strengthening of the
Modi'in region occurred within the boundaries of Judah (M. Stern 1973: 109 and n. 44).

59. On Judahite presence in the Lydda–Gezer region, see Na'aman 1995c: 23–24.

list of the returnees to Zion (Ezra 2, Nehemiah 7) and our knowledge of its fortification, we have no information about its conquest by the Hasmoneans.[60]
The conclusion from these data is that there was a large Judean population in
the northern Shephelah during the Hellenistic Period. However, before the
time of the Hasmoneans, this area was not part of Judah, except for temporary
border changes that took place from the time of Alexander the Great through
the end of the Ptolemaic Period.[61] It was only during Hasmonean rule and as a
result of Hasmonean activity that the province of Judah expanded to include
the districts of Ekron, Lod, Ramathaim, and Ephraim.

For our purposes, the important information is the geopolitical situation in
the Babylonian and Persian Periods. The major differences between the borders
of the kingdom of Judah in its last years and its borders in the Hellenistic Period
were in the southern and southwestern sections. In this region, the Negev, the
Hebron Mountains, and the southern and central Shephelah were separated
from the province of Judah. These areas became the center of another national-
territorial unit: Idumea. This change was the result of a long process that may
have begun in the early sixth century b.c.e.; however, the destruction of Jerusalem undoubtedly marked the point in time when the process accelerated. The
invasion of Arabian and Edomite groups through the Beer-Sheba and Arad Valleys toward the Hebron Mountains and the southern Shephelah took place
throughout the time of Babylonian rule. As will be demonstrated later, this invasion ended during the Persian Period, when Persian fortresses were built at
key junctions, and the boundaries of the Yehud province were fixed. These
boundaries, to the best of our knowledge, are identical to those that existed during the Hellenistic Period.

3.3. *Demographic and Geopolitical Processes under Babylonian Rule*

3.3.1. *The Time and Distribution of* mwṣh *Seal Impressions*

There are 42 *mwṣh* seal impressions known at the present time, either with the
full spelling with four letters (*mwṣh*) or with the vowel-letter omitted (*mṣh*).
Thirty seal impressions (more than 70% of the total number of seal impressions)
were found in Mizpah,[62] which was the administrative seat of Gedaliah and the

---

60. 1 Macc 12:38; 13:13. See also Josephus, *Ant.* 13.5.10; 6.5. For a discussion, see Kasher
1988b: 98–99 and n. 149; Schwartz 1991: 51, 58, and n. 29.

61. Several scholars have argued that temporary border changes took place between the
time of Alexander the Great and the end of the Ptolemaic Period; see in particular Kasher
1975: 204–8; 1993: 31–35; Mor 1980: 76–81. For a different perspective, see M. Stern 1981:
97. I accept Goldstein's argument (1976: 410–11) that Judean claims to ownership of Lydda,
Ramathaim, and Ephraim were based on a grant made to them during the rule of Alexander
the Great.

62. There are 28 *mwṣh* stamp impressions with 3 letters (מצה) and 2 others with plene spelling (מוצה).

center of the Babylonian province after the destruction of Jerusalem. Four additional seal impressions have been found in Jerusalem, 4 in Gibeon, 2 in Jericho,
and 1 each in Ramat-Raḥel and Belmont (Tzubah; see the map in Zorn, Yellin,
and Hayes 1994: 166). The date and significance of the seal impressions have

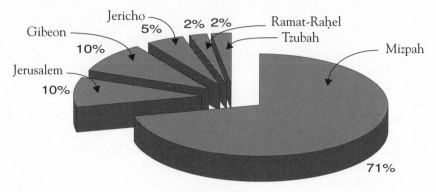

Fig. 3.1. Distribution of mwṣh *seal impressions.*

been accorded lengthy discussions in the archaeological, paleographical, and historical literature.[63] Most scholars agree that the seal impressions should be dated
to the Babylonian rule in the sixth century B.C.E.,[64] and this is based primarily on
an analysis of the evidence from Tell en-Naṣbeh.[65] The seal impressions from
Gibeon[66] and Jerusalem (see Zorn, Yellin, and Hayes 1994: 168–69) serve as supporting evidence of this, as do the ceramic analysis and paleography.[67]

The 42 extant *mwṣh* seal impressions were all made by only 6 stamps (Zorn,
Yellin, and Hayes 1994: 171–74). This implies that these stamps were in use for

---

63. For a survey of the research on the *mwṣh* stamps, see Stern 1982: 208–9; Zorn, Yellin,
and Hayes 1994, especially pp. 162–63, 174; Christoph 1993: 83–85.

64. The first person who suggested this theory for the *mwṣh* seal impression was McCown
1947: 6, 202. He was followed by Avigad 1972b: 8–9; Stern 1982: 205–9, 213; Zorn, Yellin, and
Hayes 1994: 166–69.

65. For a detailed analysis of the discoveries at the tell, see Lipschits 1999a: 165–70. On
this subject, see also the analysis by Zorn, Yellin, and Hayes (1994: 167), which relies partly on
the discussion by Stern (1982: 207–9) and which is based entirely on data reported by Wampler (1941; 1947: 137). It is worth noting the information reported by Avigad 1976a: 20 and
nn. 90–94; and the comments by Graham 1984: 56.

66. Stern (1982: 207–9) argues that there is a gap from the beginning of the fifth century
B.C.E. to the Hellenistic Period at el-Jib. In this light, it is significant that the 4 *mwṣh* stamp impressions, but no *yhwd* stamp impressions, were found at the site; this also serves as evidence of
the chronological relationship of the stamp impressions. See the analysis of the archaeological
material from Gibeon (Lipschits 1999a: 172–76) and the discussions of the date of the *yhwd*
stamp impressions (below, §3.4.2, pp. 174–179).

67. For a summary of the ceramic materials, see Zorn, Yellin, and Hayes 1994: 169–70, and
for a summary of the paleographic discussion, see pp. 170–75.

a limited time and served a specific purpose. Three possible interpretations of the seal impressions have been proposed by Avigad.[68] Two of these should be combined, because they are essentially complementary:

1. The seal impressions were used to identify the manufacturer of (apparently) wine or oil (Cross 1969c: 22–23; Graham 1984: 56).
2. The place where the pottery vessels were manufactured and the impressions were made was apparently a crown estate that supplied agricultural products to the governor who resided in Mizpah.[69]

If we adopt the second interpretation, it explains why most of the seal impressions were found in the provincial capital. It also explains the difference in distribution between the *mwṣh* seal impressions and the *gbʿn gdr* inscriptions. On the basis of an analysis of the evidence from the site, it appears that Gibeon was the location of wine production for the army and the Babylonian bureaucracy stationed in the country; it was not a crown estate (Lipschits 1999a: 172–76).

Zorn, Yellin, and Hayes (1994: 166) claimed that the distribution of the seal impressions and the land allocation of the tribe of Benjamin are concurrent. I do not think that this connection should be accepted, because there is no historical evidence that Benjamin had independent administrative status in the sixth century B.C.E., especially because 5 of the seal impressions (about 12% of the total found) were discovered outside this area (4 were found in Jerusalem, and an additional example was found in Ramat-Raḥel). I think that it would be more useful to compare the similarities between the distribution of the seal impressions with the area where "those who remained" were active after the destruction (Jer 40:7–41:18). This, according to the archaeological analysis, is the area that was not destroyed during the destruction of Jerusalem (Lipschits 1999b; 1999c; see also below, §4.3.3, pp. 237–258), and according to the analysis of the historical data, it was also the arena of activity of "those who remained" during the rule of Gedaliah.[70] Thus, this area may be considered the place where the "remnant" in Judah gathered, either because it was possible to continue to live there safely or

---

68. See Avigad 1958b; 1958c. For a review of these proposals, see also Stern 1982: 207–9; Zorn, Yellin, and Hayes 1994: 163.

69. The seal impression *hmṣh šʿl*, also on the jar handle (Avigad 1972b: 5–9), supports this theory. On the meaning of the name and its geographical context, see p. 7. On the appearance of the name *šwʿl* on bullas from the end of the First Temple Period, see Avigad 1986: 56, and nn. 72–74. See also the bullas numbered 79, 123, 164, 175. Avigad preferred the idea of the crown estate (1958c: 119; 1972b: 7–9), and he was followed in this by Stern 1982: 207–9; see also Zorn, Yellin, and Hayes 1994: 183. See also the comments by Graham 1984: 56. It is likely that Moṣah's status as a crown estate was the basis for several traditions preserved for several centuries afterward (*m. Moʿed* [*Sukkah* 4:5]; *y. Sukkah* 18:2; *b. Sukkah* 45a).

70. See above, §§2.3.1–3 (pp. 98–112), the comprehensive discussion reconstructing historical data; and see below, §3.3.2 (pp. 152–154), a compilation of data and the discussion of its geopolitical significance.

because official Babylonian policy permitted the "remnant" to continue living in that region.

3.3.2. The Geographical-Historical Evidence for the Immediate Period after the Destruction of Jerusalem

The sole biblical evidence for the history of the Judean community after the destruction is the two versions of the story of Gedaliah (2 Kgs 25:22–26 and Jer 40:7–41:18).[71] In both accounts, the events are limited to a narrowly defined geographical area, with Mizpah at the center. In the 2 Kings version, Mizpah is mentioned twice (vv. 23, 25), and around it either the land of Judah (v. 22) or "the land" (v. 24) is mentioned in conjunction with Mizpah. In the version in Jeremiah, Mizpah is mentioned 13 times (40:8, 10, 12, 13; 41:1 [twice], 3, 6, 7 [the city], 10 [twice], 14, 16), and in the context are the "cities" (40:10) of the land of Judah (40:12). At the center of these cities is Gibeon (41:12, 16), the house of the Lord in Jerusalem is mentioned (41:5), and there is the statement that people were "halted at Geruth-Kimham, which is by Bethlehem, on their way to Egypt" (41:17).[72]

Apart from accounts that some of the residents of the fallen kingdom remained in the Benjamin region and in the environs of Bethlehem, there is no information about the status of the area after the destruction of Jerusalem. We do not even know whether the presence of Judeans was the result of an official decision by the Babylonians. This state of affairs has given rise to much, often contradictory, speculation that is reflected in the scholarly literature. Some have thought that Judah had an independent administrative status within the Babylonian structure.[73] In contrast, Alt postulated that, after the destruction of Jerusalem, the area north of Bethlehem was separated from the areas south of it and was annexed to the province of Samaria.[74] Noth offered a compromise:

---

71. As stated, there is very little evidence from this period that matters for demographic and geopolitical research. This section is based on an analysis of historical events at the end of the First Temple Period and during the time of Gedaliah (above, §§2.2.2–5, pp. 72–97). Any repetition of discussions found in previous chapters is intended to support the discussion of the size of the territory and the fate of the population. On the ideology and date of the biblical sources for this period and the historiographical trends, see the discussion in chap. 5 below.

72. On the various proposals for an interpretation of the verse and identification of the place, see Thompson 1980: 662; Holladay 1989: 298.

73. See, e.g., the opinion of Oesterley and Robinson 1934: 51–52; Avi-Yonah 1949: 18.

74. In contrast to conventional scholarship and the archaeological picture discussed below, Alt (1925a: 108–16; 1934a: 14–18) thought that it was precisely the rural area south of Bethlehem that suffered less damage in the Babylonian deportation. He argued that, in contrast to this, the land of Benjamin and the area of Jerusalem merged even before the destruction, thus creating an expanded "royal city," the fate of which was different from that of the rest of the kingdom. See also Kochman 1980: 100 and nn. 9–10; McEvenue 1981; Bedford 2001: 45. For other opinions, see Albright 1932c: 172; Kallai 1960: 84; Malamat 1964: 309–10. See also the opinion and criticism of Williamson 1985: 34, and cf. Lemaire 1990: 32–36; Blenkinsopp 1998: 37; Lipschits 1999b: 483; Mittmann 2000: 28–42, with further literature.

Judah was an independent administrative unit only for the short period of Gedaliah's reign and later became a subprovince of Samaria (Noth 1954: 286–88).[75] Meyers has accepted the opinion of Noth and Alt, but argues that the annexation of Yehud to the province of Samaria was not official (Myers 1965a: xx–xxi). Liver has objected to the idea that Judah's territory was reduced and has maintained that there was no administrative reorganization after the destruction of Jerusalem (Liver 1958: 116; 1959: 67–68).[76]

In my opinion, given the biblical description of Gedaliah's rule, the region between Benjamin and the northern Judean hills[77] was the area where the Babylonians permitted "the people left in the land of Judah" to remain (2 Kgs 25:12a, 22a; Jer 39:10, 40:7, 52:16). This conclusion is based, first and foremost, on a reconstruction of the events that took place around Jerusalem during the Babylonian siege, when the Babylonians were establishing an administrative alternative to the kingdom of Judah. The process they initiated at this stage was designed to establish a Babylonian province in Judah, with Mizpah at the center, headed by a governor who was not of the Davidic line. Support for this historical reconstruction is found in the archaeological data. An analysis of the evidence shows that the area of Benjamin and the environs of Bethlehem suffered less damage than other parts of the kingdom, and thus a reconstruction of the full, uninterrupted life of the population of Judah is possible there. This is also precisely the area where the 42 *mwṣh* seal impressions previously discussed were found, all of which are dated to the sixth century B.C.E. and are connected with the Babylonian provincial administration.

In the middle lay Jerusalem, between the region of Benjamin and the city of Bethlehem. We may theorize that, as part of the Babylonian policy, settlement in Jerusalem and its immediate environs was prohibited (Lipschits 2001). The city was laid waste, its inhabitants deported, and the surrounding area devastated. On the other hand, there is no information about the status of the area south of Bethlehem or the Shephelah or the Negev. Taking into consideration the information we have about the devastation brought on the entire southern area and the dwindling population in these areas, followed by the gradual incursion of the Edomite-Arabian population, we may conclude that the area's status had not been defined. Even if it had been, it is doubtful either that the administration of these border areas could have been enforced. In any event, considering this general historical-archaeological picture, there is no escaping the conclusion that the political and demographic vacuum created in the southern

---

75. This opinion was adopted by J. Weinberg 1972: 51.

76. This was also the opinion of B. Mazar, *EncMiq* 1.732–33 (1950); cf. the opinions of the scholars cited above in n. 74.

77. The exact limits of this region are not clear, especially in the south. The historical data contain no hint of what was happening in the sixth century B.C.E. south of Jerusalem, except for a reference to Bethlehem in Jer 41:17. See also the discussion following.

and southwestern areas of the kingdom of Judah attracted the migration of the population that had previously inhabited the periphery of the area. This populace either replaced or assimilated the sparse Judean population living in the region, which was a mere remnant of the densely populated settlement that had existed there in the eighth century B.C.E.

3.4. Evidence regarding the Boundaries of the Province of Yehud under Persian Rule

There is no information in the sources from the Persian Period about the boundaries of the province of Yehud.[78] The information in the biblical sources is problematic, limited,[79] and betrays a certain amount of confusion between the places where Judeans lived and the official limits of the province.[80] To overcome this difficulty, we will examine the biblical sources and the picture that emerges from the distribution of seal impressions dated to this period. All of the data will later be brought together to present as comprehensive a picture as possible.

3.4.1. The Historical Reliability of the Geographical Lists in Ezra–Nehemiah and Their Significance for Geographical-Historical Research

3.4.1a. Introduction

There is widespread agreement in modern scholarship that the book of Ezra–Nehemiah is based on three separate original works that were composed at different times and for different purposes.[81] The author/editor had a large share in the writing and editing of the final composition, and this makes it difficult to analyze the geographical lists embedded in the work.[82] These lists present many

---

78. In the Greek and Persian sources, there is no treatment of the internal geopolitical division of *Eber Nāri* ('Beyond the River'), except for some accounts of events in the coastal region. For a discussion of these sources, see Stern 1982: 237–39, with further literature on p. 278 n. 8; 2001: 360–72.

79. In the books of Ezra and Nehemiah, there is only a general reference to the boundaries of Yehud (Ezra 5:8). Except for references to the province as one of the provinces 'Beyond the River' (Ezra 8:36; 4:10, 11, 16, 17, 20; 5:3, 6, 8, 13; 7:21, 25; Neh 2:7, 9), there are only general geographical indications, most striking among them the general outline of the borders of Judah and Benjamin and an emphasis on the centrality of Jerusalem. See, e.g., Ezra 1:2, 3; 2:1; 10:9; Neh 5:14; 13:15, etc.

80. The Bible explicitly refers to Judeans outside the borders of Yehud province in the Persian Period. For example, Ezra is described as teaching the Torah "to all the people that are Beyond the River" (Ezra 7:25); there is a reference to "the Jews who lived near them" in Neh 4:6[12]; and references to Israelites from outside Judah in 2 Chr 30:11; 35:18, texts that are ascribed to the period before the destruction. The epigraphic and archaeological evidence also provides data in regard to this; see below.

81. For a summary of the process of writing and composing, see Japhet 1993b: 111–21, with further literature.

82. In Ezra and Nehemiah, there are five geographical lists, two of which are almost identical (the list of the returnees to Zion in Ezra 2:1–67; Neh 7:6–68). The third list is the list of

problems, among which are their authenticity, the date they were written, and the extent to which they were adapted when they were incorporated into the historical work. An independent analysis of each of the lists is required, as well as an investigation of the period to which it belongs and its sources, insofar as this is possible. Furthermore, the objectives of the composition and the redaction of each unit must be examined, as well as the motives of the author/editor who incorporated the various units into the final edition.

A comparison of the contents of the lists reveals their literary dimension, as well as the biases of the redaction (see table 3.1 below). In all of the lists together, a total of 50 towns are mentioned. Of these towns, 30 are mentioned only in one list; 15 towns (most in the region of Benjamin) are mentioned in two lists; Geba, in the region of Benjamin, is mentioned three times; and only Jerusalem is mentioned in all of the lists (or their titles).

Table 3.1. *Appearance of Regions Belonging to the Province of Yehud in the Geographical Lists*

Region	List of the Returnees	List of Builders of the Wall	List of the Sons of the Singers
Benjamin	+	+	+
Jerusalem	+	+	+
Jordan Valley[a]	+	+	−
Ono-Lod	+	−	−
Judean hills	−	+	−
Shephelah	−	+	−

a. There are two main approaches to the explanation of הכיכר, which is mentioned in Neh 3:22 and 12:28. According to one approach, this term refers to the area near the Jordan River; according to the second, it refers to the area close to Jerusalem. I will explain below why I prefer the first approach, rather than that of Williamson (1985: 198, 208), who advocates the second approach and adds that mentioning the region was intended to distinguish the priests who lived near Jerusalem from those who lived in the city.

The most distinctive of the lists is the list of חצרים (*ḥăṣērîm*, i.e., small settlements dependent on a major city and belonging to a defined territory; Neh 11:25–36).[83] It is a utopian list of a pronounced literary and ideological nature, closely related to the list of cities in the book of Joshua. It consists of 33 placenames, 20 of which are not mentioned again in Ezra–Nehemiah, and most are

---

towns and districts incorporated in the list of the "builders of the wall" (Neh 3:1–32); the fourth is the list of settlements referred to as חצרים (Neh 11:25–35); and the last is the list of the origins of the sons of the singers in Neh 12:28–29.

83. On the characteristics and biases of this list, see Lipschits 2002c.

Table 3.2. *The Settlements in the Yehud Province according to Lists in Ezra–Nehemiah*

Region	List of Returnees (Ezra 2 + Nehemiah 7)	List of Builders of the Wall (Nehemiah 3)	List of the Sons of the Singers (Nehemiah 12)	List of ḥăṣērîm (Nehemiah 11)
Jerusalem	Jerusalem	Jerusalem	Jerusalem	Jerusalem
Judah	Bethlehem Netophah	Beth-Hakkerem Tekoa Beth-zur	Netophah	Kiriath-Arba
Shephelah		Zanoaḥ Keilah		Zanoaḥ Zorah Jarmuth Adullam Lachish Azekah
Negev				Dibon Jekabzeel Jeshua Moladah Beth-Pelet Hazar-Shual Beer-Sheba Ziklag Meconah Ein-Rimmon
Benjamin	Gibeon (?)[a] Anathoth Azmaveth Kirjath-Jearim Chephirah Beeroth [Ha]-Rama Geba Michmash Bethel Ai Nebo (Nob)[b]	Gibeon Mizpah	Azmaveth Geba Beth-Hagilgal	Anathoth Rama Geba Michmash Bethel Aija Nob Ananiah Hazor

Table 3.2. *The Settlements in the Yehud Province*
according to Lists in Ezra–Nehemiah (cont.)

Ono–Lod Valley	Lod Hadid Ono			Lod Hadid Ono Zeboim Neballat Gai-Harashim Gittaim
Jordan Valley	Jericho Senaah[c]	Jericho Senaah		

a. The people of Gibeon are mentioned only in Neh 7:25; Ezra 2:20 has "the children of Gibbar." There are scholars (see, e.g., Myers 1965a: 13) who prefer the version in Ezra, assuming that Gibeon belonged to the province Beyond the River and not to Yehud. Others (Batten 1913: 79; Bowman 1954: 43) supported this idea because there is no geographical continuity in the list and concluded that a correction was made in Nehemiah, because Gibeon is absent from the list. In refutation of this hypothesis, we might point out that there is also no geographical continuity later in the list (Williamson 1985: 25); furthermore, the number of immigrants listed in this group, as well as the fact that Mizpah is missing from the list, reinforce the authenticity of the version in Nehemiah (Blenkinsopp 1988: 81–82). For a discussion, see also Kallai 1960: 84–85; and, see also Batten's (1913: 79) problematic proposal.

b. Neh 7:33 says, "the men of the other Nebo," which does not change the geographical and historical fact. For a convincing explanation of this verse, see Williamson 1985: 26.

c. The name "Senaah" occurs in the Bible only three times: in the double list of the returnees to Zion (Ezra 2:35; Neh 7:38) and in the list of the "builders of the wall" (Neh 3:3). For an interpretation of the name, see Zadok 1988: 483. In addition to these three references to the town, note also the reference to "Judah the son of Hassenuah" in Neh 11:9 and "Sallu the son of Meshullam, son of Hodaviah, the son of Hassenuah" in 1 Chr 9:7. For a summary of the history of scholarship on this subject, see Zadok 1988: 483–84 and nn. 10, 11. The main question is whether a settlement was established by this family and named for them during the Persian Period. In my opinion, given the variety of the accounts, we cannot rule out the possibility that there was a settlement named "Senaah" near Jericho. The various proposals for identifying this site are listed by Zadok (1988: 484), but it should be remembered that none of them has been proved archaeologically.

located far from the borders of the province (the Beer-Sheba–Arad Valleys, the southern Shephelah, and the coast region).[84] If we omit the names of towns that are mentioned only in this list, there would be 28 town names in the 4 remaining lists. Approximately 20 are mentioned in the lists of the returnees, and almost all of them lie within the borders of Benjamin (12 towns). The other towns are located in the nearby region south of Jerusalem (3), in the Ono–Lod Valley (3), and in the Jordan Valley (2). The list of the wall-builders completes

---

84. An analysis of the list shows that it does not reflect the reality of the Return to Zion period and should not be relied upon to reconstruct either the borders of the province or the settlement situation. On this subject, see Lipschits 2002c.

the picture in Judah and adds other, more-southerly towns (Beth-Hakkerem, Tekoa, and Beth-zur) as well as 2 in the southern Shephelah (Zanoaḥ and Kei-lah). This list also parallels the lists of the returnees with regard to towns in the Jordan Valley, and only 2 towns from the region of Benjamin are mentioned: Gibeon (repeated) and Mizpah (added). In the list of the sons of the singers, there is a parallel to the lists of the returnees in the Jerusalem area (Netophah) and in the Benjamin region (Azmaveth and Geba); the list adds another town in Benjamin: Beth-Hagilgal.[85]

Out of 28 towns mentioned in the three historical-geographical lists under discussion here, 20 are mentioned in one list only; they lack a reference in any other list. Seven towns appear in two of the lists, and only Jerusalem is men-tioned in all three lists (or in their headings). Thus, all of the lists mention the region of Benjamin and Jerusalem, two lists mention the Jordan Valley, and only one list mentions the Ono–Lod Valley, the Judean hills, and the Shephelah. In my opinion, this is a reflection of the true status of the Yehud province in the Persian Period, when Jerusalem served as the political and religious center and the Benjamin region continued to serve as the major demographic center, de-spite the serious decline it suffered in the early sixth century B.C.E. (paralleling the beginning of the Return to Zion era).

In the following sections, I present a separate discussion of each of the lists, focusing on each list's geographical significance, with an attempt to understand the settlement history lying behind each list.

3.4.1b. The Double List of the Returnees to Zion (Ezra 2; Nehemiah 7)

The lists of the returnees to Zion appear in parallel versions in Ezra 2:1–67 and Neh 7:5–68.[86] Modern scholars accept the premise that the list in Ezra 2 is later and secondary to the list in Nehemiah 7. This premise conforms to the overall conclusion that the literary unit Ezra 1–6 is later than the other two units in the book of Ezra–Nehemiah and secondary to them; however, it is also based on a detailed analysis of both lists.[87] This point is important when we

---

85. Because this list is of minor importance to the geographical-historical discussion, it will not be given a separate discussion.

86. For a thorough comparison of the lists, see Batten 1913: 71–103; Galling 1951a: 149–59; Allrik 1954: 21–27.

87. On this subject, see the discussion by Rudolph 1947: 13; Japhet 1982: 84; 1993b: 112; Clines 1984: 44–45; Williamson 1983: 1–30; 1985: 29–30; Blenkinsopp 1988: 43–44, 86–87. For additional bibliography and an itemization of the literary rationale for preferring the ver-sion in Nehemiah over that in Ezra, see Williamson 1985: 29–30. For a different opinion, see Batten 1913: 71–72; Noth 1943: 128–29; Allrik 1954: 21–27; Mowinckel 1964–65: 1.30–31; Pohlmann 1978: 60–61; Blenkinsopp 1988: 83. For detailed criticism of these opinions, see Williamson 1983: 29–30; 1985: 2–7. The question of the authenticity of the list is important for two reasons. (1) From a literary perspective, the list of the returnees serves as a central, of-ten decisive fact in examining the connection between Ezra 1–6 and the book of Nehemiah. (2) From a historical perspective, these lists have been used as primary data for estimating the size of the population of the province at the beginning of the Persian Period. On this subject, see below, §4.4 (pp. 258–271).

consider the historical credibility of the list, because those who believe that the Ezra 2 list is original (i.e., that it lists those who returned to Judah immediately after the proclamation of Cyrus) must postulate that the original version of the list was preserved for dozens of years until it was finally inserted in Ezra, no earlier than the mid-fifth century B.C.E.[88] Despite this difficulty (and apart from minority opinions that claimed that the list had no historical value; Meyer 1896: 105–8, 148–52; Torrey 1910: 66), most scholars argued that the source on which the list was based was reliable, reflecting the reality of a specific time during the Return to Zion. Some scholars believed that the list reflectd the waves of immigration that reached Yehud at the beginning of the Return to Zion (Galling 1951a: 150–51; Myers 1965a: 15–16; Kochman 1980: 118, with further literature), and they based this idea primarily on the identification of the original title of the list[89] and on details in the text itself that seem to support the list's originality and reliability.[90] Nowadays, however, there is a marked tendency in contemporary scholarship to think that this was a condensed list, summarizing lists of several waves of immigration before Nehemiah's time.[91]

---

88. See, e.g., Hölscher 1923b: 42–43; Alt 1934a: 25–26; Rudolph 1949: 7–17; Kaufman 1959–60: 8.167–68. It is noteworthy that scholars who regard this as an authentic list and believe it to be historically credible base their conclusion specifically on interpreting the title of the list according to its simple meaning; on several details that it contains, which they believe point to its antiquity; and on seeing Ezra 2 as the authentic, reliable source of the list of the returnees. For a summary of the points raised by critics of this opinion, see Williamson 1985: 30–31.

89. Apart from the literary heading at the top of the list (Ezra 2:1 = Neh 7:6), which can be connected to the placement of the original list in its present position, the main reference is to the subhead. The subhead was apparently preserved in Neh 7:7a, הבאים עם זרובבל ('those who came with Zerubbabel') and was adapted to the literary heading in Ezra 2:2a, אשר באו עם זרובבל ('they were the ones who came with Zerubbabel'). This heading is also linked to Neh 7:7, which, according to vv. 5–6 is a statement regarding those who came to Judah in the early days of the return, before the time of Nehemiah. See the opposing views presented by Mowinckel 1964–65: 1.63 and Williamson 1985: 32.

90. Two major leaders of the returnees were from the second generation after the destruction: according to 1 Chr 3:19, Zerubbabel was the grandson of Jehoiachin and the son of Pedaiah, one of the younger brothers of Shealtiel (see below a discussion of the problems involved in this reconstruction); Jeshua, who elsewhere (Ezra 3:2; Hag 1:1, etc.) is referred to as the son of Jehozadak, was the grandson of the last high priest before the destruction (2 Kgs 25:18; 1 Chr 5:40–41). There is additional proof that this list was earlier: a reference to the fact that the family of Hakkoz was disqualified from the priesthood (Ezra 2:61 = Neh 7:63), though during the time of Ezra a member of this family was one of the important priests of Jerusalem (Ezra 8:33; Neh 3:4, 21); the combined listing of different groups of settlements without any convincing geographical rationale and the assumption that groups of immigrants arrived together and then were dispersed throughout several settlements; the fact that the list includes 5,022 (5,021 according to Nehemiah) priests, Levites, and other temple functionaries; the list of gifts donated to the temple (Ezra 2:68–69; Neh 7:70–71); the fact that the list records animals used for travel but not cattle and sheep (Ezra 2:66–67 = Neh 7:68–69, and see the questions and theories suggested by Blenkinsopp 1988: 93). For additional points that support this hypothesis, see Williamson 1985: 31.

91. Batten (1913: 72–73, 74–75) proposed dating the list later, to the time of Ezra, primarily on the basis of the parallel between the names of those who immigrated with Ezra and the

In contrast to these theories, I find it difficult to accept the notion that this was the list of those who returned from Babylon, even if it referred to several waves of immigration. There is no supporting evidence in the archaeological and historical record of demographic changes of the proportions reflected by this list. There is no evidence of a deportation of these dimensions at the beginning of the sixth century B.C.E., nor is there any evidence of a massive return at the end of the sixth and beginning of the fifth centuries B.C.E. or even during the course of the fifth century B.C.E. (Lipschits forthcoming; cf. Becking forthcoming). On the contrary, the archaeological data from the end of the sixth and beginning of the fifth centuries B.C.E., which will be discussed in chap. 4, show that there was a decrease in the population, particularly in Benjamin, and a reduction of the population living in Jerusalem at that time. The implication is that the list of the returnees to Zion is a literary construction based on various lists, perhaps a list derived from a census of all residents of the province at various intervals.[92] It appears that the earliest of these secondary lists belongs to the first generation of the returnees to Zion, and the latest belongs to the days of Ezra;[93]

families of immigrants who appear in the list of the returnees. Liver (1959: 117–19 and n. 40) tried to demonstrate this theory from a historical perspective: during the early days of the Return to Zion, major waves of immigration arrived, and these were joined by new waves at the beginning of Darius's reign, when the situation in Babylon worsened. See also Myers 1965a: 15–16; Schultz 1980; Williamson 1985: 31. Rudolph proposed that the list was a summary of immigration that took place within a relatively short period during the rule of Cyrus and the beginning of Darius's rule (1949: 17; and cf. Dyke 2000: 134). This is, to some extent, a continuation of Alt's proposal (1934a: 24–25); Alt had also postulated that this list was intended to regulate the rights of the returnees with regard to the land. Williamson limits the date of the list to the time of Cyrus and Cambyses (1985: xxxiv, 31–32, with further literature). On this subject, see also Blenkinsopp 1988: 83; and the opinions listed in Liver 1959: 117, and n. 30; Kaufman 1959–60: 8.167–68, and n. 10. One proof of the variegated composition of the list is the difference between the numbers reported in the two versions of the list of the "men of the children of Israel," when compared with the slight differences in the lists of priests, Levites, and other temple functionaries. The occurrence of the Persian name Bigvai has served as a major argument for dating the list later. Hölscher (1923b: 32) identified Bigvai as a Persian tax official; for a critique of this proposal, see Blenkinsopp 1988: 83.

92. This argument is not new and has been expressed by many scholars. See, e.g., the arguments of Albright 1949a: 87–88, 110–11; 1950: 64 n. 122; Bright 1959: 376–77; Blenkinsopp 1988: 83. Hölscher (1923b: 504) claimed that this was a list of taxpayers, composed ca. 400 B.C.E. Against this proposal, see Blenkinsopp 1988: 83. Alt (1934a: 24–25) linked the list to the regulation of the rights of the returnees. Galling (1951a; 1964: 89–108) connected this census to the event described in Ezra 5:3–4. For counterarguments, see Kaufman 1959–60: 8.168 n. 11; Kochman 1980: 118. Despite the problematic nature of these proposals, the general approach is correct in trying to place the list on a realistic historical footing. Considering the complex structure of the list, Albright's proposal seems plausible: the list should be seen as the summary of several censuses that were conducted from the early days of the Return to Zion onward. See more on this subject below.

93. Along with the rather cogent arguments raised by scholars for dating this list earlier, there are many parallel points between other parts of the list and the list of those who went up with Ezra (Ezra 8:3–14). See the detailed comparison between those who came with Ezra and

in any event, the list appears to be composed of several parts (two major sections?) with at least a 50-year gap between them. It is likely that these lists described the affiliation of the residents of the province ("the whole congregation together"; cf. Ezra 2:64 and Neh 7:66), who for the author/editor were identical with the "the children of the province who went up out of the captivity"[94]—the legitimate continuation of the nation of Israel (Blenkinsopp 1988: 83; and cf. Dyke 2000).

The range of opinions concerning the nature and time of the original list demonstrates the difficulties scholars have had in analyzing it. These difficulties are not only the product of the processes of composing and consolidating the list but also the result of the intensive editing and adaptation by the author/editor of Ezra–Nehemiah, whose objective was to adapt the list to fit the literary sequence in which it is found. The list was placed in Nehemiah 7, where it serves as the basis for the casting of lots by Nehemiah, with the aim of settling Jerusalem with every tenth family from among the returnees (11:1).[95] Aside from the linguistic and topical connection between Neh 7:73a (cf. Ezra 2:70) and Neh 11:1, there are two additional proofs of the literary function of the list:

1. The numerical summary in the list (Ezra 2:64–65 = Neh 7:66–67; see also 1 Esd 5:41) states that "all of the congregation together" numbered 42,360 and in addition, 7,337 arrived, "male servants and female servants and two hundred singing men." However, this summary does not correspond to the total enumerated in the list. Adding up the number of people "who went up" according to Ezra 2 produces a sum of 29,818, in contrast to 31,089 in Nehemiah 7 and 30,143 in 1 Esdras. Inasmuch as it would be difficult to postulate that an arithmetical error was registered in the list

---

the list of returnees to Zion, parallel to the rest of the lists in the books of Ezra and Nehemiah, assembled by Heltzer and Kochman 1985: 26–27.

94. The term מדינה occurs in the Bible 53 times in Hebrew and another 10 times in Aramaic. Most of the occurrences (38, which is more than 60%) are in Esther. Nine more are in Daniel (twice in Hebrew and 7 times in Aramaic), 8 in Ezra–Nehemiah (Ezra 2:1; 4:15; 5:8; 6:2; 7:16; Neh 1:3; 7:6; 11:3); 4 in 1 Kings 20 (vv. 14, 15, 17, and 19; and see Burney 1903: 234–35); twice in Ecclesiastes, and once each in Ezekiel and Lamentations. On the word מדינה as an Aramaic term cognate with the Assyrian-Babylonian-Persian term for "province" or "satrapy," see Shalit 1960: 103–6; Avi-Yonah 1949: 17; Stern 1982: 238. This suggests that the title of the list, "Now these are the children of the province who went up out of the captivity," refers to those who were in the province and who had immigrated to it from the Babylonian exile, in distinction from those who had been there previously (Kallai 1960: 84; Heltzer and Kochman 1985: 34). See additional literature in Blenkinsopp 1991: 36 n. 1; Hoglund 1992: 75–76.

95. See Blenkinsopp 1988: 83–84. Most scholars call attention to the disruption in the literary continuity of Nehemiah's Memoirs (from chap. 7 to chap. 11) because of the insertion of chaps. 8–10. See Meyer 1896: 94–102; Torrey 1910: 255–61; Batten 1913: 266–67; Rudolph 1949: 181; Myers 1965a: 186; Fensham 1982: 242; Clines 1984: 211; McConville 1985: 136; Blenkinsopp 1988: 281; Grabbe 1998: 59–60, 168. For a different view, see Japhet 1993b: 120 and n. 14. On this subject, see the summary in Lipschits 2002c.

(and the various identical numerical summaries can only attest to the original summary of the list), we may assume that the sum was the original total of a more-expanded list, which served as the redactor's source of information. He abridged this list and adapted it for his composition.[96]

2. According to the list in Neh 11:3–24, a total of 3,044 people came to live in Jerusalem. This number is the product of the lots cast by Nehemiah and is supposed to be exactly "one out of ten to dwell in Jerusalem, the holy city" (11:1). Thus, it should come as no surprise that the calculation of the numbers of those who arrived in Nehemiah 7 (not including the servants and priests who could not prove their family relationship and are not counted or considered "Israel") adds up to 30,477 immigrants. This number demonstrates the serious and deliberate editorial-computational effort made by the author/editor of this unit in Nehemiah, for whom it was important to create agreement between the lists.

The conclusion to be drawn from these accounts is that the author/editor of Nehemiah compiled some of the numerical data from a list or several lists available to him to present the total number of all the "sons of the exile." By placing the list in his final work, he wished to show that Nehemiah's act of casting lots took place precisely as stated: exactly one-tenth of those who returned came to settle Jerusalem. This demonstrates the importance that the author attributed to the settling of Jerusalem and shows that he chose to present the inhabitants of the province as having come from Babylon, at the same time ignoring those who had remained in the land after the destruction.[97]

The conclusions concerning the character of the list highlight its limitations in the context of the geographical-historical discussion. It is possible to postulate that additional immigrants and additional towns were mentioned in the original list but were later omitted by the author/editor, whose aim was to achieve his numerical target: he needed a total ten times the number who settled Jerusalem. To arrive at this conclusion, however, requires that another difficulty be solved, namely, the structure of the list, which has always been put forward by scholars as proof that it is authentic and that it reflects a realistic historical picture.[98] The structure of the list appears in other literature of the period, and the point re-

---

96. On the theme of the redaction and composition of this part of the book of Nehemiah, see Lipschits 2002c. See the discussion by Blenkinsopp 1988: 93, 282.

97. See Blenkinsopp 1988: 83, and Lipschits 2002c.

98. The editor of the list summarized the immigration according to a classification system: First are those who are included in the general category of "the people of Israel" (Ezra 2:3–35 = Neh 7:8–38). After them are the priests (Ezra 2:36–39 = Neh 7:39–42) and the other temple functionaries: the Levites, the singers, and the sons of the gate-keepers (Ezra 2:40–42 = Neh 7:43–45). Closing the list are the "temple servants" and "the children of the servants of Solomon" (Ezra 2:43–58 = Neh 7:46–60), as well as those who came "who could not tell whether their father's house and descent were of Israel" and the priests "who sought their genealogical register but they were not found, and therefore they were excluded from the priesthood as unfit"

garded as decisive in the historical reconstruction is that some of "the men of the people of Israel" (Ezra 2:2b = Neh 7:7a) are counted by families, and some are counted by towns.[99] A more or less systematic division between these two groups may be discerned:[100]

1. Those counted by families (Ezra 2:3–19 = Neh 7:8–24)
2. Those counted by towns (Ezra 2:20–29 = Neh 7:25–33)
3. Addition to those counted by families (Ezra 2:32–33 = Neh 7:34–35)
4. Addition to those counted by towns (Ezra 2:33–35 = Neh 7:36–38).

In my opinion, Rudolph and Galling are correct in seeing the third section as a later addition to the list.[101] Deleting this section produces a more orderly list, with two major groups that are distinguished by their various affiliations: using the term בני ('the children of . . .') in the lists of families and אנשי ('the men of') in the list of towns.[102] There is another clear difference in the number of people who belong to each group: most of the groups counted by families add up to numbers in the hundreds and even the thousands, while most of the groups counted by towns add up to only scores or a few hundred.[103]

Most scholars have connected the evidence contained in the list of the returnees with the consequences of the destruction and exile. In their opinion,

---

(Ezra 2:59–63 = Neh 7:61–65). This classification of those registered appears elsewhere in the literature of the period, for example, the list of "the builders of the wall" (Nehemiah 3); see Myers 1965a: 17–22.

99. On this subject, see the analysis by Galling 1951a: 152. See also Naʾaman 1995c: 22, with further literature in n. 41.

100. The division presented here is slightly different from the division made by Zadok 1988: 483–86.

101. See Rudolph 1949: 17; Galling 1951a, and see there the rationale for this simple solution.

102. The phrasing is more systematic in Nehemiah, although it is not complete and does not include the family of Gibeon (v. 25), the inhabitants of Jericho, Lod, Ḥadid, and Ono (vv. 36–37), and perhaps even the inhabitants of Senaah (v. 38). On this subject, see Myers 1965a: 17–18 and see the explanations offered by Batten 1913: 76–78. Despite this, we must not necessarily see these terms as rigidly connected to families or members of a certain settlement; compare this list to the list of wall-builders (Nehemiah 3). The inhabitants of Jericho and Gibeon in the list of the returnees are referred to as the men of Jericho and the men of Gibeon in the list of wall-builders; the inhabitants of Senaah are referred to as such in both places; and alongside this, the people of the other towns are referred to in other ways, either as "the Tekoaites" (Neh 3:5, 27) or as "those who live in Zanoaḥ" (v. 13).

103. The numerical average of families reaches 912 people per group (with slight differences between the lists in Ezra and Nehemiah—these groups include an average of 861 people according to Ezra 2 and 963 according to Nehemiah 7); the average in the groups listed by settlement reaches some 249 people per group. In effect, this number is even lower, because these groups consist of an average of 213 people (according to Ezra 2) and 284 (according to Nehemiah 7), but some of them include 2 or 3 settlements in a group, which lowers the average to 166 people per group. It should be noted that including the large number of "the inhabitants of Senaah" (3,630 according to Ezra or 3,930 according to Nehemiah) changes the statistical picture (see below).

there was a selective deportation from the settlements in the Benjamin region; therefore, only small numbers returned to Benjamin from the exile. In comparison, the deportation from the Judean hills was on a larger scale, and this region remained desolate throughout the exilic period. Consequently, the exiles returned in larger numbers to areas that were relatively devoid of population, south of Jerusalem and north of Hebron, and it is these people who were counted by family.[104] This is the background against which Alt and Noth theorized, each according to his own logic, that the difference between the returnees who were listed by towns and those listed by families was a function of the political and demographic situation prevalent in the area.[105] Galling also followed this line of reasoning to infer that the division according to place-names and family names reflected two phases of settlement during the Return to Zion era: in the first phase, people returned and settled in the area around Jerusalem; in the second, they settled the rest of the territory of Judah (Galling 1951a: 152). Kallai thought that the area between Beth-zur and Bethlehem, which was settled in Nehemiah's time, was populated by families who originally came from the south and had been displaced from lands seized by the Edomites (southern Hebron hills and the Negev).[106]

However, there is insufficient evidence for the historical background that these hypotheses require. The premise underlying all of them is that there were extensive deportations in the early sixth century B.C.E. and that the Return to Zion was numerically significant. But a totally different picture emerges from an analysis of the evidence, which shows that the Babylonians deported primarily the elite and the residents of Jerusalem; there were no extensive deportations

104. Examples of this theory can be found in nineteenth-century scholarship, and it became established in twentieth-century geographical and historical scholarship almost unchallenged. See Alt 1925a: 108–16; Kittel 1927–29: 2.341; Abel 1933–38: 2.120; Klein 1939: 2–3; Kallai 1960: 83; Kochman 1980: 98–116.

105. See the arguments by Alt 1934a: 24–25 and Noth 1954: 286–88. In my opinion, this interpretation, which was once accorded a consensus, should no longer be accepted; see the arguments put forward by Kaufman (1959–60: 8.178–79) and the discussion above on the history of the era of destruction and exile.

106. See Kallai 1960: 83–84 and n. 10. In contrast to this view, Kaufman (1959–60: 8.171–74) argued that there was a very large deportation from the entire region between Bethlehem and Benjamin and portrayed this region as remaining desolate from the Babylonian era onward. Kaufman tried to account for both the desolation of the region and the lack of invasion by other nations such as the Edomites and Samaritans by claiming that the Babylonians had decided that the area belonged to the Judahite province and therefore protected the region. He saw this as part of "Nebuchadrezzar's policy of suppression and pacification" (p. 174). In this connection, the "sociological theories" cultivated by Meyer (1896: 152–54), Kittel (1927–29: 2.359–60), and Rudolph (1949: 20–21) should be rejected. These theories claim that those who were listed by family name included all of the well-born families, landowners who possessed full rights and citizenship; those who were listed by the name of the town were the poorest people, devoid of property and bereft of rights, who banded together into groups in Babylon and returned to existing towns. Against these opinions, see the arguments by Kaufman 1959–60: 8.175–76.

from other areas of Judah and Benjamin. The latter historical reconstruction corresponds to the biblical descriptions of the time of the Return to Zion, with the renewed status of Jerusalem, even though there was no dramatic change in the demographic profile of the region (see the discussion below, §4.4, pp. 258–271). For this reason, we cannot draw any inference from the structure of the list about the historical reality in Judah during the period of the Return to Zion and at the same time connect the list to the days of exile and destruction. It is preferable to explain the difference between the various parts of the list—some by family and some by place—as a literary rather than a historical difference, stemming from the nature of the source used by the editor of the list, as well as the time and purpose of its writing.

At this point, it is necessary to point out that this list was composed of various census registers that come from various periods and that it reflects various ways of listing groups, some by families and some by towns. A natural assumption is that this reflects different censuses that were carried out for different purposes. The recording of people by place, particularly those in the Benjaminite region who may have been landowners in specific places, is different from the recording of family members (including women and children?) by genealogy. We may presume that the counting of the sons of Lod, Ḥadid, and Ono in the list, even if they did not belong to the administrative borders of the province, is evidence that some of the lists were written or preserved in the temple and they may have been connected to times of pilgrimage, various donations to the temple, and so forth. In any case, the editor of these lists, who incorporated them in the text for his literary purposes, was not interested in reflecting the historical reality of a specific period but in creating a comprehensive literary framework, a list of provincial residents that could be used as the basis for casting lots for the settling of Jerusalem.

Now we may examine the geographic and demographic reality that stands behind the list. Of 29,702 "people of the province" listed in Ezra 2 or 30,996 listed in Nehemiah 7, the residence of only about 10% is known.[107] Even if we add the religious and cultic functionaries who apparently lived in Jerusalem[108] and the children of Senaah,[109] we are still left with 17,870 Judeans (according to Ezra) or

---

107. The lists cite the residence of approximately 3,180 Judeans (according to Ezra 2) or 3,085 (according to Nehemiah 7). More than 60% of them lived in the Benjaminite region (1,931 according to Ezra 2, or 1,831 according to Nehemiah 7), some 23% in the northern Shephelah (725 according to Ezra 2; 721 according to Nehemiah 7), 11% in Jericho (345 according to both versions), and less than 6% near Jerusalem, south of the city (179 according to Ezra 2 and 188 according to Nehemiah 7).

108. Among the religious and cultic functionaries are the priests (4,289 in both lists), the Levites (74 in both lists), and the various temple functionaries (659 according to Ezra 2 and 680 according to Nehemiah 7).

109. The inhabitants of Senaah numbered 3,630 in Ezra and 3,930 in Nehemiah. There is no evidence that they settled north of Jericho, but for the purpose of the theoretical discussion

18,911 Judeans (according to Nehemiah) whose place of residence is not listed. These figures are evidence that, geopolitically and demographically, this list conceals more than it reveals, and it is doubtful that any kind of geographical-historical profile can be based on it.

If we wish to create a geographical picture of the province of Yehud in this era, we may begin by comparing these figures and the archaeological picture derived from excavations (to be discussed below).[110] This comparison (see table 3.3) is based on two fundamental premises:

1. The numbers in the list of the returnees are partial and represent an unknown phase (or unknown phases) within the process of demographic and settlement change in the province from the early days of the Return to Zion (the last third of the sixth century B.C.E.) until the days of Nehemiah (the middle of the fifth century B.C.E.).
2. The archaeological data reflect the settlement "heyday" of the province of "Yehud," which was apparently in the mid-fifth century B.C.E.

A comparison of the data from archaeological discoveries with the list of the returnees shows a significant absence of correlation in all data relating to Jerusalem and its environs. These data indicate that *Jerusalem* was the focal point of the list, and yet the emphasis on the priests and other temple functionaries does not correlate with the demographic proportions revealed by the archaeological data. This disjunction in the data regarding Jerusalem has a counterpart in the absence of any reference to the existence of a settlement in the *Judean hills* by the returnees to Zion. Many scholars have explained this absence as evidence of the destruction suffered by the area and that the area attracted massive settlement by those returnees who were listed by family. However, this explanation does not correlate with either the archaeological profile, which indicates that this area also was characterized by continuous settlement, or with information in the list of the "builders of the wall," which implies that there was a well-established settlement in this region. This leads me to prefer the hypothesis that the contrast between the archaeological data and the lists is a chance result of the lists' having been copied and edited: the author/editor selected the parts of the lists that were best suited to his literary purposes.

---

on this point, they can be omitted. This addition raises to 12,484 the number of those whose place of residence is known (according to Ezra) and to approximately 12,700 according to Nehemiah. This calculation raises the proportion of settlement in the Jericho region to 32%, with 45% of the returnees living in Jerusalem, approximately 15% in Benjamin, about 6% in the northern Shephelah, and 1.5% south of Jerusalem.

110. Despite the caution required in use of the archaeological data, the data reflect a profile of major settlement concentrations in Yehud province in the Persian Period. On the basis of the data, one can create a picture of the settled and empty areas at that time and compare them with figures in the lists of the returnees to Zion.

Table 3.3. *Comparison of the Settlement Profile
Reflected Both in the List of the Returnees and in Archaeology*

Region	Estimate of settled area (in dunams)	% of total	Number of immigrants acc. to Ezra	% of total	Number of immigrants acc. to Nehemiah	% of total
Benjamin	500	46.75%	1,931	24.1%	1,831	23.1%
Jerusalem environs	110	10.30%	5,022	62.6%	5,043	63.5%
Judean hills	300	28.00%	–	–	–	–
N. Shephelah	150	14.00%	725	9.0%	721	9.1%
Eastern strip	10	0.95%	345	4.3%	345	4.3%
Total	1,070	100.0%	8,023	100.0%	7,940	100.0%
Unknown place of residence	–	–	21,697	73.0%	23,056	74.4%

In contrast, the data in the list of the returnees reinforce the impression that the *Benjamin region* had a central demographic role in the Persian Period. According to the archaeological data, Benjamin had nearly half of all the settled dunams within the limits of the province, and it is likely that most of the residents of Benjamin were the "remnant"—those who had not been exiled.[111] In the list of the returnees as well, Benjamin is the primary locus of Judean habitation, apparently because one passage embedded in the list cataloged those who lived in this region according to the name of their settlement. Later, it appears that a decline in settlement in the region of Benjamin was a major factor in renewed Judean settlement in the *northern Shephelah*, particularly in the Ono–Lod Valley. We may reasonably conclude that settlement in the northern Shephelah, which was not within the borders of Yehud, gained momentum in the fifth century B.C.E. and attracted at least some residents who were abandoning the

---

111. On this process, see Lipschits 1999a. It should be noted that there is no satisfactory explanation for the absence of Mizpah in the list of the returnees. Perhaps this is due to Mizpah's status as the center of the province before and after the days of the Return. This status required the presence of officials, administrators, and military personnel in numbers unknown to us, which might have discouraged settlement in the town or the adjacent area (Ginsberg 1948a: 21–22; Kallai 1960: 85). The list of "the builders of the wall" (Nehemiah 3) suggests that Mizpah continued to be a district capital even during the time of Nehemiah.

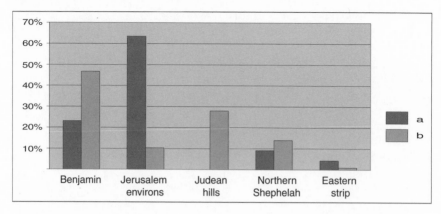

Fig. 3.2. Comparison of number of immigrants with information from the archaeological profile, region by region: (a) immigrants whose residence is known (Nehemiah 7); (b) the archaeological profile (in %).

region of Benjamin.[112] It is likewise reasonable to conclude that the Judean residents of this region maintained some sort of connection with Yehud province; however, the nature of this connection and its longevity are not clear from the narrative in Nehemiah (Schwartz 1988: 3–7; Naʾaman 1995c: 22–23; Lipschits 1997, with further literature). In the *Jordan Valley and along the littorals of the Dead Sea*, settlement was extremely sparse, and most of the population must have been located at En-Gedi and in the Jericho region.

3.4.1c. The List of "The Builders of the Wall" (Nehemiah 3)

The list of "the builders of the wall" in Nehemiah 3 is not a geographical list,[113] but an administrative register that includes all of those who assumed responsibility for rebuilding one of the 41 segments of the wall of Jerusalem.[114] Usually, the text connects those responsible for building a specific segment of the wall by means of the verb חזק (in third-person singular).[115] The author/editor's

---

112. On this historical process, which also is accompanied by convincing archaeological evidence, see Lipschits 1997.

113. In contrast to the interpretation of some scholars, see, e.g., Stern 1982: 245–46.

114. See Heltzer and Kochman 1985: 115; Naʾaman 1995c: 21. For a summary discussion of the list, see Williamson 1985: 195–202; Carter 1991: 56–57.

115. In the description of the building of the wall, there are 6 occurrences of the root בנה 'build' in the 3rd-person sing. or pl. (ויבנו, בנו, יבננו), compared with 33 occurrences of the root חזק in the 3rd-person sing. or pl. (החזיקו, החזיק). Most scholars translate חזק as 'reconstructed', e.g., Myers (1965a: 107) or 'repaired', e.g., Ryle (1907: 174); Rudolph (1949: 114); Williamson (1985: 200); Blenkinsopp (1988: 227); and they do not attribute any special significance to the verb except for its technical sense.

intention probably was to set forth the responsibility of these people or groups: they were supporters, financiers, and organizers, though not necessarily those who actually built the wall. This meaning of the root חזק is particularly evident in Neh 3:13, where the difference between Hanun, who החזיק "the valley gate," and the inhabitants of Zanoaḥ, who "rebuilt it, and set its doors, bolts, and bars in place," is highlighted. This sense is also evident in v. 5, where it is noted that the men of Tekoa built the segment assigned to them; however, "their nobles did not put their necks to the work of their Lord."[116]

Apart from a few exceptions (for those who took part in building two segments of the wall), there is a noticeable division of responsibility for the building of segments of the wall among specific people or well-defined groups: 22 segments were built with the support of people who are listed only by name;[117] 8 segments of the wall were built with the support of official functionaries who were in charge of districts, subdistricts, or settlements;[118] and 5 segments of the wall are said to have been built with the support of people who had ritual functions (priests, Levites, and temple servants).[119] One segment of the wall was built with the support of another Jerusalem functionary, "the keeper of the east gate";[120] 4 segments were built with the support of the settlements from the periphery of the province;[121]

---

116. The use of the root חזק in the meaning 'to give support and assistance' is widespread in biblical literature of all genres. The use made of it in Neh 3:19 is also significant and reinforces the conclusion that it refers not only to construction activity but also to support and assistance (Ryle 1907: 174; Batten 1913: 221–22).

117. Zaccur, son of Imri (Neh 3:2b); Meremoth, son of Uriah, son of Hakkoz (two segments: vv. 4a, 21); Meshullam, son of Berechiah, son of Meshezabel (two segments: 4b, 30b); Zadok, son of Baana (4b); and Joiada, son of Paseah, and Meshullam, son of Besodeiah (6a); Melatiah the Gibeonite and Jadon the Meronothite (7a), who came from Gibeon and Mizpah, "the seat of the governor of Beyond the River" (7b); Uzziel, son of Harhaiah (8a); Hananiah, one of the perfumers (8a); Jedaiah, son of Harumaph (10a); Hattush, son of Hashabniah (10b); Malchijah, son of Harim, and Hasshub, son of Pahath-moab (11); Hanun (13a); Baruch, son of Zabbai (20); Benjamin and Hasshub (23a); Azariah, son of Maaseiah, son of Ananiah (23b); Binnui, son of Henadad (24); Palal, son of Uzai (25a); Pedaiah, son of Parosh (25b); Zadok, son of Immer (29a); Shemaiah, son of Shechaniah (29b); Hananiah, son of Shelemaiah, and Hanun, son of Zalaph (30a); Malchiah, one of the goldsmiths (31).

118. Rephaiah, son of Hur, ruler of half the district of Jerusalem (v. 9); Shallum, son of Hallohesh, ruler of half the district of Jerusalem (Neh 3:12a); Malchiah, son of Rechab, ruler of the district of Beth-Hakkerem (14); Shallun, son of Col-hozeh, the ruler of the district of Mizpah (15); Nehemiah, son of Azbuk, ruler of half the district of Beth-zur (v. 16); Hashabiah, ruler of half the district of Keilah (17b); Ezer, son of Jeshua, ruler of Mizpah (v. 19).

119. Three segments of the wall were rebuilt with the support of the priests: Eliashib the high priest and his fellow priests (Neh 3:1); the priests from the surrounding region (v. 22); the priests (as an inclusive group), who built "each one opposite his own house" (v. 28). One segment of the wall was rebuilt with the support of a family of Levites headed by Rehum, son of Bani (Neh 3:17a). Another segment of the wall was rebuilt with the support of the temple servants who were living in the Ophel (Neh 3:26).

120. This is the description of Shemaiah, son of Shechaniah (Neh 3:29b).

121. Of the 4 segments of wall built by groups that are listed by settlement name, 2 segments were built by the Tekoites, and their virtue in taking on this responsibility is emphasized by the

one segment of the wall was rebuilt with the support of the goldsmiths and the merchants, two groups who are mentioned only by profession.[122]

The great diversity among the people who supported the building endeavor shows that there is no significant connection between the role, status, and position of the individuals and groups and the support that they gave to building a segment of the wall.[123] It is, therefore, reasonable to assume that those mentioned in the list with no title were well-off individuals who were capable of financing the construction of a segment of the wall.[124] We can also make inferences from this information about the positions held by official functionaries who bore the title שׂר and who were in charge of districts,[125] parts of districts, or

---

fact that they bore the burden alone: "their nobles did not put their necks to the work of their Lord" (Neh 3:5); and that they were not satisfied with one section: they "rebuilt a second section" (v. 27). Alongside them, the men of Jericho rebuilt one section (v. 2a), and another segment was rebuilt by the sons of Hasenaah (v. 3, and see the discussion above). The fact that the sons of Hasenaah worked alongside men from Jericho connects them with a settlement located north of Jericho, a settlement that had probably been established after the return. The inhabitants of Zanoaḥ (v. 13a) are not listed in this category because they were partners in the rebuilding with Hanun, who apparently financed the relatively large building project on that segment of the wall.

122. See Neh 3:32. These probably were some of Jerusalem's merchants, who had a clear financial interest in building the wall. Compare also the professions of those listed in v. 8.

123. There is no way of knowing why this task was assigned to these people specifically (because there is information available about the activity of other important personages in the days of Nehemiah) and whether it was of their own free will, imposed on them, due to understanding the need for a wall, or for any other reason.

124. It must be emphasized that, except for two people, nothing is known about the geographical origin of most of the financiers. Nonetheless, it is likely that some of them lived in Jerusalem and thus had a clear personal interest in building the wall. Only Melatiah the Gibeonite and Jadon the Meronothite are described (Neh 3:7) as having come from "Gibeon and Mizpah, the seat of the governor of Beyond the River." Both of these names, with the unique reference to their origins and their relationship to the "seat of the governor of Beyond the River," have preoccupied many scholars, who find geographical and political significance in the reference. For a survey of the research on this subject, see Kallai (1960: 89–91), who follows the theory suggested by Batten (1913: 210–11) for solving the problem by attributing the second part of the verse to Jerusalem and to the part of the wall that was built by these people. On this subject, see also Heltzer and Kochman 1985: 116.

125. Most scholars understand the term פלך, which occurs only in Nehemiah 3 (vv. 9, 12, 14–18), in the sense of 'district'; compare the interpretations of Williamson 1985: 206; Blenkinsopp 1988: 235–36; Weinfeld 2000: 249. Demsky (1983), followed by Graham (1984: 57), maintained that this is an administrative term for a group of conscripted laborers. Bowman commented on this subject (1954: 267) and has been supported by Carter (1999: 80); but see the critique by Williamson (1985: 206). In addition to a methodological problem with the sources that Demsky uses, this interpretation cannot be accepted, because only seven sections of the wall were built by "group leaders" of this type. This definition of the term also necessitates the assumption that there was a complex administrative system, with every district having officials supervising the conscripted work, implying that there was much labor of this sort available. For a critique of this interpretation of the term פלך, see Carter 1991: 75–76, and n. 71; Na'aman 1995c: 21 n. 39; Weinfeld 2000.

settlements.[126] Whether these officials resided in these specific areas or whether they built a segment of the wall with the help of someone from each area is not mentioned.[127] As was the case with the main group of supporters, these officials probably bore the financial burden of the construction, paying for it personally and organizing the work. The difference between these officials and the individuals who are mentioned by name but not by title probably is that the heads of the districts were subordinate to the governor, a fact that may have obligated them to bear the expenses.[128]

From a literary perspective, we can say that the list was incorporated by the editor into the narrative in Nehemiah 2–4. Most scholars consider it to be an original list that reflects the building process,[129] despite the linguistic and technical problems it contains and despite the fact that it underwent significant editing (Myers 1965a: 112–16; Williamson 1985: 195–202; Blenkinsopp 1988: 231–33). Accordingly, this list has been assigned a great deal of importance for the history of Jerusalem during this period,[130] for understanding the internal administrative structure of the province (Kallai 1960: 87–94; Stern 1982: 245–48), and for learning about its size and boundaries.[131]

126. We should not be surprised by the mixing of the roles and dwelling places of those responsible for building segments of the wall. This confusion reinforces the hypothesis that positions and titles were not connected to any specific assignment in the building endeavor, and this has ramifications for geographical and historical interpretations based on this list.

127. This point is the basis of the theory that conscripted teams of laborers were used, which is connected more closely to what is described in Nehemiah 4 (see below).

128. This is the group that is the focus of the discussion about the place, extent, and status of the districts; the manner in which the information is presented demonstrates that caution is required when considering the geographical and administrative significance of these districts.

129. The striking exception is Torrey 1896: 37–38; 1910: 225, 249. The full description of the size of the wall, in comparison with the breakup and reduction in size of the area from which the builders came, is the main evidence for the credibility and authenticity of the list. The extent of the detailed portrayal is said to show that the account is not tendentious. To this, scholars have added the technical character of the list, the use of unique administrative terminology, and the geographical picture it portrays, which corresponds to the information derived from the *yhwd* seal impressions. On this subject, see Kochman 1980: 119–21; Williamson 1985: 201; Blenkinsopp 1988: 231–32. Nonetheless, Kochman's conjecture (in Heltzer and Kochman 1985: 112), following Myers (1965a: 112) and others, regarding the source and date of the list prior to the time of Nehemiah, seems farfetched and not well grounded.

130. The subject relates to the status of the city as well as its size, area, and the position of its walls. See Burrows 1933–34; Tsafrir 1977; Blenkinsopp 1988: 232–39; Eshel 2000: 337–42, with further literature.

131. The list has been seen by scholars as the chief geographical and historical evidence for Judah during the Persian Period. This is largely because of the relative ease of establishing its time and background, as well as because of the detail it contains; because it refers to a relatively large area; and because it only incidentally hints at the settlement picture. See Meyer 1896: 107–11; Kittel 1927–29: 1.49–53; Kallai 1960: 87–94; Stern 1982: 245–48; Ofer 1993: 1.37. The main opposition to dating the list to Nehemiah's time, by those who redate it to the preceding period (Heltzer and Kochman 1985: 112), relies on arguments that are not convincing and that are unable to justify taking the list out of its present placement. As most scholars have

However, scholars have not given enough weight to the fact that the list does not necessarily mention all of the districts that existed within the province's boundaries[132] and that some of the wealthy people and leaders of the nation did not agree to take part in the endeavor.[133] This has led to a dispute among scholars concerning which districts should be added to the list,[134] the internal structure of the province, and the borders to assign to each district. The controversy among scholars over these questions is evidence that the list offers very little clear-cut information about the geography and administration of the province.[135] This also reveals that scholars have often tried to find in the list data that simply do not exist.

I believe that the only geographical conclusion to be drawn from the information that does appear in the list is that there were 5 districts in Judah. There is no evidence of any additional districts and, methodologically, one may certainly not add districts on the pretext of "filling in gaps" or with a preconceived notion of the borders of the province or the borders of the districts that it comprised. There is certainly no basis for the assumption that the borders of the province extended beyond the boundaries of the preexilic kingdom of Judah, particularly to the west (see, e.g., Stern 1982: 245–49; in contrast, see Schwartz

---

emphasized (see, e.g., Myers 1965a: 112–13), the list does not relate the entire building process; it has a specific goal, and we should not draw conclusions from the list based on information that it does not contain.

132. Along with a reference to the Beth-Hakkerem district (Neh 3:14) and the Mizpah district (v. 15), as well as the two half-districts of Jerusalem (vv. 9, 12) and the two half-districts of Keilah (vv. 17, 18), only one half-district of Beth-zur is mentioned. See also Naʾaman 1995c: 21. Kallai's deliberation (1960: 93) on the possibility that there was only one half-district of Beth-zur is surprising.

133. This sheds light on the emphasis placed on the Tekoites and the gap between them and "their nobles" (3:5), especially considering that the Tekoites managed to finance "another section" (v. 27). Furthermore, the reference to the priests as of הַכִּכָּר (v. 22) may be an allusion to the other groups of priests (from Jerusalem?) who did not support the project.

134. Thus, for example, Klein 1939: 3–4; Avi-Yonah 1949: 21; Blenkinsopp 1988: 232–33; and many others add one more district (Jericho), and Stern (1982: 248–49; 2001: 430–31) adds two (Jericho and Gezer), extending the borders of the province westward. Researchers have suggested diverse ways of reconstructing the administrative division of the province, and the huge difference between these reconstructions demonstrates that their basis is quite shaky. Thus, for example, Aharoni (1962b: 338) divided the district of Mizpah into 2 parts and postulated that only the Beth-Hakkerem district was not divided. Blenkinsopp (1988: 232–33), on the other hand, proposed that there were 6 districts, each divided into 2 (12 half-districts). Kallai (1960: 93) raised the possibility that in the district of Beth-zur there was only one half-district. On the borders of each district, see also Abel 1933–38: 2.120–22.

135. We must remember the numerical data indicating that 31 out of 41 sections of the wall (some 75%) were built by people whose place of origin was unknown, which leaves only 11 sections of wall built by people known to have been affiliated with a specific place or region within the province. This makes it difficult to see the list as a representative sampling of the settlements existing at that time or to draw any clear-cut conclusions from it (against the views of Klein 1939: 3–4; Demsky 1983: 242; Ofer 1993: 1.37–38).

1988: 4–5; Naʾaman 1995c: 19–23) or north.[136] Any reconstruction must assume that the borders remained stable throughout the period; those who maintain differently must assume the burden of proof.[137]

These facts, combined with a geographical analysis of the region, the information about the border of Judah at the end of the Iron Age, and knowledge of the historical events in the Persian Period, allow for the following reconstruction of the districts that existed in the province of Yehud in the mid-fifth century B.C.E.

The Mizpah District was largely congruent with the region of Benjamin. This conclusion is based on the continuity of the region's boundaries between the seventh and the fifth centuries B.C.E. The people of Jericho and Hasenaah probably also belonged to this district;[138] attempts to include the Ono–Lod region or parts of Samaria in this district should be rejected.[139] The hypothesis suggested by some that Mizpah belonged to the imperial authority has no basis. Mizpah's status as a major city in the district is evidence enough that it belonged to the territorial and administrative framework of the province.

The Jerusalem District lay south of the Mizpah District and probably included the city limits and its immediate environs. Taking into account the surrounding districts, we may assume that the Jerusalem District continued eastward to the edge of the desert but did not extend greatly beyond the borders of Jerusalem in the north and south. The existence of an independent district of Jerusalem reinforces the assumption of continuity between the structure of the districts in the province, which I believe drew on the internal structure of the districts of the kingdom of Judah in the seventh century B.C.E. (Naʾaman 1991a: 14–15).

The Beth-Hakkerem District lay south of Jerusalem and apparently included the western slopes of the hill country.[140] The men of Tekoa were probably included in this district that, like the two districts north of it, reached the Shephelah on the west and was bordered by the Keilah District (Kallai 1960: 92–93, with further literature). We reject Avi-Yonah's theory that the Emmaus and Chephirah regions are to be included in this district as well (Avi-Yonah 1949:

---

136. See the attitudes expressed above regarding the status of this region at the end of the kingdom of Judah and during the rest of the Babylonian Period.

137. Some would take exception to this statement, trying to account for geographical difficulties by resorting to explanations involving temporary changes in borders. On the Lod–Ono region, see Bright 1959: 384. On the area of Gezer, see Kochman, in Heltzer and Kochman 1985: 113.

138. This conclusion is in contrast to the attempt by Klein (1939: 3–4), Avi-Yonah (1949: 21), and Blenkinsopp (1988: 232–33) to make the Jericho district into the 6th district in the province of Yehud, as well as Stern's attempt (1982: 247–48; 2001: 430–31) to add Gezer as another district in addition to Jericho.

139. See, e.g., Kallai's proposal 1960: 87–94; in contrast, see Naʾaman 1995c: 20–24, with further literature.

140. There is no longer any basis for the view that Meyer (1896: 107) tried to establish. See Avi-Yonah 1949: 21; Kallai 1960: 91, 93–94.

21). These two regions were definitely a part of the Mizpah District. Similarly, Kallai's proposal that the northeastern Shephelah (the region of Gezer and Ekron) is to be included in this region must be rejected (Kallai 1960: 94).

The Beth-zur District is the southernmost in the hill country. On the east is En-Gedi, and the district is bounded on the west by the Keilah District. It is reasonable to assume that the boundary between the districts ran east of the Adullam–Zanoaḥ line. The southern boundary probably ran along the narrow strip between Beth-zur and Hebron, in the same location, where it continued until the days of the Hasmoneans.

The Keilah District was the only stronghold that the province of Yehud had in the Shephelah. It was bounded on the southwest by Mareshah and on the west by Ekron.On the north, the boundary did not extend beyond the Gezer line, which lies outside the borders of the province (Na'aman 1995c: 16–24).

* * * * *

It is noteworthy that there is a the clear continuity between the districts of the Yehud province and the districts of the kingdom of Judah in the seventh century B.C.E., as depicted in the biblical sources. This continuity reinforces the role and importance of the Babylonian Period in the process of creating and maintaining an administrative system that continued into the Persian Period.

3.4.2. *The Date and Distribution of the YHWD Seal Impressions and Their Significance for Geographical and Historical Research*

3.4.2a. The Date and Distribution of the *YHWD* Seal Impressions[141]

The study of the *yhwd* seal impressions, which were stamped on handles or on sides of jars, has extended for more than 100 years.[142] Nonetheless, until the exhaustive study by Stern (1973), who gathered, classified, and catalogued the extant seal impression, research was characterized by the publication of new seal impressions and discussion of invidual impressions or groups of impressions.[143]

---

141. At the beginning of this discussion, some cautionary comments about methodology are appropriate: we should not rely on the discovery of single or isolated seal impressions as clear-cut evidence that the site or the entire region belongs within the borders of the province. In this chapter, I will focus only on the *yhwd* seal impressions that were found in archaeological excavations. For reservations about the authenticity of the discovery of 65 bullas and 2 seals published by Avigad (1976a), see Bianchi 1993.

142. For a detailed review of the history of the research on the *yhwd* seal impressions, see Christoph 1993: 8–16, 37–74.

143. It must be noted that even today we do not have the full collection of *yhwd* seal impressions. The most complete corpus appears in the English edition of Stern's (1973) book, which was published in 1982. The English edition includes more than the list that appears in the original Hebrew edition (1973), and the bullas published by Avigad (1976a) were added. Nevertheless, the book lacks the seal impressions discovered in excavations in Jerusalem and Tell el-Fûl, as well as in the surveys and excavations conducted in the 1980s (see, e.g., Ariel and Shoham

The well-thought-out classification of the seal impressions proposed by Stern has been generally accepted by scholars. According to this classification, there are three major types: [144]

1. Nearly 60% of the stamp impressions (206 out of 342 in Stern's list) have the name of the province either in plene spelling (יהוד) or defective (יהד). Subdivisions of this category are:
   a. *yhwd* on either one line or two, without a monogram [145]
   b. *yhwd* on one line, with the letter ו above
   c. either the plene or defective spelling of *yhwd* in a circle + a monogram (including יהד on one line + monogram).
2. In nearly 32% of the seal impressions (110 out of 342 on Stern's list), the name of the province appears in abbreviated form. It is usually abbreviated to two letters (יה), [146] and in only 5 seal impressions is it abbreviated to one letter (ה).
3. In nearly 8% of the seal impressions, a 4-letter word is added to the name of the province (פחוא); the meaning is assumed to be 'governor', with or without a proper name. [147]

2000). We now know of about 408 seal impressions, 66 more than the 342 presented by Stern. There is no information on some of them, beyond the fact of their discovery or a general description. The discussion in Christoph's doctoral thesis (1993), which is devoted to this topic, is based on a corpus of 412 stamp impressions (p. 121), but the source of many of the stamp impressions in his dissertation is not clear.

144. See Stern 1982: 202–3; 2001: 548. Since the publication of the bullas discovery (Avigad 1976a), the bullas and the stamp impressions have been discussed together, on the assumption that both were used for similar administrative purposes. Discussing the bullas and stamp impressions together is methodologically justified, because the name *ḥnnh* appears both on the impressions on the jars and on the bulla (Avigad 1976a: iii–iv; Kochman 1982: 10–11; Stern 1982: 202–3). Nevertheless, the questions raised regarding the authenticity of the bullas (Bianchi 1993) demand special caution when we consider the epigraphic and chronological implications. The classification discussed here is based on the data that appear in Stern 1982 and that had been established prior to the publication of the bullas find.

145. The difference between writing the name of the province on one line or on two reflects, in my opinion, variant forms of writing and has no functional or chronological significance.

146. On the subtypes of this group, see Christoph 1993: 110.

147. The known stamp impressions of this type are: two stamp impressions that read *yhwd/ ʾwryw* (Jericho; Gezer?); five stamp impressions that read *yhwd/ḥnnh* (three from Ramat-Raḥel and two on bullas nos. 3–4 published by Avigad 1987); four stamp impressions that read *yhwd/ yhwʿzr/phwʾ* (all from Ramat-Raḥel); three stamp impressions that read *lyhwʿzr*[?] (from Jericho and Ramat-Raḥel); six stamp impressions that read *lʾhzy/phwʾ* (five from Ramat-Raḥel and one from Mizpah); four stamp impressions that read *yhwd/hphh* or *yhd/hphh* (all from Ramat-Raḥel); one stamp impression that reads *yʾz/br yšb/yhd* that was found at Tzubah (Millard 1989: 60–61); one stamp impression that reads *lḥnwnh yhwd* found at Tell Ḥarasim (Naveh 1996: 44–47), and a similar stamp impression found at Ramat-Raḥel, though scholars are in dispute about how to read it (Avigad 1976a: 15). There are no parallels to the stamp impression *lʾlntn/phwʾ* published by Avigad (1976a: 4–5).

This classification of the seal impressions shows that more than 90% of them in-clude only the name of the province, with or without a monogram, and this re-inforces the theory that has become rooted in the research from its inception—that these are official seal impressions of the provincial administration and are chiefly related to tax matters. [148] In my opinion, this conclusion is also supported by the fact that the stamp impressions come from four major centers (96.9% of the 412 discovered thus far): [149]

Ramat-Raḥel (194 seal impressions, 47.1% of those found);
Jerusalem (170 seal impressions, 41.3% of those found);
Mizpah (19 seal impressions, 4.6% of those found);
Jericho (16 seal impressions, 3.9 % of those found).

Inasmuch as most of the seal impressions were found near Jerusalem, [150] these sites may be seen as collection centers for taxes that were sent to the Judean center in Jerusalem and to the Persian center in Ramat-Raḥel. [151] Just like the *lmlk* jars and rosette jars, all of the *yhwd*-stamped jars were apparently manufac-tured in one center, distributed to the settlements in the province, and sent to the provincial tax collection centers when the jars were full. [152]

---

148. Impression on jars, and especially jar-handles, is a well-known Judean administrative phenomenon, beginning in the late eighth century b.c.e. and continuing at least until the sec-ond century c.e. Despite general agreement among scholars about the economic and adminis-trative context of the *yhwd* stamp impressions, their precise significance is unclear, and different explanations are given by the various researchers. On the basis of the parallel to the *lmlk* stamp impressions, the accepted hypothesis is that the impressions on the jars were official marks sym-bolizing that their contents were part of the tax collection system in the province (Stern 1982: 205–6; Avigad 1976a: 3, 4, 6, 8, 9–11, 23–24; Kochman 1980: 54; Naveh 1996: 47). For a de-tailed review of the various proposals, see Stern 1982: 205–6; Christoph 1993: 176–77. On pro-posals concerning the role of the *yhwd* coins, beginning in the late Persian Period, see Stern 1982: 225–26.

149. The data are based on the material presented by Christoph 1993: 132. Additional single stamp impressions were found at Jericho, En-Gedi, Gezer, Tell Jarmuth, and Azekah. On the finds at Jarmuth and Azekah, see the reservation expressed by Stern 1982: 246. It should be noted that, because no *yhwd* stamp impressions have been found in the border areas of the province (especially significant is the absence of *yhwd* stamp impressions at Beth-zur), Chris-toph (1993: 194) has ruled out the idea that the *yhwd* stamp impressions are connected with the province's taxation system.

150. Note that the *lmlk* jars and rosette jars were found primarily in the northern section of the highland and the Shephelah. See Kletter 1995: 223–29; Cahill 1995.

151. On Ramat-Raḥel as the Assyrian and Persian administrative center in Judah, see Na'aman 2001: 260–80; see further §4.3.2a, esp. pp. 213–215, below.

152. Theories regarding the role of the *yhwd* stamp impressions are not fully explored here, and they deserve further research. There are three possible connections between the *lmlk* and *yhwd* impressions: (1) the places where the *yhwd, lmlk,* and rosette stamp impressions were im-pressed; (2) the centers where the *yhwd* stamp impressions were found and the distribution of the *mwṣh* stamp impressions; (3) the uninterrupted use of the *yhwd* stamps in the Hellenistic Period (including the use of *yhwd* coins).

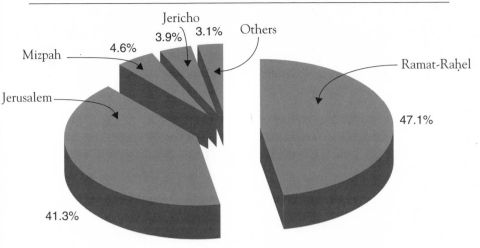

Fig. 3.3. Graph showing relative proportions of yhwd *stamp impressions.*

In contrast to the prevailing general agreement regarding the meaning and function of the *yhwd* seal impressions, the date of the impressions is disputed.[153] Even whether the impressions should be assigned to the Persian Period has been questioned,[154] although the name *yhwd* ('Yehud') and the term *pḥw'* ('province') and the title *hpḥ'* ('the governor') clearly are at home in this period. A chronological determination has been made more difficult by the absence of clear stratigraphic associations for the seal impression discoveries.[155] Some attempts to date the material have grasped at any chronological straw and have proved fruitless, including attempts to identify the names found in the seal impressions or to compare a monogram appearing on them to a monogram familiar

153. For a review of the various opinions, see Stern 1982: 205.

154. For a discussion of whether the *yhwd* seal impressions date to the Persian Period, see Kochman 1980: 142, with references to other researchers who have dated the stamp impressions to the Hellenistic Period. The reconstructions that date the *yhwd* stamp impressions later fit well with the historical reconstructions that emphasize the secondary status of Judah and its annexation to the province of Samaria, at least until the time of Nehemiah (Alt 1934a: 5–28; Galling 1964: 92 n. 3). Noth (1954: 286–88) supported this view, at least for the time following Gedaliah's rule. For a review of the reconstructions and their bases, see McEvenue 1981: 353–64. For a critique of the reconstructions, see Kochman 1980: 104–9, 136–39. For critiques of Cross's proposal (1969c: 24), that the word *phr'* in these stamp impressions should be understood as 'potter', see Stern 1982: 204–7; Avigad 1976a: 4–5, 9; Kochman 1980: 140–43; Meyers 1985: 34. On the meaning of the word *pḥw'*, see Kutscher 1960: 112–19; Naveh 1996: 44–45, with further literature.

155. For a compilation of the analyses of the stratigraphy connected with these stamp impressions, see Avigad 1976a: 19–21. In my opinion, Christoph (1993: 96–97) attributes excessive chronological significance to the evidence from Ramat-Raḥel, which is unclear, because there are no unequivocal archaeological data from this site (see the discussion by Aharoni 1962a: 39, 59, and n. 52).

from the Elephantine papyri.[156] For this reason, I have limited my discussion of the date of the seal impressions to their paleography.[157]

The paleography of the seal impressions must be situated against the background of the conventional understanding of language and script development: the status of Hebrew weakened after the fall of Jerusalem and Aramaic and the lapidary Aramaic script increasingly replaced Hebrew.[158] At the beginning of the Hellenistic Period, there was a minor renaissance of the use of ancient Hebrew script; this was due to a nationalistic impulse and found its major expression in the Hasmonean coins.[159] Inasmuch as some of the *yhwd* seal impressions are in Hebrew script and some in Aramaic,[160] most scholars have assigned a later date to the seal impressions. The generally agreed-upon date for the Aramaic seal impressions is the second half of the fifth century and the early fourth century B.C.E., and the Hebrew seal impressions are usually dated to the Hellenistic Period.[161]

This general discussion of the *yhwd* seal impressions demonstrates that they have practically no significance for the geographical-historical study of the Persian Period. The site distribution of the *yhwd* seal impressions has consistently been claimed by researchers as evidence for the extent of the Yehud province, but this is a methodological error: the chance discovery of a single seal impression in Kadesh Barnea, Tell Ḥarasim, or Gezer, or the lack of any seal impres-

---

156. See Stern 1982: 205. The attempt by Albright, Avigad, Yadin, Aharoni, and others to identify the names in the stamp impressions with people who are known from the Bible (*'wryw-'wryh* or, from other writings, *yḥzqyw-yḥzqyh*) has not been successful. See Avigad 1976a: 11, 17; Kochman 1980: 140–41, 151; Stern 1982: 204–5.

157. For a review of the research in this field, see Stern 1982: 202–7; Kochman 1980: 139–52; 1982: 3–23; Christoph 1993: 93–98.

158. See Lapp 1963: 26 n. 20; Cross 1969c: 22; Avigad 1976a: xvi; Naveh 1989a: 115–16; 1992: 12, 23; Hoglund 1992: 81. For the archaeological foundation for this theory, see Avigad 1976a: 19–21.

159. See Avigad 1974: 57–58; 1976a: xvi, xix; Garbini (in Aharoni 1962a: 8); Lapp 1963: 31; Cross 1969c: 22–25; Naveh 1989a: 113, with further literature in 116–17 n. 99; 1992: 13–14, 23–24.

160. For a discussion of the parallel existence of Aramaic and Hebrew stamp impressions, see Garbini (in Aharoni 1962a: 66–68). However, on the basis of Christoph's analysis (1993: 178–80), one may draw some conclusions about the chronological differences. See more on this subject below. With regard to the date of the seal impressions, see Stern 1977: 18; 1982: 202–5, with further literature. For an example of reliance on the transition stage from Aramaic to Hebrew, see Garbini (in Aharoni 1962a: 67, and n. 40); Christoph 1993: 97.

161. See Stern 1977: 18; 1982: 202–5; 2001: 547; Christoph 1933: 95, 176. Attempts to assign an earlier date to the appearance of the stamp seals have been based mainly on the 65 bullas and 2 stamps that were published by Avigad (1976a: ii–xv). However, the unique nature of the script on the bullas that Avigad examined (1976: 13) has aroused reservations about this judgment (Stern 1982: 206). In light of the suspicions raised by Bianchi (1993) concerning the authenticity of the find, we apparently should not rely on it to date the first appearance of the *yhwd* impressions. In any case, we cannot accept Kochman's (1980: 139–51; 1982: 9–23) results: he dates the appearance of the stamp impressions even earlier.

sions from Bethel should not be accepted as unequivocal evidence for the boundaries of the province.[162] Using the distribution of the seal impressions to determine the province's borders is faulty for two methodological reasons:

1. Most of the maps used as a basis for geographical-historical reconstruction mark the sites where many seal impressions have been found along with sites where only one seal impression has been found, without making any distinction. It would be more appropriate to note the number of seal impressions found at each site.[163]
2. The distribution of the *yhwd* seal impressions has been used to aid in the analysis of information from the geographical lists embedded in the books of Ezra and Nehemiah and for evaluating their reliability. A somewhat marginal piece of archaeological information (e.g., a single seal impression) should be used neither to evaluate the reliability of a biblical list nor to determine the course of a political border.

Given the current state of the data, the usable geographical-historical information contained in the seal impressions is scanty and limited. It does reflect the administrative importance of Jerusalem and Ramat-Raḥel. In addition, two other sites where a significant quantity of seal impressions were uncovered (Mizpah and Jericho) apparently were important centers of administration, at least regionally. A more complete understanding of the geographical-historical development in Judah during this era may be obtained from a comparison of the distribution of the *yhwd* seal impressions with the distribution of the *mwṣh* seal impressions, as the next section will show.

3.4.2b. A Comparison of the Distribution of the *YHWD* Seal Impressions with the Distribution of the *MWṢH* Seal Impressions

On the assumption that the *yhwd* seal impressions were first created somewhere near the middle of Persian rule and that the *mwṣh* seal impressions were made during Babylonian rule, we may compare the distribution data from four key sites: Tell en-Naṣbeh, Gibeon, Jerusalem, and Ramat-Raḥel (see table 3.4 and fig. 3.4, p. 180).[164]

A comparison of the distribution data of the *mwṣh* and *yhwd* seal impressions shows that during the Persian Period a sharp change took place in the settlement pattern and the location of the province's primary center. The region of

---

162. See, e.g., McCown (1947: 171–72), who states that, because there are no *yhwd* stamp impressions from Bethel, the site must not have been a part of the province; or Cohen (1986: 40–45), who states that the single impression that was found at Kadesh Barnea is evidence that the southern border of the province ran through the line of fortresses unearthed in the Negev.

163. See Carter 1991: 63–64. For maps that organize the information about the places where stamp impressions were found, see Stern 1982: 202–3, and 246–47 n. 32; Kochman 1982: 17.

164. The data are based on Christoph's presentation (1993: 132), together with data presented and discussed in previous chapters.

Table 3.4. *Quantitative and Qualitative Comparison of the* yhwd *and* mwṣh
Seal Impressions Discovered at Key Sites

Name of Site	No. of *mwṣh* Seal Impressions	% of Total Seal Impressions (42)	No. of yhwd Seal Impressions	% of Total Seal Impressions (412)
Mizpah	30	71.4%	19	4.6%
Gibeon	4	9.5%	0	0.0%
Jerusalem	4	9.5%	170	41.3%
Ramat-Raḥel	1	2.4%	194	47.1%
Others	3	7.2%	29	7.0%

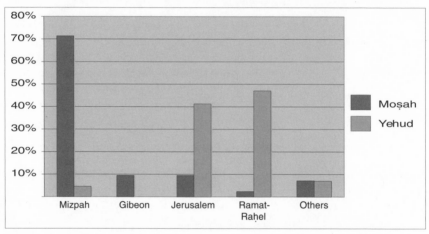

Fig. 3.4. Graph showing the distribution of yhwd *and* mwṣh *seal impressions (in %).*

Benjamin lost its importance as an administrative center: though approximately
80% of all the *mwṣh* seal impressions were found there, only 5% of the *yhwd* seal
impressions were discovered in Benjamin. In contrast, Jerusalem reverted to its
former importance, because 80% of the *yhwd* seal impressions were discovered
in Jerusalem and Ramat-Raḥel (Christoph 1993: 187–89, and additional literature there). This set of data was one of Na'aman's main arguments for his theory,
according to which the Persian rulers favored Ramat-Raḥel as an administrative
center instead of Mizpah, after Jerusalem once again became the center of the
Persian province (Na'aman 2001; see also §4.3.2a, esp. pp. 213–215).

The data in table 3.4 are also of importance for dating the *yhwd* seal impressions in Aramaic and Hebrew. In chap. 2, I tried to show that the settlement at Mizpah steadily declined during the early days of the Persian rule. Thus, it is important to note that it was at Tell en-Naṣbeh that 1 Hebrew and 18 Aramaic seal impressions were found and at Jericho 16 Aramaic seal impressions were found but not even 1 in Hebrew.[165] These figures reinforce the conclusion that the Aramaic seal impressions had already begun to appear at the (end of?) the first half of the fifth century B.C.E.[166] We may also conjecture that the use of this type of seal did not continue after the fifth century B.C.E. and that the use of Hebrew seal impressions began later, when Mizpah had declined in importance and was the site of a small, impoverished, unwalled settlement.

3.5. Shaping the Boundaries of Judah under Babylonian Rule: Demographic and Geopolitical Processes between the Seventh and the Fifth Centuries B.C.E.

We can summarize the processes by which the borders of Judah were shaped between the seventh and the fifth centuries B.C.E. as follows:

1. In the second half of the seventh century B.C.E., there was a marked expansion and consolidation process of the kingdom of Judah in its eastern sector. The establishment of En-Gedi and the founding of the settlement in Jericho turned the Judean Desert into an integral part of the kingdom's system of settlement because of the dozens of encampments and forts that were built along the major roads leading from the top of the mountain ridge eastward. Apparently there was some northward expansion of the kingdom of Judah, and its boundary was fixed north of Bethel. It is reasonable to assume that it was during this period that the fortresses along the border of the Negev were founded. The objective of the fortresses was to guard the border of the kingdom of Judah. The archaeological evidence shows that there was increasing pressure on this border because of the heightened presence in the region of seminomadic tribes, and prominent among these were the Edomite and Arabian elements.

2. At the beginning of the sixth century B.C.E., particularly after the Babylonian campaign of 598 B.C.E., the kingdom showed signs of weakening and had diminished ability to withstand the pressure of migration from the south. Nonetheless, there is no evidence that the fortresses on the southern border of the kingdom of Judah were destroyed before 587 B.C.E.

---

165. On this subject, see Christoph 1993: 121 and the discussion on pp. 122–23. The source of Christoph's data is unclear, and it is not clear why, for example, he does not mention the En-Gedi discoveries.

166. This is supported by the statistical evidence presented by Christoph 1993: 187–89.

3. The eve of the destruction saw the establishment of the Babylonian province of Judah. Most of the inhabitants of the province gathered in the region of Benjamin and in the environs of Bethlehem. Historical accounts
   of this appear in the two biblical narratives from the time of Gedaliah.
   From an archaeological standpoint, this region was less affected than
   others during the destruction of Jerusalem. Archaeological evidence from
   the Benjamin region covers the entire sixth century B.C.E. and reveals almost complete settlement continuity from the end of the Iron Age to the
   Babylonian and Persian Periods. This area is also where the *mwṣh* seal impressions were found.

4. It is likely that, after the destruction, the status of the southern hills of Judah as well as the southern Shephelah was not defined, and these areas remained sparsely populated and relatively desolate. At this stage, a
   distinction between the area south of Hebron and Mareshah developed:
   the southern portion remained relatively desolate, but the area north of
   Hebron and Mareshah was less affected and a large share of the settlements continued there as they had before. The separation between these
   two regions began during the campaign of Sennacherib (701 B.C.E.), when
   the Assyrian campaign damaged primarily the southern hills of Judah and
   the Shephelah. Settlement in these areas dwindled noticeably and never
   fully recovered. In the Judean highland, a clear distinction emerged between the areas north and south of Hebron. North of Hebron, the settlement had returned to its previous dimensions by the mid-seventh century
   B.C.E. South of Hebron, the process of rebuilding was slower, and the size
   of the settlement never reverted to what it had been before the Assyrian
   campaign. In the Shephelah, the settled area was concentrated at the foot
   of the hill country, and the population grew thinner toward the western
   and southern parts of the region.

5. The "collapse of systems" in the Beer-Sheba and Arad Valleys had probably begun during the Babylonian siege of Jerusalem and came to an end
   with the fall of the city. Following the destruction, pastoral groups who
   lived in the south began to invade the Negev, and prominent among these
   were the Edomite and Arabian groups. In a gradual process that was partly
   violent and partly quiet incursion, these groups began to advance northward toward the Shephelah and the Hebron highland. This migration
   may be linked to the apparent devastation as well as decreased population
   in the Negev, southern Judean highland, and southern and central Shephelah. Notwithstanding this, sources contemporary with the Persian
   Period and later sources indicate that at least part of the Judean population remained in these areas.

6. The population flow toward the north was curbed only in the Persian Period. At some time during this period, the boundaries of the provinces in

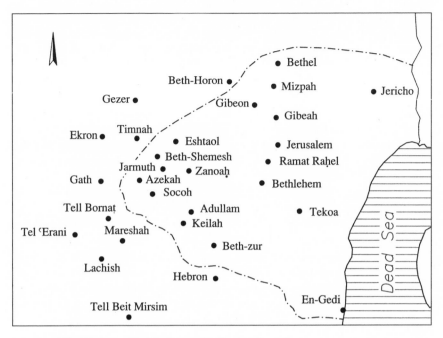

Map 6. The Borders of Judah during the Persian Period.

the region were redefined, apparently on the basis of the borders that had previously existed, with minor adjustments to fit the demographic situation. Thus, the southern and southwestern borders of the provinces of Yehud were shaped. This border alignment continued until the Hellenistic Period, when the Hasmonean expansion began. The information available on the regions occupied by the Hasmoneans or granted to them supports the evidence we have on the borders that remained the same until this period. The archaeological finds show evidence of settlement in the central hill region, demonstrating that a new settlement prototype had developed, different from settlement types of the Iron Age. We can assume that, in the mid-fifth century B.C.E., the southern boundary of Yehud had already been charted, and settlement in this area grew.

7. The system of fortresses in the southern part of the Yehud province attests to the desire of the Persian authorities to stabilize the province's southern border. Based on the archaeological and historical evidence, it appears that this took place at the end of the fifth and maybe only at the beginning of the fourth century B.C.E.

One of the critical questions in this discussion is whether a specific area was provided by the Persian authorities for settlement of the returnees to Zion (this was the view of, e.g., Kittel 1927–29: 2.341; Kaufman 1959–60: 171; and others) or whether, during the Persian Period, Judeans settled wherever they were permitted, and the areas they settled in later became the border of the province (this was Alt's theory [1931: 68; 1935: 94–95], and many followed him).

The theory that a predefined area of settlement was assigned to the returnees is problematic and requires us to assume that the borders of the province had already been defined by the Babylonians[167] or that the Persian authorization to return to Judah had an appendix that determined the area within which the Judeans were allowed to live (Kittel 1927–29: 1.49–53; Kochman 1980: 100 and n. 9). The principal problem with all of these conclusions is that they are predicated on the idea that the Return to Zion brought about a significant change in the demographic and geopolitical situation in Judah. This flies in the face of the combined archaeological and historical data, which attest to uninterrupted development and a lengthy process that molded the demographic character of the country. Another problem with these conclusions is that there is no information that either the Babylonians or the Persians at the beginning of their rule established or defined administrative borders. It was only when border disputes arose among neighboring provinces that the ruling authorities were compelled to intervene and resolve the disputes by determining, or approving, specific boundaries. There is no historical evidence that any dispute of this kind erupted before the middle of the fifth century B.C.E. Therefore, we can assume that the limits of the area settled by the returnees to Zion were not delineated until the fifth-century dispute. If this is true, then the borders of the province were determined *post factum* on the basis of the limits of the settlement of "those who remained" and those who returned to Zion, and thus the borders are in fact an outgrowth of the realities that devolved from the revolt, destruction, and 65 years of Babylonian rule.

This lengthy process highlights the importance of the events that took place in the sixth century B.C.E. This period was crucial in shaping the human landscape and political borders of the Hebron highland and the Negev, as well as the central and southern Shephelah. The collapse of the kingdom of Judah left these border regions vulnerable to invasion by nomads from the south, and in a slow process that lasted throughout the entire century, the border of Judah receded and was established north of the Hebron–Mareshah line.

---

167. This assumption is one of the factors that have led many scholars to attribute reductions in the territory of the Judean kingdom to the time before the destruction, particularly in the Negev; see, e.g., the views of Alt 1925a: 104–7; Noth 1954: 282–83, 288; Aharoni 1962b: 328, 332; Kochman 1980: 100–102.

Chapter 4

The Significance of Material Culture for Understanding the History of Judah under Babylonian Rule

4.1. The Study of the Babylonian Period in Archaeological Research of Palestine

Archaeologists generally have not focused their attention on the period when Babylon ruled Israel.[1] In summary works, scholars tend to deal with the Babylonian Period in brief, either as the concluding chapter of the Iron Age[2] or as the opening chapter of the Persian Period.[3] Many archaeologists see these 65 years[4] as the period when there was a genuine cultural gap in Israel.[5] The main

---

1. It is for good reason that many scholars still refer to Weinberg's summary work (1970); see, e.g., Stern 2000: 46–47 nn. 1, 3. Weinberg based his resume on the results of excavations conducted before the 1960s in Judah and surrounding areas, some of which are no longer relevant. Furthermore, Weinberg was unable to report on surveys carried out in Judah, Samaria, and Golan at the end of the 1960s. Since the publication of these important surveys (Kochavi 1972), the survey method has played an increasingly important role in archaeological discussion. Weinberg himself (1970: 215–16) was aware of this, and in his plan for excavating the sixth-century B.C.E. sites, he proposed a comprehensive survey that would have the objective of "learning about the material culture of Palestine in the sixth century (B.C.E.)."

2. On this subject, see, e.g., the concluding chapter in Kenyon's book (1960: especially 305–6); the last paragraph in Aharoni 1962b; the definitions proposed by Dothan (1985: 140–41); the last chapters of Miller and Hayes 1986; A. Mazar's short summary (1992: 548–49); and the last two chapters of Ahlström 1993. It is interesting to note that Ruth Amiran chose to end her book on the ancient pottery of the Holy Land (Amiran 1971) with the destruction of the First Temple, thus supporting the idea that this date signifies a break in the material culture. Wright (1961: 96) took a similar approach.

3. See, e.g., Stern (1982: 225), who writes: "Before summarizing our discussion of the finds of the Persian Period, we should note some features of the Babylonian Period which preceded it (586–538 B.C.)." For similar statements, in which the Babylonian Period is little more than a prelude to the Persian Period, see the encyclopedias of archaeology edited by Negev (1972), Avi-Yonah (1975), and Stern (1992 = NEAEHL), as well as Lapp 1970: 179–97. A recent exception to this approach can be found in Stern's recent book (2001); Stern discusses the material culture of Israel in the context of three eras—the Assyrian, Babylonian, and Persian Periods.

4. This interval is calculated as the time between the conquest of "Ḫatti-land" by the Babylonians in 605/4 B.C.E. and the fall of Babylon to Cyrus and his armies (539 B.C.E.).

5. See, e.g., the title of Stern's (1999: 19–20) article, "Is There a Babylonian Period in the Archaeology of the Land of Israel?" as well as his (2000) article "The Babylonian Gap." As will

contention is that many sites in Judah, in the Shephelah and along the coastal plain, in the Beer-Sheba–Arad Valleys, the Jordan Valley, the Jezreel Valley, and in Galilee were destroyed by the Babylonians and remained desolate until they were rebuilt during the Persian Period.[6] The fact that no administrative records of any kind have been uncovered from the time of Babylonian rule, coupled with the rarity of accounts of international trade, has been interpreted as evidence that the limited population that remained in the land during that time lived a wretched existence (Stern 1999: 19–20; 2000: 47; 2001: 309–31; Vanderhooft 1999: 110–12).

The sharp drop in economic activity and the lower quality of the government of the land during the Babylonian Period are facts that can be understood as consequences of two fundamental differences in the nature of imperial rule administered by Assyria and Babylon:[7] the difference in duration of the two empires and the difference in imperial administration that each empire brought to bear in its rule of Ḥatti-land.

The Babylonian Empire lasted for a total of approximately 70 years—from the great victory over Egypt and Assyria (609 B.C.E.) until the fall of Babylon at the hands of the Achaemenids (539 B.C.E.). We cannot accept Stern's comparison of the Babylonian Empire with the "positive" period of Assyrian rule in Palestine, which lasted a similar period of time, from the end of the eighth century B.C.E. to the last third of the seventh century B.C.E. (Stern 1999: 19–20; 2000: 45–51, 76; 2001: 307–8). Assyria had already begun to develop patterns of imperial administration in the ninth century B.C.E. and continued to refine them until the empire reached its high point in the *Pax Assyriaca* of the seventh century B.C.E. In contrast, the Babylonian Empire grew within a few years from a disjointed band of cities and tribes fighting for their survival and uniting to resist Assyrian hegemony to the status of a colossal empire. During the last years of Nabopolassar's rule and at the beginning of Nebuchadrezzar's reign, Babylon in-

be discussed later, this perception has had a powerful influence on modern archaeological research; see, e.g., Vanderhooft 1999: 106–7. Amiran (1975: 129) and N. L. Lapp (1975: 48, 137 n. 10) took a minority viewpoint by defining this period as one whose material culture provided it with its own raison d'être. Wright (1961: 96) also provided this period with a distinct label ("Iron Age IIC"), although he did not include it in his discussion (see Barkay 1993: 106–9). A distinct characterization of the material culture of this period was provided, in particular, at the excavations at Bethel by Sinclair (in Kelso et al. 1968) and at Gibeah (Tell el-Fûl) by N. L. Lapp (1981); see also the discussion following.

6. Albright (1932a: 103–4) had already reached this conclusion, and this is also the basic argument made by Weinberg (1970: 204–11), who was followed by Stern (1999: 19; 2000: 46–47; 2001: 308–11), Vanderhooft (1999: 106–7), and others. The impact of this perspective is noticeable in many studies; cf., e.g., Waldbaum and Magness 1997: 26. This point was well established archaeologically by Lehmann (1998), who identified a distinct break in the development of local pottery in Syria and Lebanon ca. 580 B.C.E.

7. For a characterization of the differences in policy between Assyria and Babylon and its significance for the border areas, see Naʾaman 1995a: 114–15; 2000: 42–43; Stager 1996a: 69; 1996b: *71; Vanderhooft 1999: 109.

herited large parts of the Assyrian Empire, without being afforded the time to develop effective and systematic tools of administration that would have enabled Babylon to make better use of the territories it had gained.[8]

A more significant difference between Assyria and Babylon was in the approach that shaped the establishment of authority and patterns of imperial government in the lands they each controlled. Massive destruction and two-way deportation of populations characterized the Assyrian conquest of the region in the second half of the eighth century B.C.E. Large populations were deported from their native lands to remote areas of the empire, and other populations were imported to replace them.[9] The goal of the Assyrians was to assimilate the nations under their control, to discard the national administrative frameworks that had existed for centuries, to crush national and religious spirit, and to create a homogenized population with an Assyrian orientation. In the first half of the seventh century B.C.E., the Assyrian kings, who then ruled the world, brought their imperial, military, and economic power to bear in order to rehabilitate the provinces and protectorate kingdoms, to build a well-ordered administrative and military system, and to establish an extensive network of trade.

The Babylonians, on the other hand, conquered vast territories: the inhabitants of these territories had already lost their national and cultural identity, and they had lived in areas that had had the status of a province since the second half of the eighth century B.C.E.; only in the periphery did there remain kingdoms with distinctive national characteristics. These kingdoms were relatively small and had well-defined political and religious centers, where the elite resided. Consequently, the Babylonians were able to establish their control over these centers or, alternately, to destroy them and deport only the elite.[10] When they did so, they left in place large sectors of the population, particularly the rural sector, and made no effort to rehabilitate the economy and administration.

No evidence has been found of imperial Babylonian construction projects anywhere in the empire or even of the building of a network of border fortresses and way-stations.[11] This absence may be explained by the relatively short time

---

8. We may also assume that the constant threat to Babylonian rule by the Egyptians in the southern part of Ḥatti-land hindered the Babylonians from clearly establishing their authority over the southwestern parts of the empire, which would have enabled them to develop these areas. This may well have been another factor in the sharp decline of the southern part of the Shephela and the coastal area and the total collapse of the border regions.

9. For an extensive discussion of the nature of Assyrian deportations, see Oded 1979.

10. See also Eph'al 1978: 81, with further literature; Vanderhooft 1999: 110–11; see also the summary by Lipschits 1999b.

11. Stern 1999: 20; 2000: 47; 2001: 307–11. The archaeological data presented below are not compatible with the reconstruction proposed by Graham (1984: 56); he argues that the Babylonians pursued a deliberate economic and agricultural policy in Judah. The data presented by Barstad (1996: 48–60) on the extent of continuity in the culture of Judah during the sixth century B.C.E. also seems exaggerated. For a critique of this, see Vanderhooft 1999: 106 and n. 179; Na'aman 2000: 43; and also see the discussion below.

that Babylon existed as an empire. However, it is more reasonable to conclude that, in contrast to the Assyrian kings, Nabopolassar and Nebuchadrezzar did not consider themselves rulers of the world and did not develop an imperial ideology like that of the Assyrian kings.[12] The consequence was that they did not invest great resources in establishing their rule in the areas they conquered; they did not formulate an imperial system of administration; and they were content to carry out periodic campaigns designed to ensure stability and the regular payment of taxes.[13]

This policy led to a drastic decline throughout the Levant in the economy and in trade, as well as in urban life. At the same time, we may assume that the Babylonians allowed local populations to carry on their lives and even develop, if they had the capability of doing so. Given these factors, the sharp drop in economic activity and decline in the quality of government in Palestine after the Babylonian conquest fits the context; however, it is unlikely that there was, at this time, a sharp, general decline in material culture throughout the country (see also Barkay 1992a: 372–73; 1993: 106–9; 1998: 25; A. Mazar 1992: 548).

The notion that there was a demographic and material-culture gap throughout the sixth century B.C.E. is too sweeping. Barkay points out the fallacy of this generalization when he writes:

> The date of the destruction 587/586 B.C.E. is not at all relevant to the history of most parts of the Land of Israel—the Galilee, the Samarian Hills, the coastal plain, the Negev, and eastern Transjordan . . . it seems that the destruction of the Temple and the fall of Jerusalem influenced modern scholarship which fixed the date of the end of the Iron Age according to a historical fact and not on the basis of the archaeological picture.[14]

Indeed, it appears that historical considerations are what stand behind the dating of destruction layers in sites in Judah to approximately 587/6 B.C.E.[15] As a result, there has been a lack of appropriate attention to the possibility that a large population continued to exist in Judah even after the destruction of Jerusalem.[16] Paradoxically, these associations of the archaeological evidence with

---

12. See the summary in Vanderhooft 1999: 9–59, with extensive literature there. See also the discussion above, §1.5 (pp. 29–31).

13. This is the view also taken by Stager (1996: 71*) and Vanderhooft (1999: 109, 111).

14. See Barkay 1998: 25. Compare also Barkay's previous comments: 1992a: 372; 1993: 106.

15. See, e.g., the statement by Shiloh 1989: 102; cf. Barstad 1996: 50–51. See also the examples Barstad provides, as well as additional literature.

16. One of the striking examples of this is in the analysis of the finds from the Benjamin survey (Magen and Finkelstein 1993). Even in this region, for which there is general consensus that most settlements continued to exist throughout the sixth century B.C.E., scholars have explained the survey results from an erroneous historical perspective: "this decline in settlement is undoubtedly related to the destruction of Judah in the early sixth century B.C.E." (1993: 27). For a critique of these conclusions and a fresh discussion of the material from the survey, see Lipschits 1999a: 180–84.

the date of Jerusalem's fall have provided material for historical studies, which in turn are based on dating the strata of the destruction, thus providing a historical profile of the Babylonian destruction throughout Israel.[17]

The archaeological data provide neither absolute dating of nor reasons for the destruction evident in most parts of the country. Historically, there is no imperative to attribute all destruction layers to the early days of the Babylonian presence. In fact, we should differentiate the fate of the Assyrian provinces in the northern and central parts of the land (as well as the provinces of Syria) from the fate of the smaller kingdoms in the southern coastal plain, the periphery of the hilly regions, and Transjordan. The former existed as provinces from the time of Assyrian rule,[18] while the latter were conquered by the Babylonians in the late seventh and early sixth century B.C.E. and were then annexed and turned into provinces.

It is unlikely that the Babylonian conquest had any effect on the Assyrian provinces in the central and northern parts of Palestine (Samaria, Megiddo, and Dor). There is evidence of continuity in the material cultural, demography, and settlement patterns in these regions[19] and no sign of the struggles that took place there during the shifts in power from Assyrian to Egyptian, Babylonian, and Persian control. It may well be that some of the imperial cities and administrative centers in these regions were sacked at some date during this time.[20] However, most of these regions show cultural continuity between the seventh and fifth centuries B.C.E., and it appears that the short duration of Babylonian rule did not leave any significant impression.[21]

In a discussion of the fate of the kingdoms that were subjugated by the Babylonians, we must be careful not to generalize but to evaluate independently the extent of continuity or discontinuity in the material culture of each region. For example, we cannot evaluate the small, relatively isolated kingdoms located on the edges of the hilly regions and Transjordan according to the same criteria

---

17. An example of this may be seen in Vanderhooft 1999: 106–7.

18. See above, §1.2, esp. pp. 3–8, for a review of this process and an extensive discussion of the borders of the provinces and the history of the region under Assyrian and Egyptian rule.

19. Compare the significant continuity in Dor from the Assyrian through the Persian Periods (Stern 1990a: 154), as well as the continuity that is evident in the results from the survey of Samaria (Zertal 1990: 11, 14–15).

20. A strong case may be made that some of the destruction of the administrative centers and imperial cities in these regions took place during the great upheaval that beset all of Syria–Palestine in the last third of the seventh century B.C.E., when Assyria retreated from its holdings and Egypt gradually established itself as the heir apparent. From the archaeological viewpoint, however, there is nothing to rule out the theory that some of this destruction took place during Babylonian rule or even in the early Persian Period.

21. See, e.g., Zertal 1990 and Stern 2001: 49–50 regarding the provinces of Samaria; and Stern 1990a regarding the provinces of Dor. I support A. Mazar's view (1992: 549) that in the Babylonian Period the coastal area began to flourish and that this process continued and even intensified in the Persian Period.

that we use for the coastal kingdoms, which could have continued to maintain
marine and commercial contact with Egypt and other parts of the Mediterranean basin. It is likely that the Babylonians found it more important to establish
a stable government and maintain strict supervision over the coastal region,
thus blocking the Egyptians from reestablishing their economic, political, and
military power in this area.

If we focus the discussion on Judah, the most conspicuous archaeological phenomenon after the destruction of Jerusalem is a sharp decline in urban life,[22]
which is in contrast to the continuity of the rural settlements in the highland of
Judah, particularly in the area between Hebron and the territory of Benjamin.[23]
This settlement pattern continued throughout the Persian Period when, despite
the rebuilding of Jerusalem and the restoration of its status as the capital of the
province, urban life remained insubstantial; settlement in Judah continued to be
largely rural.[24] The unavoidable conclusion is that a marked change in the nature of the settled areas took place during the Babylonian Period: Jerusalem was
destroyed, as were the border cities in the west of the kingdom, and as a result
there was a gradual collapse of the border regions in the southern and eastern sectors of Judah. In contrast, in the Benjamin region and in the highland of Judah,
there was no destruction, and some of the rural population remained in place.[25]
The center of gravity of settlement moved from the core to the periphery, and a
new pattern was created: the core was depleted and the nearby periphery
continued almost unchanged. The population of Benjamin and the highland of
Judah contained most of the inhabitants of the kingdom in the twilight of its
existence, and these inhabitants preserved the material culture that was known
from the predestruction period (see below, §§4.3.3, pp. 237–258).

The simplistic assertions often made regarding the cultural gap in Judah in
the sixth century B.C.E. apply primarily to the urban centers and culture but are

---

22. Barstad's perspective on this (1996: 61–82) cannot be sustained; see the criticisms of
Vanderhooft (1999: 110) and Na'aman (2000: 43). It is important to stress that this phenomenon characterizes the entire hill region in the Persian Period; see also Lipschits 1997a: 190–95;
2003: 326–38; 2004c.

23. On this subject, see Carter 1994: 106–45; Milevski 1996–97; Lipschits 1997a: 171–336;
1999a; 2004c (contra Faust 2003); Na'aman 2000: 43; Albertz 2003: 95–96. It is difficult to understand the archaeological/historical basis for Barstad's conclusions (1996: 47–48) regarding
the difference between the area north of Jerusalem and the area south of it.

24. A study of the material culture of the hill country during the Persian Period shows a surprising paucity of architectural finds, even at sites where there are rich remains of pottery and
other artifacts (Stern 1982: 47; Lipschits forthcoming). At some of the sites, not even vestiges
of buildings were found, and at others, the remains are so poor that scholars sometimes have
doubted whether they constitute evidence of any structure at all. For a detailed survey and discussion of the significance of the finds, see Lipschits 1997a: 190–95; 2003: 326–38; forthcoming.

25. Barkay 1992a: 372; 1998: 25; A. Mazar 1992: 548–49; Barstad 1996: 47, with further literature in n. 1; Lipschits 1999a: 155–90; 1999b: 467–87; 1999c: 115–23; 2001: 129–34; 2004c
(contra Faust 2003); Na'aman 2000: 43–44. On the demographic estimates, see the discussion
below.

not valid for the demographics or for the material culture of the rural population. Examination of the material culture of the Babylonian Period must focus on a few sites, particularly in the Benjaminite region, where there is clear continuity between the seventh and sixth centuries B.C.E., and on characterization of the culture that existed in these areas. At the same time, the thrust of research must shift from the studying of urban culture toward a more comprehensive study of the rural population, particularly in the region of Benjamin and the northern part of the Judean highlands (between Hebron and Bethlehem).

An examination of these regions should take into account the fact that the settlement patterns of the Babylonian Period continued into the Persian Period, resulting in a continuity of settlement and material culture from the seventh through the fifth centuries B.C.E. (contra the conclusions of Faust 2003, see Lipschits 2004c). We must treat the sixth century B.C.E. as an intermediate phase, linking the end of the Iron Age to the beginning of the Persian Period.[26] Gradual changes took place in the material culture of this period that are harbingers of the cultural markers of the Persian Period.[27]

That the sixth century B.C.E. was a phase intermediate between the Iron Age and the Persian Period will be demonstrated below through a discussion of the continuity in the pottery assemblages in Judah (§4.2). The consideration of the archaeological evidence of the Babylonian destruction (§4.3.2) alongside the archaeological evidence for the "remnant" in Judah (§4.3.3) will serve as the basis for reconstructing the process of destruction and collapse, on the one hand, and for reconstructing the areas where the population remained in place, on the other. Following this is a summary discussion of the demographic changes and the shifts in settlement pattern that took place in the various regions of Judah during these two periods (§4.4).

---

26. Despite the fact that Stern later argued for a cultural gap in Israel in the sixth century B.C.E., it was he (1982: 229) who first described the characteristics of the culture of this period. Additional descriptions have been provided by Barkay 1992a: 304–5, 372–73; A. Mazar 1992: 548–49; Lipschits 1997a: 171–98; 1999a; 1999c: 121–23; 2003; 2004c.

27. Stern (1982: 229) had noted this continuity early on and defined it cogently: "in the Babylonian period, despite the destruction of the Temple, the culture of the Israelite period continued. Some 70–80 percent of every pottery group from this time consists of vessels, which are usually attributed to the latest phase of the Israelite Period. The other vessels represent new types, which are considered to belong to the Persian Period. During the course of the sixth century B.C.E., an increase in the number of 'Persian' vessels and a decrease in the number of 'Israelite' vessels can be witnessed. By the end of the century, at the beginning of the Persian Period, the new types constitute the majority. It is therefore clear that a proper study of the finds of the Babylonian Period is impossible without the examination of entire groups or assemblages, and not of isolated finds, for while each vessel separately can be attributed to either the

4.2. Continuity in the Pottery Assemblages as a Link between the Iron Age and the Persian Period

The object of this section is to show the continuity of features in the pottery assemblages in Judah from the end of the Iron Age into the Persian Period and to highlight the role of the sixth century B.C.E. as an intermediate link connecting these two periods. The central thesis is that the characteristics of the well-known local pottery assemblages dating from the end of the Iron Age and from the Persian Period exhibit continuity and that, therefore, these patterns document an unbroken material cultural tradition in Judah from the end of the seventh century B.C.E. to the fifth and fourth centuries B.C.E.[28] This means that the population of Benjamin and the northern highland of Judah at the end of the Iron Age survived, even after the destruction of Jerusalem, and continued to produce the same pottery vessels. Local traditions of pottery production persisted throughout the sixth and early fifth centuries B.C.E., even though there are observable innovations and gradual changes that resulted from internal developments, interaction with both neighboring regions and neighboring cultures, and interaction with the cultures of the Persian Empire and Hellenistic civilization. Only in the mid-fifth century B.C.E. do the pottery repertoires begin to include types and forms considered to typify the local culture of the Persian Period.

The characteristics of the pottery assemblage from the end of the Iron Age in Judah are well known and clearly defined, and they date to the time between the mid-seventh century B.C.E. and the beginning of the sixth century B.C.E.[29] The distinction between the assemblages in Strata 3 and 2 at *Lachish* serves as a chronological and stratigraphic key.[30] The characteristic pottery vessels of the strata belonging to the destruction level at Lachish II are familiar from other sites in Judah, among them[31] the *City of David* (particularly Stratum 10 of

---

Israelite or the Persian Period, no typical characteristics have been distinguished so far for vessels of the Babylonian Period." On this subject, see also Stern 2001: 342–44.

28. For a discussion of similar continuity in the pottery assemblages of Edom, see Bienkowski 1995: 43–45, 54–62; 2001b: 198–213; also see Bartlett 1989: 163–74. For cultural continuity in Ammon, see the summary in Lipschits 2004b, with further literature.

29. Stratum 3 at Lachish was destroyed during Sennacherib's campaign (701 B.C.E.), and the common assumption is that Stratum 2 was built following a considerable interval of time in the early seventh century B.C.E. In light of this, the pottery assemblages typical of this stratum may be limited to the second half of the seventh and the beginning of the sixth centuries B.C.E. On this subject, see, e.g., Ussishkin 1977: 28–60; *NEAEHL* 3.863; Zimhoni 1990: 47; Stern 2001: 212–14.

30. The dating of Strata 3 and 2 at Lachish is based on Tufnell's excavation report (1953: 53–58). For a characterization and dating of the pottery assemblages from the two different stages, see Zimhoni 1990: 3–52; compare the pottery vessels of the late Iron Age (1990: 30–47). For a partial list of the pottery types, with a range of parallels, see Aharoni and Aharoni 1976: 76–90; N. L. Lapp 1981: 81–107; Ofer 1993: 2.48–50.

31. I will cite below only sites where complete pottery assemblages that may be correlated to Stratum 2 at Lachish have been found. My analysis is based primarily on the comparisons made by Zimhoni (1985; 1990) and other clear parallels. I will not refer to sites in which the

Area E and Strata 10C and 10B of Area G); Stratum 5a at *Ramat-Raḥel*; Stratum 3A at *Tell Beit Mirsim*; Strata 7–6 at *Tel Arad*; Stratum 6 at *Tel Ira*; and Stratum 5 at *En-Gedi* (Tel Goren).[32] Compare also the late Iron II corpus at Tell Gezer (Gitin 1996: 86–89).

The characteristics of the pottery vessels from the Persian Period in Judah are also well known and clearly defined.[33] Their distinctive shapes appear in the middle of the fifth century B.C.E.[34] There is no single clearly defined pottery

---

pottery assemblages are not clearly dated, sites in which there is a limited variety of pottery types and/or a small number of pottery vessels, or sites in which the pottery assemblage is problematic. Compare, e.g., the discussion in N. L. Lapp 1981: 81–88; and the summary table presented by I. Eshel 1995: 62, which mentions some of these problems.

32. *City of David*: See Shiloh 1984a: 9, 12, 14–16, 22–23, figs. 24:1, 30:2, and 34:2; Cahill and Tarler 1994: 34–45; I. Eshel 1995: 1–157. See also Zimhoni 1990: 38 and Ofer 1993: 2.24–25.

Ramat-Raḥel: See Aharoni 1955: 160–65; 1960a: 10–24; 1964: 23–35, 49–63; see also the review by Lipschits, 1997a: 253–56. The pottery assemblage from Ramat-Raḥel is important and central to this period, despite many problems in the stratigraphy of the site and the dating of the pottery vessels. On this subject, see also Zimhoni 1990: 42; Ofer 1993: 2.48–50.

Tell Beit Mirsim: Albright (1943: 40, 66) dated Stratum A1 at Tell Beit Mirsim to the ninth and eighth centuries B.C.E. and Stratum A2 to the seventh and beginning of the sixth century B.C.E.; he assigned most of the pottery from Stratum A to the second phase (1943: 45). A stratigraphic and chronological reevaluation of the pottery vessels from this stratum was carried out by Miriam and Yohanan Aharoni (Aharoni and Aharoni 1976: 76–90), who divided Stratum A2 into two subphases: the first subphase was destroyed in Sennacherib's campaign, and the pottery assemblages there match those in Stratum 3 at Lachish, Stratum 2 at Beer-Sheba, etc. The pottery assemblage from the second subphase parallels the pottery in Stratum 2 at Lachish and the other levels discussed here (Aharoni and Aharoni 1976: 73).

Tel Arad: See Zimhoni 1985: 63–90; Singer-Avitz 2002: 159–92, with further literature. On the dating of Strata 7–6 at Arad, see Herzog 1997: 172–79, with further literature.

Tel 'Ira: For a summary of the pottery finds from this stratum, see Freud 1999: 189–289, especially pp. 215–27. See also Zimhoni 1990: 38, 41; Ofer 1993: 2.27.

En-Gedi: See Mazar, Dothan, and Dunayevsky 1963: 24–58; Mazar and Dunayevsky 1964b: 143–52; 1966: 183–94; and see the remark by Aharoni and Aharoni (1976: 73–74) regarding the date of the destruction of this level. See the survey in Lipschits 1997a: 312–15; 2000: 32–35. Also see Zimhoni 1990: 42, 48; I. Eshel 1986–87: appendix, pp. 131–46.

33. Although Stern's study (1982: 93–136) is based on material that was known at the end of the 1960s and was updated with material that came to light in the 1970s, it continues to play a central role to this day. In effect, there can be no discussion of Persian Period pottery from Israel without referring to Stern's definitions of pottery types and the distinctions that he made; evidence for this may be found in the works of A. Mazar 1981: 229–49; Barkay 1985: 266–82, 298–305; Hizmi and Shabtai 1993: 74–79; Ofer 1993: 2.50–51. See also Carter's view (1999: 54). The chief problem with Stern's study is the scope of the discussion, both geographically (a discussion of the pottery of all the various regions of Palestine without considering political, ethnic, cultural, and other differences among the various regions within the country) as well as chronologically (a discussion of the entire period from the end of the Iron Age to the Hellenistic Period, while ignoring more narrow chronological demarcations, even while suggesting that the appearance and shape of the pottery vessels was gradually evolving, and sometimes even stating it outright).

34. Carter's attempt (1999: 116–18, as the basis for his theory throughout the book) to divide the material culture of the Persian Period into two stages cannot be sustained; his division is between the First Persian Period (538–450 B.C.E.) and the Second Persian Period (450–332 B.C.E.). Even if the historical logic behind this division is apparent, there is no archaeological

assemblage in Judah that may be used as the basis for defining the characteristics of pottery vessels from this period. However, for this purpose we may use, as a base, a composite of the archaeological picture that emerges from several sites in which pottery assemblages are clearly dated to the Persian Period: Stratum 4 at En-Gedi, Stratum 9 of area G at the City of David, Stage II at Jabel Nimrah, the early stage at Stratum 1 at Beth-zur, Stratum 4b at Ramat-Rahel, Bethany, Stratum 1 at Mizpah, Stratum 1 at Lachish, and the last stage of settlement at Jericho (Tell es-Sultan).35

basis for it, and Carter does not even try to define differences in the material culture of his two periods. Furthermore, even the division of the strata and sites into his two time periods is not properly based on archaeological data; only at a few sites are there pottery assemblages on which Carter can base archaeological discussion. As discussed above, pottery from the Persian Period evolved in a process that began in the sixth century B.C.E., and the distinction between pottery assemblages that precede the "classical" Persian Period of the mid-fifth century B.C.E. and the later pottery assemblages seems artificial and not well grounded.

35. En-Gedi: This stratum was dated to the period between the end of the sixth or beginning of the fifth centuries and the end of the fifth or beginning of the fourth centuries B.C.E. See Mazar and Dunayevsky 1966: 188–89; 1967: 137–38; Stern 1982: 38–39; N. L. Lapp 1981: 88; B. Mazar 1986: 86. Remarkably rich material remains have been attributed to this stratum, including seal impressions, local pottery characteristic of the fifth and fourth centuries B.C.E., and imported Attic vessels (Mazar, Dothan, and Dunayevsky 1963: 59; pls. D:2; E:2; G:1–2; 1966: 38–39). Structure 234 yielded an abundance of installations, pottery and stone vessels, seal impressions, and five groups of Attic pottery that were dated to the fifth century B.C.E., some from the beginning of the century but most from the third quarter (Mazar and Dunayevsky 1964b: 148; 1966: 188).

City of David: As at many other sites, at Jerusalem, too, excavations of the early twentieth century uncovered much from the Persian Period (pottery vessels and seal impressions). However, this material was not clearly linked to any specific stratum or architectural remains (Macalister and Duncan 1926: 188–201; Crowfoot and Fitzgerald 1929: 67–68; Duncan 1931: 2.139–42). For our purposes, the most important excavations are those carried out by Kenyon (1961–68) and by Shiloh (1978–85). See the first publications by Shiloh (1979b: 170); Shiloh and Kaplan (1979: 49); and see also the summary by Cahill and Tarler (1994: 31–35). The new excavations of the City of David have uncovered much from the Persian Period that also is related to architectural remains. The·most important discovery was found in Area G, where Shiloh identified a distinct stratum (Stratum 9) on top of Stratum 10A (the stratum of the Babylonian destruction) and under Strata 8–7, which are dated to the Hellenistic Period (Shiloh 1979b: 168; 1984: 23; Shiloh and Kaplan 1979: 45). In addition to "clean" ceramic material that belongs to the Persian Period, two thin walls were assigned to this stratum. Support walls and layers of fill were also discovered in Areas E-1, D-1, and D-2, and additional segments of wall were also uncovered in Area D (Shiloh 1979a: 16; 1983: 130). On the finds in Area D-1, see Ariel 2000: 59–62, and on the finds in Area D-2, see Ariel 1990: 99–100, 111–13. Despite the relatively large amount of material remains, the information available to us about the Persian Period is still very scant, and it is impossible to characterize the nature of this occupation. The stratigraphic context of the major discovery found outside of the fortification line built on the rock at the top of the eastern slope (Shiloh 1984a: 12, 23; 1984b: 57; Kenyon 1974: 182–85) has not been proven. Kenyon identified Nehemiah's wall with the remains in the upper portion of Trench I, which was excavated in 1923–25 by Macalister and Duncan (1926: fig. 11), who defined the remains as the "Jebusite wall" and the "Tower of David." The new dating of these structures as a Hasmonean fortification and identifying a segment of the adjacent wall that was founded on the bedrock at the top of the slope have confirmed the course of Nehemiah's wall (Kenyon 1963: 15 and pl. 7:b; 1964b: 45–46; 1966: 81–83; 1967a: 111; 1967b: 69; 1974: 181–

There is a gap of 150 years between the "classic" pottery vessels of the late Iron Age and the "classic" pottery vessels of the Persian Period. During this time, the population of Judah dwindled; Jerusalem and its environs were dealt a mortal blow; and the settlement array collapsed in the Judean Desert, the Jordan

---

87). In the eastern section, midden rubbish tipped over the wall, accumulating against the debris and, according to Kenyon (1967a: 107, 111), contained pottery sherds from the fifth and fourth centuries B.C.E. These pottery vessels have many parallels in the new excavations in the City of David as published by Shiloh (1984: 20). It must be noted that the date assigned to the pottery assemblage from this stratum is very general (the sixth through the fourth centuries B.C.E.), and the published assemblage is not large enough for study and comparison. For additional problems concerning the finds dated to the Persian Period in Jerusalem, see the discussion below.

Jabel Nimrah: See Hizmi 1998: 14–18; Hizmi and Shabtai 1993: 74–79. Note that according to Hizmi and Shabtai there are also pottery vessels from the sixth century B.C.E. at this site.

Beth-zur: No distinct stratum from the Persian Period was found. The site is located on terraces and, thus, most of the pottery was found in unclear stratigraphic contexts (Sellers and Albright 1931: 4; Sellers 1933: 10, 32). Based on the excavation season of 1931, Sellers and Albright (1931: 8–9; see also Sellers 1933: 43) maintained that there was a gap between Iron II and the Persian and Hellenistic Period occupations. This claim was based on the dating of the pottery and the identification of a gap lasting from the beginning of the sixth century to the fifth century B.C.E., as well as on an historical consideration—that the destruction of the Iron Age stratum took place soon after the destruction of Jerusalem (but cf. the alternative view offered by Sellers 1933: 10 and Funk 1958: 14). These conclusions were altered after the excavation season of 1957, when the Babylonian destruction was reidentified (Sellers 1968: 28, 54). The hypothesis that at least in Area II there was a large gap between the sixth and second centuries B.C.E. gained some credence (1968: 29, 54–69). In contrast to this opinion, P. W. Lapp (1970: 185) dated the pottery that was uncovered at Reservoir 44 to the last quarter of the sixth century B.C.E., and this date was also supported by N. L. Lapp (1981: 86–87). Thus, it appears that settlement on the site was renewed at the end of the sixth century B.C.E. and that the gap between the end of the Iron Age and the Persian Period was shorter than the original excavators of the site had estimated.

Ramat-Raḥel: There is no clearly defined stratum from the Persian Period at Ramat-Raḥel. However, many objects dating to this period were uncovered; conspicuous among these was the large number of seal impressions of various types dated to the Persian and Hellenistic Periods, as well as a rich assemblage of pottery, which includes several sherds of Attic vessels and perhaps also Cypriote vessels (Aharoni 1964: pl. F:1–3). On the finds attributed to Stratum 4b, see Aharoni 1955: 165–74; 1960a: 14–28; 1964: 19–23, 38, 42–48; *NEAEHL* 4.1483. Most of these finds were discovered in fills or scattered throughout the site and were dated by Aharoni to the late Persian Period. Nonetheless, Stern (1982: 35–36) has dated the earlier pottery vessels to the beginning of the fifth century B.C.E. and hypothesized that the assemblage reflects a much longer time-span. N. L. Lapp (1981: 87–88) has even suggested that some of the pottery found in Cistern 484 may be dated earlier, to the late sixth century B.C.E., despite the fact that Aharoni (1964: 18) dated it to the late Persian Period. In any case, this is an intriguing pottery assemblage and has not been dated with sufficient reliability to alter the chronological profile of the site in any significant way.

Bethany: Pottery and seal impressions dating to the Persian Period were not found within a clear stratigraphic context and cannot be associated with specific architectural elements. It is very difficult to date this pottery assemblage, which was found mainly in a fill level that was apparently created in the Middle Ages (Locus 65). This has led to serious confusion and sweeping generalizations in chronological assignment of the finds. On this subject, see, e.g., the conclusions of Saller 1957: 222, 237; cf. the critique by Barkay 1985: 303. Among the seal impressions, which were not precisely dated (1985: 192–96; see the critique by Carter 1991: 138) to

Valley, the Dead Sea region, the Negev, and the southern Shephelah. Neverthe-less, a large Judean population continued to subsist in the Judean highlands, es-pecially in the region north of Beth-zur, as well as in the territory of Benjamin. This population maintained its material culture, and because of this it is very dif-ficult for archaeologists to distinguish and define this culture. As a result, no clear-cut definition of the sixth-century B.C.E. material culture has emerged and the development of the pottery types in the course of more than 200 years of Persian rule has not been adequately described.[36] This lack of adequate defini-

---

be noted are the three *yhwd* seal impressions (Saller 1957: 192–93, fig. 37, and pl. 111:b, c) and an impression with a geometric design (1957: 195–96, pl. 111:d).

Mizpah: Among the finds dated to the Persian Period is a bronze coin that Albright and Boyse dated to 406–393 B.C.E. (McCown 1947: 229) and that Bellinger dated to the fifth to fourth centuries B.C.E. (Stern 1982: 32); seal impressions of various types; and a fragment of a limestone incense altar. See McCown 1947: 154–55, 164–72, 174, 227, 236–37, 259, 275, and pls. 1:102, 14:56–57, 84; Avigad 1958c; Cross 1969a: 19–20; Stern 1982: 31–32. Most of the finds attributed to the Persian Period were found in pits scattered throughout the site. Two of the pits are very important because they contained a more homogenous assemblage (Stern 1982: 31–32): pit no. 304, dated to the years between 600 and 450 B.C.E., and pit no. 361, dated to the late fifth and early fourth centuries B.C.E. On the finds from the first pit, see Wampler 1941: 31–36; McCown 1947: 135. A very important find, discovered in the middle of this pit, is an ostracon bearing six letters. Albright (in McCown 1947: 31–32 n. 9) proposed that the os-tracon be read [*b*]*n mrsrz*[*r*]. The date proposed by Albright and Torrey is the eighth or seventh century B.C.E., whereas Wampler tends to date it to the seventh century B.C.E. (1941: 31). An-other find from this pit is an amphora dated to 540–520 B.C.E. and two fragments of kylix dated to 490–420 B.C.E. (Wampler 1941: 31). On the finds in the second pit, see Wampler 1941: 36–43; McCown 1947: 137. The few fragments of Greek pottery found in the second pit were dated to ca. 530 or 500 B.C.E. (Stern 1982: 206). Additional finds include the *mwṣh* seal impression and another seal impression, the content of which was not reported (Wampler 1941: 36). I also consider two other pits to be very important: pit no. 183, the second stage of which was dated between 450 and 200 B.C.E. (McCown 1947: 132–33), and pit no. 191, which contained finds that were dated by the excavators to no later than the end of the sixth century B.C.E. (1947: 133–34). Conspicuous among the finds dated to the Persian Period are fragments of Attic pot-tery vessels dated between 500 and 420 B.C.E., as well as a fragment of a Clazomenaen vessel dated ca. 540–530 B.C.E. (McCown 1947: 175–79, 304, and tables 59–60).

Lachish: On Stratum I at Lachish, see the detailed discussion of Fantalkin and Tal (forth-coming).

Jericho: The vestiges of a small village dated to the fifth and fourth centuries B.C.E. had al-ready been uncovered at Jericho by Sellin and Watzinger. The pottery consisted of imported Attic vessels and fragments of vessels decorated with wedge-shaped and reed impressions; ad-ditional finds include ten *yhwd* stamp impressions and one stamp impression of a lion (Sellin and Watzinger 1913: 79–82, 147–48; fig. 186; pls. 1, 3, 42). See Stern's assessment (1982: 38) regarding the dating by Sellin and Watzinger of pottery vessels from this period. The excava-tions conducted by Garstang (1930–36) as well as those by Kenyon (1952–58) add only scant information about the Persian Period (Kenyon 1964c: 201). The major find uncovered in these excavations was the *yhwd/ᵓwryw* stamp impression (see Hammond 1957). Following Stern (1982: 38), we should assume that a settlement existed at Jericho in the fifth and fourth centu-ries B.C.E., but it is difficult to garner much information about the characteristics of the Judean pottery of this era from the limited pottery assemblages.

36. Inadequate knowledge of the ceramic finds from the Persian Period is striking at Tell en-Naṣbeh, where most loci were assigned a very broad time span (see, e.g., the list of loci in

tion has created a phenomenon such that when sites lacked archaeological evidence of the Babylonian destruction and had an apparent continuity in material culture, no distinction was made among the strata from the end of the Iron Age, the Babylonian Period, or the Persian Period.[37] Even at sites where archaeological evidence of the Babylonian destruction was found, finds from the Babylonian, Persian, and sometimes even Hellenistic Periods were not separated. The settlement continuity that prevailed throughout the transitions from Babylonian rule to Persian rule and, later, to the Ptolemaic and Seleucid Periods has made it quite difficult to distinguish these periods.[38]

The major purpose of this section is to show the continuity between the pottery assemblages familiar to us from the end of the Iron Age and the assemblages from the Persian Period and to show that this continuity strengthens our proposal that the population of the region also continued from the end of the Iron Age into the Persian Period. It seems to me that an examination of most types of pottery manufactured in Judah during the Persian Period shows that they developed from typical Iron Age forms. Examples of this cultural continuity follow, using several key pottery types to identify uninterrupted development from the Iron Age to the Persian Period, though in intermediate stage, namely, the Babylonian Period.[39]

Wampler 1947: 120–24). A review of the pottery plates shows that in many instances the authors of the report were unable to differentiate pottery of the beginning of Iron Age II from pottery dated to the end of the Iron Age and the Persian Period. Another example of problematic ceramic analysis may be seen in the debate over the dating of the Persian Period assemblages from Gezer. Albright (1932b: 76) argued that Macalister had erred in dating the pottery assemblage to the Persian Period (Gezer I: xxi; Gezer II: 224–25; Gezer III: pls. 185–87). In Albright's opinion, most of the pottery vessels should be dated to the eighth and seventh centuries B.C.E. and have comparanda from other cities in the Shephelah, where they were dated similarly by Bliss and Macalister. Stern, on the other hand, argued that, apart from some pottery that belongs to the late Iron Age, Macalister was correct in his dating.

37. This is particularly striking at sites in the Benjaminite region, such as Bethel, where Sinclair (in Kelso et al. 1968: 75–76) noted that the site continued to exist until the mid-sixth century B.C.E. At Gibeon (el-Jib) and Gibeah (Tell el-Fûl), too, Wright (1965: 167) dated the destruction 50 years later and placed it at the end of the sixth century B.C.E. See the discussion of the pottery assemblage by Lapp (1965: 6), which served as the basis for these conclusions.

38. See, e.g., the broad definition given to "the Persian-Hellenistic Period" at Gezer (500 B.C.E. to 100 C.E.); to "the late Judahite Period" at Jericho; to "the Hellenistic Period" at Beth-zur (between the destruction of the First Temple and the Roman Period); to the wide-ranging manner in which all of the meager remnants at Gibeon between the sixth century B.C.E. and the first century C.E. are characterized; to the preliminary dating of Stratum 4 at Ramat-Raḥel (between the fifth century B.C.E. and the first century C.E.), etc. Furthermore, many scholars entertain strong doubts about the internal division of these strata. See the surveys on these subjects below, particularly for Stratum 4 at Tell el-Fûl; the definition of the finds from the Persian Period at Gibeon; the debate over the duration of the Persian Period at Tell en-Naṣbeh; analysis of the two stages of settlement at Bethel; and more.

39. Due to the limited focus of this study, the discussion will not be extend to the entire pottery assemblage, despite the fact that continuity in the material culture is also represented in other types of pottery. This is a subject that would require a separate, extensive study.

1. *Large "Persian" bowls* characterized by a thick ring rim, labeled by Stern as type B-5 (Stern 1982: 96–98; cf. the discussion by Sinclair in Kelso et al. 1968: 71–72). The developmental stages of the Iron Age bowls have been discussed at length;[40] because the pottery from the end of the Iron Age has been analyzed and described quite well, it has become clear that the prototypes of these bowls go back to the eighth century B.C.E. (Lachish III) and that this "family" of bowls continued to develop until the Persian Period (see Zimhoni 1990: 9–10; pls. 3, 16–21; Ofer 1993: 2.46–48, 50, with further comparisons and literature). The major difference between classic "Persian bowls" and earlier archetypes from the Iron Age is the trumpet base.[41] The shape of the rim does not manifest any major changes.[42]

2. *Cooking pots* characterized by a globular, sack-shaped body and a short, wide neck represent an intermediate type between the Iron Age cooking pots and the Hellenistic style.[43] The indicator type for our purposes is labeled by Stern as type A (1982: 100), and it is the closest to the Iron Age type. It is primarily found in the south (Tell en-Naṣbeh, Ramat-Raḥel, Lachish, Beth-Shemesh, and En-Gedi); and a smaller version of it, without handles, exists alongside it (type G, according to Stern 1982: 102). We may conclude that type B, which has an everted ledge rim characteristic of the Persian Period, appeared only at a later stage during the Persian Period (from the fifth century B.C.E. onward; Stern 1982: 100).

3. *Hole-mouth jars* characterized by a globular sack-shaped body and an everted rim are in many respects a continuation of the Iron Age hole-mouth vessels. Examples of this type are characteristic of Strata 3–2 at Lachish, though they possess body shapes that are characteristic of the Persian Period (type B according to Stern 1982: 102–3, with further literature; Ofer 1993: 2.50). We may accept the conclusion that this hole-mouth jar is indicative of the Persian

---

40. For discussion and basic bibliography on this subject, see Stern's discussion (1982: 96–98, 264 nn. 2–11); he supports dating the early type of this pottery vessel, with the flat base, to the seventh century.

41. Stern (1982: 96) calls this base "a high ring base," but both terms refer to the same form. See also Sinclair (in Kelso et al. 1968: 70).

42. See Stern 1982: 96–98; Ofer 1993: 2.51, with further comparisons and literature. Other types of bowls found in pottery assemblages associated with the "Persian bowls" may be connected to the Persian Period. A striking example of this is the wide, flat, small bowl with the straight, ledge-like rim projecting outward. These small bowls have been labeled by Stern as type A-3 (1982: 94, and fig. 114). These bowls have parallels at Tell en-Naṣbeh (Wampler 1947: pl. 57:1293–98); Gibeon (Pritchard 1964a: pl. 48:4); Ramat-Raḥel (Aharoni 1964: fig. 12: 6, 9); Gezer (Gitin 1990b: 233–34); and the City of David (DeGroot in Ariel 2000: 98). See also Ofer 1993: 2.51; and cf. the discussion of Bennett and Blakely (1989: 196–201) for the characteristics of the Persian Period mortaria from Tell el-Hesi.

43. See Stern 1982: 100–102, with further literature. Compare the Persian cooking pot with the cooking pot that developed at the end of the Iron Age, and see the examples from Stratum 3 at Lachish (Zimhoni 1990: 11–12, and fig. 5).

Period, but Stern's type A hole-mouth jar (1982: 102), with its long, cylindrical body, pointed base, and a pair of handles extending from the shoulder to the side (cf. Wampler 1947, pls. 4:56, 5:71) belongs to the beginning of the period and is closer to hole-mouth jars of the Iron Age (Stern 1982: 102). It may well be that "intermediate types" (that is, intermediate between the Iron Age and the Persian Period) are to be found in loci that are correctly dated to the sixth century B.C.E. at Tell el-Fûl (N. L. Lapp 1981: 88–89).

4. *Store jars* typically have an ovoid or sack-shaped body, convex base, narrow neck, rounded shoulder, thick everted rim, and four loop handles that extend from the shoulder to the body (Stern type A [1982: 103]). These jars are a development from the *lmlk* jars and exhibit features characteristic of this type at the end of the Iron Age in Judah.[44] These formal characteristics continue into the Persian Period (especially the sack-shaped body, everted rim, either a ring or a convex base, etc.), and they were widespread only within the province of Judah.[45] The distribution of this jar type and the fact that it is an indicator form for the period lie behind Ofer's statement that this jar is "the most typical pottery vessel of this [= the Persian] period in the survey . . . and represents the major criterion and sometimes the only criterion to identify it" (Ofer 1993: 2.50). We may conclude that jars of this kind began to appear in Judah in the sixth century B.C.E. Later in the Persian Period, jars with a more-pronounced globular sack-shaped body and with two to four handles—sometimes with no handles at all (types B and C, according to Stern)[46]—gradually replaced this type of jar.

5. *Large pilgrim flasks* are characterized by an everted rim, a balloon-shaped body composed of two nonsymmetrical parts, and a narrow, short neck with two short handles extending to the shoulder (Stern type B).[47] This type developed from the flask known from the end of the Iron Age (some of the latter have been found in strata that have been called Persian, though the evidence is not compelling; see Stern type A).[48] The distribution of these pilgrim flasks is limited to the southern part of Israel, and the Yehud province constitutes the major distribution area.[49] The type A pilgrim flasks can be dated to the sixth century B.C.E.

---

44. See the descriptions and parallels presented by N. L. Lapp 1981: 88–90.

45. N. L. Lapp 1981: 103, with a reference to the parallel pottery types.

46. See Stern 1982: 103–4; N. L. Lapp 1981: 89–90, with a reference to the parallel pottery types. My discussion here makes no reference to the jars typical of all parts of Israel in the Persian Period. For our purposes, the jars that are characteristic and important for our discussion were labeled by Stern (1982: 104–10) as types D and E and a portion of types F and G (see also Ofer 1993: 2.50).

47. See Stern 1982: 115. For parallels to these pilgrim flasks and for literature, see Barkay 1985: 280–81.

48. See Stern 1982: 114–15, and compare with the pilgrim flasks published by Amiran 1971: 332 and pl. 95.

49. Stern 1982. The pilgrim flasks from Tell el-Fûl must be added to this list (N. L. Lapp 1981: table 59: 1–5).

and type B to the sixth to fourth centuries B.C.E.;[50] it is likely that Stern type C (1982: 115), which includes a degenerative form of Iron Age pilgrim flasks, developed from this type. On this subject, compare the pilgrim flasks found at Jabel Nimrah.[51]

6. *Jugs* characteristic of the Babylonian-Persian Period in Judah are a development of the jugs familiar to us from the Iron Age, with adaptations in features such as the globular sack-shaped body, everted rim, suspended or loop handles, and disc base. This typical jug (Stern type B [1982: 115–16]) was widely distributed primarily within Yehud province. Its date is based on Paul Lapp's analysis (1970: 179–97) and on the work of Nancy Lapp during the last season of excavations at Tell el-Fûl.[52] This jug probably belongs to the sixth century B.C.E., the time to which the globular sack-shaped body jug (Stern type A [1982: 115]) belongs and which to a great extent recalls the typical pilgrim flasks mentioned earlier.[53] Most of the other jugs discussed by Stern (1982: 115–18) seem to be later, and they first appeared no earlier than the fifth century B.C.E. Most of these jugs, except for type C, are not reliable indicators of the Persian Period in Judah. Although they do appear at several sites within the province, they appear to be more characteristic of the coastal areas (particularly types G and H)[54] and Samaria (type F), or else they are variations of Cypriote vessels (types I and J; Stern 1982: 116–18).

7. The features of the *juglets* of this period are quite similar to those of the jugs. They also evidence continuity of types from the Iron Age, with gradual but increasing adaptation to the "classic" characteristics of Persian Period vessels. This is conspicuous in the *dipper juglets* with a convex base (Stern type A-1).[55] The globular sack-shaped body juglets (types A and B) are characteristic of the Persian Period and replace the elliptical-body or cylindrical-body vessels (type

---

50. See Stern 1982: 114–15; Barkay 1985: 280–81. There is a difference between the Hebrew and the English versions of Stern's book: in the Hebrew version, he dates type A to the sixth century B.C.E. and type B to the mid-sixth to the beginning of the fourth centuries B.C.E.; in the English version, he dates type A to the mid-sixth to the fourth centuries B.C.E. and type B to the end of the fifth and the fourth centuries B.C.E. In my opinion, the earlier date in the Hebrew version has better support.

51. See Hizmi and Shabtai 1993: 78 and pl. 2:6–7. For a discussion of the development of Iron Age pilgrim flasks in the sixth century B.C.E., see Amiran 1975: 12–13 and also compare the flask published by A. Mazar 1985: ill. 11:3.

52. See N. L. Lapp 1981: 117. Compare also the finds from Bethel, and see the parallels published by Sinclair (Kelso et al. 1968: 70, 72–73).

53. On this type of jug, see also the discussion by Barkay 1985: 274–75, with further parallels and discussion.

54. On the jugs from group H, see Barkay's comment (1985: 270).

55. Stern 1982: 119, with discussion and parallels. The coastal distribution of the flat-based juglets classified by Stern (pp. 119–20) as types A-2-a and A-2-b differentiate them from the juglets found in the hill country. Apparently, a Cypriote prototype reached Judah only in the fifth or fourth centuries B.C.E. (pp. 119–20), but the globular sack-shaped juglet appears no earlier than the fourth century B.C.E.

A-1-a).[56] The latter, on the other hand, duplicate the Iron Age juglets very precisely, and it is highly unlikely that we may date their appearance later than the sixth century B.C.E.[57] In the case of the *globular juglets*, too, we may differentiate between two different types in terms of distribution and chronology. Convex-based juglets with wide, flaring rim (Stern type B-1 [1982: 120]) are typical primarily of Judah and are a continuation of the globular juglets of the Iron Age, first appearing in the sixth century B.C.E.[58] Support for this may be found in the subtype labeled type B-3 by Stern (1982: 120); this type has a spout added to the body, either at the center or side. This subtype also appears only in the highlands, and we may conclude that it is later than the basic type.[59] A similar phenomenon exists in the case of the *perfume juglets* (Stern 1982: 122). In my opinion, it is difficult to prove that the perfume juglets typical of the end of the Iron Age continued after the destruction of Jerusalem,[60] even though this is a logical conclusion. The type dated to the Persian Period (Stern 1982: 122, type C-2 [1982: 122]) preserved the basic Iron Age type, adapting the globular sack-shaped body, lifting the handle, and rolling up the rim. This type, too, is limited in distribution to Judah and has not been conclusively dated.[61] Other juglets found in the Yehud province (types C-3–8) belong to the coastal types and cannot be connected to Yehud itself or relied on as a chronological or territorial indicator.[62]

8. Among the *bottles*, there are three major types.

The *alabastron-shaped bottle* (Stern 1982: 125, type B [1982: 125]) has the globular sack-shaped, elongated, narrow body, two degenerated knob handles, and a wide outward-flaring rim.[63] These bottles, too, are a continuation of the

---

56. Compare with the pottery assemblage from Stratum 3b at Tell el-Fûl, which is dated to the sixth century B.C.E. (N. L. Lapp 1981: pl. 60:8).

57. The juglets discovered by Barkay (1985: 271–72) in the repository of the tomb near the Scottish Church in Jerusalem are of great importance in this regard. This find supports Stern's dating of this juglet type to the sixth century B.C.E.

58. Compare also the finds at Tell el-Fûl (N. L. Lapp 1981: 194, pl. 37:1–4; 237, pl. 61:1–8). The juglets found in the repository of tomb 25 at Ketef Hinnom may be added to this list (Barkay 1985: 270–71), as well as the juglets from Jabel Nimrah (Hizmi and Shabtai 1993: 78 and pl. 2:2–3).

59. Similar juglets with a flat or disc base, labeled by Stern as type B-2 (1982: 120), are typical primarily of the coastal region (with some examples in the hill country and even in Judah). They appear relatively late and may have developed from the Cypriote juglets that are familiar from the sixth century B.C.E. onward.

60. It should be noted that the juglets presented by Stern as examples of type C-1 (1982: 122) are not dated with any certainty.

61. Stern dated this type to the second part of the Persian Period (1982: 122). In my opinion, this dating is not well established, and the first appearance of these juglets may be dated back even to the end of the sixth century B.C.E. The earlier date is corroborated by the many juglets found in the repository of tomb 25 at Ketef Hinnom (Barkay 1985: 272).

62. Compare these juglets with the two juglets from Ketef Hinnom published by Barkay (1985: 272).

63. Additional parallels for bottles of these types are adduced by Barkay 1985: 278–79.

type from the end of the Iron Age, and their presence is limited to the late seventh to the fifth centuries B.C.E.[64] Their distribution is restricted to the area around Jerusalem (Gibeah, Gibeon, Mizpah, Abu-Ghosh, Jerusalem itself, Beitar, Tell el-Fûl, and a grave found between Bethlehem and Jerusalem). It is interesting to note that this same type of bottle has been found near Rabbath-Ammon as well (see Barkay 1985: 279; Macalister 1915: pl. 2).

Carrot-shaped bottles have a short neck, thick and prominent ring rim, and pointed base (Stern 1982: 125, type C). These bottles have been discussed widely in the research literature[65] and are considered one of the characteristic types of the Babylonian and Persian Periods. The accepted explanation is that the archetype of these bottles (with brown painted horizontal bands) originated in Assyria, beginning in the mid-seventh century B.C.E. The early type appears in Judah by the mid-sixth century B.C.E. and is replaced by undecorated bottles that are more crudely shaped and have knife-shaved sides. Stern (1982: 127) argued that the later type must be dated to the period between the mid-sixth and the fourth centuries B.C.E.; however, I believe Barkay's date is preferable, limiting this type to the end of the seventh through the sixth century B.C.E. (1985: 277–78). These bottles have been similarly dated by N. L. Lapp (1981: 92) on the basis of the Tell el-Fûl excavations. It is noteworthy that these bottles are found primarily around Jerusalem, with various other types appearing on the periphery of the Yehud province (see Barkay 1985: 277–78).

Small bottles with round bodies have a round or pointed base, short or narrow neck, and thick everted rim (labeled by Stern [1982: 127] as type F). Arguments for their Assyrian origin have proved inconclusive; however, they appear in assemblages that are clearly dated to the sixth century B.C.E.[66] Their distribution is limited to Judah, and the relatively large quantity that has been excavated and their distribution throughout most of the Persian Period makes them one of the indicator pottery forms of the Yehud province during the Babylonian and Persian Periods.[67]

9. *Open lamps* are one of the characteristic finds of the Persian Period and are a continuation of the lamps with elevated disc base that are typical of the late Iron Age. It is fair to assume that the lamps with the elevated disc base continued into the sixth century B.C.E. but, on the basis of Stern's investigation at En-Gedi, this lamp-form did not continue into the fifth and fourth centuries

---

64. These bottles were most common in the sixth century B.C.E. (Stern 1982: 125; Barkay 1985: 279–80).

65. For discussion, comparison, and literature on this subject, see Stern 1982: 125–27; Barkay 1985: 299–300.

66. See Lapp 1970, fig. 1:4; N. L. Lapp 1981: pl. 61:15. Compare the conclusions reached by Hadley (1984: 52) regarding the finds in the repository of tomb 25 at Ketef Hinnom.

67. See the parallels cited by Barkay 1985: 276–77 and his remarks on the chronology of these bottles.

B.C.E. (see Stern 1982: 128–29). Lamps with elevated disc base were replaced by lamps with wide rims, a flat or slightly rounded base, and a sharply pinched wick-hole.[68] This successor lamp appears chiefly in two sizes: (1) large, flat lamps with a large, flat base, straight, everted rim, and very narrow wick-hole; and (2) medium-sized lamps with a rounded body, flat base, erect rim, and a less-pinched wick-hole that is wider than that of the large lamp.[69] These two forms seem to reflect functional variations rather than chronological development (see Stern 1982: 127–28).

On the basis of the identification of these key types, we may conclude that during the sixth and early fifth centuries B.C.E. Judahite pottery began to display new features in terms of shape, processing technique, and material.[70] The sixth century B.C.E. was a transitional period (see Sinclair, in Kelso et al. 1968: 70; N. L. Lapp 1981: 86), and it is apparent that, from a theoretical standpoint, a basis exists for distinguishing the pottery of this period from both the prior and the subsequent periods.[71] Nevertheless, familiarity with the assemblages of the late Iron Age and the Persian Period is not sufficient to identify all of the characteristics of the pottery assemblage that existed in the sixth century B.C.E.[72] To analyze the entire set of characteristics of the "intermediate culture" of Judah during the period of Babylonian rule exceeds the objectives of this section; I will

---

68. It should be noted that the flat-base lamps already appear at the end of the seventh century B.C.E. and in some cases are found together with lamps with a raised disc base as early as this period. For parallels and literature on this subject, see Barkay 1985: 281–82; Barkay also provides a technical explanation of the development lamp bases. In this connection, note that A. Mazar (1985: 319) claims that the flat base appeared in Philistia during the seventh century B.C.E., before it appeared in Judah.

69. A more elongated subtype of this lamp also has been found (Stern 1982: 127–28). Comparative examples of these lamp types may be seen in the Jabel Nimrah finds (Hizmi and Shabtai 1993: 78 and pl. 2:11–15).

70. As mentioned, the features common to almost all of these vessels are: thickened, everted rim, trumpet base or raised disc base, globular sack-shaped body, and raised or "suspended" handles. These "classic" features do not appear before the fifth century B.C.E., and it is likely that the sixth century B.C.E. forms served, to some extent, as transitional types between the cylindrical-elliptical shape characteristic of the Iron Age and the shape common in the Persian Period. The status of the sixth century as a transitional period is reflected in the development of the cooking pot, hole-mouth jars, jars, juglets, bottles, and the lamps with raised disc base. With regard to processing technique, see the discussion by Sinclair (in Kelso et al. 1968: 71) and N. L. Lapp (1981: 84–85) of the disappearance of polishing on the bowls in the first half of the sixth century. The fact that these same bowl forms appear in the Persian Period unpolished is evidence for significant continuity in the pottery. On the characteristics of Persian pottery vessels in comparison with those of the Iron Age, see Stern 1982: 93; see also comments by Ofer 1993: 2.50–51.

71. See N. L. Lapp's (1981: 81–101) description of the development of pottery from the end of the Iron Age into beginning of the Persian Period.

72. Vanderhooft's methodological caution (1999: 107, and n. 184) on this subject is entirely appropriate.

simply describe below the major lines of investigation that may help us to
describe this culture.

The chief pottery assemblages dating to the sixth century B.C.E. were uncovered in a number of central sites, primarily in the Benjamin region. The key to
describing and characterizing this assemblage, in my opinion, lies in the evidence from Stratum IIIb at Tell el-Fûl—the stratum most clearly dated to the
Babylonian Period.[73] N. L. Lapp has pointed out a series of well-defined loci
where she identified homogeneous assemblages dated to the sixth century
B.C.E.[74] Similar pottery was published from tombs excavated near the tell.[75] Parallel assemblages of pottery dated to the sixth century B.C.E. were found in several discrete loci in Stratum 1 at Tell en-Naṣbeh,[76] as well as in well-defined assemblages at Bethel,[77] although at both sites no specific stratum of this period

---

73. Stratum IIIb at Tell el-Fûl is one of the keys to study of the sixth-century pottery. Tell el-
Fûl is one of the few sites where excavators have succeeded in classifying a pottery assemblage
of the sixth century B.C.E. (N. L. Lapp 1981: 40–46; see also the discussion on pp. 81–101). For
an analysis of the stratigraphy and the objects from this stratum, see Lipschits 1997a: 220–22;
1999a: 177–78; see also comments by Carter 1999: 122–24.

74. See N. L. Lapp 1981: 40–46. She has classified three loci in the northwest portion of
the site as homogeneous loci: L. XXI-28; L. III-30–31; L. X-8, as well as granary 28 in the structure located in the northeast part of the site (L. IX-13). On the group of loci that Lapp has assigned to Stratum IIIb, see N. L. Lapp 1981: appendix B.

75. On this pottery, see Macalister 1915: 35–37, which also includes the comments of Clark,
who was assigned responsibility for the pottery; note the very general date Clark assigned.

76. Pottery from the sixth century B.C.E. was found primarily in the pits and granaries, in
some instances in mixed loci of pottery from the Iron Age and the Persian Period. The most
important loci were: pit no. 166, in which the latest find was dated to the first half of the sixth
century B.C.E. (and, similarly, pit no. 183; McCown 1947: 130–31); pit no. 191, in which the
latest find was dated to the end of the sixth century B.C.E. (1947: 133–34); pit no. 325, which
was used until the middle of the sixth century B.C.E. (1947: 136); pit no. 363, which was used
until the middle of the sixth century B.C.E. (1947: 137–38); this also applies to Pits 361, 368,
369 (1947: 138–39). Wright has already discussed several of the pottery types dated after 600
B.C.E. (in McCown 1947: 225–26, and fig. 58), and N. L. Lapp has analyzed the sherds from
some of the pits and has drawn a parallel between the finds in some of them and the assemblages from the sixth century that were found at Tell el-Fûl (1981: 86; 94–95). Van Volsem
(1987: 95–103) has analyzed additional assemblages from Tell en-Naṣbeh and compared them
with assemblages from Bethel and Tell el-Fûl. A large portion of the finds originated in the
western part of Tell en-Naṣbeh, within the rooms of structure 159.07, which was reconstructed
in Zorn's plan (1993a: 966). If we accept my argument (Lipschits 1999a: 168–70) that this
building should be combined with building 177.06 and 177.07, thus, producing an additional
"open court" structure, we would have corroboration for the date of the structure as well as testimony to its administrative role in the sixth century B.C.E. The location of the building near
the wall and the warehouse area south of it supports this conclusion.

77. In the summary report of the excavations, Kelso stressed that the site was not destroyed
at the beginning of the sixth century B.C.E., and he assigned the destruction to a time between
553 and 521 B.C.E. (Kelso et al. 1968: 37). In an analysis of the pottery assemblages, Sinclair focused on locus sub-104 (Kelso et al. 1968: pl. 8, lower plan) and identified several other homogeneous loci (loci 129, 136) that he dated to the sixth century B.C.E. For arguments against this
classification of loci 129 and 136 and the dating of the pottery they contained, see N. L. Lapp

has been identified. At Gibeon, pottery that matched vessels found at Bethel, Tell el-Fûl, and Tell-en-Naṣbeh was uncovered.[78] Most of the sherds were found in the large pool, in the area of the winepresses, and in the "Israelite buildings" north of the pool.[79] An analysis of the finds at the site attests to the importance and significance of the sixth-century B.C.E. occupation at Gibeon (see Wright 1963: 211 n. 1; P. W. Lapp 1968: 391–93; N. L. Lapp 1970: 185; Lipschits 1999a: 172–76), and the analysis by van Volsem makes available a rich and diverse assemblage of pottery from this time (van Volsem 1987: 103–9). Corroboration of Gibeon's importance emerges from an analysis of the finds from the graves around the tell.[80] In the repository of tomb no. 25 uncovered by Barkay at Ketef Hinnom, there is a large assemblage of pottery much like the pottery from the intermediate period between Strata 2 and 1 at Lachish,[81] which is dated to the sixth century B.C.E.[82] The Ketef Hinnom assemblage seems to have parallels

1981: 106 n. 11. On the characteristics of the pottery assemblage from this era, see also Lapp 1970: 181 and n. 13; 1981: 84. Sinclair described the pottery assemblage from this period as similar to the ceramics that date to the period between the Iron Age and the Persian Period (in Kelso et al. 1968: 70–71), and he directed attention to the continuity between the seventh and sixth centuries B.C.E. (pp. 75–76). In all of this debate, much weight was given to Nancy Lapp's opinions (in Wright 1965: 238–41, and fig. 13) about the pottery from Stratum V at Shechem, primarily to the dating of the pottery to 525–475 B.C.E., because of the Attic pottery discovered there. On the basis of this data, Wright (1965: 167) compared the local pottery of this stratum with the ceramics from the end of the Iron Age at Bethel, Gibeon, and Gibeah and dated the destruction 50 years later (at the end of the sixth century B.C.E.). On this subject, see also the article by Lapp (1965: 6), which was published at the same time. For a critique of this approach, see Dever 1971: 469. See further Stern 1982: 31; Carter 1991: 97; 1999: 124–26; Lipschits 1999a: 171–72.

78. On this find, see, e.g., loci 135, 137, 141, 153, 211, 212 in Pritchard 1964a: 19–23. For a critique of the dating of the wine cellars and the positioning of them later in the sixth century B.C.E., see P. W. Lapp 1968: 391–93. For a discussion of the pottery in these loci, see N. L. Lapp 1981: 85; see also comments by Wright 1963: 211. In Stern's survey (1982: 32–35) of finds from the Persian Period, he devotes a considerable part of the discussion to the *gbʿn gdr* and *mwṣh* stamp impressions, which, in my opinion, belong to the sixth century B.C.E. On this subject, see the discussion above, §3.4.

79. Because Pritchard believed that the site was destroyed at the beginning of the sixth century B.C.E., he neglected to consider significant finds that date after the destruction and included within Stratum 1 all of the finds dated between the sixth and first centuries B.C.E. (cf. the later summary in *NEAEHL* 1.262–66). For a critique, see Stern 1982: 32–33; for a more general and very acerbic critique of Pritchard's excavations at Gibeon, see Barag 1967: 143; Lapp 1968: 391–93. For a discussion of this discovery, see Lipschits 1999a: 172–76.

80. See Eshel 1987: 1–16. On the finds in some of these graves, see Dajani 1953: 66–69; 1956, figs. 19–22.

81. See Barkay 1984: 104; 1985: 266–82, 298–301; 1994b. On this subject, see also the conclusion reached by Hadley 1984: 4.

82. This material from Ketef Hinnom is supplemented by a clay coffin that also, apparently, should be dated to this period, as well as three glass vessels and several potsherds (among them two juglets found in cave 34) that were formed around a core of sand. These pieces are dated to the sixth and fifth centuries B.C.E. (parallel to vessels found at Tell el-Fûl, En-Gedi, ʿAtlit, and Beth-Shean (Barkay 1984: 107; 1985: 102–3). The dating is aided by the presence of a small

with part of the assemblage of pottery found in tomb no. 5 at Mamilah;[83] with burial caves no. 106, 109, 114 at Lachish, where pottery vessels later than Stratum II were uncovered;[84] and cave no. 14 from Beth-Shemesh.[85] Barkay (1993: 108) argues that parallel assemblages have been found in several additional graves and sites, but some have not been properly published or remain completely unpublished, and some appear to be mixed assemblages, where a conclusion can only be reached in the second stage, after a precise analysis of the pottery has been performed.

4.3. Between Destruction and Continuity: The Archaeological Picture

4.3.1. Defining the Geographical Regions

The discussion of the archaeology in this section will be organized according to five distinct geographical units:[86] *The eastern strip* includes the southern region of the Jordan Valley and the western littoral of the Dead Sea. *The western strip* includes the northern part of the Shephelah, between Tarkumiya–Nahal Govrin and Beth-Horon.[87] *The highland strip* is divided into three latitudinal units: the highland of Judah, the environs of Jerusalem, and the region of Benjamin.

Clear-cut geographical boundaries separate the three longitudinal strips.[88]

---

coin, apparently from the island of Kos, dated to the sixth century B.C.E. (R. Barkay 1984–85: 1–5, with parallels and further literature; Barkay 1986: 34; 1990: 120). In addition to the discussion of the pottery assemblage, great importance is attached to the appearance of a carrot-shaped bottle base in room no. 5 of tomb no. 20 (Barkay 1985: 317, 320), a decanter with globular sack-shaped body found in tomb no. 34 (1985: 323), the pinched spout of a flat-base lamp (1985: 329), etc.

83. See Reich 1990; 1993; 1994. On the parallels between the finds at Ketef Hinnom and those at Mamillah, see Reich 1993: 106–8; 1994: 116. I disagree with Carter (1999: 145–47), who argues that the finds from tomb no. 19 should be seen as parallel to this material; see Reich 1999: 7.

84. See Tufnell 1953: 179–90; cf. discussion and parallels in N. L. Lapp 1981: 86; Barkay 1985: 299.

85. See Grant and Wright 1938: pls. 48, 68; 1939: 78, 144–45; cf. the comment by P. W. Lapp 1970: 184 n. 24 and N. L. Lapp 1981: 84–85.

86. The demarcation of the borders of the districts of the province conforms to evidence for the districts in the time of Josiah, as it emerges from an analysis of the list of the cities of Judah and Benjamin in Joshua 15 and 18 (Na'aman 1991a: 3–33, with further literature). The assumption is that this list reflects the geopolitical reality in the last third of the seventh century B.C.E., after the Assyrian withdrawal from the land. This observation is not new; the divisions seem to be based on geographical, historical, and administrative organization that had deep roots in the history of the kingdom of Judah and, before it, in the history of Canaan. On this subject, see Na'aman 1986b: 463–68; 1994d: 251–81.

87. This demarcation deviates north of the "classic" border of the Shephelah, which has traditionally been located at W. Naḥshon. On this subject, see also below.

88. On the boundary between the highland and the Shephelah, see Amiran (Kallner) 1948–49; Dagan 1992: 23–24. On the border between the highland and the Jordan Valley and Dead Sea region, see Ofer 1993: 2.2–3.

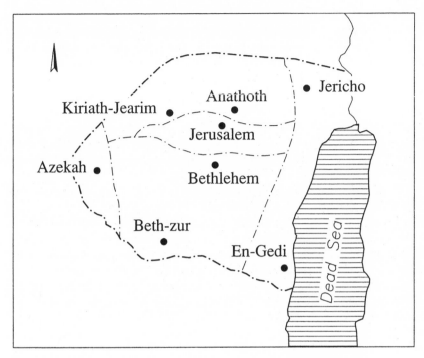

Map 7. The Geographical Units of Judah in the Babylonian Period.

The main problem in identifying the boundaries lies in defining the area of "the environs of Jerusalem," because there is no clear-cut geographical boundary between this region and the highland of Judah to the south. A distinction between the two regions is based on the historical division that existed, a distinction that perhaps goes back as far as the beginning of the second millenium B.C.E. The boundary between the area centered in the Hebron hills and the area centered in Jerusalem apparently ran south of Beth-zur. The archaeological data from the Late Bronze Age as well as information on settlement patterns from recent times reveal the deep differences between the two areas.[89]

The evolution of a separate unit known as "the environs of Jerusalem" may be connected to the growth of the city in the eighth and seventh centuries B.C.E. The city gradually expanded, and the number of residents increased; a

---

89. See Na'aman 1991c. Social and settlement parallels of recent times support the theory that the Hebron region is related to the area that reaches as far as the Beer-Sheba–Arad Valleys, and the area from Beth-zur northward is connected to the central hill country. See Ofer 1993: 1.103–4, with further literature.

large bloc of settlements consisting primarily of agricultural units developed around the city.[90] The severe crisis that beset Judah during Sennacherib's campaign highlighted the differences between the area around Jerusalem and the area south of the city. A reflection of this distinction may be found in the term "Judah and Jerusalem," which is characteristic of the literature at the end of the First Temple Period;[91] similarly, the prophecies of Jeremiah distinguish the area of "Judah" from the area known as "the cities of Judah." Jeremiah also makes a distinction between "the cities of Judah" and "the cities of the hill country" when he refers to the kingdom as existing in six regions (17:26; 32:44; 33:13).[92] In my opinion, Alt's identification of "the cities of Judah" with the Bethlehem region[93] is correct, and this identification squares with the distinction between the area surrounding Jerusalem and the area south of it.[94] The region known as "the environs of Jerusalem" conforms to the area where Gedaliah was active; it corresponds to the area where the mwṣh seals were discovered and parallels the extent of the settlements in the double list of the returnees to Zion (Ezra 2; Nehemiah 7). The geographical unit known as "the environs of Jerusalem" probably became an independent district (the district of Jerusalem) during the fifth century B.C.E. (see Neh 3:9, 12), and it is mentioned again at the beginning of the list of "the sons of the singers" (Neh 12:28–29). On the basis of these data, we may conjecture that "the environs of Jerusalem," which first came into existence as a unit in the eighth century B.C.E. (and, after upheavals and many vicissitudes, reappeared in the fifth century B.C.E.), reached all the way to Bethlehem in the south. The geographical analysis leads us to believe that this area included the Rephaim Range and the Giloh ridge; its southern boundary was defined by Wadi Heletz–Wadi Rephaim, which also encircled the central range that runs from the west of Jerusalem to the Soreq ridge (see below, §4.3.2a).

---

90. See, e.g., Barkay 1985: 399–401; 466–67; Naʾaman 1991a: 9, 13–14. The expressions that were used in connection with Jerusalem during this time, such as "this great city" (Jer 22:8) or "[a city] full of people" (Lam 1:1), support this view, as do the results of archaeological excavation (see below).

91. This term appears at the end of the eighth century B.C.E. (see, e.g., Isa 22:21), and its use continued until the end of the seventh century B.C.E. (see 2 Kgs 23:1, 24).

92. See Barkay 1985: 399–401; and Ofer 1993: 1.42. I do not think that Barkay's proposal (1985), that in the seventh century B.C.E. a separate, well-defined administrative district had developed in the area around Jerusalem, should be accepted. The facts available to us do not support Barkay's conclusion, and it is preferable to assume that the appearance of a separate district was a natural development that gained momentum on the eve of the destruction and afterward.

93. See Alt 1934a: 324–28. Despite this, I think that Alt's opinion regarding the original scope of Judah's tribal legacy and the extent of the area wrested from Judah in Sennacherib's campaign cannot be sustained.

94. See Naʾaman 1991a: 15–16. Ofer (1993: 1.44) may be right when he hypothesizes that this term was intended to define the region that remained within the limits of Judah during the Babylonian campaign or afterward, when the southern hill region had already been devastated and perhaps even cut off from the kingdom.

The boundary between the territory of Benjamin and "the environs of Jerusalem" followed a line, quite close to Jerusalem, created by connecting the southern settlements of the Benjamin tribal inheritance: Moṣah and Kirjath-Jearim are mentioned in the list of the cities of Benjamin (Josh 18:26, 28).[95] Gibeah of Saul[96] and Anathoth[97] are added to the list of the cities of Benjamin found in Isa 10:28–32.[98] A line connecting these cities lies only 5 km from Jerusalem, creating an arc running in a northeast–northwest direction; the lay of the land implies that this area was bounded on the northeast by Wadi Og and on the northwest by Wadi Soreq. The archaeological remains show that, generally, only small farms occupied the area between this arc and Jerusalem.

The conclusion that emerges from this discussion is that, in the eighth and seventh centuries B.C.E., a bloc of satellite agricultural settlements arose around the urban core of Jerusalem. This area occupied a circle of approximately 5 to 7 km around Jerusalem. Furthermore, we may estimate that it extended from south of the line of the settlements at Moṣah, Kirjath-Jearim, Gibeah of Saul, and Anathoth[99] to the area north of the Bethlehem–Beit-Ṣaḥur region. The total area of this geographical unit is some 250 sq. km at most; this estimate is based on the assumption that the natural boundary on the west was at the intersection of Wadi Soreq and Wadi Rephaim and that the western ridges up to the Soreq ridge were also included.

Between "the environs of Jerusalem" and the northern boundary of the kingdom of Judah lay the region of Benjamin. The growth of Jerusalem in the eighth and seventh centuries B.C.E. no doubt brought about a strengthening of economic relations between the two regions, inasmuch as "greater Jerusalem" needed a stable source of agricultural produce. The grains that grew in the Benjaminite plain and the olive orchards and vineyards nearby were an important

---

95. On the topic of the repeated references to Kirjath-Jearim (Josh 15:60; 18:28) in the list of cities of Judah and Benjamin, see the explanation offered by Naʾaman 1991a: 8–10. This explanation is based on a distinction between the earlier circumstances, when Kirjath-Jearim was a northern enclave of Judah even though it was near Benjamin, and the later reality, when close relations were forged between Kirjath-Jearim and its neighbors, so that it came to be considered part of Benjamin (Josh 9:17; 18:28; Ezra 2:25; Neh 7:29).

96. On the error in Josh 18:28, see Naʾaman 1991a: 8–10.

97. The affiliation of Anathoth, Jeremiah's birthplace, with the Benjamin tribal legacy is also highlighted at the height of the Babylonian siege, preceding the destruction of Jerusalem (Jer 32:7–15).

98. This list was apparently not included in the list found in the book of Joshua (Naʾaman 1986a: 229 n. 45; 1991a: 25–26).

99. My working hypothesis here is that a line from Wadi Og to Wadi Soreq was the northern boundary of the area known as "the environs of Jerusalem." The geographical basis for this judgment is that it leaves the Mt. Scopus ridge within the Jerusalem region, while it leaves out the settlements close to ʿAnata (whatever attempt is made to identify it). See King 1993: 95–96; Nadelman 1994: 62–64; Lipschits 1997a: 223–24. To make the Wadi Soreq the northern boundary on the western littorals of the mountain area is an even more obvious decision, because this line marks the entire western boundary.

source of this supply. At the same time, the distinctive political features of Benjamin that were evident on the eve of the destruction of Jerusalem and that are reflected in its different fate show that the residents of this region retained their distinction, and it is perhaps due to this distinction that the Benjamin region became the center of the new Babylonian province.

South of the "environs of Jerusalem" lay the highland of Judah. This region underwent a severe crisis during Sennacherib's campaign, and it appears that most resettlement in the seventh century B.C.E. took place from the Beth-zur line northward, in strong contrast to the marked dwindling of population in the southern hill country.

4.3.2. *Archaeological Evidence of the Babylonian Destruction*

4.3.2a. Evidence of the Babylonian Destruction in Jerusalem and Its Environs

A clear picture of the Babylonian destruction emerges from the excavations in *Jerusalem*. Evidence of the destruction has been uncovered in various parts of the city.[100] In the excavations conducted by Avigad in the Jewish Quarter between 1969 and 1982, the remains of a fire, arrowheads, and bronze "Scythian arrowheads"[101] were found close to a tower dated to the end of the Iron Age. In the excavations conducted by Kenyon in the 1960s on the eastern slope of the City of David, evidence was found of the destruction of the houses and the wall at the end of the Iron Age.[102] In excavations conducted by Shiloh in the City of David between 1978 and 1985, evidence was found of the destruction of all of the structures (including the wall) as well as of a fierce fire that sealed Level 10 in Areas D, E, and G (Shiloh 1984: 3–22). Evidence of the Babylonian destruction was also found in excavations at the citadel and in some of the buildings excavated by E. Mazar on the Ophel.[103]

Based on her excavations in the City of David, Kenyon hypothesized that the Babylonians did not destroy all sections of the city. In her opinion, some of the residents continued to live in the city after the conquest and even maintained

---

100. For a summary of the archaeological picture of the Jerusalem region at the end of the seventh and during the sixth century B.C.E., see Lipschits 1997a: 246–52; 2001.

101. Avigad (1980: 52–54) claims that this arrowhead-type was used by Mesopotamian armies at this time—a claim that I find difficult to accept. For evidence of the destruction, see Geva 2000: 82, 155–58, 215; 2003: 199.

102. See Kenyon 1974: 170–71; Franken and Steiner 1990: 57; Steiner 2001: 80, 106. According to Kenyon, the rubble remaining from the devastation of the late Iron Age buildings and city wall influenced Nehemiah to erect his wall higher, on top of the eastern hill. In her opinion (1963: 15; 1964c: 45; 1967a: 107–11; 1974: 181–87), very few inhabitants could live within the limited area enclosed by the city wall in the mid-fifth century B.C.E.; also see the estimate by Weinberg 1970: 204.

103. On the citadel, see Johns 1950: 130, and fig. 7, no. 1; Geva 1983: 56–58. On the Ophel, see E. Mazar 1991: 139; 1993: 25–32.

some of the temple rituals (Kenyon 1963: 15; 1966: 81–83; 1967a: 105–11). Barkay expanded on Kenyon's opinion, basing his conclusions on the results of his excavations at Ketef Hinnom: he believes that families of the nation's elite continued to live in Jerusalem after the destruction.[104] However, it is difficult to accept this conclusion. Note that Kenyon wrote before the large excavations in Jerusalem that began at the end of the 1960s. The main evidence of the Babylonian destruction was found in excavations conducted by Shiloh on the eastern side of the City of David; furthermore, additional evidence of the destruction at the end of the Iron Age has now been found in every part of the city. Moreover, the City of David excavations showed that there was a gap in settlement after the conquest; only some pottery—no architectural remains—was found in a few excavations conducted on the western hill; this pottery is parallel to the pottery found at Ketef Hinnom and may be dated to the sixth century B.C.E.[105] The significance of this is that there is no archaeological evidence of settlement in Jerusalem from the time of the Babylonian destruction until the middle of the Persian Period. In contrast to Barkay's opinion, I argue that the best explanation for the archaeological evidence is that Jerusalem was destroyed by the Babylonians and was emptied of most of its population. The finds from the Ketef Hinnom repository are unusual, as are those in the tombs at Mamillah.[106] It appears that, with regard to Jerusalem, the interpretation given by Weinberg to the finds of Kenyon's excavations still stands: Jerusalem was wretchedly poor, not only in the period after the destruction but even at the height of the Persian Period.[107]

---

104. See Barkay 1985: 266–82, 301–5; 1994b: 85–106. Despite the fact that Barkay's conclusions seem reasonable and well grounded, I do not think that one can use these scant archaeological remnants as evidence that life in Jerusalem continued after the destruction and, specifically, that the elite of the nation continued to reside in Jerusalem. See also, along this line, the views of Barstad (1996: 53–55) and Albertz (2003: 93). Consequently, I reject outright the view expressed by Laperrousaz (1981: 56) that 12,000 people lived in Jerusalem during the period of exile, before the Return to Zion. It is not clear which archaeological finds Laperrousaz is using to support his theory, but his conclusion does not even conform to the "most expansive" view regarding continued life in Jerusalem in this era. A population of this size would have required some 500–600 dunams as living space, and the figures available to us from the peak occupation during the Persian Period are only 20% of that number.

105. See the summary by Barkay (1993: 107). Even if we accept his ceramic distinctions and agree that the scant and scattered finds that he identified as belonging to the sixth century B.C.E., at most, this material attests only to the existence of a small, indigent population that lived in the area of the historical City of David and the Temple Mount, inside the boundaries of the city as it was at the end of the Iron Age.

106. It is impossible to draw any unequivocal conclusions regarding the continued presence of elites in Jerusalem on the basis of the finds in the repository. Aside from the fact that the finds are exceptional and unusual, it is also possible that those buried in this tomb survived the conquest of Jerusalem and afterward went to live in the area surrounding the city (perhaps in the Benjamin region or in the environs of Bethlehem) but were interred in family burial plots in Jerusalem. On this subject, see also the view of Jamieson-Drake (1991: 161).

107. See Kenyon 1967a: 105; Weinberg 1970: 204. See the summary by Lipschits 1997a: 272–75; 2001. See also Ackroyd 1968: 25–29; Miller and Hayes 1986: 426; Na'aman 2000: 43.

The settlement that was rebuilt in Jerusalem at the beginning of the Persian Period was small. In light of the scant materials from the Persian Period found outside the narrow limits of the historic City of David, it appears that the area occupied by the city at the height of the period did not exceed 60 dunams (cf. Carter 1991: 150, table 2; 1999: 190, 201–2), and the western hill was abandoned entirely until the beginning of the Hellenistic Period.[108] Some investigators include the Temple Mount and its environs within the city limits and pos-

---

Barstad had a different view (1996: 53–54), but it is not clear to me what he means, or on what basis he says that the destruction was "enormous and probably impossible."

108. In the area around the Temple Mount, only scanty remains from the Babylonian and Persian Periods have been found: one *yhwd* stamp impression was found in the Western Wall excavations, under the flooring of the Herodian Period (Mazar 1969: pl. 46:3). South of the Temple Mount, only a very few potsherds from the Persian Period were found in the landfills from the Hellenistic Period, together with two Attic sherds and one *yhwd* stamp impression (Mazar 1972: 88; 1980: 49). Ben-Dov adds to these a clay figurine from the Persian Period, though he also emphasizes the nearly complete absence of any objects from the Persian Period (1982: 63–64). When we consider the scope of construction carried out later on the Temple Mount, it is surprising that anything at all has been found. Nevertheless, beneath the strata of the Hellenistic–Roman Period, a relatively large Iron Age II find was uncovered, which reinforces the fact the Persian Period remains are relatively minor. Only a few sherds from the Persian Period, with no clear stratigraphic context, were found in landfill from the Roman Period. In the area of the Armenian Garden, several sherds from the Persian Period were found in the layers of silt overlying the debris of the Babylonian destruction (Kenyon 1967a: 105–12; Tushingham 1967: 72; 1985: 38, 72); Barkay (1985: 181), however, dates these objects later, to the beginning of the Hellenistic Period. Broshi's excavations at Beth Keifa on Mt. Zion uncovered two *yhwd* stamp impressions and a small silver coin of the *yhwd* type, similar to the coin found by Negbi on French Hill (Broshi 1972: 105; 1976: 82–83; *HA* 45 [1973] 22). The dating of these finds to the Persian Period is dubious. In the excavations conducted by Lux at the Church of the Redeemer in the northwest section of the Muristan, mixed sherds were found in the landfill underneath the wall, which was dated to the late Roman Period. Among these sherds were many from Iron Age II, and alongside these, a few sherds from the Persian Period. A striking example of the latter is the rim of a hole-mouth jar with wedge-shaped impressions (Lux 1972: 191–95; cf. Stern 1982: 133–36). Within the Citadel (the Tower of David), a *yršlm* seal impression was discovered (Amiran and Eitan 1970: 65); however, it is unlikely that this type of seal impression can be dated to the Persian Period. Avigad reports "very few" seal impressions of the *yršlm* and *yhwd* types from all of the extensive excavations in the Jewish Quarter, and he concludes that the entire area was abandoned from the end of the Iron Age until the beginning of the Hellenistic Period (1972a: 95; 1980: 62–63). G. Barkay (1985: 43) provides details about the salvage excavations conducted by Kloner and Bahat on Ha-Guy Street. Within the line of the wall, which is oriented north–south, potsherds from the Second Temple Period were found, and at the foot of the wall, on the natural rock, some sherds from the seventh century B.C.E. were discovered, together with a large bowl dated to the Persian Period. In this connection, we should note two places, slightly more removed from the boundaries of Jerusalem during the Persian Period, which also yielded pottery from the Persian Period: at the foot of French Hill, Negbi uncovered a small fort, notable especially for a *yhwd* coin dated to the fourth century B.C.E. (*HA* 31–32 [1970] 18, and cf. Barkay, Fantalkin, and Tal 2002). At Givat Ram, too, an Attic coin was found that was dated to the middle of the sixth century B.C.E. (Meshorer 1961: 185).

tulate that the settled area totaled as many as 130 or 140 dunams,[109] but in my opinion it is a mistake to include the Temple Mount in calculations of the inhabited area. The Temple Mount was an area of religious ritual, and the inhabited area was concentrated on the narrow ridge of the City of David, where most of the finds from the Persian Period also have been unearthed.[110] Even in this area, the evidence from the Persian Period is meager and poor, and the fact that hardly any architectural evidence has been uncovered reinforces the interpretation that Jerusalem did not become a large urban center at any time in the Persian Period.[111] The best way to describe the city during this period is that it was basically a temple with a settlement alongside for those who served in the temple, as well as a small number of additional residents.

In contrast to the archaeological picture of the end of Jerusalem, at *Ramat-Raḥel* there is no clear evidence regarding the time and circumstances of the destruction of the Judean fortress (Stratum Va).[112] The earliest stratum (Vb) must

109. The accepted estimates of Jerusalem's size during the Persian Period range in the area of 130–140 dunams, of which 80 are on the Temple Mount and some 50–60 on the Ophel and the City of David. See Tsafrir 1977: 34; Kenyon 1974: 182–85; Broshi 1977: 68, 71; 1978: 10–15; Williamson 1985: 81–88; Ofer 1993: 2.204–5; Carter 1991: 109–20; 1999: 148, 201–2.

110. See also Carter 1999: 201–2. Most of the material excavated at the City of David at the beginning of the twentieth century was not associated with a clear stratigraphic context (Macalister and Duncan 1926: 188–201; Crowfoot and Fitzgerald 1929: 67–68; Duncan 1931–32: 139–42). Additional finds from the Persian Period were also found in Kenyon's excavations on the eastern slope of the City of David and, naturally, in Shiloh's excavations. It was only in Shiloh's excavations on the eastern side of the City of David that for the first time a clearly-defined settlement layer from the Persian Period (Stratum 9) was found (Shiloh 1979b: 168; 1984: 20; Shiloh and Kaplan 1979: 45). This stratum, discovered mainly in Area G, is located above Stratum 10A (the stratum of the Babylonian destruction) and under Strata 7 and 8, which are dated to the Hellenistic Period. In addition to the "clean" ceramic material from the Persian Period, east of the fortification line, two thin walls were also found in this section that are attributed to this period and that may have functioned as supporting walls. Supporting walls and layers of landfill were also uncovered in Areas E-1, D1–2, and B. In Area D, a section of the city wall was also unearthed, corroborating its course along the top of the ridge's slope and confirming that the size of the city was greatly reduced in this period (Shiloh 1979a: 16; 1983: 130; Ariel 2000: 97–98). Shiloh also confirmed Kenyon's correction to the date of the segment of the city wall unearthed by Macalister and Duncan (1923–25) on the top of the eastern slope; this fortification was leaning against debris from the sixth-century B.C.E. destruction (Macalister and Duncan 1926: 235; Kenyon 1974: 181–85; Shiloh 1984a: 14, 29; 1984b: 57). See also Kenyon 1963: 15 and pl. 7:b; 1964b: 45–46; 1966: 81–83; 1967a: 111. Although Shiloh's excavations uncovered major evidence of the Persian Period, the stratum belonging to this period has only meager remains, and the primary material attributed to it comes from outside the new line of fortification (Kenyon 1974: 182–85; Shiloh 1984a: 14, 29; 1984b: 57). The dating of the stratum was primarily based on the pottery and on the seal impressions, which are typical of this period; an important object that helped to establish the date of this stratum is a small silver coin dated to the first half of the fifth century B.C.E. (Ariel 1990: 99–100, 111–13).

111. Also see the estimates of Weinberg 1970: 204 and Stern 1982: 34.

112. Ramat-Raḥel is located at the western edge of Kibbutz Ramat-Raḥel, on top of a hill, 818 m above sea level. The main road leading from Jerusalem to Bethlehem cuts directly through the site, some 4 km from Jerusalem, near the road that climbs up from Beth-Shemesh

be dated to the late eighth–early seventh century B.C.E.[113] Naʾaman suggested
that the early edifice of this stratum was the seat of an Assyrian official, built either in the late years of Tiglath-pileser III or in the early years of Sargon. This
official supervised the affairs of the kingdom of Judah and specifically the city of
Jerusalem. This early edifice was either destroyed or abandoned as a result of
Hezekiah's rebellion against Assyria (704 B.C.E.). After the suppression of the
rebellion (701 B.C.E.), the Assyrians imposed on Hezekiah the task of rebuilding
the site. The new residence of Stratum Va was rebuilt on a larger scale and of a
quality befitting the seat of an imperial representative, together with his staff
and guard. The storerooms of the palace were built to house the tribute paid
by the vassal kingdom, and this of course explains the many *lmlk* and rosette
stamped handles at the site (see Naʾaman 2001: 273–74, with further literature).

The edifice of Stratum Vb was either destroyed or abandoned after the Assyrian retreat from Judah during the last quarter of the seventh century B.C.E.
(Naʾaman 2001: 273–74). It is possible that a smaller settlement continued to
exist at Ramat-Raḥel during the sixth century B.C.E., when Jerusalem lay in ruins.[114] It was only during the fifth century B.C.E., after Jerusalem had regained its
status as the center of the province of Yehud, that the Persian authorities rebuilt
and resettled Ramat-Raḥel, making it their governmental center, designed to
supervise the affairs of the province and, in particular, the city of Jerusalem.[115]
The transfer of the Persian center of government from Mizpah to Ramat-Raḥel
is marked by the relative number of *mwṣh* and *yhwd* seal impressions found at
the two sites (Lipschits 1997a: 362; Naʾaman 2001: 274–75; see §3.4.2b above,

---

to Emeq Rephaim. The first excavation season at the tell was conducted in 1954, and four
additional seasons were undertaken between 1959 and 1962, all under the direction of Y. Aharoni. An additional season was conducted by Barkay in 1984.

113. For a summary of the various opinions on dating Stratum Vb, see Naʾaman 2001: 270–
71, with further literature.

114. Barkay (1993: 108) argued that pottery from the sixth century B.C.E. could be identified within the Stratum IV finds.

115. See Lipschits 1997a: 362; Naʾaman 2001: 274–75. The Persian Period material was
found mostly in fills and scattered across the tell; the main concentration was on the eastern
side of the fortress and in the courtyard of the earlier Israelite fortress. In most cases, the finds
were mingled with other pottery and objects from the Hellenistic and Herodian Periods (Aharoni 1955: 165–74; 1960a: 28–41; 1964: 19–23, 42–48). During the first three seasons, the excavators found it difficult to separate the various settlement layers and to isolate the Persian
Period pottery assemblage. As a result, they assigned all of the material from the fifth century
through the first century B.C.E. to Stratum IV (Aharoni 1956a: 151; 1960a: 2; see also the
stratigraphic and chronological division in Aharoni 1962). It was only during the fourth excavation season that Stratum IV was divided into two stages (Aharoni 1964: 14). The later stage
(IVa) was dated to the Herodian Period, and the early stage (IVb) was dated to the end of the
Persian Period and the transition to the Hellenistic Period (*NEAEHL* 1482–83). Stern objected to this schema and argued that some of the pottery and seal impressions should be dated
to the fifth century B.C.E. He found further support for this view in the fragments of Attic pottery (1982: 35–36).

pp. 179–181). Out of a total of 42 *mwṣh* seal impressions, dated to the sixth century B.C.E., 30 were unearthed at Tell en-Naṣbeh and only 1 at Ramat-Raḥel. Of the 412 total *yhwd* seal impressions dated to the fifth–fourth centuries B.C.E., 194 (47.1%) were unearthed at Ramat-Raḥel and only 19 (4.6%) at Tell en-Naṣbeh. In spite of the importance of Ramat-Raḥel as the administrative center of the province, the architectural remains from Stratum IVb, as in other sites of the period, are remarkably poor, and there is almost no evidence for the plan and layout of the site.[116]

Corroboration of the evidence from the excavations at Jerusalem emerges from the archaeological survey conducted in modern-day Jerusalem and its immediate environs.[117] However, no direct evidence of the Babylonian destruction can be derived from the data of this survey. The main implications of the survey come from comparing the settlement pattern at the end of the Iron Age with the settlement pattern during the Persian Period and evaluating the extent of the continuity and of the change.[118]

The data from the survey are crucial to establishing a settlement profile of the Jerusalem region at the end of the Iron Age.[119] What emerges is that, in the eighth and seventh centuries B.C.E., Jerusalem expanded, its population grew, and a large settlement area formed around the city (Barkay 1985: 399–401, 466–67; Naʾaman 1991a: 9, 14). The boundary of the fortified part of the city is defined principally by the many tombs that encircled it.[120] Unfortified neighborhoods

---

116. The remains of the few buildings from this stratum were found some 2–3 m south of the wall of the Israelite fortress. However, because the entire area was damaged by large-scale Byzantine construction, only three rooms remain. Apart from one small section of the flooring that survived, the other rooms were sealed with a fill that was dated mostly to the Hellenistic Period (Aharoni 1964: 17–19, figs. 2, 11–15; pl. 17). In addition to these rooms, a massive wall was discovered on the eastern side of the excavation area. On the basis of pottery from its foundation trench, dated as "Persian-Hellenistic," Aharoni dated the wall to the fifth to third centuries B.C.E. (1964: 18–19).

117. I would like to thank Prof. Amos Kloner for kindly enabling me to study information from the archaeological survey of Jerusalem before its publication.

118. The picture obtained from the data in the survey requires some sifting, because disproportionate weight is given to the various time periods by the length that is assigned to them. There is no differentiation of subperiods within Iron Age II; as a result, this period spans some 400 years (from the tenth century to the beginning of the sixth century B.C.E.). In contrast, the Persian Period spans only some 200 years (fifth–fourth centuries B.C.E.). Furthermore, in light of the data from the excavations in Jerusalem and at Ramat-Raḥel, we may conclude that the data from the fifth and fourth centuries B.C.E. reflect some recovery in settlement compared with the situation in the sixth century B.C.E., before the Return to Zion and the renewal of settlement in the city and near environs.

119. The profile of settlement in the Jerusalem region at the end of the Iron Age has been discussed at length in the literature. See, e.g., discussion by Gibson and Edelstein 1985; Barkay 1985; Edelstein and Milevski 1994; Lipschits 1997a: 246–75; 2001: 132–34; Feig 2000.

120. Barkay collected data on some 115 burial caves in various parts of the necropolis (see, e.g., 1985: 472; 1991: 103; 1994a). There are some 50 burial caves in the eastern cemetery in the village of Siloam, approximately 15 north of the Shechem Gate (Damascus Gate), about

were built north of the city walls,[121] and agricultural farms lay in the area around it.[122] Large villages constituted the more remote ring and apparently delineated the territory known as "the environs of Jerusalem" (Barkay 1985: 367–71; Feig 2000: 388–94, 398–409). A well-planned array of forts was built in a wide circle around the city.[123] On the basis of this compilation of data, Barkay hypothesized that the built-up area of Jerusalem, including the neighborhoods outside the wall (and, in my opinion, including the farms that were scattered throughout "the environs of Jerusalem"), reached a size of some 900–1,000 dunams.[124]

When Jerusalem and its environs began to be resettled at the end of the sixth or first half of the fifth century B.C.E., a completely different settlement pattern resulted. Most of the population was concentrated in the historic City of David, in an area that did not exceed 60 dunams. Around the city, a very small number of small farms were established, mainly characterized by a small number of structures (from a single building to no more than three or four buildings); alongside these were agricultural installations and terraces. Approximately half of these settlements were south of Jerusalem, in the area west of Ramat-Raḥel and Bethlehem, and their presence here can be attributed both to the administrative center at Ramat-Raḥel and to the growth that characterized the entire northern highland region of Judah (see more on this below, §4.3.3b, pp. 250–258). North and east of Jerusalem proper, in the area between Pisgat Zeʾev / French Hill and el-ʿAzariya, there were a total of 14 farms, compared with the more than 60 that had been there during the late Iron Age. All of the area northwest and west of Jerusalem, which had been a mosaic of small farms in the late Iron Age, remained desolate throughout the Persian Period. The overall area occupied by settlements around Jerusalem may be approximated at some 50 dunams at most, so the total of the settled area in Jerusalem and its environs at the height of the Persian Period did not exceed 110 dunams.

---

38 throughout the Ben-Hinnom Valley, and 12 in the neighborhoods outside of the city wall and in the villages and farms around the city.

121. The neighborhoods outside the city wall in the hills north of the city apparently were founded at the end of the eighth century B.C.E. and reached their highest development in the seventh century B.C.E. (Barkay 1985: 161–65, 500, with further literature).

122. The accepted interpretation is that the new city occupied the entire area of the agricultural hinterland of ancient Jerusalem. This area reached as far as 10 km west of the city, some 5 km north, 3.5 km to the south, and much less to the east (Barkay 1985: 366). Barkay (1985: 367–71) attributes to the farms several burial caves that are located in the modern city of Jerusalem. See most recently Feig 2000: 388–94, 398–409.

123. See A. Mazar 1981: 246–48; Barkay 1985: 371–73. There is a good parallel to this in Samaria: around the capital, at least three forts (of which we know) were built, and they continued in use during Assyrian and Babylonian rule (Zertal 1990; Barkay 1985: xi, 373).

124. See Barkay 1985: xiv, 165, 487. In my opinion, an estimate of this entire settled area must include all of the small farms that were included in the archaeological survey in the territory of "the environs of Jerusalem." The estimates accepted in the literature for the limits of Jerusalem at the end of the Iron Age reach approximately 600 dunams (Broshi 1974; 1991: 66; Geva 1979; 1991; Finkelstein 1994: 175). Cf. also the estimate by Shiloh (1981a) of the limits of the fortified city; and in this context, see also the doubts raised by Tushingham (1987).

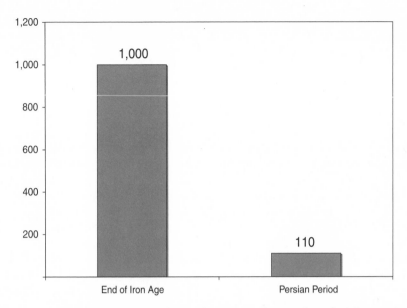

Fig. 4.1. Settled dunams in Jerusalem and its surroundings at the end of the Iron Age and during the Persian Period.

When we compare the data from the Iron Age with the data from the Persian Period, we find that there was a decline of 83.5% in the number of settlements, from 170 in Iron Age II[125] to 28 in the Persian Period.[126] The region close to Jerusalem, within 3 km of the city, saw an even sharper decline: 89% of the number of settlements.[127] Estimates of the total settled area reveal a parallel decrease, from approximately 1,000 dunams at the end of the Iron Age to approximately 110 dunams in the Persian Period). These data are reinforced by a cessation of use of the family tombs around Jerusalem and a sharp decline in the amount of pottery from the Persian Period found at the various sites. Both of

125. In the survey data, 197 sites from the Iron Age are listed. Of these, 27 sites are registered as burial caves, and the latter were not taken into account here. See the table of sites in Lipschits 1997a: table D-4-C-2 and fig. 6.

126. In this region, 30 sites from the Persian Period were listed (in addition, of course, to the city itself). One site was classified as a burial cave, and pottery from the sixth century B.C.E. was found in it (Ketef Hinnom). Two sites are of uncertain date, because the pottery assemblage discovered in them was not clearly classified. For the purpose of calculation, 28 sites are classified here as belonging to the Persian Period. See the table of sites in Lipschits 1997a: table D-4-C-2 and fig. 7.

127. In this area, 134 Iron Age sites were surveyed (not including the burial caves). Only 15 sites were classified as dating to the Persian Period (not including the tomb at Ketef Hinnom and Site 7, where the pottery assemblage was not classified clearly). See the table of sites in Lipschits 1997a: table D-4-C-2 and figs. 6–7.

these sets of data confirm that there was a very low level of human activity during this period.[128]

The first conclusion that arises from the survey data is that between the Iron
Age and the Persian Period there was a sharp decline—more than 90%—in occupation in the environs of Jerusalem. If we assume (based on the data from the
excavations in Jerusalem and at Ramat-Raḥel) that the finds from the Persian
Period reflect a demographic recovery that began in the fifth and fourth centuries B.C.E., we may safely conclude that the drop in settlement in the sixth century B.C.E. was even more drastic and that Jerusalem and its environs experienced a veritable settlement vacuum. The implication is that the region closest
to Jerusalem suffered a mortal blow at the end of the Iron Age, resulting in the
displacement of most of its population. This drop must be related to the Babylonian attack on Jerusalem and the impact that it had on the immediate environs
of the city during the long siege.[129] The fact that this region was not resettled
until the Persian Period, and even then only partially, is evidence of the extent
of the damage that the area suffered. The demographic evidence thus supports
the previous hypothesis, that Jerusalem remained desolate throughout the time
of Babylonian rule. Until the city itself recovered and was reoccupied, there was
no economic basis for villages and farms in Jerusalem's immediate environs; the
villages and farms that did exist in this period were located in the Benjamin
region, north of the city, and in the Bethlehem district to the south.

In light of the demographic evidence, it is also possible that, like Hadrian in
later times, who prohibited the Jews from living in Jerusalem after the Bar-
Kochba revolt, the Babylonians prohibited Jews from settling in Jerusalem. If
this were not the case, it is difficult to explain why at least some of the refugees
did not return to the city and why the city did not experience any recovery before the beginning of the Persian Period.

4.3.2b. Evidence of the Babylonian Destruction in the Shephelah

The destruction of the fortified cities in the Shephelah in the early sixth century B.C.E. probably was the "opening of the door" to the heart of the kingdom
of Judah by the Babylonian army. Military logic dictated that the conquest of
these cities was prerequisite for the army's thrust into the hill country and that
control of the Shephelah and the major supply routes that connected the coast
with the central ridge was necessary for the long siege of Jerusalem.

The major evidence of the invasion comes from excavations in Stratum II at
Lachish (*Tell ed-Duweir*).[130] The intensity of the devastation in this stratum was

---

128. These two points arose in a conversation with Prof. Kloner and Alon DeGroot, and I
wish to thank them for pointing this out.

129. On this subject, see my summary, in Lipschits 1997a: 272–75; 2001. See also Ackroyd
1968: 25–28; Miller and Hayes 1986: 426; Naʾaman 2000: 43.

130. In addition to Tufnell's conclusions (1953: 56–58), see the description of Stratum II at
Lachish in Ussishkin 1978: 53–54, 64–67; 1983: 134–36, 146 ; NEAEHL 3.863; Barkay 1993:
108.

apparent to the excavators; there were traces of a raging fire, arrowheads, evidence of breaches in the city wall, and total destruction of the buildings (Tufnell 1953: 56–58). The site has no evidence of rebuilding or renewed settlement until the mid-fifth century B.C.E.; it clearly was abandoned for an extended period (Tufnell 1953: 48; Fantalkin and Tal forthcoming). Nevertheless, it is difficult to accept the opinion of those who link the renewal of settlement at the site with those who returned to Zion from the exile at the beginning of the Persian Period.[131] Lachish never reverted to being a part of Judah; the plan of the residency built at the center of the site, as well as the architectural remains, pottery, and other finds excavated in it, demonstrate that it was built by the Persian ruler as a Persian governmental center.[132]

No conclusive archaeological connection can be made between the destruction of the other cities of the Shephelah and the Babylonian military campaign. Nevertheless, this region displays evidence of a drastically dwindling population and, in most of the sites, there are indications of a gap that lasted at least until the beginning of the Persian Period. These two archaeological facts can even be connected to the contents of several of the Lachish Letters and to the text of Jer 34:7: "When the army of the king of Babylon fought against Jerusalem, and against all of the cities of Judah that were left, against Lachish and against Azekah, for these fortified cities were the only ones that remained of the cities of Judah."

No clear-cut evidence of the destruction of *Azekah* (*Tel Zakariya*) has been found.[133] Bliss and Macalister assigned long periods to the strata they excavated, and the dates suggested by Albright for these strata were based primarily on historical considerations.[134] There are only scanty remains from the Persian Period, but conspicuous among these is a rare Athenian coin dated to 526–430

---

131. See Tufnell's judgment (1953: 48), and see also the conclusion reached by many scholars (*NEAEHL* 3.864).

132. For conclusions that can no longer be sustained, given the standards of modern scholarship, regarding the construction features of the palace at Lachish and its parallels, see Amiran and Dunayevsky 1958; Aharoni 1967a; 1975: 33–40. For a critique of these discussions, see Reich 1987: 182, 185; see also Fantalkin and Tal forthcoming.

133. The site was excavated in 1898–1899, under the direction of Bliss (assisted by Macalister), and the excavation results were published in preliminary reports (Bliss 1899a; 1900a) as well as in a summary report of the excavations at the four tells in the Shephelah (Bliss and Macalister 1902: 9–26). For a review of the history of excavations at the site and the major discoveries, see *NEAEHL* 3.1165–67; Dagan 1992: 27–34. On the fate of Azekah, cf. Jer 34:7 and ostracon no. 4 at Lachish; see also Albright's appraisal (1960: 30–31).

134. See the comparative table of the dating of the strata at this site in *NEAEHL* 3.1167. The "Jewish Stratum" was dated by Bliss and Macalister to a period from the eighth to the third centuries B.C.E. Albright (1965: 28) identified a gap of approximately 200 years between the destruction of the "Israelite period" stratum (which he places between 1000 and 587 B.C.E.) and the Seleucid Period stratum (400–100 B.C.E.). However, it seems clear that he based this conclusion on historical considerations, and he also ignores the few sherds from the Persian Period that were found on the site. See also the conclusions of Dagan (2000: 86–89), in contrast to his own arguments (1992: 33–34).

B.C.E. (Bliss 1900a: 7–16; Bliss and Macalister 1902: 26, pl. 56:44). Thus, it appears that settlement activity was renewed at Azekah at the end of the sixth century or at the beginning of the fifth century B.C.E. It is possible that Azekah survived into the period that Bliss and Macalister called "the Seleucian Period," but the beginning of this phase should probably be moved back to the fourth century B.C.E. (Bliss and Macalister 1902: 19–23; Albright 1965: 28).

At *Tel Goded* (*Tell Judeideh*), the gap apparently lasted longer, throughout the entire Persian Period. Notably, pottery assemblages at the site are parallel to those found in Strata III and II at Lachish; in addition, there is evidence of a small Hellenistic settlement.[135] At *Mareshah* (*Tell Sandahannah*), too, there was a large gap between the city that was destroyed at the end of the Iron Age and the Hellenistic city. Finds from the Persian Period are very sparse.[136]

Data from the *archaeological survey* that has been conducted in the Shephelah since 1979 supplement the picture obtained from archaeological excavations.[137] The survey results show that, during the ninth and eighth centuries B.C.E., the Shephelah experienced a flowering of settlement activity.[138] Population density increased; many new settlements were established (particularly small, agricultural sites); and the settled area extended to new regions, primarily in the western part of the Shephelah (for discussion and additional literature, see Dagan 1992: 252–63; 2000: 200–207; Finkelstein 1994: 172–73). Sennacherib's campaign (701 B.C.E.) dealt the Shephelah a severe blow from which it did not recover.[139] It is also likely that the problematic economic, political, and security

---

135. Tel Goded was excavated in 1899–1900, under the direction of Bliss (assisted by Macalister), and the excavation finds were published in preliminary reports (Bliss 1900c) as well as in the summary report of the excavations at the four tell sites in the Shephelah (Bliss and Macalister 1902: 44–51, and see also pp. 7–8, 89–90, 107, 195, 199). For a general review of the excavation results, see *NEAEHL* 1.273–75; see also the analysis by Dagan (1992: 41–45; 2000: 91–93, with further literature). For a contrasting perspective, see the discussion of Gibson (1994: esp. p. 230), who claims that the site was destroyed already in 701 B.C.E.

136. Mareshah was excavated in 1900, under the direction of Bliss (assisted by Macalister), and the excavation finds were published in preliminary reports (Bliss 1900d: 319–41) as well as in the summary report of the excavations at the four tell sites in the Shephelah (Bliss and Macalister 1902: 52–61). For a summary of the excavation results, see *NEAEHL* 3.1015–17; Dagan 1992: 45–47; 2000: 94–95; Kloner 1991; Kloner and Eshel 1999: 150.

137. The discussion in this section, as well as in §4.4 below, is based primarily on Dagan's M.A. thesis (1992: 259–63; see also 1996) and Ph.D. dissertation (2000: 207–28).

138. The quantity of pottery parallel to the Stratum III pottery at Lachish is significant at almost every one of the Shephelah sites and constitutes evidence of the intensity of human activity, particularly during the eighth century B.C.E.

139. In the survey, 277 sites were found to have pottery from the end of the eighth century B.C.E. (parallel to Stratum III at Lachish). The overall area of these sites is estimated at 4,187 dunams. In contrast, pottery from the seventh century B.C.E. (parallel to Stratum II at Lachish) was found only at 84 sites. The overall area of these sites is estimated at 1,388 dunams. These data reflect a decline of 70% in the number of sites and 67% in the total size of the settled area. It is important to note that, even at the sites where seventh-century B.C.E. pottery was found, it is remarkably poor compared with the relative wealth of the eighth century B.C.E. material. On

conditions in the region, which grew more serious as the seventh century B.C.E. advanced (the rending of territory from Judah, the presence of the Assyrian army, the destruction of forts on Judah's border, and the growth of the kingdom of Ekron) caused the population to continue to dwindle.[140] The decline in settlement is most evident at the smaller sites, and it appears that, as the seventh century B.C.E. progressed, settlement was greatest in the eastern parts of the Shephelah, with the population concentrated mainly in major cities (Dagan 1992: 261–62; 2000: 211–12; Finkelstein 1994: 173). These cities were refortified and again became the kingdom's western border forts. The total built-up area in this region in the second half of the seventh century B.C.E. may be estimated at approximately 900 dunams.[141]

The number of settlements in the Shephelah continued to decrease in the sixth century B.C.E.[142] We do not know whether the farms and small villages in this region were destroyed in a single military campaign, at the same time as the

---

these data and their significance, see Dagan 1992: 252–63; 2000: 200–228. The significance of these data is emphasized by the congruence between them and the number of exiles cited in Assyrian sources for Sennacherib's campaign. On this subject, see Naʾaman 1989: 57–60; 1993b: 112–15; 1994a: 25–26.

140. See Naʾaman 1987: 11–15; 1989: 57–61; 1993b: 112–15; 1994a: 25–26; Dagan 1992: 259–63; Finkelstein 1994: 173, 176. It is reasonable to conclude that, after the grave blow that the Shephelah suffered during Sennacherib's campaign, especially during the siege of Lachish, there was insufficient manpower to rebuild and populate the settlements (Naʾaman 1993b: 112–15).

141. This estimate is lower than Dagan's estimate (1992: 259–60; 2000: 210–11) that the maximum settled area was 1,388 dunams. Dagan (p. 260) admits that he calculated the entire area of tells, despite not knowing whether a tell's entire area was occupied. For a lower estimate than that given here, see Finkelstein 1994: 173; he puts the total at 800 dunams. At the same time, it is not clear why Finkelstein totally omitted the Shephelah when calculating his grand total (pp. 176–77); see also the summary on this subject, §4.4 below.

142. When considering the changes in settlement pattern between the late Iron Age and the Persian Period, we must remember that the borders of Judah had shrunk and extensive areas of the Shephelah were no longer inside its boundaries. See the discussion above in chap. 3, esp. pp. 138–140, 146–149, 181–184. On the basis of historical facts concerning the borders of the kingdom of Judah and the Yehud province and taking into account the data that have been published so far in the Shephelah survey, we can define the Shephelah as covering some 360 sq. km. This area is bounded by: longitude 140° (west of Tell Batash and Mareshah); longitude 152° (mountain slope line, east of Wadi ha-Elah); latitude 137° (Latrun junction line); latitude 109° (the line between Tarkumiya and the Hebron junction). It is possible to compare the settlement patterns within this area, although in order to make sense of the demographic data, the areas compared must include both the kingdom of Judah prior to the destruction of Jerusalem and the area that was part of the Yehud province during the Persian Period. We must also remember that it is problematic (and disproportional) to compare sites that yielded a pottery assemblage parallel to the assemblages typical of Lachish Stratum II with sites that have a pottery assemblage from the Persian Period. This is because the time covered by Lachish Stratum II is relatively short, during the late seventh and early sixth century B.C.E., and the pottery assemblage from the Persian Period comes from a long period of occupation throughout the fifth and fourth centuries B.C.E.

Babylonian offensive against the major border forts, or whether they were destroyed gradually during the sixth century B.C.E., when the Shephelah became a
geopolitical frontier. In any event, it appears that, during the course of the sixth
century B.C.E., there was a major settlement vacuum in the Shephelah because,
apart from the evidence of a settlement gap in the sites that have been excavated, the archaeological survey reveals an entirely new settlement pattern in
the region during the Persian Period.

At the end of the Iron Age, the settled area was concentrated in the eastern
parts of the Shephelah, in the area at the foot of the western slopes of the hill
country. The settled area extended along the mouths of the large wadis, where
settlers made use of the silt deposits and water sources. In contrast, during the
Persian Period, the settled area was concentrated in two major locations:

1. In the area north and east of Mareshah and Beth-Govrin was a fairly
   dense block of sites. It is likely that these sites belonged to the rural zone
   of Mareshah, for which there are accounts from the Hellenistic
   Period. [143]
2. In the area between Beth-Shemesh and Wadi ha-Elah are four "clusters"
   of small sites that create a settlement block bounded by Wadi Zanoaḥ
   and Wadi Nativ on the east, Wadi ha-Elah on the south, and the road
   between Beth-Shemesh and ha-Elah junction on the west. [144]

This array of settlements, which sprang up in the Shephelah during the Persian Period and continued to develop during the Hellenistic Period, resulted
from a settlement vacuum that arose in the region during the sixth century B.C.E.
This vacuum enabled new ethnic groups—known in the Hellenistic Period as
Idumeans—to penetrate gradually into the region from the south as far as the
area north of Mareshah. This incursion was halted only when Judean settlements were reestablished in the northeastern Shephelah during the Persian
Period. [145] The distribution of sites during this period evinces a focusing of settle-

---

143. On the basis of this evidence, we can conclude that the border of the province of Yehud ran west and north of this area; see further below.

144. These settlement "clusters" consist of three to four sites each, in the area of Zanoaḥ;
the confluence of Wadi Sansan and Wadi Nativ; Tell Yarmut and its environs; and the Wadi
ha-Elah region. There are three other salient sites, located on the Tarkumiya–Adullam line,
mainly on the upper part of Wadi ha-Elah. Prominent among these is the Persian fort at Kh. er-
Rasm, which may have been part of the line of Persian forts in the hill region and probably was
the fort established opposite Mareshah and the rural area that crystallized around it. Alongside
it is Qeʿilah (Kh. Qeile), which historical sources identify as the center of the southwestern district of the Yehud province.

145. More than 70% of the Persian Period settlements were established on sites that were
not occupied at the end of the Iron Age. This demonstrates that there was a settlement gap
during the sixth century B.C.E. and that the new settlements that were created during the
Perisan Period were not encumbered by the constraints that arose from locating the sites on
sites that had been occupied in previous periods.

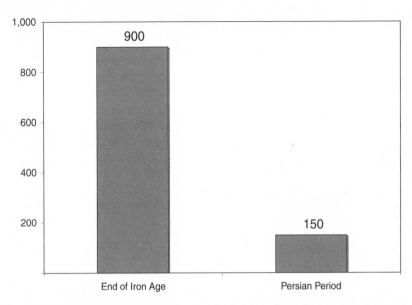

Fig. 4.2. *Settled area (in dunams) in the Shephelah at the end of the Iron Age and during the Persian Period.*

ment in the area between Beth-Shemesh and Wadi ha-Elah. If all of the sites in this area did in fact belong to the Judahite province, then this is evidence for the western boundary of the province on the Beth-Shemesh–Azekah line, up to Wadi ha-Elah. The Judahite settlement at this time was concentrated in large and medium villages, and the major tells of the Iron Age have not yielded any evidence of settlement strata from the Persian Period.[146]

There was, then, a very small population in the Shephelah portion of Yehud province. According to the survey results, a total of 22 Shephelah sites may be assigned to Judah (Dagan 2000: 222–24 and fig. 20). At most of the sites, very little pottery from the Persian Period was found, witnessing a very low level of human activity. Even taking into account a large margin of error, and taking into consideration the areas not included in the survey, the total area of the entire region occupied by settlements never exceeded 150 dunams. There was a settled area of similar size at Mareshah and its environs, but this was outside of the limits of Yehud.

---

146. Considering this state of affairs, the establishment of the Persian palace at Lachish is even more remarkable. This palace was located outside the boundaries of Yehud province, and we may conclude that it served as the Persian administrative center of the region.

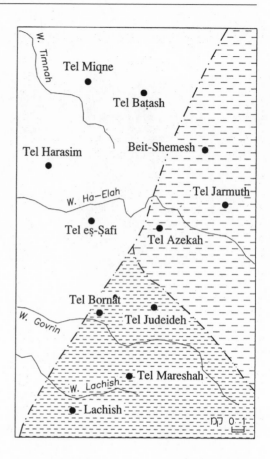

Map 8. A Reconstruction of
the "Triangle Region" formed by
the borders of the Provinces of
Judah, Edom, and Ashdod.

4.3.2c. Evidence of the Babylonian Destruction in the Southern Part
of the Judean Hills and the Negev

The unprecedented settlement activity in the Beer-Sheba and Arad Valleys
during the course of the seventh century B.C.E. was short lived.[147] At most of
the Negev sites, clear evidence of the destruction that took place at the end of
the Iron Age is detectable. At least one of the five forts in the Negev (Ḥorvat
Radum) has evidence that there was an orderly abandonment before the place
was destroyed.[148] In contrast, clear-cut evidence of the destruction at the beginning of the sixth century B.C.E. was found at the fort at Ḥorvat ʿUza and in a

---

147. See, e.g., Beit-Arieh 1985a; 1995a: 310–15; 1999a: 1–3; Naʾaman 1987; 1991a: 48–49;
Halpern 1991: 62; Finkelstein 1994: 176–78; Meshel 1995: 173–74.

148. The excavators of Ḥorvat Radum detected three different strata of the same fort, all
dated to the seventh and early sixth centuries B.C.E. The area of the fort has been estimated at
approximately 0.6 dunam. See Beit-Arieh 1992: 107, 111; cf. 1991b: 88.

small settlement nearby,[149] as well as in Stratum VI on the tell at *Arad*.[150] A gap in settlement followed the destruction of the fortress of Stratum VI, and the excavators date the next occupation level (Stratum V) to the fifth and fourth centuries B.C.E. This stratum yielded mostly pits, in which a large quantity of ostraca have been discovered.[151] Excavations at Ḥorvat Tov (*Khirbet*

149. The fortress of Stratum IV was built during the seventh century B.C.E. It is 42 × 51 m, with an area of 2.1 dunams. A settlement of 7 dunams was built north of it. The excavators distinguished two stages of construction in this stratum. However, there is a clear architectural connection between them, and their pottery assemblages show no differences (Beit-Arieh 1986a: 38; Beit-Arieh and Cresson 1991: 129–33; *NEAEHL* 3.1158). The primary evidence of the destruction of the fortress comes from some sections of the wall and the area near the gate, where evidence of a fierce conflagration, with large piles of burned wooden beams, was found. Along the slope, a pile of ash mixed with potsherds from the late Iron Age was also discovered, and this was interpreted as evidence that the new settlers who arrived at the site in the Hellenistic Period cleared the fortress of the destruction debris. See Beit-Arieh 1986a: 37–39; 1995c; Beit-Arieh and Cresson 1991: 129–33; *NEAEHL* 3.1157. Six excavation seasons at the site uncovered 35 ostraca, most of them written in Hebrew, as well as a jar bearing 2 inscriptions (Beit-Arieh 1985b: 94–96; 1986a: 37–39; 1993: 55–63; 1995c; 1999b; Beit-Arieh and Cresson 1985; 1991: 133–34). An Edomite ostracon that was found together with 4 Hebrew ostraca at the fortress gate, is of particular importance, because it became the basis for Beit-Arieh's theory that the fortress fell to the Edomites close to the time of the destruction of Jerusalem or shortly afterward (Beit-Arieh 1995a: 311; 1995b: 36–37; Beit-Arieh and Cresson 1985; see also remarks by Misgav 1990: 215–16). This hypothesis may be sustainable, but it is important to remember that the Edomite ostracon was found together with many Judahite ostraca, and there is no architectural or ceramic evidence of two distinct stages within the last period of the fortress's existence. Furthermore, if the fortress was controlled by Edom in its last days, then some other group must have destroyed it shortly after Edom gained control.

150. The fortress of Stratum VI is the last in a line of fortresses that go back to the tenth century B.C.E., and it has been dated to the end of the seventh and beginning of the sixth centuries B.C.E. It measured 50 × 55 m, and its area may be estimated at 2.75 dunams. These figures should be supplemented by the few structures found outside the fortress, whose total area may be approximated at 2 dunams (Beit-Arieh: private communication). It is likely that this last fortress existed for only a short time, as a direct successor to the fortress of Stratum VII. Few changes were made in the plan of the fortress, and these primarily consisted of several places where the interior of the wall was strengthened and the addition of a tower in the western wing; this tower was apparently intended to reinforce the wall where there was no internal buttress (Herzog 1997: 177–79; 2002: 41–49, with further literature). In one of the clusters of rooms along the southern wall in Stratum VII, three seal impressions bearing the name of Elyashib, the son of Ashyahu were found; this Elyashib is also mentioned in the Arad Letters found in Stratum VI. These seal impression are further evidence of the continuity in the function and occupation of the site throughout these two strata. Strata VII and VI have been discussed at length in the literature; see the summary in Herzog 1997: 172–79; 2002: 41–49; and see the critique by Naʾaman (2003, with further literature). On the destruction of Stratum VI, see also Herzog et al. 1984: 29; 2002: 102.

151. See Aharoni 1976: 5. On the basis of the ostraca, Aharoni thought that there had also been a fortress at Arad during the Persian Period. This is a reasonable conclusion and has been generally accepted by scholars, but there is no archaeological evidence to support it (see Cohen 1995a: 114, with further literature). On Stratum V on the tell where the fortresses lie, see also Herzog 1997: 245–49. The ostraca from this strata were published by Naveh (1976); they mainly contain instructions for supplying foodstuffs for the animals and personnel—evidence of Arad's major role as a central administrative city in the Persian imperial system.

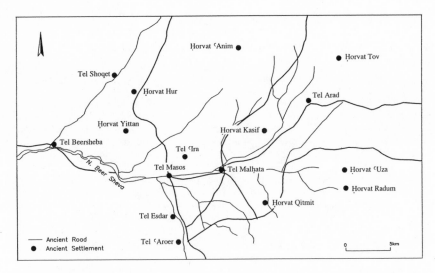

Map 9. Major Sites in the Beer-Sheba–Arad Valleys at the End of the Iron Age (after Beit-Arieh 1999).

Tov)[152] and at Ḥorvat ʿAnim (*Khirbet ʿUweina et-Taḥta*)[153] have revealed evidence that their destruction occurred under circumstances parallel to the events at ʿUza and Arad.

Clear-cut evidence of the destruction was also found in the three settlements in the center of the region, close to the junction of the Beer-Sheba and Arad

---

152. Very little data are available about the excavations at this fort, but the information we do have shows that the plan of the fort was similar to the plan of the Arad fortress. It was 38 × 38 m and had an area of approximately 1.5 dunams. The fort had two or three stages during the late Iron Age, when it was surrounded by a 1.5-m-thick wall. This fort also was destroyed at the same time as the fortress at Arad (Cohen 1995a: 115–16; cf. HA 92 [1988] 56–57).

153. Ḥorvat ʿAnim (Khirbet ʿUweina et-Taḥta) is located on the southern slopes of the Hebron Hills, close to the border with the Beer-Sheba–Arad Valleys; see Ofer 1993: 2.84–85; Cohen 1995a: 117–18. This site had already been surveyed as part of an emergency survey (Kochavi 1972: 82, Site 250), and a burial cave from the late Iron Age was excavated (Lander, HA 96 [1991] 35). Cohen excavated the fortress, the dimensions of which are 21.5 × 21.5 m, with very thick external walls (some 5 m); its interior area was approximately 11 × 11 m. The built-up area of the fort may be estimated at 120 sq. m (Cohen 1995a: 118). It is not clear how large the settlement around the fort during the late Iron Age was, but Ofer's estimate, that it extended over an area of 20 dunams, cannot be supported. A relatively poor, limited quantity of pottery was discovered on the site (Ofer 1993: vol. 2, appendix 2A, 62, no. 8; pl. 27:c), and the excavation itself uncovered only a few vestiges of walls and floors from the late Iron Age in widely separated areas. It is difficult to imagine that the area of the settlement during this period ever was more than a few dunams.

Valleys. In Stratum VI at *Tel 'Ira*, there is conspicuous evidence of violent destruction and fire at the beginning of the sixth century B.C.E. in all of the excavated areas.[154] There are remains of pits and buildings (Stratum V) belonging to a new settlement that was established during the Persian Period. This seems to have been an unfortified settlement at the edge of the tell that was abandoned at the end of the Persian Period.[155] At this site, too, there seems to have been a gap between the occupation of the site at the beginning of the sixth century B.C.E. and the settlement of the fifth century B.C.E. However, Beit-Arieh contends that one of the 20 tombs that were in use during the Iron Age (tomb T23), which were hewn into the eastern slope of the site, shows evidence of continued use in the Persian Period, and it is possible that it was also in use during the sixth century B.C.E. (Beit-Arieh 1999a: 173; for an analysis of the finds from this tomb, see pp. 162–65).

The remains from the end of the Iron Age in Area G near *Tel Masos* (*Khirbet el Mšaš*) may be attributed to Tel 'Ira.[156] The scant remains did not permit the excavators to determine conclusively whether the site had been a fort, way station, or settlement (see Kempinski et al. 1981: 165–68; Fritz and Kempinski 1983: 1.123–37; NEAEHL 3.1025). However, the absence of massive fortifications, like those found in the other five known forts in the Negev, rule out the possibility that this was a fort. The proximity of the site to Tel 'Ira (only 2.5 km distant) and its strategic location on the crossroads in the center of the Beer-Sheba–Arad Valleys and close to wells that were the most important source of water in the region lead us to accept Beit-Arieh's conjecture that the site was associated with Tel 'Ira.[157] There is no clear evidence that the site was destroyed at the end of the Iron Age,[158] and we can accept Beit-Arieh's hypothesis that the site was abandoned under pressure and that its inhabitants retreated to the fortifications at nearby 'Ira before the latter was eventually also destroyed. A

154. Stratum VI was built in the first half of the seventh century B.C.E. and is a continuation of Stratum VII, which was destroyed at the end of eighth century B.C.E. (Singer-Avitz 2004: 86, with further literature and discussion). The built-up area at the end of the Iron Age is estimated at 25 dunams (Biran 1985b; 1987: 26–29; Beit-Arieh 1985a; 1987; 1999a: 176–77, with further literature). On the evidence of the destruction in Areas C, E, and L, see Beit-Arieh 1999a: 45–49, 76–77, 115.

155. See Beit-Arieh 1999a: 177–78. On the evidence from the Persian Period in Areas B, C, and M, and on another finds from the Persian Period that had no stratigraphic context, see pp. 35, 49, 126, and 173.

156. Remnants from the second half of the seventh century B.C.E. were uncovered in limited excavations carried out at a small tell of 4 dunams in an area located some 200 m west of the Iron Age I settlement (Area G).

157. This point was discussed in conversation with Prof. Beit-Arieh, and I wish to thank him for it.

158. On the various hypotheses regarding the end of the small settlement at Tel Masos, see Kempinski et al. 1981: 167–68; Fritz and Kempinski 1983: 1.124–27, and see also remarks by Zimhoni on p. 130; NEAEHL 3.1025.

smaller settlement was rebuilt at Tel Masos at some stage during the Persian Period.[159]

Conclusive evidence of destruction was found in Stratum III at *Tel Malḥata*, particularly on the eastern side of the city.[160] In some of the small structures built close to the city wall, excavators found indications of violent destruction, which included piles of bricks that had collapsed inward from the walls of rooms or from the outside wall and signs of an intense fire (Beit-Arieh 1998: 34–35). After the destruction, there was a gap in occupation at the tell of approximately 300 years; the settlement was rebuilt only in the Hellenistic Period (1998: 38; *NEAEHL* 3.949–50).

No traces of destruction were found at *Tel ʿAroer*, apparently because the Iron Age remains (Stratum II) were badly damaged by construction activity during the Herodian age.[161]

The survey data further reinforce the evidence of a dramatic process of destruction and abandonment at the border forts and the central settlement sites of the Beer-Sheba–Arad Valleys. In the survey conducted by Beit-Arieh, pottery from the end of the Iron Age was found at 30 additional settlement sites, most of them quite small; their total area can be estimated to be 15 dunams at most (Beit-Arieh, private communication). In the survey conducted by Govrin, 7 additional sites were found, and their total area may be estimated at 8 dunams at most.[162] An additional settlement, a bit larger in area, apparently existed at Bir es-Sabaʿ, and the area of the buildings that extend from the Bedouin market of modern-day Beer-Sheba can be estimated at approximately 10 dunams (see Gophna and Yisraeli [in Aharoni 1973: 115–19]; Herzog 2002: 101). The sum total settled area of the sites excavated and surveyed in the Beer-Sheba–Arad Valleys is estimated at 116 dunams.

All things considered—the nature of the settlements, the characteristics of the region, and the areas not yet surveyed—it appears that we must be satisfied

---

159. Only a scant quantity of pottery from this period was found; see also Fritz and Kempinski 1983: 1.127.

160. Stratum III at Tel Malḥata had two stages dating to the seventh century B.C.E. (Beit-Arieh 1998: 34–35). The few remaining vestiges of this stratum do not permit a reconstruction of the plan of the settlement, but it seems that, generally, this stratum maintained the contour of Stratum IV, which was destroyed at the end of the eighth century B.C.E., as was Stratum II at Tel Beer-Sheba (1998: 35). The size of the city at the time of this stratum is estimated to have been some 15 dunams. On the evidence for the destruction of the the the late Iron Age stratum, see also Kochavi 1970: 23–24.

161. The area of the settlement during this period may be estimated at 20 dunams. See Biran 1987: 29–33; Biran and Cohen 1981: 253, 264; *NEAEHL* 4.1274–75.

162. See Govrin (1992: 27–29, 31–32, 37, 56–60, 104–8, 135–36, 162) for information about Sites 3, 10, 11, 63, 162, 216, 271. Apart from Site 162, which had an area estimated at some 5 dunams, the meager, sparse pottery at the rest of the sites is evidence that the settlements were small and poor.

with a rounded estimate of approximately 120 dunams.[163] Compare this with the Persian Period, during which the entire region had only 11 sites that have been identified as such (a decline of more than 75%). The total area of these sites may be estimated at a maximum of 30 dunams (a decline of some 75%).[164]

Archaeological criteria cannot determine the precise moment when the wave of devastation overtook the sites in the Negev (597 B.C.E., 586 B.C.E., 582 B.C.E., or perhaps even later?); the length and nature of the gaps after the destruction of each site (one short period of destruction following a planned military campaign; sporadic episodes of destruction following a series of offensives by various forces?); or the identity of those responsible for the destruction (Babylonians, Edomites, seminomadic tribes?).[165] The answer is dependent primarily on historical interpretation of the biblical accounts, as noted above (§3.1, pp. 140–146). At the same time, evidence that the process was prolonged and complex becomes evident when we cautiously examine the process through the course of as long a period of time as possible, from the end of the Iron Age until the Hellenistic Period. We also must consider the complex of factors that played a role in this process. On the one hand, it is doubtful that the Babylonians had any reason to expend effort to conquer border forts in remote districts when they would have collapsed anyway once the army was defeated and the central administration of the kingdom incapacited. On the other hand, it is also unlikely that the destruction can be fully explained as an activity initiated by the kingdom

---

163. The Tel ʿIra excavations (Beit-Arieh 1999a: 173) have shown that construction in the fortified settlements was not dense, leaving many areas available for processing agricultural produce, storage of grain (including many granaries), and other uses. It appears that this was the situation in the unfortified settlements as well. This fact must be taken into consideration when we make demographic estimates, because the total area of these sites is approximately half the settled area in the region. Compare this estimate (120 dunams) with Finkelstein's estimate (1994: 176), which suggested that the settled area included approximately 100 dunams in the sites excavated. Data from the surveyed sites (discussed previously) would have to be added to Finkelstein's estimate. Cf. also Herzog's (2002: 101) estimate.

164. The data on sites from the Persian Period in the Beer-Sheba–Arad Valleys were presented as part of this section's discussion of the major excavations in the region. Following is a brief summary of the results. Additional literature is cited only when new data are presented. At Tel ʿIra, pits, meager remains of walls, and potsherds were found in an area of less than one-half of the site (in particular, close to the northern and southern walls; Beit-Arieh 1999a: 173). At Tel Arad, only pits and pottery were found, including ostraca. At Tel Masos and Tel Malḥata, meager sherd scatters were found; at Tel Beer-Sheba, pits, pottery, and ostraca were discovered (Aharoni 1973: 79–82). In the survey, small amounts of pottery were found at several sites (Govrin 1992: Sites 3, 63, 87, 162, 174, 205). Apart from the fort (Site 205), which had an area of 150 × 300 m (4.5 dunams), all of the other sites consisted of isolated structures and small amounts of pottery.

165. Compare, for example, the opinions of Beit-Arieh (1985a) and Biran (1985b: 27) regarding the destruction of Tel ʿIra with the perspective of Biran and Cohen (1981: 265) and Meshel (1995: 174) regarding the destruction of ʿAroer, or with the controversy over the destruction of ʿUza (see above, p. 225 n. 149).

of Edom. There is no evidence that the Edomite army took action so far from its own borders, and it is difficult to imagine what Edom might have gained by this, apart from establishing its control over the entire region. It is even more difficult to understand what Edom would have gained during the time when the Babylonian army was a permanent fixture in this region.

In light of these facts, a gradual collapse of the array of forts and settlements in the Beer-Sheba–Arad Valleys is the best explanation for the archaeological evidence, taking into account at the same time the historical, demographic, and geopolitical processes—even though this explanation cannot be proved archaeologically or historically. Settlement in this region was contingent on the ability of the kingdom of Judah to defend the settlers. When Judah was no longer able to provide defense (whether on the eve of the destruction of Jerusalem or as part of a process that continued after the destruction), the border forts collapsed and, with them, the entire array of settlements. After the destruction, evacuation of the area continued for most of the sixth century B.C.E., and a much smaller settlement began to be reestablished only in the fifth century B.C.E. Nonetheless, the fact that a sparse Judean population lived in the Beer-Sheba–Arad Valleys in the Persian Period, occupying the area together with an Arab and Edomite population,[166] permits us to speculate that the area was not totally abandoned during the sixth century B.C.E.: while tribes from the south were making their incursion, a sparse Judean population continued to subsist in the region.

A process like that which took place in the Negev is paralleled in the southern highland of Judah (throughout the entire region between Hebron and the Beer-Sheba–Arad Valleys). No large-scale archaeological excavations have been conducted in this region. However, the data of the Judean highland survey[167] show that, as in the situation in the Negev and the Shephelah, there was a conspicuous desertion of the southern highland of Judah, a gap in settlement during the sixth century B.C.E., a drastic dwindling in the size of settlements being rebuilt in the Persian Period, and an obvious change in the pattern and characteristics of the new settlements.[168] Between the end of the Iron Age and the Persian Period, however, there was a significant drop—about 60%—in the number of sites in the southern highland of Judah, south of Hebron, at a time when there was almost no change in the number of sites in the area north of Hebron (Ofer 1998: 46–48). Moreover, the data of the survey reveal that the farther north one goes in the highland of Judah and the closer one gets to Jerusalem,

---

166. Evidence for the presence of people bearing Judahite names is found in the Aramaic ostraca from the Persian Period; the ostraca also demonstrate the great diversity of the population in this region. See more on this in the discussion above, §3.1.

167. For an extensive discussion of the fate of the Judean highland in light of the excavation data and survey, see the discussion below (§4.3.3b, pp. 250–258).

168. See also the summary in Ofer 1993: 2.128.

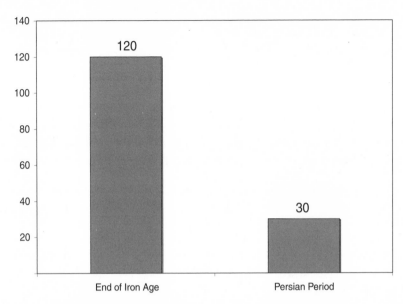

Fig. 4.3. Settled dunams in the Beer-Sheba–Arad Valleys at the end of the Iron Age and in the Middle of the Persian Period.

the more dramatically the settlement picture changes. In the southern Hebron hills, in the area bordering the Beer-Sheba–Arad Valleys, there was a drop of about 80% in the total of settled dunams; in the Hebron hills area, the decline was about 30%; and in the *northern* region of the highland of Judah, the trend was reversed—settled dunams increased approximately 65% (Ofer 1993: 2.131). Conversely, the total settled area in the *southern* region of the highland of Judah at the end of the Iron Age can be estimated at approximately 300 dunams, but in the Persian Period settlement had declined to about 85 dunams (a drop of 71.6%, in contrast to a drop of about 60% in the number of sites).[169]

The implication of these changes is that, practically speaking, the northern and southern Judean hills became different settlement units. The northern unit was clearly connected with the areas to its north, and parallels in settlement processes in the northern unit should be sought in the region of Benjamin. Settlement processes in the southern unit were clearly connected with the Negev and

---

169. These estimates are based on data collected in the Judean highland survey conducted by Ofer (1993: 2.127–31; 1998: 47–48). Nonetheless, Ofer's estimates generally seem extravagant (Finkelstein 1994: 174–75) and are not consistent from publication to publication. See, for example, Ofer's discussion of Horvat ʿAnim and the criticism it has drawn (above, p. 226 n. 153) regarding the estimate of settled area in the region. The raw data reported by Ofer (1993: vol. 2, appendix 2/a) and a cautious estimate produce a much more modest total than that reached by Ofer.

the southern part of the Shephelah, discrete from settlement processes that took place in the northern highland (Ofer 1998: 46–48; Lipschits 1997a: 298–99). In light of this settlement pattern, it is easy to understand why, when the border forts in the Beer-Sheba–Arad Valleys collapsed, the vast, relatively empty areas of the southern Judean highland attracted seminomadic groups that began to penetrate the area from the south.

4.3.2d. Evidence of the Babylonian Destruction in the Jordan Valley,
            Judean Desert, and along the Western Littorals of the Dead Sea
At the end of the Iron Age, the eastern regions of the kingdom of Judah experienced an unprecedented flowering (Stern 1993; 2001: 134–38; Lipschits 2000). Jericho and En-Gedi were agricultural and industrial centers that supported a whole array of settlements, particularly along the routes that connected these centers with the economic and political centers on the central ridge.[170] The most prominent discovery from this period has been uncovered at Tel Goren (Tell el-Jurn), which is identified as ancient En-Gedi.[171] It has been established that the beginning of settlement at the site (Stratum V) was in the second half of the seventh century B.C.E.[172] An industrial-type settlement was built on an area of roughly 2.5 dunams; at the base of the tell there may have been a lower city of indeterminate size (see comments by Stern 1993: 194–95). This settlement is remarkable for its many unique features: buildings with a uniform plan, industrial installations (particularly ovens and large clay containers), and pottery vessels that attest to a special industry—manufacturing perfumes, apparently.[173] The settlement at Tell es-Sultan (ancient Jericho) also gradually expanded in the second half of the seventh century B.C.E., and the site's immediate environs witnessed extensive agricultural activity that were the result of the establishment of irrigation systems, agricultural farms, and forts (Magen 1983: 57; Stern 1993: 192; 2001: 134; NEAEHL 2.738). On the basis of the rich finds exposed on the slopes of the tell and a four-room house unearthed on the eastern slope, it appears that the settlement extended over the entire area of the

---

170. On the importance and significance of this region, see Lipschits 2000, which includes a reconstruction of the trade routes in this area (and with further literature).

171. Mazar, Reifenberg, and Dothan had surveyed the site in 1949. Aharoni and Naveh conducted additional surveys in the immediate vicinity. Five excavation seasons were carried out between 1961 and 1965, conducted by Mazar, Dunayevsky, and Dothan (in the first two seasons). For a review of the history of the excavations at Tel Goren, see NEAEHL 3.1189.

172. For a summary of the various opinions in the literature about the date of the founding of Stratum V and a discussion of the material remains from this stratum and their significance, see Lipschits 2000: 31–33; Stern 2001: 136–37.

173. See Mazar, Dothan, and Dunayevsky 1963: 24–58; NEAEHL 3.1191–92. On the unusual products manufactured at En-Gedi and their importance for the Judean economy at the end of the seventh and beginning of the sixth centuries B.C.E., see Lipschits 2000.

tell (approximately 40 dunams). It is also possible that the buildings extended beyond the limits of the tell itself during this period.

The entire array of settlements in the eastern hinterland of the kingdom of Judah was destroyed at the end of the Iron Age,[174] apparently as a result of the collapse of the military and economic systems after Jerusalem was destroyed.[175] After a period marked by the total absence of settlement activity in the entire region, Jericho and En-Gedi show evidence of reoccupation during the fifth century B.C.E. The industrial site established at Tel Goren at the end of the sixth or beginning of the fifth century B.C.E. was spread out over the entire area of the tell (which occupies only 2 dunams). The buildings overflowed the top of the tell and were built on the slope as well, so that the settlement's total size may be placed at approximately 4 dunams—perhaps even a little more.[176] At Tell es-Sultan, however, there is almost no information about the small settlement of this same period. The pottery reveals that it was a small settlement: remains were discovered on only part of the tell, making it unlikely that the site was larger than a few dunams.[177]

The data from the surveys conducted in this region provide conclusive evidence that settlement activity was intense and that the collapse of that activity

---

174. There are no data that would permit us to connect the destruction of the sites in the Jordan Valley and along the western littoral of the Dead Sea with the date of the destruction of Jerusalem (contra Stern 2001: 137–38). On the date of the settlement at Jericho at the end of the Iron Age, see Stern 1993: 192 and 196 n. 9, with further literature. See also Stern's discussion in *NEAEHL* 2.738. On the date of the destruction of the settlement at Tel Goren, see Lipschits 2000: 32, with further literature. Many sites that had existed at the end of the Iron Age were no longer occupied in later periods; see, e.g., the comments of the excavators regarding the following sites: Ḥorvat Shilḥa (Mazar, Amit, and Ilan 1984); Vered Jericho (Eitan, *HA* 82 [1983] 43); Kh. Abu-Tabak, Kh. e-Samrah, and Kh. el-Maqari (Stager 1976).

175. One could conceivably argue that the total devastation of all of the sites in the eastern part of the kingdom of Judah was the result of a well-planned military offensive mounted by the Babylonian army or auxiliary forces. Nonetheless, at some of the sites in the region, we can detect an orderly process of abandonment and gradual destruction (see, e.g., the conclusion reached by Mazar, Amit, and Ilan [1984] regarding the circumstances of the destruction of Ḥorvat Shilḥa). This orderly process and the lack of rationale for an organized military campaign to the border areas support the idea that the entire settlement array in this region collapsed after the destruction of Jerusalem, though the process may have begun during the Babylonian siege.

176. On the date of the building of this site, see Mazar 1986: 86; for another opinion, see Stern 1982: 38–39. On the structure, design, and features of the settlement of this period, see the summary in Lipschits 1997a: 312–15; 2000a: 36–37, with further literature.

177. As previously stated (p. 196 n. 35), this settlement was first excavated by Sellin and Watzinger, and they correctly dated it to the fifth and fourth centuries B.C.E. (Sellin and Watzinger 1913: 79–82, fig. 186; pls. 1, 3, 42; see also Stern 1982: 38). In Garstang's excavations (1930–36), as well as in Kenyon's (1952–58), only scant information about the Persian Period was added (Kenyon 1964c: 201). On the settlement of the Persian Period, see Stern 1982: 38; Bartlett 1982b: 101–2; see also Hengel 1974: 20, 22.

in the early sixth century B.C.E. was dramatic.[178] At the end of the Iron Age, the area between Jericho and En-Gedi was relatively densely populated. Most of the 59 sites that have been identified were small settlements with few buildings. Several forts were situated on strategic sites,[179] and many encampments[180] were located near them. The locations of the settlements during this period are important for understanding the organization of the region (Lipschits 2000: 32–35 and figs. 1–2). There were 6 sites in the area near Jericho, within 3 km of Tell es-Sultan.[181] The importance of this region during the Iron Age is also reflected in the large number of sites located along the central roads.

1. From the northwest, a road ran down from Mt. Ba'al Ḥaṣor to Jericho. There were 6 Iron II sites located along the upper part, in the northeastern part of the region of Benjamin (see further §4.3.3a, esp. pp. 245–249). There were 11 additional sites along the road (listed in the Judean Desert and Jericho Valley survey).[182]

2. From the west, the road ran down to Jericho from the area of Michmash. Along this road, there are 7 known Iron II sites.[183]

3. From the south-southwest, the road ran to Jericho from the Bethlehem–Tekoa region, through the Horkania Valley. Along its route lie 17 sites from Iron Age II.[184]

---

178. The most important and comprehensive survey in this region was conducted by Bar-Adon, as part of the "emergency survey" (Kochavi 1972). Despite the difficult terrain, the survey was rigorous; evidence of this is the fact that, though the survey was conducted some 30 years ago, only a few additional sites have been discovered. On these sites, see Eitan, *HA* 82 (1983) 43; Mazar, Amit, and Ilan 1984, and further literature in nn. 1–3; Cross and Milik 1956; Stager 1976. On the fieldwork carried out before the 1950s, see the summary in Naveh 1958: 4–8. For a summary of the settlement picture in the Jordan Valley and along the western littoral of the Dead Sea, see Lipschits 2000: 38–39, with further literature, p. 40 n. 5.

179. Sites 23, 35, 43, 45, 50, 51, and 59 (in Lipschits 1997a: table D-4-F-1 and fig. 17, the list of sites in the Jordan Valley and Dead Sea region) were forts. It should be noted that other sites could also be considered forts. However, at these sites, either the plan was not sufficiently clear, or their pottery was insufficient to provide a precise date.

180. Many of the sites in the Jordan Valley and Dead Sea region (listed in Lipschits 1997a: table D-4-F-1 and fig. 17) may be classified as encampments; they typically have one or more structures, along with a fence or several fences.

181. See sites 1–6 in the Jordan Valley and Dead Sea region in Lipschits 1997a: table D-4-F-1 and fig. 17.

182. For a description of the discoveries at these sites, see Kochavi 1972: 111–13, site nos. 39, 40, 41, 42, 43(?), 44, 45, 49, 51, 52, and 57. In this connection, note that all along the road that connects this route with the Michmash region there are 7 additional Iron Age sites, which were surveyed in the Benjamin survey. On these sites, see Mazar, Amit, and Ilan 1984: 236–50.

183. Also see the discussion in the Benjamin survey, below, in §4.3.3a, esp. pp. 245–249. See also Mazar, Amit, and Ilan 1984: 236–50.

184. Some of these sites are discussed as part of the Judean highland survey (below, §4.3.3b, esp. pp. 250–258, and in the list of sites in the Judean highland in Lipschits 1997a: table D-4-F-1 and fig. 17), and some are listed among the Iron Age II sites in the Jordan Valley and

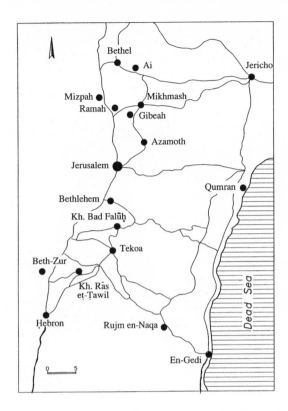

Map 10. A Reconstruction
of the Main Roads in the
Judean Desert.

4. From the south, the road to Jericho ran along the western littoral of the
   Dead Sea and connected Jericho with En-Gedi. There were 14 sites along
   this road during Iron Age II.[185]

As noted above, there was a second major center during this period at En-
Gedi. There was a small fort nearby,[186] and a major road through Wadi Arugot
led to the site from Tekoa (D. Amit 1992: 345–62). There are 13 sites known to
be from Iron Age II along this route.[187] One branch of this road ran down

the Dead Sea area; see Sites 13, 14, 16, 18, 19, 20, 21, 22, 23, 25, 26, 29, and 31 in the list of
Iron Age II sites in the Jordan Valley and Dead Sea region (1997a: table D-4-F-1 and fig. 18).

185. See Sites 7, 8, 9, 10, 11, 12, 15, 17, 24, 27, 28, 30, 32, and 35 in the list of Iron II sites
in the Jordan Valley and Dead Sea region (Lipschits 1997a: table D-4-F-1 and fig. 17; cf. Lipschits 2000: 40–42).

186. See Site 59 in the list of sites in the Jordan Valley and Dead Sea region from the late
Iron Age (Lipschits 1997a: table D-4-F-1 and fig. 17).

187. See Sites 36, 38, 44, 47, 48, 49, 51, 52, 53, 54, 55, 56, and 57 in the list of Iron II sites
in the Jordan Valley and Dead Sea region (Lipschits 1997a: table D-4-F-1 and fig. 17; 2000a:
40–42).

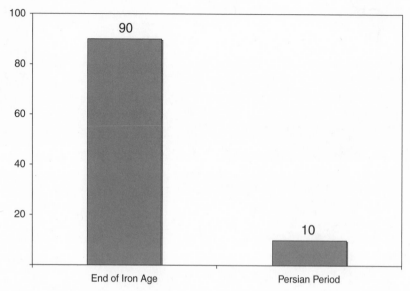

Fig. 4.5. Settled dunams in the eastern strip at the end of the Iron Age and during the Persian Period.

through Wadi Ḥaṣṣaṣon, and along it were 4 Iron II sites.[188] Another road con-nected these two roads and the longitudinal road that crossed into the Horkania Valley and Jericho; there were 3 sites along this road during Iron Age II.[189]

A comparison of the settlement array described above with settlements dur-ing the Persian Period leads to the conclusion that the collapse of settlement at the end of the Iron Age was drastic. The drop in settlement is estimated at 95%, a rate without parallel in other regions of Judah at that time. There were 59 sites throughout the entire region between En-Gedi and Jericho at the end of the Iron Age, but there were only 3 sites in this region (Jericho, Ketef Yericho, and En-Gedi) during the Persian Period. The decline in the total number of settled dunams was about 89% (from approximately 90 dunams at the end of the Iron Age to some 10 dunams during the Persian Period). However, if there was a settlement gap during the sixth century B.C.E. at the 3 sites that were occupied during the Persian Period, it is probable that the collapse of the settlement array

188. Along the road that ran through Wadi Ḥasaṣon stood settlement nos. 39–42 in the list of Iron II sites in the Jordan Valley and Dead Sea region (Lipschits 1997a: table D-4-F-1 and fig. 17).

189. This connecting road ran down the course of Wadi Ḥaṣṣaṣon and crossed through the upper part of Wadi Tekoa. It entered the southern opening of the Horkania Valley, where it joined the road running down from Wadi Dragot (Darage). The sites that existed alongside this road are sites 43, 45, and 46 on the list of sites in the Jordan Valley and Dead Sea region from Iron Age II (Lipschits 1997a: table D-4-F-1 and fig. 17; 2000a: 40–42).

in this region at the beginning of the sixth century B.C.E. was universal—the area was depleted of its entire population.

4.3.2e. Summary
The conclusion that must be drawn from the data assembled in this section is that the Babylonian campaign brought about complete destruction in Jerusalem and its immediate environs. The region was almost completely emptied of its population and remained so until the beginning of the Persian Period. As part of the Babylonians' military activity, the forts along Judah's western border were also destroyed; the Shephelah, which had not yet recovered from the grave blow dealt by Sennacherib's campaign, suffered yet another trauma and was likewise emptied of its inhabitants. In contrast, it appears that the hinterland areas in the south and to the east of the kingdom fell in a longer, more-complex process that eventually led to consequences just as ruinous. The thriving array of settlements present in the Judean Desert, Jordan Valley, and Dead Sea environs gave way completely. At the beginning of the Persian Period, after an extended gap, only the settlements at En-Gedi and Jericho were reestablished, alongside a new settlement at Ketef Yericho. The Judean kingdom's border forts in the Beer-Sheba–Arad Valleys collapsed as well, together with the settlements that had existed under their protection. Tribal groups that had previously resided near the border began to make incursions into the vast, relatively empty space north of the Negev and into the southern part of the Shephelah and as far as the Hebron Hills.

4.3.3. *The Archaeological Evidence for a "Remnant" in Judah after the Destruction of Jerusalem*

4.3.3a. The Archaeological Evidence for a "Remnant" in Benjamin
Many scholars have noted the different fate that befell the Benjamin region and the archaeological reality that prevailed there after the destruction of Jerusalem.[190] This region, which according to the biblical accounts was the center of Judah in the period following the destruction of Jerusalem, had four important settlements that were not destroyed and that in fact flourished during the sixth century B.C.E.[191] The primary, most important settlement in Judah at this time was *Tell en-Naṣbeh*, which is identified with biblical Mizpah.[192] Excavations at this site have

---

190. See, e.g., Malamat 1950: 227; Wright 1957: 199; Lapp 1965: 6; Weinberg 1970: 206; Weinberg 1972: 47–50; Stern 1982: 229; 2000: 51; Barstad 1996: 47–48; Milevski 1996–97; Lipschits 1999a; 2001: 131–35. This view has been adopted by most of the histories that deal with this period; see, e.g., Miller and Hayes 1986: 416–17; Ahlström 1993: 795; Stern 2001: 321–23; Albertz 2003: 95–96.

191. For a detailed discussion of the excavation sites and the resulting archaeological profile, see Lipschits 1999a.

192. For a review of the geographical and historical research on Tell en-Naṣbeh, including the intense controversies surrounding the identity of the site, see McCown 1947: 13–49; Muilenburg 1954; Diringer 1967: 329–30; see also the summary in Lipschits 1997a: 203. I reject the attempt recently made by Magen and Dadon (1999: 62) to return to Albright's proposal

produced results indicating unbroken settlement continuity throughout the Iron Age (Strata 3–4) and the Babylonian Period (Stratum 2).[193] In Stratum 2, apparently at the beginning of the sixth century B.C.E., the plan of the city and the fortification system underwent a significant change. The inner gate and the western wall (which connected the inner and outer gates) fell into disuse, and the circular plan of the site, which had characterized the city plan from the ninth century B.C.E. onward, disappeared. It appears that this change was not a result of the capture and razing of the city, because there is no archaeological evidence of a destruction level: very few sherds were found on the floors of the buildings, the walls were preserved to a relatively high level, and many pillars were found in situ. These finds may be construed as evidence that the site was abandoned; only later was the area within the walls leveled, and the houses of Stratum 2 were erected on the leveled ruins of the site (Zorn 1993a: 151, 161–63, 175–76; 2003).

The city of Stratum 2 continued to use the wall and the outer gate that had been built at the end of the Iron Age (Stratum 3B). The foundations of some of the buildings in Stratum 2 were based on walls of the structures of the previous stratum, and there is clear continuity in the pottery assemblages found in the two strata.[194] Nevertheless, the general plan of the city in Stratum 2 is different in

---

(1923: 110–12) to identify Nebi-Samuel as Mizpah. At Tell en-Naṣbeh, there were five excavation seasons (1926, 1927, 1929, 1932, and 1935) directed by Badé. McCown and Wampler, who published the final reports of the excavations were unable to present a clear stratigraphic picture; because of the way the reports were published and the data presented, only a few additional studies have attempted to reexamine the results of the excavation. For a critique of the excavation reports, see Wright 1947: 70; Albright 1948: 202; McClellan 1984: 53–54; Finkelstein 1986: 57. Because of the sad state of the final reports, Zorn's doctoral dissertation (1993) is especially important: he processed much of the raw material left by Badé and attempted to present a well-formulated stratigraphic profile of the site. For a summary of the stratigraphic picture, see Lipschits 1999a: 165–70.

193. McCown (1947: 181–203) detected two major strata from the Iron Age. Stratum 2 is dated to the period between the eleventh century B.C.E. and the seventh century B.C.E. Stratum 1 is divided into two stages: the early stage is dated to the seventh and early sixth centuries B.C.E., and the late stage is dated to a period after the Babylonian destruction. Meager remnants of walls were found on top of various parts of the Iron Age city wall and were dated to the Persian Period. Zorn (1993a: 103–62, 312–36) also has emphasized the continuity of settlement at Mizpah throughout the entire Iron Age. Zorn argues that McCown's Stratum 2 (Zorn's Stratum 4) is limited to the twelfth and eleventh centuries B.C.E.; he makes the beginning of the early stage of McCown's Stratum 1 ("early 1") much earlier, in the tenth century B.C.E. (Zorn's Stratum 3); he expands the chronological span of this stratum to the end of the Iron Age; and he divides it into three substages. Stratum 3C is to be dated to the tenth century B.C.E., Stratum 3B to the first half of the ninth century B.C.E., and Stratum 3A to the time between 850 and 586 B.C.E. Zorn divides McCown's later stage of Stratum 1 ("late 1") into two secondary stages: The earlier stage he labels Stratum 2 and dates to the Babylonian and Persian Periods. The later stage, his Stratum 1, dates to the Hellenistic Period (1993a: 163–85).

194. McCown (1947: 198, 202) had detected this phenomenon, particularly in the area of the Stratum 3 gate, on which several structures belonging to Stratum 2 were built; see also Zorn 1993a: 154. We may speculate that the change in the gate system was the result of a different

orientation from the plan of the city from the beginning of the Iron Age (Zorn 1993a: 155, 163–64, 167, 172, 336–37; 1997: 29–38, 66; 2003: 419–33). A comprehensive "master plan" is conspicuously absent: there is no connection between the orientation of the buildings and the orientation of the wall and the natural topography of the site.[195] Also conspicuously absent are the dwelling units that were a major part of the plan of Stratum 3. Instead, Stratum 2 had several large, central buildings, testimony to the fact that Mizpah had ceased to be a Judean border city with a diverse Judean population[196] and had become a governmental and administrative center, noteworthy for its storehouses and the number of relatively large residential buildings.[197] Most of the dwelling units in Stratum 2 were built according to the classic "four-room house" plan, which is evidence that at least some of the people who lived there were Judeans. Nevertheless, the quality of the construction in this stratum is superior to that of Stratum 3 in its various phases,[198] and this can be considered proof of the status and wealth of the inhabitants of this stratum. The Babylonian finds from this stratum strengthen this conclusion (Zorn 2003: 433–38; cf. Vanderhooft and Horowitz 2002).

The circumstances surrounding the end of Stratum 2 are unclear, but it appears that the transition to Stratum 1, like that from Stratum 3 to Stratum 2, was unaccompanied by destruction.[199] Presumably, the settlement at Mizpah

conception of the city's defense; however, it may also be that this change reflects a different evaluation of the external dangers that faced the city. In the later stage, when the external threat to the city apparently intensified, the external gate was narrowed. Zorn (1993a: 176) connects this development with the location of Mizpah on the northern boundary of the province and interprets it in the context of (Persian) imperial disputes.

195. The assumption is that this is the result of filling and leveling large sections of Stratum 3, which blurred the natural contour lines on which the earlier strata were founded.

196. Zorn estimated that approximately 800–1,000 residents lived in the city of Stratum 3, and in Stratum 2 this number shrank to half (400–500 residents).

197. See Zorn 1993a: 167–83, and the plan on p. 966; 2003: 419–33; Lipschits 1999a: 167–70. It appears that the city's main residential area was on the eastern and southern side, close to the wall. This area included Judahite structures having three or four rooms, alongside other structures whose function is not clear; some of these structures can be classified as large storehouses and workshops. There were additional structures in the center and western part of the site. Buildings that may be construed as Mesopotamian palaces of the "open court" style were found in the northern and southwestern part of the city, and the area between them, in the center of the site, apparently was used for storage.

198. Evidence of the fine quality of construction in Stratum 2 may be found in the construction techniques used for the inner walls, the widespread use of stone and monoliths, and the larger size of the houses in this stratum. See Zorn's (1993a: 167–83) discussion of this; he also claims (pp. 173–74) that the average area of Stratum 2 structures was larger by a significant percentage, almost double the average area of Stratum 3 structures. See also Zorn 2003: 419–33.

199. Zorn (1993a: 184; 2003: 419–33) bases his conclusions on the height of some of the preserved walls and pillars that remained standing, as well as the absence of pottery on the floors (except for three rooms). McCown (1947: 62–63) did not find any evidence of destruction or ruin in this stratum either, and he concluded that the settlement was abandoned when its strategic and political status had declined.

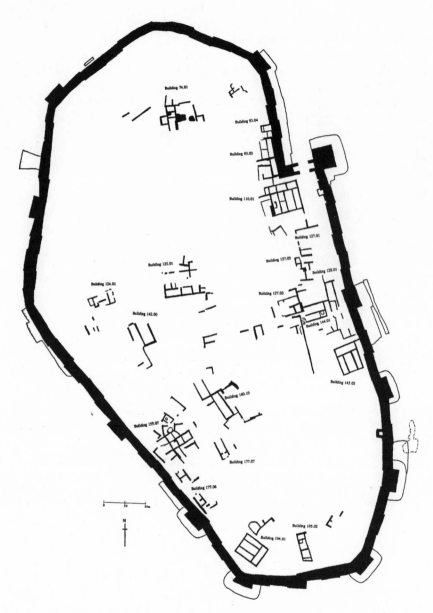

Fig. 4.6. A plan of (Zorn's) Stratum 2 at Mizpah. Courtesy J. R. Zorn.

was occupied at least until the mid-fifth century B.C.E. There is even a small amount of material remains that attests to continued occupation throughout the Persian Period, accompanied by a prolonged process of abandonment that was not complete until the beginning of the Hellenistic Period (McCown 1947: 63, 185–86, 202, 225–27; Zorn 1993a: 184–85).

There is also marked settlement continuity at *Tell el-Fûl*, which is identified as *Gibeah*.[200] It is at Tell el-Fûl that the most important stratum for learning about the material culture of this region during the sixth century B.C.E. was excavated.[201] The destruction at this site at the end of the Iron Age was only partial. In most of the occupied area, there is full settlement continuity. We may even assume that, in the first half of the sixth century B.C.E., the built-up area extended beyond the city wall, and the local population was growing. Tell el-Fûl was deserted only at the end of the sixth century and the beginning of the fifth century B.C.E.; the settlement remained unoccupied after that until the beginning of the Hellenistic Period.[202]

---

200. For a summary of the reasons for identifying Tell el-Fûl with Gibeah, see Arnold 1990: 39–60, with further literature. Four excavation seasons were conducted at the site, directed by Albright (1922–23; 1933) and Lapp (1964). For a discussion of the excavation results for the period between the end of the Iron Age and the Persian Period, see Lipschits 1999a: 177–78.

201. As discussed previously (§4.2, pp. 204–205), Fortress IIIb at Tell el-Fûl serves as one of the main keys for understanding the material culture of the sixth century B.C.E. in Benjamin (N. L. Lapp 1981: 40–46; see the discussion of the pottery on pp. 81–101). Albright (1924a: 20, 25–27; 1933: 10), followed by Sinclair (1960: 33–35), first dated Fortress IIIa to the early seventh century B.C.E. Fortress IIIb was dated to the second half of the seventh century, and the date of its destruction fixed at the beginning of the sixth century B.C.E. Although a large amount of material dated to the Persian Period was uncovered during the first excavation season, Albright did not classify any specific stratum as belonging to this period and believed that, after the Babylonian destruction, the site was abandoned and rebuilt only in the fourth century B.C.E. (Stratum IV). These conclusions drew sharp criticism, which was directed at the stratigraphic analysis, chronological assignments of strata, and historical interpretation (Franken 1961: 471–72; Amiran 1963: 263–64). Sinclair (1964: 60–62) subsequently revised some of his earlier conclusions and proposed that Stratum IV be divided into two stages and that the beginning of new settlement on the site after the destruction of Fortress IIIb (Stratum IVa) be dated to the end of the sixth century B.C.E. N. L. Lapp (1981: 59) accepted this conclusion and, accordingly, changed her identification of Stratum IVa, now referring to it as Stratum IIIb. Her concern was to reflect the fact that this sixth-century B.C.E. stratum is a direct continuation of the last Iron Age settlement stratum (Stratum IIIa). N. L. Lapp did not accept P. Lapp's interpretation of the 1964 excavations regarding the end of this stratum and the transition to Stratum IIIb; according to P. Lapp, the site was destroyed by the Babylonians at the beginning of the sixth century B.C.E. (Lapp 1965: 2–10). N. L. Lapp showed that the Babylonian destruction was selective, and except for the destruction of the fortress and one of the buildings in the northeast part of the site, the settlement continued uninterrupted in the sixth century B.C.E. (N. L. Lapp 1976: 25; 1981: 39).

202. See N. L. Lapp 1981: 39, 59. Lapp connected the abandonment of the site with the relocation of the residents to Jerusalem at the beginning of the Persian Period. See also Stern 2001: 321–22.

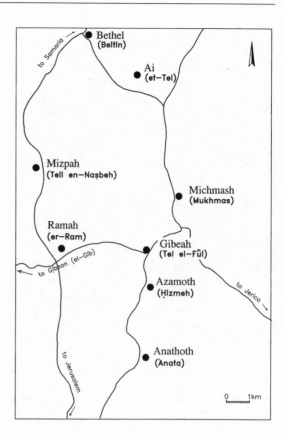

Map 11. Major sites in the region of Benjamin.

Similarly, at *Bethel* (identified with the site of Beitin),[203] no evidence of Babylonian destruction was found, and Albright concluded that the settlement remained occupied until later in the sixth century B.C.E.[204] This view is supported by the final reports, which date the destruction of the last Iron Age stratum to the last third of the sixth century B.C.E.[205] It is not clear whether Bethel

---

203. On the identification of Bethel, see Albright 1928: 9–11; Kelso et al. 1968: 1–2; and cf. Koenen 2003: 3–26. Four excavation seasons were held at Beitin, with a gap of 20 years between the first season conducted by Albright (1934) and the next three, conducted by Kelso (1954, 1957, and 1960).

204. Albright (1949a: 142) based his conclusions largely on the dating of pottery to the sixth century B.C.E.; he identified the pottery as intermediate between late Iron Age pottery and Persian Period pottery.

205. See Sinclair 1964: 62; P. Lapp 1965: 6; Kelso 1968: 75–76. Kelso (p. 37 n. 6) tried to suggest an even more specific time for the destruction of the site: between the 3rd year of Nabonidus (533 B.C.E.) and the early days of Darius (521 B.C.E.). This dating is based on his interpretation of the pottery assemblage from the Iron Age II burned buildings and the fact that this material is, in his opinion, later than the pottery assemblages from the destruction

was abandoned for any amount of time, and the remains on the site from the beginning of the Persian Period are scant. In any event, it appears that during the
fifth century B.C.E. the settlement recovered. The major evidence for this recovery comes from the central section of the site (Area II), which contains remains
of structures that continued to exist until the Hellenistic Period.[206]

Another site that apparently was not destroyed at the beginning of the sixth
century B.C.E. is Gibeon, identified as the site associated with the village of
el-Jib.[207] An analysis of the excavated materials reveals that, at this time, Gibeon was thriving and increasing in prominence.[208] There is no archaeological

---

levels at Tell Beit Mirsim, Lachish, Tell el-Fûl, and other sites destroyed by the Babylonians.
Dever (1971, followed in part by Koenen 2003: 27–68) has disagreed with Kelso's conclusions,
particularly his ceramic comparisons and laid greater emphasis on the the eighth and seventh
centuries B.C.E. ceramic parallels available from comparing the Beitin material. He criticized
Kelso's generalizations, but stressed that his criticism in no way rejected the possibility that
Bethel was destroyed later than Jerusalem. Nonetheless, additional support for the continued
occupation of the site during the sixth century B.C.E. may be found in Nancy Lapp's discussion
of Attic pottery from Shechem; she concludes that Shechem Stratum V should be dated to
525–475 B.C.E. On the basis of these conclusions, Wright (1965: 137, 238–41, and fig. 113)
compared the local pottery of this level with the pottery found at Bethel, Gibeon, and Gibeah
and dated the destruction of these sites to the mid-sixth century B.C.E. at the earliest. Despite
the consensus among most scholars regarding the question of continued settlement at Bethel
after the destruction of Jerusalem, it is noteworthy that there is no clear settlement stratum at
this site dated to this period, and most of the reconstructions are based on what dating is assigned to several pottery vessels from the Iron Age pottery assemblage.

206. See Kelso et al. 1968: 37–38, 52, pl. 7. This conclusion is problematic, because, at least
according to Lapp's analysis (in Kelso 1968: 77), the pottery from this stratum does not belong
to the fourth century B.C.E.; see also Dever 1971: 466. It should be noted that Albright's excavations produced almost no pottery from the Persian Period, and in some of the excavation
areas, there was a Hellenistic stratum directly above the remains from the late Iron Age. The
first evidence of resettlement in the Persian Period is a wall found in Area I. The wall was
roughly built from large stones that, according to Albright, were taken from the Iron Age city
wall. It should be remembered that, apart from the fact that these remnants are on top of the
Iron Age destruction level, there is no specific evidence for dating the material. Even in the final report of the excavation, only pottery that can be dated late in the Persian Period is published. See Albright 1934b: 25; 1934c: 14; 1935b: 198; Kelso 1955: 9–10; Kelso et al. 1968: 5–
7, and pls. 7, 28. Because no architectural evidence from the Persian Period was found on the
site, Kelso theorized that the settlement from this period was not located on the tell but in the
lower areas, near the springs, south of the major areas of excavation. With regard to the possibility of reconstructing a monumental building of the Persian Period on the eastern part of the
hill, on the basis of two damaged pillar bases found there, see Kelso 1955: 9–10 and fig. 3, and
see the quotation of Albright's comment there, in n. 5 (Stern 1982: 31).

207. On the identification of the site, see Albright 1924: 94; Abel 1933–38: 2.347–73; Pritchard 1960b: 1–2. Five major excavation seasons were held at Gibeon under the direction of
Pritchard (1956–57, 1959–60, 1962), but the method of excavation and the published reports
do not allow us to make clear stratigraphic distinctions. It is impossible to date satisfactorily either the structures or the objects that belong to the various stages of settlement. For a criticism
of Pritchard's method of excavation and his publications, see P. Lapp 1968: 391–93.

208. In 1964, a final report on the winepresses and fortifications that were excavated in
the 1959–60 seasons was published, and for the first time it became possible to conclude with

evidence of destruction of the city wall or other structures at the end of the Iron Age.[209] An analysis of the pottery assemblage and *mwṣh* seal impressions found in the winepresses and pits in the northwest area of the tell are evidence for continued occupation during the sixth century B.C.E.[210] The uninterrupted occupation of Gibeon is supported by the objects found in the "Israelite" structures in Area 17, all of which are dated to the sixth century B.C.E.,[211] and by the 56 *gbʾn gdr* inscriptions on pilgrim flask handles,[212] which were discovered in the fill of the large pool.[213] Based on the stratigraphic, paleographic, and ce-

---

certainty that the site was occupied at the end of the Iron Age and in the Persian Period. Pritchard (1964a: 27) tried to argue that Gibeon was destroyed at the beginning of the sixth century B.C.E. and that there was a settlement gap until the first century B.C.E., but it appears that Pritchard's opinion was based on historical considerations and has not been archaeologically validated (de Vaux 1966: 130–35). A careful analysis of the materials reveals the opposite picture: the settlement continued throughout the sixth century B.C.E. and flourished even more during this period than it had in earlier times. For an extensive discussion of the evidence for this period and its significance, see Lipschits 1999a: 172–76.

209. Pritchard's conclusion (1956: 73–75; 1964a: 35–40) has no archaeological support at all. See the criticisms of Albright 1966: 32–33; Barag 1967: 143; Lapp 1968: 391–93. For a discussion of this subject, see Lipschits 1999a: 173–74.

210. For discussion of these materials, see Lipschits 1999a: 173. Pritchard dated the entire assemblage to the eighth and seventh centuries B.C.E. On the pottery, see, e.g., Loci 137, 141, 211, and 212 in Pritchard 1964a: 20–23; and see P. Lapp's analysis (1968: 391–93); N. L. Lapp 1981: 85; van Volsem 1987: 103–9. On the *mwṣh* seal impressions, see Locus 136 (Pritchard 1964a: 20, and fig. 50:4, 7). One *mwṣh* seal impression was published by Pritchard (1959a: 27) among the private seal impressions, and it is parallel to the 28 *mwṣh* seal impressions found at Tell en-Naṣbeh and the single example found at Jericho. Four additional *mwṣh* seal impressions were discovered in the 1959 season, and Pritchard dated them to the Persian Period, together with a gold ring and a silver ring with an obscure inscription (1959a: 25; 1960: 11).

211. The finds from the sixth century B.C.E. include pottery decorated with wedge-shaped and reed impressions, and *mwṣh* seal impressions. See Pritchard (1964a: 20, 21, 23; figs. 32:7; 33:13; 34:14; 48:17, 22; pls. 50:1, 4, 7; 51:6).

212. Classifying these vessels as pilgrim flasks follows the system developed by Stern 1982: 32, 114–15 and Amiran 1975.

213. The first full report published by Pritchard (1959a) was devoted to the epigraphic material and included 56 *gbʾn gdr* inscriptions on the handles of the pilgrim flasks, some 80 seal impressions of various types, and 8 private seals. All of the material (except for 5 seal impressions) was found in the fill of the large pool, which, according to Pritchard (1959a: v–vi) was filled from the area south of the pool. The discussion of the *gbʾn gdr* engravings is important for our purposes. According to Pritchard (1959a: 15–16), the flasks were filled with wine or oil, and the produce was intended for export—this is the only explanation for their being marked with the site name. The recording of the place of production and name of the manufacturer was meant to guarantee that the vessels would be returned after the contents were received. This explains the absence of inscriptions of this kind at other sites in Judah and Benjamin. Alternatively, he proposed that the inscriptions be seen as a sign guaranteeing the quality of the product, on the premise that Gibeon enjoyed the status of a quality wine producer and that the names of the people inscribed on the handles were well known (1959a: 16). On this subject, see also a separate essay by Pritchard (1959b: 22–24) devoted to the wine industry, in which he describes at length the role of the inscribed pilgrim flasks and the way they were used.

A new approach to understanding the significance and date of the inscriptions appeared in an article by Demsky (1971), who says that the inscriptions should be divided into two groups ramic analyses,[214] all of these inscriptions should be dated to the sixth century B.C.E., and this date should also be applied to the large cemetery unearthed at the foot of the tell.[215]

In summary, the archaeological results from the major sites excavated in the Benjamin region reveal no evidence of a destruction at the beginning of the sixth century B.C.E., apart from a partial destruction at Tell el-Fûl. In all of the excavated areas, occupation continued uninterrupted during the seventh and sixth centuries B.C.E., throughout the years of Babylonian rule. At the end of the sixth century B.C.E. and during the fifth and fourth centuries B.C.E., these four major sites gradually declined in population. This decline may be connected to the transfer of the center of activity to the Jerusalem region after the Return to Zion, which resulted in the decline in status of Mizpah, along with the entire Benjamin region.

The data from the archaeological survey conducted in the territory of Benjamin help complete the picture obtained from an analysis of the archaeological finds at the central sites. These data enable us to understand the demographic processes at work in the region between the sixth and fifth centuries B.C.E. and also help us to sketch a broad settlement profile for each of these periods. In addition, the survey data can be used to obtain a wider perspective on the agricultural and military systems in the region and on its periphery.[216]

---

representing two families of wine producers in villages near Gibeon. The wine was sent to Gibeon, which was the center of production and trade. Each of the families wrote its name on the pilgrim flasks so that they would be returned, and the vessels found at Gibeon were those that had been damaged and were therefore discarded.

214. For an extensive discussion of the *stratigraphic analysis*, see Lipschits 1999a: 174–76, with further literature. See especially the view of Wright 1963: 211. Regarding the *paleography*, some scholars have argued that the inscriptions should be dated earlier, in the seventh century B.C.E.: Avigad 1959: 131; Demsky 1971: 23; in contrast, most scholars date all of the inscriptions to the sixth century B.C.E.: Albright 1960b: 37; Cross 1962b; Wright 1963: 210–11. In terms of *ceramic analysis*, it appears that the pilgrim flask with inscribed handles should be dated to the sixth century B.C.E. Pritchard (1959a: 3, 12–13, fig. 6:2) postulated that most of the flasks belong to one type; because he was unable to find an exact parallel to the inscribed flask, he proposed seeing it as a special type that was manufactured for a specific purpose and therefore was not common at other sites. A comprehensive discussion of ceramics parallel to the pilgrim flask with inscribed handles has been presented by Amiran (1975): she found parallels at Megiddo, Beth-Shemesh, and particularly in tombs from the end of the Iron Age at Beth-Shean—all of which are very close to the type of flask found at Gibeon. Amiran theorized (1975: 129, 132, and pl. 2:1–5) that this flask was the last link in a chain of flasks that went back to the tenth to ninth centuries B.C.E. and that their development may be traced through the eighth and seventh centuries B.C.E. For parallels to the flask from Gibeon, see Amiran 1975: fig. 1:4 and pl. 11; see also Amiran 1971: pls. 81:15; 82:13. Another vessel of the same type was found at Tel Batash (A. Mazar 1985: 319, and fig. 11:3).

215. See Eshel 1987: 14. On the finds in some of the graves, see Dajani 1953: 66–69; cf. Eshel and Kloner 1990: 39.

216. For an analysis of the survey results, see Milevski 1996–97; Lipschits 1999a: 180–84.

Nonetheless, the unique fate of the region of Benjamin during Babylonian rule requires us to approach the survey's results with particular caution. The survey data must be interpreted through the lens of data from the excavations, which show that the central settlements in the Benjamin region continued without interruption throughout the years of Babylonian rule and diminished gradually, beginning at the end of the sixth century B.C.E. and continuing throughout the fifth century B.C.E. Thus, because there is settlement and ceramic continuity in the Benjamin region throughout the transition from the Iron Age to the Babylonian and Persian Periods, the evidence from the sixth century B.C.E. is included in the survey data as part of the broad description of Iron Age II. This is significant, because, according to the survey data, no evidence is assigned to the sixth century B.C.E. (not even as evidence of a settlement gap), and Iron Age II spanned a period of more than 500 years.[217] Furthermore, the picture of the Persian Period that emerges from the survey largely reflects the fifth century B.C.E., when the Benjamin region was in the middle of a process of depopulation and settlement decline. If this is true, then the evidence assigned to the Persian Period by the survey reflects a low point, rather than a peak in settlement activity or a reconstruction stage, such as the rebuilding that took place in Jerusalem during the Return to Zion.[218]

The first fact that emerges from the survey is the sharp drop in the number of sites (60%, from 146 during Iron Age II to 59 in the Persian Period.) A parallel drop is estimated in the number of settled dunams (56.5%, from 1,150 in Iron Age II to approximately 500 in the Persian Period).[219] An analysis of the excavation results shows that, for both parameters (number of settlement sites and estimated total size of the settled area), the area was more thoroughly settled during the sixth century B.C.E. than during the Persian Period.[220]

---

217. See the remarks by the surveyors in Magen and Finkelstein 1993: 138, 346.

218. See the comment by Finkelstein in Magen and Finkelstein 1993: 27. The paucity of pottery from the Persian Period at sites covered by this survey demonstrates that activity was lower at these sites during the Persian Period than during the Iron Age. The scarcity of pottery from the Persian Period must be taken into account when the size of settlements from one period is compared with the other.

219. See Lipschits 1999a: 180–84. For a different appraisal—that the decline in the number of sites was approximately 75%—see Milevski 1996–97: 18. The fundamental difference between these two appraisals is due to the fact that Milevski included the area close to Jerusalem in the Benjamin region, although it historically had a fate different from the fate of the Benjamin region. Including the area near Jerusalem results in a significant increase in the number of sites from the late Iron Age and heightens evidence for destruction in the Benjamin region; see Lipschits 1997a: 246–75; also see the discussion above, in §4.3.2a (pp. 210–218).

220. This hypothesis is contrary to the theory expressed by Finkelstein (in Magen and Finkelstein 1993: 27). Finkelstein argued that, in the early sixth century B.C.E., at the time of the destruction of Jerusalem, a severe crisis beset settlement in the Benjamin region—the picture being even more grim than the survey reflects. In the fifth and fourth centuries B.C.E., on the other hand, some recovery occurred—which is what the survey reflects. In my opinion,

The sharpest decline in number of settlements occurred in the eastern part of the region of Benjamin, especially the northeastern sector.[221] East of a line running through Bethel-Michmash-Gibeah-Anathoth, approximately 71 sites from Iron Age II were found in the survey,[222] compared with only 14 sites from the Persian Period (a drop of about 80%). The major decline in number of sites is registered in the area between Michmash and the slope running down toward Jericho. In this area, 27 sites from the Iron Age were surveyed, compared with only 1 site from the Persian Period—a site that was located in the northern part of the area.[223] These data show that settlements totally disappeared from this region, which only began to be settled at the end of the Iron Age.[224] A marked reduction in settlement was also noted by the survey in the northern part of the Benjamin region (the area of modern Ramallah). During Iron Age II, there were about 12 sites, most of them in the western portion of the watershed, compared with only 2 sites from the Persian Period.

The primary conclusion that emerges from the data is that, apparently, by the sixth century B.C.E., the main settlements in Benjamin were at the core of the region, the narrow zone along either side of the watershed, while settlement in the northern and eastern zones ceased almost entirely. This conclusion is in accord with existing information about the complete cessation of settlement throughout the Jordan Valley and the western littoral of the Dead Sea, and it appears that this, too, is connected with the collapse of the economic, military, and political system of the kingdom of Judah.[225] Most of the surviving settlements were concentrated along the hill country ridge and its upper slopes (in

---

Finkelstein's conclusion is a general historical assessment that is not supported by archaeological evidence. There is no doubt that the settlement pattern in Benjamin reflects a crisis. However, as noted, the only possible point of comparison is between the survey data and sites excavated in Benjamin—which indicate the opposite picture. During the sixth century B.C.E., settlements in Benjamin continued to flourish and prosper; the dwindling of settlements began only in the late sixth and early fifth centuries B.C.E. The evidence regarding the centrality of Gibeon as a wine-producing center at this time also leads us to conclude that there was vigorous agricultural production in the region.

221. This point has also been well described by Milevski 1996–97: 18–19.

222. On the survey in this region, see also Mazar, Amit, and Ilan 1984: 236–50, with further literature. See also the discussion in §4.3.2d above (pp. 232–237).

223. It should be noted that the existence of this single, isolated site in the Persian Period is not certain; in any case, its size (0.5 dunam) does not materially change the picture (Goldfus and Golani in Magen and Finkelstein 1993: 279). See also the comments of the surveyors (1993: 138).

224. See also the comments of the surveyors in Magen and Finkelstein 1993: 279, 346.

225. See the discussion above, in §4.3.2d (pp. 232–237). Remember, too, that the northern region of Benjamin bordered the province of Samaria. It is unlikely that the leaders of the Yehud province or representatives of the Babylonian/Persian imperial regime could guarantee safe living conditions for residents of the border areas. This may be yet another reason for the sharp decline in settlement in northern Benjamin and the abandonment of pasture areas in the eastern part.

the central and western Benjamin region) and around the main economic and administrative centers that continued in the region.[226] The relative prosperity of this area must be attributed to the influence of the political center at Mizpah and the economic importance of Gibeon and Moṣah; it is likely that agricultural production was based around these settlements.

Settlements in the Benjamin region gradually grew more impoverished during the course of the fifth century B.C.E., possibly because of the transfer of the provincial capital to Jerusalem and the diminished status of Mizpah, as well as the reduced economic and security conditions in the region during the Persian Period (see Lipschits 1997b; 1999a: 182–85). All of these changes weakened the economic base of the settlements in the region, resulting in a sharp demographic decline. As a percentage, this decline may be estimated at about 60%: from some 1,150 settled dunams at the end of Iron Age II[227] to about 500 settled dunams in the Persian Period.

It is likely that some of the region's inhabitants moved to Jerusalem and its environs, but it is also possible that the decline in the region of Benjamin explains the growth of settlements in the northeastern part of the Shephelah (the area between Lod–Ono and Modi'in) during the Persian Period (Lipschits 1997b; cf Sapin 1991). The political stability and, even more, the growing economic activity in the coastal area during the Persian Period attracted many people from the hill country to settle nearby. The agricultural potential of the area and its proximity to the major coastal trade routes and the major roads to the Benjamin region and Jerusalem were additional incentives. In addition to this, we cannot rule out the possibility that this migration also had ideological motives. At the time of the Return, the ruling authority in Judah was transferred to those who returned from the Babylonian Exile, and they forced their religious, ritual, social, and national views upon the residents of the province. This may have pushed some of the inhabitants of Benjamin to migrate beyond the administrative limits of the province and to settle beyond its borders.

---

226. See the description and model presented by Magen and Finkelstein 1993: 20–21; see also the assessment of the surveyors as cited there, p. 138.

227. Compare this with the estimate by Broshi and Finkelstein (1990: 10; see also Finkelstein 1994: 175), who estimated that the total settled area at the end of the Iron Age was approximately 900 dunams. However, Broshi and Finkelstein included only 100 of the 146 sites that appear in the table in Lipschits 1997a: table D-4-B-2 and fig. 5. Ofer (1993: 2.217), on the other hand, estimated the total settled area at 1,100 dunams, on the basis of 135 occupied sites. However, it is not clear what basis Ofer (p. 221) used to separate late seventh and early sixth centuries B.C.E. data from data of the first two-thirds of the seventh century B.C.E. (which, according to his theory, belong to "Iron Age II D"; for a critique of this, see below). It is also unclear which data Ofer drew on to decide that settlement in Benjamin declined during the late seventh century and early sixth century B.C.E. His assessment that the Benjamin region at this time had 935 settled dunams has no archaeological basis, to the best of my knowledge; furthermore, his claim also contradicts the historical reconstruction of this period. On the grounds for the estimate given here, see the discussion in Lipschits 1999a: 180–84.

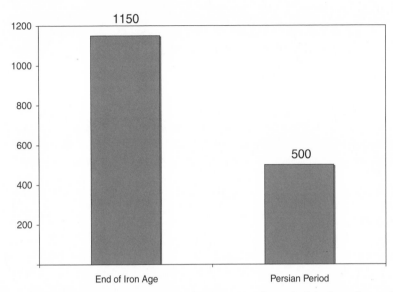

Fig. 4.7. Settled dunams in the region of Benjamin at the end of the Iron Age and during the Persian Period.

This demographic situation is the key to explaining 1 Chr 8:12–13, which states that Elpaal, whose origins were in Benjamin, "built Ono and Lod," while Beriah and Shema were "the ancestral heads of Aijalon's inhabitants." Biblical sources from the Persian Period contain several accounts that lend support to this demographic trend. Particularly striking in this regard is the account of marriages between "the people of Israel" and foreign women who came from among the "people of the lands" (Ezra 9:1–2, 12–15; 10:2–3, 10–44; Neh 10:31). This also provides the background for understanding Neh 13:23–24, where "[Nehemiah] saw Jews who had married women of Ashdod, Ammon, and Moab; and half of their children spoke the language of Ashdod and could not speak the language of Judah but spoke the language of various peoples." Relations with the people of Tyre are also important during this era; some of them even settled in Jerusalem (Neh 13:16). In addition, we have accounts of relations between "many in Judah" and Tobiah (Neh 6:17–19) and the prohibition against Ammonites and Moabites coming "into the congregation of God forever" (Neh 13:1). These turbulent social demographics also provide the background for understanding the proposition made by Sanballat, the Horonite, and Geshem, the Arabian, to meet with Nehemiah "in one of the villages in the plain of Ono" (Neh 6:2), where a Judean settlement of unclear political allegiance was located. The Jewish population known to have been in this area during the Hellenistic Period apparently goes back to this period (Lipschits 1997b: 10–11, 28–31).

4.3.3b. Archaeological Evidence for a "Remnant" in the Northern and Central Highland of Judah

The major sites excavated in the highland of Judah have not yielded any real evidence of a destruction at the end of the Iron Age, but it appears that, at least at some sites, there was a settlement gap throughout the sixth century B.C.E.[228] At *Hebron* (*Tell er-Rumeida*), the circumstances of the demise of the settlement at the end of the Iron Age have not been clarified, but it appears that the tell was abandoned in the sixth century B.C.E. and that there was a gap in occupation throughout the Persian Period.[229] At *Tel Rabud* (*Debir*), a settlement stratum dated to the seventh and the beginning of the sixth century B.C.E. was uncovered.[230] Traces of a fire may be associated with this stratum, but there is no obvious proof that the site was destroyed, and the reasons for its abandonment are not clear. Nevertheless, it appears that the gap in occupation at the site continued until the early Persian Period.[231] At *Beth-zur* (Kh. eṭ-Ṭabaqa), remains of a settlement from the end of the seventh and beginning of the sixth century B.C.E. were excavated.[232] Here, too, there was no objective evidence of a destruction at the beginning of the sixth century B.C.E.,[233] but many scholars believe that there was a gap in occupation until the beginning of the fifth century

---

228. According to Ofer (1993: 2.84–85), one of the most telling proofs of destruction at the end of the Iron Age was uncovered at Ḥorvat ʿAnim (Khirbet ʿUweina et-Taḥta), which I discussed above (p. 226 and n. 153). As noted earlier, the fortress structure and its fate are evidence that it belonged to the array of Negev fortresses and the evidence from it should be discussed in this context.

229. On this subject, see Ofer 1989: 91; 1993: 2.59–60, 132; *NEAEHL* 2.478; Chadwick 1992: 43; Jericke 2003: 31–33. There is no evidence that the settlement had already migrated to a new site in the valley at the foot of the tell in the Persian Period; the new settlement had its origin only in the Hellenistic Period.

230. On the site and its history, see Kochavi 1973: 49–54; *NEAEHL* 4.1440. On the characteristics of the settlement from the seventh to early sixth centuries B.C.E., see Kochavi 1973: 55–57. The city wall that had been destroyed in Sennacherib's campaign was rebuilt, and on the inside, an inner tower was built next to other structures (1973: 56). The density of these buildings is less than that in the previous stratum; however a "suburb" has been attributed to the site during this period, and this suburb, located on the western step of the hill, had an area of 5–7 dunams (Kochavi 1973: 53 n. 18; *NEAEHL* 4.1440).

231. On the evidence from the Persian Period, see Kochavi 1973: 55, 59, 61; see also *NEAEHL* 4.1440. Kochavi posited that there was a destruction at the beginning of the sixth century B.C.E., arguing for this from the gap in occupation; however, there is no clear-cut archaeological evidence of any destruction.

232. On the identification of the site and the history of excavation, see *NEAEHL* 1.196–98; Ofer 1993: 2.65–73; Lipschits 1997a: 276–80. On the late Iron Age materials, see Sellers et al. 1968: 24–13; see also Albright 1943: 8, and n. 9; Funk 1958: 14; Ofer 1993: 70–72.

233. After the first excavation season, the excavators concluded that the site had been destroyed by the Babylonians and was not resettled until the late Persian Period. This conclusion is rooted in a historical presumption—that the Babylonians totally devastated Judah—but this impression has no archaeological basis, and no evidence of destruction was found during the second excavation season (Funk 1958: 14; *NEAEHL* 1.197).

B.C.E.[234] However, this conclusion is problematic in terms of the archaeological data and does not seem to be based on the evidence:[235] archaeologically and historically, Beth-zur belongs to a region marked by settlement continuity throughout the sixth century B.C.E. (see also Ofer 1993: 2.73).

The data from the survey conducted in the highland of Judah bolster the conclusion that there were substantial differences in the settlement processes and demographic disposition between the southern and northern Judean highlands.[236] These facts seem to point to a steady increase in the number of settle-

---

234. Most scholars argue that the pottery evidence from Beth-zur reveals a gap between the end of the Iron Age (early sixth century B.C.E.) and the Persian Period (early fifth century B.C.E.; Sellers and Albright 1931: 9; Sellers 1933: 43). During the first excavation season, coins with the inscriptions *yhd* and *yhzqyhw*, dated to the late Persian and Hellenistic Periods, were found (Sellers 1933: 71–72, pl. 14:74, fig. 72). However, Beth-zur did not yield the seal impressions that were widespread throughout the province in the fifth and fourth centuries B.C.E., and only one fragment of Attic ware was found, which was dated to the early fifth century B.C.E. The chief evidence for this period was found during the first excavation season in Loci 58–62, especially in Room 59 (Sellers 1933: 15, fig. 5, pl. 14:1). Sellers found corroboration for the hypothesis of a gap in occupation in the results of the second season's excavations, especially in Area II, where a large gap was noticed between the sixth century B.C.E. and second century B.C.E. (Sellers et al. 1968: 29, 54–69). In support of the hypothesis, the fact that very few sherds from the Persian Period were found in Areas I and III was stressed (and see the discussion by Lapp in Sellers et al. 1968: 70–71). See the discussion by Sellers and Albright (1931: 8) and compare the different, earlier interpretation by Sellers (1933: 10). Stern agrees with the excavators' opinion (1982: 36–38; 2001: 437–38), as does Funk (*NEAEHL* 1.197).

235. From an archaeological perspective, serious doubt may be cast on the hypothesis that there was a gap between the end of the Iron Age and the Persian Period. There is no evidence whatsoever of a destruction at the site. In addition, pottery dated to the sixth century B.C.E. or the early Persian Period has been found at the site in assemblages containing pottery from the end of the Iron Age. For example, a carrot-shaped Persian bottle was found in Room 146, south of the fortress in a complex of rooms where most of the pottery can be dated to the late Iron Age (Sellers 1933: 20–35). In the water reservoir in the southern part of the site, much pottery from the Persian Period was also discovered in mixed assemblages containing pottery from the late Iron Age (1933: 27–31; Sellers et al. 1968: 69–70).

236. The first reliable archaeological information about Iron Age and Persian Period sites in the Judean highlands was collected in Albright's explorations in the 1920s (Albright 1924b: 4–5; 1925a; 1925b) and by Alt in the 1920s and 1930s (Alt 1925b; 1926b; 1932; 1934b). However, the most comprehensive and extensive information about the highland region was gathered in the emergency survey initiated in 1968 (Kochavi 1972: 19–91). Thirty-one sites from the Persian Period were surveyed in the Judean highlands (this is the number according to the survey data—not 28, as erroneously reported in the summary in Kochavi 1972: 23); the results of this survey for the first time provided a database that permitted a reconstructtion of the history of the region. A supplementary survey by Gutman (1970), together with other excavations and surveys conducted in the 1970s and 1980s (A. Mazar 1981, 1982; Amit 1992; *HA* 95 [1990] 65–66; 97 [1991] 77–78; etc.) provided much additional information. The picture has now been completed by the comprehensive survey led by Ofer (1993). For a summary of the settlement picture in the Judean highlands at the end of the Iron Age and in the Persian Period, see Ofer 1993: 4.16–18; 1998: 46–48; Lipschits 1997a: 291–99. It should be noted that Ofer took the most radical methodological approach of anyone who has published survey results with regard to the precise quantification of data (1993: 2.143ff.). A no-less problematic issue is Ofer's attempt to distinguish between pottery of the seventh century B.C.E. (Ofer's Iron

ments and in the total settled area in the entire hill country from the eleventh century to the eighth century B.C.E.[237] It appears that the entire region was dealt a severe blow during Sennacherib's campaign (701 B.C.E.), but in contrast to the rapid recovery made by the area north of Hebron (primarily in the area around Bethlehem), the area south of Hebron recovered only partially during the seventh century B.C.E., with settlement there remaining sparse.[238]

The area north of Hebron continued to be within the borders of Judah during the Persian Period. In this area as well, population diminished as one goes farther south, from Bethlehem to Beth-zur. At the end of the Iron Age, there were 63 sites in this area, most of them either near the major road that passes over the watershed line or close to the roads that branch from it eastward or westward.[239] The total settled area of these sites may be estimated at some 305 dunams.[240] This entire region, from south of Bethlehem to a little south of Beth-zur, stretches about 15 km. If we divide this into 3 equal strips oriented latitudinally, with each one 5 km wide, the decrease in the number of settlements and their normal distribution into large, medium, and small settlements is observable.[241]

- In the northernmost strip, there are 24 sites (45% of all sites in the area under discussion). The diversity in the size of these sites is remarkable, perhaps

Age IIc, 1993: 2.44–48) and pottery of the end of the seventh and early sixth century B.C.E. (Ofer's Iron Age IId, 1993: 2.48–50). I am dubious that such fine distinctions are so clear or sharp or may be maintained on the basis of archaeological surveys. For a criticism of Ofer's conclusions regarding the ceramic material, see Finkelstein 1994: 174–75.

237. Between the eleventh and eighth centuries B.C.E., virtually complete continuity may be noted at all of the sites; there is expansion into the border areas and a sharp rise in the importance of small settlements (small farms and sites of less than 5 dunams). See Ofer 1993: 2.121–26; see also the summary by Finkelstein 1994: 174–75.

238. See the data presented by Ofer 1993: 2.125–34, 138–42; 4.13–18; 1998: 46–48; see also the discussion below. See also the criticism of Ofer's conclusions by Finkelstein (1994: 174–75).

239. At most sites, there is no evidence that a topographical location convenient for defense was a consideration, and there is no evidence of fortification. The sites are scattered 1–2 km from each other (except for "blocks" of settlements consisting of 2–3 small sites) and are located in areas relatively convenient for settlement and agriculture. The number and size of the sites diminish noticeably as one moves farther east or west from the watershed divide. See Ofer 1993: 2.125–34, 138–42.

240. For the data on which this summary is based, see the table of sites in Lipschits 1997a: D-4-D-2 and fig. 10. Of these 63 sites, 6 sites are particularly important: 3 in the northwest (Kh. Zakandaḥ—21 dunams; Kh. Ḥubeilah—20 dunams; Kh. Judūr—19 dunams) and 3 in the southeast (Kh. et-Tuqū'—28 dunams; Kh. ez-Zāwiyye—18.4 dunams; Kh. Rās eṭ-Ṭawil—40 dunams). The total area of these sites is 146 dunams, which is 48% of the entire settled area in the region. To these primary sites we may add 10 more with an area of more than 5 dunams and that together total some 96 dunams (approximately 31.5% of the settled area). Most of the sites (47, which is approximately 75% of the sites) are identified as farms or small agricultural settlements, and their total settled area is 63.4 dunams (approximately 20.5% of the total settled area in this region).

241. Ten small, isolated sites were removed from this list. They are located in the western or eastern edges of the region and cannot be assigned to the subregions identified within it.

reflecting diversity of function (2 large settlements, 5 medium-sized, and 17 small ones). The settled area in this strip is estimated at 122 dunams, which is 40% of the entire settled area in the region under discussion.

• In the central strip, there are 16 sites (about 30% of all sites in the area under discussion). This strip does not have any medium-sized settlements but does have 3 large settlements (Kh. Zakandaḥ—21 dunams; Kh. Ḥubeilah—20 dunams; Kh. Judūr—19 dunams) and 13 small sites, most of them farms of 1 dunam or less. The total settled area is estimated at 81 dunams, which is about 26.5% of the total settled area in the region under discussion.

• The southern strip has 13 sites (about 25% of all sites in the area under discussion). The total settled area in this strip is estimated at 102 dunams (approximately 33.5% of the total settled area in the region under discussion). Almost half of this total area is at Kh. Rās eṭ-Ṭawil (40 dunams), and there are 5 sites of medium size with a total combined area of 48 dunams. In addition, there are 7 small sites (about half of the number of small sites in the other two strips).

The data from the settlements in the area north of Beth-zur exhibit an obvious continuity throughout the Persian Period.[242] There was an 11.5% drop in the number of settlement sites (56 sites in the Persian Period in contrast to 63 at the end of the Iron Age). However, there was hardly any change in the extent of settled area (299 dunams in the Persian Period compared with 305 dunams at the end of the Iron Age, a decline of less than 2%). No settlement larger than 5 dunams was abandoned, and the main difference between the two periods is in the distribution and nature of the settlements. Three major changes took place in the settlement pattern during the transition from the Iron Age to the Persian Period:

1. There was a dramatic decline in the importance of the larger sites. This decline is reflected in the quantity of large sites (from 6 to 3) and the estimated size of their occupation area (from 146 dunams to 69 dunams, a decline of about 53%). Before the destruction, the large sites represented 48% of the total settled area in the Judean highland; in the Persian Period, they represented only 23%.

2. There was a marked increase in the importance of the medium-sized sites, that is, sites larger than 5 dunams. There was a sharp increase of 60% in the number of these sites (from 10 sites at the end of the Iron Age to 16 during the Persian Period). There was also an increase of 50% in the total occupied area of these sites (from 96 dunams at the end of the Iron Age to 145 dunams during the Persian Period). This shift is also reflected in the

242. Ofer studied this phenomenon (1993: 2.131); see also the discussion by Lipschits 1997a: 291–99.

proportion of these sites to the total of settled dunams, which increases
from 31.5% at the end of the Iron Age to 48.5% during the Persian Period.
3. A significant increase in the location and importance of sites smaller than
   5 dunams. There is no change in the number of sites that belong in this
   category (37 sites in both periods), but there is an increase of 36% in the
   total estimated area of settled dunams (from 61.9 dunams at the end of the
   Iron Age to 85.2 dunams during the Persian Period). This is also reflected
   in the relative weight of the small sites as a portion of the entire settled
   area, which increased from 20.5% at the end of the Iron Age to 29% during the Persian Period.

Ofer (1993: 2.134) explains these changes as due to weakening of the internal security in the region; however, it is unlikely that any change can be detected in either the nature and location of the sites or the fortifications around
them. There is no evidence that the population was concentrated in strong, fortified settlements; on the contrary, the importance of large sites declined in this
period. In my opinion, the settlement patterns of the Persian Period must be explained as precisely the opposite of this: they reflect a prolonged period of quiet
during which the population was able to develop small settlements without
concern for security. The dispersal of settlement and the sites' continued occupation over an extended period of time attests to a respite from preoccupation
with defense and an ongoing internal stability in the land during the Persian
Period.

The data from the latitudinally-oriented strips in the northern highland of
Judah (as defined previously) reveal a striking continuity between the Iron Age
and the Persian Period *in the northern strip* from Bethlehem southward. There is
no evidence here of destruction by the Babylonians or of the transition to the
Persian Period. The number of sites remained unchanged and the same settlement pattern was maintained, and the total settled area in both periods is estimated at about 40% of the total settled area in the Judean highlands. Nevertheless, the southeastern section of this strip, together with the northeastern
section of the central strip, experienced a significant change in settlement pattern. The 21 small sites that had existed in this region during the Iron Age no
longer existed during the Persian Period. Almost all of them are located east of
the watershed divide, and most of them (approximately 15) are within a radius
of about 4 km of Tekoa.[243] It is likely that this profile reflects the economic and
security situation that prevailed at the end of the Iron Age, when settlements

---

243. These sites are found in two major "blocks": 6 sites are located north of Tekoa (Sites 10,
15–18, and 21 in the list of Iron Age sites in the Judean highland, listed in Lipschits 1997a:
table D-4-D-2 and fig. 10). Two additional sites may be added to these in Wadi Darga (Darage)
in the northeast (Sites 22, 23), as well as a small fortress located some 5 km east of Tekoa (Site
30). An additional 6 sites are scattered, fan-like, east of Beit-Fajjār (Sites 34, 36–38, and 43).

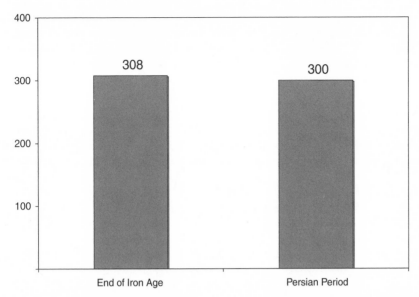

Fig. 4.8. Settled dunams in the northern part of the Judean hills at the end of the Iron Age and during the Persian Period.

were able to expand more effectively to the edge of the desert near Tekoa, especially along the main roads leading from the mountain ridge eastward.[244]

The thriving of the desert frontier at the end of the Iron Age parallels the flourishing of the desert frontier in Benjamin at that same time. This situation may be related to the establishment of En-Gedi, the growth of Jericho, and the establishment of the array of sites in the Jordan Valley and along the western littoral of the Dead Sea (see D. Amit 1992: 347; and the discussion above, §§4.3.2d and 4.3.3a, pp. 232–237 and pp. 245–249). It may well be that this

244. As demonstrated in Map 10 (p. 235), the main road from the mountain ridge east-northeast ran from the area south of Bethlehem toward Jericho and passed through Wadi Darga and the Horkaniah Valley. Farther toward Jericho along this road, 13 Iron Age sites were discovered, apparently from the end of this period, reflecting the importance of this road. A branch of this road led toward En-Gedi, and additional Iron Age sites were found along this route (see above, §4.3.2d, pp. 232–237). The road southwestward passed through Wadi Arugot toward En-Gedi; it has been surveyed by Bar-Adon (Kochavi 1972: 94, 130–35, 139–45). A secondary fork in this road left Kh. el-ʿArūb and connected to the main road in Wadi Arugot (Amit 1992: 345–62). An additional parallel road went down eastward through Wadi Ḥaṣṣa-ṣon and then ascended north toward the Horkaniah Valley. On the main road, which a modern road follows (through Tekoa and Rujm en-Nāqa), 9 Iron Age sites were found. There were 7 more sites along the parallel road that ran through Wadi Ḥaṣṣaṣon. Although all of these are small sites, they are evidence that the road was used in the late Iron Age.

settlement array collapsed due to changing economic, military, and political conditions that eliminated the economic base on which most of the settlements relied. It is likely that, bereft of security in these frontier regions and the disappearance of means of livelihood, the local populace abandoned many of these sites as early as the sixth century B.C.E.

During the Persian Period, this area experienced renewed settlement activity, and the pattern of settlement was different from the pattern of the Iron Age.[245] Evidently, settlements in the Tekoa area, which had spread to the eastern frontier too diffusely at the end of the Iron Age, migrated westward during the Persian Period, resulting in more densely-packed concentrations near the watershed divide. Apparently, the lack of brisk commercial traffic over the roads leading toward the Judean Desert and the Jordan Valley made it impossible to maintain densely populated settlements east of the divide. Most of the settlements were established where more-reliable water resources and more-diverse possibilities for livelihood based on agriculture existed. This region is the heart of the Beth-Hakkerem district (see above, pp. 173–174 and Map 6, p. 183), which is known from the days of Nehemiah and whose importance with regard to settlement in the fifth century is significant.

During the Persian Period, the total number of sites in *the central strip* increased to 21 (compared with 16 sites during the Iron Age). Within this total, the most dramatic change was in the establishing of medium-sized sites (those larger than 5 dunams): where there were none at the end of the Iron Age, 6 medium-sized sites were founded, comprising an area estimated at 56 dunams (about 54% of the total settled area in the region). The total settled area in this strip reached 104.2 dunams (an increase of about 28%), and this strip had approximately 35% of the total settled area in the Judean highland (compared with 26.5% at the end of the Iron Age). This increase was at the expense of *the southern strip*, whose importance diminished considerably. The decline in the number of sites is estimated at 15% (11 sites during the Persian Period, versus 13 at the end of the Iron Age). However, the decline in the total settled area, about 25%, is more significant (77.1 dunams during the Persian Period, compared with 102.8 dunams at the end of the Iron Age). The ratio of this strip to the total occupied area in the Judean highland decreased from 34% at the end of the Iron Age to about 26% in the Persian Period. The decrease was most dramatic in the reduced area of medium-sized sites that had been occupied in the Iron Age, from 5 sites with a total area of approximately 48 dunams to 4 sites with a total area estimated at about 36 dunams. This decrease is coupled with a sharp drop in

---

245. The survey data indicate that in 21 sites pottery from the Persian period was found and that there was no evidence of Iron Age pottery (or least not from the end of the period). A rather small circle south of Bethlehem contains 15 of these sites. See Sites 17, 18, 24, 27–30, 34–39, 43, 44 in the list of Persian Period sites in the Judean highland (in Lipschits 1997a: table D-4-D-2 and fig. 10).

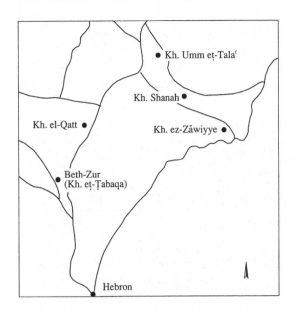

Map 12. Persian forts in
the southern part of
Judah.

estimated settled area at Kh. Rās et̯-Tawil (from 40 to 23 dunams—though I believe that the total was even lower in the Persian Period).[246]

One theory for the decline in the southern zone is that it was a frontier area, opposite the southern Judean highland and the Negev. Apparently, during the Persian Period, this area experienced instability due to incursions of peoples from the south. This hypothesis is supported by the fact that there are no known Persian fortresses in the southern part of the province, south of Beth-zur (which probably was an imperial Persian fortress). In contrast, north of Beth-zur, there are four known fortresses along the two major north–south roads: Kh. ez-Zāwiyye and Kh. Shanah are located on the southeastern road, coming from Wadi Siʿir; and Kh. el-Qatt lies on the main mountain road, about 2 km north of Kh. et̯-Tabaqa. Kh. Umm et̯-Talaʿ is situated at the vertex of the "triangle of fortresses" and also controls the road running east, toward Tekoa. In my opinion, these fortresses mark the course of the southern boundary of the province of Yehud; this line was established to exclude the peoples that lived south of it. Thus, it is reasonable to conclude that the area of Wadi Siʿir and the Beth-zur line in the west were the southernmost settlements of the province and that the area south of them was outside the province boundaries.

With this settlement pattern as background, we may theorize regarding the stabilization of the southern border of Yehud province during the Persian Period:

---

246. See the data on the sites in this strip in the list of sites in the Judean highland in Lipschits 1997a: table D-4-D-2 and fig. 10.

In the sixth century B.C.E., seminomadic groups gradually began to invade the
Beer-Sheba–Arad Valleys and from there moved toward Mt. Hebron and the
southern Shephelah. The gradual intrusion of these groups into the area may explain the massive destruction that beset the entire region. At the same time, the
settlement of "Yehud" province steadied in the area north of the Beth-zur line,
and most settlements there persisted unchanged from the Iron Age to the Persian Period. The intervening area was, therefore, the latitudinal zone between
Beth-zur and Hebron. This helps to explain the establishment of Persian fortresses during the second half of the fifth or during the fourth century B.C.E.: they
apparently were intended to preserve order in the region and perhaps were even
intended to mark and defend the southern boundary of the province.

4.3.3c. Summary
   The conclusion to be drawn from the data presented in this section is that
the Benjamin region, as well as the vicinity of Bethlehem, did not suffer destruction during the Babylonian campaign against Judah. The biblical description and the distribution of the *muṣh* seal impressions lead to the conclusion
that the limits of the "early nucleus" of the Babylonian province of Judah were
established during the siege of Jerusalem, under Gedaliah's rule. In contrast to
the total devastation of Jerusalem and its environs, the severe blow dealt to the
border fortresses in the Shephelah, and the collapse of the southern and eastern
hinterland, the continuity in Benjamin and the northern highland of Judah is
all the more striking. There is no doubt that it was in the Babylonians' best interest to permit most of the Judean population to remain. In addition, perhaps
the nucleus that they created, to which the "remnant" of Judah attached themselves, became the core of the province during the days of Babylonian rule and
Persian domination. The process of rebuilding settlement in the central Judean
highland (to the Beth-zur line) and in the Shephelah had its origin in this limited area. The date this process began is unknown, but by the second half of the
fifth century B.C.E. a new settlement pattern throughout the area between Bethlehem and Beth-zur is already detectable and the establishment of Judean settlement in the eastern part of the Shephelah is underway.

4.4. Demographic Changes in Judah between the Seventh and Fifth Centuries B.C.E.

4.4.1. Introduction
   The possibility of formulating an independent historical picture that does
not depend on the Bible and is as unfettered as possible by prior historiographical and theological perceptions is a privilege of modern research and is of prime
importance even for an examination of the biblical descriptions themselves.[247]

---

247. Nonetheless, see Dever (1985) on the use of archaeological data for interpreting the
biblical text and validating it historically. See also Meyers and Meyers 1994: 268–69.

In this section, I review the demographic status of the kingdom of Judah at the end of the Iron Age (second half of the seventh century B.C.E.) and compare it with the demographic situation in the province of Yehud at the height of the Persian Period (mid-fifth century B.C.E.), using archaeological tools. By presenting the well-established data from these two periods, which are also chronologically well defined (see §4.2), it is possible to demonstrate that there was a long, complex settlement and demographic process, at the center of which are the changes that took place during the Babylonian rule.

The methods of estimating population size on the basis of archaeological data, as controversial as they may be, have become better established in recent years, both in terms of theory and in terms of the database on which such estimates may be based for any specific period.[248] Some of the major essays in which the population of ancient Syria–Palestine has been investigated are the work of Gophna and Portugali (1988) on the population of the coastal area from the Chalcolithic Period through the Middle Bronze Age; of Broshi and Gophna (1984; 1986; Finkelstein and Gophna 1993; Gophna 1995) on the Early Bronze Age and the Middle Bronze Age; of Finkelstein (1989) on the Intermediate Bronze Age; of Finkelstein (1984) and Sharon (1994) on the Israelite population during Iron Age I; of Shiloh (1981a) on the Iron Age; and of Broshi and Finkelstein (1990; 1992) on the population of Israel in the eighth century B.C.E. To these, we must add Broshi's work (1974; 1978) on the size of the population of Jerusalem during the Iron Age, additional studies considering various aspects of the demographic situation during the Bronze and Iron Ages (London 1992: 75, 78 nn. 27–29), and many studies on the population of the land in later periods (see, e.g., the literature compiled in Zorn 1994b; Carter 1999: 195–205).

Most scholars have based their population estimates on a combination of excavation and survey results in a specific region and from a specific period; from these data they tried to arrive at an estimate of total settled dunams. This type of estimate is largely speculative, because the vast majority of sites (especially small and medium-sized sites) have not been excavated, and the numerical results are based on the general impressions of surveyors and estimates of the total area of a site, weighted against the relative quantity of sherds from the various periods.[249] Despite these limitations, an estimate of total settled dunams is of

---

248. This is not the place to discuss models and the theoretical background of demographic studies. References to these may be found in many of the articles, mentioned below, that deal with the Bronze and Iron Ages. See also Portugali 1988; 1989. For literature on various methods of estimating population, see Zorn 1994b: 32–35; Carter: 1999: 195. For a theoretical discussion and review of the literature on the Bronze and Iron Ages, see London 1992: 71–79; and for a summary of studies of population density per dunam, see Carter 1999: 195–99, with further literature.

249. Survey publications tend to leave out many facts, which makes it difficult to evaluate the accuracy of those surveys. Among missing data may be such details as (1) the size of the area relative to the number of surveyors (the overall area of the site; extent of the area surveyed;

great importance, because it serves as a figure that permits comparisons among various periods, thus helping to identify the changes in settlement pattern and population size. Converting the number of settled dunams into an estimate of population size is a function of the estimate and is dependent on the coefficient of the number of people per dunam.[250] In the latest studies, the figure of 25

number of surveyors; the number of times they went over the area and the pace at which they walked; the dexterity of the surveyors, etc); (2) data regarding visibility and an evaluation of the relative ability of the surveyers to make finds while conducting the survey (the season when the survey was conducted; the weather on the day it was conducted; vegetation covering the site; and evidence of human activity in later periods); (3) general data on the survey's discoveries (number of sherds collected; their size, color, and density; the relative number of identifiable pieces of pottery; the relationships among the various archaeological periods; the manner of documenting the finds and the degree of precision in registering the items); etc. The need to regularize the data also makes it difficult to collect and process the data, because the various survey reports are separated by large time gaps and are characterized by a conspicuous absence of uniformity, which is reflected even in the terminology assigned to the periods surveyed and the subdivisions that were made. Ofer (1993) distinguishes between Iron Age IIc, which corresponds mainly to the seventh century B.C.E., and the period that he calls Iron Age IId, which corresponds to the late seventh and early sixth century B.C.E. In most other surveys, this period is discussed only generally as Iron Age II, and, in some of the surveys, even more general classifications were used. Sometimes the lack of uniformity in survey data is partly the result of differences in the types of areas being surveyed. This phenomenon is particularly striking if we compare the survey of the built-up area of Jerusalem and its environs with a survey of Judah and Benjamin. Lack of uniformity is also evident in the survey data coming from sites that are located underneath existing villages; similarly, the problem of uniformity looms when we consider data obtained from areas of high settlement density with data obtained from areas of low settlement density. For our purposes, the main problem is the different perspectives of the surveyors, which are reflected primarily in the way data is quantified and the manner in which statistics are used to estimate the area and vigor of the settlement. This is not the place for a discussion of survey theory or for evaluating different survey techniques. However, inasmuch as these estimates are, ultimately, one of the focal points of our discussion, it is important to note that there are serious methodological problems hampering our ability to estimate the relative size of settlements in any given period on the basis of survey data alone. In my opinion, contemporary survey methods are insufficient to allow us to arrive at precise estimates of the area of most types of sites. Any attempt to use mathematical calculations or fixed formulas is based on data that are themselves surveyors' estimates—a circular pattern of argumentation. Accordingly, it is better to be aware of the limitations of the information gathered by the survey and to make do with a general evaluation of the nature of the site: to which classification of the main types the site belongs, an estimate of the area of the site at its peak size, and as precise a calculation as possible of the quantities of indicator pottery from each period. This information can serve as the basis of an evaluation of the intensity of human activity at the site throughout different eras. Attempts to quantify data of this kind via mathematical formulas needs to take into account many additional variables (such as, e.g., proximity of materials to the surface, the extent of cover from later periods, the amount of cultivation of the area, built-up areas, etc.). These variables can undermine the accuracy of formulas and even influence the results. Therefore, it is preferable to state at the outset that the results are only an estimate and to be aware that estimates contain elements of speculation. On this subject, see also London 1992: 71; Zorn 1994b: 32, with further literature; as well as Broshi and Finkelstein 1990: 5, who favor the descriptive phrase "educated guess."

250. On the problems related to this subject, see the review by London 1992: 74–77, with further literature.

people per dunam has been accepted as a growing standard.[251] This figure is based primarily on ethnoarchaeological studies in traditional societies and data from rural Arab villages during the British Mandate. Although the figure seems quite high for the population of small villages and quite low for the population of walled cities, it has gained acceptance as an average appropriate for estimating the total population of specific regions, at least the maximum population of the inhabited area.[252]

4.4.2. Between the End of the Iron Age and the Persian Period: Total Settled Area

Table 4.1 presents a summary of the total settled dunams in Judah, based on excavation data and on the results of surveys and predicated on the discussion in previous sections of this chapter. The main conclusion that emerges from the data is that between the end of the Iron Age and the Persian Period there was a decline of approximately 70% in settled area. Even if the figures presented for one or more regions in either of these periods is not exact, the aggregate figures are sufficient to show the general trend: between the end of the Iron Age and the Persian Period there was a major demographic change that reflects a settlement crisis. The crisis probably occurred during the time of Babylonian rule, and the epicenter of the crisis was the destruction of the kingdom of Judah. It is not surprising that the sharpest decline in population occurred in Jerusalem and

---

251. This is the formula used by Shiloh and most researchers whose studies I have cited above—to which many more can be added (see the references in London 1992: 75, 78 nn. 27–30). See also Zorn 1994b: 32–35, and the comparative table on p. 34; Carter 1999: 194–99, with further literature.

252. For the primary references to these methods and discussions of various formulas for calculating population size, see the prefaces to the studies cited previously, as well as Portugali 1988; London 1992: 74–77; Zorn 1994b; Carter 1999: 195–98, with extensive further literature. All of the comparisons with the demographic situation in Arab villages during the British Mandate show that the ratio of 25 people per dunam is quite high. This was also London's (1992: 74–75) primary criticism; she also argued that a single ratio could not be applied to the entire region. In her opinion, the ratio of people per dunam should be adjusted to the characteristics of each individual site. Additionally, she said that the location and function of each site must be taken into account. London's criticisms were followed by Biger and Grossman (1992), who also rejected the idea that a fixed density ratio could be used to calculate the area of settlements in various regions and in different historical periods. In their study, Biger and Grossman presented two central principles for evaluating population density ratios: (1) There is an inverse relationship between the size of the built-up area and the density ratio: the smaller the site, the greater the population density (1992: 114, table 10). (2) The connection between the area in which the settlement is located and the average density there must be taken into account (1992: 116, table 3). The first principle may be criticized, because it appears that population density was lower in small farms and villages during the late Iron Age and Persian Period than in large villages and cities. In any event, because most of the sites have not yet been excavated for the periods with which this study deals, and the estimates of settled area are only general, we have to make do with an estimate of population based on a fixed ratio of 25 people per dunam. The use of this ratio makes it possible to compare the demographic data from the end of the Iron Age and the Persian Period with the data from other periods in the history of the land.

Table 4.1. A Comparison of Settled Area in the Iron Age
and the Persian Period by Region

Region	Settled dunams, end of Iron Age	Settled dunams, Persian Period	% decrease in settled area
Benjamin	1,150	500	56.5%
Jerusalem environs	1,000	110	89.0%
Northern Judean hills[a]	306	300	2.0%
Southern Judean hills[b]	300	85	71.7%
The Shephelah	900	150[c]	83.3%
Beer-Sheba–Arad Valleys	120	30[d]	75.0%
Eastern strip	90	10	88.9%
Total	3,866	1,185	69.3%

a. As defined above (§4.3.3b), this refers to the entire region between Jerusalem and Beth-zur.

b. As defined above (§4.3.2e), this refers to the entire region between Hebron and the Beer-Sheba–Arad Valleys.

c. The settled area of this region only includes the northern border (consisting of 150 settled dunams), which, according to the preceding analysis, was included in the borders of the Yehud province during the Persian Period. An area of similar size near Mareshah and south of it was not included either in this total or in the total settled area during the Persian Period.

d. This region was not included in the boundaries of Yehud province during the Persian Period; thus, it is reasonable to assume that it was not considered part of Judah during Babylonian rule. Consequently, the settled area of this region in the Persian Period was not included in the overall total of settled areas during this period.

its environs (89%), the area which was the focus of Babylonian activities (see §4.3.2a). A similar rate of decline took place in the Judean Desert, Jordan Valley, and the western littoral of the Dead Sea, implying that the process of collapse in these regions was rapid, once the kingdom's administration and army had ceased to exist (see §4.3.2d). The heavy devastation in the Shephelah (83% decrease in settled area) may be explained by the concentrated Babylonian campaign against the fortresses on the western border of the kingdom of Judah and the rapid collapse that took place, particularly in the southern Shephelah, after the destruction and in the subsequent years of Babylonian rule (see above, §4.3.2b). The southern border of Judah also capitulated rapidly, and the semi-nomadic groups that had inhabited the area south of the Judean border for many

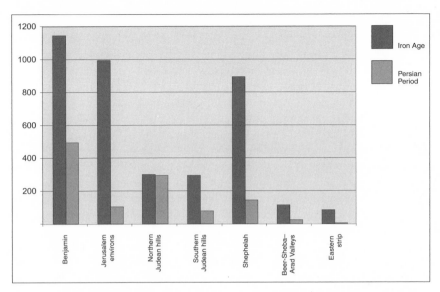

Fig. 4.9. Comparison of settled dunams in the Persian Period with settled dunams at the end of the Iron Age.

years quickly invaded the empty expanses of the southern Judean hills and the southern Shephelah (see §4.3.2c). These areas were no longer considered part of Yehud province during the Persian Period; in this region, a population was gradually consolidating that eventually would become part of Idumea in the Hellenistic Period.[253]

In the Benjamin region, the decrease in size of the settled area between the Iron Age and the Persian Period was more moderate—approximately 55%. An analysis of the central sites in the region leads us to conclude that this decrease took place gradually at the end of the sixth and the beginning of the fifth centuries B.C.E.[254] In contrast, the region between Jerusalem and Beth-zur was marked by thoroughgoing settlement continuity; there was an impressive increase in the number of small sites, evidence of a prolonged period of stability and security.[255]

---

253. For a reconstruction of the historical processes and an analysis of the archaeological evidence from these areas, see the discussion above, §3.1; §4.3.2–3.

254. For a discussion of this subject, see above, §4.3.3a; and for a detailed discussion of settlement processes and their historical background, see Lipschits 1997a: 196–245; 1997b; 1999a.

255. For a detailed discussion of the data from this region, see Lipschits 1997a: 276–99; see also above, §4.3.3b.

The data presented above are significantly different from the data that have been presented by earlier researchers, and several words should be offered in explanation. Apart from Finkelstein's summary of the archaeological situation in the days of Manasseh, almost no other studies have been published on the size of the population at the end of the kingdom of Judah.[256] Historical evaluations based on lists and descriptions in the Bible have resulted in exaggerated, far-fetched numbers, double or more than double the most "generous" archaeological estimates.[257] Past estimates of population size in Yehud province during the Persian Period also were based only on the biblical accounts, especially on the lists of the "returnees to Zion" (Ezra 2; Nehemiah 7), because most scholars speculated that this list reflected the different waves of immigration to the province during the days of Cyrus and his descendents until as late as the days of Nehemiah.[258] Previously, Carter was the only one who had attempted to estimate the population of Yehud on the basis of archaeological data,[259] but his archaeological method for the Persian Period is problematic. Accordingly, his final figures are significantly lower than those presented here.

A comparison of the summary data from the end of the Iron Age with the data collected by Finkelstein (1994) reveals striking differences in the overall totals (3,866 settled dunams in the estimate presented here compared with 2,250

256. On the difficulty of estimating the population of Judah at the end of the Iron Age, see Meyers and Meyers 1994: 281–82. These difficulties make even more important Finkelstein's (1994) compilation of evidence in order to summarize the archaeological and demographic situation of the seventh century B.C.E. Nevertheless, his summary is incomplete, and his demographic estimate is significantly lower than the one presented here (see more on this below).

257. See, e.g., the view of J. Weinberg (1972: 45–50) who, using the biblical accounts and general appraisals as a basis, estimated the population of Judah at 220,000–250,000 people. This is further evidence that caution must be exercised when population estimates are based either on historical accounts or on lists preserved in secondary sources that underwent reworking and adaptation for historiographical purposes.

258. On this list, see the discussion above, §3.4.1b. It should be noted that this list contains the only historical census of all the inhabitants of the province. The total count given in the list is 42,360 (Ezra 2:64; Neh 7:66; 1 Esd 5:41), but this total does not agree with the numbers given in the list itself (29,818 according to Ezra 2; 31,089 according to Nehemiah 7; 30,143 according to 1 Esdras 5). For various explanations of these numerical discrepancies, see Zer-Kavod 1949: 39–40; Myers 1965a: 20–21; Blenkinsopp 1988: 93; 1991: 44. On the basis of these lists, most estimates of the province's inhabitants range around 50,000. For this estimate, see, e.g., Albright 1949a: 87–88, 110–11; Bright 1959: 376–77; Blenkinsopp 1988: 83; Smith 1989a: 31–35. J. Weinberg (1972: 47–50) has offered an out-of-range estimate of about 200,000 people, and on this based his interpretation of the list in Nehemiah 7 (= Ezra 2); see above, §3.4.1b, as well as the criticism by Blenkinsopp 1991: 42. Heltzer and Kochman (1985: 34) arrived at an assessment similar to Weinberg's, and they estimated that the numbers in the list of returnees refer to males. Therefore, they suggested that the "number of males" be multiplied by four per family (thus providing a total of 200,000 people). The theoretical basis for this ratio of males to family size is unclear, and thus the demographic estimate is aberrant and without basis.

259. See Carter 1991: 2.150–65; 1999: 195–213. Meyers and Meyers (1994: 268–85) followed the direction taken in Carter's doctoral dissertation.

dunams according to Finkelstein's estimate).[260] The major difference is in the settled area of the Shephelah (which, according to Finkelstein, was 800 dunams—close to the estimate made in this study), which Finkelstein omitted from his calculations. In my opinion, this omission lacks both archaeological and historical justification. Finkelstein himself is aware that, despite the harsh blow that the Shephelah was dealt by Sennacherib's campaign, settlement in the region did recover, partially, during the seventh century B.C.E. Other differences in estimates of the settled area are the result of new data from the Jerusalem survey, which attest to the strength of settlement in the immediate environs of the city (a total of some 1,000 settled dunams, in contrast with Finkelstein's estimate, which was based on the accepted—at the time—estimate of 600 settled dunams in the city). Finkelstein also did not take into account the total settled area in the Jordan Valley, Judean Desert, and along the western littoral of the Dead Sea (approximately 90 dunams). In addition, the estimate of total settled area in the Negev is missing 20 dunams of settled area that must be added on the basis of new survey data.

A comparison of the summary data from the Persian Period with Carter's data (1991, 1994, 1999) shows striking differences, most of which stem from Carter's archaeological methodology and from the distinction he makes between the two segments of the Persian Period.[261] Thus, for example, Carter concludes that the total settled area during the Babylonian(?) and Persian Periods (including an allowance for margin of error that he adds to his figures) is approximately 868 dunams (about 75% of the estimate given above). At the same time, the distinction he attempts to make between the two different phases of the Persian Period requires a manipulation of the data—injecting different error ratios for each of the periods and adding general estimates of the size of Jerusalem at these two stages on the basis of the biblical descriptions in Nehemiah, Haggai, and Zechariah. The data from the archaeological surveys do not permit more than a general dating of evidence to the Persian Period, and even in this there are significant limitations, given that the pottery indicative of that period has not been

---

260. See Finkelstein 1994: 173–77. Finkelstein mentions the Jordan Valley, Judean Desert, and western littoral of the Dead Sea but neither cites the total number of settled dunams nor includes it in the grand total.

261. My criticism of Carter's work chiefly relates to his method of classifying the archaeological evidence from the Persian Period into two subdivisions: Persian Period A (from 539/8 to the mid-fifth century B.C.E.) and Persian Period B (from the mid-fifth century to 332 B.C.E.). This division is problematic from almost every angle, but especially because it attempts to define a material culture using historical data. The notion that a parallel for a change in the local material culture can be found in historical information—for instance, changes in imperial rule (which is largely the thesis of Hoglund 1992: 202–5)—cannot stand the test of reality. Carter did not even attempt to provide a methodological basis for the model that he presented, which would require clearly defined assemblages of pottery that are from definitive stratigraphic contexts and that may be dated decisively. To a large extent, Carter's approach is an example of a theoretical model that should not be adopted.

well defined. The division of data between two different "phases" of the Persian Period requires speculative manipulation of the survey data. Carter himself (1999: 199–201) acknowledges this: based on his assumption that many sites were abandoned in the first third of the fifth century B.C.E., he decides on a lower error margin for the first "phase" (10%) than the margin he uses for the second "phase" (20%). Furthermore, because he is unable to provide evidence of a well-established archaeological profile in Judah for both phases of the Persian Period, he projects the settlement picture in Benjamin onto Judah, although he is conscious of the risky, speculative nature of this measure; as a result, he creates a general picture that raises doubts about its conformity with the archaeological data.[262] An additional problem with Carter's study is the manner in which he created regional divisions, which is based on an analysis of ecological niches (1999: 202; and see the basis for his geographical discussion, pp. 100–113) rather than on a historical and geographical basis reflecting the areas that had existed throughout the long history of Judah, from the time of the kingdom through the Persian Period. As a result, it is impossible to understand either the historical or the archaeological significance of his geographical divisions or to compare them with the regional divisions that I have presented in this chapter.

4.4.3. The Babylonian Period and the Settlement Process between the End of the Iron Age and the Persian Period

On the basis of the discussion in this chapter, and taking into account the comparison of data from the end of the Iron Age and the Persian Period, it is possible to arrive at an estimate of the settled area in Judah after the destruction of Jerusalem and throughout most of the sixth century B.C.E. Jerusalem and its environs were thoroughly razed by the Babylonians, and there is no evidence of any settlement whatsoever in the region until the Persian Period. This archaeological picture corresponds to the biblical description and to the historical reconstruction above, and it is likely that many of the exiles taken to Babylon came from the city and the area surrounding it.

In contrast to the settlement picture in Jerusalem, the archaeological data provide unequivocal evidence that decline in settlement in Benjamin only began to occur at the beginning of the Persian Period. It appears that settlement in this area continued without interruption throughout the sixth century B.C.E., and it may even be that population density was greater than it had been just before the destruction of Jerusalem. This means that the total settled area during

---

262. Carter 1999: 200–201. Thus, Carter concludes (I think without justification) that 25% of the sites in Benjamin existed in his Persian Period B. Then, he projects this relative proportion onto all of the sites in Judah, while omitting from the discussion the Persian fortresses whose date he determines separately. It is, therefore, not clear how he decides that 41 out of 55 sites in Judah were in existence in Persian Period A and how he divides the total settled area on this basis.

the sixth century B.C.E. may be estimated at approximately 1,600 dunams (a decline of about 60% when compared with the size of the settled area at the end of the Iron Age). The dwindling population in the Benjamin region at the beginning of the Persian Period led to an additional reduction (approximately 25%) in the size of settled area, while the rebuilding of settlements in Jerusalem had almost no demographic significance.

The facts indicate that the "Return to Zion" did not leave an imprint in the archaeological data or in the demographic evidence. Probably, a few thousand of the nation's elite, especially from the priestly caste, returned to Judah and settled in Jerusalem and its environs at the beginning of the Persian Period. Nonetheless, the city remained poor, and the returnees found it difficult to recruit the resources and manpower required to build the temple.

Paralleling this, because of the shift of the political and religious hub to Jerusalem, a rapid dwindling in population took place in the region of Benjamin, especially beginning about the middle of the fifth century B.C.E. Apparently, part of the region's inhabitants emigrated out of the province, either to the Ono–Lod area or to other parts of the Shephelah, most likely the eastern sectors (see above, §4.3.3a, esp. pp. 245–249; Lipschits 1997b).

4.4.4. Demographic Changes in Judah between the End of the Iron Age and the Persian Period

To complete this discussion, I am providing an estimate of the total settled area in Judah at three distinct points in time: the end of the seventh and beginning of the sixth century B.C.E. (end of the Iron Age); the mid-sixth century B.C.E. (Babylonian Period); and the mid-fifth century B.C.E. (Persian Period). In order to give these figures demographic significance, a reasonable range of deviation designed to fill in known gaps in the archaeological surveys must be taken into account.

Some scholars have cited a fixed deviation of 20% to the final figures,[263] while other scholars have attempted to estimate the range of deviation for each region separately.[264] The second approach seems preferable to me, because it permits us to take into account the extent of coverage and quality of the survey, the characteristics of the area surveyed, and the characteristics of the settlement pattern in each region when applying a "standard" deviation. Likewise, we must remember that any "standard deviation" applied to speculative estimates may need to be altered periodically as the archaeological picture becomes clearer and the amount of data from each region increases.

In the *Benjamin region*, all of the major sites were excavated, and a comprehensive survey was conducted throughout most of the region. The area as yet

---

263. See, e.g., the range of deviation used by Broshi and Gophna 1984: 42; 1986: 74.

264. A similar method was employed by Broshi and Finkelstein 1990; Finkelstein 1994; Ofer 1993: 2.135–37, 216–21.

unsurveyed primarily includes the western slopes of the mountain ridge, an area with nearly no water resources and with very few settlements throughout history (Magen and Finkelstein 1993: 19–21). Little pottery from the Persian Period was found at most of the sites, which shows that there was a lower level of activity than had been the case at the same sites during the Iron Age. Thus, the estimate for Benjamin during this period seems to be realistic or, perhaps, even too high. The estimate of the settled area at the end of the Iron Age also seems quite realistic, because 80% of the total settled area comprised 14 settlement sites with an area of more than 30 dunams and 32 settlement sites with an area greater than 10 dunams. It would be difficult to argue that additional sites of this size went undiscovered in the archaeological survey; furthermore, even if some smaller sites were not discovered by the survey, their overall area would be insignificant in relation to the total settled area of these larger sites (cf. Finkelstein 1994: 176).

In *Jerusalem and its environs*, the surveyors encountered great difficulty, because a large part of the survey was conducted in a built-up area. It must be assumed that the survey's coverage was low; much of the time, the discovery of a site in this region is casual. Many small villages and farms surrounded the city, particularly at the end of the Iron Age, which seems to require that a high margin of error be added. Nevertheless, about 90% of the total settled area in this region was included within the line of Jerusalem's fortified walls (encircled on all sides by burial caves of that period), which is evidence that the small farms were not very important within the total estimate of the settled area in this region. The total estimate of settled area in the Iron Age given here is one of the highest cited in the literature, and it seems unnecessary to add any margin of error whatsoever. The quantity of pottery from the Persian Period at most sites is very small, which attests to a much lower level of activity in this period than in parallel sites from the Iron Age. In this period, too, most of the settled area was within the city wall, and this leads us to conclude that for this period, as for the Iron Age, there is no need to take a possible margin of error into account.

In the *Judean hills*, there are great gaps in our knowledge (Ofer 1993: 2.218). About one-third of the area has not been surveyed, including large areas south of Jerusalem, which probably was settled relatively densely. However, it is difficult to assume that large, important sites did not come to light in the archaeological survey; the major gaps in our information are with regard to the small sites in the region. It seems sufficient to add a margin of error of 30% for both periods, which were settled with a similar density (see also Broshi and Finkelstein 1990: 11–12; §§4.3.2c, 4.3.3b above).

In the *Shephelah*, there are large gaps in our knowledge. However, the main sites in this region are well known; the major gap in our information relates only to the medium-sized and small sites. Additionally, Dagan's estimates of settled area state the maximum area of each site, and his ceramic estimates are only

Table 4.2. A Comparison of Settled Area in the Iron Age
and in the Persian Period, by Region, plus Margins of Error[a]

Region	Added margin of error	Settled dunams, end of Iron Age	Settled dunams, Persian Period
Benjamin	none	1,150	500
Jerusalem environs	none	1,000	110
Northern Judean hills	30%	400	390
Southern Judean hills	30%	390	110
The Shephelah	30%	1,170	390/195
Beer-Sheba–Arad Valleys	none	120	30
Eastern strip	none	90	10
Total		4,320	1,345

a. See the notes to table 4.1 above, p. 262.

general, which implies that in this region the total settled area has been over-estimated. The 30% margin of error for the two periods seems to be an appropriate ratio in light of the state of our knowledge.

The conditions of the terrain coupled with the quality of surveys conducted in the *Beer-Sheba–Arad Valleys and the Jordan Valley, the Judean Desert, and the western littoral of the Dead Sea* have resulted in solid evidence that most of the settlement sites that existed in these regions are well known and familiar.[265] Almost all of the key sites have been excavated, and the size of the settled area in the sites has been discussed above, including the problems raised by this estimate. The gaps in these surveys do not appear to be significant, because the overwhelming majority of settlements were at large sites; thus, it seems unnecessary to add any margin of error.[266]

The corrected figures, including the margins of error proposed above, are presented in table 4.2. As discussed previously, the accepted density ratio in demographic studies is an average of 25 people per settled dunam. Table 4.3 presents

265. For an evaluation of the survey conducted in the Judean Desert, Jordan Valley, and along the western littoral of the Dead Sea, see Lipschits 2000: 31–42. Regarding the survey conducted in the Beer-Sheba–Arad Valleys, it appears that the data cited above, including the oral information from Beit-Arieh, accurately reflect the settlement picture in the periods in question. The main unknown in this region concerns the size of the ancient site under modern-day Beer-Sheba (the area of the Bedouin marketplace). See the discussion above on this point.

266. See a similar assessment by Broshi and Finkelstein 1990: 12–15.

Table 4.3. Estimate of Total Population of Judah at the End of the Iron Age
and in the Persian Period by Regional Distribution

Region	Estimated population, end of Iron Age	Estimated population, Persian Period
Benjamin	28,750	12,500
Jerusalem environs	25,000	2,750
Northern Judean hills	10,000	9,750
Southern Judean hills	9,750	not included in province
The Shephelah	29,250	4,875[a]
Beer-Sheba–Arad Valleys	3,000	not included in province
Eastern strip	2,250	250
Total	108,000	30,125

a. In the Shephelah, only the settlement sites within the limits of Yehud province
during the Persian Period were taken into account; see the discussion in §3.4.

a comparison of the total population for both periods on the basis of estimates of
the settled area multiplied by the accepted coefficient.

On the basis of these figures, and rounding the totals, the number of inhabitants of the kingdom of Judah as it came to an end was approximately 110,000,
and the population of Yehud province was approximately 30,000. On the basis
of the discussion above, one may estimate the population of Judah during the
Babylonian Period at 40,000.

These demographic analyses have great significance for reconstruction of the
history of Judah between the seventh and fifth centuries B.C.E., because they
cast a different light on the biblical descriptions that, until now, have served as
the primary, virtually exclusive source for all historical research. Thus, for example, it appears that the destruction of Jerusalem and the end of the kingdom
of Judah brought about the gravest demographic crisis in the history of the kingdom of Judah, with much more severe results than the Sennacherib campaign of
701 B.C.E.[267] The Babylonians concentrated their effort on Jerusalem and its
environs, while the region of Benjamin and the northern Judean hills were
hardly touched and continued almost unchanged in terms of settlement patterns and demography.

267. These data do not leave any room for Barstad's (1988; 1996) conclusions, expressed as
"the myth of the empty land." The data further show unequivocally that the destruction and
exile were indeed historical events, described in their full harshness in the biblical historical
record and reflected in the lamentations and prophecies of this period. See also Albertz 2003:
95–96.

The data on settlement and demography may lend support to the idea that most of the exiles to Babylon had been residents of Jerusalem. It is also reasonable to conclude that the Babylonians dealt a major military blow to the inhabitants of the Shephelah, and residents of this region also probably were deported to Babylon. As I have noted, the processes of the collapse and destruction of the settlements on the kingdom's eastern and southern border areas are still unclear, but it is doubtful that they were destroyed as a result of a Babylonian military campaign or that a significant portion of the population from these small sites was taken into exile. Similarly, there is no evidence of deportation from either the Benjamin region or the northern Judean hills. It appears that, even if there were such an exile, it was quite small and was demographically insignificant.

One of the most noteworthy conclusions to emerge from the demographic data is that the "Return to Zion" left no archaeological evidence. At the end of the sixth and beginning of the fifth centuries B.C.E., there was a notable dwindling of settlements (particularly in the Benjamin region), and there is no indication whatsoever of either a population increase or any change in settlement pattern, apart from a renewal of settlement in Jerusalem and its environs. The demographic figures from the Jerusalem region also demonstrate that, even at the height of the Persian Period, the city's population was only 3,000, which is about 12% of the population of the city and its environs on the eve of the destruction. Even if all of the residents of the region were part of the Return to Zion, these returnees only amounted to several thousand.

The demographic figures also indicate that, at the height of the Persian Period, the territory of Benjamin and the Judean hills continued to serve as home for most of the population of the province (75% of the total population). Less than 15% of the populace of the province lived in the Shephelah, while some 10% lived in Jerusalem and its environs. This fact is proof of the long-term effect of the blow that Jerusalem suffered at the hands of the Babylonians at the time of its destruction and the extent to which Jerusalem was unsuccessful in recovering and once again becoming a large, significant urban center; Jerusalem was not again a major city until the beginning of the Hellenistic Period. This conclusion accords with the book of Nehemiah, which describes Jerusalem as bereft of populace. Furthermore, Nehemiah's claim, that the city had a tenth of the province's inhabitants (approximately 3,000 people), matches our population estimate, that the province had approximately 30,000 inhabitants.

Chapter 5

Babylonian Rule, the Destruction of Jerusalem, the Exile, and the "Remnant" in Judah

Perceptions and Trends in
Biblical Historiography

5.1. The Description of the Destruction of Jerusalem and Its Causes in 2 Kings: The Date of Composition, Place of Writing, Sources, and Purposes

5.1.1. Introduction to the Deuteronomistic Historiography [1]

Noth, in his seminal 1943 study, offered a new model for seeing the set of books from Deuteronomy to Kings as a single unit, which may be called the "Deuteronomistic history." In his view, this set of books was written to describe and to explain the history of the people of Israel from Horeb to the Babylonian exile (Noth 1943: 4–11). The work was written by an author-compiler (whom Noth labeled "Dtr") who lived in Judah in the mid-sixth century B.C.E. (1943: 12, 79, 85, 141 n. 9) and who had a variety of sources available from different eras of the kingdoms of Israel and Judah (pp. 75–88). He edited some of these sources and placed them in his work. He wrote other parts in his own words (pp. 9–11, 75–78) and integrated the entire account into one schema express-ing his theological-historical conception of the history of the people of Israel (pp. 18–25, 84–88).

Noth based his thesis on the consistent presence of characteristic Deuterono-mistic language; [2] however, he also highlighted the ideological unity of the entire work. In his opinion, the covenant between God and his people lay at the core of the description. The author emphasized, repeatedly, that the people had vio-lated this covenant, despite constant warnings from God, until God decided to

---

1. I prefer the term *historiography* to *history*, as Van Seters (1983: 1) has defined it, because it better accounts for the fact that the world view of the author/editor is part and parcel of the narrative, and that what is reported is not necessarily the factual course of events. See Brettler 1995: 2, in contrast to Römer 2003: 248–50.

2. Noth 1943: 4–5. See also Weinfeld 1972: 320–65; H.-D. Hoffmann 1980: 323–63.

cast them out from before him and send them into exile in Assyria and Babylon (Noth 1943: 89–99; cf. Knoppers and McConville 2000: 20–30). In addition to linguistic and ideological-theological unity, Noth also highlighted the structural consistency that reflected the historiographical perception of the author (1943: 18–25). The author divided history into subperiods, and he expressed his opinion through repetitive, stylized summaries in the form of speeches that he used to introduce or conclude these subperiods.[3] These speeches were inserted at key historical junctures and were designed to highlight the message that underlay the composition: the deportation to Babylon was the result of centuries of religious transgression; the history of the people of Israel was to be seen as a gradual decline toward destruction and exile (1943: 89–99).

On the basis of the unity and consistency of the composition, Noth attempted to reconstruct the sources on which it had drawn.[4] He theorized that ancient sources were embedded in the work by the author as they had originally been written and are central to the composition (1943: 76–77). However, Noth did not find any evidence that the composition had undergone later systematic revision; in his opinion, only marginal additions, at most, had been made.[5]

The main points of Noth's theory were widely accepted,[6] and the debate among scholars in the following decades has focused primarily on two questions: (1) Which parts of the composition were from earlier sources, and which were written by Dtr? (2) What was the extent of the original composition, and what were the stages of later additions?

Thus, for example, some accepted Noth's basic theory regarding the date of the composition but developed a different theory about the identification of the sources embedded in it and the role of the author. Among these, the contributions of Hoffmann, Van Seters, and Long are notable. Hoffmann was the first to

---

3. Noth 1943: 5–6, 34. See also Weinfeld 1992: 189–233, with further literature.

4. Noth dealt extensively with the ancient sources and the stages in the creation of the composition (see, e.g., his commentary on the book of Joshua, 1953), but he almost never dealt directly with the material discussed here.

5. Noth 1943: 6–10, 87–90. He (1943: 40 n. 61) identified an abundance of passages within the Deuteronomistic work that, in his opinion, were later additions; some of them are extensive and significant (Joshua 13–22; Judg 1:1–2:5, and chaps. 17–21; most of 1 Samuel; 2 Samuel 21–24; 2 Kgs 17:34b–40, etc.). But Noth did not try to arrange them into organized units or to attribute them to specific sources. See also McKenzie's (1991: 144–50) observation and Knoppers's summary (in Knoppers and McConville 2000: 1–2).

6. For many years, especially before the 1970s, Noth's theory received almost complete acceptance; see the extensive literature listed in Weippert 1985; Eynikel 1996: 10–12, esp. n. 21. Two notable exceptions were Eissfeldt (1965: 241–48) and Fohrer (1965, especially his conclusions on pp. 210–12). Comprehensive and incisive criticism of Noth's theory has appeared primarily during the past two decades; see especially the arguments summarized by Westermann (1994); but see also van Keulen's (1996: 9) reasoned response to the main problems raised by this critique, as well as a critique of the alternate thesis presented by Westermann. For another critique of Noth's thesis, see also Knoppers 1993: 17–56; 1994: 229–54; Auld 1998: 63; and for further bibliography, see Knoppers and McConville 2000: 2 and n. 7; Person 2002: 1–29.

grant a more important role and greater significance to Dtr than Noth had.[7] He identified Dtr as an independent author (one or more) who presented his view of the history of the people of Israel by incorporating diverse sources (including oral traditions) into his composition and fusing them so thoroughly that literary tools can no longer be used to distinguished them (1980: 15–21, 154–270, 316–18). Hoffmann's view of the nature of the Deuteronomistic composition (although not his view of its purpose) was reinforced by Van Seters (1981, 1983).[8] Van Seters compared Dtr's work with familiar historiographical works from the ancient Near East and the Hellenistic-Roman world, particularly Herodotus's history, and concluded that Dtr reworked his material in such a way that it cannot be dissected into its components. In Van Seters's opinion, the Deuteronomist had diverse sources but treated them with complete freedom, integrating them into a coeherent running history that reflected his own world view (1981: 137–85; 1983: 292–321, 354–62, especially pp. 357–59). Long's work was largely an expansion of Van Seters's; like Van Seters, he saw in Herodotus a model for the method of composition found in the Deuteronomistic work (Long 1984: 15–30). He supported Noth's theory that there was a single major redaction and argued that various theories reconstructing several Deuteronomistic redactions are without basis in the historiography of the ancient world:[9] texts were not modified by addition or revision; instead, works of this kind were completely rewritten. According to Long, the manner in which the book of Chronicles was written can serve as a model for the writing of the Deuteronomistic history.[10]

The studies by Hoffmann, Van Seters, and Long have been of great importance in biblical research. They have highlighted the close connection between biblical historiography and the historiographical works of the Hellenistic and Roman Periods, in terms of genre and literary technique. These scholars argued against the distinction, made by other researchers, between the sources and the Deuteronomistic redaction. This distinction is important, even if it has not become central to Deuteronomistic research. The distinction has not gained much ground, primarily because these studies have not proved the ideological homogeneity of the composition or that it is a linguistic and literary unity, both of

---

7. H.-D. Hoffmann 1980. See the summary and critique of this theory in Mayes 1983: 10–14; O'Brien 1989: 16; van Keulen 1996: 9–14; Eynikel 1996: 13–14, with further literature and references to scholars who have adopted Hoffmann's thesis.

8. Since, according to Van Seters, the Deuteronomistic work was written before the Yahwistic and Priestly works, he could distinguish many contributions and later additions to the Deuteronomistic history.

9. On these theories, see the discussion below.

10. Long also interacted with the specific arguments of scholars who posited multiple redactions, some of which were dated before the destruction of Jerusalem. Thus, for example, Long (1984: 16–17) maintained that the promise of an enduring Davidic dynasty is not evidence for the date of writing of either the entire composition or parts, because this language is hyperbole typical of a monarchy wishing to establish its legitimacy and well known in the ancient Orient.

which would have to be the case if the composition were the work of one (or more) author(s). These scholars also have not offered an adequate explanation for the conceptual and literary contradictions in the composition or for the variety of literary layers. Van Seters's suggestion that the work contains later additions[11] is unconvincing.[12] The composition's uniformity or lack of uniformity can be ascertained only after a thorough discussion of the linguistic, literary, and ideological-theological features of the Deuteronomistic work, as well as a systematic analysis of each of its parts. Accordingly, it is not surprising that, in most studies of Deuteronomistic history, a discussion of the sources of Dtr, his redactional style, and identification of the passages that he himself wrote continues to be at the heart of research.[13]

At almost the same time as the publication of Noth's monograph, two other important studies were published that influenced later scholarship, though in two different directions. In 1947, von Rad began an examination of two of the central themes in Deuteronomistic history: the idea of prophecy and fulfillment and the idea of everlasting kingship for the House of David.[14] On one hand, von Rad's work corroborated Noth's thesis; von Rad's research revealed a pattern of prophecy and fulfillment in the Deuteronomistic historiography that became the literary-conceptual device for explaining the destruction of Jerusalem. He concluded that this pattern served Dtr because it led to the inevitable conclusion that the fall of Jerusalem was the fulfillment of prophecies that portended destruction if the people failed to repent of their evil ways.[15] On the other hand, the unconditional promise to David and his line offered a theoretical basis for a challenge to Noth's thesis:[16] the promise of the Davidic line's continuity

---

11. See, e.g., the conclusions reached by Van Seters (1983: 277–91) following his discussion of 2 Sam 2:8–4:12; chaps. 9–20; 1 Kings 1–2, and McKenzie's expansion of the idea (1991), arguing that the text contains many post-Deuteronomistic additions. Long's attempts (1984: 16–17) to connect central motifs (such as the promise of an enduring Davidic dynasty) to the period of the Babylonian exile are not convincing. See the critique by Provan 1988: 96; and McKenzie 1991: 132–34.

12. See the critiques by Polzin 1989: 13–17; van Keulen 1996: 11–14; O'Brien 1989: 16–17; McKenzie 1991: 16–17; and Knoppers 1993: 32–36.

13. See also the comprehensive critique by Halpern (1988: 186–94) of the theories proposed by scholars who have adopted this approach.

14. See von Rad (1958: 189–204); and compare the chapter in his book (1966a: 205–21); see also 1953: 74–91; 1962: 334–47.

15. See von Rad 1958: 189–99; 1966a: 205–16; and see, e.g., the prophecies and their fulfillment (according to von Rad): 1 Kgs 11:11–13, 29–39 → 12:22–24; 1 Kgs 13:1–3, 31–32 → 2 Kings 16–18; 1 Kgs 14:5–16 → 15:25–32; 1 Kgs 16:1–5, 6–7 → 8–14; 1 Kgs 21:17–29; 2 Kgs 9:1–11 → 9:15; 2 Kgs 1:15–16 → 17–18; 2 Kgs 13:14–19 → 23–25; 2 Kgs 20:16–19; 21:10–16 → 24:2–4, 13. See also Weippert 1991.

16. See von Rad 1953: 74–91; 1958: 199–203; 1996a: 216–20. On this subject, see Wolff 1961; cf. the discussion by Zeligman 1969–74: 298–313. It should be noted that Noth did not discuss this theme, which essentially goes against his thesis. However, even von Rad did not

could not coexist with the idea of prophecy and fulfillment, unless this series of prophecies was oriented toward the destruction of Israel and had no connection with the destruction of Jerusalem.[17] The conclusion that naturally followed from von Rad's two ideas is that the two themes originated in two schools of writers who worked at cross-purposes and did not write at the same time. Consequently, the coexistence of these two themes presents a serious dilemma: Dtr could not minimize the extent of the punishment, because the destruction of Jerusalem and the deportation of the nation's elite were obvious facts that could only be explained by recourse to a religious rationale. On the other hand, he could not acknowledge that the promise to David was empty.

Although von Rad's literary-conceptual distinction was the beginning of a more general theory regarding two stages in the composition of the Deuteronomistic history,[18] the distinction did not lead him to the logical chronological conclusions. With this perspective in mind (and following Noth, who believed that Dtr was active after the destruction of Jerusalem), von Rad postulated that the book's conclusion—a description of the release of Jehoiachin from prison—resolves the conflict between the prophecy-fulfillment motif and the promise of everlasting kingship to the House of David. The future, therefore, is optimistic: the continued existence of the House of David allows God to begin his people's history anew.[19]

---

consider the chronological significance of the presence of this theme for the Deuteronomistic historiography—although he did not accept the idea that the history was monolithic (see, e.g., von Rad 1962: 347). For a critique, with an emphasis on the chronological significance, see Cross 1973: 276–77; McKenzie 1991: 122–23; Knoppers 1993: 24–27.

17. In principle, one could argue that the prophecy to Manasseh (2 Kgs 21:11–16) should not be included in the series of prophecies and that the prophecy in 1 Kings 9 (especially vv. 6–9) is a later addition. If this were the case, the general message of the prophecies would be different, and they could be seen as in harmony with the promise of eternity to the Davidic line. Accordingly, it comes as no surprise that these prophecies (especially the prophecy to Manasseh) have been at the center of many studies on the Deuteronomistic historiography. See, e.g., the book by van Keulen (1996), with further literature.

18. See below for discussion of the "dual redaction" theory (or the "blocks model") proposed by Cross, which takes precisely this idea as its point of departure.

19. See von Rad 1958: 203–4; 1966a: 219–21. In this connection, it is worth recalling Wolff's thesis (1961). In many respects, Wolff developed von Rad's line of thought further, but discarded several of its postulates and founded his approach on the lack of consistency in the book of Kings. Wolf did not assume that the promise to the Davidic line was enduring and also disagreed with Noth's view that the Deuteronomist's goal was to provide a rationale for the destruction. He identified several texts as containing a "message of optimism" (Judg 2:11–19; 1 Sam 7:3–4; 12:19–22; 1 Kgs 8:46–53; 2 Kgs 17:13; 23:25), the central theme of which was not the restoration of the House of David but the restoration of divine mercy to the nation in exile. Two additional passages, Deut 4:25–31; 30:1–20, are, in Wolff's opinion (1961: 179–83), later additions to the Deuteronomistic composition and were inserted under the influence of traditions and ideas from the book of Jeremiah. These notions, introduced by Wolff, had significant influence on the thesis propounded by Cross (1973: 278) and his students (see, e.g., McKenzie 1991: 12, and n. 7); for a catalog of criticism of this thesis, see Knoppers 1993: 24–25.

In 1953, from another perspective, Jepsen published a complex analysis of the development of the Deuteronomistic historiography.[20] Unlike Noth, Jepsen focused on the book of Kings. Jepsen argued that two sources composed during the days of the kingdom of Judah form the basis of the book. One source was a synchronistic chronicle from the eighth century B.C.E. that recounted the history of the kings of Israel and Judah from the days of David to the days of Hezekiah. The second source was a series of annals composed in Judah during the seventh century B.C.E. that narrated roughly the same period (1956: 8–9). These sources underwent three major redactions during the Babylonian exile. The priestly redaction was first (R^I); it was carried out shortly after the destruction of Jerusalem (about 580 B.C.E.) and narrated the history from Solomon through Hezekiah. It incorporated a recounting of Solomon's reign and the synchronistic chronicle of the kings of Judah and Israel, along with a composition recounting the history of religious ritual at the temple in Jerusalem.[21] The prophetic redaction came next (R^{II}), approximately in the middle of the sixth century B.C.E. (about 550 B.C.E.; Jepsen 1956: 95–101, 105); at the end of the sixth century, a final redaction of the book of Kings took place (R^{III}). This final redaction was carried out by Levites, who incorporated material of a midrashic nature into the text (1956: 102–5).

Despite the weaknesses in Jepsen's theory and the criticism to which it has been subjected,[22] the theory's chief importance is that it presented the development of the Deuteronomistic history as a complex process. This process may be contrasted with Noth's one-dimensional approach and von Rad's and Wolff's rather obscure theories, at least in terms of the historical process of text development. This explains why Jepsen's theory has formed the basis for further studies and has become one of the foundations of the "layers model."

In the 1970s, research began to focus precisely on the lack of uniformity of the elements of the Deuteronomistic composition and the long and complex process of its formulation. The major developments took place in two opposing directions. In Göttingen, Smend and his students have developed the *layers model*, building on the foundation of Jepsen's studies. Most scholars from this "school" (also known as the "Göttingen School") accept Noth's fundamental premise that the Deuteronomistic history was composed after the destruction of Jerusalem.

---

20. See Jepsen 1956. It should be noted that Jepsen's manuscript was completed in 1939, before Noth's, which was published in 1943. Jepsen's theory shares identical axioms with Noth's approach. One of these axioms is that all of the redactional activity came after the destruction of Jerusalem.

21. Jepsen 1956: 30–40, 54–60; see also pp. 10, 22–23, 106. For a critique of the basis of this redactional stage, see Weinfeld 1992: 186.

22. The major criticisms of Jepsen's theory have noted his simplistic approach to the two sources that form the basis of the first redaction and to the distinction, which was not made sufficiently clear, among the three redactions, their character, and purpose. See Knoppers 1993: 20; and see also the discussion below.

They disagree with him chiefly regarding the uniform nature of the work, emphasizing its three different stages of composition and redaction: (1) the stratum of the historical author-redactor (Dtr^H), (2) the prophetic stratum (Dtr^P, which is chiefly concerned with the prophecies embedded in the account), and (3) the nomistic stratum (Dtr^N, which emphasizes the Torah and its laws).[23]

Parallel to this, a new "school" developed in the United States: the *blocks model* (the theory of the "dual redaction"), according to which the Deuteronomistic history developed in two chronological stages: preexilic and exilic. Frank Moore Cross was at the heart of this "school" (1968; 1973: 274–89), which in some respects revived opinions that had been current before Noth's monograph was published.[24] In Cross's view, the first stage in the Deuteronomistic composition (Dtr^1) occurred in the days of Josiah, and it ended with 2 Kgs 23:25a.[25] A later redactor (Dtr^2), who was active ca. 550 B.C.E., expanded this work with the objective of adapting the book to the historical and conceptual reality of the

---

23. See below on the central elements of this theory and the main criticisms that can be leveled against it. I will not discuss here some of the "trends" in German scholarship, which have a strong tendency toward fragmentation of the Deuteronomistic history; see, e.g., Westermann 1994; Würthwein 1994: 1–11; Rösel 1999.

24. In this "school," there was a return to the basic assumption popular at the end of the nineteenth and beginning of the twentieth centuries, especially in the studies of Wellhausen, Kuenen, Stade, Cornill, Wildeboer, Steurnagel, Eissfeldt, Weiser, Pfeiffer, and others. These scholars identified two redactional layers in the book of Kings: (1) an already existing text, not composed by a Deuteronomistic author-redactor, followed by (2) a later redaction (by a redactor who also was responsible for the last part of the book). See the surveys of Eynikel 1996: 14–15; and van Keulen 1996: 22–24, with further literature.

25. Following von Rad and Wolff, Cross (1973: 279–85) identified two central motifs in the first Deuteronomistic layer. The first motif, which is interwoven throughout most of the book of Kings, placed the sin of Jeroboam and the wickedness of the Northern Kingdom at the center, noting that God had promised the North "a sure house, as I built for David" (1 Kgs 11:38). For a general discussion of this idea and its place in the ancient Near Eastern context, see Evans (1983: 97–125), and see also the debate between Provan (1988: 70–73) and McKenzie (1991: 123–25), who interpret this idea in the setting of their general theories. The divine promise to Jeroboam was not fulfilled because Jeroboam "returned not from his evil way" (1 Kgs 13:33) and committed two major transgressions: (1) he built centers for religious worship in Dan and Bethel, and (2) he appointed priests "from all ranks of the people, who were not of the sons of Levi" (1 Kgs 12:31). The effect of Jeroboam's sins continued throughout the entire span of the kingdom of Israel, when most of the kings "did not depart from the sins of the house of Jeroboam, who made Israel to sin" (2 Kgs 13:6, and more than 20 additional times in various forms). Punishment befell every dynasty; the destruction of the Northern Kingdom was the ultimate punishment. The second motif in Dtr^1 is David's unqualified fidelity to God and the promise to him of an enduring dynasty. Cross (1973: 283, 287) thought that the only era suitable for the cultivation of this idea was during Josiah's rule. He argued that the author saw Josiah as "the new David" and wished to promote the ideas that were the basis of his reform, promoting Josiah as a king who "was unlike any king before, who turned to the Lord with all his heart and all his might" (2 Kgs 23:25). See also the discussion in Nelson 1981: 119–32; and Friedman 1981a: 7–8; 1981b: 171–73. Following Naʾaman (1995d: 46–47), a third major theme must be added: the continuity of the original cult in the Jerusalem temple. See also Albertz 2003: 280–81, who in many respects opposes the conclusions of Römer 1997: 5–6.

destruction of Jerusalem and the time of the Babylonian exile.[26] This redactor's work begins with the account of the end of the life of Josiah (2 Kgs 23:25b) and continues with the history of the kingdom of Judah until the destruction of Jerusalem.[27] Paralleling this history and as an integral part of it, Dtr[2] revised the existing work, updated it, and inserted passages that introduced a condition for the fulfillment of the promise of an enduring dynasty.[28] Speeches and summaries that presuppose imminent destruction were also inserted, and a call for the exiles to repent was sounded (Cross 1973: 285–89). A major feature of these passages is the message that they contain; from this perspective, Cross's appraisal, that Dtr[2] is a laconic account lacking the creativity of the Dtr[1] composition (1973: 288), is justifiable. Dtr[2]'s account lacks the literary and ideological characteristics that were central to the earlier edition: the promise of an enduring dynasty to the Davidic line and the motif of prophecy and fulfillment.[29] According to Cross, this redaction is primarily a supplement to the historical account. He finds only three theological comments (23:26–27; 24:3–4, 20) in it, two of which lay the blame for Jerusalem's destruction on Manasseh; he also highlights that there is no reference to prophets in this version and no treatment of the centralization of the cult in Judah.[30] The distinctions made by

26. Cross (1973: 285–87) contended that at this stage a third motif was added to the Deuteronomistic work: the destruction came as a result of the sins of Manasseh, who was portrayed as the most iniquitous of the kings of the Davidic line. Inasmuch as this motif could not have been contemporary with the previous two central motifs but had to be later, Cross placed it at the center of the later composition (Dtr[2]), expressing the idea that the kingdom of Judah was in a continuous state of decline, heading toward destruction. The idea that the destruction was punishment for the sins of Manasseh expresses a pessimistic tone that is in sharp contrast to the positive tone that characterized the history of Judah until that time. For a discussion of this subject, see Nelson 1981: 123; Levenson 1984: 353–61; Becking 1990: 292–93.

27. Friedman (1981a: 7–8; 1981b: 171) has examined this point, connecting 2 Kgs 23:25b to Dtr[1] and showing the ideological importance of the link between Josiah and Moses. See also on this McKenzie 1991: 136–37. For the question of the end of Dtr[1] and beginning of Dtr[2], see the discussion by van Keulen (1996: 43–48), which includes a critique of the conclusions of Cross and his followers, as well as extensive literature, including a consideration of various scholarly approaches to the problem. See also the critique of Albertz (2003: 277–78).

28. Against this claim, see Nelson 1981: 65–69. On the central passages that Cross believes were reedited, see Cross 1973: 285–87, and n. 49; and following him, McKenzie 1991: 7 n. 11, 135–45; Eynikel 1996: 16. For a survey of research, see O'Brien 1989: 6–7 n. 17.

29. Von Rad already had identified these motifs; see the summary by Friedman 1981a: 6–10; 1981b: 167–72. Regarding the motif of prophecy and fulfillment, see the cogent critique of van Keulen (1996: 46) and his reference to the fulfillment of the prophecy in 2 Kgs 24:2.

30. On this subject, see the studies by Friedman (1981a: 6; 1981b: 174). Vanoni (1985) also has discussed the later composition's different use of terms related to religious ritual; however, in relation to this, see Camp 1990: 18–20; Ackerman 1992: 37–99; Knoppers 1993: 4, 9; van Keulen 1996: 46–47. McKenzie (1991: 127) also found that the prevalence of religious ritual terminology decreases dramatically after 2 Kgs 23:24, that the Deuteronomistic language in the last part of the book evinces small changes in the intent of the words, and that there are signs of imitation and repetition of the language characteristic of Dtr[1]. On this subject, see the critique of van Keulen (1996: 46) and his explanations for the disappearance of some of the religious terminology and theological comments.

Cross have been supported by scholars who have examined the development of the opening and closing formulas that become more rigid and stereotyped in Dtr[2],[31] by scholars who have investigated the literary and conceptual uniformity of Dtr[1],[32] and by those who have explored the unique expressions and linguistic characteristics of Dtr[2].[33] Many other studies further support Cross's theory from different directions, expanding upon it linguistically and conceptually and defining the scope of the redaction and additions belonging to Dtr[2].[34] On the basis of these studies, the major texts that belong to Dtr[2] have been defined:[35] the historical account from Josiah's death (2 Kgs 23:25b) onward;[36] the passages that blame Manasseh for the destruction (2 Kgs 21:2–15; 23:26; 24:3–4);[37] the passages that address the exiles or that call for repentance (1 Kgs 8:46–53; 9:6–9);[38]

---

31. See Weippert 1972: 333–39; as well as Nelson 1981: 29–42; McKenzie 1985: 184. Against this approach, see Provan 1988: 48–49; and van Keulen 1996: 47–48.

32. One of the latest examples of this direction is the work of Geoghegan (2003). The basic works are still those of Friedman 1981a: 7–10; 1981b: 171–73. See also Knoppers 1993; 1994.

33. A lengthy chapter was dedicated to this subject in the book by Nelson (1981: 43–98).

34. See Boling 1975: 29–38; 1982: 216; Levenson 1975; 1981; 1984; Friedman 1981a: 7–10; 1981b; Nelson 1981: 29–42; Mayes 1983: 136; Peckham 1983; Vanoni 1985: 358; O'Brien 1989: 227–34, 266–87; Knoppers 1993: 51–52. For additional literature, see Eynikel 1996: 14–20.

35. Cross did not establish clear-cut criteria for attributing passages to Dtr[2]; this was mainly done by others who have pursued this theory. See the texts identified by McKenzie (1991: 136) and the criteria that he summarized for picking out these passages (p. 135). In later studies, it has become clear that Cross had not attempt to justify the attribution of various passages to Dtr[2], such as, e.g., the addition of a condition to the unconditional promise given by God to the House of David during Solomon's rule (1 Kgs 2:4; 6:11–13; 8:25b; 9:4–5). See the arguments supplied by Nelson 1981: 100–105; Friedman 1981a: 12–13; 1981b: 175–76; McKenzie 1991: 137–38. All of the instances to be discussed below refer to Dtr[2] additions to the book of Kings, even though Cross (1973: 287) attributed isolated passages in the book of Deuteronomy (4:27–31; 28:36–37, 63–68; 29:27; 30:1–10, and perhaps also vv. 11–20) and in the books of Joshua (23:11–13, 15–16) and Samuel (1 Sam 12:25) to the postexilic composition. Cross concluded that Dtr[2] only rarely injected himself into these books. A detailed discussion of these texts is beyond the purpose of this study.

36. The starting point of Dtr[2] is hotly debated; see n. 27 above.

37. Blaming Manasseh for Jerusalem's destruction is a central theme of the later redaction within the account of the last days of Judah. This idea is so central that the verses containing this indictment play a crucial role in the discussions of researchers of almost every approach and "school" (see the summary discussion of van Keulen 1996, with further literature). Within the "dual redaction school," various scholars agree regarding the attribution of the central passage (2 Kgs 21:10–15) and, subsequently, all other related passages to Dtr[2]. See, e.g., Cross 1973: 285–86; Nelson 1981: 66–67; Friedman 1981a: 10–12; 1981b: 176–78; Lohfink 1984: 184–85; Knoppers 1994: 106. In the "multiple redaction school," most scholars have been inclined to attribute vv. 10–15 to Dtr[P], and some have attributed part of this passage to Dtr[N]. On the first, see, e.g., Dietrich 1972: 31–34 and Ben-Zvi 1991a, with further literature. On the second, see Würthwein 1984: 440, who attributed only vv. 10–13 to Dtr[P], contending that vv. 14–15 belonged to different circles of the Dtr[N] stratum. Spieckerman (1982: 421–22) is an exception, in that he assigns vv. 10–15 to a later redaction of Dtr[N]. For a criticism of these approaches, see Lowery 1991: 181–82, 189; van Keulen 1996: 122–39, 191–206.

38. Attributing 1 Kgs 9:6–9 to Dtr[2] is accepted by most scholars (see Cross 1973: 276; Nelson 1981: 73). Nelson (1981: 69–73), following Cross, ascribed 1 Kgs 8:44–51 to Dtr[2];

and passages that presuppose the coming of the exile (2 Kgs 17:19; 20:17–18; 22:15–20).[39]

*   *   *

At the same time that Cross proposed his "dual redaction" theory, Helga Weippert posited her own thesis regarding the Deuteronomistic composition.[40] She, too, distinguished between preexilic and postexilic stages within the Deuteronomistic composition.[41] She maintained that the last stage in the composition (R[III]) occurred during the exile and consisted chiefly of a description of the final days of the last four kings of Judah (in many respects, parallel to Cross's Dtr[2]). However, in contrast to Cross, Weippert rigorously analyzed the introductory and closing regnal formulas, concluding that the preexilic version (Cross's Dtr[1]) was created in two major stages of development. In the first stage, dated to the time of Hezekiah, there is a description of the history of Judah from Jehoshaphat to Ahaz and the history of the kingdom of Israel from Jehoram to Pekah or Hosea. The second stage, during the reign of Josiah, frames the first stage with a description of the history of Israel from Jeroboam to Ahaziah and a description of Judah from Hezekiah to Josiah.

In my opinion, there is no basis for this division or for Weippert's idea that there was a gradual evolution within the preexilic Deuteronomistic historiography. No proof of developmental stages of an earlier complete composition written at the end of the eighth century B.C.E. has been provided; and discussions of

Levenson (1981: 143–66), on the basis of various arguments (pp. 157–58), ascribed vv. 23–53 and 56–61 to Dtr[2]. In contrast, Friedman (1981a: 21) did not assign a single verse from this chapter to Dtr[2], largely following the view of Gray 1964: 197–213. See also the arguments presented by McKenzie 1991: 139–40.

39. Cross (1973: 287) attributed 2 Kgs 17:19 to Dtr[2] and was followed by Lohfink (1984: 185). Friedman (1981a: 24–25) reasoned that vv. 35–40a might also be additions, and Nelson (1981: 53–69) maintained that Dtr[2] should be credited with most of this chapter (vv. 7–20, 23b, 40–44). See McKenzie's (1991: 141–42) analysis of these conclusions, and see also the subsequent remarks of Knoppers (1993: 64 n. 36). There is sharp debate among scholars of the "multiple redaction school" about where 2 Kgs 17:19 should be assigned. Thus, for example, Dietrich (1972: 24) ascribes it to Dtr[N], and Würthwein (1984: 396) sees it as an even later addition. For a broad survey of the research and literature, see Eynikel 1996: 88–94. On the literary unit in 2 Kgs 20:12–19, see Nelson 1981: 88; Begg 1986b.

40. See Weippert 1972; 1983; 1985; 1988: 457–79. In their basic conclusions regarding the source of the composition and the long process of its development, Weippert and her followers continued in the path blazed by Nicholson (1967), which had been buttressed and expanded by other scholars taking a variety of approaches: see the works by Debus 1967: 114; Weinfeld 1972: 7–9; 1985: 91; 1992: 134–95; Barrick 1974: 257–59; Jones 1984: 44; McKenzie 1985: 174–76; Campbell 1986: 126–28; Lemaire 1986; Provan 1988: 28, 131–32; Rofé 1988: 99–101; O'Brien 1989: 272–92; Halpern and Vanderhooft 1991; Moenikes 1992; Eynikel 1996. For a critique of this theory, see McKenzie 1991: 6; and for responses to some of the objections raised by McKenzie, see Halpern and Vanderhooft 1991: 241–44.

41. Weippert herself (1985: 215) has stated that, apart from the subdivision that she posited in the preexilic stage, there is no great difference between her "triple redaction theory" and Cross's "double redaction theory."

the developmental stages of the work taking into account the opening and ending regnal formulas in the book of Kings have not arrived at definitive conclusions.[42] I believe that it is preferable to leave the question of Deuteronomistic redaction prior to the Josianic period open and to assume that, up until the time of Josiah, there were diverse sources and, perhaps, even some processes of consolidation of these sources—but there is no way for us to determine the chronological stages or to identify the underlying conceptual plan. Thus, in accord with Cross's theory, the established starting point for the Deuteronomistic history is the activity of Dtr[1], who is to be dated to the time of Josiah (Na³aman 2002: 55–60). The major questions about this edition are: which sources were available to the redactor at that stage, and to what extent were the sources consolidated?[43]

At the same time, Cross's theory is not without its own difficulties.[44] There are various additions within the Dtr[2] composition, and there are additions to the early version (Dtr[1]) that do not fit Dtr[2]. Cross's definition of the two major blocks of the composition have proved to be too general: his criteria do not provide answers to the comprehensive text-analytical works written by scholars affiliated with the "layers model" of the school of Jepsen, Smend, and their followers (Albertz 2003: 277–78). It would be worthwhile to integrate this school's analysis with Cross's theory of the "dual redaction" to create a more complex synthesis—that the composition was created in three major stages. (1) The

---

42. I will not treat the preexilic composition (Dtr[1]) in this work. At this point, I will note only that, in my opinion, Weippert's theory—that the composition evolved gradually in the time between Hezekiah and Josiah—should be discarded, along with theories based on it that developed subsequently (see, e.g., Eynikel 1996). The major innovation in Weippert's theory was the attempt to identify the precise stages of development of the Deuteronomistic history and to anchor them in specific historical contexts. However, the attempt to make sharp distinctions between the various sources and to classify the sources' contents is the major weakness of this theory. The distinctions in the opening and closing regnal formulas between R[I] and R[II] are not necessarily criteria supporting a chronological distinction or even a distinct existence of these two hypothetical compositions. It is more reasonable to see the formulas as related by content and by the editor's attitude toward Asa, Hezekiah, and Josiah. There are also difficulties with the scope of the compositions as defined by Weippert, the points at which they have their origins, and their ending points (particularly if they were written at the time that she proposes). On these weaknesses, see also Cortese 1975; Van Seters 1983: 316 n. 84; Provan 1988: 39–41, 50–53; McKenzie 1991: 112–19; Knoppers 1993: 44–46. On the importance of the במות in this context, see Provan 1988: 57–89; McKenzie 1991: 119–22.

43. We assume that this composition was created in the period of religious reform as part of the propaganda of the House of David and against a backdrop of the national revival that accompanied the era of reform. See Na³aman 2002: 55–60.

44. For example, the acerbic criticism that Halpern (1988: 113–14, 118) leveled at Cross regarding the criteria for identifying texts to be assigned to Dtr[2] has not received sufficient attention among scholars (and cf., in this regard, the critique of Albertz 2003: 277–78). On the other hand, Provan's (1990: 20–23) criticism is not well founded (see the response by Knoppers 1993: 52), and the same may be said for Provan's (1988: 28, 131–32) criticisms. Despite these critiques, Knoppers (1993: 51) has aptly identified the advantages of Cross's theory: "it is this confluence of literary and ideological features which make Cross' theory by far the most convincing of the various multiple redaction hypotheses" (cf. Fretheim 1983: 17).

basic edition (Dtr¹) was created in the time of Josiah; (2) the Dtr² edition was devised after the destruction of Jerusalem, as a supplement; and (3) the third stage was finalized during the Babylonian exile and the time of the Return to Zion, when secondary additions were inserted into the work and the text went through further stages of editing.[45]

The roots of the "layers model" are found in Jepsen's study (1956) and have been reinforced by Smend's work.[46] Smend accepted Noth's basic position regarding the exilic authorship of the Deuteronomistic history and designated this stage Dtr^H (= "Historie").[47] In his view, the composition was redacted once more at a later stage (Dtr^N (= "nomist")) by someone whose main interest was the laws in the Torah (the book of Deuteronomy).[48] Dietrich expanded the role of the last redactor, assigning greater weight to the relatively small Dtr^N posited by Smend

---

45. Many scholars have followed this line. O'Brien (1989), Knoppers (1993; 1994), and van Keulen (1996) stand closest to the basic viewpoint that I support. O'Brien (1989: 227–34, 266–87) identified three strata of redaction dating to the exilic period within the basic Deuteronomistic text that came from Josiah's time: the addition of the account of the last four kings of Judah; the redactional layer that was designed to explain the exile as divine retribution for Manasseh's iniquity; and the nomistic layer, in which the emphasis shifted from the kings to the people, with its stress on the people's persistent refusal to obey the law. Knoppers (1993: 51–52 and in the discussion in chaps. 2–3, pp. 57–134) accepts Cross's fundamental understanding of both the basic Deuteronomistic work from the days of Josiah (Dtr¹) and the redactional layer from the exilic period (Dtr²) and shows the presence of later additions within this unit. Van Keulen (1996) accepts the fundamental understanding of the preexilic composition and identifies 2 Kings 21–25 as a "redactional block" added after the destruction of Jerusalem (1996: 199–200). In his opinion (pp. 200–201), the nomistic redactional layer is responsible for additional short passages inserted into the early composition at a later date. Lohfink (1981; 1984: 40; 1987: 462) pursues a similar direction, but it is difficult to accept his reconstruction of two pre-Deuteronomistic works from the days of Josiah (one was a pre-Deuteronomistic version of Deuteronomy–Joshua and the second, of Kings) that were consolidated after the destruction and underwent two stages of redaction. It is also difficult to accept McKenzie's perspective (1991: 135–50); he accepts the premise that a basic version of the book of Kings was created in the days of Josiah but rejects the idea of a single major redactional layer after the destruction (Dtr²) and instead identifies various secondary additions that stem from a variety of sources.

46. See Smend 1971; 1978: 69–81, 110–39. Smend himself (1978: 123) maintained that Jepsen was the first to express these ideas. On the centrality of Smend's work and the basis of the "layers model," which is identified with the "Göttingen school," see the comprehensive survey by van Keulen (1996: 14–22), with further literature and criticism. For an analysis of this "school" (focusing on 2 Kings 22–23), see also Eynikel 1996: 20–31, with further literature.

47. Smend, and subsequently Dietrich and Veijola, designated the basic composition Dtr^G (= Dtr^{Geschichte}). Later, Dietrich adopted the more common terminology and called it Dtr^H (= Dtr^{Historie}). See the critical review by Dietrich (1977a), as well as his essay (1977b). Smend (1978) and other scholars of the "layers model" school followed Dietrich.

48. It should be noted that Smend restricted his discussion to the books of Joshua and Judges and relied on Dietrich's analysis of the book of Kings (see Auld 1998: 61, with further literature). Veijola (1975), another of Smend's students, dealt primarily with the book of Samuel (see below, n. 51). Smend named the additional redactor Dtr^{Nomist} because of his specific interest in and concentration on the laws of the book of Deuteronomy. For a critique of this approach, see Weinfeld 1992: 186, and n. 30, and see also below.

and also finding evidence for this redactor's work within the prophetic speeches in the book of Kings.[49] He also exposed another stratum of redaction between Dtr[H] and Dtr[N], which he identified as prophetic and named Dtr[P] (= "Prophet").[50] He believed that this stratum included prophetic stories and speeches inserted into the historical account (Dtr[H]). He dated Dtr[H] to the first years after the destruction of Jerusalem; the prophetic redaction level (Dtr[P]) was added a decade later (Dietrich 1972: 110–34), and the third redaction level (Dtr[N]) is to be dated approximately 560 B.C.E. According to Dietrich, this stratum reflects a tendency to compromise between the antimonarchist Dtr[P] and the pro-Davidic Dtr[H]. Dtr[N] expresses this compromise by providing hope for the continued existence of the Davidic line through obedience to the laws of God.

The central ideas of the "Göttingen School" may be summarized as follows: the Deuteronomistic history was created during the exilic age in three stages:[51] Jepsen thought that the basic historical account was created by an author/redactor from among the priests (K = R[I]); this account is identical to Smend's Dtr[H] and Noth's basic Deuteronomistic composition. The second stratum of redaction, which Jepsen maintains has prophetic-Deuteronomistic features (Dtr = R[II]), is identical to Dietrich's Dtr[P].[52] The third stratum of redaction, which had nomistic characteristics, was assigned by Jepsen to the Levites and is parallel to Smend's Dtr[N].[53]

---

49. Dietrich (1972: 9–36) assigned a long line of passages to Dtr[N] but did not delineate them thoroughly enough. Some of the verses that he ascribed to Dtr[N] have no discernible relationship, or only marginally refer, to the law. See, e.g., the discussion below on 2 Kgs 23:26–27; 24:3–4, 20a; 25:22–30.

50. See Dietrich 1972: 110–34. In the first chapters of his book, this layer is known as Red[P], and only after Dietrich proves the distinction between this layer and Dtr[G] does he refer to it as Dtr[P]. On the later priestly redaction, see the discussions in García Lopez 1987; Begg 1989; Christensen 1992; also see the survey by van Keulen 1996: 16–17, with further literature.

51. For additional studies that take this approach, see Klein 1983; Würthwein 1976; 1984; Jones 1984; Spieckermann 1982. See also Spieckermann's analysis (1982: 153–200) of 2 Kings 22ff. within the approach of the "Göttingen school"; compare the different conclusions reached by Würthwein (1984: 440–43) and Ben-Zvi (1991a), who also used the same basic approach. For additional literature, see O'Brien 1989: 7–8 n. 22; 10 n. 30; Eynikel 1996: 13. Veijola (1975; 1977) applied the triple redaction theory to the book of Samuel and limited sections of the book of Judges (8:22–23; chaps. 17–21). He also supplemented Dietrich's theory with his own perception that the source of the antimonarchist idea in the DH is the product of the additions and revisions made by Dtr[P]. It should be noted that, although many accept the existence of Dtr[N], only a few accept Dietrich's understanding of the role of Dtr[P]. For additional literature on this subject, see Ben-Zvi 1991a: 355–56 and n. 2.

52. I consider this layer to be the major flaw in the "layers model"; in effect, Smend himself (1978: 123–24) acknowledged that the textual basis for it is shaky. See Provan 1988: 24 and van Keulen 1996: 21; see also below.

53. Dietrich and Smend do not agree regarding the time of Dtr[N]. According to Dietrich (1972: 147), this portion of the redaction process ended ca. 560 B.C.E., but Smend (1983a: 257) was of the opinion that it was a generation or more later, perhaps during the early days of the Return to Zion.

The "layers model" is open to criticism on three levels.[54] First, there are difficulties with assigning the entire composition to the exile (see Knoppers 1993: 40–41). The historical realities of this brief period do not provide an adequate background to explain several of the composition's central themes (such as the emphasis on the sins of the kingdom of Israel) as well as the evolution of other ideas (i.e., the development of the concept of the eternal promise to the Davidic line).[55]

The second, and more important, criticism has to do with the separation of ideological-theological attitudes from the historiographical scheme, as though the writing or redaction of a historical account cannot include well-formed ideas, speeches, and prophetic stories.[56] According to Weinfeld, Dtr[N] is an integral part of the conceptual background of the author of the historical account.[57] Similarly, one could, as an alternative, posit Dtr[P] as the central literary motif that the author used to help convey his message.[58] This is not to suggest the other extreme—that there are no secondary additions to the Deuteronomistic redaction. On the contrary, it is my opinion that Dtr[N], in contrast to Dtr[P], played an important role in the evolution of the Deuteronomistic school during the Babylonian exile and the Return to Zion (see also Provan 1988: 24; van Keulen 1996: 20–21). However, as will be demonstrated below, both Dtr[N] and

---

54. For a further critique of this school, see Provan 1988: 24–26; O'Brien 1989: 8–10; McKenzie 1991: 9; and Knoppers 1993: 38–42.

55. Thus, for example, when Veijola (1975: 127–30) was engaged in identifying the development of attitudes toward the king in the Deuteronomistic composition, he decided that the unconditional promise to the Davidic line belongs to Dtr[H], not to Dtr[N] (this differs from the "classic" view of Smend and Dietrich). In Veijola's opinion, the idea was so important in Dtr[H] because of the doubts raised about the future of the Davidic line in the period immediately following the Babylonian destruction. In contrast to Dtr[P]'s negative attitude toward the Davidic line, Veijola (1975: 142; 1982: 62–65) postulated that Dtr[N] developed a compromise position. In all of this, it never occurred to Veijola to assign an earlier date to the Deuteronomistic redaction or, at minimum, to assign the time of formulation of the Davidic promise to the period that preceded the destruction. Historically, at least, it is logical to assume that such an idea was necessary in that period. See, e.g., Veijola 1975: 150–58; in contrast, see Knoppers 1993: 40–41; and Würthwein 1984: 91–103. For another angle, see the view of Gerbrandt 1986: 14–15.

56. See O'Brien's (1989: 8) criticism regarding the need to mark the boundaries of Dtr[H] clearly, because it is the basic historical account on which the later redactional layers are overlaid; compare Kenick's (1983: 17) comments regarding the artificial distinction between Dtr[N] and Dtr[P], and see also Knoppers's (1993: 39–40) criticism.

57. As early as 1972, Weinfeld (1972: 137; 1992: 182–88, and n. 30) had identified a secondary layer that had been inserted into the text of the Deuteronomistic history, and he identified the subject of this layer as the written Deuteronomistic law; however, he argued that this should not be seen as a separate, later development but as a trend that characterized the Deuteronomistic school from its beginning.

58. This is in contrast to the view of Ben-Zvi (1991a: 371–74); see also below. For a comprehensive critique, see Campbell 1986: 5–16. Similarly, with an emphasis on the attitude toward Huldah's prophecy, see Spieckermann 1982: 58–71. Building on Spieckermann's criticism of the assignment of 2 Kgs 22:15–20 to Dtr[P], see Knoppers 1993: 39 concerning 2 Samuel 7.

other conceptual additions and interpretations found in the text do not add up
to a unified redactional stratum (Albertz 2003: 276).[59]

The third criticism relates to literary-ideological matters: the removal of prophetic speeches from the historical account, leaving the entire composition
without message or motive. By doing this Dietrich (1972) and others ignore important elements that Noth understood: the meticulous organization of the material and the thematic, structural, and linguistic uniformity of the entire work.
Differentiating among and separating the different elements of the redaction
come at the expense of the message and leave the composition merely a con-
glomeration of redactions having no unifying central strand and no organizing
principle.

The attempt to identify and catalogue the thematic, linguistic, and literary
variations in the various layers of the Deuteronomistic history is the "Göttingen
School's" contribution to scholarship. However, its weakness becomes apparent
when we note that it tried to go one step too far by attaching labels to different
aspects of the same text, thus permitting them to be detached from each other as
distinct "layers." In my opinion, redactional layers in the Deuteronomistic history
can be identified as independent layers only to the extent that one can textually
prove the existence of later insertions into Dtr^2 or one can prove the ideological
goals behind insertions into Dtr^1 that are later than Dtr^2. Any argument along
these lines must be supported, insofar as possible, with linguistic arguments.[60]

The "dual redaction" theory fulfills these requirements. It creates the necessary distinctions among the disparate redactional strata and also distinguishes
the later passages that were inserted into the Dtr^1 edition. Accepting the distinctions identified by the "layers model" enriches this theory and provides tools
for understanding the complex picture presented by the Deuteronomistic literature, including explanations both for the lack of uniformity in Dtr^2 and for the
later insertions in Dtr^2 (both within Dtr^2 and Dtr^1).

Modern scholars tend to distinguish several types of additions that constitute
the later, tendentious insertions into Dtr^2. These additions were inserted at different times and for various purposes, and the nomistic stratum (Dtr^N) is the
most important of these additions.[61] The nomistic stratum is characterized by its

---

59. Mayes (1983: 133–39) persuasively pointed this fact out when he examined the strong
"nomistic" trends and conspicuous hallmark of Dtr^N within the redaction of Dtr^2; see an expansion of this point in the theory proposed by Cortese (1990).

60. See Ben-Zvi (1991a: 357) and van Keulen (1996: 48–51) concerning the identification
of the later insertions (in this case, of Dtr^2) into the Dtr text. Compare also Halpern (1988:
168–71) on the identity of the author of 1 Kgs 8:33–34, 46–51.

61. The term "nomistic" was coined by Smend (1978: 68, 115) and it is important to specify
its denotation: it does not refer to a specific nomistic editor, as the "classic" school of Smend theorized (see above), but refers to a variegated layer having several specific linguistic and thematic

legal-Deuteronomistic language,[62] which emphasizes the transition from religious ritual to acceptance of the Torah laws as a way of life. The ideology behind this stratum implies that the center of gravity moves from the royal house to the people; in addition, one can detect a change in the definition of the prophet's role.[63] Many of the passages attributed to the nomistic stratum are located at key junctures in the Deuteronomistic history. Thus, the interpretive and ideological intention is achieved, and the central lesson is taught: the history of the people is the lasting consequence of obedience—or disobedience—to the Deuteronomistic law.[64]

O'Brien dates the nomistic redaction layer to the last third of the sixth century B.C.E. (the end of the exilic period and the beginning of the Return to Zion; O'Brien 1989: 284). He chiefly bases his arguments on the latest additions inserted into the nomistic redaction, as well as on its attitude toward the Davidic line and the temple. This conclusion seems appropriate for at least some of the additions, but even in this case there is a noticeable tendency to reduce the time allowed for the additions to be written, integrated, and redacted into the Deuteronomistic composition.[65] If one can detect a change in attitude toward the temple after it was built, there is surely no reason to postulate that other nomistic characteristics disappeared after the early days of the Return to Zion. It is reasonable to assume that the exposition of the king's role, which was a central component of the nomistic insertions, developed only at a much later stage (perhaps the middle of the fifth century B.C.E.), when the House of David had lost the last vestiges of its prior status.[66]

Additional later insertions into the Deuteronomistic composition may be found in three passages that deal with Shechem (Deut 11:26–30; 27:4–10; Josh

---

features that accompanied the insertion of several verses into the earlier composition (O'Brien 1989: 280 n. 15). See Ben-Zvi 1991a: 368–71; Eynikel 1996: 21; van Keulen 1996: 200–201.

62. For a list of the verses characterized by this language, see O'Brien 1989: 280–83; and see an expansion of this in van Keulen 1996: 197–200, as well.

63. See Dietrich 1972: 42, and n. 80; see also the summary by O'Brien 1989: 280–83.

64. Key passages, such as Deut 4:29–30 or 2 Kgs 17:7–19, spell out the main message: the history of the people is contingent on its obedience to God. There is an emphasis on God's control and self-restraint in the face of the people's disobedience throughout history. This provides the usual explanation for events, as well as the constant admonition against certain behaviors. For a summary, see O'Brien 1989: 281–82.

65. There are nomistic characteristics in the insertions into the nomistic sections of 2 Kings 8 (O'Brien 1989: 284) as well. These insertions are later than the Return to Zion, and this fact is sufficient to prove the length of time required for the redactional layer to be consolidated.

66. From the sparse textual material available, we may reconstruct a gradual process. During the early portion of the Return to Zion, great importance was still assigned to the Davidic line. In the period immediately before the temple was built, the House of David still enjoyed a certain status that was preserved throughout the exile in Babylon and at least until Ezra's time.

8:30–35),[67] in a few additions that are suspected of being Priestly,[68] in texts containing polemics against the Samaritans (in 2 Kgs 17:24–41),[69] and a few others.[70]

My main conclusion regarding the history of the Deuteronomistic composition can be summarized as follows. The basic Deuteronomistic composition (Dtr[1]) was created during the time of Josiah's reform (622 B.C.E.), as part of the dominant ideology of the time. We have no information about what happened to the literary and ideological-theological circles that created the basic Deuteronomistic text during the period leading up to the destruction of Jerusalem,[71] but after the crisis of the destruction, an ideological, historical, and even linguistic-terminological change took place in the Deuteronomistic school. During this time, more than two generations after the completion of the work of Dtr[1], the need arose to update the historical account ending with Josiah.[72] This update was indispensable, because the destruction of Jerusalem and the deportation of the nation's elite had called the central ideologies, as well as the Deuteronomistic theological interpretation of national events, into question. The adherents of the Deuteronomistic school were obliged to interpret events on these terms but also in accord with ideas current among the people after the destruction of Jerusalem; this was their main purpose (O'Brien 1989: 272–73, 291). However, this was not the cessation of Deuteronomistic literature. In ways that parallel the creation of postexilic books such as Jeremiah or Ezra–Nehemiah, history in its Deuteronomistic guise continued to occupy writers, thinkers, and commentators at a later

---

67. See L'Hour 1962: 182; Anbar 1985; 1992: 7–20; Koopmans 1990: 1–95. Naʾaman (1993a) went one step further and tried to identify the precise historical moment of these three texts. He concluded that they were written after the destruction of Jerusalem but before the temple in Jerusalem had been rebuilt. At an even later stage, additional texts were inserted, contradicting these and having the objective of opposing the "Shechem tradition."

68. On the insertions suspected as being Priestly, especially in Deuteronomy 32 and 34 and in Joshua 13–22, see Boling 1982: 58–67; Van Seters 1983: 331–37; the latter also attributed Judg 1:1–2: 5 to this source. On Deuteronomy 34, see von Stoellger 1993.

69. On the theological controversy between the Judeans and the Samaritans during the postexilic period, see Frevel 1991; Macchi 1992; Walsh 2000, with further literature.

70. See, for example, the list presented in O'Brien 1989: 285–86. We must emphasize that most of these insertions are found, predictably, in the Dtr[1] text.

71. On this point, I do not accept Weippert's dating of R[II]'s work to Jehoahaz's reign. My opinion is that we can differentiate the passages that belong to Dtr[1] and the passages that belong to Dtr[2] in its various stages (see below), but it is impossible to identify the passages that belong to the stage between the end of Josiah's rule and the period after the destruction of Jerusalem (609–586 B.C.E.). There is a gap between the major stages of the composition's formation, and there is no evidence that any editing took place in between. Accordingly, I also cannot accept Seitz's thesis (1989: 189–202) that the original book of Kings ended with 2 Kgs 24:20a and was written a short time after the deportation of Jehoiachin. For a criticism of this perspective, see van Keulen 1996: 43–44.

72. I do not accept the generally accepted date for Dtr[2], which holds that Jehoiachin's release from prison (ca. 562 B.C.E.) is the terminus post quem of the composition and the Persian defeat of Babylon (539 B.C.E.) is the terminus ante quem, because both additions in 2 Kgs 25:22–30 are later than Dtr[2] (Halpern and Vanderhooft 1991: 182). See also the discussion below.

time as well. It may be that basking in the eminence of this glorious history intensified the significance of the increasingly distant events. The implications of
these historical accounts for fundamental issues—such as the right of the people
to its land; the status of Jerusalem; the role of the House of David versus the status
of the priesthood; relations between the Diaspora and Israel; and the importance
of immigration to Judah—preoccupied earlier and later generations, all of whom
wished to convey a moral message to their contemporaries (see also the comment
by Ben-Zvi [1991a: 368]).

Polemics and the interpretation of Holy Scriptures were legitimate means of
transmitting these messages, as were interpreting the remote events of the past
and exploring their ramifications for current issues. This process became increasingly refined over time, metamorphizing into one of the principal features
of Jewish literature throughout the generations.

5.1.2. Dtr²: Date, Purpose, and Place of Writing

The basic premise of this section is that the exilic Deuteronomistic edition
(Dtr²) is a supplement that was added to the preexilic edition (Dtr¹). The author[73] of this account was active after the destruction of Jerusalem,[74] he was familiar with the first version,[75] and, apart from the historical narrative that he
wrote to extend the previous composition, he only inserted in it passages that
were important to him ideologically. He added a new color that he utilized to
achieve his own ends: the Deuteronomistic narrative from the time of Josiah,
which described the history of the nation until the religious reform, was extended up to the destruction of Jerusalem, which it now served to explain. The
message is now addressed to the first generation of exiles in Babylon, and events
are described meticulously, explained clearly, and presented through the eyes of

---

73. By using the title "author" (third person, singular) to refer to the creator of the postexilic
work, I do not intend to imply that one person created the historical composition that supplements Dtr¹ and was responsible for inserting the additions into the Dtr¹ edition. Technically,
the limited scope of the work would allow us to make this assumption, but the ideological and
theological depth of the later composition and the way it incorporates the older composition are
evidence, in my opinion, of extensive literary activity during a discrete span of time immediately after the destruction of Jerusalem. For a very clear description of the Deuteronomistic
circles of the sixth century B.C.E., see Albertz 1994: 382; 2000: 10–11, with further literature.

74. The characteristics of this composition fit well with the first generation after the destruction. Babylon is described in all its might, there is no mention of Persians, and even the
liberation of Jehoiachin is still a distant vision. See also the discussion below.

75. Dtr²'s familiarity with the work of Dtr¹ is reflected in the minute details of the Deuteronomistic narratives, formulas, ideas, and language. Frequently, this familiarity is characterized
by refinement of familiar elements and adaptation of them to Dtr²'s needs. His language is either
a direct continuation of the Dtr¹ style or, with variations in terminology, is based on his familiarity, and apparently his audience's familiarity, with conventional Deuteronomistic language.
See especially the discussion below of the roots שלח, שוב, אבד, נגש, ענש, מאס, שלך, סור, חרה,
קצף, חנה, בקע, שחת, נפץ, etc. See also the discussion of the expressions לא שב ה' מחרון אפו;
הלך לקראת; בעת ההיא; בימיו; על פי ה'; על כל הכעסים אשר הכעיסו; etc.

a narrator whose primary purpose is to convey a message rather than to present the details of the narrative.[76]

In the later edition, the last years of the kingdom of Judah are described as an accelerated process of decline from the death of Josiah until the destruction. Because this work was written post factum, with a knowledge of the conclusion of events, the perspective put forward is that the die had been cast ever since the days of Manasseh;[77] even the righteous King Josiah was unable to alter the kingdom's fate. The sin "of the innocent blood that [Manasseh] shed, for he filled Jerusalem with innocent blood" (2 Kgs 24:4) is mentioned as the main reason for divine wrath during that king's reign.[78] The connection between God's punishment and Manasseh's actions is also highlighted by linguistic-literary devices, by the references to warnings given in the days of Manasseh ("and the Lord spoke

76. This is not the place to go into detail. However, I think that the author's adherence to the ideological line that he imposed on himself and the brevity with which he described the events from Josiah until the destruction show that his audience knew the events, implying that they lived only a short time after the events occurred. His objective was to interpret the events and to explain why things happened as they did.

77. Blaming Manasseh for Jerusalem's destruction is one of the striking and central features of the later work of Dtr². It seems to be an extension of the blame placed on Jeroboam by Dtr¹. Compare also the explicit culpability placed on Manasseh in Jer 15:4 (Smelik 1992: 166–68). For a discussion of 2 Kings 21 and its attribution to Dtr², see van Keulen 1996, with further literature.

78. On the passages connected to Manasseh, see O'Brien 1989: 227–34, 266–71, 272–87; see van Keulen's criticism (1996: 185–91, 193) regarding the connection between 2 Kgs 24:4 and 21:1–18 (following Würthwein 1984: 469, who attributes vv. 3–4 to two different nomistic redactors). The sin of shedding "innocent blood" is the major sin attributed to Manasseh in 2 Kgs 21:16: "Manasseh shed very much innocent blood, till he had filled Jerusalem from one end to another." The expression "innocent blood" relates to violation of the Deuteronomistic law regarding the murder of innocents (Deut 19:1–13; 21:1–9, and see also 27:25, which I believe to be a later addition to the whole series of curses). For a discussion of this expression, see Garbini 1988: 111–20, 196–98. Garbini's suggestion that this sin should be connected with the practice of sacrificing children to Molech is problematic, because the latter practice is based on Ps 106:37–38, and it is doubtful that "innocent blood" should be understood this narrowly; the Molech cult practice is not directly connected to the shedding of innocent blood in any passage. Smelik's proposal (1992: 151–53 and n. 81) that the phrase refers to the murder of the poor is likewise questionable, because it is based mainly on a single passage (Jer 2:34) and has no parallels elsewhere. For additional suggestions on this subject and reactions to them, see Smelik 1992: 151–52 nn. 80, 88. The centrality of this specific sin, with its linguistic and legal contexts, is the result of its significance in the prophecies of Jeremiah (Šanda 1911–12: 2.376; Cogan and Tadmor 1988: 307). This explanation makes good sense, especially given the reference to "innocent blood" in Jer 19:4–5, in the context of a prophecy that was spoken at the Topheth in the valley of Ben-Hinnom (Jer 19:1–15) and that also describes the ritual sacrifice of children (Smelik 1992: 151–53). This phrase recurs in five other places in the prophecies of Jeremiah (2:34; 7:6; 22:3, 17; 26:15), and we may assume that this idea influenced Dtr², because the centrality of this sin is not characteristic of the Deuteronomistic version that existed before the destruction. Compare this with the simple, uncompounded sense that the phrase has in 1 Sam 19:5. For speculation about the later development of the law, see Garbini 1988: 113–15, 196, and n. 4; Smelik 1992: 151–52. On the first Deuteronomistic book of Jeremiah, see Albertz 2003: 327–32.

by his servants the prophets"—21:10), and in the description of the fulfillment of prophecies, "according to the word of the Lord that he spoke by his servants the prophets" (24:2b; compare 17:23a).[79]

The description of the destruction (2 Kgs 25:1–21) is both the climax of the story and the goal toward which the author aimed his composition. In this account, two circles are closed:

1. **From the historical perspective**—the destruction of the kingdom of Israel and the deportation of its inhabitants are linked to the destruction of Jerusalem and the deportation of the inhabitants of the kingdom of Judah. This connection is created by the use of parallel language in both descriptions;[80] the language makes the theological explanation for the destruction of Israel explicit (17:7–23) and highlights the fate of Judah, which was inserted into the explanation (vv. 19–20).[81]

2. **From the literary perspective**—The threats of impending destruction (threats that were part of the later version [Dtr²], as well as those that were inserted into the earlier version [Dtr¹]) were connected to the description of Jerusalem's destruction. The connection was accomplished by the repetition of identical expressions,[82] which also allowed the ideological message to be conveyed clearly and directly.[83]

---

79. On the connection between 2 Kgs 17:23; 21:10; and 24:2, see Gosse 1994: 168. For a discussion of the function of the phrase and its authenticity, see Seitz 1989: 176; see also Cross 1973: 285–86; Nelson 1981: 88; O'Brien 1989: 270. On the connection of Dtr² with Nathan's oracle, see Lohfink 1990: 368–69.

80. Compare the language of these two verses:

| 2 Kgs 17:23b: | ויגל ישראל מעל אדמתו אשורה עד היום הזה |
| 2 Kgs 25:21b: | ויגל יהודה מעל אדמתו |

The Dtr² version ends with this verse (in my opinion; see also below). Furthermore, the addition in 17:23b is significant for understanding the historical situation at the time of its writing. In addition to an allusion to the time of its writer, it may point to the geographical proximity of the two communities in exile.

81. See, for this purpose, the references above, in nn. 78–79; Brettler 1989: 268–82.

82. The condemnation of Manasseh, who is cited as the reason for the destruction (23:26–27; 24:2b–4, 20a), is repeated thrice, at the beginning of each stage of the decline toward destruction. The expression that recurs in all three instances is הסיר מעל פניו or השליך מעל פניו. These phrases can be compared with the Dtr² or later insertions into the early Deuteronomistic composition (2 Kgs 13:23; 17:18, 20, 23), though it must be noted that they are characteristic of the Deuteronomistic literature in various layers; see the comment by O'Brien 1989: 270. The element of divine wrath is also common to all three passages: 23:26; 24:3–5; and 24:20. See the discussion on this in van Keulen 1996: 148–55.

83. Evidence that Dtr² was building a systematic historiography may be found in his use of the phrase ומאסתי את העיר הזאת (23:27b). The use of the root מאס is restricted to three additional episodes, and the connection between them is deliberate. (1) In the episode in which the people demand a king and Saul is anointed (1 Samuel 8–10), the root מאס appears three times (1 Sam 8:7 [twice]; 10:19). This is intended to indicate that the people no longer wanted their God and instead demanded a king. (2) In the description of the transfer of the monarchy from Saul to David, this root appears six times (1 Sam 15:23 [twice], 26 [twice]; 16:1, 7). Its

Scholars are divided about where the author of the exilic edition of the Deu-teronomistic history resided.[84] Noth and Janzen[85] have presented the major arguments in favor of Judah (Mizpah?) as the location of the Deuteronomist fol-lowing the destruction of Jerusalem. The main problem with this persepctive is that both Noth and Janzen treat this work as a single piece, without distinguish-ing the preexilic and exilic editions, and most of their arguments are connected to Dtr[1] or later additions to Dtr[2] (such as the two appendixes at the end of the book).[86] Only two of their supporting arguments have to do with Dtr[2] as defined in the previous paragraph, and neither of these is sufficient to support the asser-tion that the Deuteronomistic history was written in Judah.

---

centrality to the story is evident: Saul rejected the word of the Lord, and the Lord rejected his kingship and ordered the anointing of David as king. (3) In the theological rationale for the de-struction of Israel (and Judah), this root is used twice in order to show the direct connection between the behavior of the people and their downfall. Because "they rejected his laws and covenant," "the Lord rejected the whole seed of Israel." The expression in 2 Kgs 23:27b comes as a direct consequence of this, and the verdict "I will remove Judah also out of my sight as I re-moved Israel" (23:27a) is the direct outgrowth of "I will cast off this city of Jerusalem that I have chosen." These segments are directly connected, at least on the linguistic and redactional level. The use of these components creates a link between the destruction and the initial "sin" of demanding a king, as well as the transfer of the monarchy to the House of David and the downfall of the nation. At the heart of these events are the conditions under which the House of David and Jerusalem are chosen, and the main purpose is to show the ephemeral nature of these choices and that their continuance depended on obedience to God's commands. Here, too, the impact of Jeremiah's prophecies is felt: this terminology plays a central role in the prophet's book (esp. 2:37; 7:29; 14:19; 18:9). It is likely that Jeremiah's prophecies included in the early parts of the book (and see below) are the source of influence on the Deuteronomist, who was active after the destruction. For a review of various scholarly perspectives and a discus-sion of this subject, see O'Brien 1989: 98–120; McKenzie 1991: 10–14; Weinfeld 1972: 324–25, 347; 1992: 94–99, 108–9. A significant question in this context (to be discussed below as well) is the place of the Davidic kings within the ideological system of Dtr[2]. Friedman (1981b: 187–88) sees this as the most difficult ideological problem that faced the later author in handling the earlier text. According to Friedman, Dtr[2] attempted to resolve the ideological problem by plac-ing the blame on the people, not on the kings of David's house. As will be demonstrated below, this solution is only partially valid because, along with the author's positive attitude toward the Davidic kings, especially Jehoiachin (which is evidence of the time when Dtr[2] wrote), the au-thor identified three kings as transgressors whose behavior led to the nation's destruction: Ma-nasseh, Jehoiakim (in particular), and, along with them, Zedekiah.

84. For a summary of the opinions of scholars on this subject, see Nicholson 1970: 117–22; Eynikel 1996: 7–31; Albertz 2003: 282–84.

85. See Noth 1943: 73–99, 141 n. 9; Janssen 1956: 49–56; cf. Wolff 1961: 172. For a sum-mary of the arguments put forward by Noth and Janssen, see Ackroyd 1968: 65–68; Nicholson 1970: 117–22, who also provides a critique of these arguments. For a different view, see Nichol-son 1970: 120–22; Soggin 1975.

86. On the two appendixes (2 Kgs 25:22–29), see the discussion below. A thorough exami-nation of Noth's and Janssen's arguments (from the standpoint of an "improved version" of the "dual redaction" theory as previously presented) leads to the conclusion that most are not ger-mane to Dtr[2]. Thus, for example, the argument that there were many local traditions con-nected with the Mizpah region (including the story of Gedaliah) is irrelevant, because there is no reference to this region in Dtr[2] (see the following discussion).

1. Janzen claimed that the Deuteronomistic history does not recount the Babylonian exile or refer to the status of the exiles, and this follows Noth's argument that it has no vision of a Return to the land of Israel. In my opinion, these are the most telling arguments that can be adduced to prove that the work was written in Judah. However, aside from the fact that they cannot be sustained on other grounds,[87] they ignore the objectives and nature of the composition itself. The Deuteronomistic history was not written to recount a contemporary historical situation but to explain a process the consequences of which were known. If we assume this perspective, a description of the situation of the people in exile would be irrelevant; the author did not need such a description, either for ideological or literary reasons. Furthermore, a discussion of the possibility of a return and references to exiles would not serve the purposes of someone who wished to present the exile as the end of a historical process. This is true apart from any judgment about whether opinions of this sort were prevalent among the people in the first half of the sixth century.

2. Noth maintained that sufficient sources for the Deuteronomistic composition were available only in Judah. However, if we take into account the thesis that Dtr[2] merely completed the description of the history as outlined in the earlier work (Dtr[1]), then the only source he required was the account of the days of Josiah, and there is no reason to believe that this work was not available to the exiles in Babylon. Perhaps a version had already been carried to Babylon during the deportation of Jehoiachin (Seitz 1989: 189–202), or had arrived in Babylon at some time between the deportation of Jehoiachin and the destruction of Jerusalem, or was brought to Babylon after the destruction.[88] It is important to remember that the elite of the nation resided in Babylon. Furthermore, extensive literary activity took place there, and we know that letters between those in exile and those in Jerusalem were exchanged and that emissaries traveled between the two countries.[89]

In addition to the literary and theological arguments raised and summarized by Albertz (2003: 282–85), some additional arguments tip the balance in favor

---

87. See the arguments of Nicholson (1970: 118–20; see also the textual discussion on pp. 75–87). Wolff (1961: 92–94) already saw the difficulty in Noth's opinion, even though he in principle accepted Noth's position.

88. Information on the exchange of letters and passage of emissaries during this time can be gleaned from the prophecies of Jeremiah and Ezekiel. See the discussion below.

89. Regarding the sources of the postexilic composition, it should be noted that Noth does not produce evidence of any sources embedded in the account of the destruction, nor is proof to be found in the work of other scholars (such as Cogan and Tadmor 1988: 321). I surmise that Dtr[2] based his work primarily on firsthand knowledge and what he himself saw. The details found in his account were certainly also known to the generation that experienced the destruction, and these details were reported precisely, in keeping with the ideological perspective defined by the author, in a style that reflects his intimate familiarity with the Deuteronomistic history and other biblical texts.

of the conclusion that the later redaction of the Deuteronomistic history (Dtr²) was carried out in Babylon.

1. The narrative focuses on the elite of the nation who went into exile both at the time of Jehoiachin (2 Kgs 24:12, 15–16) and following the destruction of Jerusalem (25:11). The exiles are presented as "the people of Judah" (25:21b), totally ignoring the people who remained in Judah.[90] In the only historiographical account written in Judah, which describes the reign of Gedaliah in Mizpah,[91] a completely different perspective toward those "remaining in Judah" appears. The stance toward the remnant in Judah distinguishes the two components of the nation after the destruction and also differentiates other texts created in the exile (for example, the prophecies of Ezekiel) from those that were composed in Judah (part of Jeremiah's prophecies and the account of the reign of Gedaliah; see §5.2 below).

2. In the opening formulas to the accounts of the last four kings of Judah, blame is assigned to Manasseh and Jehoiakim,[92] skipping over Josiah.[93] Apparently, the guilt laid at the feet of Jehoiakim is an act of historiography resulting from the need to explain events that have already occurred, among them the fact that he was the only king of the last four who died in Jerusalem and was not deported.[94] This gives expression to the special relationship that Dtr² had with Jehoiachin, who was exiled in Babylon; an entirely different attitude toward the royal house is reflected in the account about Gedaliah.[95]

3. Literary activity among the exiles in Babylon after the destruction of Jerusalem was widespread.[96] Indeed, what we know of this is primarily prophecy and

90. See below (§5.1.4, pp. 299–304) for a discussion of the only two references to those who remained in the land (24:14b; 25:12). For the moment, it is enough to note that these texts are later insertions having identical objectives and coming from the same hand, a person who wrote at the height of the exile. On this subject, see also Rofé 1998: 226.

91. For a discussion of the two preserved versions of this source, see below, §5.2.2d (pp. 339–347.

92. Assigning the blame to Jehoiakim is particularly striking in the last two opening formulas: in 2 Kgs 24:9, Jehoiachin is blamed for doing evil in the sight of the Lord "according to all that his father had done," and in 24:19, Zedekiah is blamed for doing evil in the sight of the Lord "according to all that Jehoiakim had done." See Weippert 1972: 333–34; Nelson 1981: 36–41; Mayes 1983: 123; Vanoni 1985: 359; O'Brien 1989: 268–69; Halpern and Vanderhooft 1991: 209–11. For a different perspective, see Provan 1988: 48–49; and for a critique of these views, see O'Brien 1989: 269 n. 142.

93. The opening formulas of Jehoahaz (2 Kgs 23:31) and of Jehoiakim (23:36) are identical; in both, the blame is directed at אבותיו rather than אביו, the usual form.

94. On the story of Jehoiakim's death and its historiographical aims, see Lipschits 2002b, with further literature.

95. On Jehoiachin's place in the literature created in Babylon, see the discussion below, §5.4.1d (pp. 354–356).

96. See, e.g., the surveys by Ackroyd 1968: 62–137. On the importance of this literary activity, see Noth 1954: 296. It is difficult to accept Janssen's theory (1956); he argues that Isaiah 21; Obadiah; and Psalms 44, 74, 79, 89, and 102 were all written in Judah, together with the entire Deuteronomistic history. See the more balanced theory of Albertz (2003); and see below.

poetry, and we have no additional historiographical material composed in Babylon during the exile. However, we may hypothesize that historiographical activity also took place (Albertz 2003: 283–85, with further literature). On the other hand, there is almost no information about literary activity in Judah after the destruction of Jerusalem, except for a description of the days of Gedaliah (see below). The Deuteronomistic editions of Jeremiah bear a different ideology (see below). The exilic activity, I believe, was partially a result of self-justification, coupled with the profound religious, social, and national changes that the elite had to undergo in order to adapt to life in exile. The "remnant in Judah," by comparison, underwent a less-drastic transformation, because they remained in the family, settlement, and regional contexts that they had always known. Thus, it is likely that the historiographical account, which purported to give the reasons for the destruction, was written in Babylon by one of the exiles.

4. The use of Babylonian dates—events dated to the years of Nebuchadrezzar's reign (2 Kgs 24:12; 25:8)—and apparent parallels between the description of the destruction and the Babylonian Chronicles tend to reinforce the argument that the work was composed in Babylon.[97] The method of dating used in 2 Kings 24–25 has only one parallel in the Bible (Jer 52:28–30), and its use there shows that the author was familiar with Babylonian practice.[98]

5.1.3. The Appendixes in 2 Kgs 25:22–30: Their Date, Place of Composition, and Purpose

The description of the destruction of Jerusalem (2 Kgs 25:1–21) is an integral part of the postexilic Deuteronomistic work (Dtr²). It is precisely this narrative that underscores the question regarding its conclusion: the destruction (which should have been the author's goal and which was supposed to be the climax of the description—its finale) is buried in the account and becomes merely another milestone. The narrative continues with a description of what happened to the "remnant" in Judah (25:22–26) and the story of Jehoiachin's release from imprisonment 26 years later (25:27–30).[99] These events are placed immediately

---

97. I state this, despite reservations about the conclusions reached by Van Seters 1983: 295.

98. See Montgomery 1951: 555; Freedman 1956: 56; Bright 1965: 691; Gray 1964: 753, 759–60; Freedy and Redford 1970: 463; Malamat 1983: 263–64; Cogan and Tadmor 1988: 311; and Rofé 1997: 180–84; 1998: 225–26. It is difficult to accept Mowinckel's opinion (1932: 199–200) that using Babylonian dating is, in all instances, evidence of later additions. I prefer the view expressed by Rofé (1997) that vv. 28–30 were deleted from the LXX version.

99. On the first "appendix," see the discussion below. On the second "appendix," see Zenger 1968; Levenson 1984: 353–61; Begg 1986a: 49–56; Murray 2001: 245–65; Albertz 2000: 6–8; 2003: 103–4. Noth did not ascribe much importance to the description of Jehoiachin's release from imprisonment and saw it as the original conclusion of the Deuteronomist's narrative, providing the last pieces of information available to him. Von Rad, however, recognized in the second appendix a "message of optimism" regarding the House of David (1953: 90; 1962: 1.334–47; 1966a: 220). Many scholars have followed von Rad; see the survey of Murray 2001: 245–46, with further literature, as well as Albertz 2003: 293.

after the account of the destruction of Jerusalem and the deportation of the nation's elite: surprisingly, there is no theological summation of these events or any emphasis on their historical significance.[100] The perspective in both of these appendixes appears to be later than the perspective of the description of Jerusalem's destruction and is separated from it textually, conceptually, and thematically.[101] The descriptions revolve around events distant in space and time from the destruction of Jerusalem;[102] the city, the temple, and the exiles in Babylon are not mentioned at all. Support for the later dating of these accounts may be found in the various perceptions that they express, especially on two subjects:

1. *The Attitude toward the Babylonians.* In the description of Jerusalem's destruction (2 Kgs 25:1–21), the Babylonians destroy, burn, smash, kill, and deport. Their cruel treatment of Zedekiah, Jerusalem, the temple, the king's officers, and the residents of the kingdom is blatant. In contrast, in vv. 22–30, the Babylonians appoint Gedaliah governor at Mizpah, and Gedaliah promises that if the people submit to the Babylonians "it shall be well with you" (v. 24). The Babylonians also release Jehoiachin from imprisonment and set his throne "above the throne of the other kings who were with him in Babylon" (v. 28).

2. *The Attitude toward the "Remnant" in Judah.* In the description of the destruction, there is no mention of the "remnant." The only comment (in v. 21b) creates the impression that no one remained in Judah. In contrast, in vv. 22–26, the "remnant" was organized under the protection of the Babylonians. Because

---

100. As noted above, the only ideological statement regarding the fate of Judah (2 Kgs 17:18–20) was appended to the summary of the fate of the kingdom of Israel. This fact highlights even further the absence of a summary treatment of the royal house and the temple, at least as a fulfillment of the prophecy in 2 Kgs 21:10–16; see also Seitz 1989: 173–74. It is difficult to accept Cross's opinion (1973: 288) regarding the absence of a summary editorial comment or the thesis developed by O'Brien (1989: 280–82), who explains the deportation of Jehoiachin as the fulfillment of this prophecy. See also below.

101. *Textually:* the language of this account is different from the Deuteronomistic language that characterizes both the earlier edition (Dtr¹) and the later edition (Dtr²). It is lacking the prototypical Deuteronomistic expressions and does not use conventional figures of speech. The conclusion that the source for this first appendix is an independent source composed in Judah (see more on this below, §5.4.2d) reinforces its linguistic difference from the Dtr² composition.

Conceptually: this account is striking, because there is no reference to God's activity in history, direct or implied retribution, or any theological explanation for events. In addition, the events are not connected ideologically with the description of the destruction. Furthermore, the account of Gedaliah's reign contains an anti-Davidic note unique to the entirety of biblical historiography (see the discussion in §5.4.1d below). The only possible conceptual link to the Deuteronomistic description touches upon Jehoiachin's release from prison, but even in this regard the story is remote from the intent of Dtr² (see below).

102. The account of Gedaliah's rule (2 Kgs 25:22–26) focuses on the area around Mizpah and the Bethlehem region. This is in stark contrast to the account that deals only with the siege of Jerusalem and focuses on the fate of the city, the temple, the king, and the people living there. On this subject, see the discussion that follows, in §5.2.2b. It also deals with the short time span after the destruction; Jehoiachin's liberation from prison (2 Kgs 25:27–30) takes place after 37 years in exile, 26 years after the destruction of Jerusalem (561 B.C.E.).

the "remnant" was willing to accept the authority of Babylon, these Judahites discovered an alternative to the rule of the House of David.[103]

If this is the case, we may conclude that the original ending of the postexilic Deuteronomistic history (Dtr[2]) was at 2 Kgs 25:21b.[104] Thus, the destruction of Jerusalem and the deportation of the nation's elite were the climax of the narrative, paralleling the description of the end of the kingdom of Israel (2 Kgs 17:23b). The message is unequivocally pessimistic: "So Judah was carried away out of their land." The destruction of the land is total, the deportation of the nation is complete, and there is no one left in the country.

It was only a generation or more later that two "appendixes" were added to the description of Jerusalem's destruction.[105] My discussion of the account of Gedaliah's time (below, §5.2.2d) will establish this hypothesis textually and will also deal with the question of the source of this "appendix."[106] However, at this point, I wish to state my hypothesis that both "appendixes" were added at one time, under the impetus of a single ideological purpose:[107] to show the possibility of continued life under Babylonian rule, both in Judah and in the exile.

This ideological intention is reflected in two episodes:

1. 2 Kgs 25:22–26 records the tragedy of a missed opportunity, because Ishmael, son of Nethaniah, "of the seed royal" (v. 25), murdered Gedaliah, after the Babylonians had made it possible to reestablish life after the destruction of Jerusalem.

2. 2 Kgs 25:27–30 provides a description of Jehoiachin's release from prison by Evil-merodach, king of Babylon; the account accentuates Jehoiachin's special status among the kings held captive in Babylon.

---

103. On 2 Kgs 25:12, see the discussion below; see also Ackroyd 1968: 57.

104. This was the conclusion of Montgomery 1951: 564; Nelson 1981: 61, 86, 89; Cogan and Tadmor 1988: 324; and O'Brien 1989: 268–73.

105. On the reasons for the addition of these two "appendixes" to the Deuteronomistic composition and their sources (including the connection between 2 Kings 25 and Jeremiah 39–41), see the discussion following. Among the scholars who have established the later dating of one or both of the "appendixes," Pohlmann's work (1979) is of great importance textually, as are Friedman's publications (1981a: 35–36; 1981b: 189–92). See also Jones 1984: 648; Seitz 1989: 196 n. 197, 198; O'Brien 1989: 272, 287, and n. 32; and McKenzie 1991: 152. On this subject, I reject the idea proposed by García López (1987: 222–32) and Begg (1989: 49–54) as a development of Würthwein's thesis (1984: 477–78).

106. As I will discuss below, the account of Gedaliah's rule is based on an independent source composed in Judah a short time after the destruction and embedded in the book of Jeremiah. On the other hand, the sources for the second "appendix," which describes Jehoiachin's release from prison, are not clear; see Cogan and Tadmor 1988: 329–30; Seitz 1989: 199; Albertz 2003: 284.

107. This conclusion is different from O'Brien's (1989: 271); he believes that the appendixes originated from different redactional stages. See also Cross 1973: 277–89; and Friedman 1981b: 189–92. Cf. Seitz 1989: 175, 193; and see the critique by van Keulen 1996: 43–44.

It is likely that both of these episodes were known to the people of that generation and that the events described were among the most important in the history of the Jewish people, both in the period immediately after the destruction
of Jerusalem and during the heart of the exilic period, some 25 years later. But
the brevity of the description of both events, their proximity, and the lack of
chronological and geographical connection between them demonstrate the
weight that the author assigned to his message but not necessarily to the details
of the events he described. In both the abridged version of the account of Gedaliah's reign (2 Kgs 25:22–26) and in the expanded version (Jer 40:7–41:18),
there is an emphasis on the opportunity that "the people who remained in Judah" were given to rebuild national life under Babylonian authority. The condemnation of Ishmael, son of Nethaniah, "of the seed royal," for the murder of
Gedaliah is also prominent. The act of murder, a single irrevocable deed, cost
the "remnant" in Judah the opportunity to rebuild the nation. The moral lesson
is obvious: the Babylonians would permit the nation to continue in its land only
on the condition that the nation acknowledge Babylonian authority. The main
message of the story is found in Gedaliah's words (2 Kgs 25:24): "Fear not the
servants of the Babylonians; dwell in the land and serve the king of Babylon,
and it shall be well with you."[108]

A parallel message is conveyed by the account of Jehoiachin's release. Theoretically, one could see it as a fulfillment of the promise of an enduring dynasty
to the House of David.[109] However, as will be discussed below, this account has
a larger goal than merely to locate the king in the Deuteronomistic historiography: the story wishes to highlight the king's status in the Babylonian exile. Historically, the story is connected to Jehoiachin's surrender in 597 B.C.E. (see Seitz
1989: 219–24; Murray 2001: 256–60), and ideologically, its aim is to emphasize
that, "though he be delayed, he will surely come."[110] Jehoiachin's release and
the honor he was accorded demonstrated that, eventually, things could change,
if only the people practiced patience.

It is likely, then, that in the mid-sixth century B.C.E., after Jehoiachin's
release and before the fall of Babylon and the rise of Persia, this message was
transmitted by adding these two "appendixes" to the end of the Deuteronomis-

---

108. See Wolff 1961: 171–86; Levenson 1984: 353–61; and Becking 1990: 283–93. On the
linguistic problems with this verse, see §5.2.2d below.

109. This has been, with minor variations, the opinion of most scholars; see, e.g., Noth
1943: 107–8; von Rad 1953: 90; 1962: 1.343; 1966a: 220; Cross 1973: 277; Levenson 1984:
353–61. For further literature, see Murray 2001: 245–46; Albertz 2000: 6–7; 2003: 293.

110. In this regard, see Long's (1984: 29) interpretation of 1 Kings: he follows von Rad and
notes the importance of this episode within the Deuteronomistic ideology regarding the Davidic House. Nonetheless, in his commentary on 2 Kings (1991), Long adopted the approach
taken in this book, indicating that the supplement describing Jehoiachin's release from prison
was added to the earlier work as an open message to the exiles in Babylon, with the aim that
they embrace the message—that to be exiles in Babylon also meant learning to get along with
the Babylonians (1991: 289).

tic history. According to this new message, one should no longer talk of total destruction and complete deportation (2 Kgs 25:21b), but, instead, one must speak of hope for continued life under Babylonian rule. This can be seen as evidence of a national sobriety, a reconciliation with the status quo, and a desire to keep going, based now on a realistic understanding of existing limitations. This reflects an entirely different perception of the status of the "remnant in Judah" and of the exiles in Babylon.

It is difficult to know where these perceptions developed and where they were written. If we consider the story of Jehoiachin's release and the attitude toward him, we might postulate that the appendix was composed in Babylon. Although the source for the account of Gedaliah is Judean (below §5.2.2d), the emphasis of the supplement regarding his reign is on the mass departure from the land after the flight of the "remnant" of Judah to Egypt. The later additions (2 Kgs 24:13–14; 25:12) seem to "answer" the appendixes in 25:22–30, perhaps intending to counterbalance them with the viewpoint of the Babylonian exiles—which supports the theory that these texts comprise a dialogue conducted entirely in Babylon. (For more on this subject, see §5.4 below.)

5.1.4. The Additions to Dtr² (2 Kgs 24:13–14; 25:12):
Date, Place, and Purpose[111]

The brief account of the deportation of Jehoiachin is divided into three parts: the siege of the city leading to its capitulation (24:10–11);[112] the deportation of the nation's elite and removal of the spoils of war to Babylon (vv. 12–16); and the coronation of Mattaniah-Zedekiah (v. 17). This schematization is logical, the description is in agreement with the Babylonian Chronicle from the seventh year of Nebuchadrezzar, and it seems to be precise and purposeful.[113]

The main problems with this description are its redundancy and its awkwardness in numbering the exiles. In vv. 12, 14, 15, and 16, six verbs describing surrender and exile occur.[114] It is striking that the deportation of Jehoiachin is

---

111. Two supplements dealing with the "remnant" in the land were inserted into the account of the deportation of Jehoiachin (2 Kgs 24:10–17) and the destruction of Jerusalem (25:1–12). The purpose of this section is to provide grounds for dating these additions to a later time and to clarify the reason for their insertion. On the historical duration of this period, see the discussion above (§§2.1.3–4, pp. 49–62).

112. Jehoiachin's capitulation is described in v. 12a but not explained. It is possible to explain Jehoiachin's action in terms of the historical context: his father, Jehoiakim, was the one who had rebelled, and his death created an opportunity to obtain better terms of surrender (Lipschits 2002b).

113. For a reconstruction of this campaign, see the discussion in §2.1.3 (pp. 49–55), with further literature. On the logic and credibility of this narrative, see the discussion in §2.1.4 (pp. 55–62), with further literature. See also Noth 1954: 282–83; and Malamat 1983: 260–62.

114. See the repetition of the verbs describing the surrender and exile in these verses: ויביאם . . . גולה . . . ;גולה ;הוליך גולה ;ויגל את ;הגלה את ;ויקח אותו ;ויצא יהויכין . . . על. On the connection between the deportation of Jehoiachin and Ezekiel's prophecy in chap. 19, see Duguid 1994: 35–37.

recounted twice (vv. 12b, 15a), and the deportation of החרש והמסגר (v. 14aβ, 16aβ) and גבורי החיל (v. 14aα; compare אנשי החיל in v. 16aα) is also related twice.[115] The repetition is especially pronounced in vv. 14aα, 15–16, and, from the literary point of view, it appears that the descriptive sequence of vv. 12 and 15–16 is interrupted by vv. 13–14.[116] Apart from the sequence of vv. 12 and 15–16 and the thematic parallel between these two verses,[117] the exiles are num-bered in Jer 29:2 in exactly the same order,[118] which provides additional evidence of the historical accuracy of these descriptions or of their common source.

In addition, 2 Kgs 24:13–14 has linguistic, conceptual, and redactional diffi-culties.[119] The topic in v. 13 (removing the treasures of the house of God and the house of the king and cutting them up in pieces)[120] is out of place in the descrip-tive sequence and interrupts the narrative sequence begun in v. 12. Furthermore, the beginning of v. 13 ("and he carried off") does not fit the current context, be-cause Jerusalem and/or the temple is last mentioned in v. 11 (see Nelson 1981: 88; Brettler 1991: 549–50). The generalizations stated in this verse, too, are evi-dence of its tendentiousness (see Cogan and Tadmor 1988: 312; Seitz 1989: 168; Brettler 1991: 546). Information from the Babylonian Chronicle[121] as well as the record of Jer 27:16–22 and 28:3 imply that the Babylonians took spoils from the

115. For a discussion of the significance of these repetitions, see above, §2.4.1 (pp. 57–58), with further literature.

116. Stade (1884) had already recognized the secondary nature of vv. 13–14 and the conti-nuity between v. 12 and v. 15. This conclusion is accepted by nearly all scholars; see, e.g., Bur-ney 1903: 366; Montgomery 1951: 555–56; Bright 1964: 692; Gray 1970: 760; Jones 1984: 637; Nelson 1981: 88; 145 n. 157; Rehm 1982: 233; Würthwein 1984: 473; O'Brien 1989: 268; Seitz 1989: 168; Brettler 1991: 541–52; Albertz 2003: 90.

117. See the comparison in n. 74, pp. 56–57 above.

118. For this comparison, see also n. 74, pp. 56–57 above. Using those texts, it is possible to reconstruct a historical picture in which the first to leave Jerusalem were Jehoiachin, his mother, and the entire ruling elite of the city (Jehoiachin's servants, officials, and eunuchs). They all surrendered to the Babylonians and thus brought about the end of the siege of Jerusa-lem. At this stage, the king's wives remained in the palace, and the social and economic elite awaited their fate in the city. This is when the Babylonians decided who would go into exile and who would remain in Jerusalem. They appointed Zedekiah king, exacted heavy tribute, and returned to their land.

119. For a summary of the problems and arguments against the originality of these verses, see Montgomery 1951: 555–65; Gray 1970: 760–61; Dietrich 1972: 140; Nelson 1981: 88; Jones 1984: 637; Würthwein 1984: 473; and Seitz 1989: 178–79.

120. On the use of the root קצץ, see 2 Kgs 16:17 (cf. 2 Chr 28:24); 2 Kgs 18:16; Ps 46:10. In the Deuteronomistic history, there are five additional instances of removal of treasure from the temple and the royal palace (1 Kgs 14:26; 16:18; 2 Kgs 12:19; 14:14; 18:15). The description closest to 2 Kgs 24:13 is 1 Kgs 14:26. Compare:

1 Kgs 14:26: ויקח   את   אוצרות בית ה' ואת   אוצרות בית המלך ואת הכל לקח
2 Kgs 24:13: ויוצא משם את כל אוצרות בית ה' ו   אוצרות בית המלך
ויקח את   כל מגיני הזהב אשר עשה שלמה.
ויקצץ את כל כלי הזהב אשר עשה שלמה.

121. See the discussion above, in §2.1.4 (pp. 55–62); see also line 13 in the Babylonian Chronicle (B.M. 21946; Wiseman 1956: 72–73; Grayson 1975a: 102).

temple and the king's palace, but it is unlikely that "all of the treasures of the house of the Lord and all of the treasures of the house of the king" were actually removed or that "all the vessels of gold were cut in pieces."[122] The end of the verse, which states that the treasures were plundered "as the Lord had said," has led the majority of scholars to treat the verse as a secondary insertion created under the influence of the description of the destruction in chap. 25.[123]

Verse 14 is also out of place in the sequence describing the deportation of Jehoiachin because, not only does it repeat information found in vv. 12 and 15–16, but also it is worded as a very broad generalization (Gray 1964: 760; Würthwein 1984: 473). It is the only verse that generalizes the deportation with four 'all's (וכל החרש והמסגר . . . כל גבורי החיל . . . כל השרים . . . כל ירושלים),[124] and it summarizes with the sweeping statement that לא נשאר זולת דלת עם הארץ, proof that its author was familiar with the parallel descriptions in 2 Kgs 25:12 and Jer 52:15.[125] This portrayal is not realistic,[126] and the location of the summary statement is odd, because the details of the deportation come after it. Therefore,

122. Jer 27:21 makes explicit reference to "the vessels that remained in the house of the Lord and in the house of the king of Judah and of Jerusalem"; the statement is repeated three times (vv. 19, 20, 21). On the ideological objective of the LXX version of these verses, see Rofé 1997; 1998: 225–26. In 2 Kgs 25:13–15, an additional report of removal of temple vessels appears.

123. This point was, as noted above, made by Stade (1884) and has been accepted by most scholars. For a survey of opinions in the scholarly literature, for critiques, and extensive literature, see Seitz (1989: 168–73, 177–89), who sees this verse as an important element supporting his theory that the Deuteronomistic history was composed after the deportation of 597 B.C.E. Cogan and Tadmor (1988: 313–14) have challenged this conclusion, emphasizing the fact that the removal of vessels mentioned in v. 13 corresponds to the information in Jer 27:18 and 28:3 and that this verse is also linguistically and thematically related to 2 Kgs 20:16–18. On this basis, they hypothesized that the historical kernel of this verse might be authentic. For a critique of this theory, see Brettler 1991: 543–45. In my opinion, the source of these two verses is not to be sought in chap. 25, nor should these verses be relied on as a historical source for this period (contra Brettler 1991). It is reasonable to think that this insertion was influenced by the description of the removal of the temple vessels in 25:13–17: it filled in a critical lacuna in the description of the deportation of Jehoiachin, particularly with regard to the removal of the *golden* vessels, because the description of the plundering by the Babylonians after the destruction refers mainly to *copper* vessels. See Nelson 1981: 129–30.

124. The only generalization in this account outside of vv. 13–14 appears in the description of the removal of "all of the men of might" (v. 16a). This generalization is made for a totally different reason (see the discussion on this below) and serves as one of the central arguments put forth by Burney (1903: 366) for this verse's being an expression of the historical reality ten years later.

125. Talmon (1964: 119) analyzed the expression דלת עם הארץ as a composite of two familiar expressions: דלת הארץ (2 Kgs 25:12) and דלת העם (Jer 52:15); he also compared it to the expression מרום עם הארץ in Isa 24:4. Along these lines, Cogan and Tadmor (1988: 312) emphasized that, in any case, it does not refer to עם הארץ here. On the omission of Jer 52:15 from the LXX, see Rofé 1997; 1998: 225.

126. The description found in 24:14 is not realistic, not only because the deportation of these officials is not mentioned anywhere else. There could not have been a deportation of "all of Jerusalem," because Zedekiah was appointed king over the city, which continued to exist for another 11 years (cf. 2 Kgs 24:18). Furthermore, "the rest of the people that were left in the

it is reasonable to conclude that v. 14 was inserted to support the ideological goals of a later redactor, who was interested in expanding the description to enhance the value and number of those deported and to depreciate the value of those who remained.[127]

The later date of the additions in v. 14 and the verse's tendentiousness are also reflected in the citation of the number of exiles taken to Babylon. According to this verse, the deportation included "all Jerusalem, all the officials, and all the mighty warriors—ten thousand exiles"; to this was added "all the craftsmen and smiths." According to v. 16, the exile encompassed "all the mighty—seven thousand"; to this was added "craftsmen and smiths, one thousand." These passages should be compared with Jer 52:28, which states that, "in the seventh year, three thousand and twenty three men of Judah" were deported. All attempts to reconcile these numbers seem forced and ignore the objectives of the different authors (who number at least three) and variations in the sources that were available to them.[128] Perhaps the round number in 24:14 is part of the tendency to exaggerate and generalize—characteristics that are typical of this insertion. We cannot rule out the possibility that the author was familiar with both 2 Kgs 24:16 and the later expansion in Jer 52:28 (Rofé 1997; 1998: 225) and thus arrived at the round number of 10,000, in addition to the "craftsmen and smiths."[129]

In summary, 2 Kgs 24:13–14 may be considered misplaced in the description of the deportation of Jehoiachin (24:10–17) and may have been inserted into Dtr² at a later stage, apparently after the Return to Zion. Both verses share the tendency to generalize (the word כל appears six times in these two verses) and also share a lack of historical reality, signaled specifically by hyperbole concerning the importance and status of the exiles. This tendentiousness matches the inflated importance assigned to the temple vessels in v. 13, which matches the importance of the vessels in the Return to Zion. Given these facts, vv. 13–14 may be identified as an insertion that reflects attitudes prevalent at the end of the Babylonian exile and during the Return to Zion; similar attitudes may have been current in the biblical literature of the Persian Period as well.[130]

---

city" were removed after the destruction of the city, and the killing of some officials and leaders during this time is described in 25:18–21.

127. This is Seitz's central conclusion (1989: 178–80); however, I do not accept his general conclusions about the place and time of the Deuteronomistic author.

128. See, e.g., the solutions proposed by Janssen 1956: 28–40; Thompson 1980: 782; Malamat 1983: 264–65; Cogan and Tadmor 1988: 312; and Smith 1989a: 31–32. For a survey of the literature, see Seitz 1989: 181–84.

129. There is an additional rationale for dating the insertion in 2 Kgs 24:13–14 later: its author was familiar with the accounts of the deportation of Jehoiachin, as well as the description of the destruction in Kings and Jeremiah. As noted above, additional support for this hypothesis is found in the expression דלת עם הארץ (24:14b), which seems to be a combination of 2 Kgs 25:12 and Jer 52:15.

130. On the features of biblical literature from the early days of the Persian Period, see the summaries by Ackroyd 1968: 62–137; and Weinfeld (in Tadmor 1983: 165–75).

A similar insertion, displaying the same motifs and expressing the same tendencies, occurs in the description of the destruction of Jerusalem (2 Kgs 25:1–21). Verse 12 is the only text within the entire description that does not deal with the fate of Jerusalem and its inhabitants[131] but, rather, focuses on the "remnant" that was allowed to remain in Judah and did not go into exile. The contents of the verse are clear: it deals with the part of the group (. . . ומ in the sense of 'part of . . .') known as דלת הארץ ('the poorest people of the land'). This group is identified in the parallel version in Jer 39:10 as העם הדלים אשר אין להם מאומה ('some of the poor people who had nothing'),[132] and, according to 2 Kgs 25:12a, this group was left in Judah to serve as כורמים ויוגבים ('vinedressers and field-workers')[133] at the instruction of Nebuzaradan (compare the role of Nebuzaradan in Jer 40:1–16).

The phrase "the poorest people of the land" appears in the Bible only four times—twice in 2 Kings (24:14; 25:12) and twice in Jeremiah (40:7; 52:16). Assuming that Jer 40:7 is a later insertion and that it does not appear in the LXX (see below), it appears that this phrase is used uniquely in the context of the exile. The connection between these two events is conspicuous: after the deportation of Jehoiachin, "only the poorest people of the land were left," and, after the destruction of Jerusalem, those who were left were "some of the poorest people of the land." In light of this parallel usage and the identification of 2 Kgs 24:13–14 as a later insertion, we may conclude that this phrase was a later insertion, expressing an ideology prevalent among the Babylonian exiles and, later, the returnees to Zion, namely, that the elite of the nation went into exile, and those who remained in Judah were a handful of paupers whose existence was marginal and insignificant.[134]

This addition also continues the message of 24:14. It opposes the presentation of "the remnant in Judah" in 25:22 as a group holding status and authority who continued to live in Judah. After the addition of both "appendixes" (2 Kgs 25:22–30) to the Deuteronomistic composition during the exilic period, this addition challenged the message of both: "and the people who remained in Judah" (25:22) are merely "some of the poorest people of the land" (v. 12); "the captain of the guard" (v. 12) left them there, not Nebuchadrezzar, king of Babylon (v. 22); they were not left behind in order to renew national life under the

---

131. Dtr² included the events that corresponded to his ideas and that justified the perspective that he wished to express. For this reason, he focused on what was happening in Jerusalem, ignoring events in other parts of the country at that time.

132. This verse is part of an extensive later addition (39:1–2, 4–13) to the MT that does not appear in the LXX. See the discussion below, §5.2.1b.

133. On the significance of this expression, see the discussion above (§2.3.2, pp. 102–107), with further literature.

134. See the extensive discussion below on the prevalence of this idea in biblical literature from the Persian Period.

leadership of Gedaliah (vv. 22–23) but only to serve as "vinedressers and field-workers" (v. 12) for the Babylonian authority.

5.1.5. Summary
The discussion in this section results in the following conclusions:

1. The description of the destruction in 2 Kgs 25:1–11, 13–21 (as a continuation of the description in 2 Kgs 23:22–23, 26–37; 24:1–12, 15–20) is part of the work composed by Dtr². It was created in Babylon a short time after the destruction of Jerusalem and reflects the perceptions of the exiles at that time.
2. Approximately one generation later, in the middle of the sixth century B.C.E., the "appendixes" were added (2 Kgs 25:22–30). The "appendixes" reflect the people's reconciliation with the Babylonian authority, and there is a marked propensity to encourage the possibility of continued life under Babylonian rule, both in exile and in Judah. It is reasonable to conclude that both supplements were written in the Babylonian exile.
3. Apparently, in the early days of the Return to Zion, additions were formulated, giving sharper expression to the viewpoint of the Babylonian exiles (2 Kgs 24:13–14; 25:12). The emphasis in these verses is on the importance of the exiles and the temple vessels, and the attitude toward the "remnant" of Judah is reflected in the description of them as a small group of paupers whose continued existence in Judah is of little importance.

5.2. Jeremiah 37–44: The Date, Location, Sources, and Purposes of the Composition

5.2.1. Introduction to the Book of Jeremiah

5.2.1a. The Process of the Writing, Consolidation, and Redaction of the Book

The major body of scholarly literature concerning the creation of the book of Jeremiah[135] was written at the beginning of the twentieth century and laid the groundwork for understanding the book's complexity, the extended period of time during which the various versions came into being, and the various stages

---

135. The purpose of this introduction to the book of Jeremiah is to clarify two basic questions: the process of writing, consolidation, and editing of the book (§5.2.1a); and the problems of its textual transmission while it was taking on the various shapes familiar to us today (§5.2.1b). These questions are some of the most difficult and complex in the history of biblical research. A concise survey will be presented here, and several conclusions will be formed as the basis for a discussion of the "biography" of the prophet. For a summary of these conclusions, see §5.2.1c below.

of redaction of the book.[136] Mowinckel's study (1914), in which he defined four basic sources upon which the book was based, is of special importance.[137]

Source A includes the original prophecies and admonitions of the prophet (chap. 1 through 25:14; and 25:15–38, as a prologue to the prophecies in chaps. 46–51). These prophecies were collected and drafted in a scroll that was written in the fourth year of Jehoiachin's reign. It was edited in Egypt during the sixth or early fifth century B.C.E. Mowinckel considered this source highly authentic and reliable (Mowinckel 1914: 17–23, 48, 56).

Source B includes biographical-historical accounts (Jer 19:1–20:6; 26; 28; 29; 36; 37–43; 44). It is not a genuine biography in the modern sense but a collection of stories that were transmitted orally over time. The stories were collected by one of the prophet's adherents during the same period when source A was being edited. Mowinckel emphasized that the author of this source was not Baruch son of Neriah.[138]

Source C is connected to the Deuteronomistic stratum and consists mainly of the prose speeches scattered throughout the book.[139] The major feature of this source is a tendency to use a uniform style and fixed formulas, and the central ideology behind the source is the sin of Judah and consequent punishment. Mowinckel maintained that there is conceptual and literary affinity between this document and the Deuteronomistic source and concluded, on this basis, that this source is less reliable than sources A and B (1914: 31–40, 46–53). He found

---

136. During the nineteenth century, a theory arose concerning the composition of the book of Jeremiah: the book came from two major sources and a third, later source that was mainly additions and that was also connected to the editorial reworking of the other sources. For a summary, see Lundbom 1975: 2–5. Giesebrecht (1907) composed his comprehensive commentary on the basis of this theory. Research continued into the early twentieth century, when Duhm (1901: xii–xx) proposed the following classifications: 280 verses in the book of Jeremiah (and particularly the Lamentations) should be assigned to the prophet himself; 220 verses were written by Baruch; and 850 verses were later additions, in which the Deuteronomistic viewpoint predominates (especially chaps. 26–29; 46–51; and 52). However, these sections contain many disparate elements, some of which were added only in the first century B.C.E. The commentaries of Cornill (1905) and Peake (1910) continued to elaborate on these definitions, and on this base Mowinckel grounded his magisterial work (1914).

137. It is noteworthy that Mowinckel later changed his opinion (1946: 105–6) regarding the classification of the sources as collections of traditions that were written down and edited independently, emphasizing the process of oral transmission of the material. See also the discussion below.

138. Mowinckel 1914: 24–30, 56. It should be noted that Mowinckel later changed his views (1946: 61–65) regarding the author of source B; see the discussion below.

139. According to Mowinckel, this source included the following: 3:6–13; 7:1–8:3; 11:1–5, 9–14; 18:1–12; 21:1–10; 22:1–5; 25:1–11; 27; 29:1–23; 32:1–2, 6–16, 24–44; 34:1–22; 35:1–19; 39:15–18; 44:1–14; 45. It should be noted that this document parallels the "secondary additions" of Duhm (1901: xxff.). Some short passages should be assigned to the redactor or redactors of the book, as Mowinckel himself has noticed (and cf. Rudolph 1947: xix–xxi; Albertz 2003: 305–6).

it difficult to determine the date of the third document but theorized that it was no later than the end of the fifth century B.C.E. (1914: 57).

Source D is, according to Mowinckel, an independent source, which he entitled "The Book of Consolation" (30:1–31:28). According to Mowinckel, later additions, such as part of chaps. 46–51, the supplement in 52, and so forth, were appended to this source (1914: 46–47, 52–57).

The approach taken by Mowinckel had a central role in shaping scholarship on the book of Jeremiah and, with various revisions and emendations, has been considered the solution to most of the problems related to the processes leading to the final form of the book.[140] Many scholars linked source A to the scroll described in Jeremiah 36 (although Mowinckel did not do so) and attributed the writing of source B to Baruch son of Neriah (even though Mowinckel rejected this idea, at least initially).[141] Criticism of Mowinckel's work mainly concerned the identity of the various sources that lie behind the book,[142] the original form of these sources, and the manner in which they were preserved (with an emphasis on oral tradition),[143] as well as their historical credibility (see, e.g., Hyatt

---

140. See, e.g., Pfeiffer 1941: 500–511; Eissfeldt 1951: 151. See also the basic opinion in the main commentaries on the book of Jeremiah: Rudolph 1947; Hyatt 1956b; Bright 1965; Carroll 1986; McKane 1986, 1995; Hoffman 2001.

141. See, in this regard, Robinson's opinion (1924) on Baruch's contribution to the composition. See also May (1942a), who ruled out Baruch as the editor or author and connected source B to an early-fifth-century person connected with the Deuteronomistic tradition. The question of Baruch's connection with source B was central in the discussions of the 1950s. The issue remained without a clear-cut resolution and was forgotten until the 1970s, when Wanke's key research (1971) was published. For a summary of this subject, see below.

142. Much of the criticism of the views of Duhm and Mowinckel and their followers was directed at the perception of the identity, place, and date of source C; the extent of the material to be assigned to it; and particularly at its attribution to the Deuteronomist. Two pivotal articles were published in 1951; see Hyatt 1951: 251; Cazelles 1951: 89–91; for a detailed review of this stage of critical investigation of the book of Jeremiah, see Holladay 1989: 12–14. In the same year, Bright (1951) argued that the language of source C was not unique to the Deuteronomist and that it is typical of all prose of the seventh century B.C.E.; see also his commentary on the book of Jeremiah (1965: especially pp. lxvii–lxxiii). Some scholars followed Bright; see, e.g., Weinfeld 1972: 135–38; and Holladay 1975: 408–12. In contrast, other scholars suggested that the language of source C was a reflection of Jeremiah's own language; see, e.g., Weippert 1973: 228–29; and Thompson 1980: 34. For a survey of these various hypotheses and a critique, see K. M. O'Connor 1988: 151. Despite these differences of opinion, most scholars agree that at least the editing of the book must be closely connected to the Deuteronomistic circles (Hyatt 1942; 1951; and cf. Albertz 2003: 305–12). This is a point of great importance for this study, and the question of the nature of the connection between the accounts of the destruction in the book of Kings and the book of Jeremiah, as well as the account of the rule of Gedaliah (2 Kgs 25:22–26; Jer 40:7–41:18), will be discussed below.

143. This point has been highlighted mostly by scholars from the "Scandinavian School." They have formulated an alternative view regarding the oral transmission of the traditions that were written down and edited after the destruction. The scholars who belong to this school do not consider it worthwhile to identify the various sources within the prophetic books and claim that they were assembled from several tradition systems that were consolidated after a

1942; 1956b: 777–93; Rudolph 1947: xiv–xxiii; Bright 1965: lxiii–lxxviii). The main scholarly debate, however, has been about the redaction of the book and the various stages of its formation (Albertz 2003: 304).

For the purpose of this study, the main points of Mowinckel's approach should be accepted, specifically, the points that were substantiated by Hyatt in a series of articles[144] and subsequently supported by May, Nielsen, Rudolph, Rofé, Tov, and others.[145] According to this view, source C has no identifiable independent traits, is secondary in nature, and should be seen as a level of adaptation and re-daction carried out by the exilic Deuteronomistic school, several phases from the days of the exile until the days of the Return to Zion.[146] This was a complex process that was not concluded before the beginning of the fifth century B.C.E.[147] Albertz has very clearly described the development in scholarship since the 1940s and especially the transformation from source criticism to redaction-historical criticism, tracing the work of Hyatt (1942; 1951; 1956b), Thiel (1983; 1981), Rudolph (1947), and others. To this list we should add Thompson (1980), as well as Hoffman's exegesis of the book of Jeremiah (2001), which continues in the same vein. The place of some of the "biographical chapters" will be discussed below (§5.2.2), following this approach, and I will present there my view concerning the different stages of editing and the various prose materials that were included in it.

5.2.1b. The Transmission Process of the Text and Its Various
          Stages of Editing
Many scholars have studied the transmission processes and the various stages of editing of the book of Jeremiah. The vast differences between the Masoretic

---

long process of oral transmission. Engnell applied this perception to the book of Jeremiah; see the summaries by Hobbs 1972: 265–66; and Lundbom 1975: 11–14. However, this is a rad-ical idea that totally ignores the existence of writing on a large scale at the end of the First Temple Period; scholars of this school do not adequately contend with the texts' internal evi-dence, such as, e.g., the account in Jeremiah 36, the connection between some of the prophe-cies and some of the prose passages, the evidence of different redactional stages within one text, etc. See the critique by Rietzschel 1966: 21–24; Lundbom 1975: 14–16; Hobbs 1985: 180–84, with further literature.

144. Hyatt's research (1942, 1951, 1956b) is the main basis for this theory.

145. May 1942a: 139–55; Rudolph 1947: xvii–xx; Nielsen 1954: 78; Rofé 19865; and Tov 1999: 61, with further literature. See also Albertz 2003: 306–7.

146. For a detailed discussion of the different Deuteronomic phases, see Albertz 2003: 312–45; and see further below.

147. This text contains evidence of several historical strata. There are signs of editorial reworking, involving different sources that were "planted" around ideas prevalent during the Return to Zion; see the discussion by Hoffman 1996: 179–89, with further literature; Albertz 2003: 312–45. The transformations and editorial reworking of the text, including the various expansions, are also noticeable when the MT is compared with the LXX, which is considerably shorter and more concise; see Tov 1972: 279–87; 1981: 154–55; see also below.

Text and the LXX[148] and modern-day comparison of both texts with other versions of the book allow us a more extensive look at these processes. This textual
investigation has decisive importance here,[149] because the differences in the
various versions reflect the different perspectives held by the various redactors
on the events described in the book (for an exhaustive review of this subject
and further literature, see Stulman 1985: 12–17).

In the history of scholarship, there have been four principal theories explaining the differences between the MT and LXX Jeremiah. Eichhorn's *two-editions
theory* is the earliest of these, and it postulates that the differences exist because
each is based on a distinct edition of the original book written by Jeremiah himself (Eichhorn 1824: 137ff.). The first (earlier) edition was composed in Egypt
and became the basis for the LXX version. The second edition was sent to the
exiles in Babylon; it had its origin in Judea and eventually became the Hebrew
version. This theory has not won much support (see Kuenen's remarks).[150]

Alternatively, the most popular theory at the end of the nineteenth century
was the *abridgement theory*, proposed by Spohn, Graf, and Keil, as well as by
others.[151] According to this theory, the LXX resulted from an abridgement of
the MT. The LXX was translated from a text very much like the MT, and the
abridgement process took place either during translation or later, at some other
stage in its transmission.

A third theory, parallel in time but opposite in trend, was the *expansion theory*
(see, e.g., Streane 1896: 1–18). According to this theory, the text preserved in
the LXX is evidence of the original version of the book of Jeremiah. After the
LXX translation was made, during the course of transmitting the text, the MT
was expanded and modified.

---

148. Differences between the two versions are substantial, including the length of the text
(3,097 fewer words in the LXX, some 14.7% of the entire Hebrew text, mostly in the prose sections of the book; Tov 1999: 56–57; for an earlier numerical estimate that has been quoted in
many studies—that the LXX is missing approximately 2,700 words—see Graf 1862: xliii). The
organization of the chapters is markedly different as well; see Janzen 1973: 1, 87; Tov 1981:
151–52; 1999: 56–58. On these differences, see also the introductions to most commentaries
on the book of Jeremiah: Rudolph 1947; Bright 1965; Thompson 1980; Feinberg 1982; Davidson 1985; Carroll 1986; Herrmann 1986; McKane 1986; Clements 1988; Holladay 1986, 1989;
Keown, Scalise, and Smothers 1995; Hoffman 2001; see also Soderlund 1985.

149. I will not discuss the internal problems of the LXX of Jeremiah here, particularly the
problem of the conspicuous differences between the two parts of the book (chaps. 1–28; 29–52,
according to the LXX arrangement). Tov devoted an entire chapter in his doctoral thesis
(1973) to this question; also see his book, 1976: 162. For a survey, discussion, and evaluation of
this subject, see Soderlund's doctoral thesis (1985); see also Holladay 1989: 5–6.

150. See Kuenen 1890: 239. Despite these facts, in the 1960s and 1970s new supporters of
Eichhorn's theory emerged (with specific changes); see, e.g., the view of van Selms 1976; see
also Overholt 1968.

151. See, e.g., Graf 1862: 12–14. For foundational support of this theory (with revisions
and incorporating modern research techniques), see Soderlund 1985.

In recent decades, a new approach has evolved. It is difficult to define this approach, because its major characteristic is that it represents a *middle way*. The main point made by scholars who take this approach is that no conclusive arguments supporting any of these theories as a comprehensive solution has emerged and, therefore, each individual pericope must be judged on its own merits.[152]

Publication of passages from Jeremiah in the Dead Sea Scrolls from Qumran has provided additional evidence: most of them parallel the MT, but some corroborate the LXX.[153] Study of these data was the basis for Janzen's doctoral thesis (1963) and the book that followed (1973),[154] which, in many ways, once again turned the focus to the "expansion theory."[155] Janzen revised the expansion theory and incorporated modern research methods into it, methods that had been employed in the "middle way" theory, and meticulously examined each passage in the book. Janzen believes that the Greek translator of the book of Jeremiah had a much shorter Hebrew text than the MT, and this shorter version was both earlier and more reliable.[156] Another copy of the book of Jeremiah was expanded in a long, gradual process until it achieved the familiar form of the MT and its parallels. The expansion process involved adding single words (especially titles), sentences, and entire passages (33:14–26; 39:1–2, 4–13, etc.), as well as relocating the prophecies to the Gentile nations within the book (and reordering several other verses).[157] The additions are characterized by: the systematic expansion of names and titles; the addition of editorial headings to certain prophecies or the extension of existing headings; the addition of details, which, in most cases, were taken from nearby passages; a tendency to clarify texts that are difficult or problematic; some grammatical changes and editorial additions (some of these harmonistic and some intended to suit the text to the

---

152. The foundation was laid for this approach in early-twentieth-century studies (Duhm 1901 and others). This approach has also appeared in some of the important commentaries of the twentieth century (Rudolph 1947; Bright 1965; and Thompson 1980); see also Hyatt 1956b: 791; Schmid 1996; Albertz 2003: 312.

153. For a detailed and updated list, see Hoffman 2001: 4–8. Two out of three passages in the 4QJer^b scroll (parallel to 9:22–10:18; 43:3–9), which are dated to the first half of the second century B.C.E., support the text of the LXX. See Cross 1961: 187 n. 38; Janzen 1973: 181–82; and Tov 1981: 146–49; 1997: 302–12; 1999: 55.

154. In many respects, Janzen followed the direction laid out by Cross; see the introduction to his book (Janzen 1973: 2–9).

155. The continuation of this approach may be found in a series of studies by Emanuel Tov: 1981; 1989; 1991; 1999, and in additional studies. For further literature, see Tov 1999: 62 nn. 5, 22; Piovanelli 1995.

156. The superiority of the LXX is proved throughout the text, except for places where it is obvious that it has deliberate abbreviations, errors, and minor omissions and (mostly short) additions (Janzen 1973: 67; Tov 1976: 149; 1985: 211–37; 1999: 55–58). On the likely nature of the Hebrew version that was used for translating the book into Greek, see Holladay 1989: 7, with further literature.

157. For a discussion of each of these phenomena, see Tov 1981: 150–67; 1985: 215–37; 1999: 57–61. For a summary of these phenomena, see Hoffman 2001: 8–12.

editor's ideological message); repetition of familiar texts; and an interpretation of texts, some on the basis of other books in the Bible.[158]

The expanded version is parallel to all of the known Hebrew versions (including most of the passages in the Dead Sea Scrolls from Qumran and several passages from the Cairo Genizah), the presumed Vorlage of the Syriac translation (the Peshiṭta), the Aramaic translations, the Vulgate, and various adaptations and late versions of the LXX (see Tov 1981: 145–46, 149; 1997: 302–12; 1999: 55, with further literature). Tov theorizes that one editor was responsible for the expanded revisions and alterations to the MT.[159] However, Holladay contends that the change in literary technique in the expansion and editing of the text appears to be evidence of two different editors (Holladay 1989: 38). Stulman has aptly identified the later redaction as resulting from a desire to highlight the continued disobedience of the people, which led to the divine retribution of the exile.[160]

Examination of the traits of the two parallel versions of the book of Jeremiah makes it possible to deduce where they were composed and transmitted. Inasmuch as some of the passages in the Qumran scrolls (those that are parallel to the shorter LXX version) are near in time to the estimated date of the translation into Greek, we surmise that the Vorlage for this translation was meticulously preserved and existed independently, probably in Egypt.[161] Alternately, the MT reflects harmonistic tendencies that are also characteristic of the Samaritan Pentateuch, and this is the main argument for the theory that the MT reflects a Judean tradition (see Holladay 1989: 6–7, with further literature).

The attributes of these two versions also permit us to theorize about their date. The shorter, earlier version was apparently composed during the exile (with a small amount of material that may belong to the postexilic period and with a few later supplements; see Piovanelli 1995: 35–49, with further literature). The longer, later version was revised over an extended period of time, beginning with the early days of the Return to Zion (it contains an account of the fall of the Babylonian Empire; see Lust 1981: 119–42; Tov 1999: 60–61), into the fifth century B.C.E., and ending in the Hellenistic or Roman Period.[162]

---

158. For a characterization of these additions, see Tov's articles (in the preceding note).

159. Tov 1981: 152, and see the ideological and editorial characterization of these additions by the same author (1999: 60–61).

160. See Stulman 1985a: 142–44. On additional trends in the later redactions, see Tov 1999: 60–61.

161. See Janzen 1973: 127–28; and Tov 1976: 165. The existence of texts at Qumran that are close to LXX Jeremiah is interesting in itself, and it opens the way to much speculation about the connection between the Jews in Judah (or at least the Jewish community at Qumran) and the Jewish community in Egypt and the way the ancient scrolls were preserved. See also Rofé 1998: 220.

162. Rofé 1986: 310; 1991: 307–15; Schencker 1994: 281–93; Piovanelli 1995: 35–49; and Ferry 1998: 69–82. In this regard, compare the central ideas of and the places mentioned in Jer 17:19–27; 31:37–39 with those in the book of Nehemiah (with regard to geography, compare mainly with 13:15–22). See Lundbom 1975: 5–6; Tov 1981: 166–67; and Holladay 1989: 8.

5.2.1c. Summary

1. Jeremiah's prophecies are the basis of the book of Jeremiah. It can be assumed that some of his speeches were recorded shortly after Jeremiah delivered them; they were gathered and grouped into collections. These collections may have been organized around special events or at key junctures in the history of the nation and the life of the prophet.

2. The scrolls containing these collections were reworked before they were incorporated into the book of Jeremiah. At the stage when the book was being consolidated, the scrolls underwent a fundamental redaction as well. Some of the prophecies were incorporated into the conceptual framework of the Deuteronomistic redaction, even if the ideas expressed in the redaction did not conform to the spirit of the prophet's words.

3. Most of the prose passages were composed after the prophecies themselves were put into writing.[163] These passages incorporated popular traditions alongside stories that were intended to authenticate the importance of the prophet and the veracity of his prophecies. The prose is quite similar to the prophetic writing, both in language and in ideas; it was influenced by the prophetic writing and, in some cases, even based on it. The later date of the biographical-historical accounts also is demonstrated by the consolidation of duplicate accounts and the incorporation of popular traditions already in the primary text (see below, §5.2.2b).

4. It is likely that some of the events surrounding Jeremiah on the eve of the destruction and afterward were written by one of the prophet's adherents and admirers. The context suggests that it was Baruch son of Neriah,[164] but it is also likely that the final integration of the biographical-historical accounts took place later and incorporated other traditions, more remote in time and place.

5. The redaction of the book extended over a period of many years, taking place in at least three different historical stages: (1) at the end of the kingdom of Judah, (2) during the Babylonian exile, and (3) during the Return to Zion. It is clear that ideas that were consistent with one period did not always accord with another. The need to adapt earlier ideas to a new reality is typical of the various revisions that were made to the book. These revisions are primarily reflected in attitudes—attitudes toward those living in Babylon, Egypt, and Judah; toward the Return to Zion; toward the Davidic line; and toward the priesthood and the temple.

6. It is difficult to determine the extent of the material that belongs to each of the original scrolls, to determine which passages are additions to these scrolls, or to determine a date for them. More than one editor was responsible for the book. The process was complex, and we must closely examine the characteristics

---

163. See the correct distinction that Hoffman (2001: 62–63) makes between the different types of prose passages.

164. For arguments supporting this hypothesis, see below, §5.2.2.

of each of the texts and the supplements added during the various stages of revision, as well as their purposes.

7. I accept the opinion that the LXX reflects an earlier edition of the book of Jeremiah, which was written mainly during the exile and the Return to Zion. The supplements in the MT version were a by-product of the ongoing process of consolidating the book. The consistent characteristics of these supplements (literarily, emphasizing the credibility of the story; ideologically, emphasizing the exile as a punishment for the ongoing sin of disobedience) support the theory that two or more authors were at work.

8. It is reasonable to conclude that the earlier copy of the book of Jeremiah was preserved in Egypt until it was translated into Greek, in a form close to the original and with only minor revisions. Another copy was kept in Judah, and it is difficult to know whether a version of it spent any time in Babylon. This copy was expanded gradually during the Persian, Hellenistic, and even Roman Periods and now is known to us as the MT version.

5.2.2. The "Biography" of Jeremiah: The Place, Sources, and Purposes of Writing

5.2.2a. The Structure and Sources of the Composition

In contrast to the various individual stories about Jeremiah, scattered primarily throughout chaps. 19–29,[165] chaps. 37:1–43:7 present a continuous, coherent narrative of the events that befell Jeremiah during the Babylonian siege of Jerusalem and the period after the destruction of the city.[166] This narrative is composed of six sections, each distinct in its narrative, linguistic, and thematic features:[167]

---

165. The generally accepted view among scholars is that the main stories in this category are found in 19:1–20:6; chaps. 26–29; see also 32:1–15. See the various perspectives expressed by Rudolph 1947: 172–73; Koch 1969: 200–210; Wanke 1971: 91–133, 151–54; March 1974: 174–75; Rofé 1988: 106–22; Holladay 1989: 282; Hoffman 2001: 57.

166. In terms of language, as well, chap. 37 introduces a new episode; as a result, most scholars see 36:32 as the end of a section (scroll, unit, or chronological chapter, etc.; Kessler 1965: 247–48; Holladay 1975: 395–96; 1989: 280, with further literature). Holladay (1989: 282–83) proposed that the new section began with the king's request to the prophet, "Pray for us to the Lord our God" (37:3), and its corresponding end was the paraphrase of this request, "when you sent me . . . saying, Pray for us to the Lord our God" (42:20). In Holladay's opinion, the continuation of the narrative in chaps. 43–44 is the concluding section, describing the prophet's descent into Egypt. On chaps. 37–43, see also Pohlmann 1978: 132–35; Stipp 1992: 239–41; Perdue 1994: 247–59; Albertz 2003: 323–24; and see below.

167. See the similar division made by Kremers (1953: 131) and Wanke (1971: 94–95) of 5 sections and 10 passages, which is based on Duhm's analysis (1901). For a criticism of this division, see Holladay 1989: 282; and see also below. Rudolph (1947: 1) characterizes chaps. 36–45 as an independent unit and divides it much like that cited above. The division suggested by Carroll (1986: 669–721) is essentially similar, but in two instances he makes no reference to the question of whether the subdivision has a literary basis or has an origin in various compositional sources. See Hoffman's (2000: 1–2 n. 3) criticism of this point and the division he has offered (2001: 679–747).

1. the history of Jeremiah in the time of Zedekiah (37:1–38:28a)
2. the history of the people at the time of the destruction of Jerusalem by the Babylonians (39:1–2, 4–10), containing no reference to Jeremiah
3. the duplicate description of the transfer of Jeremiah to Mizpah (38:28b; 39:3, 11–18; 40:1–6)
4. the description of the time of Gedaliah (40:7–41:18), containing no reference to Jeremiah
5. the history of Jeremiah before the flight to Egypt (chap. 42)
6. the history of Jeremiah during the flight to Egypt (43:1–7).

Despite the complexity of the "biography," it has substantial thematic unity and a coherent narrative sequence, evidence of a comprehensive, systematic redaction. Pervading the account is a message for the "remnant" of Judah,[168] as well as for the exiles in Egypt and Babylon, that no one should resist submitting to Babylon; instead, everyone should try to live under Babylonian authority and take advantage of the possibilities for restoration.

This narrative is perceived by scholars as an example par excellence of "prophetic biography."[169] Some have attributed the account to Baruch son of Neriah, Jeremiah's scribe, seeing it as a unified literary work with only hints of minor, late editorial changes.[170] Other scholars, in contrast, have emphasized its episodic nature and enlarged on the importance of the redactional additions.[171] An analysis of part of the biographical section (as demonstrated below) supports the latter approach. The process of integrating and consolidating this narrative was complex and prolonged. It embodied at least three stages during the sixth and fifth centuries B.C.E. A fourth stage can be posited at the end of the Persian Period or even later, after the division between the MT and LXX, and evidence

---

168. Hoffman (2000: 103, and n. 1) has analyzed the significance of the root שאר (especially in the nominal form שארית 'remnant') as a key word in the literary unit Jer 40:1–43:7.

169. For a fundamental definition of *prophetic biography*, see Rofé 1988: 106–22, with further literature; also see Nicholson 1970: 2, 17, 51; Hoffman 1997b: 90 n. 1, with further literature; 2001: 57.

170. See the opinions of: Duhm 1901: xiv–xvi; Volz 1928: xlvi; Rudolph 1947: xiv–xvi; Kremers 1953: 123; Eissfeldt 1965: 354; Bright 1965: lxvii; Muilenburg 1970: 215–38; Holladay 1989: 24, 286, 287. It is interesting to note that Mowinckel (1914: 24–30) ruled out, at least initially, the possibility of attributing this source to Baruch because he believed that it was written after the people fled to Egypt, during the sixth century B.C.E.

171. Rietzschel (1966: 95–96) put greater emphasis on the episodic nature of the composition and downplayed the influence of a single author in the development of the traditions. Nicholson (1970: 8) followed Rietzschel's study, coming to a different conclusion: basing his theory on von Rad's work (1962: 2.14–25), Nicholson compared the description of Jeremiah's personal history with the accounts of Elijah and Elisha. He argued that underlying the biography was a broad circle of traditions that were assembled later and consolidated into a single uniform narrative system. In addition to the works cited above, see also Kremers 1953: 120–24; Wanke 1971: 94–95; Lohfink 1978: 331–34; Stipp 1992: 239–41; and Hoffman 1996: 179–89; 1997b: 90–103. Pohlmann (1978: 48) expressed an even-more radical view; see Seitz's critique 1989: 236 and n. 65. For more about these approaches, see the discussion below.

of this has been preserved only in the MT. These stages may be characterized as follows.

1. The basis for the composition and its primary source was the history of the prophet's life just prior to the destruction of Jerusalem and after the assassination of Gedaliah.[172] This section displays a firsthand familiarity with the milieu of the period in general and the history of the prophet in particular, so we may assume that the author was close to Jeremiah and we may even identify him as Baruch son of Neriah. Support for this theory may be found in Jer 36:19, 26, and especially 43:2–3, in which Azariah son of Hoshaiah and Johanan son of Kareah "and all the malicious men" oppose Jeremiah, who speaks out against the flight to Egypt; they accuse Baruch of inciting the prophet "to hand us over to the hands of the Chaldeans that they might kill us or carry us into exile to Babylon." The personal animosity that these people displayed toward Jeremiah and Baruch corresponds with the narrative's description of the attitude toward the prophet (see additional discussion below). The original ending of the book in chap. 45 of the MT, as it was preserved in the LXX, may be understood to imply that the editors of this section wished to grant Baruch due respect.[173] Assigning the composition of this section of the biography to Baruch is based on an evaluation of the time it was written[174] as well as of the ideas expressed in it, which accord with the period immediately after the destruction of Jerusalem. The author portrays Jeremiah's behavior and cites his words as a model of behavior toward the Babylonian occupiers; he expresses the view that resistance should be eschewed and that the people should choose the path of submission to Babylonian authority. An additional reason for attributing this document to Baruch is that the author relies on the prophecies as a way of understanding and interpreting events (see the summary in Holladay 1989: 286). This vision is appropriate for someone who accompanied the prophet for many years, saw reality through the prism of these prophecies, and tried to convince the nation of their truth.[175]

2. At a fairly early stage, this composition was supplemented by two folkloristic stories. One story recounts an event in the life of the prophet during the Babylonian siege of Jerusalem (38:6–13), and the second provides an additional description of the transfer of Jeremiah to Mizpah.[176] There is no reason not to

---

172. See units 1, 5, and 6, identified above (p. 313).

173. On the date and setting of this chapter, see Taylor 1987; Holladay 1989: 307–11; Hoffman 2001: 748–49.

174. See Weiser (1961: 329) and Nicholson (1970: 112). Their opinions contrast with most of the opinions expressed in the scholarly literature (such as, e.g., May 1942: 139–55), which are an attempt to date the composition of the entire story to the fifth century B.C.E.

175. It is not necessary to accept the view of Wanke, who postulates that, if these things had been written by Baruch in Egypt, he would have included information about Jeremiah's personal history in Egypt, thus concluding the book.

176. See unit 3 as defined above (p. 313). On the two versions of this description, see the discussion below, §5.2.2b.

believe that these stories and the narrative of the prophet's history were created at the same time and coexisted for some time. This is because the basic ideologies—assigning blame for the destruction of Jerusalem to the king's officials; the weakness of the king, who was not able to muster the courage to surrender and, thus, prevent the destruction; the isolation of Jeremiah inside the besieged city of Jerusalem, etc.—are common to both sources; in fact, in these two stories they are even more sharply accentuated. Nonetheless, these stories seem more remote from Jeremiah and his prophecies; more "popular"; more prone to hyperbole; and, we may presume, also less accurate in their recounting of events. It is likely that the editor, and perhaps his contemporaries as well, assigned great importance to these traditions, which explains why they were incorporated in the narrative sequence of the biography, even though their incorporation meant duplication and incompatibility with some of the material included in the "biography."[177]

3. Because of thematic and chronological agreement between the narrative of the prophet's life and the account of the days of Gedaliah, a later editor synthesized these two sources, with the object of providing supplementary information about the prophet, even though Jeremiah himself was never mentioned in the narrative.[178]

4. A description of the destruction of Jerusalem was added at a much later stage of the text's development, after the split between the MT and LXX versions. A later editor, who sensed a gap in the information regarding the history of the prophet during the destruction era, copied a passage from Jeremiah 52 to fill this lacuna.[179]

5.2.2b. The Source and Purpose of Jeremiah's History during the Destruction of Jerusalem

The "backbone" of the biography—its central chapters[180]—were composed and edited a short time after the flight to Egypt, evidently by a writer close to Jeremiah and among his adherents (Baruch son of Neriah?). These sections describe what happened to the prophet in the last months preceding the destruction of Jerusalem and in the first months after it. This biographical material, into which Jeremiah's prophecies were embedded and which was composed factually and sequentially, was supplemented at a later stage with several popular stories that dealt with central events in the life of the prophet.

---

177. Nicholson's opinion (1970: 17–20) regarding the didactic, interpretive, and homiletic motivations for the editor's incorporating these stories, in addition to the historiographical motive of preserving the words of the prophet and the accounts about him, seems well-founded.

178. On the source of the account of the reign of Gedaliah and the way it was embedded in 2 Kings and Jeremiah, see the discussion below, in §5.2.2d.

179. On the source of the account of the destruction in Dtr²'s composition, see the discussion above (§5.1.2). See also the discussion of how the description was embedded in Jeremiah 52 and later in the biography, in §5.2.2e below.

180. See units 1, 3, 5, and 6 as defined above (p. 313).

One object of this section is to examine the extent of the biographical chapters and supplemental stories, and to identify their source, time, and purpose. A
second goal is to examine the way these supplemental stories were embedded
within the biographical chapters (37–38). This will enable us to clarify the
objectives of the first redactor, who created the first version of the biography,
which was later supplemented with an account of the destruction of Jerusalem
(below, §5.2.2c) and an account of the days of Gedaliah (below, §5.2.2d). This
section will be divided into two parts: (1) a discussion of the biographical chapters and supplemental stories that deal with Jeremiah's history before the destruction of Jerusalem, and (2) a discussion of the biographical chapters and
supplemental stories that deal with Jeremiah's history immediately after the destruction, until he was transferred from Jerusalem to Mizpah.[181]

(1) The Source of Jeremiah's History before the Destruction of
    Jerusalem and the Purpose of Its Writing

The episode recounted in chaps. 37–38 is literarily quite unified, and its objectives are well defined ideologically. It is composed of four subunits (37:3–16;
37:17–21; 38:1–13; 38:14–28a),[182] in each of which we may discern four parallel elements:

- a. *A well-defined prologue.* Three of the passages begin with the expression
  וישלח המלך צדקיהו (37:3, 17; 38:14), and only 38:1 has a different beginning: וישמע (on this topic, see also the discussion below).
- b. *Uniform closing.* All four sections end with an expression that includes
  reference to a specific place where Jeremiah remained (= וישב). In 37:16,
  the place described is "the pit and the cells," and the narrative reports that
  "Jeremiah remained (= וישב) there many days." In the other three closing
  passages (37:21; 38:13, 28a), the same language is used: "Jeremiah remained (= וישב) in the court of the guard" (Kremers 1953: 106; Wanke
  1971: 92; Hoffman 2001: 679–81, 688, 690).
- c. *Parallel structure.* Each of the four passages includes a prophecy or segments of a prophecy by Jeremiah, as well as a description of his imprison-

---

181. Except for touching briefly on the editing of the section and the ideas expressed in it, I
will not discuss the descent into Egypt (42:1–43:7). On the conventional scholarly opinion regarding the sources of these chapters and the locale where they were edited, see Kremers 1953:
126–31; Hyatt 1956b: 1088–92; Wanke 1971: 116–31; Pohlmann 1978: 136–41; Thiel 1981:
62–66; Seitz 1989: 277, with further literature. On the structure of the section and its objectives, see also Hoffman 2000; 2001: 725–26.

182. Compare this with the organization suggested by Kremers (1953: 122–25) and by
Wanke (1971: 94–95), who without justification further subdivides 38:1–13 into two parts
(vv. 1–6 and 7–13); see Holladay's (1989: 282) critique. There is also no justification for Hoffman's subdivision of 37:3–16 into two parts (vv. 3–10 and 11–16; 2001: 685–88); see the discussion below.

ment (or a reference to his imprisonment) and his rescue, followed by his transfer to a more secure location (Holladay 1989: 283).

d. *Consistent attitude toward the three protagonists of the narrative: Jeremiah, Zedekiah, and the officials.*[183] At the center of the narrative is Jeremiah, who opposes rebellion against Babylon and calls for surrender, hoping to save Jerusalem from destruction. Opposing him are the officials, who are described as leaders of the rebellion who believe that it will succeed; therefore, they force it on others, harming their opponents and intimidating the king. The king is portrayed as a coward who does not dare (or perhaps is unable) to stand up against the officials, even though he is convinced of the justice of Jeremiah's words. The king's weakness is reflected in his encounters with Jeremiah (37:17; 38:14; Bright 1965: 244); in his capitulation to the officials' demand that the prophet be put to death (38:5); in that he makes a vow to Jeremiah, but only "secretly" (38:16; Janzen 1973: 530); and in his instruction to the prophet regarding his answer to the officials, should they ask him about the subject of their meeting (38:24–25). The criticism that is repeatedly directed at the officials (e.g., in 38:9a, 16b) is also intended to accentuate the king's weakness and his capitulation to their influence. This point is also expressed in the words of the women "who were brought out of the king's house" (v. 22b; Holladay 1989: 290); they addressed the officials, who persuaded the king not to take the right course of action.[184]

This story appears to be literarily well-structured and meticulously edited;[185] it displays a gradual decline in the king's self-confidence, paralleled by his increasing anxiety about the officials. This is most clearly reflected in the king's three requests to Jeremiah for a prophecy:

a. The first request is delivered to Jeremiah by messengers (37:3, 7). It is an open, public request (v. 3) delivered poetically: "Pray for us to the Lord our God."[186]

b. The second request is delivered by the king himself, with great apprehension, when Jeremiah is brought to the palace and is asked, "in his house secretly, 'Is there any word from the Lord?'" (37:17).

---

183. Duhm (1901: 301) had commented that the shaping of the characters in this story is essential to understanding the message it conveys.

184. See the comments by Kessler (1965: 273). For a proposed revision of this text based on the LXX, see Streane 1896: 246; and Holladay 1989: 268.

185. The editor's activity in shaping the story is also reflected in the prefatory comments embedded in the description, in the summaries of the episodes, and in the spaces created between the different parts of the story. In these comments, the editor repeats fixed idioms and uses them to advance the narrative and highlight each stage. See also Hoffman 2001: 682–83.

186. Cf. 42:20. See 2 Kings 20 and compare with the parallel situation described in 2 Kgs 19:2–4 = Isa 37:2–4. On Jeremiah's prayers, see Hoffman 2001: 366–69, with further literature.

c. For the third prophecy, the king sends for Jeremiah and has him brought
"to the third entrance of the house of the Lord" (38:14). At this time,
Zedekiah very fearfully asks Jeremiah for his words: "I will ask you some-
thing; hide nothing from me." He also swears "secretly" to Jeremiah that
he will safeguard his life and not hand him over to "those who are seeking
your life" (i.e., the officials, v. 15). At the end of the encounter, he instructs Jeremiah to hide what he has said from them (Rudolph 1947: 222;
Thompson 1980: 631; Holladay 1989: 287; Hoffman 2001: 698–99).

The structure of the episode is gradual, eventually making the officials the principal protagonists accountable for the destruction of Jerusalem. They "triumph"
over Jeremiah in his attempt to persuade the king to surrender to Babylon and
save the city. It becomes unequivocally clear from the story that the king's fear of
the officials is what causes him to prolong the war until Jerusalem capitulates.[187]

It is precisely against this background of literary unity that the lack of unity
of the story's sources is so striking. The first 10 verses (37:1–10) seem to be of
the author's own making, because they do not add anything to the narrative and
are based on information that appears later in the story (except for the description of the delegation sent to the prophet in v. 3).[188] On this basis, we may con-

---

187. Seitz (1989: 240–41) has cogently described the purposes of the redaction: to explain
the fate of the king, the nation, and the city because they had sinned and because they did not
heed the prophet's admonitions; the redaction also reinforces the impression that the land was
being comletely emptied of its inhabitants. The original story—the biography of the prophet—
is presented from a sympathetic angle in order to justify Jeremiah's campaign for submission to
Babylon both in Judah and in the Babylonian Diaspora (see primarily chaps. 27–29). According to this story, then, there was an ongoing struggle with the officials and the false prophets,
lasting from the deportation of Jehoiachin until after the destruction of Jerusalem (Seitz 1989:
241). This struggle helps to explain why Rudolph (1947: xix, 195–96) described the biography
as a tale of the prophet's suffering. For a differing viewpoint, see Thompson 1980: 41–42.

188. This is similar to the views of Holladay 1989: 282; and Seitz 1989: 237, 242–44, 247–
48; see also Wanke 1971: 100–102. At the center of this literary unit is Jeremiah's prophecy
(vv. 6–10). Two editorial comments (vv. 4–5) were added to provide historical background,
and they come after the introduction to the entire episode (vv. 1–2). The purpose of the introduction is the chronological location of the story and the presentation of the characters who
appear later in the story. On the historical and linguistic problems raised by the opening remark, see Janzen 1971: 107, 142, 155; 227 n. 70. On the connection between the comment in
37:4, where the prophet "came in and went out among the people" (or "within the city" according to the LXX), "for they had not put him into prison," and the description of the
prophet's imprisonment later on in the narrative, see Holladay 1989: 287. The term בית הכליא,
as is generally understood, probably is a late phrase for any place where the accused would be
detained prior to sentencing. There was no special building for this purpose, and the terms
בית הבור and החנויות were also used (vv. 15–16); on these terms, see Hoffman 2001: 682–83,
688. The lack of a specific detention facility also explains why the house of Jonathan, the
scribe, was used as a prison; on this subject, see also below, n. 191. A context similar to this one
also serves as the background for the purchase of the field in Anathoth (cf. Jer 32:1–5, 34:1–7).
Accordingly, we may conclude that around this time (and perhaps against a background of the
departure of many of Jerusalem's population and the imprisonment of Jeremiah) the various
traditions concerning the prophet's fate developed.

clude that they were intended to allow the editor to express his perspective at the beginning of the story: Zedekiah and the officials are responsible for the destruction of Jerusalem because "neither he, nor his servants, nor the people of the land listened to the words of the Lord that he had spoken through Jeremiah the prophet" (37:2).[189]

The first sources recounting the history of Jeremiah, compiled and edited on the eve of the destruction, were 37:11–38:28. The narrative begins at the height of the Babylonian siege, when the Egyptians rallied to the aid of Judah (37:11) and brought about a temporary lull in the siege.[190] Against this backdrop, Jeremiah left Jerusalem "to go to the land of Benjamin" (v. 12), but he was captured (v. 13), brought before the officials (v. 14b), beaten, and imprisoned in the house of Jonathan, the scribe (vv. 15–16).[191] This is the context for the meeting, held "secretly" (v. 17a), between the king and the prophet in the palace and Jeremiah's unequivocal prophecy: "you will be delivered into the hand of the king of Babylon" (v. 17b). Only after the prophet's request and his attempt to

---

189. In general, Wanke's view (1971: 100–102) that this unit is a later expansion of 21:1–7 seems to be accurate, although, in my opinion, the sources for these verses is varied and also includes 34:1–7 and the sequel to the story in chap. 37. In this connection, see also the distinction between the two literary units made by Holladay (1989: 283).

190. On the historical background of this era, see the discussion above, §2.2.2 (pp. 72–84), and see there also the discussion of the terms לחליק and בעל פקידות. Verse 11 repeats the historical background provided in v. 5b and thus also appears to be an editorial comment intended to clarify the background of Jeremiah's deed and to give chronological context for the interval between the two parts of the siege. These events must precede the period described in 32:2 and make good sense as the background of the situation described there. Accordingly, the attempts by Pohlmann (1978: 62–63) and Seitz (1989: 239, 255–57) to identify the original beginning of the story are futile; the beginning was, in any case, composed by the editor.

191. The expression בית האסור בית יהונתן הסופר 'the house of the imprisoned, the house of Jonathan, the scribe' is problematic, particularly in light of the LXX translation, which reads only 'the house of Jonathan, the scribe.' There is the possibility of haplography in the LXX, but the clarification provided at the end of the verse, כי אותו עשו לבית הכליא ('for they had made that the prison'), and the words of Jeremiah in v. 20 make the LXX preferable to the "duplicate reading" of the MT's editor (Janzen 1973: 22). One may assume that Jeremiah's attitude toward this place as "the prison" (v. 18) led to this addition. Verse 16 is more problematic in the terminology it uses and in its relation to v. 15. Two other places where Jeremiah stayed are reported: בית הבור 'the house of the pit' and the החנויות (a unique occurrence of this term). In this case, another verb describes Jeremiah's arrival (כי בא or in the LXX 'he went'). The use of an active verb does not seem appropriate to describe the prophet's imprisonment (cf. to 37:4, 15, 21; 38:6); the proposals by Holladay (1989: 288) as well as other commentators attest to the difficulty of understanding this verse. In my opinion, v. 16a is the editor's note, which was intended to describe Jeremiah's location accurately and to adapt the story to 38:6–13 and the prophet's words in vv. 18, 20. There is support for this notion in the citation of his name in the second half of the verse: "And Jeremiah had remained there many days" (v. 16b), which can be understood only if it came immediately after v. 15; it now appears to be a duplication after the addition of v. 16a. In the LXX, the name of the prophet does not appear, and this reinforces the hypothesis regarding the original sequence: *ויקצפו השרים על ירמיהו והכו אותו ונתנו אותו בית יהונתן הסופר כי אותו עשו לבית הכלא וישב שם ימים רבים. See also Wanke 1971: 94; Janzen 1973: 147.

prove the accuracy of his words in the past (vv. 18–20; Thompson 1980: 634–35) did the king give the order to release him, and he was transferred to "the court of the guard" (v. 21).[192]

In 38:1–4, the officials again imprison Jeremiah, after interpreting his subsequent prophecies to the people as intended to undermine the morale of "the soldiers who remain in the city and all the people."[193] The king is apprehensive about resisting his own court officers (v. 5: "for the king can do nothing against you")[194] and allows the prophet to be cast into the pit of Malchiah, the king's son,[195] which is in the court of the guard; Jeremiah sinks into the mud in the bottom of the pit (v. 7). Ebed-melech the Cushite[196] rescues Jeremiah (as described in detail in vv. 7–13), and Jeremiah returns to the court of the guard.

After rescuing Jeremiah, the king calls him again and asks to hear his prophecy. This time, the encounter takes place in "the third entrance of the house of the Lord" (v. 14). Jeremiah tries to avoid answering, but after the king has sworn "secretly" that he will neither put him to death nor hand him over to "these men that seek your life" (v. 16), Jeremiah offers him two alternatives: to surrender and go on living or to continue rebelling against the Babylonians and bring about destruction and death (vv. 17–18). The king expresses his fear that, if he surrenders, he will be handed into the hands of the "Jews who deserted to the Chaldeans," who will abuse him (v. 19); but in response, Jeremiah repeats the two choices in more detail, with greater emphasis on the personal fate of the king and his household (vv. 20–23). At the end of this episode, the king instructs Jeremiah about how he is to reply if asked by the officials about the contents of their meeting (vv. 24–26). The officials do indeed ask Jeremiah about the meeting, and Jeremiah, for the first time, does not speak his mind, "for the matter was not

---

192. I do not accept Pohlmann's opinion (1978: 69) that 37:17–21 are late and secondary. For additional literature, see Seitz 1989: 238.

193. Against the background of Jeremiah's two prophecies (vv. 2–3; cf. the complete version of the prophecies in 21:9; 32:2 and also 34:2), the officials accuse Jeremiah on two counts. The first is that he is "weakening the hands of the soldiers who remain in the city and the hands of all the people," and the second, graver charge is that the prophet is motivated by malice: "for this man seeks not the welfare of this people but their hurt." There is only one parallel to this expression in the Bible, in Ezra 4, though it also appears in one of the Lachish Letters (letter 6, line 6): דברי הנביא לא טובים לרפות ידיים ולהשקיט ידי הארץ ('The words of the prophet are not good, to weaken the hands of the people and to silence the strength of the land').

194. On the verb יוכל and on suggestions for emending it, see Rudolph 1947: 220. On the linguistic problems later in these verses, see Holladay 1989: 266.

195. On the phrase "the king's son" in this context, see Holladay 1989: 289. For a comprehensive discussion of the significance of this title, its role, and its status, see Fox 2000: 43–53.

196. The description of Ebed-melech the Cushite as "a eunuch," is not found in the LXX (Janzen 1973: 73; Tov 1981: 57); cf. 29:2; 40:16. It is likely that the additional information was provided to explain his presence in the king's palace, as in 2 Kgs 20:18 (Holladay 1989: 266). On the title "the Cushite," see Jer 13:23; on his accusation against the king (according to the LXX) or against the officials (according to the MT), see Holladay 1989: 266–67.

overheard" (v. 27). The prophet's silence allows him to return to the court of the guard and to remain there "until the day Jerusalem was taken" (v. 28).

Many scholars have noticed the similarity between the episodes described in chaps. 37 and 38: In both stories, there is a description of Jeremiah's imprisonment for the crime of treason (37:13b, 15) or incitement (38:4), and in both stories he is accused by the officials (37:15; 38:1, 4) and cast into a cell in a pit (37:16) or into a pit (38:6). In both cases, the king intervenes on Jeremiah's behalf, rescues him (37:21; 38:10), and asks for counsel and a prophecy (37:17a; 38:14). In both cases, the prophet advises the king to surrender and thereby to prevent the destruction of Jerusalem (37:17b–19; 38:17–18, 20–23). In both stories, Jeremiah's request not to be sent back to the house of Jonathan, the scribe, is repeated (37:20; 38:26). Both stories end with exactly the same situation: "and Jeremiah remained in the court of the guard" (37:21; 38:13, 28), and in both cases the narrative suggests that Jeremiah remained there until the end of the siege (37:21; 38:28).

Despite the similarity between the episodes, most scholars have reconstructed events according to the simple meaning of the text and emphasized the differences between the stories, as well as their continuity.[197] I am of the opinion that this approach is unconvincing, because these are not two supplementary stories in a single chronological sequence, nor even two parallel stories describing the same event (Hoffman 2001: 680). From a literary viewpoint, this narrative contains a single main story on which the biography is based (37:11–21; 38:14–28); into this biography, another story from a variant source has been inserted (38:1–13). This second story describes events from a different viewpoint: the distance from the prophet in time and space seems much greater, and there is a markedly different perspective informing the depiction of the characters. Some of the arguments corroborating this thesis were first suggested by Skinner (1926: 256–60; Hoffman 2001: 680–81), and to these additional arguments can be added:

a. The main difference between the story in 37:11–21 and 38:14–28 and the story in 38:1–13 is the shaping of the characters. It appears that the primary characteristics of the personages in the first story have been made more extreme in the second story. Thus, for example, the officials' hostility toward Jeremiah, which in the first story leads to his being arrested and even beaten (37:15–16), is described in the second story as an attempt to murder him (38:6). A similar phenomenon can be noticed in the shaping of the character of the king, who is described in both narratives as being fearful of the officials (38:5, 24–26); however,

---

197. Skinner 1926: 256–60; Pohlmann 1978: 69–70; Eph'al 1993: 20; and Hoffman 2001: 679–81 hold a minority view about this section; see also the debate in Bright 1965: 232–34; 1976: 185–86 n. 25. See also Thompson 1980: 636–37; Rofé 1988: 116–17; and Clements 1988: 220. See the counterarguments provided by Holladay (1989: 282–84), who uses the differences between the two accounts to prove that they are continuous and sequential.

his weakness is more pronounced in the second story, as is his vacillation (compare vv. 5 and 10).

b. Both encounters between the king and the prophet (37:17–20; 38:14–26) were originally part of a unified, sequential narrative. The second encounter is not connected to the story of Jeremiah's imprisonment, which was added in 38:1–13, and it takes place after his rescue. The insertion of the imprisonment story forced the editor to create a repetition to link 37:21b and 38:13b, and this "wraps" the narrative around 38:1–13a. From the literary perspective, the resumptive repetition was designed to make the insertion of the imprisonment narrative imperceptible and to restore the protagonists to the places they had at the end of the narrative in 37:21.

c. The encounter between Jeremiah and the king, as described in 38:14–26, is linked to the story in 37:11–21. According to the first story, Jeremiah was thrown into the house of Jonathan, the scribe, which was transformed into a prison. According to the text, Jeremiah remained there in a pit of some kind (37:15–16). In the second story, he was thrown into a pit belonging to Malchiah, son of the king, located in "the court of the guard" (38:6). After Jeremiah was rescued from the pit, he met with the king a second time. During this meeting, the king proposed to Jeremiah that he tell the officials that he had requested of the king "that he would not send [him] back to Jonathan's house to die there" (38:26). But, in fact, the house of Jonathan is not mentioned at all in the account in chap. 38.[198]

d. The continuation of the story in 38:1–13 is found in 39:15–18.[199] This point reinforces the hypothesis that this story was interpolated between the two encounters between Jeremiah and the king. The end of the story was shifted from its original place and embedded in the episode of Jeremiah's rescue by the Babylonians,[200] and the editor duplicated the summary from 38:21a in 38:28a, while creating a transition between these two accounts.[201]

e. The narrative in 37:11–21 is influenced by "Akkadianisms," as pointed out and identified by Eph'al (1993: 18–22, especially p. 20).

The literary and conceptual differences between the two stories support the idea that the narrative is composed of a main story into which a story of a different origin has been interpolated. The sequential account in 37:11–21 and

---

198. The attempt by scholars to provide an explanation of this difficulty does not resolve the problem; the solutions tend to interfere with the continuity of the narrative. For the generally accepted opinion, see Bright 1965: 234.

199. Bright 1965: 232–35; and Rudolph 1947: 198. Holladay (1989: 284, 293) adds the editorial comment in 38:28a to this sequence.

200. On the reasons for this, see below, in the next section.

201. The structuring of this episode relies on 2 Kgs 25:3–4 and Jer 52:6–7. The episode points to the famine in the city as the reason for its surrender. The conclusion is that the editor composed these two verses, thus bringing the events closer to each other in time.

38:14–28 seems to be part of a continuous "biography." The account focuses on a description of the events that befell the prophet throughout a significant period, incorporates passages from his prophecies, and interprets the events from this perspective. In contrast, the story in 38:1–13 is episodic, detached from its context, and focuses on a single event: the story of Jeremiah's rescue from the pit in which he was about to drown.[202] The emphasis in this story is on its dramatic tempo, which is created by the abundant use of verbs and the rapid shift between scenes.[203] In terms of linguistics and literary style, the story uses colloquial language,[204] and the characters are portrayed as one-dimensional stereotypes in order to serve the purposes of the editor.[205] This served to heighten the tension

202. The episodic nature of the narrative explains why it expands on various details that the parallel story hardly discusses—and which may not necessarily have occurred. See, for example, the elaboration on the harsh conditions of Jeremiah's imprisonment, in a pit filled with mud, and the danger to his life (v. 6b), a topic that is not mentioned again later in the story (compare the words of Ebed-melech, the Cushite [v. 9] with the words of the king [v. 10]).

203. This story makes lavish use of the literary device of controlling the pace of the story by rapid changes in the number of verbs and the extent of details used in the descriptions, as well as by rapid shifts of scene. In v. 6, for example, which describes the prophet's descent into the pit, the pace of events is accelerated by a sequence of four verbs (וישלחו . . . וישליכו . . . ויקחו . . . ויטבע . . .). At the same time, there is a wealth of details about the pit (the location, ownership, condition) and even a description of how the prophet is lowered into the pit by ropes (a prelude to the way he is later taken up, in vv. 11–14). Immediately at the end of this description, at the dramatic climax, the story moves to a new scene, in another locale, presenting a new protagonist (Ebed-melech, the Cushite), and the pace slows, maintaining a complete blackout of what is happening to Jeremiah at the same time.

204. The folkloristic nature of the narrative is reflected in the ironic quotation of the confused speech of Ebed-melech, the Cushite (Jer 38:9), when he says that Jeremiah "may well die of hunger here, seeing there is no more bread in the city." See Janzen 1973: 52; Tov 1981: 158; and Holladay 1989: 267. A similar confusion is found in the directions for rescue that Ebed-melech gives Jeremiah (v. 12), which begin, "Put now . . . under your armpits," and which end with, "under the ropes"—which clashes with the beginning. The detailed account of the rescue (vv. 11–13) was intended to highlight the difficulty of the salvage operation, to describe Jeremiah's danger, and to draw out the dramatic tension until the rescue itself. The text describes the place (תחת האוצר) from which the rescue equipment was taken (see the emendation by Rudolph 1947: 221; Holladay 1989: 267, on the hypothesis that the word האוצר is a gloss), as well as the equipment itself (according to the Qere: בלוי סחבות ובלוי מלחים), and the way Ebed-melech threw it to Jeremiah in the pit (וישלחם אל הבור בחבלים; see the emendation by Janzen 1973: 52) and explained to Jeremiah the best way to hold it שים נא בלואי הסחבות והמלחים תחת אצילות ידיך מתחת לחבלים). Jeremiah's response is presented very concisely in v. 12b (ויעש ירמיהו כן; see Kessler 1965: 91 about this expression). It is noteworthy that v. 12 in the LXX is much shorter and that the MT was expanded on the basis of the information in v. 11 (Janzen 1973: 53, 147, 152; Holladay 1989: 267).

205. The folkloristic style of the story and its focus on a single episode are also reflected in other ways, such as: the way the characters are shaped, stereotypically and one-dimensionally (good, bad, etc.); the clear-cut role that each character fills; and the characters' disappearance when they are no longer needed. The officials are mentioned only in the imprisonment scene, Ebed-melech only in the rescue scene, the prophet only in connection with the pit into which he was thrown; the king is only mentioned at two critical junctures in the story: he authorizes the imprisonment of the prophet, and he authorizes the release. Thus, for example, after the

between Jeremiah, who represents the people supporting surrender to Babylon, and the officials, who support continued resistance. The antipathy toward Jeremiah is pronounced, the desire to murder him is unmistakable, and it is clear that he is standing alone on the battlefield. His rescue by a foreigner underscores his isolation (Volz 1928: 339), and the king does not function independently: on the one hand, he capitulates to the demands of the officials and abandons Jeremiah to them; on the other, he orders Ebed-melech to save Jeremiah *after* the situation has been brought to his attention and Ebed-melech admonishes him to act. Furthermore, there is no specific prophecy or particular deed for which Jeremiah is imprisoned and, in contrast to the parallel story, in which the prophecies play an important role, the character of the prophecies here is totally different: they were compiled from well-known prophecies, embedded in the literary context (which was designed to highlight the officials' assignment of blame to Jeremiah), and constituted the basis on which he was suspected of sedition.[206]

Because of the qualities of the story in 38:1–13, it may be identified as a folktale that focuses on a specific event in the life of Jeremiah.[207] This story existed alongside the broader description of what befell Jeremiah on the eve of the destruction (37:11–21; 38:14–28), and in the course of the redaction of the biography, it was interpolated between Jeremiah's two encounters with the king. Thus, a symmetrical story was created: the prophet was imprisoned three times, and after each imprisonment he met with the king, who then released him. The interpolation of the story created a chain of events that was ostensibly the reason for the next meeting, but the main problem created by the insertion is the inappropriate excuse that appears in 38:26.[208]

---

king "disappears" in v. 5, he is mentioned seven times in vv. 7–9, with the climax coming when Ebed-melech, the Cushite, addresses him: ויצא עבד־מלך מבית המלך וידבר אל המלך לאמר אדוני המלך. In this connection, note that some of these expressions seem to be secondary overlay (Holladay 1989: 266–67).

206. There is an exact parallel for both the first prophecy (Jer 38:2; cf. 21:9) and the second prophecy within the broader context (32:2; cf. 34:2; Mowinckel 1914: 6; Kessler 1965: 262). For the prophecy in 38:2, see Janzen 1973: 43–44, 205 n. 19. Rudolph (1947: 220) sees this verse as an addition, and Wanke (1971: 94–95) agrees and sees v. 3 as an original part of the preface to the second chapter. It is reasonable to conclude that both prophecies are not an original part of any narrative unit, and their connection to chap. 21, including the mention of Pashhur, is evidence that chap. 21 was the background for this part of the story. Also see Bright on this subject (1965: 233).

207. The parallels between this story and the opening verses of the account of the purchase of the field in Anathoth (32:1–5) support the theory that details of the prophet's history circulated before the destruction of Jerusalem and that in certain circles various versions developed around this information.

208. This problem is evidence, in my opinion, of the great importance that the editor attributed to the meetings between the prophet and the king, especially in that he used the meetings as forums for the prophecies spoken on those occasions. This importance also is manifest in the two prophecies embedded in the introduction to the story (37:6–10).

The duplication created by the appearance of both stories reinforces the historical credibility of the event they describe. The basic facts reported in both accounts supplement the information found in other sources concerning the time of the destruction of Jerusalem; the principal historical detail that has been added regards the Egyptian campaign that led to a temporary cessation of the Babylonian siege.[209] This is the background for Jeremiah's attempt to leave the city for Benjamin (37:12–14) to join the Judahite populace residing there. The picture that emerges from a reconstruction of the Babylonian siege (see above, §§2.2.2, pp. 72–84) shows that the people who assembled in that region either were reconciled to Babylonian authority and opposed to revolt or, at least, saw revolt as futile. It is likely that, during the lull in the siege, people who did not believe that the revolt would succeed left the city. They thereby created two camps in the nation, politically and socially: the advocates of surrender to Babylon were outside of Jerusalem, and the advocates of continued resistance, mainly residents of Jerusalem and the elite, remained in the besieged city. This state of affairs may explain the isolation of Jeremiah, and this is supported by the rhetorical question addressed to the king (37:19): "Where are your prophets now?" This question is meant to direct attention to Jeremiah's truthfulness in the past (compare 2:28; 17:15), and it apparently reflects a situation in which the "optimistic" prophets continued to speak freely, even though they were wrong when they predicted that "the king of Babylon will not come against you or against this land." In contrast, the prophet who foresaw the Babylonian campaign and spoke of it was imprisoned (Thompson 1980: 637).

(2) The Source and Purpose of the Description of Jeremiah's
     History after the Destruction

In literary style, the duplicate description of Jeremiah's release from the "court of the guard" (38:28b; 39:3, 11–18; 40:1–6) is the most problematic, complex section of the biographical narrative. The major problems are:

a. The fusion of two stories is also detectable in this description. However, in contrast to the redaction of chaps. 37–38, in which a folktale is imbedded within the biographical sequence (see above, §5.1), here the two stories of Jeremiah's release from the "court of the guard" have been combined in such a way as to make it difficult to isolate them and to identify the narrative thread of each.

---

209. I believe that there is no reason to doubt the information in the editorial notes in 37:5, 11, because it was this military foray that formed the basis of Jeremiah's prophecy in vv. 6–10, as well as providing the background for the story of the prophet's attempt to leave Jerusalem in vv. 12–16. The prophecy in 34:12–22 can also be linked to this event, because the Egyptian campaign explains the violation of the covenant and the reenslavement of the slaves (34:8–11). See Clements 1988: 288; Hallo 1995: 79–94; Hoffman 2001: 648–51, with further literature. For a reconstruction of the events of this time, see above, §2.2.2.

b. Within this description, additional sources have been integrated at various stages of the account's development. Among these are the fate of Zedekiah and the account of Jerusalem's destruction by the Babylonians (39:1–2, 4–10; see above, §5.2.2c); the prophecy to Ebed-melech, the Cushite (39:15–18); the prologue to Jeremiah's prophecy (40:1); and the reason for the destruction (40:3b).

c. A large section of this episode is missing in the LXX (38:28b; 39:1–2, 4–13; see above, §5.2.1).

In the scholarly literature, the accepted understanding of Jeremiah's release by the Babylonians is the *theory of two versions*.[210] *One version* opens with the editorial heading that identifies the date of the events (38:28b). It is interrupted at the beginning of chap. 39 and continues with the assembling of the Babylonian officials "in the middle gate" (39:3). It is again interrupted by a later addition, in 39:4–13, and ends with the story of Jeremiah's transfer to Gedaliah (39:14). *The second version* begins with Nebuchadrezzar's instructions to Nebuzaradan regarding the treatment of Jeremiah (39:11–12).[211] It continues with the description of the prophet walking among the exiles departing Ramah, where he is located by Nebuzaradan (40:1aβ–b). The latter addresses a speech to Jeremiah marked by Deuteronomistic features (40:2–3) and offers to have Jeremiah accompany him to Babylon (40:4aα) or go to any other place he might choose (40:4b MT). Nebuzaradan finally recommends that the prophet join Gedaliah, even providing him "with an allowance of food and a present" (40:5 MT). Jeremiah joins "Gedaliah, son of Ahikam, at Mizpah and stayed with him among the people that were left in the land" (40:6).

The two stories are different in content, style, and language, but the most striking difference between them relates to their concreteness and the measure of their concurrence with the well-known historical data. The *first version* is closely linked to the time of Jerusalem's destruction and is sharp and clear-cut regarding the time and location of the events. It begins immediately after the fall of Jerusalem (38:28b), with a listing of "all of the officials of the king of Babylon" (39:3aα), who enter through "the middle gate" (v. 3aβ). Three of them are mentioned by name (v. 3bα), along with "all of the remainder of the officials of the king of Babylon" (v. 3bβ); they take Jeremiah from "the court of the guard" (v. 14aα) and send him to Gedaliah, son of Ahikam, in Mizpah (v. 14aβ–b). The *second version* begins at an indeterminate time but describes a later period, when

---

210. The two-version interpretation is found in Duhm (1901) and Giesebrecht (1907) and was accepted by most modern scholars and commentators as well. See, e.g., Wanke 1971: 110; Rofé 1988: 208–9; Eph'al 1993: 20; Hoffman 2001: 712. For counterarguments, see Thompson 1980: 651–52; Clements 1988: 229.

211. These two verses are part of a later addition to the MT that does not appear in the LXX. They were probably added to the narrative to enhance Jeremiah's importance even further and to present his treatment as Nebuchadrezzar's personal order, even prior to Jeremiah's departure from Jerusalem with the rest of the exiles.

Jeremiah already was at Ramah, bound in chains, walking in the column of ex-iles to Babylon. The text focuses only on the figures of Nebuzaradan and Jere-miah, giving them speeches of a clearly ideological nature. Jeremiah receives an offer to leave for any place that he chooses. Eventually, he is sent to Gedaliah, who, according to the narrative, has already been appointed over "the cities of Judah" (40:5aα).

There are a few points of contact between the two versions;[212] nonetheless, we must reject the idea that there is continuity between them, as well as the attempt to find a historical basis for the "duplicate release" of Jeremiah by the Babylonians.[213] In my opinion, a secondary story of a popular nature has been incorporated into the biographical sequence, very much like the insertion in the description of Jeremiah's history before the destruction. The first version is a di-rect continuation of the biography that describes events that befell Jeremiah be-fore the destruction, and there is a marked connection between the stories, both linguistically[214] and literarily.[215] The chronological transition between the description of Jeremiah's personal history in the pre-destruction period and the

---

212. The first point of contact is in the description of the taking of Jeremiah. In both sto-ries, use is made of the paired verbs שלח and לקח, the preposition מ or its equivalent מן is used, and Jeremiah is the direct object (את, אותו):

40:1aβ	39:14
אחר שלח אותו	וישלחו ויקחו את ירמיהו
נבוזראדן רב טבחים	
מן הרמה בקחתו אותו ...	מחצר המטרה ויתנו אותו

In addition to the parallels that relate to Jeremiah's release, there are even finer parallels in the concluding verses of both episodes. Both say that Jeremiah came to "Gedaliah, son of Ahi-kam," and both say that he stayed with him "among the people":

40:6	39:14
ויבא ירמיהו	ויתנו אותו
אל גדליהו בן אחיקם	אל גדליהו בן אחיקם
	בן שפן
המצפתה	
	להוציאהו אל הבית
וישב אתו	וישב
בתוך העם	בתוך העם
הנשארים בארץ	

213. For a survey and literature on this subject, see Rofé 1988: 209–11, and nn. 37–38; Hoffman 2001: 712.

214. The repetition and the play on the words ויבאו כל השרים (38:27a) and ויבאו כל שרי מלך בבל (39:3a) are important evidence of the connection between the two parts of the story. The word-play is paradoxical, setting the "wicked" officials of Judah, who imprison Jeremiah, against the "good" officials of Babylon, who release him. The message is that the tables have turned: the strong of yesterday are no longer mighty, and the weak one who persevered in his policy of loyalty to the Babylonians receives his appropriate reward.

215. The connection between both parts of the first description is evident in the first ver-sion when, on the eve of the destruction, Jeremiah is sitting in the court of the guard (38:28a), and, according to 39:14aα, he is taken from there and sent to Gedaliah. However, according to the second version, Jeremiah is taken from Ramah (40:1aβ) and sent to Gedaliah.

description of his life immediately after the destruction occurs in 38:28. In v. 28a, Jeremiah's pre-destruction history comes to an end and the history of his life after the destruction begins (28b). The narrative linking of the two parts of this verse is apparent in another play on words (עד יום אשר and והיה כאשר). The author/redactor ignores the destruction of the city and emphasizes the events that befell the prophet.[216] We may hypothesize that "omitting" a description of the destruction of Jerusalem was unacceptable to the later redactor of the narrative. Thus, the redactor inserted the two opening verses as an account of the destruction (39:1–2); these verses are a quotation from chap. 52.[217] It may be that he then decided to delete the words of v. 28b.[218]

The original continuation of 38:28 was the report of the arrival of "all the officials of the king of Babylon . . . and the remainder of the officials of the king of Babylon," with the report that they sat in "the middle gate" (39:3). This verse contains the only deviation from the dry, concise description of Jeremiah's history: the names of the officials are cited, as well as the place where they sat. Many scholars think that the specific notice of the gathering of the officials of the Babylonian king in "the middle gate" is evidence of a historical situation: the Babylonians were about to judge the people and determine the fate of those who had been caught.[219] However, I have strong doubts that the historical plau-

216. The play on words and the sharp temporal shift between the two parts of the verse attract attention, because the first part of the verse is parallel to the way in which all other "chronological chapters" end in the narrative of Jeremiah's imprisonment and release by the Babylonians (37:21b; 38:13b; compare also with 37:16b; 38:6b; 39:14b; 40:6). All of these verses have a literary function in the redaction, and they do not seem to be an original part of the story. The second part of 38:28 sounds like a paraphrase of the first part of the verse. Considering this, the uniformity of the wording, and the placement of this verse as a bridge between descriptions of Jeremiah's history before and after the destruction of Jerusalem, I believe that v. 28 is original within the biography of Jeremiah. Furthermore, it may be seen as the source of the uniform version, which was penned by the editor: he embedded the same words in the conclusions of the secondary scenes in order to give the account a uniform outline.

217. On the source of the destruction accounts, see the discussion above, §5.2.2c. It seems likely that the editor had no information about Jeremiah's life during the capture of the city, and in this respect, the narrative in 39:1–2 serves to fill in the gap; in terms of the contents, it also fits well into the narrative sequence.

218. Verse 28b is missing in the LXX. This omission may be explained by the similarity between the two parts of v. 28, but labeling them as a dittography seems too easy a solution (Holladay 1989: 268). In my opinion, the major reason for the deletion is the insertion of 39:1–2, which created a chronological problem for the editor. After 38:28b mentions the conquest of Jerusalem, 39:1–2 returns to the beginning of the siege and concludes with a description of the breaching of its walls as the introduction to the fate of the city and its inhabitants (Mowinckel 1914: 24; Volz 1928: 333; Rudolph 1947: 224–25). The deletion of v. 28b did not resolve this difficulty, but doing so did make it easier to create a chronologically acceptable sequence of events (Bright 1965: 224–46). In any event, the stylistic and thematic contrast between 38:28 and 39:1–2 is striking, and the different origins of these two verses is clearly evident (Holladay 1989: 268). See also Hoffman 2001: 701, 703.

219. See, e.g., Rudolph 1947: 224; Wanke 1971: 110; Rofé 1988: 208–9. With regard to the credibility of the list of officials as well as their appearance in the Babylonian list of officials

sibility of this detail is decisive regarding our interpretation of the story. It seems to me that the primary issue here is how we should see these circumstances in light of Jeremiah's prophecies in 1:13–18 (especially vv. 15–16): "I will call on the families of the kingdoms of the north, says the Lord, and they shall come, and they shall set everyone his throne at the entrance of the gates of Jerusalem, against all its walls round about and against all the towns of Judah, and I will utter my judgments against them regarding all their wickedness, in that they have forsaken me." These words are fulfilled as they were spoken, and their message is clear-cut: the prophet who was imprisoned by the king of Judah's officials was released by the king of Babylon's officials, because "today, I have made you [Jeremiah] a fortified city, and an iron pillar and wall of copper to stand against the whole land—against the kings of Judah, its officials, its priests, and the people of the land; they will fight against you, but they will not overcome you, for I am with you, says the Lord, to rescue you" (1:18–19). It is likely that 39:3 is the continuation of the biography that was written by someone close to the prophet who knew his prophecies and his political views (Baruch?). Ideologically, this is one of the climaxes of the narrative, containing one of the important messages that the author wishes to convey.

The end of the first version is 39:14. This verse describes Jeremiah's being removed from the court of the guard; his transfer to Gedaliah, son of Ahikam;[220] and his living "among the people."[221] Linguistically and thematically, this verse is a direct continuation of the description of the assembly of the Babylonian officials.[222] The conclusion is, therefore, that the first version of the account of Jeremiah's release from prison by the Babylonians after the fall of Jerusalem is an integral part of the description of his experiences during the Babylonian siege. The account of this time is distinctly concise and pithy, which focuses attention on the ideological content that the author wishes to deliver: the prophet's words have been proved true—Jerusalem was conquered, the Babylonians are inside, and it is they who are now deciding the fate of the city and its inhabitants.

(*ANET*, 308), see Rudolph 1947: 244–45; Hyatt 1956: 1079; Rofé 1988: 210–11 n. 40; Holladay 1989: 268–69, 291; Hoffman 2001: 706.

220. The expression להוציאהו אל הבית seems disjointed, and the fact that the last two words do not occur in the LXX supports this notion. Rudolph's proposal, that the phrase be read (parallel to 37:4) להוציאהו ולהביאו seems reasonable.

221. Wanke (1971: 110) argued that v. 14b was a secondary overlay. In my opinion, this cannot be supported, because the purpose of the comment is to describe the situation of Jeremiah and his adversaries after the Babylonian conquest, in contrast to their situation before the conquest. The focus is on Jeremiah, who is staying among the people, not in isolation in the court of the guard.

222. Linguistically, 39:14 describes the first action of the Babylonian officials after they assembled in "the middle gate" (39:3). The verbal sequence is clear: "And all of the officials of the king of Babylon came, and they sat in the middle gate . . . and they sent and took Jeremiah . . ."). In terms of plot development, 39:14 describes Jeremiah being removed from the pit in the court of the guard, where he had been kept on the eve of the destruction (38:28).

The second version of the story of Jeremiah's release by the Babylonians is much more problematic. The two opening verses of the narrative (39:11–12) do not appear in the LXX (nor do vv. 4–10), the continuation in 40:1–6 seems disjointed, and the connection between the two parts of the narrative and the original sequence between them is not clear. In my opinion, the disjointedness and awkwardness of this version resulted from the fact that three supplements were added after the story was already written:

a. The two opening verses of the story (39:11–12) are a supplement created by a later redactor.[223] We may speculate that Nebuchadrezzar's instructions to Nebuzaradan (commanding him to take Jeremiah, safeguard him, and do his bidding) were interpolated as part of a later addition to the story about the time of the destruction. This command now concludes the sequence of events during the destruction and forms a pronounced gap between the fate of the king, Jerusalem, its inhabitants, and the fate of Jeremiah.[224] The implication is that the major reason for the placement of vv. 11–12 is the sequence that preceded these verses. They contribute no new information, apart from the fact that the command to release Jeremiah is attributed to Nebuchadrezzar.[225]

b. A later redactor also added the heading in 40:1 for editorial reasons that are not directly related to this story. In the LXX, the phrase והוא אסור באזיקים ('and he was bound in chains') does not appear, nor does the generalization

---

223. This hypothesis is based on the fact that they are missing from the LXX, together with vv. 4–10 (which are also missing).

224. This comparison is one of the ideological goals of the account, and it is reinforced by the later redaction. The focus is on the fact that Nebuchadrezzar, the king who destroyed, deported, burned, killed, blinded, and imprisoned, is the one who ordered his senior officers to safeguard Jeremiah and do his bidding. The message here is plain: those who did not heed the word of God and who rebelled against the Babylonians were punished. Those who acted according to God's commands and responded to the call for submission to Babylon were saved and accorded merciful treatment.

225. In my opinion, all of the information in 39:11–12 is drawn from the narrative itself. The heading of the episode was written on the basis of this description, and a relationship between Nebuchadrezzar's commands and Nebuzaradan's actions was created:

- The command קחנו 'take him' is matched by 40:2, which begins with the verb ויקח 'he took'.
- The command ועיניך שים עליו 'look after him well' is matched by 40:4, which cites the promise ואשים את עיני עליך 'I will look after you'.
- The command ואל תעש לו מאומה רע 'do him no harm' is matched by 40:4, which presents the structure: אם טוב בעיניך . . . ואם רע 'if it seems good to you . . . if it seems ill'.
- The command כי אם כאשר ידבר אליך כן עשה עמו 'do to him as he asks you' is matched by 40:2–3 with its sophisticated statement attributed to God but also expressing the idea that ה' אלוהיך דיבר . . . ויעש כאשר דיבר 'the Lord your God pronounced . . . has done as he said'.
- The unique occurrence of the word אזיקים (40:1, 4) reinforces the connection between the story and the heading added to it.

[כל] גלות [ירושלים ו]יהודה ('[all] the exiles of [Jerusalem and] Judah').[226] The reconstruction of 40:1b in its original wording (based on the LXX) is, therefore, "*The word came to Jeremiah from the Lord after Nebuzaradan, commander of the imperial guard, sent for him, when he took him from among the captives of Judah, who were in Ramah, being carried off to exile in Babylon." The structure and language of this verse are parallel to various editorial captions in the book. These captions were intended to supply information about the time and place that the prophecies were spoken. The problem is that, after this heading, there is no prophecy and, thus, any attempt to assign part of vv. 2–5 to Jeremiah ignores the structure and purpose of the text.[227] Rudolph offered a different explanation,[228] maintaining that this verse must be connected with the introduction to the book (1:1–3), where a chronological outline for the words of Jeremiah up until the destruction of Jerusalem is provided. In view of this, the later redactor of the book felt a need to begin the postexilic material with a new heading, which, to him, began at this point. The similarity to editorial comments inserted at other places (32:1; 33:1; 34:1; 36:27; etc.) and the fact that this verse is a continuation of the prophecy in 39:15–18 both corroborate this suggestion. This prophecy must also be treated as a later interpolation created by the redactor (Kessler 1965: 288–89).

c. The language and contents of 40:3 are out of place in the sequence of Nebuzaradan's words, particularly because in v. 3a there is a shift to second-person plural (in contrast with the second-person singular in the rest of the narrative).[229] Most scholars and commentators who have confronted this dilemma have proposed a reconstruction of two original, independent versions that have since been integrated:[230] (1) the account of Nebuzaradan's words to Jeremiah and (2) Jeremiah's prophecy. Bright (1965: 244), followed by Holladay (1989:

226. See Janzen 1973: 53, 65–67; and Holladay 1989: 269–70. It is likely that the MT is an expansion based on information that was available in the same story, such as, e.g., 29:1, 4, 20 (see also 24:5; 28:4; 29:22; Janzen 1973: 53). The expansion on the "chains" appears to be incorporating information available later in the story: see the beginning of the second part of Nebuzaradan's words (40:4). The fact that these are the only occurrences of this word corroborates the hypothesis stated above. On the phrase בקחתו אותו and its context in v. 2, see also the comment by Duhm 1901: 313.

227. For attempts to resolve the conflicting accounts or to emend the text in vv. 2–6 and see part of it as the prophecy of Jeremiah connected to the introduction in v. 1, see Bright 1965: 244–46; Thompson 1980: 651–52; and Holladay 1989: 293–94. On the controversy in the scholarly literature over whether Jeremiah's prophecy begins in 42:7, or whether a passage from his prophecy may have been embedded in vv. 2–3, see the summary by Kessler 1965: 288.

228. See Rudolph 1947: 227. In fact, this interpretation was also proposed by Rabbi David Qimḥi (Radaq) in his commentary on 42:7.

229. On the linguistic problems raised by the speech and its possible connection to the heading in v. 1, see Janzen 1973: 22, 53; and Holladay 1989: 270. On Nebuzaradan's speech, see the comment by Duhm (1901: 313).

230. On the proposals of Volz, Rudolph, Bright, and others, see the survey by Holladay 1989: 281.

281), proposed that Jeremiah's prophecy began in v. 2b (emending the singular possessive suffix אלהיך to the plural possessive suffix אלהיכם) and continued in v. 3. However, this proposal is also problematic.[231] It is more reasonable to suggest that only v. 3b has been interpolated from Jeremiah's prophecy ("because you have sinned against the Lord and have not obeyed his voice; therefore this thing is come upon you"); the second half of it is lacking in the LXX. The presence of an exact parallel to this segment in the more complete prophecy in 44:23 supports this proposal.[232] A reconstruction of this kind makes good sense in terms of the overall sequence as well, because it implies that Nebuzaradan's speech compared the fate of the city with the fate of the prophet, though the interpolation included only the rationale for the grim fate of Jerusalem. The insertion of this section from Jeremiah's prophecy in the middle of Nebuzaradan's speech is of great ideological importance, because it would have done much to explain the disaster that the Lord brought on his city and his people: he brought the disaster because of the sins of the people and their refusal to heed warnings. This is the message woven into the narrative; incorporating it in the description of the event makes use of a familiar technique in Deuteronomistic literature. The redactor no doubt thought it important to underscore the message, and so he embedded it in the transition from the fate of the city to the fate of the prophet. In the original story Nebuzaradan's speech is addressed to Jeremiah using second-person singular, which emphasizes the different fates of the city—retribution from the Lord (vv. 2–3, except for the interpolation in v. 3b)—and of the prophet, which was also determined by God.

The conclusion regarding these three later additions, created by a later redactor, is that the original story added to the "biography" consisted only of Nebuzaradan's speech to Jeremiah (40:2–3a, 4–5), as in the abridged version preserved in the LXX. The prologue to Nebuzaradan's words (v. 2a) is unique linguistically. The preposition ל should be understood as having the sense of את (compare 2 Sam 3:30; Job 5:2) and the phrase should be read ויקח רב טבחים את ירמיהו

---

231. Despite the close connection between the words דיבר and כאשר דיבר, this prophecy is nevertheless truncated and detached from its original context. Thus, for example, there is no explanation for the words הדבר הזה (v. 3b), which seem detached from any context. Accepting Bright's and Holladay's proposal also requires emendation of the beginning of Nebuzaradan's speech in v. 4.

232. The language of the phrase, the idea it expresses, and even its linguistic character parallel the prophecy in chap. 44; but more than the immediate parallel of this specific phrase is involved. Note a comparison of 40:3b and 44:23a:

. . . כי חטאתם לה' ולא שמעתם בקולו והיה לכם הדבר הזה.
. . . ואשר חטאתם לה' ולא שמעתם בקול ה' . . . על כן קראת אתכם הרעה הזאת.

On the phrase חטאתם לה', compare also with Deut 9:16, and on the expression ולא שמעתם, see also Jer 42:21 (and cf. Deut 1:43; 9:23). It should also be noted that the expression הדבר הזה is characteristic of the book of Jeremiah, occurring in the book 16 times.

('and the commander of the guard took Jeremiah'). The parallel to 39:14 makes it clear that the text's intention is to allude to Jeremiah's removal from prison; however, neither the release itself nor the place where Jeremiah is brought is described, and the sequence of verbs in 40:2 ("and he took . . . and said . . .") demonstrates that the focus is on Nebuzaradan's speech.[233] Nebuzaradan's opening words are that the fate of the city has been decided by God (v. 2bβ), and what God has determined is exactly what has come to pass (v. 3a).[234] This is the backdrop for the release of Jeremiah from his chains (v. 4a)[235] and the presentation of his options.[236] The first option: to go with Nebuzaradan to Babylon and receive preferential treatment there. The second option: to remain in the land of Judah and join Gedaliah, son of Ahikam.[237] It appears that the third option offered to Jeremiah, "or go wherever you please" (v. 5aβ), is simply exaggeration: it deviates from the circumscribed framework of the first two offers.

Without waiting for the prophet's answer, the captain of the guard sends for Jeremiah, and gives him a "present."[238] We are not told what Jeremiah decided until the summary in v. 6: "Then Jeremiah went to Gedaliah, son of Ahikam, at Mizpah." This verse connects the story to the account of what happens to

---

233. The justaposition of the two verbs ויקח and ויאמר emphasizes the direct speech of the prophet after his release from prison. The similarity between this sequence of actions and the sequence in Jeremiah's meetings with Zedekiah (37:17; 38:14) cannot be ignored. This parallel again underscores the intention of contrasting the behavior of Nebuchadrezzar and his officials to the actions of Zedekiah and his officials.

234. The verb ויבא at the beginning of v. 3 is difficult to explain. It may be connected to the verb ויקח at the beginning of v. 2. The fact that it is omitted from the LXX may be because it was deleted precisely because it was a problem. It is also hard to explain the deletion of the words כאשר דיבר; see the solutions suggested by Janzen 1973: 22, 53; and Holladay 1989: 270.

235. The verb פתחתיך is unique here. For the word אזיקים, see also 40:1. The fact that the word occurs only in these two verses supports the idea that the expansion of the heading (40:1) is borrowed from here (40:4).

236. There is linguistic symmetry between the two options: "If it seems good to you to come with me to Babylon . . . if it does not seem good to you to come with me to Babylon. . . ." In the LXX, everything after the second condition ("if it does not seem good . . .") is missing, and the result is that Jeremiah's second option is presented in v. 5. It is reasonable to conclude that, in the course of later editing, the sentence offering options was expanded, and both parts of it were blended into a single structure, followed by a sentence intended to emphasize the difference between Jeremiah's fate and the fate of the nation (Holladay 1989: 270). The hyperbole that Nebuzaradan employed in his offer "behold, all the land is before you" also appears to be a later addition, as does the phrase אל הטוב ואל הישר. It should be noted that the word-pair טוב and ישר is widespread in Deuteronomistic literature and almost without exception may be taken as an identifying marker peculiar to this literature. The expansion in v. 5 is also very hyperbolic: Gedaliah is appointed "over the cities of Judah."

237. For suggestions for emending the text, see Holladay 1989: 270–71.

238. Compare this phrase with Gen 43:34; 2 Sam 11:8; Ps 141:2; Esth 2:18; etc. It appears that the specific sense of the term is a gift from a man of high rank to someone of lower rank (Hoffman 2001: 715). The food is missing from the LXX and again appears to be an editorial elaboration intended to emphasize even more the honor lavished upon the prophet and the importance attached to him by the Babylonians.

Gedaliah in Mizpah (40:7–41:18), which was probably composed by the first redactor of the biography.

I conclude, then, that Jeremiah's history after the destruction is presented in
a brief, focused, concise account. It incorporates Nebuzaradan's speech, which
included an additional version of Jeremiah's release from prison and his transfer
to Mizpah by the Babylonians. The linguistic similarity between the descriptions
and the similar details that they incorporate are evidence that both were based
on a known fact: Jeremiah was taken from his place of imprisonment by senior
Babylonian agents, sent to Gedaliah, son of Ahikam, who was in Mizpah,[239] and
finally, "[Jeremiah] stayed with him among the people [who were left in the
land]" (39:14; 40:6). The difference between the two accounts is a result of the
time when the source was written, the author's knowledge of the details of the
events, and the extent to which he reported details—for example, the Babylonian personalities who were involved, the exact place from which the prophet
was taken, and so on.[240] Both of these sources had already been integrated at the
time of the redaction of the biography. At a later stage, a more extensive redaction took place, in which the story was edited as part of the general redaction
and organization of the entire book.[241]

The main goal of the editor of the biography was to contrast the fate of Jeremiah with the fate of the House of David, Jerusalem, and its inhabitants. To
achieve this purpose, the editor placed 39:11–12 immediately after the description of the destruction of Jerusalem and before the account of Jeremiah's release
from prison. Both versions of Jeremiah's release were included, in vv. 13 and 14.
These different versions were blended by changing the names of the officials and
adding the name of Nebuzaradan. In consequence, a scenario was created in

---

239. At this point, there is a problem with the historical reconstruction because, from this
time onward, the prophet "disappears," and he reappears only in chap. 42, when the "remnant"
of the people is found, apparently in the area of Bethlehem (according to 41:16). There is no
suggestion that the prophet was present at the assassination of Gedaliah, and he was not the
person who sounded the warning of danger. Accordingly, one might ask whether Jeremiah
really was at Mizpah. On the other hand, transferring Jeremiah to Mizpah fits the Babylonian
inclination to support moderate elements after they conquered Judah. The Babylonian objective was to restore the land to a normal status as quickly as possible while assuring fealty to
themselves. A person of Jeremiah's stature, who apparently was highly influential at least among
certain circles in the country and who they knew was the person who led the campaign against
war with Babylon, advocating submission, was certainly the right person for the Babylonian
plan. By sending Jeremiah to Mizpah, the Babylonians intended to encourage popular support
for the new government and to give Gedaliah religious and moral support.

240. The possibility that both authors knew the details of the event, but only one of them
incorporated it into his narrative, must be considered. For the purposes of the discussion here,
however, there is no significant difference between the two possibilities.

241. This stage of redaction is marked by clear Deuteronomistic features and can be connected with the the the fifth century B.C.E. redaction, when the structure of the book and its essential shape were formulated. I connect it to Albertz's second Deuteronomistic book of Jeremiah
(2003: 315–18, 332–39); and see below.

which the "captain of the guard" acted in concert with "all the officials of the king of Babylon" to secure Jeremiah's release from prison in the "court of the guard."[242]

Jeremiah had called for surrender to the Babylonians. To underscore the difference between those who opposed and those who supported Jeremiah's call, the prophecy to Ebed-melech the Cushite (39:15–18) was added at a later stage. The interpolation of this prophecy created a problem in the narrative sequence because, according to the heading (v. 15b), it was spoken when Jeremiah was still incarcerated in "the court of the guard."[243] However, this difficulty only serves to highlight the central message of the prophecy: Ebed-melech was rescued from the fate shared by the city and the people in it because he had trusted in the Lord (v. 18bβ).[244]

The prophet's fate is portrayed in the narrative as an extremely important sign of the justice of his ways, and his release therefore demonstrates "divine justice." The destruction is presented as retribution to those who did not heed repeated warnings. God's concern for the fate of those who followed Jeremiah (including Ebed-melech, the Cushite) emphasizes the importance of Jeremiah's position. It seems, then, that the prophet's release from prison was ideologically important. No doubt other people, perhaps even groups, received similar treatment; however, the focus on Jeremiah's experiences, detached from the wider historical context, is evidence of the importance that the author assigned to the prophet's fate.

In light of the message at the center of the narrative, we may conclude that it was written during the exilic period, perhaps very shortly after the destruction of Jerusalem. The story is ambivalent toward the Babylonians. The major attitude promoted is acceptance of their authority because there was no way to contest it. Any attempt to resist would have been a futile risk of lives. The Lord would reward those who waited patiently and did not try to fight, so *patience* and *forbearance* were the key words. In my opinion, this text should be assigned to the first edition of the book of Jeremiah, parallel to Albertz's first Deuteronomistic edition, even though Albertz has made a distinction between the main corpus of oracles in chaps. 1–25 and the narrative tradition about Jeremiah in chaps. 26–45 (Albertz 2003: 312–18; 327–39, with further literature). I see it only as a difference in genre, and Albertz himself, while noting this, admits that "it [= the first edition] was probably [from] the same group of Deuteronomistic redactors" (2003: 315).

---

242. The repetition of the verb—וישלח (v. 13a) and וישלחו (v. 14a)—highlights the editor's purpose, which was to create a coherent sequence of events (Rofé 1988: 209–10). On the place of v. 13 in the redaction of the text, see Janzen 1973: 118; and Holladay 1989: 269.

243. There are two places where this prophecy could have been inserted: after 38:13 (Rudolph 1947: 229) and before 38:28a (Holladay 1989: 281).

244. A generally-accepted conclusion is that the prophecy was moved here to emphasize its fulfillment and also to underscore the difference between the fate of Jeremiah and Ebed-melech, the Cushite, and the fate of Zedekiah and his supporters (Volz 1928: 344; Rudolph 1947: 229; Kessler 1965: 285–86; Clements 1988: 226–27; Hoffman 2001: 704).

The origins of the second narrative are more popular, and its content reveals the great importance that its author attributed to Jeremiah. The difference in the portrayal of Jeremiah is so great that it is clear that the stories were written at two different times. The later story was written when the prophet's image had expanded to dimensions unknown in the earlier stories (Rofé 1988: 211–12).

No allusion to the fall of the Babylonians occurs in Nebuzaradan's speech; they are depicted as being at the pinnacle of their power. On this basis, we may theorize that this story also originated not later than the middle of the sixth century B.C.E. Apparently it was a popular tradition among Jeremiah's followers and admirers in the years after the flight to Egypt.[245] This fact may also imply an earlier date for the first redaction of the entire sequence and, furthermore, that the sources available to the redactor were diverse. Some of these sources no doubt were a biography of Jeremiah, folktales about him, passages from his prophecies, and segments of the Deuteronomistic narrative about the fate of the king, temple, and capital city—all incorporated into a single narrative sequence.

5.2.2c. The Source and Purpose of the Descriptions of the Destruction of Jerusalem

We possess three works describing the destruction of the kingdom of Judah, and they are similar in language and content (2 Kgs 25:1–21; Jer 39:1–10; 52:4–30). The descriptions of events in 2 Kgs 25:1–21 and Jer 52:4–30 are identical in most respects, and the differences between them are not significant.[246] Jer 39:1–10 parallels the other two texts only in the description of the destruction of Jerusalem, but it does not have the accompanying lists. This text is clearly inferior when compared with the other two sources, and the only additional information it contributes concerns the actions of the Babylonian king's officials during the conquest, which is in effect part of the account of Jeremiah's transfer to Mizpah (39:3).[247]

In my opinion, the original description was composed by Dtr² a short time after the destruction of Jerusalem in order to complete a historical supplement to the earlier Deuteronomistic composition. The text of Jeremiah 52 was based on Dtr²'s narrative and was secondary to it.[248] The description in Jeremiah 39 is

---

245. If so, this second edition should stand in the middle, between Albertz's second and third editions (2003: 315–27, 332–45). In my opinion, assuming that his first and second editions are simply two faces of the same, first Deuteronomistic edition, dated to the first generation of the exile, this second edition should be dated to the second generation of exiles. I agree with Albertz regarding the third edition.

246. In Jeremiah 52, a census of the deportation was added (52:28–30), as well as information on Zedekiah's fate (52:11b). This information is not present in the LXX, for ideological reasons (Rofé 1997: 180–84; 1998: 225). The list of temple vessels carried off to Babylon is more complete in the 2 Kings version (25:17–22).

247. This piece of information has generally been seen by scholars as an addition by the editor of Jeremiah's biography (and see below).

248. The prevalent theory is that chap. 52 is a "historical supplement" and should be seen as such (Hoffman 2001: 869–70). The theory that the author of this supplement made use of

later,[249] is dependent on the description in chap. 52,[250] and drew upon it some time later, after the revisions of Jeremiah 52 and 2 Kings 25 had already been made (Rudolph 1947: 243; Clements 1988: 223–24; and Holladay 1989: 280). The objective of the editor who interpolated this passage into the description of Jeremiah's history (chap. 39 of the MT) was to fill in the information on a period for which the editor had no information on the fate of the prophet.[251] At the same time, the editor's objective was to show how the prophecies that spoke

the Deuteronomistic account contrasts with the view that there is no connection between the descriptions of the destruction of Jerusalem in Kings and Jeremiah or that both texts quote a common source (Rofé 1988: 116–19, 208; Cogan and Tadmor 1988: 320–21). In my opinion, there was no chronistic source embedded in the accounts in 2 Kings 25 and Jeremiah 52. The argument that there was a systematic, uniform chronistic body of writing that described the Babylonian siege, the destruction of Jerusalem, the Babylonian exile, and the short time of Gedaliah's rule in Mizpah (Noth 1954: 74) is based on the analogy that scholars drew between the description of the destruction (2 Kgs 25:1–21 and Jer 52:4–27), the description of the era of Gedaliah (2 Kgs 25:22–26 and Jer 40:7–41:18), and the assumption that both descriptions originated from the same source. On this subject, see, e.g., Rofé 1988: 116–19; and Seitz 1989: 264. I do not believe that there is any evidence either of chronistic writing of this type or of the insertion of such a document into the Deuteronomistic history.

249. It was Noth (1943: 74, 137–38 n. 60) who first argued that the description of the destruction of Jerusalem in 2 Kings 25 was later, secondary, and dependent on Jeremiah 37–39 (see: Thiel 1981: 54 n. 12 and Seitz 1989: 240–73). This position is no longer accepted by most scholars. As stated, vv. 1–2, 4–13 are missing from the LXX and are apparently a very late addition to the text (Janzen 1973: 118; Tov 1981: 154; Holladay 1989: 269, 280; see also above, in §5.2.1). Many have explained the lack of this section as the result of homoioteleuton, the copiest's eye having skipped from the words שרי מלך בבל to the words רבי מלך בבכל (Kessler 1965: 287; Rofé 1988: 209–10, and n. 36). It is difficult to accept this argument, not just because of the size of the missing text or the problem with assuming that the MT is superior to the LXX, but primarily because of the character of the section and the need for it that was created by the lack of information about the fate of Jeremiah during this period.

250. The major dispute has focused on the question of whether this account was taken from 2 Kings 25 (see, e.g., the opinion of Mowinckel 1914: 24 n. 2; Volz 1928: 342; Pohlmann 1978: 105; Thiel 1981: 54–55, and n. 12; Cogan and Tadmor 1985: 321; Seitz 1989: 240, 263) or from Jeremiah 52 (see, e.g., Rudolph 1947: 243; Wanke 1971: 110; Clements 1988: 223–24). A comparison of the texts suggests that the second possibility is better. In Jeremiah 39, the king of Babylon is נבוכדראצר (as in 52:4), not נבוכדנאצר (as in 2 Kgs 25:1); see Janzen 1973: 70. In the description of the siege in v. 1, the verb is plural (ויצורו) as in 52:4 (ויחנו), in contrast to 2 Kgs 25:1, in which it is singular (ויחן). The use of the verbs יברחו ויצאו in v. 4 is parallel to 52:7; they do not appear in 2 Kgs 25:4. The use of the third-person singular וידבר in v. 5 is parallel to v. 9 and contrasts with the plural person used in 2 Kgs 25:6. The mention of חורי יהודה 'nobles of Judah' in v. 6 is parallel to שרי יהודה in 52:10; they are not mentioned in 2 Kings 25. The citation of the place where the sons and officials of Zedekiah were slaughtered (v. 6) is parallel to 52:10 and is not mentioned in 2 Kings 25. There is only one parallel between 2 Kings 25 and Jeremiah 39: the use of the third-person singular in v. 4 (ויצא), parallel to וילך in 2 Kgs 25:4 and in contrast to the plural form (וילכו) in Jer 52:7. This parallel can be explained as a reworking and adapting of the text to fit the sequence.

251. The information contained in Jeremiah's life story is relevant to the account of his stay in the court of the guard on the eve of the destruction and following the destruction of Jerusalem (see Jer 37:21; 38:28; 39:14). Bearing this in mind, it is likely that, seeing a gap in information, the author wanted to expand Jeremiah's story at the time of the destruction.

of the burning of the city and Zedekiah's unsuccessful attempt to escape the Chaldeans were being fulfilled (38:17–18, 22–23; Clements 1988: 223–24). The section recounting the fate of the king (vv. 4–7) was reworked for this purpose and the part that describes the fate of the city (v. 8) focuses on how the Babylonians burned it.[252] In view of this, it is difficult to accept Pohlmann's view that the author of this description (the biographer) had no interest in the destruction of Jerusalem but wanted to move on quickly to the story that took place afterward. Jeremiah is not mentioned in the account of the days of Gedaliah either, which is an extended section that also seems to be supplying the missing passages that preceded the flight to Egypt (Pohlmann 1978: 106). The explanation offered by Lohfink—that the account is very selective and therefore skips the story of the destruction—also ignores the nature of the biographical source, which is characterized by filling in gaps in information and using a combination of other sources (Lohfink 1978: 332).

The development of the destruction narrative may be described as follows:

> A description of the destruction of Jerusalem was written by Dtr² in Babylon, a short time after it took place.

> The description of Dtr² was placed in the concluding chapter of the book of Jeremiah. The "appendix," telling of the release of Jehoiachin, is also drawn from the Deuteronomistic work. Alongside these, another source is embedded, summarizing part of the deportation from Judah. These are the bits of information with which the redactor chose to end the description of the life of the prophet; if this be the case, it appears that the redaction was completed some time after the release of Jehoiachin but before the Return to Zion. We may conclude that this chapter was written in Judah or in Egypt after 560 B.C.E. but before the collapse of the Babylonian Empire (539 B.C.E.).

> A later redactor of the version that eventually evolved into the Masoretic version noticed that information concerning the prophet's life at the time of the destruction of Jerusalem was missing from the biography. He inserted passages from the account of the destruction that he found in chap. 52 into the right place in the "biography."

---

252. The fundamental reworking of the text is noticeable in the abridgement and conciseness of the description, the translation of terms from 2 Kings 25 and Jeremiah 52 (ויצררו instead of ויחנו; חורים instead of שרים), an inclination to be overly precise (in the description of the king leaving the city in 39:4a; adding Nebuchadrezzar and the name of the city, Riblah, in v. 5; attributing the slaughter of the sons of Zedekiah to Nebuchadrezzar himself in v. 6), and

5.2.2d. The Source and Purpose of Writing the Descriptions of
   the Time of Gedaliah

The period during which Gedaliah ruled in Mizpah is recounted in two versions: a brief version, consisting of 5 verses (2 Kgs 25:22–26), and a longer version, consisting of 28 verses (Jer 40:7–41:18).[253] From the beginning of research
on this subject, scholars have investigated the linguistic and literary connection
between the two versions. Opinion has been divided on the source, date, and
nature of the connection between the versions as well as on the purpose for
which they were written.

(1) The Source and Date of the Description

Scholars take three primary approaches to determining the source of the
account of Gedaliah's reign. Wanke contended that the version preserved in
2 Kings is reliable and original and preferable to the version found in Jeremiah
(Wanke 1971: 114–15). His line of argument has not been accepted by others,
most of them seeing the version in 2 Kings as a later supplement and not part of
the story of Jerusalem's destruction. This "appendix" is foreign to the preceding
chapter, both linguistically and in literary style, but is connected to the "appendix" that follows it (2 Kgs 25:27–30), which describes the release of King Jehoiachin.[254] In addition, others have noted the linguistic and thematic unity of the
version in Jeremiah, and this tends to witness against the possibility that it was
an expansion of the brief version in 2 Kings.[255]

These points formed the basis for the theory commonly accepted by scholars
that the version preserved in Jeremiah is original and that it also served as the

an evident desire to make the story more fluent and readable. This type of reworking is characteristic of the later editor of MT Jeremiah. This editor was especially skilled at adding names
and titles and attempted to improve the credibility of the tale through the precision of the description (see above, §5.2.1a). Nonetheless, the later insertion of the destruction account created a problem for the editor with regard to the chronology of the account because, according
to this version, Zedekiah escaped from Jerusalem only after the officials of the king of Babylon
sat in the middle gate (39:3). This event took place after the city wall was breached (v. 2). The
attempt to incorporate the addition, beginning in v. 4, by means of the story of Zedekiah's
flight only "when he saw them" (i.e., the officials of the Babylonian king, who were sitting in
the gate of Jerusalem) is forced and demonstrates the sort of adjustment that this later editor
was forced to make when he inserted the description.

253. There is a clear connection between the two episodes; cf. 2 Kgs 25:23–24 = Jer 40:7–9;
2 Kgs 25:25 = Jer 41:1–3; 2 Kgs 25:26 = Jer 41:16–18 (and cf. also 43:5–7).

254. See the discussion above, §5.1.3 (pp. 295–299). As stated, the two "supplements" at
the end of the book of Kings were added to the account of the destruction during the middle of
the sixth century B.C.E., in order to demonstrate the need to accept Babylonian supremacy.
Both supplements present the benefits of following this policy: the continued presence of the
nation in Judah under the rule of Gedaliah and the release of Jehoiachin after 37 years of imprisonment.

255. See Rofé 1988: 114–15. An analysis of parallel verses in 2 Kings 25 and Jeremiah 40–
41 supports this view, because it shows that the later editor of 2 Kings needed to adapt and create connections for the principal verses that he selected from the expanded story (see below).

basis for the summary in 2 Kings 25.[256] The major problem with this viewpoint is that the literary features of the account of Gedaliah are different from those of Jeremiah's biography. The prophet himself is never mentioned,[257] and none of his prophecies are incorporated into the account.

With this in mind, I find a third theory preferable, namely, that the two versions in 2 Kings and Jeremiah are based on a single source (de Boer 1970: 71–79; Cogan and Tadmor 1988: 326; Rofé 1988: 114–15). The redactor of the biography used this source in its entirety, or perhaps a fuller version of it,[258] and the author of the later "appendixes" of the book of Kings apparently adapted that same source and abridged it to just a few verses.[259]

---

256. Many scholars have subscribed to this view: Montgomery 1951: 564–65; Kremers 1953: 126–28; Gray 1964: 770; Nelson 1981: 86; Jones 1984: 630; Würthwein 1984: 479–80; O'Brien 1989: 271; Smelik 1992: 98; Hoffman 2001: 716. Even those who supported 2 Kings 25 as the original source emphasized the superiority of the version of Gedaliah's reign as it was presented in Jeremiah; see Baltzer 1961: 37; Zenger 1968: 17; Dietrich 1972: 140; Pohlmann 1978: 110–11; 1979: 94–109; and Thiel 1981: 54–55 n. 12, 61. Note that the occasional argument that, if the author of 2 Kings had been quoting from the book of Jeremiah, we would have expected him to mention the prophet's name cannot be sustained (Klausner 1949: 8–23; 1953; Seitz 1989: 219). It should be noted that Noth (1981: 74, 138 n. 71) also was part of this stream of scholarship, if we consider his view that the entire destruction account was written by Dtr, based on the description in Jeremiah (except for the account of Jehoiachin's release from prison in vv. 27–30, which he believed was based on the author's personal knowledge). A direct derivative of Noth's opinion is presented by Seitz (1989: 198–200, 274 n. 190) as part of his theory of the late composition of 2 Kings 25, based on sources available to the author in Babylon. According to Seitz, the account of Gedaliah's reign is based on an exilic chronicle preserved in an expanded (and perhaps complete) version in Jeremiah and in an abridged version in 2 Kgs 25:22–26. See below for counterarguments to this theory.

257. Jeremiah is not mentioned even at the story's climax, that is, either on the eve of Gedaliah's murder or after the murder; see de Boer 1970: 71–79; Cogan and Tadmor 1988: 326; Rofé 1988: 114–16; Seitz 1989: 219.

258. See the discussion of the biography below, which identifies the biography as the outcome of a complex process of redaction that involved bringing together different sources in order to create a unified, sequential account of the prophet's life story. Jeremiah himself appears only within the frame of the narrative: in two versions describing his arrival in Mizpah (39:14 and 40:1–6) and in the account of his descent to Egypt with the Judeans escaping from Benjamin after the murder of Gedaliah (chaps. 42ff.). If this is correct, then the account of Gedaliah's rule may be seen as supplementing information missing from the prophet's biography, similar to the destruction account, when Jeremiah was in the court of the guard. In my opinion, another factor that led to the account's being incorporated into the biography is that the period was characterized by great hopes for restoration of the nation, hopes that were contingent on the personal qualities of Gedaliah. The information about the prophet's presence in Mizpah, the known connection between the family of Shaphan and Jeremiah, and the ideological and political sympathy shared by the two families explain why this extensive chapter does not seem out of place within the narrative sequence of Gedaliah's reign. It also serves the literary and ideological purposes of the biography's editor, and more than anything else, provides justification for the policy that Jeremiah had urged from the beginning of his career. This point is of great importance when we consider the attitudes expressed toward the province of Judah and the the "remnant" of Judah, in contrast with the Babylonian exiles.

259. Theoretically, one could postulate that the book of Kings contained a revision that was then embedded in the biography of Jeremiah. However, in my opinion, a linguistic analysis

Identifying the account of the Gedaliah's rule as an independent source raises several questions. What was the original form of the account? Where was it written? Where was it preserved until its incorporation into Jeremiah's biography and into the supplement to the destruction account in 2 Kings? Rofé identified this source as "a chronicle of the kind written by royal scribes, which in this case recorded the events of the destruction of Judah" (1988: 116–17). However, I think that this identification should be rejected for three major reasons:

a. It is difficult to argue that the writing of chronistic accounts continued to be connected to the House of David after the status of the Davidic line in Judah was neutralized and the elite of the nation were sent into exile.

b. This source is not connected, either thematically or linguistically, to the account of the destruction of Jerusalem, and it does not deal with this event. Its focus on the period immediately after the destruction highlights its uniqueness and underscores its difference.

c. Ideologically, this source presents a different point of view, one that is even opposed to the perspective of the account of the destruction of Jerusalem composed by Dtr[2]. I will return to this point in my discussion of the various historiographical approaches to the period, but it must be said, at this point, that the account of the days of Gedaliah is unparalleled in its "anti-David" attitude.[260]

I believe that this source can be viewed as a story written to articulate an idea: those who remained in the land under the leadership of Gedaliah had an excellent chance to rebuild life in Judah and put it on a firm footing. Gedaliah's leadership generated a popular response among the "remnant of Judah," including a willingness to pay the price for life under Babylonian rule. However, the opportunity vanished when Ishmael assassinated Gedaliah.

This idea is expressed in the narrative's heading,[261] especially in the protago-

---

of the episode in 2 Kings and Jeremiah shows that the version in Kings is based on the original source. In several respects, this version represents the source most reliably. An example of this may be seen below, in the discussion of the language of Gedaliah's oath in the two versions. This evolution of the source's form in Jeremiah and Kings was examined by Seitz (1989: 198–200, 274 n. 190).

260. This bias is echoed in biblical literature from the Persian Period (see below, §5.4), but I think that this is the most definitive example of anti-Davidic ideology in the book of Kings. See also Hoffman 2000: 108–9.

261. On the basis of a comparison of the headings in 2 Kgs 25:23a and Jer 40:7 and a comparison of the MT with the LXX of Jeremiah (Janzen 1973: 53), we may conclude that the original heading of the episode was similar to the heading preserved in 2 Kings: *וישמעו כל שרי החילים המה ואנשיהם כי הפקיד מלך בבל את גדליה. When the heading was inserted into Jeremiah's biography, geographical details were added (אשר בשדה . . . . בארץ . . .), as well as the expansion in v. 7b. At a much later stage, after the split between the MT and the original Hebrew source of the LXX, the name of Gedaliah's father (בן אחיקם) was added to the book of Jeremiah, and the description of the remnant in Judah was expanded, with the addition of 'טף' and 'דלת הארץ' (cf. 41:16; 43:6; etc.). The purpose of the redaction of Jeremiah is reflected in the last addition:

nists upon whom it focuses:[262] Gedaliah symbolizes those who were willing to accept Babylonian rule in order to ensure continued life in Judah; the *army officers* symbolize the remnant of Judah's military force[263] who chose to join the restoration process;[264] *Ishmael, son of Nethaniah*, was a scion of the royal family and an associate of the king of Ammon, and he turns out to be the person responsible for stopping the restoration process.

to make it match the description of the remnant of Judah in 2 Kgs 25:12; Jer 39:10; 52:16, while ignoring the initial purpose of the redaction, which was to present the remnant as a nation whose chances for restoration were good and as a "trust" committed to Gedaliah.

262. The story focuses only on Gedaliah, the army officers, and Ishmael, while neglecting others who were present at Mizpah and took part in the events. The stereotyping of the characters, who are presented as representatives of various ideological camps prevalent among the people, reveals the author's objective, and his aim is to highlight the message: the chance that once existed for restoration was destroyed by the murder of Gedaliah. For a literary analysis of this episode, with a study of the motif of inversion among the main protagonists, see Hoffman 2000: 109–13.

263. On the title שר, see the discussion above, p. 57 n. 78. The title שר החיל (plural, שרי החיל or שרי החילים) appears twice in the abridged version in 2 Kings (25:23, 26) and five times in the expanded version in Jeremiah (40:7, 13; 41:11, 13, 16; cf. their occurrence in the next chapter of the biography: 42:1, 8; 43:4, 5). Apart from these occurrences, the title appears seven times in 2 Samuel (24:2, 4); 1 Kings (15:20); 2 Kings (9:5); Nehemiah (2:9); and 2 Chronicles (33:14). These occurrences indicate that the term refers to army officers of various ranks. It is likely that the term did not refer to a senior officer, for whom the title שר הצבא was reserved (see Josh 5:14; Judg 4:7; 1 Sam 14:50; 2 Kgs 5:1; etc.), but rather to various ranks under his command. See the discussion by Rütersworden 1985: 34–38, with further literature. In view of this identification and the information on the שרים later in the story, I think that the term here referred to leaders of small combat groups that roamed throughout Judah after the defeat, perhaps refusing to accept the Babylonian victory or perhaps out of fear of a Babylonian reprisal. It is also possible that some of these groups engaged in guerilla warfare against the Babylonians (Bright 1965: 253; Harrison 1973: 160; Feinberg 1982: 272; Thompson 1980: 654; Davidson 1985: 135). There is no information on the location of these groups during the long Babylonian siege of Jerusalem: they may have been scattered throughout Judah; they may have been in Jerusalem during the siege and escaped from the city at some point (cf. 2 Kgs 25:5; Jer 52:8); and they may have managed to survive near the city after it fell (Holladay 1989: 295; Hoffman 2001: 720). Logically, and on the basis of historical parallels, we may conjecture that the main area where they roamed was on the eastern fringes of the Judean highland, the Judean Desert, and Transjordan; at least for the Transjordanian area, there is additional evidence of the presence of Jewish refugees (see Jer 40:11, 13; 41:10, 15).

264. The sweeping generalization כל שרי החילים intends to encompass the entire military force remaining in Judah after the destruction. The author chose to focus on these army officers as symbolic of those who opposed Gedaliah. By reporting their willingness to join Gedaliah in Mizpah (especially given the risk that they were taking upon themselves, inasmuch as the Babylonian reaction was unknown), the author finds support for the path of national rehabilitation upon which Gedaliah had embarked, and he emphasizes the broad popular support that this policy enjoyed. In reality, it is clear that the situation was different, because it is known that other military officers arrived in Mizpah. Conspicuous among these was Jezaniah/Azariah, son of Hoshaiah, who is mentioned in Jer 42:1; 43:2 (see also Jer 40:11–12 and its parallel to the story, linguistically and ideologically). The attitude of the army officers toward Ishmael and his actions is not clear from the account in 2 Kings, but from the brief note that associates Ishmael with the House of David, it appears that his interests were different and that he did not represent the rest of the officers, who later went to Egypt.

The theme of restoration is conveyed primarily in the words of Gedaliah's oath:[265] life in Judah under the Babylonians is possible if there is willingness to accept their authority. The key sentence appears almost unchanged in both versions (2 Kgs 25:24aβ–b; Jer 40:9aβ–b):[266] "Do not be afraid of the Chaldean officials; dwell in the land and serve the king of Babylon, and it will be well with you." It appears that this statement correctly reflects the reality in Judah immediately after the destruction of Jerusalem.[267]

---

265. The idea of rebuilding life in Judah under Babylonian rule is contained in both the abridged (2 Kgs 25:24) and expanded versions (Jer 40:9–12) of Gedaliah's oath. It should be noted at this point that an oath is usually presented in the Bible to reinforce a certain fact or a promise that has been made. The usual wording in such cases is . . . להשבע ב, with the name of God as the object of ב, and/or . . . ל להשבע, in which case the individual or group of people (Num 14:23; Josh 9:19–20; etc.) marked by ל is the one(s) to whom the oath is given (Gen 26:3; Ps 132:11; etc.). Linguistically, there is a significant difference between the version in 2 Kings ("and he swore to them . . . and he said to them . . .") and the version in Jeremiah ("and he swore to them . . . saying . . ."). The former could mean that the wording of the oath is not actually reported—only the statement after the oath is reported; the latter, however, contains the reported speech, that is, the wording of the oath itself. On this basis, scholars have reasoned that the wording of the oath is not given in 2 Kings (Bright 1965: 253). However, this is difficult to accept, because the combination of the two verbs להשבע and לאמר appears frequently before the actual words of an oath, both in the form that the two verbs take in 2 Kings (parallels in 1 Sam 20:3; 1 Kgs 1:29; etc.) and in the form they have in Jeremiah (parallels in Num 31:10; Deut 1:34; Josh 14:9; 1 Sam 28:10; 2 Sam 3:35; 1 Kgs 2:23; etc.). I think it likely that there has been a corruption of the text in 2 Kings, resulting from the second verb being forced into a form that mimics the first (וישבע להם . . . ויאמר להם); on this point, the version in Jeremiah is closer to the original source. The repetition of the pronoun in Kings (להם . . . להם) seems superfluous, but it also does not necessarily indicate that the wording of the oath was not reported, and it is more likely that it points to a textual corruption in Kings. Finally, note that in Gedaliah's oath there is no mention of ritual activity or reference to the name of a deity. Holladay (1989: 296) proposes linking the oath to the meal mentioned in Jer 40:1, but this proposal has no support. The absence of religious elements in the oath highlights the nature of the story and the fact that Gedaliah was the Babylonian king's appointee; his authority originated with the Babylonians, and it was in their name that he also took his oath.

266. Apart from the marginal difference between ויטב in 2 Kgs 25:24b and וייטב in Jer 40:9b, the significant difference between the two versions is in the phrase אל תראו מעבוד הכשדים 'Fear not the servants of the Chaldeans' (2 Kgs 25:24a), in contrast to אל תראו מעבוד הכשדים 'Fear not to serve the Chaldeans' (Jer 40:9a). Many scholars prefer the version in Jeremiah (see, e.g., Cogan and Tadmor 1988: 326), but, in my opinion, the version in 2 Kings is closer to the original source—because LXX Jeremiah supports the text in Kings (Streane 1986: 250; Holladay 1989: 271), and the phrase in Jeremiah does not flow smoothly with the rest of the text, creating an unnecessary redundancy: אל תראו מעבוד הכשדים שבו בארץ ועבדו את מלך בבל 'Fear not to serve the Chaldeans; dwell in the land and serve the king of Babylon'. In contrast, the narrative logic in Gedaliah's speech in the Kings version is straightforward, and it harmonizes with the source's goal of emphasizing the need to overcome fear of עבדי הכשדים 'the servants of Babylonians' and to accept their rule as a condition for continued life in the land (see below). Compare the expression עבדו את מלך בבל with the words of Jeremiah in 27:12 and 17.

267. I note that with these words Gedaliah is also expressing a literary objective that apparently derives from the original story: this is an introduction to the story of Gedaliah's murder and the flight to Egypt that followed, with an emphasis on the importance of conquering fear of

In my opinion, it is very likely that a story of this kind was written close to the time these events took place, and that most of it is based on firsthand observation. This conclusion is based on details that appear in the story:[268] on the sympathy expressed toward Gedaliah and the restoration that he represented, on the deep disappointment over his murder, and on the hostility expressed toward the murderer and those who had sent him.[269] The fact that God is not mentioned in the account is connected to the time and place where it was written as well.[270] Additional support for the idea that the account's origin is temporally and spatially near the destruction may be found in the fact that the entire episode took place within a short period of time, immediately after the destruction of Jerusalem, and ended quickly after the murder of Gedaliah and the flight of some of the inhabitants of Mizpah and its environs to Egypt.

We have no way of knowing whether the author of this narrative was one of those who fled to Egypt, because the description of the flight to Egypt was already part of the biography of Jeremiah, which placed the prophet and his experiences at the center of the narrative. However, the pessimistic ending of the account, emphasizing that the land was being emptied of its inhabitants, the various details about those who left the country, and the account's concentration on the Bethlehem region all support this conclusion.

---

the Babylonians so that the restoration can proceed. This account also meshes well with the description of the consequences of the murder: the main motive for the flight to Egypt is "because they feared the Chaldeans." Thus, Gedaliah's terrible failure to achieve the primary goal that he set for himself is emphasized.

268. My conclusion is based on the list embedded in the story: the names of the army officers who arrived at Mizpah. Some of the officers are mentioned later in the story and others are not, which creates the appearance that the list was compiled on the basis of the personal knowledge of someone who was there and who described the events he witnessed. Even the description of the actual number of soldiers that came to Mizpah could have been written by someone who was there and saw what happened. Ishmael, son of Nethaniah, arrived in Mizpah with ten men (2 Kgs 25:25; Jer 41:1–2); after a battle with the men of Johanan, son of Kareah, "and all the army officers who were with him" (Jer 41:11), Ishmael fled to the king of the Ammon with eight men (Jer 41:15).

269. The description of events is vivid, and the author clearly identifies with the feelings of the protagonists whose exploits he describes. Thus, for example, fear of the Babylonians is portrayed with great intensity, both in the context of Gedaliah's need to calm the army officers who arrived in Mizpah (2 Kgs 25:24; Jer 40:9) and in the great fear that gripped them after the murder of Gedaliah (2 Kgs 25:26; Jer 41:17–18). Presumably, the general mood that prevailed during the period of Gedaliah's rule was great apprehension toward the Babylonian forces, who had recently devastated Jerusalem and deported its inhabitants.

270. There is a striking difference between Dtr²'s theological judgment regarding the last kings of Judah and the avoidance of mentioning God by the compiler of Gedaliah's. If the hypothesis that each of these accounts was written in a different location is correct, then we might be able to draw a distinction between the different theological views that prevailed among the remnant of Judah and among the exiles. On this subject, see the discussion below; for another perspective, see the views of Albertz (2003: 282–84, 322–27).

(2) The Purpose for Placing the Account in the Books of
Jeremiah and Kings

The account of the rule of Gedaliah has been preserved, apparently close to
the original version, in Jer 40:7–41:18. The redactor of Jeremiah's biography inserted it from a source available to him and used it to supplement a lacuna in information about the prophet. As mentioned, there is no reference to Jeremiah
himself even once in the story. However, linguistically[271] and narratively[272] it
was deftly embedded within his biography.

The redactor's expansions of the text in the heading of the story (Jer 40:7a)
and the addition of v. 7b were intended to serve his ideological purpose: emphasizing the contrast between the advocates of surrender to Babylon and those
who opposed it. In keeping with the generalizing tendency of the source, according to which "all" of the army officers heard that the king of Babylon had
appointed Gedaliah governor (2 Kgs 25:23a; Jer 40:7a), the redactor of the biography created a geographical separation between the two sides by precisely defining the place over which the Babylonians had appointed Gedaliah ("in the
land")[273] and the location of the army officers when they heard of the appointment ("in the fields = open countryside").[274]

---

271. The beginning of the story in question (וישמעו) is linguistically parallel to the sequence of images related in 38:1, 7 and the beginning of the passage in 40:11–12. The description of Gedaliah's role in Nebuzaradan's speech (40:5) connects well with the description of his
role in the narrative itself (v. 7). On the theory that, in both cases, this is an editorial comment, I conclude that it is a link created by the editor between the two stories he embedded.

272. In terms of narrative sequence, the editor found two versions of Jeremiah's arrival at
Mizpah immediately after the conquest of Jerusalem (see §5.2.2b). In the parallel stories of the
prophet's release—both the biography and the popular tale—there is a description of Jeremiah's transfer to Mizpah, his being delivered to Gedaliah, and his stay with Gedaliah בתוך
העם 'among the people' (39:14; 40:5–6). Later on, the descent to Egypt, which is also described
beginning with chap. 42, is connected with the time of Gedaliah because, according to this account, the flight to Egypt came about due to the people's fear of Babylonian reprisal for the
murder committed by Ishmael, son of Nethaniah. First among those fleeing to Egypt was Johanan, son of Kareah, who had fought Ishmael (see below). The prophet himself, who "disappears" before the beginning of the story of Gedaliah's rule at Mizpah (41:7), is mentioned again
only during the journey to Egypt (chap. 42); thus, the sequence is well laid out. This chapter is
chronologically located at a pivotal point between the fall of Jerusalem and Jeremiah's journey
to Egypt together with some of the remnant of Judah (chaps. 42ff.).

273. In the prophetic language, as in the prose language of the book of Jeremiah, the word
ארץ has a specific meaning whenever it follows the prepositional ב 'in': it refers to the settled
part of the country, both agriculturally and demographically (cf. 3:16; 4:5; 7:7; 14:4; 16:3; 23:5;
32:15; 42:10).

274. The word שדה appears in the story several times. The word mainly was used for remote
and isolated places, generally contrasting with centers of settlement. In the case here, the objective is to juxtapose those who were "in the field" with Gedaliah, who was appointed "in the
land" (see previous note). In 40:13, the meaning is even more explicit: to describe the coming
of "the army officers who were in the field . . . to Gedaliah in Mizpah." This may have been the
meaning also in 41:8, where "the stores in the field" were set off against the pit in the midst of
the city (41:7, and see below). This usage is also found in the language of Jeremiah's prophecies;

The addition of the heading (v. 7b) highlights Gedaliah's camp. The redactor repeats the verb הפקיד 'appointed', which was used in relation to the news that the army officers had just heard (v. 7a) and gives it additional significance, defining the population over which Gedaliah had been appointed.[275] The reference to the men and women who had been committed to his jurisdiction[276] stands opposite the general statement about "all the army officers" and reinforces the impression of two parties confronting one another. The object of this addition was to highlight the new motif on which the story is based: the motif of restoration. The appointment of Gedaliah over the land and the commitment to him of "men and women . . . who were not carried away captive to Babylon" marks the beginning of the restoration in the land under Babylonian rule.

*   *   *

The narrative of the time of Gedaliah's rule in 2 Kgs 25:22–26 is one of two "appendixes" added to the account of Jerusalem's destruction (see above, §5.1.3). In both of these "appendixes," the viewpoint expressed is later and different from the perspective found in Dtr²: it appears that the shock of the destruction of Jerusalem and the deportation of the nation's elite has passed. Thus, for example, there is no reference to the fate of either Jerusalem or Zedekiah, the destruction and deportation are portrayed as faits accompli, the time of Gedaliah is described in the past tense, and Jehoiachin is depicted as both the leader of the nation and the hope for renewed national life. Nonetheless, these two "appendixes" belong

---

thus, for example, he sets the "field" in opposition to Jerusalem in order to demonstrate the scope of sin (13:27). The field in 14:5 is presented as a wild uncultivated place, compared with "the land," which is the agricultural area (v. 4), etc. Compare these verses with, e.g., 2 Sam 11:11; 14:18.

275. The meaning of the phrase הפקיד אתו is 'to deposit for safekeeping' (cf. Lev 5:23; 1 Kgs 14:27; Isa 10:28; Jer 36:20; 37:21; Ps 31:6; 2 Chr 12:10). The literal meaning of the sentence is that the "poorest people" were committed to Gedaliah for safeguarding. The play on words involving הפקיד, used of Gedaliah's appointment as governor, and the same word used for committing the people into his custody is important for the ideological point that the editor wished to make: it emphasizes the role that the Babylonians intended for Gedaliah to play in restoring life in Judah after the destruction and the great hope invested in him by the remnant in Judah. This beginning suggests the direct connection between Gedaliah's murder (chap. 41) and the flight of the remnant to Egypt (chaps. 42–44) later in the story.

276. In the LXX, the words וטף ומדלת הארץ are lacking, and the text refers only to "the men and women who were not carried off to Babylon" (Janzen 1973: 53). We might conclude that the intention of the original text was to emphasize that there was a civilian population with Gedaliah and that his main objective was to rehabilitate this population (Bullah 1984: 498). This could be a later expansion based on 41:16 (with its emphasis on "women and children"; cf. also the expansion in 43:6 and later in 39:10), the purpose of this expansion being to elaborate on the picture and to describe the remnant as precisely as possible. Bright's suggestion (1965: 237), connecting the expression דלת הארץ with accounts of the destruction and seeing it as an attempt to identify those who remained in Judah, cannot be supported. As previously stated, this phrase is a later addition to the entire narrative, and this definition of the remnant in Judah is contrary to the narrative's general purpose.

to exilic times: the Babylonians are portrayed as the only political power in the region, and there is no reference to the rise of the Achaemenid dynasty, the fall of Babylon, or the Return to Zion (cf., e.g., Ezra 1; 2 Chr 36:20–23).

The release of Jehoiachin from prison, after 37 years (2 Kgs 25:27), points to the central ideological message that the author wished to convey to the exiled generation: to be patient is advantageous; it is profitable to accept the Babylonian yoke; and hope for the future depends on the nation's ability to understand and accept its circumstances. The summary of the more extended narrative about Gedaliah (25:22–26) contains a similar message and was also intended for the second generation of the exile.[277] It presents the possibility of restoration for those who remained in Judah, should they decide to accept Babylonian hegemony and Gedaliah's leadership. Nonetheless, the structure of this episode[278] and its emphasis on the end of Gedaliah's time and the flight to Egypt is, in my opinion, evidence that these "appendixes" were redacted in Babylon as an extension of the composition of Dtr². The message, too, is aimed primarily at those living in Babylon. The emphasis on the remnant's fear of the Babylonians after the murder of Gedaliah and the remnant's flight to Egypt is different from the message addressed to the remnant in Judah in the book of Jeremiah and from the depiction in the biography of Jeremiah.

---

277. The heading of the account of Gedaliah in 2 Kgs 25:22 is the only part that has no parallel in the more expanded narrative in Jeremiah, and it is at this point that the reason for the story's embedding becomes most clear. All of the details presented in the heading also appear in the introduction to the story in its full version, Jer 40:7; this also points to the source for the abridged story in 2 Kings and its connection to the expanded version in Jeremiah. In addition, the heading and the narrative framework that it creates is different from the summary of the story that appears in the middle. The remnant of Judah referred to in the heading as the subject of the story ("and the people that remained . . . whom Nebuchadrezzar had left . . . he appointed over them . . .") and also mentioned at the end of the story when the land was emptied by the flight to Egypt (vv. 26: "And all the people arose . . . and went . . . for they were afraid") is not mentioned in the body of the story at all. The account concentrates on what happened to Gedaliah and the army officers (Gedaliah is mentioned five times in three verses, and the army officers and their men, including a reference to them in third-person plural, are mentioned five times; in addition to this, they are cited by name). All of these details highlight the sharp shift between the heading (v. 22) and the summary of the story. The tendentiousness of the heading and the way that the editor used it to make his objectives evident by incorporating the supplement into the destruction account are clear from three additional points: (a) the disproportionate ratio between the relatively long introduction (a whole verse) and the short story that follows; (b) the exaggerated importance attributed to the remnant of Judah, reflected in their detachment from the destruction events and the change in attitude toward them in v. 22, in contrast with the attitude toward them in vv. 12, 21b; (c) the assertion that the person who left the remnant in the land and appointed Gedaliah over them was Nebuchadrezzar, not the "captain of the guard," as reported in v. 12.

278. In terms of the structure of this story, it is striking that it is composed of two short, different stories that revolve around the person of Gedaliah and the fate of the remnant of Judah, although the temporal relationship between them is not clear: the appointment of Gedaliah and his early activities (vv. 22–24); the murder and the flight of the remnant of the people to Egypt that followed (vv. 25–26).

5.3. *Summary: The Date of the Historiographical Accounts*

In §5.1, I discussed the development of 2 Kgs 23:22–25:30. The main conclusions drawn were that Dtr² composed the basic work in Babylon soon after the destruction of Jerusalem. This text was supplemented by two "appendixes" in the middle of the sixth century B.C.E., apparently between 560 and 539 B.C.E. It is not clear where these two "supplements" were composed, but it seems likely that both came into being in Babylon. However, in §5.2.2d, the description of Gedaliah's era was attributed to a different source, which was also written a short time after the destruction of Jerusalem (at the same time as Dtr²), but apparently in Judah. The account of Jehoiachin's release from prison was written after the event, but before Persia conquered Babylon. The logical conclusion is that it was written in Babylon. At a later stage, after a long interval beginning with the Return to Zion, various nomistic supplements were added to the text, as well as reactions to the account in the appendixes. It is not clear where these supplements were created, but they reflect the viewpoint and interests of those who returned to Zion.

In §5.2, I discussed the development of Jeremiah 37–44. The main conclusions were that Jeremiah's biography was based on the work of an author who was part of the prophet's inner circle, perhaps Baruch. We postulated that the source materials for the biography were composed in Egypt[279] a short time after the murder of Gedaliah. Alongside the biography were other traditions and stories about the prophet. We hypothesized that these stories grew gradually and eventually crystallized into what is now known as the "biography." However, because they contain no allusion to the decline of the Babylonian Empire, which is still portrayed as the primary power in the region, it appears that they were written before Babylon's rapid collapse and conquest by Persia (539 B.C.E.). The redaction of the biography was also completed before the fall of the Babylonian Empire; its objective was to stress the need to accept Babylonian sovereignty and to continue life under Babylonian rule. A later redactor used the sources available to him. One source was the account of the destruction of Jerusalem in Jeremiah 52 that had been copied previously from a description by Dtr². Another source was the account of Gedaliah's time, which, as stated, was composed in Judah a short time before he was assassinated. The basic text of the biography was composed in Egypt, and the stories about the prophet also circulated there. It is difficult to know for certain where the text was edited but, considering the unequivocal message about the population leaving the country, it is not likely

---

279. Theories regarding the sources of stories composed in Babylon and in Egypt can also be based on the differences between genres. Apart from the story of Gedaliah, there is no contact between the two works; each follows its own course and is based on its own sources.

that the redactor lived in Judah; it may have been edited either in Egypt or in Babylon.[280]

The sources and dates of the texts are summed up in Table 5.1 (p. 350).[281]

5.4. Babylonian Rule, the Destruction of Jerusalem, the Exile and the Remnant in Judah: Perceptions and Trends in Biblical Historiography

5.4.1. The Compositions from the First Generation after the Destruction of Jerusalem

Authors from the first generation after the destruction of Jerusalem who lived in Judah, Egypt, and Babylon perceived Babylonian rule, the destruction, the exile, the remnant in Judah, and the status of the House of David in different ways. The objective of this section is to identify these perceptions and to pinpoint their time and place.

5.4.1a. Perceptions about and Attitudes toward the Rule of Babylon

The account of Gedaliah's time and the biography of Jeremiah reflect a tendency toward reconciliation with Babylonian authority. These sections emphasize the possibility of national rehabilitation under Babylonian rule immediately after the destruction of Jerusalem. The centrality of this message in both descriptions was stressed above, and it is clear that their authors opposed all kinds of political activism.[282] Jeremiah supported this ideology and may have been one of the party's leaders before the destruction of Jerusalem.[283]

---

280. For a summary of the history of research on this question, see Seitz 1989: 289–91. Identifying and interpreting the "Akkadianisms" tends to support claims that the story was composed in Babylon (Eph'al 1993: 20).

281. This table is designed to summarize the discussion above in §§5.1–2. The chronological division is arbitrary and schematic and is intended to distinguish three time periods: the first generation after the destruction of Jerusalem, the second generation of exile (between the mid-sixth century B.C.E. and the fall of the Babylonian Empire), and the period of the Return to Zion (primarily the late sixth and early fifth century B.C.E.). As the table shows, there was extensive literary activity during the exile, when the biography of Jeremiah was composed in the form familiar to us today. The implication is that the date 560 B.C.E. is a decisive chronological limit for the creation of Jeremiah 52, though it is possible that the biography was composed several years earlier.

282. That both compositions had a common objective is what enabled the first editor of the biography to combine them into a single literary sequence. The emphasis on this idea is evidence that the author of the account of Gedaliah's rule was part of the ideological circle to which both Jeremiah himself and, later on, the editor of the biography belonged; however, it may also show that this ideological perspective was prevalent among a much wider circle of the remnant in Judah.

283. Anti-political activism had characterized Jeremiah's prophecies from the beginning of Babylon's appearance in the region (605 B.C.E.).

Table 5.1. Summary of the Dates and Sources
of the Historiographical Descriptions

	586–560 B.C.E.	560–538 B.C.E.	538 B.C.E. and onward
Babylon	The account by Dtr²: 2 Kgs 23:22–23 23:26–37 24:1–12 24:15–20 25:1–11 25:13–21	2 Kgs 25:22–26 (?) (the source for these verses was written in Judah) 2 Kgs 25:27–30	2 Kgs 23:24–25 (nomistic addition) Supplements to Dtr²: 2 Kgs 24:13–14 25:12
Judah	The source for the account of Gedaliah's rule in Mizpah. Apparently, this source is reflected in Jer 40:7–41:18, except for the expansions and supplements added by the redactor of the biography.		Final Deuteronomistic edition of the book of Jeremiah.
Judah/ Egypt	The biography of Jeremiah (the basic text): Jer 37:11–21 38:14–28 39:3, 13–14 Chaps. 42:1–43:7 (except for editorial comments and later supplements)	Addition of the story of Gedaliah to the biography of Jeremiah: Stories added to the biographical text: Jer 38:1–13 40:2–3a, 4–5. Redaction of the biographical text, including the source text, stories that were added, and various supplements: Jer 37:1–10 39:1–2 39:4–12 39:15–18 40:1, 3b, 6. Jeremiah 52 (the source for this account was composed by the Deuteronomist in Babylon—2 Kings 25).	

In both accounts, the idea is expressed in a similar fashion. The narrative of
Gedaliah's time tells of the Babylonians' positive relationship with the remnant,
and the opportunities for restoration are presented in sympathetic detail.[284]

---

284. The Babylonians' positive attitude toward the remnant in Judah is expressed in the
account of the "rumor" heard by the military officers, "that the king of Babylon had made Gedaliah governor" (2 Kgs 25:23; Jer 40:7) and in the rumor that reached the refugees in Transjordan, "that the king had set over them Gedaliah, son of Ahikam, son of Shaphan" (Jer
40:11).

This perspective is expressed in Gedaliah's words to the army officers (2 Kgs 25:24; Jer 40:9); it is a characteristic motif of the entire story, the theme being the beginning of the restoration process—until the assassination of Gedaliah brings the process to a brutal end. It is nevertheless obvious that the army officers who come to Gedaliah are apprehensive of the Babylonians. This fear impels them to flee to Egypt after the assassination, and I think that the text reflects this fear as being prevalent among "the people who remained." Their attitude toward the Babylonians immediately after the destruction of Jerusalem had two focal points: fear, based on their knowledge of the past, coupled with hope for the future.

Within the biography, the prophecy of Jeremiah delivered just before the flight to Egypt (Jeremiah 42, particularly vv. 10–12) reflects his attitude toward the Babylonians. The prophet outlines the opportunity for restoration. Just like the narrative about Gedaliah's time, this prophecy also attributes to the Babylonians a favorable attitude toward restoration. On the basis of the chronological sequence, we may theorize that these words were spoken after the assassination of Gedaliah. This attitude toward the Babylonians is also reflected in the stereotypical description of the central characters[285] and in the emphasis on Jeremiah's efforts to convince the king to surrender and thus prevent the destruction of the city.[286] Jeremiah states unequivocally: if the king surrenders, the city will not be destroyed, the king will not be put to death, and his household will be saved (Jer 38:17–18, 20–23). The officials are portrayed as radicals who consistently refuse to reconcile themselves to capitulation to the Babylonians. These officials are victorious over Jeremiah; they succeed in silencing him (v. 27) and preventing the king from surrendering (vv. 24–26). According to the biography, the officials are to blame for the destruction of Jerusalem, and the Babylonians are almost "compelled" to conquer Jerusalem.

After Jeremiah acknowledges that no one has succeeded in convincing the king to capitulate, he calls on the people to accept a reality that cannot be altered. For many years, he struggled to convince the people of his perspective, speaking fearlessly, even when he knew that he was endangering his own life. But when he realized that he had failed and that continued struggle would be fruitless, he gave in and chose to remain silent (Jer 38:27). His choice of silence at this stage reflects a political reality: there was no longer any point in mounting a hopeless struggle, and Babylonian authority must therefore be accepted.

Dtr², in contrast, does not make peace with Babylonian rule. In his composition, there is no expression of positive attitude toward the Babylonians. On the contrary, this account, which had its origin in the Babylonian exile, reveals

---

285. As previously noted, the account focuses on three figures, each of whom represents a one-dimensional perspective.

286. The three encounters between Jeremiah and the king, when he tried to convince Zedekiah to surrender, are pivotal.

strong hostility toward those responsible for the destruction of the land and the deportation of the people,[287] even though both events were carried out at God's command.[288] Dtr² notes that the Babylonians are, after all, an instrument of retribution sent by God. This is not stated to create a positive attitude toward the Babylonians but out of a need to provide a historical, moral, and theological explanation for the destruction.[289] A similar message appears in the consolation prophecies of Ezekiel (chaps. 33–38). The Vision of Dry Bones is his response to the words of "the whole house of Israel," spoken after the destruction of Jerusalem: "Our bones are dried up and our hope is lost; we are completely cut off" (Ezek 37:11b).

5.4.1b. Perceptions about the Extent of the Destruction, and the Purpose behind the Description

Dtr² focuses on the fate of the king and his family, the destruction of Jerusalem, the deportation of those who lived in it, the plundering of the temple vessels, and the murder of 72 of the city's distinguished citizens. Dtr² does not report what was happening in other parts of the country and, thus, I doubt that the summary statement "so Judah was carried away from its land" (2 Kgs 25:21b) faithfully reflects the true state of affairs. In light of the biblical description, in light of the historical reconstruction proposed above (chap. 2), and in light of the archaeological evidence (chap. 4), we know that the Babylonians dealt Judah a severe blow, but we also know that this blow did not entirely empty the land of its inhabitants. The basis for this sweeping conclusion lies in Dtr²'s historiographical and literary objectives (see §5.1.2), which also provide us with a rationale for concluding that the account was composed in Babylon.

This portrait of a land emptied of its inhabitants is also unusual when we compare it with other descriptions from the same period that come from Judah and Egypt. The story of Gedaliah is based on sources from the remnant in Judah. Although it focuses on Gedaliah, son of Ahikam, on a specific group of army officers, and the story of the assassination in Mizpah and its consequences, the story contains evidence of the beginning of the restoration process. Many Judahites returned to the territory of Benjamin and began to settle there, and there is even indirect evidence of the renewal of some kind of ritual activity in the destroyed temple (Jer 41:5). Note that this account contains no reference to the fate of Jerusalem, apart from indirect evidence regarding the fate of the temple

---

287. The attitude toward the Babylonians is reflected, among other things, in the verbs Dtr² chooses to use in his description of the destruction of the city (2 Kgs 25:8–11; 13–21): וישרוף, שרף, נתצו, הגלה, שברו, וישאו, לקחו, לקח, ויקח, ויקח, לקח, ויקח, ויולך, ויך, וימיתם, ויגל.

288. The Babylonians are the שוסים 'spoilers' who bring evil upon Jerusalem (2 Kgs 21:10–16); it is their function to remove Judah from the sight of the Lord (23:26–27).

289. These words refer primarily to the ideological, theological, and historiographical dilemma of the exiles in Babylon.

(see §2.3.4). This is the only point of contact between Gedaliah's story and the version of Dtr², which focuses on the destruction of Jerusalem.

A parallel portrait emerges from the biography of Jeremiah. After the fall of Jerusalem and after the officials of the Babylonian king gather in the gate of the city (Jer 39:3), the prophet is removed from confinement and sent to Mizpah, where Gedaliah, son of Ahikam, is already placed in authority (v. 14). This sequence probably contains some time-gaps, the result of the nature of the story, but it also contrasts the destruction of Jerusalem and deportation of its residents with the ongoing life at Mizpah. This difference between the fate of Jerusalem and the fate of the Benjaminite region is also implied by the verses about the lull in the Babylonian siege of the city, during which Jeremiah tried to leave the city for Benjamin. According to the narrative, he was not alone (see Eph'al 1993: 18–22; §2.2.2 above).

5.4.1c. Perceptions about the Exiles and the Remnant and Intentions behind the Accounts

In the story of the destruction of Jerusalem, Dtr² concentrates on the deportation event itself; there is no reference to "a remnant," and the impression is that the land was emptied of all its inhabitants. The compositions created in Judah and Egypt, in contrast, make no reference to the deportees and focus only on those who remained in the land (at least until some of them leave for Egypt). These distinctions completely expose the difference between the compositions, a difference that stems from the different audiences toward whom the compositions are aimed and the historiographical biases of their authors. In effect, the message resides in the very choice of things on which the accounts focus or ignore. This discrepancy is especially pronounced in a comparison of the beginning of Jeremiah 42, which describes those who remained in Judah (vv. 1–2, 8, etc.) with a section later in the story, which describes the flight into Egypt and the final emptying of the land of its inhabitants (43:4–7). Here, too, we must remember that the account is intended for those who went to Egypt—the very people among whom and for whom the composition was written.[290] The gap between the exiles who went to Babylon and the people who remained is reflected, in all of its bitterness, in the prophecies of Ezekiel, particularly 11:15–21; 33:23–29,[291] and it is against this background that we should understand the prophecy of The Two Baskets of Figs (Jeremiah 24; Hoffman 2001: 483–85).

These prophecies reflect the two main arguments of "those who remained":

---

290. This tendentiousness, which becomes clear from the texts themselves, only reinforces the problematic nature of the reporting and exposes the author's historiographical perception.

291. On these prophecies, see Fohrer and Galling 1955: ix–x; Zimmerli 1969: 201, 817; Eichrodt 1970: 142–44, 436–61; Greenberg 1983: 203–4; Japhet 1983b: 107–10; Tadmor 1988: 50–52; and Rofé 1998: 226. Regarding the date of the prophecy in chap. 11, see Japhet 1983b: 123 n. 19. For the historical background of this prophecy, see Tadmor 1988: 51–52.

1. "Those who remained" viewed the exiles as having sinned and therefore being punished by being deported from their land. This argument recalls Jer 2:5 and highlights the source of the Judahite world view (see the references in Japhet 1983b: 123 n. 21), which apparently was Isaiah's prophecy (6:11–13). In response to this argument, Ezekiel promised (11:17–21) that those deported from their land are destined to return to Israel (vv. 17–20); he prophesied a grim future for "those who remained" (v. 21).
2. "Those who remained" saw themselves as "the people of God." Their presence in the land was fulfillment of the promise given to Abraham (Ezek 33:24). In reply, Ezekiel prophesied that they would be utterly destroyed (vv. 25–29).[292]

Both of these arguments, as well as the prophet's harsh reply to them, reveal the profound ideological rift between the two parts of the nation at this time (see also Rofé 1998: 226). In my opinion, the rift stemmed primarily from the blow to the status of the nation's leaders, who were deported to Babylon, and the attempt by "those who remained" to usurp the leaders' place and their property (see comments of Gedaliah in Jer 40:10) and to continue life without them. It is likely that economics played a decisive role in creating the rift between the "head" of the nation and its "body." Socially, this involved a remarkable shift on the part of the people, who shook themselves free from those who, only a short time before, had been their leaders. It is also likely that the most severe crisis took place in Babylon, the crisis in Judah being less intense (see below).

5.4.1d. Perceptions regarding the Status of Jehoiachin and the Davidic Line, and Tendencies in Portraying Them

In the account of Gedaliah's rule in Mizpah, an anti-David bias clearly emerges. It is prominent in the negative stress placed on the origins of Ishmael, son of Nethaniah, "of the seed royal" (2 Kgs 25:25; Jer 41:1). Positive stress is correspondingly placed on Gedaliah, as though the chances for restoration after the destruction of Jerusalem were completely dependent on him. In any case, the murder of Gedaliah is perceived as eradicating any chances for restoration, and blame is placed unequivocally on a person "of the seed royal."[293] An obvious tendency to criticize the Davidic line also appears in Jeremiah's biography.[294] Zedekiah is portrayed as a weak king who does not have the courage to

---

292. On the connection between these arguments and the prophecies of Second Isaiah and the change these arguments underwent during the exile, see below and see also Japhet 1983b: 110; and Tadmor 1988: 52–53, 54. On the connection to the promise in Genesis 15, see Tadmor 1988: 53 n. 12, with further literature.

293. Ishmael's motives are not made explicit in the account. The text does not elaborate on this subject at all, although there is an allusion to it when he arrives from Ammon (Jer 40:15).

294. On the general tendency in the book of Jeremiah to blame the House of David for the destruction of Jerusalem and the temple, see Hoffman 2000: 108–9.

capitulate to the Babylonians and in doing so save Jerusalem, the temple, and the kingdom. He behaves this way because of his fear for himself (Jer 38:19) and his fear of his own officials (vv. 24–26).[295]

Dtr², who was active among the exiles in Babylon after the destruction and reflected the opinions prevalent among them, evinced a totally different attitude toward the royal house. Although the last four kings of Judah play a central role in the description of the decline leading to the destruction and deportation, the House of David is not mentioned even once in the threats of destruction and deportation. The punishment threatened in these verses generally includes destruction and deportation (2 Kgs 17:19–20; 21:12–16; 23:26–27; 24:3) and refers to the nation, to Jerusalem, and to the temple, but makes no explicit reference to the fate of the royal house. I believe that this demonstrates that, at the time of composition, shortly after the destruction of Jerusalem, Jehoiachin's status was still secure; his close relationship with the nation's elite demonstrated the continuing existence of the royal house and the hope for his ongoing rule. This is also the reason for Dtr²'s literary and ideological contrast between the isolated Zedekiah, on the one hand, whose army was scattered, whose sons were slaughtered before his very eyes, and who was brought blinded to Babylon (25:6–7), and Jehoiachin, on the other hand, who was also brought to Babylon, but was accompanied by his mother, his wives, eunuchs, and soldiers (24:15). The author of the later supplements, who was active in Babylon one generation after Dtr², added a phrase about the fate of Zedekiah: in contrast to וידברו אתו משפט 'and they passed judgment on [Zedekiah]' (25:6b), the release of Jehoiachin is described with the words וידבר אתו טובות 'and he spoke kindly to him' (25:28a).

The continuation of this bias may be seen in the prophet Haggai's paraphrase (2:23) of Jeremiah's words to Jehoiachin (22:24–30). In contrast to the anti-David tendency expressed by Jeremiah, "even though Coniah, son of Jehoiakim, king of Judah, were the signet ring on my right hand, still I would tear you off . . . for none of his offspring shall prosper in sitting on the throne of David and ruling again in Judah," Haggai states, "On that day, says the Lord of hosts, I will take you, my servant Zerubbabel, the son of Shealtiel, says the Lord, and make you like a signet ring; for I have chosen you, says the Lord of hosts."

In summary, it may be said that, after the destruction of Jerusalem and the deportation of the nation's elite, a gap appears between the perception of events in Judah and the outlook prevalent in Babylon. This finds expression in the work of Dtr² in Babylon, and the viewpoint prevalent in Judah and Egypt is expressed in the description of Gedaliah's rule in Mizpah and Jeremiah's "biography." Dtr² expressed reservations regarding the Babylonians, stressed the fact that the land of Judah had been totally emptied, and focused on the destruction of Jerusalem,

---

295. The design of the story, formed by three encounters between the king and Jeremiah and an emphasis on the increasing pressure on the king, only serves to highlight this viewpoint further.

totally ignoring the existence of the "people who remained," and expressing support for Jehoiachin and the House of David. We may assume that these attitudes were influenced in no small degree by the place in which they were written (Babylon), the author's target audience (the exiles), and the time when the composition was written (soon after events took place).

In contrast, the compositions that were written in Judah (the description of Gedaliah's rule) or in Judah/Egypt (the "biography" of Jeremiah) expressed utterly different historiographic purposes. They focused on the "remnant" in Judah and made no mention of those who had been deported to Babylon. There is no mention of Jerusalem, and the arena of events is the Benjamin region. Here we find the first significant evidence of an anti-Davidic tendency and identification of the House of David as being responsible both for the destruction of Jerusalem and the failure of the restoration process afterward. These writings call for accepting the yoke of the ruling power and underscore the futility of actively resisting its supremacy. The composition written in Judah outspokenly acknowledges Babylonian authority as a condition for rebuilding national life under its domination. According to this work, rehabilitation is an option recognized by the Babylonians and may occur at any time.

5.4.2. *Writings from the Second Generation after the Destruction of Jerusalem*

During the second stage of literary development, an ideological rapprochement between texts composed in Babylon and those composed in Judah and Egypt developed. It is likely that this reflected an extended process of adjustment to the need to acknowledge, accept, and live with Babylonian authority. The most obvious expression of this development is in the addition of the "appendixes" (2 Kgs 25:22–30) to the account composed by Dtr². This addition was made between Jehoiachin's release from prison and the rise of Persia and decline of Babylon, and its central message is the need to accept Babylonian domination, which would permit life to go on.

A synopsis of Gedaliah's reign reveals that it focused on the possibility of restoration offered to the remnant in Judah, on condition that they submit to Babylon and obey the primary directive (v. 24): "Fear not to be the servants of the Chaldeans; live in the land and serve the king of Babylon, and it shall be well with you." The assassination of Gedaliah caused the flight of the people to Egypt and the loss of this opportunity. In the description of Jehoiachin's release from prison after 37 years (2 Kgs 25:27), with its emphasis on his elevated status (vv. 28–30), an important message was delivered to the exiles in Babylon: accepting Babylonian authority and demonstrating the patience and willingness to continue to live in exile under Babylonian rule can be profitable. In exile, too, it is possible to live in dignity and to rehabilitate national life. In this short description, there are suggestions of the great expectations that were stirred among the exiles when Jehoiachin was freed, and it may have been this event that impelled the exiles to make peace with life in exile, at least temporarily.

These data show that the exiles in Babylon in the mid-sixth century B.C.E. expressed historiographical messages similar to the ones that were transmitted in Judah in the first generation after the destruction of Jerusalem. For the author of the "appendixes," it was important to emphasize the possibility of ongoing life under Babylonian rule. He demonstrated this by reporting one episode that took place in Judah and one that took place in Babylon, which demonstrates the all-inclusive nature of the message: it was not contingent on living in one place or the other. Furthermore, this is the first time that "the people who remained" are mentioned in a passage connected with the destruction of Jerusalem, as part of a historiographical text composed in the Babylonian exile. In fact, the author of the "appendixes" acknowledges the existence of people who remained in Judah.

It is also likely that Jeremiah's biography was edited in the middle of the sixth century B.C.E.; during this time, the folk stories and supplements composed by the redactor were appended to it. If this is true, it is evidence that during the mid-sixth century B.C.E., literary material was being sent to the various Judahite diaspora, and texts were being copied and reworked. Both in the folk stories and in the redaction of the text, the central message was that the people should accept Babylonian rule and take advantage of the opportunities for restoration that the Babylonians afforded (Jer 39:15–18; 40:1, 2–3a, 4–5, 6). Opposing Babylonian rule was hopeless and would lead inevitably to disaster.

In summary, it may be said that a great change took place during the Babylonian exile in the perception of Babylonian rule and in the ways that authors and editors described it. The portrayal shifts from a terminal view of the destruction and deportation to a recognition of the possibility of restoration under Babylonian rule, both in the exile and in Judah. A realization began to dawn on the second-generation exiles: opportunities for rehabilitation hinged on their willingness to accept Babylonian rule. In this way, Deuteronomistic historiography at a later stage "adopted" Jeremiah's political world view: if the reality was that there was no realistic chance of fighting a superpower, Judah was obliged to maintain a moderate stance and not be drawn into activism of any kind.[296]

This realization has resulted in the ideological unity that is reflected in the historiographical texts, which probably also reflects the ideological unity of the various segments of the people. This unity did not contradict hope for the fall of Babylon, which some of the people felt, but it marked a return to the moderate

---

296. Similar perceptions, although from different perspectives and in another literary form, may be found in the consolation prophecies of Second Isaiah. The idea that Jerusalem "has received of the Lord's hand double for all her sins" (Isa 40:2) attests to the process of adjustment and the growth of unconditional hope for future redemption. Some moderation is reflected in Isaiah's words on the debate between the remnant and the exiles regarding who "the people of God" are.

and sober political thinking that had characterized the kings of Judah during most of the life of the kingdom.

5.4.3. *Additions to Biblical Historiography after the Return to Zion*

After the Return to Zion, the reworking of ancient biblical historiographical sources and the books of prophecy continued. New ideological nuances were added, and ancient messages were interpreted according to the spirit of the era.

In the biography of Jeremiah, there are no specific verses or stages that can be attributed to this period. In contrast, within the Deuteronomistic account, several later additions have been identified. Most were inserted into the original composition (Dtr¹), most conspicuously the nomistic redactional layer (DtrN).[297] Most of the supplements that belong to this redactional layer were inserted into major historical junctures that already existed in this ancient work (Dtr¹), but two central verses that belong to this layer (2 Kgs 23:24–25) were inserted into the later Deuteronomistic text (Dtr²). These verses explain the decline toward destruction and the nomistic understanding of the Josianic reform.

Two other primary supplements to this text (Dtr²) have been identified in the passage about Jehoiachin's deportation (24:13–14) and in the description of the destruction of Jerusalem (25:12). The subject of these verses is unusual, as are their language and intent. Except for a pronounced preoccupation with the temple vessels, their significance lies in their marked polemic regarding "those who remained in the land." The specific point made is that the leadership went into exile with Jehoiachin, while in Judah only the "the poorest people of the land were left" (24:14b). The remainder of the elite was deported after the destruction of Jerusalem, and those who were left behind were again "some of the poorest people of the land," left to serve as "vinedressers and fieldworkers" (25:12). These verses were added into an existing "seam" in the text, between two earlier statements (2 Kgs 25:21b and 22).[298] The verses describe the status of those who remained in the land in a fashion diametrically opposed to the "appendix" that begins in 25:22. Instead of the comment that "the people remained in the land of Judah" (v. 22a), the later supplement states that only "some of the poorest people of the land" were left (v. 12a). Instead of describing Nebuchadrezzar, king of Babylon, as the one who permitted the people to remain (v. 22a), the later supplement states that it was the chief of the guard (v. 12a). Instead of reporting that the king of Babylon had given permission for the people to maintain autonomous life under Gedaliah's rule (v. 22b), the later supplement states

---

297. For a summary of the verses that belong to this layer, see O'Brien 1989: 281–84.

298. On the one hand, the account penned by Dtr² ends with the general statement that the land was completely emptied of its inhabitants (25:21b). On the other hand, the later "supplement" begins with the simple statement that "the people that remained in the land of Judah" were permitted to maintain autonomous life in Judah (25:22).

that the poorest people of the land were allowed to remain for a limited economic reason only: to be "vinedressers and fieldworkers" (v. 12b).

The perspective of those who returned to Zion is represented in these verses. Their goal was to minimize the significance of those who remained in Judah and to amplify the importance of those who returned (Seitz 1989: 178–80). I believe that an ideological development, unknown in earlier texts, was underway at this juncture. It was not a confrontation about rights to the land or about the punishment of those who went into exile and or about those who remained in the land. Instead, this was a struggle regarding the role of the elite, who were trying to return and assert themselves over those who remained. This confrontation could have developed only after the Return to Zion, and it is evidence that the remnant of Judah was unwilling to accept the leadership of the returnees.

Summary

The main purpose of this summary is to synthesize the various subjects and themes discussed in this book: to integrate the major historical processes of the ancient Orient between the late seventh and late sixth centuries B.C.E. with the processes in Judah; to present the relationship between the major geopolitical processes and the primary stages evident in the material culture; to highlight the sixth century B.C.E. as the period that connected the late First Temple Period with the Persian Period; and to describe the historical background of the historiographical accounts and to discern the context of the ideological, religious, and national messages expressed in these works.

*   *   *

During Assyrian rule over the region comprising Syria and Palestine (740–627 B.C.E.), the national and political system was altered—shaped by the economic, military, and strategic interests of the empire. The Assyrians destroyed most of the kingdoms of the region, including the largest territorial kingdoms (among these, the kingdom of Israel), annexed their territory, and turned them into provinces, exiling extensive segments of the population and settling exiled people from other remote areas in their stead. Thus were these kingdoms obliterated from the annals of history. It was only near the border of Egypt that the Assyrians permitted some small vassal kingdoms an independent existence, though only under constant supervision and while forcing them to pay high taxes. The economy of these states was part of the economic system of the Assyrian Empire. Philistia and Transjordan were kingdoms of this kind—as was Judah, a small, marginal, mountainous kingdom. The harsh blow that Judah suffered in the expedition led by Sennecherib (701 B.C.E.) left it smaller and weaker than ever before.

The long reign of Manasseh (698–642 B.C.E.) witnessed the golden days of the Assyrian Empire. Judah benefited from the economic prosperity of the entire region and participated in the wide-ranging commercial opportunities that had developed with the encouragement of the Assyrians. The economic boom climaxed in the border regions: the Jordan Valley, the Judean Desert, and the Beer-Sheba–Arad Valleys. In the southern Judean hills and in parts of the Shephelah that remained within the jurisdiction of Judah, a slow rebuilding began after the devastating consequences of Sennacherib's campaign. The northern part of the

Judean highland recovered more quickly, and the Benjamin region thrived, reaching its peak in the late Iron Age. During this period, Jerusalem maintained its status as the primary city of the kingdom. The number of residents grew, as did the city's wealth and splendor. Around the city, a large, densely-populated block of settlements was established, including unwalled neighborhoods, farms, large villages, and forts. Jerusalem and its environs became a separate district within Judah, and this reality became part of the memory of the miraculous deliverance of the city during Sennacherib's expedition. Within the circles of the Jerusalem elite, there was increasing support for the idea that Jerusalem was chosen by God and that his eternal promise protected it from affliction and foe.

Nonetheless, the borders of the kingdom of Judah during the reign of Manasseh were more constricted than during the time of Hezekiah. The western border of the kingdom ran through Eshtaol–Azekah–Lachish, the same line that existed after the expedition of Sennecherib. In the east, the border of Judah remained the Jordan River–Dead Sea line; in the north, the boundary ran from Geba to Mizpah; and in the south, the border ran through the line of fortresses in the Beer-Sheba and Arad valleys.

The Assyrian Empire collapsed in a rapid series of events, primarily because it failed to put a complete end to the uprisings that repeatedly broke out in Babylon. Assyria's domination of Babylon (747–626 b.c.e.) accelerated the unification of the inhabitants of the ancient urban centers with the Aramean and Chaldean tribal groups who lived in and around the southern Mesopotamian cities and eventually led to the formation of a coalition during Nabopolassar's reign. The death of Aššur-etel-ilāni (627 b.c.e.) marks the "point of no return" in the collapse of Assyria. Several months later, Nabopolassar formally ascended the throne (the 26th of Marheshvan, Nov. 22/23, 626 b.c.e.), establishing the Neo-Babylonian kingdom. By 620 b.c.e., Nabopolassar had managed to extend his rule over the entire land of Babylonia, and with this base he was able to threaten Assyria's very existence. The Assyrian Empire's collapse accelerated during the rule of Sin-šar-iškun (627–612 b.c.e.), and it is likely that, by the beginning of his rule, Assyria had retreated from all of its holdings in Ḫatti-land.

At this time, the 26th (Saite) Dynasty, which had been created with Assyrian aid, was in power in Egypt, and it became stronger under Psammetichus I (664–610 b.c.e.). Within a few years (perhaps as early as 656 b.c.e.), Psammetichus succeeding in uniting all of Egypt under his control; he was sufficiently powerful to make the transition from protectorate of Assyria to independent king and was apparently regarded an ally. As Assyria collapsed, beginning in the second decade of the seventh century b.c.e., the 26th Dynasty succeeded in imposing itself as the heir to Assyrian power throughout Syria and Palestine.

In the period between Assyria's decline and withdrawal from its holdings in Ḫatti-land and the establishment of Egyptian control over the region, Josiah (640–609 b.c.e.) took advantage of the resulting void in the political arena to impose his religious reforms. During this time, in support of the ideology prevalent in Jerusalem after the collapse and retreat of Assyria, the Deuteronomistic history (Dtr¹) was created, narrating the history of the nation from Joshua until Josiah and expressing a world view based on the legal principles found in Deuteronomy, stressing the importance of observing them. At the center of this composition is the explanation for the destruction of the Northern Kingdom, Israel, and faith in God's eternal promise to the House of David—both of which are an outgrowth of a long ideological development that began with the destruction of the kingdom of Israel and Sennecherib's invasion and ended in the optimistic era between the rule of Assyria and the rule of Egypt.

Notwithstanding, the "intermission" granted to Judah was brief indeed. It is likely that, in the first years following Assyria's retreat from Ḫatti-land, the Egyptians rapidly extended their own control over the small kingdoms that had managed to survive Assyrian rule, among them the kingdom of Judah. Josiah was apparently an Egyptian vassal in his final years. It is likely that, even so, he was granted some latitude with regard to the central highland region, because Egypt had a special interest in the coastal area, and the inhabitants of Samaria had not yet crystallized into any permanent political framework. Nonetheless, we should not assume that there were any real changes to the kingdom's boundaries, particularly in the Shephelah, because Egypt would not have permitted a foreign power to rule an area of such strategic importance. At best, Josiah may have been able to extend Judah's northern border slightly, to the Bethel–Ofra line.

By 616 B.C.E., Psammetichus I had come to the aid of the Assyrians, apparently because Egyptian interests favored the existence of a weakened, reduced Assyria as a buffer between the areas it controlled in Syria and the rising forces of Babylon and the Medes. Egyptian assistance was not sufficient. In the summer of 614, the army of the Medes destroyed the city of Aššur, and, two years later, in the summer of 612, the Babylonians and Medes destroyed Nineveh. The last Assyrian king, Aššur-uballiṭ II, took the throne in Ḫarran, and the Babylonians quickly established their rule over all Assyria. In the winter of late 610–early 609, the last Assyrian center was captured, after the Egyptian king, Necho II, failed in his attempt to come to the aid of the Assyrians, a few months after he took the throne. Assyria bowed off the stage of history, and the Euphrates became the boundary between Egypt and Babylon.

The year 609 was the beginning of a new era, with Egypt and Babylon now struggling for ascendancy in Ḫatti-land. The two powers faced each other on opposite sides of the Euphrates; as Babylon continued to extend its control over the areas east of the Euphrates, the Egyptians continued to position themselves as the only empire in Syria–Palestine. They concentrated most of their attention on Philistia, the land corridor to Egypt; the "Via Maris," that is, the coastal ports of Palestine; and Phoenicia. It is not clear what steps were taken by Psammetichus and Necho to solidify their rule in central and southern Syria, but it seems that, after the final disappearance of Assyria, they did not have enough time to consolidate their control all the way along the Euphrates. The military initiatives that Necho II took in 608–605 attest to the great importance that he attributed to this region. However, the rapid conquest of the entire region of Syria and Palestine by Nebuchadrezzar (605–604) is evidence that, when the first Egyptian line of defense was penetrated along the Euphrates, the entire line of defense fell, and Necho was forced to withdraw inside the borders of Egypt.

The beginning of direct Egyptian-Babylonian conflict in 609 B.C.E. was also the beginning of the decline toward destruction for the kingdom of Judah, a direct result of its geopolitical position between the two mighty empires. However, this slide was assisted by the reckless policies pursued by the kings of Judah, as well as the political and religious unrest among the various circles of the Jerusalem elite. The nationalistic activism of these people, who were unwilling to accept Egyptian hegemony, probably was what set in motion the events that led to the killing of Josiah at Megiddo by Necho II, his goal being to aid the Assyrians in their final battle for survival at Ḥarran (August/September 609). This orientation toward nationalism also led to the choice of Shallum-Jehoahaz, the younger son of Josiah, as successor instead of Eliakim, his older brother. When Necho II returned from the battle at Ḥarran three months after Josiah was killed, he did not allow Jehoahaz to remain on the throne but instead exiled him to Egypt. He then appointed Eliakim in Jehoahaz's stead, changed his name to Jehoiakim, and levied a heavy tribute on Judah. Nothing is known of what happened in Judah during the 4 years between 609 and 605 B.C.E. However, the tiny Judean kingdom's proximity to Egypt, which controlled the entire region, gave Judah no political or military latitude. Thus, Jehoiakim was left with no choice other than to be a loyal vassal of Egypt.

The events of the summer of 605 B.C.E. dramatically affected the history of the region for the next 66 years. The heir to the Babylonian throne, Nebuchadrezzar, defeated the Egyptian army at Carchemish and managed to advance as far as central Syria. His first 2 years of rule, after the death of his father in late summer of 605, were marked by the Babylonian assumption of control over all of Ḥatti-land. Because the political administrative structure of Syria and the northern part of Palestine were already deeply engrained, and there were no longer any kingdoms or population-groups with distinct national identities, Nebuchadrezzar succeeded in establishing his control in this region with relative ease. In the latter half of 604, all of the remaining kings in the western section of the Empire capitulated, including Jehoiakim, the king of Judah. Apparently, after Egypt retreated from the region, and in the absence of any counterweight to Babylonian power, all of the potentates in the region understood that they had no other choice. The king of Ashkelon was the only one who did not correctly evaluate the shift in the international balance of power, and the bitter fate of that city was useful to the Babylonians as a lesson to other kingdoms of the region.

There is no evidence to suggest that Nebuchadrezzar attempted either to develop the area that he occupied in 604 B.C.E. or to introduce new political or geopolitical administrative forms. He apparently permitted the administrative structures that had been put in place during Assyrian and Egyptian rule to continue, exhibiting as little involvement as possible in the affairs of the petty kingdoms that remained in the corner of the Empire and investing little effort in strengthening his control, mainly through annual military campaigns. As part of this policy, Nebuchadrezzar chose to leave Jehoiakim on the throne, although he had been placed there just a few years earlier by Necho II. By this action, Nebuchadrezzar hoped to preserve stability in Judah, assuming that anyone who was wise enough to remain loyal to Egypt for 5 years and then capitulate to the new rulers unconditionally would also be sensible enough to remain loyal to the new ruler.

In his second year, after taking control of Hatti-land, Nebuchadrezzar made preparations to conquer Egypt—which was his primary goal. There is no information about what was happening in Judah during this time, but it appears that Jehoiakim, like the rest of the region's kings, remained loyal to Babylon. Nonetheless, when he campaigned against Egypt (November/December 601 B.C.E.), Nebuchadrezzar failed to surprise Necho II's army, and the Babylonian army retreated without having achieved its objective. In consequence, the Babylonian grip on the southern part of Hatti-land was weakened, and Egypt was able to return and regain its influence in the region that it had controlled a mere three years earlier. Apparently, during this time, the Egyptians succeeded in regaining a foothold in Philistia, capturing Gaza. The Egyptian advance would have required Jehoiakim again to seek the protection of his former masters, which implied rebellion against Babylon. At this particular time, Nebuchadrezzar was unable to muster the forces required to put down the uprising. However, after he rebuilt his army and reequipped it (600–599 B.C.E.), he began to reestablish control over Hatti-land by raids on the nomads (winter 599–598). The Babylonian hold on the region was completed during Nebuchadrezzar's seventh year (598–597). At the center of Babylonian activity that year was the conquest of the "city of Judah," namely, Jerusalem (2nd of Adar, March 16/17, 597 B.C.E.).

Initially, the Babylonians had set out to punish Jehoiakim. However, he died during the early stages of the expedition or immediately after the Babylonian force had set out, and he was succeeded by his son Jehoiachin, who surrendered to Nebuchadrezzar's army. The Babylonians did not destroy Jerusalem. They left Judah as a subject kingdom, left the House of David on the throne, and Judah thus survived another 11 years. Nonetheless, for the first time since taking control of Hatti-land, Nebuchadrezzar intervened in the governance of Jerusalem. He exiled the young king, Jehoiachin, along with 10,000 others; among them were many of the nation's elite, some of the top military units, and craftsmen with technical skills. The Babylonians had a special interest in transferring the exiles to desolate regions in Babylonia that, in the battles against Assyria, had been laid waste, with most of their population deported. In place of Jehoiachin, Nebuchadrezzar appointed Mattaniah-Zedekiah, leaving the heads of government and important office-holders in the royal administration with him, apparently intending not to upset the kingdom excessively and to preserve stability and continuity of rule. It is likely that practical considerations informed these measures, and this reflected the Babylonian policy to intervene only minimally in vassal kingdoms in the hope that minimal intervention would enhance stability and encourage loyalty to Babylon.

During the ninth decade of the sixth century, problems on the eastern border of his Empire began to plague Nebuchadrezzar (596–595 B.C.E.), followed closely by a revolt in his palace (595–594). During this time, Egypt again began to take an interest in the Levant, and during the reign of Psammetichus II (595–589), the kingdoms of the region came to believe that Egypt was capable of counterbalancing Babylon. Nebuchadrezzar failed to check the growing instability, and apparently at this time a regional anti-Babylonian pact was formed under the protection of Egypt; and Zedekiah, king of Judah (597–586 B.C.E.), played a primary role. Hophra's ascent to the throne in Egypt (589 B.C.E.) and the sense that Nebuchadrezzar's control over Ḫatti-land was weakening were unquestionably the major reasons for Zedekiah's decision to rebel against Babylon. However, this decision also had domestic support—social; political; and, especially, ideological-theological reasons—that encouraged the leaders of Judah to persist in their rebellion against Babylon until the city capitulated and was destroyed. It is reasonable to posit that Zedekiah was influenced by activists in Jerusalem, including the prophetic circles who urged him to rebel against Babylon, believing that Jerusalem would live in peace forever and would never fall prey to affliction or foe. This world view led to a relaxation of some of the inhibitions that had characterized the small kingdom during most of its history and had produced a large measure of its political, diplomatic, and military freedom—at a time when prudence was more essential than ever.

Apparently, the palpable threat to Babylonian rule over Ḫatti-land when Hophra ascended to the Egyptian throne convinced Nebuchadrezzar that he could no longer rely on the loyalty of vassal kingdoms and that he had to change the administrative governance of the region. He decided to conquer these kingdoms and annex their territory, making them provinces under direct Babylonian control. In the next 18 years, he implemented this new policy and thus solidified his control all the way to the Egyptian border. On the border between the Babylonian and Egyptian empires, a buffer zone consisting of impaired and weakened provinces was created. It also appears that the Babylonians used the devastation of this region to leverage the rebuilding of areas in Babylon that had been laid waste by the Assyrians during their long years of war against Babylon. This they accomplished by deporting large groups of the administrative, economic, and

religious elite from the local kingdoms and settling them in desolate and uninhabited regions of Babylonia proper.

Judah was the first target of the Babylonians. The beginning of the siege of
Jerusalem must be dated to early January 587 B.C.E. During the siege of Jerusalem, the Babylonians destroyed most of the population centers in the Shephelah, apparently as a way of "opening the gates" from the coast toward the hill-
country ridge and as part of the Babylonian interest in maintaining open roads
from east to west. The local population continued to decline during the Babylonian control of this region, which became a geopolitical and settlement frontier.
The areas closer to Jerusalem on the north and south were not destroyed; the
Babylonians founded their new center in Benjamin, made Mizpah the capital of
the province, and chose Gedaliah, son of Ahiqam, to be the first governor. Gedaliah was a scion of the family of Shaphan, which was known for its moderate
political and national views and had a long tradition of public service in high-
ranking positions. It is quite likely that, before the beginning of the siege, Gedaliah served as one of the high-ranking officials of Judah ("who was over the
household"). Accordingly, the Babylonians calculated that Gedaliah would rebuild the country quickly, preserve governmental stability, and remain loyal to
the Babylonian regime.

During Gedaliah's term, and apparently during the siege of Jerusalem, Mizpah's inhabitants were evacuated. Mizpah was transformed from a Judean frontier town into a Babylonian administrative center that served as the capital of
the province and the seat of the bureaucracy, some of whose members were
Babylonian. Alongside Mizpah, Gibeon continued to serve as a wine-producing
center. Surrounding Gibeon and Mizpah lay expanses of rich agricultural land,
which apparently also produced olive oil and grain, and intensive agricultural
activity developed here in central and western Benjamin. The *muṣh* seal impressions and the *gbʾn gdr* inscriptions are probably evidence of the orderly management of the agricultural system under the auspices of the Babylonian administration. Nevertheless, there is no historical or archaeological evidence of any
attempt by the Babylonians to develop the region or to establish a logistical
scheme to reinforce their control.

The migration of the Judahite population to the Benjamin region prior to the
destruction of Jerusalem reached its climax during the respite in the Babylonian
siege of Jerusalem that resulted from the Egyptian expedition to Palestine. Many
of those who did not believe that the rebellion could succeed took advantage of
the respite to "go to the land of Benjamin" (Jer 37:12). They joined the residents of the Benjamin region who had from the start practiced a policy of capitulation to the Babylonians. Jeremiah of Anathoth also tried to escape from
Jerusalem "among the people." However, the supporters of rebellion against
Babylon feared the results if a person of Jeremiah's stature were to join those living in Benjamin, and they captured and imprisoned him within the city. When

the siege of Jerusalem was renewed, some of those remaining in the city continued to be convinced of the justice of their cause and remained confident that the city would not fall to the Babylonians. For the first time in the history of the kingdom of Judah, two warring political factions, apparently from different social backgrounds, confronted each other.

On the 9th of Tammuz (end of July 586 B.C.E.), after 18 months of siege, Jerusalem fell. Zedekiah was punished severely for violating his personal oath of fealty to Nebuchadrezzar, and the House of David's rule in Judah was abolished. About one month after the fall of the city, it was systematically laid waste, and most of its residents, including the elite of the nation, were sent into exile in Babylon. The temple was also destroyed, its priests put to death, and some of the ritual vessels smashed and others sent to Babylon. The Babylonians also destroyed the unwalled outlying towns, villages, farms, and forts that had belonged to the Jerusalem district. For the remainder of Babylonian rule, the city and its environs remained completely empty. It is reasonable to conclude that, as in the case of Hadrian's policy toward the Jews after the Bar-Kokhba war, the Babylonians issued a prohibition against rebuilding the city; however, it is unlikely that they could have prevented pilgrimages to the site of the temple ruins. It also seems that, even though the temple had been destroyed, many in Babylon and Judah continued to regard it as the primary, even exclusive, site for religious ritual and hoped for its speedy rebuilding. On the ruins of the destroyed temple, limited rituals apparently continued to take place; individuals and small groups came to the site of the temple to lament, pray, and sacrifice meal offerings and incense. It is even possible that these pilgrimages reinforced the Babylonians' purpose of demonstrating the galling fate of a city that had rebelled and the punishment of citizens who had relied on their God's eternal protection.

The destruction of Jerusalem and the forcible deportation of the elite of the nation from their homeland to Babylon effected grave religious, national, and personal crises for the exiles living in Babylon—both those who were exiled during the time of Jehoiachin and those who had recently joined them. Additionally, for the first time, the nation was split along social and class lines; an important segment of the nation (in numbers and even more in quality) now had to live far from its homeland and temple; the threat of physical, spiritual, and cultural annihilation was real. To cope with this harsh reality, the exiles first and foremost had to explain the events that led to the destruction, and thus quickly developed a new social, national, and religious system.

The system of beliefs manifested in the Deuteronomistic History from the time of Josiah, the core of which was the promise of eternity for the House of David and God's enduring choice of Jerusalem as his city, was no longer relevant for the exiles. The historical narrative that ended in the "optimistic period" when Josiah was king also ceased to be relevant for them. To understand the destruction and the events that led to it, the leaders of the exiles and the carriers of the Deuteronomistic historiographical ideas had to complete the historical narrative and update the ideological and theological messages embedded in it.

The goal of the supplementary Deuteronomistic History (Dtr²), written soon after the beginning of the Babylonian exile, was to make the entire composition contemporary and relevant for the exiles. This objective was achieved when the historical narrative was updated, according to the spirit of the times, by adding a description of the events from the death of Josiah until the destruction (2 Kgs 23:22–23, 26–37; 24:1–12, 15–20; 25:1–11, 13–21) and by inserting passages into the earlier Deuteronomistic History (Dtr¹), including statements that included the condition under which God would ensure the eternity of the Davidic line. The result of this redaction is a Deuteronomistic History that was written, in its entirety, in accordance with a single program—to show that the history of the Jewish people led inevitably to the destruction of Judah. The purpose of the account was to explain how this course of events came to be; thus, the die was cast in Manasseh's time, and even Josiah's righteousness was not able to alter the kingdom's fate. The account of the destruction of Jerusalem became the climax of the account and interpreted the entire history of the Jewish people, particularly of the kingdom of Judah, in light of the destruction and exile, thus explaining prior events for the Babylonian exiles.

The composition evinces strong hostility toward the Babylonians and highlights the historical, moral, and theological distress that accompanied attempts to understand the disaster. The emphasis of the record is on the destruction's scope; the focus is on what happened in Jerusalem among the royal family and the people who would be exiled to Babylon; and there is no account of what happened in other parts of the country. The conclusion is that the entire nation was deported to Babylon, leaving the land completely uninhabited.

However, the land was *not* left uninhabited. Following the destruction of Jerusalem, Judah apparently registered a decline of 60% in settled area. This means that, although 110,000 people lived in Judah at the end of the kingdom, only 40,000 remained in the Babylonian province that was established in the same area. The archaeological evidence shows that the time of the Babylonian war against Judah is a sharp cut-off point marking the termination of one of the characteristic features of Judean settlement: large, important cities were laid waste, and urban life effectively came to an end. In contrast, the majority of rural settlements had been in the Judean highlands, particularly in the area between Beth-zur and the Benjamin region; this continued almost unchanged. As a result, the center of gravity of settlement shifted from the center to the periphery, and a new settlement pattern appeared: the center was empty, the remote periphery was desolate and barren, and the inner periphery nearest Jerusalem continued life almost unaltered. The destruction in the kingdom's frontier region (the Negev, Jordan Valley, and the southern Shephelah) was apparently a by-product of the collapse of the central structure. It is likely that the ability of the settlements in these areas to survive had been dealt a mortal blow by the Babylonian campaign of 597 B.C.E. Additionally, nomads apparently began to encroach, at the very beginning of the Babylonian siege, upon the regions that Sennacherib's campaign (701 B.C.E.) had first laid waste. These nomadic incursions gathered intensity after the destruction of Jerusalem and throughout the sixth century B.C.E. When the commercial network upon which these settlements based their economy was destroyed, they were no longer able to survive, and when no army capable of defending these settlements remained in Judah, Arabian and Idumean tribes were able to invade unimpeded. These tribal groups either pushed out the impoverished Judahites or assimilated them and gradually took over the area stretching from the Beer-Sheba and Arad valleys to Mareshah in the Shephelah and Hebron in the highlands.

There is no way of knowing whether the Babylonian regime created an official geopolitical designation for the Benjamin region and the northern Judean highland—the area to which most of "those remaining" rallied after the destruction of Jerusalem. We may presume that the status of the hill country south of Bethlehem, the southern Shephelah, and the Negev was never formalized. It is doubtful that the Babylonians had either the interest or the ability to enforce their own administration on these areas. Only in the Persian period were the boundaries of the provinces in the region redefined, apparently on the basis of preexisting borders that had been adapted to take into account changes in the demographics. At this time, the southern and southwestern borders of Yehud were allocated, taking into account the borders of the province of Ashdod and Idumea/Arabia. These borders remained unchanged until the second century B.C.E., when the Hasmoneans began to expand their territory.

According to one historical reconstruction, Gedaliah had served as the Babylonian governor only slightly more than seven weeks after the destruction before he was assassinated, apparently on the 3rd of Tishri. Thus, he did not live long enough to stabilize the country after the destruction; the crisis brought on by his assassination followed very closely on the heels of the trauma of the destruction of Jerusalem. At that time, only a few refugees from the war had returned to Judah, and those who had remained in the area had not yet recovered or adjusted to the new situation, nor had they begun to rebuild. Some of the officials in the provincial bureaucracy and administration, both Jews and Babylonians, had been murdered at Mizpah by Ishmael, the son of Nethaniah, who was a scion of the House of David. The motive for the killing is not clear, but we may hypothesize that Gedaliah and the residents of Mizpah were regarded as collaborating with the Babylonians. The assassination is a symbol of failure to come to terms with Babylonian rule, even though killing Gedaliah could not have brought about a significant change in the reality that had been evolving since the destruction of Jerusalem.

Fear of the Babylonian reaction to Gedaliah's assassination motivated several of Gedaliah's followers to escape to Egypt. It appears that this group of escapees was not large: perhaps they were certain individuals who had good reason to fear the Babylonian response. The projection of this group's behavior onto "all of the people" is part of the later redaction of this episode, and it is likely that the population of the Benjamin region and the northern Judean highlands continued, without any obvious change, into the last third of the sixth century B.C.E.

Shortly after the assassination of Gedaliah, during the time when the supplementary Deuteronomistic History (Dtr²) was being composed in Babylon, an account of the rule of Gedaliah in Mizpah was being written in Judah (as preserved in the expanded version, Jer 40:7–41:18). This account was embedded in the "biography" of Jeremiah (Jer 37:11–12; 38:14–28; 39:3, 12; 42:1–43:7), which was composed in Judah or in Egypt a short time later. The biography was primarily an account of the prophet's life from the eve of the destruction onward. Two popular stories (38:1–13; parts of the story in 40:1–6) and the prophecy to Ebed-Melech, the Cushite (39:15–18), were added to the biography. Later, it was edited, apparently also in Judah or in Egypt, and some short additions, particularly quotations from the prophet's words, were appended.

There are striking differences between these two compositions and the supplementary Deuteronomistic history (Dtr²) with regard to the narrative's goals and messages. The variations are the result of the compositions' different locations and target audiences. These historiographical works were formulated to explain the destruction and exile by selectively reporting events of the time. Therefore, each work focuses on a different time-span, on a different geographic region, and on different personalities.

Gedaliah's history focuses on the fate of the "people who remained" and their prospects for rehabilitation in Judah under Babylonian rule. It appeals to those who remained in Judah or went down to Egypt and emphasizes that, as a result of Gedaliah's assassination, an opportunity to rebuild was irretrievably lost.

The "biography" of Jeremiah focuses on the prophet's life from the time of the destruction until his journey to Egypt, which was a sign of the justice of his cause and the truth of his prophecy. It highlights the difference between the fate of the prophet and the fate of the House of David, Jerusalem, and its residents—who are sent to exile in Babylon. Zedekiah is presented as a weak king, and the blame for the destruction of Jerusalem is assigned to him and his wicked officials. Harsh criticism is directed against those who fled to Egypt after the assassination of Gedaliah.

In both of these sources, the fact that "the people who remained" had a chance for rehabilitation after the destruction is emphasized, and the focus is primarily on the fate of those who remained in the land. There is no allusion to the exile, and the destruction itself is scarcely mentioned. In addition, these accounts display a strong anti-Davidic tendency (also present in Jeremiah's prophecies), as well as opposition to any kind of political activism.

The different interpretations of the destruction and exile found in these two works reflects the ideological gap and controversy that continued to develop between the exiles in Babylon and the "people who remained." Those who remained in the land were deprived of the elite class that had shaped their way of life for centuries, the institutions of government to which they had been accustomed, and the major site of their familiar religious rituals. However, they were able to remain in their own homes and on their own land, with their own local leadership, in the context of the local centers that had long served them. It is even possible that, in many respects, the situation of those remaining in Judah actually improved: in the restructuring of the province after the destruction, new possibilities for social mobility emerged and new elites came into existence; perhaps some became owners of homes and property for the first time. It is also likely that the absence of a central government ensuring Jerusalem's place at the center, particularly as the only legitimate place for religious ritual, precipitated the development of alternate places of worship. Local traditions may have emerged into the open, including some that were quite ancient, having gone "underground" during the Jerusalem monopoly. It is also possible that new traditions arose regarding the importance and endurance of the House of Saul, the primacy of the major cities in Benjamin, and the sanctity of religious sites such as Bethel, Mizpah, Gibeon, and even Shechem.

The exiles in Babylon, on the other hand, underwent an ideological and religious melting-pot experience, and within a short time a new national, religious, and ethical world view took shape in which Jerusalem and the House of David continued to be central components. The anger expressed by Ezekiel in his furious prophecies against those who remained in Judah (particularly in 11:14–21; 33:23–29) shows that the exiles did not accept the ideological "liberation" of those who stayed in the land, namely, their attempt to found life in Judah on a leadership independent of the House of David and with unacceptable (to the exiles) moral perspectives. According to the Judeans' moral perspective, whoever had sinned had been punished by exile, and those who remained in Judah were "the people of God," entitled to realize the promise given by God to Abraham. Furthermore, the exiles were quite naturally angry that those who remained had seized their lands and property: the exiles continued to regard themselves as the legal owners of those assets, which also surely played a part in their longing to return to Palestine.

It was only among the second generation of the exiles to Babylon, in the mid-sixth century B.C.E., that a note of reconciliation with Babylonian rule and with the reality of life in exile can be discerned—as well as an acknowledgment of the existence of the remnant in Judah. There is evidence of a new perspective emerging, with the exiles acknowledging their loss, adjusting to their situation, and making peace with the new reality, and even expressing views that were similar to beliefs prevalent in Judah and Egypt a generation earlier. This new perception was expressed in two supplements "appended" to the Deuteronomistic History

(2 Kgs 25:22–30), both of which were apparently appended in Babylon after Jehoiachin was released from prison (560 B.C.E.) and before Persia's rise to power
(539 B.C.E.). These supplements relate two separate episodes in the history of the
relationship between the people and the Babylonian government: the story of
Gedaliah and the story of Jehoiachin's liberation. The summary of the story of
Gedaliah (vv. 22–26) is based on the Judahite source, rather than on the version
integrated into the "biography" of Jeremiah, and the source for the account of Jehoiachin's release from prison (vv. 27–30) is unknown. It is reasonable to conclude that the second episode's writer had firsthand information and was one of
those who remained faithful to the House of David. He even emphasized the fact
that Jehoiachin was favored over Zedekiah, enhancing his royal legitimacy by
adding the phrase "and he spoke kindly to him" (2 Kgs 25:28) while describing
the fate of Zedekiah with the words "he passed sentence on him" (25:6). The object of these supplements was to deliver a message to the populace in exile in
Babylon and perhaps also to those remaining in Judah or who went into exile in
Egypt: it is possible to live under Babylonian rule; there is no choice but to be patient, to demonstrate willingness to accept the Babylonian yoke, and to make
peace with being a subject people.

It is likely that the province of Judah continued under Babylonian rule as an
administrative unit of the Babylonian Empire ruled by local governors, and Mizpah continued to be its capital perhaps until Jerusalem's walls were rebuilt in the
middle of the fifth century B.C.E. There is no evidence that the proclamation of
Cyrus and Persian rule altered the status of the province; its organization remained a legacy from Babylonian rule. The major changes that took place during Persian rule were the appointment of governors who were relatives of the
royal family and the restoration of the reins of government to the elite who had
been in exile in Babylon. The latter is the most important hallmark of the new
era that began with the Return to Zion, because it meant that once again the
old-time elite ruled over the people who had remained in Judah.

The "Return to Zion" appears to have had no demographic impact on the
land of Judah: no change in population density is detectable between the end of
the sixth century and the beginning of the fifth century B.C.E. Moreover, the
dwindling of the total population of the province after the destruction of Jerusalem continued into the beginning of the Persian Period: the population of the
province of Judah in the middle of the fifth century B.C.E. may be estimated at
approximately 30,000 people. It is likely that at the beginning of the Persian Period several thousand returned of the nation's elite to Judah, particularly members of the priestly caste and those who served in the temple worship, and they
settled in Jerusalem and its environs. At the same time, the city continued in
poverty, and those who returned were unable to reestablish it as a true urban
center. Jerusalem at this time was little more than a temple, alongside of which
were residences for those who served in the temple and perhaps a few others.

The archaeological data show that the population of the northern Judean highland during the Persian Period remained as it had been during the sixth century (about one quarter of the total population of the province). Also unchanged was the population density of the northern Shephelah (some 15%). The Jordan Valley, like the western shore of the Dead Sea, was almost totally uninhabited, except for sparse settlement around the agricultural and industrial centers at En-Gedi and in the Jericho region. It may be that there was demand in the Persian Empire for luxury goods from Judah, and the Persian government perhaps integrated these economic centers into the imperial commercial structure. However, new settlements were not established in the region, a fact that may reflect the centralized control maintained by the Persians.

Approximately one-half of the population of the province during the Persian Period continued to live in the Benjamin region. Most of the population no doubt consisted of the people who had remained in Judah. At the beginning of the Persian Period, the region of Benjamin shows a dramatic drop in the number of settlements, and it is likely that this area was the principal source of people who began to settle in the northern Shephelah, particularly in the Ono–Lod Valleys. The northern Shephelah was part of the province of Samaria and attracted inhabitants from the Benjamin region, either for the economic opportunities it offered or for religious and ideological reasons—those who remained wishing to distance themselves from the returnees to Zion. We may conjecture that the Judahite residents of the northern Shephelah maintained their connection with their countrymen, the residents of Yehud, and the temple in Jerusalem, but the nature of this connection and its permanence is not clear. In any event, one of the results was that residents of the northern Shephelah were apparently a mediating factor, strengthening the connection of the Judahites with the peoples of the region: the Tyreans, Ammonites, and Moabites. The descendants of Judahites who spoke "the language of Ashdod" were one of the results of this intermingling.

There is clear archaeological-cultural continuity between the province of Yehud in the Persian Period and the region occupied by the kingdom of Judah in the seventh century B.C.E., which implies that the Babylonian Period was little more than an interim period linking the two epochs. The Mizpah district was the province's northernmost, and its area roughly corresponds to the boundaries of the tribe of Benjamin. The Mizpah district extended south to the northern edge of Jerusalem, to Jericho on the east, and as far as Beth-Horon in the west. The district of Jerusalem encompassed the city and its environs. The Beth-Hakkerem district lay south of Jerusalem and extended from Tekoah and the edge of the desert east of it to Keilah in the west. The Beth-zur district was the province's southernmost, and its area extended from En-Gedi in the east to Keilah in the west. The Keilah district was the province's only foothold in the Shephelah, and its borders stretched from near Mareshah to Ekron and to Gezer. It seems likely that the border between the Keilah and the Beth-Hakkerem and Beth-zur districts ran east of the Adullam–Zanoaḥ line.

The sixth century B.C.E. was also the bridge between the material culture of Judah at the end of the Iron Age and that of the Persian Period. Throughout the sixth century and the beginning of the fifth century, the population that continued in the Benjamin region and in the northern Judean highlands after the destruction of Jerusalem preserved local traditions of pottery manufacturing, and within this tradition gradual changes took place: new shapes, processing techniques, and materials emerged. It was only in the middle of the fifth century B.C.E. that the pottery assemblage typical of the Persian Period in Judah begins to appear.

*   *   *

The days of the Return to Zion brought to an end a brief, exceptional epoch in the history of Judah. The elite returning from Babylon were unable to come to terms with the fact that the people remaining in Judah had managed their lives without the elite, that their inheritance had been taken from Jerusalem, that the central (or only) temple was standing in ruins, and that alongside these ruins other ritual sites were springing up. Consequently, upon their return to Zion, they expunged the history of the community that had stayed in the land from biblical history, and a "dark age" was created, with the land empty, desolate, and ruined; the history of this period now became merely an account of the exiles in Babylon. As far as the returnees were concerned, the only Jewish presence in Judah was the result of their arrival in the land, and Cyrus's proclamation was the basis for the founding of the Yehud province.

However, the historical, geopolitical, and archaeological research presented in this book affirms the fact that in every respect the circumstances at the beginning of Persian rule in Judah were a direct continuation of the situation during Babylonian rule. The changes that occurred at the time of the Return to Zion were the reestablishment of the temple and the renewed acknowledgment that the Jerusalem temple was the official site of religious ritual in the Persian province—in other words, the establishment of Jerusalem as the uncontested political, social, and religious center of the nation and, therefore, the reestablishment of the elite that had been in exile in Babylon as the nation's leadership. This leadership leveraged the support of the Persian imperial administration to impose its agenda and perspective as they had taken shape during the Judahites' 50 years of Babylonian exile.

It is against this background that the later additions to the Deuteronomistic History (2 Kgs 24:13–14; 25:12) may be explained. In these additions, the reality of the "people who remained" is not denied, but they are presented as a sparse assemblage of impoverished people whose presence in Judah was of little significance. In these additions, those who remained have no standing or authority and, furthermore, the conciliatory attitude toward Babylonian rule that emerges from the two appendixes to the Deuteronomistic History (Dtr²) is undermined. Given these factors, the rapid disappearance of the alternate ritual sites that had begun to develop during the sixth century is quite understandable; memory of the sites quickly faded. These developments are articulated in the sharp polemics, added at this time to the Deuteronomistic History, against the ritual centers that had sprung up in Benjamin during the 50 years of exile.

The religious and national ideology that the returnees brought back with them was innovative and shaped the character of the province until the Hasmonean Period. Jewish fanatical society closed in upon itself, set itself apart from its neighbors, and diverted most of its efforts to rallying around Jerusalem, the center. The constant tension between the realities of the small, weak province, which was nationalistic and isolated, and memories of the past and longing for the future is a central characteristic of the prophetic literature from the early days of the Return to Zion and the later historiographical literature. The Deuteronomistic historiography continued to preoccupy writers, commentators, and thinkers, who found genuine topical significance for their times in it and attempted to adapt the account for the benefit of their contemporaries. This was the time that was decisive in formulating the nomistic layer (Dtr^N), which treated the history of the people as a product of obedience or disobedience to the Deuteronomistic law. At the center of the nomistic layer were the importance of Torah-based laws as a way of life and a shift of the center of gravity from the royal house to the people. During the Return to Zion, this composition was systematically redacted again by members of the priestly class, who incorporated additions, some of which are extensive. In this edition, they emphasized the centrality of the temple and the status of the priests and Levites, expressing their perspective regarding the land and the people throughout history.

* * *

Although in this book I have tried to present the major historical processes of the sixth century B.C.E., the geopolitical focal points, and the stages of ideological and historiographic development, what remains unknown overshadows what is certain. A blackout continues to overshadow major chapters of the history of Judah and the Judahites during the sixth century, and many questions, some of them fundamental and central, remain unanswered—open to further research and exploration. Some should be given separate, individual attention, some await new epigraphic and archaeological data or further reworking of the current information, and some will never be answered. Following are some of these questions (organized by category):

The patterns of Egyptian administration from the middle of the second decade of the seventh century to the year 604 and the administration's effect on events in the kingdom of Judah, the Transjordanian kingdoms, and the province of Samaria.

What were the stages by which Egypt consolidated its rule in Syria–Palestine after the Assyrian withdrawal in the second decade of the seventh century? What were the traits of Egyptian imperial rule and the nature of its relations with the kingdom of Judah and with Transjordan? Ancillary to this, how much freedom of action did Josiah have in the highland region when Assyria retreated and during the consolidation of Egyptian rule? What sort of relationship was there between the kingdom of Judah and the Israelite population in Samaria during this time? To what extent did the Northerners share the national aspirations that awakened in Judah at this time, and were they involved in these aspirations? How did the general populace react to the new religious and ritual ideas that were expressed in the Deuteronomistic ideology and the ritual reform imposed by Josiah, and to what extent were they committed to these changes?

The patterns of Babylonian administration from 604 to the 580s and their impact on the small kingdoms of the highlands and Transjordan.

How tight was Babylonian control over Judah and Transjordan during the first years of Babylon's rule in the region (604–601 B.C.E.)? How much freedom of action did the Babylonians permit these small kingdoms? To what extent were these kingdoms able to maintain their ties with Egypt during this period? To what extent did the Babylonians alter this policy after they reestablished control (597 B.C.E.), and did they then begin to develop an apparatus for tighter supervision of the region?

The political and diplomatic processes at work in Palestine and Egypt in the last decade of the sixth century.

What were the factors that led to renewed Egyptian interest in Philistia, Phoenicia, Judah, and Transjordan in the early sixth century, during the reigns of Psammetichus II and Hophra? What were the processes and thinking that motivated the local kingdoms to join in an anti-Babylonian alliance and rebel against Babylon?

The patterns of Babylonian administration in Judah during the siege of Jerusalem and after its destruction.

What was the relationship between the Babylonians and the leaders of the remnant Judahites in Mizpah during the siege of Jerusalem, after the destruction of the city, and after the murder of Gedaliah? How did the Babylonians supervise the province? What governmental apparatus was set up, and how restrictive was it? To what extent was the local population part of the administrative structure, and to what extent did they merely cooperate with it? Were any of the ritual sites that developed during the sixth century B.C.E., after the Jerusalem "monopoly" ended, accorded a preferred status by the Babylonians or by the people who remained in Judah? What was the status of the exiles in Babylon at this time? What influence did the exiles have on events in Judah, and what kind of relationship did they have with the Babylonian rulers? What was the Babylonians' reaction to the assassination of Gedaliah, and what changes, if any, did they make in the administration of the province as a result?

Relationships among the various Judahite communities that existed after the destruction.

How, to what extent, and at what level of intensity were connections maintained among the exiles in Babylon, those remaining in Judah, and the exiles in Egypt? How did each of these communities regard ideological developments and the historical works that were composed in the other communities, and how well did they accept them? To what extent were the communities influenced by these compositions? When was the primacy of the exile community in Babylon recognized?

Connections between the Judahite communities in Palestine and the Israelite population in Samaria.

How did the Israelite population in Samaria react to the destruction of Jerusalem? What was the nature of the relationship between this population and those who remained in Judah after the destruction of Jerusalem? What was the nature of the relationship between these two groups at the beginning of the Return to Zion? How were connections maintained, if indeed they were, with the few Judahites who continued to live in the Negev, the southern highlands of Judah, and the southern Shephelah? To what extent did these people assimilate to Arabian-Idumean groups that had consolidated there, and to what extent was their relationship with Judah maintained?

Processes that took place in Judah after the Return to Zion.

At the beginning of the Return to Zion, what was the relationship between the elites returning from Babylon and the people who had remained? Over what issues did these two communities contend with each other, and to what extent did they battle? How did those who remained accept the idea of rebuilding the temple? Did the leaders of the returnees take specific action against the worship sites that had arisen in Judah during the exile? Did they take action against the settlements of those who remained and against their leaders? During this time, was there a battle over the restoration of property and lands to their former, lawful owners?

Development of the material culture in the sixth century B.C.E.

What were the major changes in the types of pottery during the period from the early sixth century to the middle of the fifth century B.C.E.? Is it possible to isolate well-defined settlement layers or loci from this "interim period," particularly in the Benjamin region, and identify their characteristics? On the basis of these characteristics, is it possible to identify the material culture of tombs or small agricultural sites from this time in the Judean highlands and the Shephelah?

I hope that, following the publication of this book, many more studies on topics introduced here will illuminate the history of Judah and the Judeans under Babylonian rule, including their culture, the major geopolitical processes of this brief yet decisive period in their history, and the way that all of these are reflected in the biblical literature.

Abbreviations

Reference Works

AASOR	Annual of the American Schools of Oriental Research
AB	Anchor Bible
ABD	Freedman, D. N. (ed.). *Anchor Bible Dictionary*. 6 vols. New York, 1992
ABR	*Australian Biblical Review*
AcOr	*Acta Orientalia*
ADAJ	*Annual of the Department of Antiquities of Jordan*
AfO	*Archiv für Orientforschung*
AION	*Annali dell'Istituto Orientali di Napoli*
AJA	*American Journal of Archaeology*
AJBA	*Australian Journal of Biblical Archaeology*
AJBI	*Annual of the Japanese Biblical Institute*
AJSL	*American Journal of Semitic Languages and Literature*
ANES	*Ancient Near Eastern Studies* (formerly *Abr-Nahrain*)
ANET	Pritchard, J. B. (ed.). *Ancient Near Eastern Texts Relating to the Old Testament*. 3rd ed. Princeton, 1969
AOAT	Alter Orient und Altes Testament
AoF	*Altorientalische Forschungen*
ArOr	*Archiv Orientální*
AThANT	Abhandlungen zur Theologie des Alten und Neuen Testaments
AUSS	*Andrews University Seminary Studies*
BA	*Biblical Archaeologist*
BaghM	*Baghdader Mitteilungen*
BAR	*Biblical Archaeology Review*
BASOR	*Bulletin of the American Schools of Oriental Research*
BBR	*Bulletin for Biblical Research*
BDB	Brown, F.; Driver, S. R.; and Briggs, C. A. *Hebrew and English Lexicon of the Old Testament*. Oxford, 1907
BETL	Bibliotheca ephemeridum theologicarum lovaniensium
Bib	*Biblica*
BibOr	Biblica et Orientalia
BJRL	*Bulletin of the John Rylands University Library of Manchester*
BJS	Brown Judaic Studies
BN	*Biblische Notizen*
BSac	*Bibliotheca Sacra*
BZ	*Biblische Zeitschrift*
BZAW	Beihefte zur Zeitschrift für die alttestamentliche Wissenschaft

CAD	*Chicago Assyrian Dictionary*
CAH	*Cambridge Ancient History.* Cambridge
CB	Century Bible
CBQ	*Catholic Biblical Quarterly*
CBQMS	Catholic Biblical Quarterly Monograph Series
CdÉ	*Chronique d'Égypte*
CHJ	*Cambridge History of Judaism*
CTM	*Concordia Theological Monthly*
EncMiq	*Encyclopedia Miqra'it*
ErIsr	*Eretz-Israel*
ETL	*Ephemerides theologicae lovanienses*
EvT	*Evangelische Theologie*
ExpTim	*Expository Times*
FOTL	Forms of the Old Testament Literature
FRLANT	Forschungen zur Religion und Literatur des Alten und Neuen Testaments
GAG	W. von-Soden. *Grundriss der Akkadischen Grammatik.* Rome, 1969
HA	*Archaeological News* [Hebrew]
HSM	Harvard Semitic Monographs
HSS	Harvard Semitic Studies
HTR	*Harvard Theological Review*
HUCA	*Hebrew Union College Annual*
IB	Buttrick, G. A., et al. (eds.). *Interpreter's Bible.* 12 vols. New York, 1951–57
ICC	International Critical Commentary
IDB	*Interpreter's Dictionary of the Bible*
IDBSup	Crim, K. (ed.). *Interpreter's Dictionary of the Bible: Supplementary Volume.* Nashville, 1976
IEJ	*Israel Exploration Journal*
INJ	*Israel Numismatic Journal*
Int	*Interpretation*
IOS	*Israel Oriental Studies*
JANES	*Journal of the Ancient Near Eastern Society*
JAOS	*Journal of the American Oriental Society*
JARCE	*Journal of the Archaeological Research Center in Egypt*
JBL	*Journal of Biblical Literature*
JBR	*Journal of Bible and Religion*
JCS	*Journal of Cuneiform Studies*
JEA	*Journal of Egyptian Archaeology*
JEThS	*Journal of the Evangelical Theological Society*
JHS	*Journal of Hellenic Studies*
JJS	*Journal of Jewish Studies*
JNES	*Journal of Near Eastern Studies*
JNSL	*Journal of Northwest Semitic Literature*
JPOS	*Journal of the Palestine Oriental Society*
JQR	*Jewish Quarterly Review*
JSOT	*Journal for the Study of the Old Testament*

JSOTSup	Journal for the Study of the Old Testament Supplements
JSS	*Journal of Semitic Studies*
JTS	*Journal of Theological Studies*
KAT	Kommentar zum Alten Testament
MDOG	*Mitteilungen der Deutschen Orient-Gesellschaft*
MRS	Mission de Ras Shamra
NABU	*Nouvelles Assyriologiques Brèves et Utilitaires*
NCBC	New Century Bible Commentary
NEAEHL	Stern, E. (ed.). *The New Encyclopedia of Archaeological Excavations in the Holy Land.* Jerusalem, 1992
NICOT	New International Commentary on the Old Testament
OBO	Orbis biblicus et orientalis
OLA	Orientalia lovaniensia analecta
OLP	*Orientalia Lovaniensia Periodica*
OLZ	*Orientalistische Literaturzeitung*
Or	*Orientalia*
OTL	Old Testament Library
OTS	Old Testament Studies
OtSt	*Oudtestamentische Studiën*
PEF(QS)	*Palestine Exploration Fund (Quarterly Statement)*
PEFA	Palestine Exploration Fund, Annual of
PEQ	*Palestine Exploration Quarterly*
PJB	*Palästina-Jahrbuch*
QDAP	*Quarterly of the Department of Antiquities in Palestine*
RA	*Revue d'assyriologie et d'archéologie orientale*
RB	*Revue Biblique*
RevQ	*Revue de Qumran*
RHR	*Revue de l'histoire des religions*
SAAS	State Archives of Assyria Studies
SBT	Studies in Biblical Theology
Sem	*Semitica*
ST	*Studia theologica*
TA	*Tel-Aviv*
TLZ	*Theologische Literaturzeitung*
TOTC	Tyndale Old Testament Commentary
Trans	*Transeuphratène*
TynBul	*Tyndale Bulletin*
UF	*Ugarit-Forschungen*
VT	*Vetus Testamentum*
VTSup	Supplements to Vetus Testamentum
WBC	Word Biblical Commentary
WO	*Die Welt des Orients*
Yedi'ot	*Yedi'ot Bahaqirat Eretz-Israel Weatiqoteha (Bulletin of the Israel Exploration Society n.s.)* [Hebrew and English]
ZA	*Zeitschrift für Assyriologie*

ZÄS   *Zeitschrift für Ägyptische Sprache und Altertumskunde*
ZAW   *Zeitschrift für die Alttestamentliche Wissenschaft*
ZDPV   *Zeitschrift des Deutschen Palästina-Vereins*
Zion   *Zion: A Quarterly for Research in Jewish History* [Hebrew]
ZTK   *Zeitschrift für Theologie und Kirche*

Classical Sources

Eusebius,   *Historia ecclesiastica*
  Hist. Eccl.
Herodotus   Herodotus. *Histories*. Trans. Godley, A. D. Loeb Classical Library.
              Cambridge, Massachusetts, 1920
Josephus,   Josephus. *Jewish Antiquities*. Trans. Thackeray, H. St. J. Loeb Classical
  Ant.   Library. Cambridge, Massachusetts, 1937
Josephus,   Josephus. *Against Apion*. Trans. Thackeray, H. St. J. Loeb Classical Library.
  Ag. Ap.   Cambridge, Massachusetts, 1926
Josephus,   Josephus. *The Jewish War*. Trans. Thackeray, H. St. J. Loeb Classical Library.
  J.W.   Cambridge, Massachusetts, 1927

Bibliography

Abel, F. M.
1933–38   Géographie de la Palestine. Paris.
Abou-Assaf, A.
1981   Die Statute des HDYSʾY, König von Guzana. MDOG 113: 3–22.
Abou-Assaf, A.; Bordreuil, P.; and Millard, A. R.
1982   La Statue de Tell Fekherye et son inscription bilingue assyro-araméenne. Paris.
Abramsky, S.
1973   "Rosh Hashana" and "Pesah" in Ezekiel. Pp. 56–78 in vol. 1 of Avishur, Y.;
       Abramsky, S.; and Reviv, H. (eds.). Beer-Sheva. Jerusalem. [Hebrew, with
       English summary on p. 243]
Ackerman, S.
1992   Under Every Green Tree: Popular Religion in Sixth-Century Judah. HSM 46.
       Atlanta.
Ackroyd, P. R.
1958   The Old Testament Historical Problems of the Early Persian Period. JNES 17:
       13–27.
1968   Exile and Restoration: A Study of Hebrew Thought of the Sixth Century BC.
       Philadelphia.
1970   Israel under Babylon and Persia. Oxford.
1979   The History of Israel in the Exilic and Post-Exilic Periods. Pp. 320–50 in
       Anderson, G. W. (ed.). Tradition and Interpretation. Oxford.
1984a The Jewish Community in Palestine in the Persian Period. Pp. 130–61 in
       vol. 1 of Davies, W. D., and Finkelstein, L. (eds.). CHJ. Cambridge.
1984b The Book of Jeremiah: Some Recent Studies. JSOT 29: 47–59.
Aharoni, M., and Aharoni, Y.
1976   The Stratification of Judahite Sites in the 8th and 7th Centuries B.C.E.
       BASOR 224: 73–90.
Aharoni, Y.
1955   Excavations at Ramat Rahel. Yediʿot 19: 147–74. [Hebrew]
1956a Excavations at Ramat Rahel, 1954 (Preliminary Report). IEJ 6:102–11, 137–
       57.
1956b Additional Notes on the Ramat Rahel Excavations. Yediʿot 20: 44–47.
       [Hebrew]
1960a Excavations at Ramat Rahel (Second Session, 1959). Yediʿot 24: 147.
       [Hebrew]
1960b Hebrew Jar-Stamps from Ramat Rahel. ErIsr 6: 56–60. [Hebrew]
1961   Excavations at Ramat Rahel. BA 24: 98–118.
1962a Excavations at Ramat Rahel: Seasons 1959 and 1960. Rome.
1962b The Land of Israel in Biblical Times: A Historical Geography. Jerusalem.
       [Hebrew; citations from rev. ed., 1984]

1964 *Excavations at Ramat Raḥel: Seasons 1961 and 1962.* Rome.

1967a The "Persian Fortress" at Lachish: An Assyrian Palace? *Yediʿot* 31: 80–91. [Hebrew]

1967b Beth-Haccherem. Pp. 178–83 in Thomas, D. W. (ed.). *Archaeology and Old Testament Study.* Oxford.

1975 *Investigations at Lachish: The Sanctuary and the Residency (Lachish V).* Tel-Aviv.

1976 *Arad Inscriptions.* Jerusalem. [English version, 1981]

1978 *The Archaeology of Eretz Israel.* Jerusalem. [Hebrew]

1982 The Negev and the Southern Desert Frontier. Pp. 202–13, 266–68 in Malamat, A. (ed.). *The History of the People of Israel—The Age of the Monarchy: A Political History.* Jerusalem. [Hebrew]

Aharoni, Y. (ed.)

1973 *Beer-Sheba I: Excavations at Tel Beer-Sheba, Seasons 1969–1971.* Tel-Aviv.

Aharoni, Y., and Amiran, R.

1955 A Tour of the City Mounds of the Shephelah of Judea. *Yediʿot* 19: 222–25. [Hebrew]

Aḥituv, S.

1984 *Canaanite Toponyms in Ancient Egyptian Documents.* Jerusalem.

1993 The Missing District: A Study in the List of the Cities and Districts of Judah in Joshua 15:21–62. *ErIsr* 24: 7–11. [Hebrew]

Ahlström, G. W.

1971 *Joel and the Temple Cult of Jerusalem.* Leiden.

1982 *Royal Administration and National Religion in Ancient Palestine.* Leiden.

1993 *The History of Ancient Palestine from the Palaeolithic Period to Alexander's Conquest.* Sheffield.

Albertz, R.

1994 *A History of Israelite Religion in the Old Testament Period.* 2 vols. Louisville. [English Translation of the 1992 German edition]

2000 In Search of the Deuteronomists: A First Solution to A Historical Riddle. Pp. 1–17 in Römer, T. (ed.). *The Future of the Deuteronomistic History.* Leuven.

2003 *Israel in Exile: The History and Literature of the Sixth Century* B.C.E. Atlanta. [English Translation of the 2001 German edition]

Albright, W. F.

1922 Gibeah of Saul and Benjamin. *BASOR* 6: 8 11.

1923 The Site of Mizpah in Benjamin. *JPOS* 3: 110–12.

1924a Excavations and Results at Tell el-Full (Gibeah of Saul). AASOR 4. New Haven, Connecticut.

1924b Researches of the School in Western Judaea. *BASOR* 15: 211.

1925a The Fall Trip of the School in Jerusalem: From Jerusalem to Gaza and Back. *BASOR* 17: 49.

1925b Topographical Researches in Judaea. *BASOR* 18: 6 11.

1928 A Trial Excavation in the Mound of Bethel. *BASOR* 29: 9 11.

1931–32 Recent Works on the Topography and Archaeology of Jerusalem. *JQR* 22: 414–16.

1932a The Seal of Eliakim and the Latest Preexilic History of Judah. *JBL* 51: 77–106.

1932b   *The Excavation of Tell Beit Mirsim in Palestine, Vol. I: The Pottery of the First Three Campaigns*. AASOR 12. New Haven, Connecticut.

1932c   *Archaeology and the Bible*. New York.

1933   A New Campaign of Excavation at Gibeah of Saul. *BASOR* 52: 612.

1934a   Light on the Jewish State in the Persian Time. *BASOR* 53: 20–22.

1934b   The First Month of Excavation at Bethel. *BASOR* 55: 23–25.

1934c   The Kyle Memorial Excavation at Bethel. *BASOR* 56: 215.

1935a   Observations of the Bethel Report. *BASOR* 57: 27–30.

1935b   Beitin. *QDAP* 4: 196–98.

1942a   *Archaeology and the Religion of Israel*. Baltimore.

1942b   King Joiachin in Exile. *BA* 5/4: 49–55.

1943   *The Excavation of Tell Beit Mirsim, Vol. 3: The Iron Age*. AASOR 21–22. New Haven, Connecticut.

1948   Book Reviews. *JNES* 7: 20–25.

1949a   *The Biblical Period from Abraham to Ezra*. New York.

1949b   The Biblical Period. Pp. 14–62 in Finkelstein, L. (ed.). *The Jews: Their History, Culture and Religion*. Philadelphia.

1950   *The Biblical Period*. Pittsburgh.

1956a   The Nebuchadnezzar and Neriglissar Chronicles. *BASOR* 143: 28–33.

1956b   *Recent Discoveries in Biblical Lands*. Reprinted with additions. Pittsburgh.

1960a   *The Archaeology of Palestine*. 2nd ed. Harmondsworth. [First pub., 1949]

1960b   Reports on Excavations in the Near East and Middle East. *BASOR* 159: 37–39.

1965   *The Archaeology of Palestine*. Tel-Aviv. [Hebrew trans. of 1960 edition]

1966   Some Recent Reports and Publications. *BASOR* 183: 32–34.

Alfrink, B.

1943   L'Expression *šākab ʿim ʾābotāyw*. *OtSt* 2: 106–18.

Allrik, H. L.

1954   The Lists of Zerubbabel (Neh. 7 and Ezr. 2) and the Hebrew Numerical Notation. *BASOR* 136: 21–27.

Al-Rawi, F. N. H.

1985   Nabopolassar's Restoration Work on the Wall *Imgur-Enlil* at Babylon. *Iraq* 47: 1–13.

Alt, A.

1910   Mizpah in Benjamin. *PJB* 6: 46–62.

1925a   Judas Gaue unter Josia. *PJB* 21: 100–116. [Reprinted in: idem, *Kleine Schriften zur Geschichte des Volkes Israel*. Munich, 1953 (= KS), vol. 2: 76–88]

1925b   Das Institut im Jahre 1924. *PJB* 21: 5–58.

1926a   Anathoth. *PJB* 22: 23–24.

1926b   Das Institut im Jahre 1931. *PJB* 23: 5–47.

1928   Das Taltor von Jerusalem. *PJB* 24: 74–98.

1929   Das System der assyrische Provinzen auf dem Boden des Reiches Israel. *ZDPV* 52: 220–42.

1931   Judas Nachbarn zur Zeit Nehemias. *PJB* 27: 66–74. [Repr. KS 2 (1953) 338–45]

1932   Das Institut im Jahre 1932. *PJB* 28: 5–47.

1934a   Die Rolle Samarias bei der Entstehung des Judentums. Pp. 528 in Deichert,
         A., and Hinrichs, J. C. (eds.). *Festschrift Otto Procksch zum 60. Geburtstag.*
         Leipzig. [Repr. *KS* 2 (1953) 316–37]
1934b   Das Institut im Jahre 1933. *PJB* 30: 5–31.
1935   Zur Geschichte der Grenze zwischen Judäa und Samaria. *PJB* 31: 94–111.
         [Repr. *KS* 2 (1953) 346–62]
1945   Neue assyrische Nachrichten über Palästina. *ZDPV* 67: 128–46. [Repr. *KS* 2
         (1953) 226–41]
1951   Bemerkungen zu einigen judäischen Ortslisten des Alten Testaments. *Beiträge
         zur biblischen Landes- und Altertumskunde* 68: 193–210. [Repr. *KS* 2 (1953)
         289–305]
1953   Neue Erwägungen über die Lage von Mizpa, Ataroth, Beeroth, und Gibeon.
         ZDPV 69: 1–27.
Amiran (Kallner), D.
1948–49 The Western Border of the Hebron Mountains. *Yediʿot* 14: 112–18. [Hebrew]
Amiran, R.
1957   The Necropolis of Jerusalem in the Time of the Monarchy. Pp. 65–72 in
         Aviram, J. (ed.). *Judah and Jerusalem: The Twelfth Archaeological Convention.*
         Jerusalem. [Hebrew]
1962   Review of AASOR 34–35. *BibOr* 19/6: 263–64.
1971   *The Ancient Pottery of Eretz Yisrael from Its Beginnings in the Neolithic Period to
         the End of the First Temple.* Jerusalem. [Hebrew]
1975   A Note on the 'Gibeon Jar.' *PEQ* 1975: 129–32.
Amiran, R., and Dunayevsky, I.
1958   The Assyrian Open-Court Building and Its Palestinian Derivatives. *BASOR*
         149: 25–32.
Amiran, R., and Eitan, A.
1970   Excavations in the Jerusalem Citadel. *Qadmoniot* 10: 64–66. [Hebrew]
Amit, D.
1992   Hebron–ʿEin Gedi: Survey of Ancient Road. *ErIsr* 23: 345–62. [Hebrew]
Amit, Y.
1988   The People of the Land. P. 642 in vol. 3 of Hoffman, Y. (ed.). *The Israeli
         Encyclopedia of the Bible.* Givataim. [Hebrew]
Anbar, M.
1985   The Story about the Building of an Altar on Mount Ebal: The History of Its
         Composition and the Question of the Centralisation of the Cult. Pp. 30–49
         in Lohfink, N. (ed.). *Das Deuteronomium: Entstehung, Gestalt und Botschaft.*
         Leuven.
1992   *Josué et l'alliance de Sichem (Josué 24: 1–28).* Frankfurt.
Andersen, F. I., and Freedman, D. N.
1980   *Hosea.* AB 24. New York.
Andersen, N. E.
1983   The Role of the Queen Mother in Israelite Society. *CBQ* 45: 179–94.
André, G.
1980   *Determining the Destiny: PQD in the Old Testament.* Lund.
Ariel, D. T. (ed.)
1990   *Excavations at the City of David, II: 1978–1985, Directed by Yigal Shiloh:
         Imported Stamped Amphora, Handles, Coins, Worked Bone and Ivory, and Glass.*
         Qedem 30. Jerusalem.

2000   *City of David Excavations: Final Report V*. Qedem 40. Jerusalem.

Ariel, D. T., and DeGroot, A. (eds.)
1992   *Excavations at the City of David, III: 1978–1985, Directed by Yigal Shiloh: Stratigraphical, Environmental, and Other Reports*. Qedem 33. Jerusalem.
1996   *Excavations at the City of David, IV: 1978–1985, Directed by Yigal Shiloh: Various Reports*. Qedem 35. Jerusalem.

Ariel, D. T., and Shoham, Y.
2000   Locally Stamped Handles and Associated Body Fragments of the Persian and Hellenistic Periods. Pp. 137–69 in: Ariel, D. T. (ed.). *Excavations at the City of David, VI: 1978–1985. Directed by Yigal Shiloh: Inscriptions*. Qedem 41. Jerusalem.

Arnold, P. M.
1990   *Gibeah: The Search for a Biblical City*. Sheffield.

Auld, A. G.
1998   The Former Prophets (Joshua, Judges, 1–2 Samuel, 1–2 Kings). Pp. 53–68 in McKenzie, S. L., and Graham, M. P. (eds.). *The Hebrew Bible Today: An Introduction to Critical Issues*. Louisville.

Avigad, N.
1958a   A New Class of *Yehud* Stamps. *Yediʿot* 22: 310. [Hebrew]
1958b   New Light on the MŞH Seal Impressions. *Yediʿot* 22: 126–33. [Hebrew]
1958c   New Light on the MŞH Seal Impressions. *IEJ* 8: 113–19.
1959   Some Notes on the Hebrew Inscriptions from Gibeon. *IEJ* 9: 130–33.
1965   Seals of Exiles. *IEJ* 15: 222–32.
1970a   Ammonite and Moabite Seals. Pp. 284–95 in Sanders, J. A. (ed.). *Near Eastern Archaeology in the Twentieth Century*. New York.
1970b   Excavations in the Jewish Quarter of the Old City of Jerusalem, 1970 (Second Preliminary Report). *IEJ* 20: 129–40.
1972a   Excavations in the Jewish Quarter of the Old City. *Qadmoniot* 1920: 91–101. [Hebrew]
1972b   Two Hebrew Inscriptions on Wine Jars. *IEJ* 22: 19.
1974   More Evidence on the Judean Post-Exilic Stamps. *IEJ* 24: 52–58.
1975   New Names on Hebrew Seals. *ErIsr* 12: 66–71. [Hebrew]
1976a   *Bullae and Seals from a Post-Exilic Judean Archive*. Qedem 4. Jerusalem. [Hebrew]
1976b   New Light on the Naʾar Seals. Pp. 294–300 in Cross, F. M.; Lemke, W. E.; and Miller, P. D. (eds.). *Magnalia Dei: The Mighty Acts of God. Essays on the Bible and Archaeology in Memory of G. Ernest Wright*. New York.
1978a   The Seal of Seraiah (Son of) Neriah. *ErIsr* 14: 86–87. [Hebrew]
1978b   Baruch the Scribe and Jerahmeel the King's Son. *IEJ* 28: 52–56.
1980   *The Upper City of Jerusalem*. Jerusalem. [Hebrew]
1986   *Hebrew Bullae from the Time of Jeremiah*. Jerusalem. [Hebrew]
1987   The Contribution of Hebrew Seals to an Understanding of Israelite Religion and Society. Pp. 195–208 in Miller, P. D.; Hanson, P. D.; and McBride, S. D. (eds.). *Ancient Israelite Religion*. Philadelphia.

Avioz, M.
2003   When Was the First Temple Destroyed, According to the Bible? *Biblica* 84: 562–65.

Avi-Yonah, M.
1949   *Historical Geography of Palestine from the End of the Babylonian Exile up to the Arab Conquest.* Jerusalem. [Hebrew; citations from 4th ed., 1984]
1954   The Walls of Nehemiah: A Minimalist View. *IEJ* 4: 239–48.
1968   Jerusalem of the Second Temple Period. *Qadmoniot* 12: 19–27. [Hebrew]
1971   The Newly-Found Wall of Jerusalem and Its Topographical Significance. *IEJ* 21: 168–69.

Avi-Yonah, M. (ed.)
1975   *Encyclopedia of Archaeological Excavations in the Holy Land.* 4 vols. Englewood Cliffs, New Jersey.

Ayalon, E.
1985a   *The Iron Age II Pottery Assemblage from Hurvat Teiman (Kuntillet ʿAjrud).* M.A. Thesis. Tel-Aviv. [Hebrew]
1985b   Trial Excavation of Two Iron Age Strata at Tel ʾEton. *TA* 12: 54–62.

Badé, W. F.
1930   The Tell en-Naṣbeh Excavations of 1929. *PEF(QS)* 1930: 8–19.
1933   The Seal of Jaazaniah. *ZAW* 51: 150–56.

Baltzer, K.
1961   Das Ende des Staates Juda und die Messias-Frage. Pp. 33–43 in Rendtorff, R., and Koch, K. (eds.). *Studien zur Theologie der Alttestamentlichen Überlieferungen: Festschrift G .von Rad.* Berlin.

Barag, D.
1966   The Effect of the Tennes Rebellion on Palestine. *BASOR* 183: 6–12.
1967   Book Review on Pritchard 1964. *JNES* 26: 142–43.
1999   Owners of Two or More Seals in Judah during the First Temple Period. *ErIsr* 26: 35–38. [Hebrew]

Barkay, G.
1984   Excavations on the Slope of the Hinnom Valley, Jerusalem. *Qadmoniot* 68: 94–108. [Hebrew]
1985   *Northern and Western Jerusalem in the End of the Iron Age.* Ph.D. Dissertation. Tel-Aviv. [Hebrew]
1986   *Ketef Hinnom: A Treasure Facing Jerusalem's Walls.* Jerusalem. [Hebrew]
1989   The Priestly Benediction on the Ketef Hinnom Plaques. *Cathedra* 52: 37–76. [Hebrew]
1992a   The Iron Age II–III. Pp. 302–73 in Ben-Tor, A. (ed.). *The Archaeology of Ancient Israel.* New Haven, Connecticut.
1992b   "The Prancing Horse": An official Seal Impression from Judah of the 8th Century B.C.E. *TA* 19/2: 124–29.
1993   The Redefining of Archaeological Periods: Does the Date 588/586 B.C.E. Indeed Mark the End of the Iron Age Culture? Pp. 106–9 in Biran, A., and Aviram, J. (eds.). *Biblical Archaeology Today II.* Jerusalem.
1994a   Burial Caves and Burial Practices in Judah in the Iron Age. Pp. 96–164 in Singer, I. (ed.). *Graves and Burial Practices in Israel in the Ancient Period.* Jerusalem. [Hebrew]
1994b   Excavations at Ketef Hinnom in Jerusalem. Pp. 85–106 in Geva, H. (ed.). *Ancient Jerusalem Revealed.* Jerusalem.
1995   The King of Babylonia or a Judaean Official? *IEJ* 45/1: 41–47.

1998   The Iron Age III: The Babylonian Period. P. 25 in Lipschits, O. (ed.). *Is It Possible to Define the Pottery of the Sixth Century* B.C.E. *in Judea?* (Booklet of Summaries of lectures from the conference held in Tel-Aviv University, Oct. 21, 1998). Tel-Aviv. [Hebrew]

Barkay, G.; Fantalkin, A.; and Tal, O.
2002   A Late Iron Age Fortress North of Jerusalem. *BASOR* 328: 49–71.

Barkay, R.
1984–85   An Archaic Greek Coin from the 'Shoulder of Hinnom' Excavations in Jerusalem. *INJ* 8: 15.

Barrick, W. B.
1974   On the Removal of the 'High Places' in 1–2 Kings. *Bib* 55: 257–59.

Barstad, H. M.
1988   On the History and Archaeology of Judah during the Exilic Period: A Reminder. *OLP* 19: 25–36.

1996   *The Myth of the Empty Land: A Study in the History and Archaeology of Judah during the 'Exilic' Period.* Oslo.

Bartlett, J. R.
1972   The Rise and Fall of the Kingdom of Edom. *PEQ* 104: 26–37.

1978   From Edomites to Nabataeans: A Study in Continuity. *PEQ* 110: 53–66.

1982a   Edom and the Fall of Jerusalem, 587 B.C. *PEQ* 114: 14–24.

1982b   *Jericho.* Grand Rapids, Michigan.

1989   *Edom and the Edomites.* Sheffield.

1995   Edom in the Nonprophetical Corpus. Pp. 13–21 in Edelman, D. V. (ed.). *You Shall Not Abhor an Edomite for He Is Your Brother: Edom and Seir in History and Tradition.* Atlanta.

1999   Edomites and Idumaeans. *PEQ* 131: 102–14.

Batten, L. W.
1913   *A Critical and Exegetical Commentary on the Books of Ezra and Nehemiah.* ICC. Edinburgh.

Baumann, A.
1968   Urrolle und Fasttag. *ZAW* 80: 350–73.

Beaulieu, P. A.
1997   The Fourth Year of Hostilities in the Land. *BaghM* 28: 367–94.

Bebbett, W. J., and Blakely, J. A.
1989   *Tell el-Hesi: The Persian Period (Stratum V).* Winona Lake, Indiana.

Becking, B.
1990   Jehojachin's Amnesty: Salvation for Israel? Notes on 2 Kings 25, 27–30. Pp. 283–93 in Brekelmans, C., and Lust, J. (eds.). *Pentateuchal and Deuteronomistic Studies.* Leuven.

1994   Jeremiah's Book of Consolation: A Textual Comparison—Notes on the Masoretic Text and the Old Greek Version of Jeremiah XXX–XXXI. *VT* 44/2: 145–69.

1997   Inscribed Seals as Evidence for Biblical Israel? Jeremiah 40.7–41.15 *Par Exemple.* Pp. 65–83 in L. L. Grabbe (ed.). *Can a "History of Israel" Be Written?* JSOTSup 245. Sheffield.

1999   Continuity and Community: The Belief System of the Book of Ezra. Pp. 256–75 in Becking, B., and Korpel, M. C. A. (eds.). *The Crisis of Israelite Religion: Transformation of Religious Tradition in Exilic and Post-Exilic Times.* Leiden.

2005	"We All Returned as One!": Critical Notes on the Myth of the Mass Return. Pp. 3–18 in Lipschits, O., and Oeming, M. (eds.). *Judah and the Judeans in the Persian Period*. Winona Lake, Indiana.

Bedford, P. R.

2001	*Temple Restoration in Early Achaemenid Judah*. Leiden.

Begg, C. T.

1986a	The Significance of Jehoiachin's Release: A New Proposal. *JSOT* 36: 49–56.

1986b	2 Kings 20:12–19 as an Element of the Deuteronomistic History. *CBQ* 48: 27–42.

1989	⟨DtrP⟩ in 2 Kings 25: Some Further Thoughts. *RB* 96/1: 49–55.

Beit-Arieh, I.

1985a	Tel ʿIra: A Fortified City of the Kingdom of Judah. *Qadmoniot* 69–70: 17–24. [Hebrew]

1985b	The Ostracon of Ahiqam from Horvat ʿUza. *ErIsr* 18: 94–96. [Hebrew; for English version, see *TA* 13/14 (1986–87): 32–38]

1986a	Horvat ʿUza: A Border Fortress in the Eastern Negev. *Qadmoniot* 73–74: 31–40. [Hebrew]

1986b	An Edomite Temple at Hurvat Qitmit. *Qadmoniot* 75–76: 72–79. [Hebrew]

1987	Tel-ʿIra and Horvat ʿUza: Negev Sites in the Late Israelite Period. *Cathedra* 42: 34–38. [Hebrew]

1989a	An Edomite Shrine at Horvat Qitmit. *ErIsr* 20: 135–46. [Hebrew]

1989b	New Data on the Relationship between Judah and Edom towards the End of the Iron Age. *AASOR* 49: 125–31.

1991a	The Edomite Shrine at Horvat Qitmit in the Judean Negev: Preliminary Excavation Report. *TA* 18: 93–116.

1991b	A Small Frontier Citadel at Horvat Radum in the Judean Negev. *Qadmoniot* 95–96: 86–89. [Hebrew]

1992	Horvat Radum. *ErIsr* 23: 106–12. [Hebrew]

1993	A Literary Ostracon from Horvat ʿUza. *TA* 20: 55–63.

1995a	*Horvat Qitmit: An Edomite Shrine in the Biblical Negev.* Tel-Aviv.

1995b	The Edomites in Cisjordan. Pp. 33–40 in Edelman, D. V. (ed.). *You Shall Not Abhor an Edomite for He Is Your Brother: Edom and Seir in History and Tradition*. Atlanta.

1995c	An Inscribed Jar from Horvat ʿUza. *ErIsr* 24: 34–40. [Hebrew]

1996	Edomite Advance into Judah. *BAR* 22/6: 28–36.

1998	The Excavations at Tel Malhata: An Interim Report. *Qadmoniot* 115: 30–39. [Hebrew]

1999a	*Tel ʿIra: A Stronghold in the Biblical Negev.* Tel-Aviv.

1999b	Ostracon ʿAseret from Horvat ʿUza. *ErIsr* 26: 30–34. [Hebrew]

Beit-Arieh, I., and Beck, P.

1987	*An Edomite Shrine in the Negev: Discoveries from Ḥorvat Qitmit Excavations (Catalog Number 277)*. Jerusalem.

Beit-Arieh, I., and Cresson, B.

1985	An Edomite Ostracon from Horvat ʿUza. *TA* 12/1: 96–101.

1991	Horvat ʿUza: A Fortified Outpost on the Eastern Negev Border. *BA* 54: 126–35.

Ben-Dov, M.

1982	*The Dig at the Temple Mount*. Jerusalem. [Hebrew]

Bennet, C.-M.
1978   Some Reflections on Neo-Assyrian Influence in Transjordan. Pp. 165–71 in Moorey, P. R. S., and Parr, P. J. (eds.). *Archaeology in the Levant.* Warminster.
1982   Neo-Assyrian Influence in Transjordan. Pp. 181–87 in vol. 1 of Hadidi, A. (ed.). *Studies in the History and Archaeology of Jordan.* Amman.

Bennett, W. J., and Blakely, J. A.
1989   *Tell el-Hesi: The Persian Period (Stratum V).* Winona Lake, Indiana.

Ben-Zvi, E.
1991a   The Account of the Reign of Manasseh in II Reg 21, 1–18 and the Redactional History of the Book of Kings. *ZAW* 103: 355–74.
1991b   *A Historical-Critical Study of the Book of Zephaniah.* Berlin.
1996   *A Historical-Critical Study of the Book of Obadiah.* New York.

Berger, P. R.
1973   *Die neubabylonischen Königsinschriften: Königsinschriften des augebenden babylonischen Reiches (626–539 a. Chr.).* AOAT 4/1. Kevelaer and Neuchirchen-Vluyn.

Berquist, J. L.
1995   *Judaism in Persia's Shadow: A Social and Historical Approach.* Minneapolis.

Betlyon, J. W.
1986   The Provincial Government of Persian Period Judah and the Yehud Coins. *JBL* 105: 633–42.

Bewer, J.
1928   The Problem of Deuteronomy: A Symposium. *JBL* 47: 305–79.

Bianchi, F.
1993   *"I superstiti della deportazione sono là nella provincia" (Neemia 1,3): Ricerche epigrafiche sulla storia della Giudea in età neobabilonese e achemenide (586 a.C.– 442 a.C.).* Supplement 76 to ANNALI 53/3. Naples.
1994   Le rôle de Zorobabel et de la dynastie davidique en Judée du VIe Siècle au IIe Siècle av. J.-C. *Trans* 7: 153–65.

Bickerman, E. J.
1946   The Edict of Cyrus in Ezra 1. *JBL* 65: 242–75.
1976   *Studies in Jewish and Christian History.* Leiden.
1979–80 Nebuchadnezzar and Jerusalem. *Proceedings of the American Academy for Jewish Research* 46–47: 69–85.
1981   La seconde année de Darius. *RB* 88: 23–28.

Bienkowski, P.
1990   Umm el-Biyara, Tawilan and Buseirah in Retrospect. *Levant* 22: 91–109.
1991   Edom and the Edomites: Review Article. *PEQ*: 139–42.
1992   The Date of Sedentary Occupation in Edom: Evidence from Umm el-Biyara, Tawilan and Buseirah. Pp. 99–112 in Bienkowski, P. (ed.). *Early Edom and Moab: The Beginning of the Iron Age in Southern Jordan.* Sheffield.
1994   The Origins and Development of Edom. Pp. 253–68 in Mazzoni, S. (ed.). *Nuove Fondazioni Nel Vicino Orienta Antic: Reatà e Ideologia.* Pisa.
1995   The Edomites: The Archaeological Evidence from Transjordan. Pp. 41–92 in Edelman, D. V. (ed.). *You Shall Not Abhor an Edomite for He Is Your Brother: Edom and Seir in History and Tradition.* Atlanta.
2000   Transjordan and Assyria. Pp. 44–58 in Stager, L. W.; Greene, J. A.; and Coogan, M. D. (eds.). *The Archaeology of Jordan and Beyond: Essays in Honor of James A. Sauer.* Studies in the Archaeology and History of the Levant 1. Winona Lake, Indiana.

2001a   Iron Age Settlement in Edom: A Revised Framework. Pp. 256–69 in Daviau,
         P. M. M.; Wevers, J. W.; and Weigl, M. (eds.). *The World of the Aramaeans II:
         Studies in History and Archaeology in Honor of Paul-Eugène Dion.* Sheffield.
2001b   New Evidence on Edom in the Neo-Babylonian and Persian Periods.
         Pp. 198–213 in Dearman, J. A. (ed.). *The Land That I Will Show You: Essays
         on the History and Archaeology of the Ancient Near East in Honor of J. Maxwell
         Miller.* JSOTSup 343. Sheffield.

Bienkowski, P., and Steen, E. van der
2001   Tribes, Trade, and Towns: A New Framework for the Late Iron Age in
         Southern Jordan and the Negev. *BASOR* 323: 21–47.

Biger, G., and Grossman, D.
1992   Population Density in the Traditional Village of Palestine. *Cathedra* 63: 108–
         21. [Hebrew]

Biran (Bergman), A.
1936a   Soundings at the Supposed Site of Old Testament Anathoth. *BASOR* 62: 22–
         25.
1936b   Anathoth? *BASOR* 63: 22–23.

Biran, A.
1982   Notes and News: Aroer. *IEJ* 15: 161–63.
1985a   On the Identification of Anathoth. *ErIsr* 18: 209–14. [Hebrew]
1985b   Tel ʿIra. *Qadmoniot* 69–70: 25–28. [Hebrew]
1987   Tel-ʿIra and ʾAroʿer towards the End of the Judean Monarchy. *Cathedra* 42:
         26–33. [Hebrew]

Biran, A., and Cohen, R.
1976   Notes and News: Aroer. *IEJ* 26: 138–40.
1978   Aroer in the Negev. *Qadmoniot* 41: 20–24. [Hebrew]
1981   Aroer in the Negev. *ErIsr* 15: 250–73. [Hebrew]

Birch, W. F.
1911   Gibeah of Saul and Zela: The Site of Jonathan's Home and Tomb. *PEF(QS)*:
         101–9.
1913   Gibeah at Adaseh. *PEF(QS)*: 38–42.
1914   The Site of Gibeah. *PEF(QS)*: 42–44.

Blair, E. P.
1936   Soundings at ʿAnata (Roman Anathoth). *BASOR* 62: 18–21.

Blenkinsopp, J.
1988   *Ezra, Nehemiah.* OTL. Philadelphia.
1990   *Ezekiel.* Interpretation. Louisville.
1991   Temple and Society in Achemenid Judah. Pp. 22–53 in Davies, P. R. (ed.).
         Second Temple Studies, 1: Persian Period. Sheffield.
1995   Deuteronomy and the Politics of Post-Mortem Existence. *VT* 45/1: 1–16.
1998   The Judean Priesthood during the Neo-Babylonian and Achaemenid Periods:
         A Hypothetical Reconstruction. *CBQ* 60: 25–34.

Bliss, F. J.
1899a   First, Second and Third Reports on the Excavations at Tell Zakariya.
         PEF(QS): 10–25, 89–111, 170–87.
1899b   First and Second Reports on the Excavations at Tell Es-Safi. *PEF(QS)*: 188–
         99, 317–33.
1900a   Fourth Report on the Excavations at Tell Zakariya. *PEF(QS)*: 7–16.
1900b   Third Report on the Excavations at Tell Es-Safi. *PEF(QS)*: 16–29.

1900c First and Second Reports on the Excavations at Tell Ej-Judeideh. *PEF(QS)*: 87–101, 199–222.

1900d Report on the Excavations at Tell Sandahannah. *PEF(QS)*: 319–41.

Bliss, F. J., and Dickie, A. C.
1898 *Excavations at Jerusalem: 1894–1897.* London.

Bliss, F. J., and Macalister, R. A. S.
1902 *Excavations in Palestine during the Years 1898–1900.* London.

Boehmer, J.
1933 König Josias Tod. *Archiv für Religionswissenschaft* 30: 199–203.

Boer, P. A. H. de
1970 Some Remarks concerning and Suggested by Jeremiah 43:17. Pp. 71–79 in Frank, H. T., and Reed, W. L. (eds.). *Translating and Understanding the Old Testament: Essays in Honor of Herbert Gordon May.* Nashville.

Bogaert, P. M.
1994 Le Livre de Jérémie en perspective: Les deux rédactions antiques selon les travaux en cours. *RB* 101: 363–406.

Bogaert, P. M. (ed.)
1981 *Le Livre de Jérémie: Le prophète et son milieu. Les oracles et leur transmission.* Leuven.

Boling, R. G.
1975 *Judges: A New Translation with Introduction and Commentary.* AB 6A. New York.
1982 *Joshua: A New Translation with Introduction and Commentary.* AB 6. New York.

Borger, R.
1956 *Die Inschriften Asarhaddons, Königs von Assyrien.* Graz.
1965 Der Aufstieg des neubabylonischen Reiches. *JCS* 19: 59–78.
1969 Zur Datierung des assyrischen Königs Sinšumulišir. *Or* 38/2: 237–39.

Bowman, R. A.
1954 Introduction and Exegesis to the Book of Ezra and the Book of Nehemiah. Pp. 551–819 in vol. 3 of *IB*.

Braun, R. L.
1979 Chronicles, Ezra and Nehemiah Theology and Literary History. Pp. 52–64 in Emerton, J. A. (ed.). *Studies in the Historical Books of the Old Testament.* Leiden.

Breasted, J. H.
1962 *Ancient Records of Egypt.* 5 vols. New York.

Brettler, M. Z.
1989 Ideology, History and Theology in 2 Kings XVII 7–23. *VT* 39/3: 268–82.
1991 2 Kings 24:13–14 as History. *CBQ* 53/4: 541–52.
1995 *The Creation of History in Ancient Israel.* London.

Briend, J.
1996 L'édit de Cyrus et sa valeur historique. *Trans* 11: 33–44.

Bright, J.
1949 A New Letter in Aramaic, Written to a Pharaoh of Egypt. *BA* 12: 46–52.
1951 The Date of the Prose Sermons of Jeremiah. *JBL* 70: 15–35.
1959 *A History of Israel.* OTL. Philadelphia. 2nd ed. 1972.
1965 *Jeremiah.* AB 21. New York.

Brinkman, J. A.
1984 *Prelude to Empire: Babylonian Society and Politics: 747–626 B.C.* Philadelphia.

1990   The Babylonian Chronicle Revisited. Pp. 73–104 in Abush, Z.; Huehnergard,
            J.; and Steinkeller, P. (eds.). *Lingering over Words: Studies in Ancient Near
            Eastern Literature in Honor of William L. Moran.* Atlanta.
Brockington, L. H.
1969   *Ezra, Nehemiah and Esther.* CB. Oxford.
Broshi, M.
1972   Excavations in the House of Caiaphas, Mount Zion. *Qadmoniot* 19–20: 104–
            7. [Hebrew]
1974   The Expansion of Jerusalem in the Reigns of Hezekiah and Manasseh. *IEJ* 24:
            21–26.
1976   Excavations on Mount Zion, 1971–1972: Preliminary Report. *IEJ* 26: 81–88.
1977   The Population of Early Jerusalem. Pp. 65–74 in Broshi, M. (ed.). *Between
            Hermon and Sinai: Memorial to Amnon.* Jerusalem. [Hebrew]
1978   Estimating the Population of Ancient Jerusalem. *BAR* 4: 10–15.
1991   The Inhabitants of Jerusalem during the First Temple Period. Pp. 63–67 in
            Amit, D., and Gonen, R. (eds.). *Jerusalem during the First Temple Period.*
            Jerusalem. [Hebrew]
Broshi, M., and Finkelstein, I.
1990   The Population of Palestine in 734 BCE. *Cathedra* 58: 3–24. [Hebrew]
1992   The Population of Palestine in Iron Age II. *BASOR* 287: 47–60.
Broshi, M., and Gophna, R.
1984   The Settlements and Population of Palestine during the Early Bronze Age II–
            III. *BASOR* 253: 41–53.
1986   Palestine in the Middle Bronze II: Its Settlements and Population. *BASOR*
            261: 73–90.
Brown, J. P.
1969   *The Lebanon and Phoenicia I.* Beirut.
Brunet, G.
1965   La prise de Jérusalem sous Sédécias les sens militaires de l'hébreu *bâq'a*. *RHR*
            167: 157–76.
Bullah, M.
1984   *The Book of Jeremiah.* Jerusalem. [Hebrew]
Bunimovitz, S.
1994   Socio-Political Transformations in the Central Hill Country in the Late
            Bronze–Iron I Transition. Pp. 179–202 in Finkelstein, I., and Naʾaman, N.
            (eds.). *From Nomadism to Monarchy: Archaeological and Historical Aspects of
            Early Israel.* Jerusalem.
Burney, C. F.
1903   *The Book of Judges and Notes on the Hebrew Text of the Books of Kings.* New
            York.
Burrows, M.
1933–34 Nehemiah 3:1–32 as a Source for the Topography of Ancient Jerusalem.
            AASOR 14: 115–40.
Burstein, S. M.
1978   *The Babyloniaca of Berossus.* Malibu.
1984   Psamtek I and the End of Nubian Domination in Egypt. *The Journal of the
            Society for the Study of Egyptian Antiquities* 14: 31–34.
Cahill, J. M.
1995   Rosette Stamp Seal Impressions from Ancient Judah. *IEJ* 45: 230–52.

Cahill, J. M., and Tarler, D.
1994   Excavations Directed by Yigal Shiloh at the City of David, 1978–1985.
        Pp. 31–45 in Geva, H. (ed.). *Ancient Jerusalem Revealed*. Jerusalem.

Camp, L.
1990   *Hiskija und Hiskijabild: Analyse und Interpretation von 2 Kön 18–20*. Münster
        Theologische Abhandlungen 9. Altenberg.

Campbell, A. F.
1986   *Of Prophets and Kings: A Late Ninth-Century Document (1 Samuel 1–2 Kings
        10)*. CBQMS 17. Washington, D.C.

Cannon, W. W.
1925   The Integrity of Habakkuk cc. 1. 2. ZAW 43: 62–90.

Carroll, R. P.
1981   *From Chaos to Covenant Prophecy in the Book of Jeremiah*. New York.
1986   *Jeremiah*. OTL. Sheffield.

Carroll, W. D.
1925   Bittir and Its Archaeological Remains. AASOR 5: 77–104.

Carter, C. E.
1991   *A Social and Demographic Study of the Post-Exilic Judah*. Ph.D. Dissertation.
        Duke University.
1994   The Province of Yehud in the Post-Exilic Period: Soundings in the Site
        Distribution and Demography. Pp. 106–45 in Eskenazi, T. C., and Richards,
        K. H. (eds.). *Second Temple Studies 2: Temple and Community in the Persian
        Period*. JSOTSup 175. Sheffield.
1999   *The Emergence of Yehud in the Persian Period. A Social and Demographic Study*.
        JSOTSup 294. Sheffield.

Cavaignac, E.
1957   Sur un passage de la tablette B.M. 25127. RA 51/1: 28–29.
1960   Rev. of CCK. OLZ 55: 141–43.

Cavigneaux, A., and Ismail, B. K.
1990   Die Statthalter von Suḫu und Mari im 8. Jh. V. Chr. Anhand neuer Text aus
        den irakischen Grabungen im Staugebiet des Qadissiya: Damms (Taf. 35–
        38). BaghM 21: 319–456.

Cazelles, H.
1951   Jeremiah and Deuteronomy. *Recherches de Science Religieuse* 38: 5–36.
        [Citations taken from pp. 89–111 in Perdue, L. G., and Kovacs, B. W. (eds.).
        A Prophet to the Nations. Winona Lake, Indiana, 1984]
1983   587 ou 586? Pp. 427–35 in Meyers, C. L., and O'Connor, M. (eds.). *The Word
        of the Lord Shall Go Forth*. Winona Lake, Indiana.

Chadwick, J. R.
1992   *The Archaeology of Biblical Hebron in the Bronze and Iron Ages*. Ph.D.
        Dissertation. University of Utah.

Christensen, D. L.
1992   New Evidence for the Priestly Redaction of Deuteronomy. ZAW 104: 196–
        201.

Christoph, J. R.
1993   *The Yehud Stamped Jar Handle Corpus: Implications for the History of Postexilic
        Palestine*. Ph.D. Dissertation. Ann Arbor.

Clements, R. E.
1988   *Jeremiah*. Interpretation. Atlanta.

Clines, D. J. A.
1972   Regnal Year Reckoning in the Last Years of the Kingdom of Judah. *AJBA* 5: 9–34.
1974   The Evidence for an Autumnal New Year in Pre-Exilic Israel Reconsidered. *JBL* 93: 22–40.
1984   *Ezra, Nehemiah, Esther*. NCBC. Grand Rapids, Michigan.
Cogan, M.
1974   *Imperialism and Religion: Assyria, Judah, and Israel in the Eighth and Seventh Centuries* B.C.E. Missoula, Montana.
Cogan, M., and Tadmor, H.
1977   Gyges and Ashurbanipal: A Study in Literary Transmission. *Or* 46/1: 65–85.
1988   *II Kings*. AB 11. New York.
Coggins, R. J.
1975   *Samaritans and Jews: The Origins of Samaritanism Reconsidered*. Oxford.
1990   2 Kings 23, 29: A Problem of Method in Translation. Pp. 277–81 in Brekelmans, C., and Lust, J. (eds.). *Pentateuchal and Deuteronomistic Studies*. Leuven.
Cohen, R.
1983a   Excavations at Kadesh-Barnea, 1976–1982. *Qadmoniot* 61: 2–14. [Hebrew]
1983b   *Kadesh-Barnea: A Border Fortress from the Days of the Kings of Judah*. Jerusalem.
1986   Solomon's Negev Defence Line Contained Three Fewer Fortresses. *BAR* 12: 40–45.
1995a   Fortresses and Roads in the Negev during the First Temple Period. Pp. 80–126 in *Eilat: Studies in the Archaeology, History and Geography of Eilat and the Aravah*. Jerusalem. [Hebrew]
1995b   The Fortress at ʿEn Hazeva during the Roman Period and in the Days of the Kingdom of Judah. Pp. 150–68 in *Eilat: Studies in the Archaeology, History and Geography of Eilat and the Aravah*. Jerusalem. [Hebrew]
Cohen, R., and Yisrael, Y.
1996   The Excavations at ʿEin Hazeva / Israelite and Roman Tamar. *Qadmoniot* 112: 78–92. [Hebrew]
Cole, S. W.
1996   *Nippur in Late Assyrian Times, c. 755–612* B.C. SAAS 4. Helsinki.
Collins, J. J.
1993   *Daniel with an Introduction to Apocalyptic Literature*. FOTL 20. Grand Rapids, Michigan.
Cooke, G. A.
1936   *Ezekiel*. ICC. Edinburgh.
Cornill, C. H.
1905   *Das Buch Jeremiah*. Leipzig.
Cortese, E.
1975   Lo schema deuteronomistico per i re di Giuda e d'Israele. *Bib* 56: 37–52.
1990   Theories concerning Dtr: A Possible Rapprochement. Pp. 179–90 in Brekelmans, C., and Lust, J. (eds.). *Pentateuchal and Deuteronomistic Studies: Papers Read at the XIIIth IOSOT Congress, Leuven 1989*. Leuven.
Cowley, A.
1923   *Aramaic Papyri of the Fifth Century* B.C. Oxford. [2nd ed., 1967]
Cross, F. M.
1955   Geshem the Arabian, Enemy of Nehemiah. *BA* 18: 46–47.

1961 *The Ancient Library of Qumran.* 2nd ed. New York.

1962a Epigraphical Notes on Hebrew Documents of the Eighth–Sixth Centuries B.C.: The Murabba'at Papyrus and the Letter Found near Yabneh-Yam. *BASOR* 165: 34–46.

1962b Epigraphical Notes on Hebrew Documents of the Eighth–Sixth Centuries B.C.: The Inscribed Jar Handles from Gibeon. *BASOR* 168: 18–23.

1968 The Structure of the Deuteronomistic History. *Perspectives in Jewish Learning* 3: 9–24.

1969a Two Notes on Palestinian Inscriptions of the Persian Age. *BASOR* 193: 19–24.

1969b Aspects of Samaritan and Jewish History in the Hellenistic Period. *HTR* 59: 201–22.

1969c Judaean Stamps. *ErIsr* 9: 20*–27*.

1973 *Canaanite Myth and Hebrew Epic.* Cambridge, Massachusetts.

1975 A Reconstruction of the Judean Restoration. *JBL* 94: 4–18.

Cross, F. M., and Freedman, D. N.
1953 Josiah's Revolt against Assyria. *JNES* 12: 56–58.

Cross, F. M., and Milik, J. T.
1956 Exploration in the Judean Buqe'ah *BASOR* 142: 5–17.

Cross, F. M., and Wright, G. E.
1956 The Boundary and Province Lists of the Kingdom of Judah. *JBL* 75: 202–26.

Crowfoot, J. W., and Fitzgerald, G. M.
1929 *Excavations in the Tyropoeon Valley, Jerusalem, 1927.* Manchester.

Curtis, E. L.
1910 *Critical and Exegetical Commentary on the books of Chronicles.* ICC. Edinburgh.

Dagan, Y.
1992 *The Shephelah during the Period of the Monarchy in Light of Archaeological Excavations and Surveys.* M.A. Thesis. Tel-Aviv.

1994 W. Adorayim and Its Surroundings. *Ariel* 102–3: 180–89. [Hebrew]

1996 Cities of the Judean Shephelah and Their Division into Districts Based on Joshua 16. *ErIsr* 25: 136–46. [Hebrew]

2000 *The Settlement in the Judean Shephelah in the Second and First Millennium B.C.E.: A Test-Case of Settlement Processes in a Geographical Region.* Ph.D. dissertation. Tel-Aviv University. [Hebrew]

Dajani, A.
1953 An Iron Age Tomb at el-Jib. *Annual of the Department of Antiquities of Jordan* 2: 66–74.

1956 Errata. *Annual of the Department of Antiquities of Jordan* 3: 82, figs. 19–22.

Dalley, S.
1993 Nineveh after 612 B.C. *AoF* 20: 134–47.

Dandamayev, M. A.
1979 State and Temple in Babylonia in the First Millenium B.C. Pp. 589–96 in Lipiński, E. (ed.). *State and Temple Economy in the Ancient Near East.* OLA 6. Leuven.

1988 Wages and Prices in Babylonia in the 6th and 5th Centuries B.C. *AoF* 15: 53–58.

1989 *A Political History of the Achaemenid Empire.* Leiden.

Dandamaev, M. A., and Lukonin, V. G.
  1989   The Culture and Social Institutions of Ancient Iran. Cambridge.
Davidson, R.
  1985   The Daily Study Bible: Jeremiah II and Lamentations. Edinburgh.
Davies, G. F.
  1999   Ezra and Nehemiah. Berit Olam. Collegeville, Minnesota.
Davis, D., and Kloner, A.
  1978   A Burial Cave of the Late Israelite Period on the Slopes of Mt. Zion.
          Qadmoniot 41: 16–19. [Hebrew]
Debus, J.
  1967   Die Sünde Jerobeams: Studien zur Darstellung Jerobeams und der Geschichte des
          Nordreichs in der deuteronomistischen Geschichtsschreibung. Göttingen.
DeGroot, A.
  1991   The Excavations of the City of David. Pp. 40–50 in Amit, D., and Gonen, R.
          (eds.). Jerusalem during the First Temple Period. Jerusalem. [Hebrew]
Delcor, M.
  1971   Le livre de Daniel. Paris.
Deller, K.
  1999   The Assyrian Eunuchs and Their Predecessors. Pp. 303–11 in Watanabe, K.
          (ed.). Priests and Officials in the Ancient Near East. Heidelberg.
Demsky, A.
  1971   The Genealogy of Gibeon (I Chronicles 9:35–44): Biblical and Epigraphic
          Considerations. BASOR 202: 16–23.
  1973   Geba, Gibeah and Gibeon: An Historico-Geographic Riddle. BASOR 212:
          26–31.
  1982   The Days of Ezra and Nehemiah. Pp. 40–65, 262–67 in Tadmor, H. (ed). The
          Return to Zion: The Days of the Persian Rule. Vol. 5 of The History of the People
          of Israel. Jerusalem. [Hebrew]
  1983   Pelekh in Nehemiah 2. IEJ 33: 242–44.
  1987   The Family of Saul and the Jar-Handles from el-Jib. Pp. 22–30 in Erlich, Z. H.
          (ed.). Samaria and Benjamin: Miscellany of Studies in Historical Geography.
          Ophra. [Hebrew]
  1991   Geba, Gibea and Gibeon: An Historico-Geographic Riddle. Pp. 94–102 in
          vol. 2 of Erlich, Z. H. (ed.). Samaria and Benjamin: Miscellany of Studies in
          Historical Geography. [Hebrew]
Dever, W. G.
  1969–70 Iron Age Epigraphic Material from the Area of Khirbet el-Kom. HUCA 40–
          41: 139–204.
  1971   Archaeological Methods and Results: A Review of Two Recent Publications.
          Or 40: 466–68.
  1984   Gezer Revisited. BA 47: 206–18.
  1985   Syro-Palestinian and Biblical Archaeology. Pp. 31–74 in Knight, J. A., and
          Tucker, G. M. (eds.). The Hebrew Bible and Its Modern Interpreters.
          Philadelphia.
Dever, W. G., et al.
  1970   Preliminary Report of the 1964–1966 Seasons (Gezer I). Jerusalem.
  1986   The 1969–1971 Seasons in Field IV: "The Acropolis" (Gezer IV). Jerusalem.

Dicou, B.
1994   *Edom: Israel's Brother and Antagonist.* Sheffield.
Dietrich, W.
1972   *Prophetie und Geschichte: Eine redaktionsgeschichtliche Untersuchung zum deuteronomistischen Geschichtswerk.* FRLANT 108. Göttingen.
1977a   David in Überlieferung und Geschichte. *Verkündigung und Forschung* 22: 44–64.
1977b   Josia und das Gesetzbüch (2. Reg. xxii). *VT* 27: 13–35.
1994   Martin Noth and the Future of the Deuteronomistic History. Pp. 153–75 in Mckenzie, S. L., and Graham, M. P. (eds.). *The History of Israel's Traditions: The Heritage of Martin Noth.* Sheffield.
Dijk, J. van
1962   Die Inschriftenfunde. Pp. 39–62, pls. 20, 27–28 in Lenzen, H., et al. *Vorläufin ger Bericht über die von dem Deutschen Archäologischen Institut und der Deutschen Orient-Gesellschaft aus Mitteln der Deutschen Forschungsgemeinschaft unternommenen Ausgrabungen in Uruk-Warka, Winter 1959/60.* Abhandlungen der deutschen Orientgesellschaft 7. Berlin.
Dinur, A.
1987   Settlement Sites of the Monarchy Period between Jabaʿ and Jerusalem. Pp. 187–94 in Erlich, Z. H. (ed.). *Samaria and Benjamin: Miscellany of Studies in Historical Geography.* Ophra. [Hebrew]
Dion, P.-E.
1992   Les KTYM de Tel-Arad: Grecs ou Phéniciens? *RB* 99/1: 70–97.
1995   Les Araméens du Moyen-Euphrate au VIIIe siècle à la lumière des inscriptions des máitres de Suḫu et Mari. Pp. 53–73 in Emerton, J. A. (ed.). *Congress Volume: Paris, 1992.* VTSup 61. Leiden.
1997   *Les Araméens à l'âge du fer: Histoire politique et structures sociales.* Paris.
Diringer, D.
1934   *Le inscrizioni antico ebraica Palestinesi.* Florence.
1941   On Ancient Hebrew Inscriptions Discovered at Tell ed-Duweir (Lachish)—1. *PEQ* 73: 38–56.
1967   Mizpah. Pp. 329–42 in Thomas, W. (ed.). *Archaeology and Old Testament Study.* Oxford.
Doorly, W. J.
1994   *Obsession with Justice: The Story of the Deuteronomist.* New York.
Dothan, M.
1985   Terminology for the Archaeology of the Biblical Periods. Pp. 136–41 in Aviram, J., et al. (eds.). *Biblical Archaeology Today.* Jerusalem.
Dothan, M., and Freedman, D. N.
1967   *Ashdod I: The First Season of Excavations, 1962.* ʿAtiqot 7. Jerusalem.
Dothan, M., and Porat, Y.
1982   *Ashdod IV: Excavation of Area M—The Fortifications of the Lower City.* ʿAtiqot 15. Jerusalem.
Dothan, M., et al.
1971   *Ashdod II–III: The Second and Third Seasons of Excavations, 1963, 1965.* ʿAtiqot 9–10. Jerusalem.
Dothan, T., and Gitin, S.
1987   The Rise and Fall of Ekron of the Philistines. *BA* 50: 197–222.

1990   Ekron of the Philistines. *BAR* 16: 20–36.
1994   Tel Miqne / Ekron: The Rise and Fall of a Philistine City. *Qadmoniot* 105–6: 2–28. [Hebrew]

Drioton, É., and Vandier, J.
1962   *Les peuples de l'Orient Méditerranéen II: L'Égypt.* 4th ed. Paris.

Duguid, I. M.
1994   *Ezekiel and the Leaders of Israel.* Leiden.

Duhm, B.
1901   *Das Büch Jeremia.* Tübingen.

Duncan, J. G.
1924a   Fourth Quarterly Report on the Excavation of the Eastern Hill of Jerusalem. *PEF(QS):* 163–80.
1924b   Fifth Quarterly Report on the Excavation of the Eastern Hill of Jerusalem. *PEF(QS):* 8–24.
1931–32 *Digging Up Biblical History, I–II.* London.

Dutcher-Walls, P.
1991   The Social Location of the Deuteronomists: A Sociological Study of Factional Politics in Late Pre-Exilic Judah. *JSOT* 52: 77–94.

Dyke, J. E.
2000   Ezra 2 in Ideological Perspective. Pp. 129–45 in Carroll, R. M. D. (ed.). *Rethinking Contexts, Rereading Texts: Contributions from the Social Sciences to Biblical Interpretation.* JSOTSup 299. Sheffield.

Edelman, D. V.
1995   Edom: A Historical Geography. Pp. 1–12 in Edelman, D. V. (ed.). *You Shall Not Abhor an Edomite for He Is Your Brother: Edom and Seir in History and Tradition.* Atlanta.

Edelstein, G., and Kislev, M.
1981   Mevasseret Yerushalayim: The Ancient Settlement and Its Agricultural Terraces. *BA* 44: 36–53.

Edelstein, G., and Milevski, I.
1994   The Rural Settlement of Jerusalem Reevaluated: Surveys and Excavations in the Repha'im Valley and Mevasseret Yerushalayim. *PEQ* 126: 2–23.

Edelstein, G.; Milevski, I.; and Aurant, S.
1999   *Villages, Terraces and Stone Mounds: Manahat Excavations at Jerusalem, 1987–1989.* IAA Reports 3. Jerusalem.

Edwards, O.
1992   The Year of Jerusalem's Destruction: 2 Addaru 597 B.C. Reinterpreted. *ZAW* 104/1: 10–16.

Efron, J.
1980   *Studies in the Hasmonean Period.* Tel-Aviv. [Hebrew]

Eichhorn, J. G.
1824   *Einleitung in das Alte Testament.* Göttingen.

Eichrodt, W.
1970   *Ezekiel.* Trans. C. Quin. Philadelphia.

Eissfeldt, O.
1951   The Prophetic Literature. Pp. 115–61 in Roweley, H. H. (ed.). *The Old Testament and Modern Study.* London.
1964   *Einleitung in das Alte Testament.* Tübingen.

1965 *The Old Testament: An Introduction.* New York. [Trans. P. R. Ackroyd of *Einleitung in das Alte Testament.* Tübingen, 1964]

Eitam, D.

1990 Royal Industry in Ancient Israel during the Iron Age Period. Pp. 56–73 in Aerts, E., and Klengel, H. (eds.). *The Town as Regional Economic Center in the Ancient Near East.* Leuven.

Elat, M.

1977 *Economic Relations in the Land of the Bible (c. 1000–539 B.C.).* Jerusalem. [Hebrew]

1978 The Economic Relations of the Neo-Assyrian Empire with Egypt. *JAOS* 98/1: 20–34.

1990 International Commerce in Palestine under Assyrian Rule. Pp. 67–88 in Kedar, B. Z.; Dothan, T.; and Safrai, S. (eds.). *Commerce in Palestine throughout the Ages.* Jerusalem. [Hebrew]

1991 Phoenician Overland Trade within the Mesopotamian Empires. Pp. 21–35 in Cogan, M., and Ephʿal, I. (eds.). *Ah, Assyria . . . : Studies in Assyrian History and Ancient Near Eastern Historiography Presented to Hayim Tadmor.* Jerusalem.

Elitzur, Y.

1987 'Geb' on Mount Ephraim. *Cathedra* 45: 3–18. [Hebrew]

1994 Rumah in Judah. *IEJ* 44: 128–43.

Emerton, J. A.

1966 Did Ezra Go to Jerusalem in 458 B.C.? *JTS* 17: 1–19.

Ephʿal, I.

1971 *The Nomads on the Border of Palestine in the Assyrian, Babylonian and Persian Periods.* Ph.D. Dissertation. Jerusalem. [Hebrew]

1978 The Western Minorities in Babylonia in the 6th–5th Centuries B.C.: Maintenance and Cohesion. *Or* 47: 74–90.

1982a *The Ancient Arab Nomads on the Borders of the Fertile Crescent, 9th–5th Centuries B.C.* Jerusalem and Leiden.

1982b Assyrian Rule in Palestine. Pp. 191–201, 262–65 in Malamat, A. (ed.). *The History of the People of Israel: The Age of the Monarchy—A Political History.* Jerusalem. [Hebrew]

1982c The Babylonian Exile. Pp. 17–27, 256–58 in Tadmor, H. (ed.). *The Return to Zion: The Days of the Persian Rule.* Vol. 5 of *The History of the People of Israel.* Jerusalem. [Hebrew]

1993 'You are Deserting to the Chaldeans' (Jer. 37:13). *ErIsr* 24: 18–22. [Hebrew]

1996 *Siege and Its Ancient Near Eastern Manifestations.* Jerusalem. [Hebrew]

1997 The Philistine Entity and the Origin of the Name "Palestine." Pp. 31*–35* in Cogan, M.; Eichler, B. L.; and Tigay, J. H. (eds.). *Tehillah le-Moshe: Biblical and Judaic Studies in Honor of Moshe Greenberg.* Winona Lake, Indiana. [Hebrew]

Ephʿal, I. (ed.)

1984 *The History of Eretz Israel: Israel and Judah in the Biblical Period.* Jerusalem. [Hebrew]

Ephʿal, I., and Naveh, J.

1988 The Use of Epigraphical Sources for the Study of Biblical History. *Zion* 52: 211–13. [Hebrew]

1996 *Aramaic Ostraca of the Fourth Century BC from Idumaea.* Jerusalem.

Erbt, W.

1902 *Jeremia und seine Zeit.* Göttingen.

Eshel, H.
  1987   The Late Iron Age Cemetry of Gibeon. *IEJ* 37: 1–16.
  1992   Samaria: From the Destruction of the City of Samaria to the Beginning of the
            Second Temple Period. Pp. 27–35 in Erlich, Z. H., and Eshel, Y. (eds.). *Judea
            and Samaria Research Studies: Proceedings of the 1st Annual Meeting, 1991.*
            Jerusalem. [Hebrew]
  2000   Jerusalem under Persian Rule: The City's Layout and the Historical
            Background. Pp. 327–44 in Ahituv, S., and Mazar, B. (eds.). *The History of
            Jerusalem: The Biblical Period.* Jerusalem. [Hebrew]
Eshel, H., and Kloner, A.
  1990   A Late Iron Age Tomb between Bet Hanina and Nebi Samwil, and the
            Identification of Hazor in Nehemia 11:33. *ErIsr* 21: 37–40. [Hebrew]
Eshel, I.
  1986–87 *The Chronology of Ceramic Assemblages from the End of the Iron Age in Judea.*
            Ph.D. Dissertation. Tel-Aviv. [Hebrew]
  1995   Two Pottery Groups from Kenyon's Excavations on the Eastern Slope of
            Ancient Jerusalem. Pp. 1–157 in vol. 4 of Eshel, I., and Prag, K. (eds.).
            Excavations by K. M. Kenyon in Jerusalem, 1961–1967. Oxford.
Eskenazi, T. C.
  1988   *In an Age of Prose: A Literary Approach to Ezra–Nehemiah.* Atlanta.
Evans, C. D.
  1980   Judah's Foreign Policy from Hezekiah to Josiah. Pp. 157–78 in Evans, C. D.;
            Hallo, W. W.; and White, J. B. (eds.). *Scripture in Context: Essays on the
            Comparative Method.* Pittsburgh.
  1983   Naram-Sin and Jeroboam: The Archetypal *Unheilsherrscher* in Mesopotamian
            and Biblical Historiography. Pp. 97–125 in Hallo, W. W.; Moyer, J. C.; and
            Perdue, L. G. (eds.). *Scripture in Context II: More Essays on the Comparative
            Method.* Winona Lake, Indiana.
Eynikel, E.
  1996   *The Reform of King Josiah and the Composition of the Deuteronomistic History.*
            OtSt 33. Leiden.
Fales, F. M.
  2002   Central Syria in the Letters to Sargon II. Pp. 134–52 in Hübner, U., and
            Knauf, E. A. (eds.). *Kein Land für sich allein: Studien zum Kulturkontakt in
            Kanaan, Israel/Palästina und Ebirnari für Manfred Weippert zum 65. Geburtstag.*
            OBO 186. Freiburg.
Falkner, M.
  1952–53 Neue Inschriften aus der Zeit Sin-šarru-iškuns. *AfO* 16: 305–10.
Fantalkin, A.
  2000   *Mezad Hashavyahu: Analysis of the Material Culture and Its Contribution to
            Historical Reconstruction at the End of the Iron Age.* M.A. Thesis. Tel-Aviv.
            [Hebrew]
  2001   Mezad Hashavyahu: Its Material Culture and Historical Background. *TA* 28/
            1: 3–166.
Fantalkin, A., and Tal, O.
  2005   Redating Lachish Level I: Identifying Achaemenid Imperial Policy at the
            Southern Frontier of the Fifth Satrapy. Pp. 167–96 in Lipschits, O., and
            Oeming, M. (eds.). *Judah and the Judeans in the Persian Period.* Winona Lake,
            Indiana.

Faust, A.
2003　　Judah in the Sixth Century B.C.E.: A Rural Perspective. *PEQ* 135: 37–53.
Feig, N.
1996　　New Discoveries in the Rephaim Valley, Jerusalem. *PEQ* 128: 3–7.
2000　　The Environs of Jerusalem in the Iron Age II. Pp. 387–409 in Aḥituv, S., and Mazar, B. (eds.). *The History of Jerusalem: The Biblical Period.* Jerusalem. [Hebrew]
Feinberg, C. L.
1982　　*Jeremiah: A Commentary.* Grand Rapids, Michigan.
Fensham, F. C.
1982　　*The Books of Ezra and Nehemiah.* Grand Rapids, Michigan.
Ferry, J.
1998　　'Je restaurerai Juda et Israël' (Jr 33, 7.9.26): L'écriture de Jérémie 33. *Trans* 15: 69–82.
Finegan, J.
1950　　The Chronology of Ezekiel. *JBL.* 69: 61–66.
Finkelstein, I.
1984　　The Israelite Population of the Iron Age I. *Cathedra* 32: 3–22. [Hebrew]
1986　　*The Archaeology of the Israelite Settlement.* Tel-Aviv. [Hebrew; English trans., 1988]
1989　　The Socio-Demographic Structure of the Intermediate Bronze Age. *ErIsr* 20: 75–81.
1990　　Excavations at Khirbet ed-Dawwara: An Iron Age Site Northeast of Jerusalem. *TA* 17: 163–208.
1992　　Horvat Qitmit and the Southern Trade in the Late Iron Age II. *ZDPV* 108: 156–70.
1994　　The Archaeology of the Days of Manasseh. Pp. 169–87 in Coogan, M. D.; Exum, J. C.; and Stager, L. E. (eds.). *Scripture and Other Artifacts: Essays on the Bible and Archaeology in Honor of Philip J. King.* Louisville.
1995　　*Living on the Fringe: The Archaeology and History of the Negev, Sinai and Neighbouring Regions in the Bronze and Iron Ages.* Sheffield.
1996　　The Settlement History of the Transjordan Plateau in Light of Survey Data. *ErIsr* 25: 244–51. [Hebrew]
Finkelstein, I., and Gophna, R.
1993　　Settlement, Demographic and Economic Patterns in the Highlands of Palestine in the Chalcolithic and Early Bronze Periods and the Beginning of Urbanism. *BASOR* 289: 1–22.
Fitzmyer, J. A.
1962　　The Padua Aramaic Papyrus Letters. *JNES* 21: 15–24.
1965　　The Aramaic Letter of King Adon to the Egyptian Pharaoh. *Bib* 46: 41–46.
Fohrer, G.
1920　　*Einleitung in das Alte Testament.* Heidelberg. [References from the 10th ed., 1964]
1959　　Der Vertrag zwischen König und Volk in Israel. *ZAW* 71: 1–22.
1968　　*Introduction to the Old Testament.* Nashville. [Trans. of *Einleitung in das Alte Testament*]
Fohrer, G., and Galing, K.
1955　　*Ezechiel.* Tübingen.

Forrer, E.
1920   *Die Provinzeinteilung des assyrichen Reiches.* Leipzig.
Fox, N.
2000   *In the Service of the King: Officialdom in Ancient Israel and Judah.* Cincinnati.
Frame, G.
1992   *Babylonia 689–627 B.C. : A Political History.* Istanbul.
1995   *Rulers of Babylonia from the Second Dynasty of Isin to the End of Assyrian Domination (1157–612 BC).* Toronto.
Franken, H. J.
1961   Review of AASOR 34–35. *VT* 11: 471–74.
1994   Cave 1 at Jerusalem: An Interpretation. Pp. 233–40 in Bourke, S., and Descoeudres, J. P. (eds.). *Trade, Contact and the Movement of People in the Eastern Mediterranean.* Sydney.
Franken, H. J., and Steiner, M. L. (eds.)
1990   *The Iron Age Extramural Quarter on the South West Hill.* Vol. 2 of *Jerusalem II: Excavations in Jerusalem 1961–1967.* Oxford.
Freedman, D. N.
1956   The Babylonian Chronicles. *BA* 19: 50–60.
1963   The Law and the Prophets. Pp. 226–68 in *Congress Volume: Bonn, 1962.* VTSup 9. Leiden.
1976   The Deuteronomic History. Pp. 226–28 in *IDBSup.*
Freedy, K. S., and Redford, D. B.
1970   The Dates in Ezekiel in Relation to Biblical, Babylonian and Egyptian Sources. *JAOS* 90: 462–85.
Fretheim, T. E.
1983   *Deuteronomic History.* Nashville.
Freud, L.
1999   Chapter 6: Pottery, §2. Iron Age. Pp. 189–289 in Beit-Arieh, I. (ed.). *Tel ʿIra: A Stronghold in the Biblical Negev.* Tel-Aviv.
Frevel, C.
1991   Vom Schreiben Gottes: Literarkritik, Komposition und Auslegung von 2 Kön 17,34–40. *Bib* 72: 23–48.
Frick, F. S.
1974   Another Inscribed Jar Handle from El-Jib. *BASOR* 213: 46–48.
Friedman, R. E.
1981a   *The Exile and Biblical Narrative: The Formation of the Deuteronomistic and Priestly Works.* HSM 22. Chico, California.
1981b   From Egypt to Egypt: Dtr¹ and Dtr². Pp. 167–92 in Halpern, B., and Levenson, J. D. (eds.). *Traditions in Transformation: Turning Points in Biblical Faith* (Fs. F. M. Cross). Winona Lake, Indiana.
Fritz, V., and Kempinski, A.
1983   *Ergebnisse der Ausgrabungen auf der Hirbet el Mšāš (Tel Māśōś), 1972–1975.* Vols. 1–3. Wiesbaden.
Frost, S. B.
1968   The Death of Josiah: A Conspiracy of Silence. *JBL* 87: 369–82.
Funk, R. W.
1958   The 1957 Campaign at Beth-Zur. *BASOR* 150: 8–20.

Gadd, C. J.
1923   *The Fall of Nineveh: The Newly Discovered Babylonian Chronicle, No. 21901 in the British Museum.* London.

Galil, G.
1984   The Administrative Districts of the Judean Hill Area. *Zion* 49: 205–24. [Hebrew]
1985   The Administrative Division of the Shephelah. *Shnaton* 9: 55–71. [Hebrew]
1987   The Administrative Division of the Kingdom of Judah in the Light of the Epigraphical Data. *Zion* 52: 495–509. [Hebrew]
1991a   A New Look at the Chronology of the Last Kings of Judah. *Zion* 56: 5–19. [Hebrew]
1991b   Gebaᶜ: Ephraim and the Northern Boundary of Judah in the Days of Josiah. *Tarbiẓ* 61: 1–14. [Hebrew]
1992   Parathon, imnatha, and the Fortifications of Bacchides. *Cathedra* 63: 22–30. [Hebrew]
1993   Gebaᶜ–Ephraim and the Northern Boundary of Judah in the Days of Josiah. *RB* 100/3: 358–67.
1996   *The Chronology of the Kings of Israel and Judah.* Leiden.
2001   The Message of the Book of Kings in Relation to Deuteronomy and Jeremiah. *BSac* 158: 406–14.
2004   The Chronological Framework of the Deuteronomistic History. *Bib* 85: 413–21.

Galling, K.
1935   Assyrische und persische Präfekten in Geser. *PJB* 31: 75–93.
1951a   The "Gōlā-List" according to Ezra 2 // Nehemiah 7. *JBL* 70: 149–58.
1951b   Kronzeugen des Artaxerxes? *ZAW* 63: 66–74.
1951c   Das Königsgesetz im Deuteronomium. *TLZ* 76: 133–38.
1952   Die Exilwende in der Sicht des Propheten Sacharja. *VT* 2: 18–36.
1954a   *Die Bücher der Chronik, Ezra, Nehemia.* Göttingen.
1954b   Von Naboned zu Darius: Studien zur chaldaischen und persischen Geschichte. *ZDPV* 70: 4–32.
1964   *Studien zur Geschichte Israels im Persischen Zeitalter.* Tübingen.

Garbini, G.
1964   The Dating of Post-exilic Stamps. Pp. 68–61 in Aharoni, Y. *Excavations at Ramat Raḥel: Seasons 1959–1960.* Rome.
1988   *History and Ideology in Ancient Israel.* London.

García Lopez, F.
1987   Construction et destruction de Jérusalem: Histoire et prophétie dans les cadres rédactionnels des livres des Rois. *RB* 94/2: 222–32.

Gardiner, A.
1961   *Egypt of the Pharaohs.* Oxford.

Garelli, P.
1991   The Achievement of Tiglath-pileser III: Novelty or Continuity? Pp. 46–51 in Cogan, M., and Ephᶜal, I. (eds.). *Ah, Assyria . . . : Studies in Assyrian History and Ancient Near Eastern Historiography Presented to Hayim Tadmor.* Jerusalem.

Garfinkel, Y.
1987   The City-List: Epigraphic Evidence and the Administrative Division in the Kingdom of Judah. *Zion* 52: 489–94. [Hebrew]

Garscha, J.
   1974   *Studien zum Ezechielbuch (Ez. 1–39).* Bern.
Gelston, A.
   1966   The Foundations of the Second Temple. *VT* 16: 232–35.
Geoghegan, J. C.
   2003   'Until This Day' and the Preexilic Redaction of the Deuteronomistic History.
             JBL 122: 201–27.
Gerardi, P.
   1986   Declaring War in Mesopotamia. *ArOr* 33: 30–38.
Geraty, L. T.
   1975   The Khirbet el-Kôm Bilingual Ostracon. *BASOR* 220: 55–61.
Gerber, M.
   1998   Die Inschrift H(arran) 1.A/B und die neubabylonische Chronologie. *ZA* 88:
             72–93.
Gerbrandt, G. E.
   1986   *Kingship according to the Deuteronomistic History.* Atlanta.
Geva, H.
   1979   The Western Boundary of Jerusalem at the End of the Monarchy. *IEJ* 29: 84–
             91.
   1983   Excavations in the Citadel of Jerusalem, 1979–1980: Preliminary Report. *IEJ*
             33: 55–71.
   1991   Jerusalem at the End of the First Temple Period: The Archaeological Aspect.
             Pp. 165–76 in Amit, D., and Gonen, R. (eds.). *Jerusalem during the First
             Temple Period.* Jerusalem. [Hebrew]
   2003   Western Jerusalem at the End of the First Temple Period in Light of the
             Excavations in the Jewish Quarter. Pp. 183–208 in Vaughn, A. G., and
             Killebrew, A. (eds.). *Jerusalem in Bible and Archaeology: The First Temple
             Period.* Atlanta.
Geva, H. (ed.)
   2000   *Architecture and Stratigraphy: Areas A, W and X-2—Final Report.* Vol. 1 of
             Jewish Quarter Excavations in the Old City of Jerusalem. Jerusalem.
Gibson, S.
   1982   Notes and News: Ras et-Tawil. *IEJ* 32: 156–57.
   1994   The Tell ej-Judeideh (Tel Goded) Excavations: A Re-appraisal Based on
             Archival Records in the Palestine Exploration Fund. *TA* 21: 194–234.
Gibson, S., and Edelstein, G.
   1985   Investigating Jerusalem's Rural Landscape. *Levant* 17: 139–55.
Giesebrecht, F.
   1907   *Das Buch Jeremia.* Göttingen.
Gilboa, A.
   1996   Assyrian Pottery in Dor and Notes on the Status of the City during the
             Period of Assyrian Rule. *ErIsr* 25: 122–35. [Hebrew]
Ginsberg, H. L.
   1948a   MMŠT and MSH. *BASOR* 109: 20–22.
   1948b   An Aramaic Contemporary of the Lachish Letters. *BASOR* 111: 24–27.
   1956   Judah and the Transjordan States from 734 to 582. Pp. 347–68 in Liberman,
             S. (ed.). *Marx Jubilee Volume.* New York.

Gitin, S.

1989   Tel Miqne–Ekron: A Type Site for the Inner Coastal Plain in the Iron Age 2
Period. Pp. 23–58 in Recent Excavations in Israel: Studies in Iron Age
Archaeology. AASOR 49. Winona Lake, Indiana.

1990a   Ekron of the Philistines, Part 2: Olive Oil Supplies to the World. BAR 16/2:
32–43.

1990b   Gezer III: A Ceramic Typology of the Late Iron II, Persian and Hellenistic Periods
at Tell Gezer. Jerusalem.

1996   Formulating a Ceramic Corpus: The Late Iron II, Persian, and Hellenistic
Pottery at Tell Gezer. Pp. 75–101 in Seger, J. D. (ed.). Retrieving the Past:
Essays on Archaeological Research and Methodology in Honor of Gus W. Van
Beek. Winona Lake, Indiana.

1997   The Neo-Assyrian Empire and Its Western Periphery: The Levant, with a
Focus on Philistine Ekron. Pp. 77–104 in Parpola, S., and Whiting, R. M.
(eds.). Assyria 1995. Helsinki.

1998   The Philistines in the Prophetic Texts: An Archaeological Perspective.
Pp. 273–90 in Magness, J., and Gitin, S. (eds.). Hesed ve-Emet: Studies in
Honor of Ernest S. Frerichs. BJS 320. Atlanta.

Glazier-McDonald, B.

1995   Edom in the Prophetical Corpus. Pp. 23–32 in Edelman, D. V. (ed.). You Shall
Not Abhor an Edomite for He Is Your Brother: Edom and Seir in History and
Tradition. Atlanta.

Glueck, N.

1936   The Boundaries of Edom. HUCA 11: 141–57.

Goldstein, J. A.

1976   I Maccabees: A New Translation with Introduction and Commentary. AB 41.
New York.

Goldwasser, O., and Naveh, J.

1976   The Origin of the Tet-Symbol. IEJ 26: 15–19.

Gophna, R.

1995   The Early Bronze Age Canaan: Some Spatial and Demographic
Observations. Pp. 269–80 in Levi, T. D. (ed.). The Archaeology of Society in the
Holy Land. New York.

Gophna, R., and Portugali, J.

1988   Settlement and Demographic Processes in Israel's Coastal Plain from the
Chalcolithic to the Middle Bronze Age. BASOR 269: 11–28.

Gordon, C. H.

1965   Ugaritic Textbook. Rome.

Gosse, B.

1994   2 Rois 14:27 et l'influence des livre prophétiques sur la rédaction du deuxième
livre des Rois. Old Testament Essays 7: 167–74.

Govrin, Y.

1992   Archaeological Survey of Israel: Map of Yatir (139). Jerusalem.

Grabbe, L. L.

1998   Ezra–Nehemiah. Old Testament Readings. London.

1999   Israel's Historical Reality after the Exile. Pp. 9–32 in Becking, B., and Korpel,
M. C. A. (eds.). The Crisis of Israelite Religion: Transformation of Religious
Tradition in Exilic and Post-Exilic Times. Leiden.

2005   The "Persian Documents" in the Book of Ezra: Are They Authentic?
            Pp. 527–66 in Lipschits, O., and Oeming, M. (eds.). *Judah and the Judeans in the Persian Period.* Winona Lake, Indiana.

Graf, D. F.
1993   The Persian Royal Road System in Syria–Palestine. *Trans* 6: 149–68.

Graf, K. F.
1862   *Der Prophet Jeremia.* Leipzig.

Graham, J. N.
1984   "Vinedressers and Plowmen": 2 Kings 25:12 and Jeremiah 52:16. *BA* 47/1: 55–58.

Grant, E.
1926   Ramalla: Signs of the Early Occupation of This and Other Sites. *PEF(QS)* 1926: 186–95.

1929   *Beth Shemesh: A Report of the Excavations Made in 1928.* Haverford.

1931–32 *Ain Shems Excavations 1–2.* Haverford.

1934   *Rumeileh.* Haverford.

Grant, E., and Wright, G. E.
1938   *Ain Shems Excavations, Part IV.* Haverford.

1939   *Ain Shems Excavations, Part V.* Haverford.

Gray, J.
1964   *I and II Kings.* OTL. London.

Grayson, A. K.
1975a   *Assyrian and Babylonian Chronicles.* Locust Valley, California. [Repr. Winona Lake, Indiana, 2000]

1975b   *Babylonian Historical Literary Texts.* Toronto.

1980   Assyria and Babylonia. *Or* 49: 140–94.

1981   The Chronology of the Reign of Ashurbanipal. *ZA* 70: 227–45.

1991   Assyria: Tiglath-pileser III to Sargon II (744–705 B.C.), pp. 71–102; Assyria: Sennacherib and Esarhaddon (704–669 B.C.), pp. 103–41; Assyria, 668–635 B.C.: The Reign of Assurbanipal, pp. 142–61 in *The Assyrian and Babylonian Empires and Other States of the Near East from the Eighth to the Sixth Centuries B.C.* Vol. 3/2 of *CAH.*

1992   History and Culture of Assyria, pp. 732–55; and History and Culture of Babylonia, pp. 755–77 in vol. 4 of *ABD.* New York.

1995a   Eunuchs in Power: Their Role in the Assyrian Bureaucracy. Pp. 85–98 in Dietrich, M., and Loretz, O. (eds.). *Vom Alten Orient zum Alten Testament: Feschrift für Wolfram Freiherrn von Soden zum 85. Geburstag am 19. Juni 1993.* Neukirchen-Vluyn.

1995b   Assyrian Rule of Conquered Territory in Ancient Western Asia. Pp. 959–68 in Sasson, J. M. (ed.). *Civilization of the Ancient Near East.* New York.

Green, A. R.
1982a   The Fate of Jehoiakim. *AUSS* 20/2: 103–9.

1982b   The Chronology of the Last Days of Judah: Two Apparent Discrepancies. *JBL* 101: 57–73.

1993   The Identity of King So of Egypt: An Alternative Interpretation. *JNES* 52/3: 99–108.

Greenberg, M.
1957   Ezekiel 17 and the Policy of Psammetichus II. *JBL* 76: 304–9.

1983   *Ezekiel 1–20.* AB 22. New York.
Gressmann, H.
    1924   Josia und das Deuteronomium. *ZAW* 42: 313–37.
Griffiths, F.
    1909   *Catalogue of the Demotic Papyri in the John Rylands Library (II).* Manchester.
Grintz, J. M.
    1972   From Zerubbabel to Nehemiah. *Zion* 37: 125–82. [Hebrew]
Gross, W. (ed.).
    1995   *Jeremia und die 'deuteronomistische Bewegung'.* Bonn.
Gunneweg, A. H. J.
    1981   Zur Interpretation der Bücher Ezra–Nehemia. Pp. 146–61 in Emerton, J. A.
             (ed.). *Congress Volume: Vienna, 1980.* VTSup 32. Leiden.
    1985   *Esra.* KAT 19/1. Gütersloh.
    1987   *Nehemia.* KAT 19/2. Gütersloh.
Gutman, S.
    1969   *Survey of Jewish Sites in the Hebron Mountain.* Jerusalem.
Gyles, M. F.
    1959   *Pharaonic Policies and Administration, 663 to 323 B.C.* Chapel Hill, North
             Carolina.
Hadley, J.
    1984   *St. Andrew's Tomb 25: A Late Iron Age/Persian Tomb on the Shoulder of the
             Hinnom Valley of Jerusalem.* M.A. Thesis, Institute of Holy Land Studies.
             Jerusalem.
Haiman, M.
    1994   The Iron Age II Sites of the Western Negev Highlands. *IEJ* 44: 36–61.
Hallo, W. W.
    1995   Slave Release in the Biblical World in Light of a New Text. Pp. 79–94 in
             Zevit, Z.; Gitin, S.; and Sokoloff, M. (eds.). *Solving Riddles and Untying Knots:
             Biblical, Epigraphic, and Semitic Studies in Honor of Jonas C. Greenfield.*
             Winona Lake, Indiana.
Hallo, W. W., and Simpson, W. K.
    1971   *The Ancient Near East: A History.* New York.
Halpern, B.
    1987   "Brisker Pipes Than Poetry": The Development of Israelite Monotheism.
             Pp. 77–115 in Neusner, J.; Levin, B. A.; and Frerichs, E. S. (eds.). *Judaic
             Perspectives on Ancient Israel.* Atlanta.
    1988   *The First Historians: The Hebrew Bible and History.* San Francisco.
    1990   A Historiographic Commentary on Ezra 16: A Chronological Narrative and
             Dual Chronology in Israelite Historiography. Pp. 85–93 in Propp, W. H.;
             Halpern, B.; and Freedman, D. N. (eds.). *The Hebrew Bible and Its Interpreters.*
             Winona Lake, Indiana.
    1991   Jerusalem and the Lineages in the Seventh Century BCE: Kinship and the
             Rise of Individual Moral Liability. Pp. 11–107 in Halpern, B., and Hobson,
             D. W. (eds.). *Law and Ideology in Monarchic Israel.* Sheffield.
Halpern, B., and Vanderhooft, D. S.
    1991   The Editions of Kings in the 7th–6th Centuries B.C.E. *HUCA* 62: 179–244.
Hammond, P. C.
    1957   A Note on Two Seal Impressions from Tel el-Sultan. *PEQ* 89: 68–69.

Handy, L. K.
  1994   The Role of Huldah in Josiah's Cult Reform. *ZAW* 106/1: 40–53.
Hanson, P. D.
  1987   Israelite Religion in the Early Postexilic Period. Pp. 485–508 in Miller, P. D.; Hanson, P. D.; and McBride, S. D. (eds.). *Ancient Israelite Religion.* Philadelphia.
Harrison, R. K.
  1973   *Jeremiah and Lamentations.* TOTC. London.
Harrison, T. P.
  2001   Tell Taʿyinat and the Kingdom of Unqi. Pp. 115–32 in Daviau, P. M. M.; Wevers, J. W.; and Weigl, M. (eds.). *The World of the Aramaeans II: Studies in History and Archaeology in Honor of Paul-Eugène Dion.* Sheffield.
Hart, S.
  1986   Preliminary Thoughts on Settlement in Southern Edom. *Levant* 18: 51–58.
  1987   Five Soundings in Southern Jordan. *Levant* 19: 33–47.
Hart, S., and Falkner, R. K.
  1985   Preliminary Report on a Survey in Edom, 1984. *ADAJ* 19: 255–77.
Hawkins, J. D.
  1995   North Syria and South-East Anatolia. Pp. 87–102 in Liverani, M. (ed.). *Neo-Assyrian Geography.* Rome.
Hayes, J. H., and Hooker, P. K.
  1988   *A New Chronology for the Kings of Israel and Judah and Its Implications for Biblical History and Literature.* Atlanta.
Hayes, J. H., and Miller, J. M. (eds.)
  1977   *Israelite and Judaean History.* London.
Heltzer, M., and Eitam, D. (eds.)
  1987   *Olive Oil in Antiquity: Israel and Neighbouring Countries from Neolith to Early Arab Period.* Haifa.
Heltzer, M., and Kochman, M. (eds.)
  1985   *Encyclopedia of the World of the Bible: Ezra and Nehemiah.* Jerusalem. [Hebrew]
Hengel, M.
  1974   *Judaism and Hellenism.* London.
Hentschel, G.
  1985   *2 Könige.* Die Neue Echter Bibel Altes Testament 11. Würzburg.
Herr, L. G.
  1985   The Servant of Baalis. *BA* 48: 169–72.
  1993   What Ever Happened to the Ammonites? *BAR* 19: 26–35, 68.
  1999   The Ammonites in the Late Iron Age and Persian Period. Pp. 219–37 in MacDonald, B., and Younker, R. W. (eds.). *Ancient Ammon.* Studies in the History and Culture of the Ancient Near East 17. Leiden.
Herrmann, S.
  1986   *Jeremia.* Biblischer Kommentar, Altes Testament 12. Neukirchen-Vluyn.
Herzog, Z.
  1997   The Arad Fortress. Pp. 111–292 in *Arad.* Tel-Aviv. [Hebrew]
  2002   The Fortress Mound at Tel Arad: An Interim Report. *TA* 29: 3–109.
Herzog, Z., et al.
  1984   The Israelite Fortress at Arad. *BASOR* 254: 1–34.

Hillers, D. R.
1972 *Lamentations: Introduction, Translation and Notes*. AB 7A. Garden City, New York.

Hirschfeld, Y.
1985 *Archaeological Survey of Israel: Map of Herodium (108/2)*. Jerusalem. [Hebrew]

Hizmi, H.
1998 The Excavations of Khirbet Nimra in Hebron. Pp. 14–18 in Lipschits, O. (ed.). *Is It Possible to Define the Pottery of the Sixth Century B.C.E. in Judea?* (Booklet of summaries of lectures from the conference held in Tel-Aviv University, October 21, 1998.) Tel-Aviv. [Hebrew]

Hizmi, H., and Shabtai, Z.
1993 A Public Building from the Persian Period at Jabel Nimra. Pp. 65–86 in Erlich, Z. H., and Eshel, Y. (eds.). *Judea and Samaria Research Studies. Proceedings of the 3rd Annual Meeting, 1993*. Ariel. [Hebrew]

Hobbs, T. R.
1972 Some Remarks on the Composition and Structure of the Book of Jeremiah. *CBQ* 34: 257–75.
1985 *2 Kings*. WBC. Waco, Texas.

Hoffman, Y.
1966 *Edom in Prophecy*. M.A. Thesis. Tel-Aviv. [Hebrew]
1972 Edom as a Symbol of Evil in the Bible. Pp. 76–89 in Uffenheimer, B. (ed.). *Bible and Jewish History: Studies in Bible and Jewish History Dedicated to the Memory of Jacob Liver*. Tel-Aviv. [Hebrew]
1973 *The Prophecies against the Nations in the Bible*. Ph.D. Dissertation. Tel-Aviv. [Hebrew]
1995 On Editorial Methods in the Book of Jeremiah. Pp. 57–72 in Oppenheimer, A., and Kasher, A. (eds.). *Dor le-Dor: From the End of Biblical Times up to the Redaction of the Talmud—in Honor of Joshua Efron*. Jerusalem. [Hebrew]
1996 Aetiology, Redaction and Historicity in Jeremiah XXXVI. *VT* 46: 179–89.
1997a "I Will Know That This Is the Word of the Lord" (Jer 32:8). *Beth Mikra* 150: 198–210. [Hebrew]
1997b "And There Were Added Besides unto Them Many Like Words." Pp. 90–103 in Hoffman, Y., and Polak, F. H. (eds.). *A Light for Jacob: Studies in the Bible and the Dead Sea Scrolls in Memory of Jacob Shalom Licht*. Jerusalem. [Hebrew]
2000 Literature and Ideology in Jeremiah 40:1–43:7. Pp. 103–25 in Garsiel, M., et al. (eds.). *Studies in Bible and Exegesis, Vol. V: Presented to Uriel Simon*. Ramat Gan. [Hebrew]
2001 *Jeremiah: Introduction and Commentary*. Vols. 1–2. Tel-Aviv. [Hebrew]

Hoffmann, H.-D.
1980 *Reform und Reformen: Untersuchungen zu einem Grundthema des deuteronomistischen Geschichtsschreibung*. AThANT 66. Zurich.

Hoffmeier, J. K.
1981 A New Insight on Pharaoh Apries from Herodotus, Diodorus and Jeremiah 46:17. *The Journal of the Society for the Study of Egyptian Antiquities* 11: 165–70.

Hogenhaven, J.
1988 *Problems and Prospects of Old Testament Theology*. Sheffield.

Hoglund, K. G.
   1991   The Achaemenid Context. Pp. 22–53 in Davies, P. R. (ed.). *Persian Period.*
             Vol. 1 of *Second Temple Studies*. Sheffield.
   1992   *Achaemenid Imperial Administration in Syria–Palestine and the Missions of Ezra
             and Nehemiah*. Atlanta.
Holladay, W. L.
   1960   Prototype and Copies: A New Approach to the Poetry and Prose Problem in
             the Book of Jeremiah. *JBL* 79: 351–67.
   1966a   The Recovery of the Poetic Passages of the Book of Jeremiah. *JBL* 85: 401–
             35.
   1966b   Jeremiah and Moses: Further Observations. *JBL* 85: 17–27.
   1975   A Fresh Look at 'Source B' and 'Source C' in Jeremiah. *VT* 25: 394–412.
   1981   A Coherent Chronology of Jeremiah's Early Career. Pp. 58–73 in Bogaert,
             P. M. (ed.). *Le Livre de Jérémia: Le Prophète et son milieu, les oracles et leur
             transmission*. Leuven.
   1986   *Jeremiah 1: A Commentary on the Book of the Prophet Jeremiah, Chapters 1–25*.
             Philadelphia.
   1989   *Jeremiah 2: A Commentary on the Book of the Prophet Jeremiah, Chapters 26–52*.
             Minneapolis.
Hölscher, G.
   1922   Komposition und Ursprung des Deuteronomiums. *ZAW* 40: 161–225.
   1923a   Das buch der Könige, seine Quellen und seine Redaktion. Pp. 158–213 in
             Schmidt, H. (ed). *In Eucharisterion: Studien zur Religion und Literatur des Alten
             und Neuen Testament* (Herman Gunkel zum 60. Geburtstag). Göttingen.
   1923b   *Die Bücher Esra und Nehemia*. Tübingen.
Hollenstein, H.
   1977   Literarkritische Erwägungen zum Bericht über die Reformmassnahmen Josias
             2 Kön. XXIII 4ff. *VT* 27: 321–36.
Holmgren, F. C.
   1987   *Ezra and Nehemiah*. Edinburgh.
Holt, E. K.
   1986   Jeremiah's Temple Sermon and the Deuteronomists: An Investigation of the
             Redactional Relationship. *JSOT* 36: 73–87.
Hooke, S. H.
   1935   A Scarab and Sealing from Tell Duweir. *PEQ* 67: 195–97.
Hooker, P. K.
   1993   The Location of the Brook of Egypt. Pp. 203–14 in Graham, M. P., et al.
             (eds.). *History and Interpretation: Essays in Honour of John H. Hayes*. Sheffield.
Horn, S. H.
   1967   The Babylonian Chronicle and the Ancient Calendar of the Kingdom of
             Judah. *AUSS* 5: 12–27.
Hornung, E.
   1966   Die Sonnenfinsternis nach dem Tode Psammetichs I. *ZÄS* 92: 38–39.
Horowitz, W.
   1988   The Babylonian Map of the World. *Iraq* 50: 147–65.
   1993   Moab and Edom in the Sargon Geography. *IEJ* 43: 151–56.
Hossfeld, F.
   1977   *Untersuchungen zu Komposition und Theologie des Ezechielbuches*. Würzburg.

Hübner, U.
1987   Bücherbesprechungen. *ZDPV* 103: 226–30.
1992   *Die Ammoniter: Untersuchungen zur Geschichte, Kultur und Religion eines transjordanischen Volkes im 1. Jahrtausend v. Chr.* Wiesbaden.
Huehnergard, J.
1986   Book Reviews about La statue de Tell Fekherye et son inscription bilingue assyrro-araméenne. *BASOR* 261: 91–95.
Hyatt, J. P.
1942   Jeremiah and Deuteronomy. *JNES* 1: 156–73.
1984   The Deuteronomic Edition of Jeremiah. Pp. 247–67 in Perdue, L. G., and Kovacs, B. W. (eds.). *A Prophet to the Nations.* Winona Lake, Indiana. [Reprint of pp. 71–95 in vol. 1 of *Vanderbilt Studies in the Humanities.* Nashville, 1951]
1956a   New Light on Nebuchadrezzar and Judean History. *JBL* 75: 277–84.
1956b   *Introduction and Exegesis: Jeremiah. IB* 5. New York.
Ihromi, I.
1974   Die Königinmutter und der "ʿam haʾarez" im Reich Judah. *VT* 24: 421–29.
Iliffe, J. H.
1933   Pre-Hellenistic Greek Pottery in Palestine. *QDAP* 2: 15–26.
Ishida, T.
1975   The "People of the Land" and the Political Crisis in Judah. *AJBI* 1: 23–38.
James, T. G. H.
1991   Egypt: The Twenty-Fifth and Twenty-Sixth Dynasties. Pp. 677–747 in *Assyrian and Babylonian Empires and Other States of the Near East: Eighth to Sixth Centuries B.C.* Vol. 3/2 of *CAH.*
Jamieson-Drake, D. W.
1991   *Scribes and Schools in Monarchic Judah: A Socio-Archeological Approach.* JSOTSup 109. Sheffield.
Janssen, E.
1956   *Juda in der Exilszeit: Ein Beitrag zur Frage der Entstehung des Judentums.* Göttingen.
Janzen, J. G.
1973   *Studies in the Text of Jeremiah.* Cambridge.
Japhet, S.
1977   *The Ideology of the Book of Chronicles and Its Place in Biblical Thought.* Jerusalem. [Hebrew]
1982   Sheshbazzar and Zerubbabel. *ZAW* 94: 66–98.
1983a   Sheshbazzar and Zerubbabel. *ZAW* 95: 218–29.
1983b   People and Land in the Restoration Period. Pp. 103–25 in Strecker, G. (ed.). *Das Land Israel in biblisher Zeit.* Göttingen.
1993a   *I & II Chronicles: A Commentary.* London.
1993b   Composition and Chronology in the Book of Ezra–Nehemiah. *ErIsr* 24: 111–21. [Hebrew]
2000   The Temple of the Restoration Period: Reality and Ideology. Pp. 345–82 in Aḥituv, S., and Mazar, B. (eds.). *The History of Jerusalem: The Biblical Period.* Jerusalem. [Hebrew]
Jepsen, A.
1956   *Die Quellen des Königbuches.* 2nd ed. Halle.

1959   Die Reform des Josia. Pp. 97–108 in Herrmann, J. (ed.). *Festschrift Friedrich Baumgärtel zum 70. Geburstag, 14 Januar 1958 gewidmet.* Erlangen.

Jericke, D.
2003   *Abraham in Mamre: Historische und exegetische Studien zur Region von Hebron und zu Genesis 11,27–19,38.* Leiden.

Joannès, F.
1982   La localisation de Ṣurru à l'époque néo-babylonienne. *Sem* 32: 35–42.
1987   Trois texts de Ṣurru à l'époque néo-babylonienne. *RA* 81: 147–58.
1994   Une visite du gouverneur d'Arpad. *NABU* (March, no. 1): 21–22.

Joannès, F., and Lemaire, A.
1999   Trois tablettes cunéiformes à onomastique ouest-sémitique. *Trans* 17: 17–34.

Johns, C. N.
1950   The Citadel, Jerusalem: A Summary of Work since 1934. *QDAP* 14: 121–90.

Jones, G. H.
1963   The Cessations of Sacrifice after the Destruction of the Temple in 586 B.C. *JTS* 14: 12–31.
1984   *1 and 2 Kings.* 2 vols. NCBC. Grand Rapids, Michigan.

Kallai, Z.
1960   *The Northern Boundaries of Judah.* Jerusalem. [Hebrew]
1967   *The Tribes of Israel: A Study in the Historical Geography of the Bible.* Jerusalem. [Hebrew]
1972   The Land of Benjamin and Mt. Ephraim. Pp. 153–95 in Kochavi, M. (ed.). *Judaea, Samaria and the Golan: Archaeological Survey, 1967–1968.* Jerusalem. [Hebrew]

Kasher, A.
1975   Some Suggestions and Comments concerning Alexander of Macedon's Campaign in Palestine. *Beth Mikra* 20: 187–208. [Hebrew]
1988a   *Edom, Arabia and Israel: Relations of the Jews in Ertez-Israel with the Nations of the Frontier and the Desert during the Hellenistic and Roman Era (332 BCE–70 CE).* Jerusalem. [Hebrew]
1988b   *Canaan, Philistia, Greece and Israel: Relations of the Jews in Eretz-Israel with the Hellenistic Cities (332 BCE–70 CE).* Jerusalem. [Hebrew]
1993   Some Suggestions and Comments concerning Alexander of Macedon's Campaign in Palestine: A Rectified Version of the 1975 Text. Pp. 13–35 in Rappaport, U., and Ronen, I. (eds.). *The Hasmonean State: The History of the Hasmoneans during the Hellenistic Period.* Jerusalem. [Hebrew]

Katzenstein, H. J.
1973   *A History of Tyre.* Jerusalem.
1983   Before Pharaoh Conquered Gaza (Jeremiah XLVII 1). *VT* 33: 249–51.
1993   Nebuchadnezzar's War with Egypt. *ErIsr* 24: 184–86. [Hebrew]
1994   Gaza in the Neo-Babylonian Period (626–539 B.C.E.). *Trans* 7: 35–49.

Kaufman, I.
1959–60 *The History of Israelite Belief.* Vols. 4/1, 8. Tel-Aviv. [Hebrew]

Keil, K. F.
1857   *Commentary on the Book of Kings.* ICC. Edinburgh.

Kellermann, U.
1966   Die Listen in Nehemia 11 eine Dokumentation aus den letzten Jahren des Reiches Juda? *ZDPV* 82: 209–27.

1967 *Nehemia: Quellen, Überlieferungen und Geschichte.* Berlin.

1968 Erwägungen zum Problem der Esradatierung. *ZAW* 80: 54–87.

Kelly, B. H.

1962 *Ezra, Nehemiah, Esther, Job.* London.

Kelso, J. L.

1955 The Second Campaign at Bethel. *BASOR* 137: 5–10.

1958 The Third Campaign at Bethel. *BASOR* 151: 3–8.

1961 The Fourth Campaign at Bethel. *BASOR* 164: 5–14.

Kelso, J. L., et al.

1968 *The Excavation of Bethel 1934–1960.* AASOR 39. Cambridge.

Kempinski, A., et al.

1981 Excavations at Tel Masos, 1972, 1974, 1975. *ErIsr* 15: 154–80. [Hebrew]

Kenik, H.

1983 *Design for Kingship: The Deuteronomistic Narrative Technique in 1 Kings 3:4–15.* Chico, California.

Kenyon, K. M.

1960 *Archaeology in the Holy Land.* London. [4th ed., 1979]

1962 Excavations in Jerusalem—1961. *PEQ:* 72–89.

1963 Excavations in Jerusalem—1962. *PEQ:* 7–21.

1964a Excavations in Jerusalem—1963. *PEQ:* 7–18.

1964b Excavations in Jerusalem—1961–1963. *BA* 27: 34–52.

1964c *Digging Up Jericho.* Tel-Aviv.

1965a Excavations in Jerusalem—1964. *PEQ:* 9–20.

1965b Jerusalem. *BA* 28: 22–26.

1966 Excavations in Jerusalem—1965. *PEQ:* 73–88.

1967a *Jerusalem: Excavating 3000 Years of History.* London.

1967b Excavations in Jerusalem—1966. *PEQ:* 65–71.

1974 *Digging Up Jerusalem.* London.

Kenyon, K. M., and Holland, T. A. (eds.).

1981 *Excavations at Jericho III: The Architecture and Stratigraphy of the Tell.* London.

1982 *Excavations at Jericho IV: The Pottery Type Series and Other Finds.* London.

Keown, G. L.; Scalise, P. J.; and Smothers, T. G.

1995 *Jeremiah 26–52.* WBC 27. Dallas.

Kessler, M.

1965 *A Prophetic Biography: A Form Critical Study of Jeremiah Chapters 26–29, 32–45.* Ph.D. Dissertation, Brandeis University. Baltimore.

1966 Form-Critical Suggestions on Jer. 36. *CBQ* 28: 389–401.

1968 Jeremiah Chapters 26–45 Reconsidered. *JNES* 27: 81–88.

1975 Die Anzahl der assyrischen Provinzen des Jahre 738 v. Chr. in Norsyrien. *WO* 8: 49–63.

Keulen, P. S. F. van

1996 *Manasseh through the Eyes of the Deuteronomists: The Manasseh Account (2 Kings 21:1–18) and the Final Chapters of the Deuteronomistic History.* Leiden.

Kidner, D.

1979 *Ezra and Nehemiah.* TOTC. Leicester.

Kienitz, F. K.

1953 *Die politische Geschichte Ägyptens vom 7. Bis zum 4. Jarhundert von der Zeitwende.* Berlin.

1968   Die Säitische Renaissance. Pp. 256–82 in Cassin, E., et al. (eds.). *Die altori entalische Reiche, III: Die erste Hälfte des I. Jahrtausends.* Vol. 4 of *Fischer Weltgeschichte.* Frankfurt.

King, P. J.
1993   Archaeology and the Book of Jeremiah. *ErIsr* 23: 95*–99*.

Kitchen, K. A.
1973a   Late-Egyptian Chronology and the Hebrew Monarchy. *JANES* 5: 225–33.
1973b   *The Third Intermediate Period in Egypt (1100–650 B.C.).* Warminster. [Revised ed., 1986]
1988   Egypt and Israel during the First Millenium B.C. Pp. 107–23 in Emerton, J. A. (ed.). *Congress Volume: Jerusalem, 1986.* VTSup 40. Leiden.

Kittel, R.
1927–29 *Geschichte des Volkes Israel.* Vols. 3/1–2. Stuttgart.

Klausner, J.
1949   *The History of the Second Temple Period.* Vols. 1–2. Jerusalem. [Hebrew]
1953   Why Was Jeremiah Ignored in the Book of Kings? Pp. 189–203 in *Morecai M. Kaplan Jubilee Volume.* New York. [Hebrew]

Klein, R. W.
1979   *Israel and Exile: A Theological Interpretation.* Philadelphia.
1983   *1 Samuel.* WBC. Waco, Texas.

Klein, S.
1939   *The Land of Judah from the Days of the Return from Babylon to the Sealing of the Talmud.* Tel-Aviv. [Hebrew]

Kletter, R.
1991   The Rujm el-Malfuf Buildings and the Assyrian Vassal State of Ammon. *BASOR* 284: 33–50.
1995   *Selected Material Remains of Judah at the End of the Iron Age in Relation to Its Political Borders.* Ph.D. Dissertation. Tel-Aviv. [Hebrew]
1999   Pots and Polities: Material Remains of Late Iron Age Judah in Relation to Its Political Borders. *BASOR* 314: 19–54.

Kloner, A.
1980   *The Necropolis of Jerusalem in the Second Temple Period.* Ph.D. Dissertation. Jerusalem. [Hebrew]
1991   Maresha. *Qadmoniot* 95–96: 70–85. [Hebrew]
1992   Burial Caves from the First Temple Period in Jerusalem. *ErIsr* 23: 241–46. [Hebrew]
2000   *Survey of Jerusalem: The Southern Sector.* Jerusalem. [Hebrew and English]
2001   *Survey of Jerusalem: The Northeastern Sector.* Jerusalem. [Hebrew and English]

Kloner, A., and Eshel, E.
1999   A Seventh-Century BCE List of Names from Maresha. *ErIsr* 26: 147– 50. [Hebrew]

Knauf, E. A.
1992   The Cultural Impact of Secondary State Formation: The Cases of the Edomites and Moabites. Pp. 47–54 in Bienkowski, P. (ed.). *Early Edom and Moab: The Beginning of the Iron Age in Southern Jordan.* Oxford.
1995   Edom: The Social and Economic History. Pp. 93–118 in Edelman, D. V. (ed.). *You Shall Not Abhor an Edomite for He Is Your Brother: Edom and Seir in History and Tradition.* Atlanta.

2000   Does 'Deuteronomistic Historiography' (DtrH) Exist? Pp. 388–98 in Pury, A. de; Römer, T.; and Macchi, J. D. (eds.). *Israel Constructs Its History: Deuteronomistic Historiography in Recent Research.* JSOTSup 306. Sheffield.

Knoppers, G. N.

1992   "There Was None like Him": Incomparability in the Books of Kings. *CBQ* 54/3: 411–31.

1993   *Two Nations under God: The Deuteronomistic History of Solomon and the Dual Monarchies, I: The Reign of Solomon and the Rise of Jeroboam.* Atlanta.

1994   *Two Nations Under God; The Deuteronomistic History of Solomon and the Dual Monarchies II: The Reign of Jeroboam, the Fall of Israel, and the Reign of Josiah.* Atlanta.

2000   Is There a Future for the Deuteronomistic History? Pp. 119–34 in Römer, T. (ed.). *The Future of the Deuteronomistic History.* Leuven.

2001   Rethinking the Relationship between Deuteronomy and the Deuteronomistic History: The Case of Kings. *CBQ* 63: 393–415.

Knoppers, G. N., and McConville, J. G. (eds.)

2000   *Reconsidering Israel and Judah: Recent Studies on the Deuteronomistic History.* Sources for Biblical and Theological Study 8. Winona Lake, Indiana.

Kob, K.

1978   Noch einmal Netopha. *ZDPV* 94: 119–34.

Koch, K.

1969   *The Growth of the Biblical Tradition: The Form-Critical Method.* New York.

Kochavi, M.

1970   The First Season of Excavations at Tell Malhata. *Qadmoniot* 9: 22–24. [Hebrew]

1972   *Judea, Samaria and the Golan: Archaeological Survey, 1967–1968.* Jerusalem. [Hebrew]

1973   Khirbet Rabud: Ancient Debir. Pp. 49–76 in Aharoni, Y. (ed.). *Excavations and Studies: Essays in Honour of Professor Shmuel Yeivin.* Tel-Aviv. [Hebrew; ET: Khirbet Rabud = Debir. *TA* 1 (1974) 133]

Kochman, M.

1980   *The Status and Extent of Judah in the Persian Period.* Ph.D. Dissertation. Jerusalem. [Hebrew]

1982   "Yehud Medinta" in the Light of the Seal Impressions YHWD-PHW. *Cathedra* 24: 3–30. [Hebrew]

Koenen, K.

2003   *Bethel: Geschichte, Kult und Theologie.* Göttingen.

Koopmans, W. T.

1990   *Joshua 24 as Poetic Narrative.* Sheffield.

Krahmalkov, C.

1981   The Historical Setting of the Adon Letter. *BA* 44: 197–98.

Kremers, H.

1953   Leidensgemeinschaft mit Gott im Alten Testament: Eine Untersuchung der 'biographischen' Berichte im Jeremiabuch. *EvT* 13: 122–45.

Kuenen, A.

1890   *Historisch-kritische Einleitung in die Bücher des Alten Testament.* Vol. 2. Leipzig. [Citations are from the 1973 ed.]

Kuhrt, A. K.
  1983   The Cyrus Cylinder and Achaemenid Imperial Politics. *JSOT* 25: 83–97.
  1995   The Assyrian Heartland in the Achaemenid Period. *Pallas* 45: 239–54.
Kutsch, E.
  1974   Das Jahr der Katastrophe: 587 v. Chr. *Bib* 55: 520–45.
  1985   *Die chronologischen Datendes Ezechielbuches.* OBO 62. Göttingen.
Kutscher, F. Y.
  1960   פחוא and Its Cognate Forms. *Tarbiz* 30: 112–19. [Hebrew]
Labat, R.
  1968   Assyrien und seine Nachbarländer (Babylonien, Elam, Iran) von 1000 bis
          617 v.Chr.: Das neubabylonische Reich bis 539 v. Chr. Pp. 9–111 in Cassin,
          E., et al. (eds.). *Die alto rientalische Reiche, III: Die erste Hälfte des I.
          Jahrtausends.* Vol. 4 of *Fischer Weltgeschichte.* Frankfurt.
Landsberger, B.
  1933   Review of Unger, *Babylon. ZA* 41: 292–99.
Lang, B.
  1978   *Kein Aufstand in Jerusalem.* Stuttgart.
Langdon, S.
  1912   *Die neubabylonischen Königsinschriften.* Leipzig.
Laperrousaz, E. M.
  1981   Jérusalem à l'époque perse (étendu et statut). *Trans* 1: 55–65.
  1987   King Solomon's Wall Still Supports the Temple Mount. *BAR* 13/3: 34– 45.
Lapp, N. L.
  1975   *The Tale of a Tell.* Pittsburgh.
  1976   Casemate Walls in Palestine and the Late Iron II Casemate at Tell el-Ful
          (Gibeah). *BASOR* 223: 25–42.
Lapp, N. L. (ed.)
  1981   *The Third Campaign at Tell el-Ful: The Excavations of 1964.* AASOR 45.
          Cambridge, Massachusetts.
Lapp, P. W.
  1958   A Comparative Study of a Hellenistic Pottery Group from Beth-Zur. *BASOR*
          151: 16–27.
  1963   Ptolemaic Stamped Handles from Judah. *BASOR* 172: 22–35.
  1965   Tell el-Full. *BA* 28: 2–10.
  1968   Review of Gibeon. *AJA* 72: 391–93.
  1970   The Pottery of Palestine in the Persian Period. Pp. 179–97 in Kutsch, E., and
          Kuschke, D. A. (eds.). *Archäologie und Altes Testament Festschrift für Kurt
          Galling.* Tübingen.
Larsson, G.
  1967   When Did the Babylonian Captivity Begin? *JTS* 18: 417–23.
Latto, A.
  1992   *Joshua and David Redivivus.* Stockholm.
Lehmann, G.
  1998   Trend in the Local Pottery Development of the Late Iron Age and Persian
          Period in Syria and Lebanon, ca. 700 to 300 B.C. *BASOR* 311: 7–37.
Lemaire, A.
  1977a   *Inscriptions hébraïques, Tom. 1: Les ostraca.* Paris.
  1977b   Les Inscriptions de Khirbet el-Qôm et l'Ashérah de YHWE. *RB* 84: 595–608.

1981   *Les écoles et la formation de la Bible dans l'ancien Israel.* Göttingen.

1986   Vers l'histoire de la rédaction des livres des Rois. *ZAW* 98: 221–36.

1990   Populations et territoires de Palestine à l'époque perse. *Trans* 3: 31–74.

1994a   Les transformations politiques et culturelles de la Transjordanie au VIᵉ siècle av. J.-C. *Trans* 8: 9–25.

1994b   Déesses et Dieux de Syrie–Palestine d'après les inscriptions (c. 1000–500 Av.N.E.). Pp. 127–58 in Dietrich, W., and Klopfenstein, M. A. (eds.). *Ein Gott Allein?* Freiburg.

1996   *Nouvelles inscriptions araméennes d'Idumée au musée d'Israël.* Transeuphratène Supplement 3. Paris.

2002   *Nouvelles inscriptions araméennes d'Idumée II, Collections Moussaïeff, Jeselsohn, Welch et divers.* Transeuphratène Supplement 9. Paris.

2005   New Aramaic Ostraca from Idumea and Their Historical Interpretation. Pp. 409–52 in Lipschits, O., and Oeming, M. (eds.). *Judah and the Judeans in the Persian Period.* Winona Lake, Indiana.

Lemche, N. P.

1988   *Ancient Israel.* Sheffield.

Levenson, J. D.

1975   Who Inserted the Book of the Torah? *HTR* 68: 203–33.

1981   From Temple to Synagogue: 1 Kings 8. Pp. 143–66 in Cross, F. M.; Halpern, B.; and Levenson, J. (eds). *Traditions in Transformation.* Winona Lake, Indiana.

1984   The Last Four Verses in Kings. *JBL* 103: 353–61.

Lewy, J.

1925   Forschungen zur Alten Geschichte Vorderasiens. Pp. 68–79, 82–86 in *Mitteilungen der Vorderasiatischen Gesellschaft* 29 (Jahrgang 2). Leipzig.

L'Hour, J.

1962   L'Alliance de Sichem. *RB* 69: 161–84.

Lindsay, J.

1976   The Babylonian Kings and Edom, 605–550. *PEQ* 108: 23–39.

1999   Edomite Westward Expansion: The Biblical Evidence. *ANES* 36: 48–89.

Lipiński, E.

1971   The Assyrian Campaign to Manṣuate, in 796 B.C., and the Zakir Stela. *AION* 31: 393–99.

1972   The Egypto-Babylonian War of the Winter 601–600 B.C. *AION* 32: 235–41.

1978   The Elegy on the Fall of Sidon in Isaiah 23. *ErIsr* 14: 79*–88*.

1991   Marriage and Divorce in the Judaism of the Persian Period. *Trans* 4: 63–72.

Lipschits, O.

1997a   *The 'Yehud' Province under Babylonian Rule (586–539 B.C.E.): Historic Reality and Historiographic Conceptions.* Ph.D. Dissertation. Tel-Aviv. [Hebrew]

1997b   The Origins of the Jewish Population of Modiʾin and Its Vicinity. *Cathedra* 85: 7–32. [Hebrew]

1999a   The History of the Benjaminite Region under Babylonian Rule. *TA* 26/2: 155–90.

1999b   Nebuchadrezzar's Policy in 'Ḫattu-Land' and the Fate of the Kingdom of Judah. *UF* 30: 467–87.

1999c   The Formation of the Babylonian Province in Judah. Pp. 115–23 in *The Bible and Its World.* Division A of *Proceedings of the Twelfth World Congress of Jewish Studies.* Jerusalem. [Hebrew]

2000   Was There a Royal Estate in Ein-Gedi by the End of the Iron Age and during the Persian Period? Pp. 31–42 in Schwartz, J.; Amar, Z.; and Ziffer, I. (eds.). *Jerusalem and Eretz Israel (Arie Kindler Volume)*. Tel-Aviv. [Hebrew]

2001   Judah, Jerusalem and the Temple (586–539 B.C.). *Trans* 22: 129–42.

2002a   On the Titles ʿbd hmlk and ʿbd yhwh. *Shnaton* 13: 157–72.

2002b   "Jehoiakim Slept with His Father . . ." (II Kings 24:6): Did He? *JHS* 4: 1–23.

2002c   Literary and Ideological Aspects of Nehemiah 11. *JBL* 121: 423–40.

2003   Demographic Changes in Judah between the Seventh and the Fifth Centuries B.C.E. Pp. 323–76 in Lipschits, O., and Blenkinsopp, J. (eds.). *Judah and the Judeans in the Neo-Babylonian Period*. Winona Lake, Indiana. [Proceedings of the Conference held at Tel-Aviv University, May 2001]

2004a   From Geba to Beersheba: A Further Discussion. *RB* 111: 345–61.

2004b   Ammon in Transition from Vassal kingdom to Babylonian Province. *BASOR* 335: 37–52.

2004c   The Rural Settlement in Judah in the Sixth Century B.C.E.: A Rejoinder. *PEQ* 136: 99–107.

2005   Achaemenid Imperial Policy, the Settlement Processes in Palestine, and the Status of Jerusalem in the Middle of the Fifth Century B.C.E. Pp. 19–25 in Lipschits, O., and Oeming, M. (eds.). *Judah and the Judeans in the Persian Period*. Winona Lake, Indiana. [Proceedings of the Conference held at Heidelberg University, July 2003]

Lipschits, O. (ed.)
1998   *Can We Define the Material Culture of the Sixth Century in Judah?* (Abstracts from the Conference Held in Tel Aviv University). Tel-Aviv. [Hebrew]

Liver, J.
1958   The Return from Babylon: Its Time and Scope. *ErIsr* 5: 114–19. [Hebrew]

1959   *The House of David from the Fall of the Kingdom of Judah to the Fall of the Second Commonwealth and After*. Jerusalem. [Hebrew]

Lloyd, A.
1983   The Late Period. Pp. 263–305 in Trigger, B. G., et al. (eds.). *Ancient Egypt: A Social History*. Cambridge.

Lohfink, N.
1963   Die Bundesurkunde des Königs Josias (Eine Frage an die Deuteronomius forschung). *Bib* 44: 261–88.

1978   Die Gattung der 'Historischen Kurzgeschichte' in den letzten Jahren von Juda und in der Zeit des babylonischen Exils. *ZAW* 90: 319–47.

1981   Kerygmata des Deuteronomistischen Geschichtswerks. Pp. 87–100 in Jeremias, J., and Perlitt, L. (eds.). *Die Botschaft und die Boten (Fs. H. W. Wolff)*. Neukirchen-Vluyn.

1984   *Rückblick im Zorn auf den Staat: Voslesungen zu ausgewählten Schlüsseltexten der Bücher Samuel und Könige*. Frankfurt am Main.

1985   Zur neueren Diskussion über 2 Kön 22–23. Pp. 24–48 in Lohfink, N. (ed.). *Das Deuteronomium: Entstehung, Gestalt und Botschaft*. BETL 68. Leuven.

1987   The Cult Reform of Josiah of Judah: 2 Kings 22–23 as a Source for the History of Israelite Religion. Pp. 459–75 in Miller, P. D.; Hanson, P. D.; and McBride, S. D. (eds.). *Ancient Israelite Religion: Essays in Honor of Frank Moore Cross*. Philadelphia.

1990   Welches Orakel gab den Davididen Dauer? Ein Textproblem in 2 Kön 8,19 und das Funktionieren der dynastischen Orakel im deuteronomistischen Geschichtswerk. Pp. 349–70 in Abusch, T.; Huehnergard, J.; and Steinkeller, P. (eds.). *Lingering over Words: Studies in Ancient Near Eastern Literature in Honor of William L. Moran*. HSS 37. Atlanta.

London, G. A.
    1992   Tells: City Center or Home? *ErIsr* 23: 71*–79*.

Long, B. O.
    1984   *1 Kings*. FOTL 9. Grand Rapids, Michigan.
    1991   *2 Kings*. FOTL 10. Grand Rapids, Michigan.

Lowery, R. H.
    1991   *The Reforming Kings: Cult and Society in First Temple Judah*. JSOTSup 120. Sheffield.

Luckenbill, D. D.
    1927   *Ancient Records of Assyria and Babylonia*. Chicago.

Lundbom, J. R.
    1975   *Jeremiah: A Study in Ancient Hebrew Rhetoric*. Missoula, Montana.
    1976   The Lawbook of the Josianic Reform. *CBQ* 38: 293–302.
    1986   Baruch, Seraiah, and the Expanded Colophons in the Book of Jeremiah. *JSOT* 36: 89–114.
    1991   Rhetorical Structures in Jeremiah 1. *ZAW* 103: 193–210.

Luriah, B. Z.
    1982   Jeremiah 26 and the Shafan Family. *Beth Mikra* 89–90: 97–100. [Hebrew]
    1983   *In the Days of the Return to Zion*. Jerusalem. [Hebrew]

Lust, J.
    1981   'Gathering and Return' in Jeremiah and Ezekiel. Pp. 119–42 in Bogaert, P. M. (ed.). *Le Livre de Jérémia: Le prophète et son milieu, les oracles et leur transmission*. Leuven.

Lux, U.
    1972   Vorläufiger Bericht über die Ausgraben unter der Erlöserkirche im Muristan in der Altstadt von Jerusalem in Jahren 1970 und 1971. *ZDPV* 88: 185–203.

Macalister, R. A. S.
    1904a   Eighth Quarterly Report on the Excavation at Gezer. *PEF(QS)*: 194–228.
    1904b   Ninth Quarterly Report on the Excavation at Gezer. *PEF(QS)*: 320–57.
    1912   *The Excavations of Gezer 1–3*. London.
    1915   Some Interesting Pottery Remains. *PEF(QS)* 1915: 35–37.

Macalister, R. A. S., and Duncan, J. G.
    1926   *Excavations on the Hill of Ophel*. PEFA 4. Jerusalem.

Macchi, J. D.
    1992   Les controverses théologiques dans le judaïsme de l'époque postexilique: L'exemple de 2 Rois 17,24–41. *Trans* 5: 85–94.

Machinist, P.
    1997   The Fall of Assyria in Comparative Ancient Perspective. Pp. 179–95 in Parpola, S., and Whiting, R. M. (eds.). *Assyria 1995*. Helsinki.

Magen, Y.
    1983   The History of Jericho and Its Sites in Light of the Last Excavations. *Kardum* 28–30: 57–64. [Hebrew]

Magen, Y., and Dadon, M.
1999   Nebi Samwil (Shmuel Hanavi–Har Hasimha). *Qadmoniot* 118: 62–77.
        [Hebrew]
Magen, Y., and Finkelstein, I. (eds.).
1993   *Archaeological Survey of the Hill Country of Benjamin.* Jerusalem. [Hebrew and
        English]
Maitlis, Y.
1989   *Agricultural Settlement in the Region of Jerusalem at the End of the Iron Age.*
        M.A. Thesis. Jerusalem.
Malamat, A.
1950   The Last Wars of the Kingdom of Judah. *JNES* 9: 218–28.
1951   Jeremiah and the Last Two Kings of Judah. *PEQ* 83: 81–87.
1956   A New Record of Nebuchadrezzar's Palestinian Campaigns. *Yediʿot* 20: 179–
        87. [Hebrew]
1963   "Haserim" in the Bible and at Mari. *Yediʿot* 27: 181–84. [Hebrew]
1964   The Last Wars of the Kingdom of Judah. Pp. 296–314 in Liver, J. (ed.). *The
        Military History of the Land of Israel in Biblical Times.* Tel-Aviv.
1968   The Last Kings of Judah and the Fall of Jerusalem: An Historical-
        Chronological Study. *IEJ* 18/3: 137–56.
1973   Josia's Bid for Armageddon. *JANES* 5: 267–79.
1975a   The Historical Background of Josiah's Encounter with Necho at Megiddo.
        ErIsr 12: 83–90. [Hebrew]
1975b   The Twilight of Judah: In the Egyptian-Babylonian Maelstrom. Pp. 123–45 in
        Congress Volume: Edinburgh, 1974. VTSup 28. Leiden.
1982   The Last Years of the Kingdom of Judah. Pp. 140–51, 248–52 in Malamat, A.
        (ed.). *The History of the People of Israel—The Age of the Monarchy: A Political
        History.* Jerusalem. [Hebrew]
1983   *Israel in Biblical Times.* Jerusalem. [Hebrew]
1988   The Kingdom of Judah between Egypt and Babylon: A Small State within a
        Great Power Confrontation. Pp. 117–29 in Classen, W. (ed.). *Text and
        Context: Studies for F. C. Fensham.* Sheffield. [= *ST* 44 (1990): 65–77]
1991   The Destruction of the First Temple. Pp. 177–83 in Amit, D., and Gonen, R.
        (eds.). *Jerusalem during the First Temple Period.* Jerusalem. [Hebrew]
2000   Between Egypt and Babylon: The Destruction of Jerusalem. Pp. 85–91 in
        Aḥituv, S., and Mazar, A. (eds.). *The History of Jerusalem: The Biblical Period.*
        Jerusalem. [Hebrew]
March, W. E.
1974   Prophecy. Pp. 141–77 in Hayes, J. H. (ed.). *Old Testament Form Criticism.* San
        Antonio, Texas.
Masterman, E. W.
1913   Tell el-Full and Khirbet Adaseh. *PEF(QS)*: 132–37.
May, H. G.
1939   Three Hebrew Seals and the Status of Exiled Jehoiachin. *AJSL*: 146–48.
1942a   Towards an Objective Approach to the Book of Jeremiah: The Biographer.
        JBL 61: 139–55.
1942b   Jeremiah's Biographer. *JBR* 10: 195–201.
Mayes, A. D. H.
1978   King and Covenant: A Study of 2 Kings Chs. 22–23. *Hermathena* 125: 34–47.

1983   The Story of Israel between Settlement and Exile: A Redactional Study of the Deuteronomistic History. London.

Mazar, A.
1981   The Excavations at Khirbet Abu et-Twein and the System of Iron Age Fortresses in Judah. ErIsr 15: 222–49. [Hebrew]
1982a   Giloh: An Early Israelite Settlement Site near Jerusalem. IEJ 31: 1–36.
1982b   Iron Age Fortresses in the Judaean Hills. PEQ 114: 87–109.
1982c   Three Israelite Sites in the Hills of Judah and Ephraim. BA 45: 167–78.
1985   Between Judah and Philistia: Timnah (Tel Batash) in the Iron Age II. ErIsr 18: 300–324. [Hebrew]
1992   Archaeology of the Land of the Bible, 10,000–586 B.C.E. New York.
1994   The Northern Shephelah in the Iron Age: Some Issues in Biblical History and Archaeology. Pp. 247–67 in Coogan, M. D.; Exum, J. C.; and Stager, L. E. (eds.). Scripture and Other Artifacts: Essays on the Bible and Archaeology in Honor of Philip J. King. Louisville.

Mazar, A.; Amit, D.; and Ilan, Z.
1984   The "Border Road" between Michmash and Jericho and Excavations at Horvat Shilhah. ErIsr 17: 236–50. [Hebrew]

Mazar, A., and Netzer, E.
1986   On the Israelite Fortress at Arad. BASOR 263: 87–90.

Mazar (Maisler), B.
1941   The Family of Tuviah. Tarbiz 12: 109–23. [Hebrew]

Mazar, B.
1950   Eretz-Israel: History. EncMiq 1: 667–742.
1957   The Tobiads. IEJ 7: 229–38.
1961   Geshur and Maacah. JBL 80: 16–28.
1969   The Excavations of the Old City of Jerusalem. ErIsr 9: 161–74, pls. 39–50. [Hebrew]
1972   Excavations near the Temple Mount. Qadmoniot 19–20: 74–90. [Hebrew]
1980   Excavations near Temple Mount Reveal Splendors of Herodian Jerusalem. BAR 6/4: 44–59.
1986   Excavations and Discoveries. Jerusalem. [Hebrew]

Mazar, B., and Dunayevsky, I.
1964a   Ein-Gedi: The Third Season of Excavations (Preliminary Report). IEJ 14: 121–30.
1964b   The Third Season of Excavations at Ein Gedi (1963). Yediʿot 28: 143–52. [Hebrew]
1966   The Fourth and Fifth Seasons of Excavations at Ein Gedi. Yediʿot 30: 183–94. [Hebrew]
1967   Ein-Gedi: The Fourth and Fifth Seasons of Excavations (Preliminary Report). IEJ 17: 133–43.

Mazar, B.; Dothan, T.; and Dunayevsky, I.
1963   Ein-Gedi: Archaeological Excavations, 1961–62. Yediʿot 22: 11–33. [Hebrew]
1966   Ein Gedi: The First and Second Seasons of Excavations, 1961–1962. ʿAtiqot 5: 1–100.

Mazar, E.
1985   Edomite Pottery at the End of the Iron Age. IEJ 35: 253–69.

1989   Royal Gateway to Ancient Jerusalem Uncovered. *BAR* 15/3: 38–51.

1991   The Ophel in Jerusalem during the First Temple Period. Pp. 135–42 in Amit, D., and Gonen, R. (eds.). *Jerusalem during the First Temple Period.* Jerusalem. [Hebrew]

1993   Excavations in the Ophel: The Royal Quarter of Jerusalem during the First Temple Period. *Qadmoniot* 10–12: 25–32. [Hebrew]

Mazar, E., and Mazar, B.

1989   *Excavations in the South of the Temple Mount, the Ophel of Biblical Jerusalem.* Qedem 29. Jerusalem.

Mazzoni, S.

2001   Tell Afis and the Luʿash in the Aramean Period. Pp. 99–114 in Daviau, P. M. M.; Wevers, J. W.; and Weigl, M. (eds.). *The World of the Aramaeans II: Studies in History and Archaeology in Honor of Paul-Eugène Dion.* Sheffield.

McClellan, T. L.

1984   Town Planning at Tell en Nasbeh. *ZDPV* 100: 53–69.

McConville, J. G.

1985   *Law and Theology in Deuteronomy.* Sheffield.

McCown, C. C.

1947   *Tell en-Naṣbeh I: Archaeological and Historical Results.* Berkeley.

McEvenue, S. E.

1981   The Political Structure in Judah from Cyrus to Nehemiah. *CBQ* 44: 353–64.

McFall, L.

1991   A Translation Guide to the Chronological Data in Kings and Chronicles. *BSac* 148: 3–45.

McKane, W.

1986   *A Critical and Exegetical Commentary on Jeremiah.* Vol. 1. ICC. Edinburgh.

1995   *A Critical and Exegetical Commentary on Jeremiah.* Vol. 2. ICC. Edinburgh.

McKenzie, D.

1913   *Excavations at Ain Shemes.* PEFA 1912–13. London.

McKenzie, S. L.

1985   *The Chronicler's Use of the Deuteronomistic History.* Atlanta.

1991   *The Trouble with Kings: The Composition of the Book of Kings in the Deuteronomistic History.* VTSup 42. Leiden.

Mercer, M. K.

1989   Daniel 1:1 and Jehoiakim's Three Years of Servitude. *AUSS* 27: 179–92.

Meshel, Z.

1974   *The History of the Negev in the Period of the Kings of Judah.* Ph.D. Dissertation. Tel-Aviv.

1977   The Negev during the Persian Period. *Cathedra* 4: 43–50. [Hebrew]

1995   Iron Age Negev Settlements as an Expression of Conflict between Edom, Judah, and Israel over Borders and Roads. Pp. 169–80 in *Eilat: Studies in the Archaeology, History and Geography of Eilat and the Aravah.* Jerusalem. [Hebrew]

Meshorer, J.

1961   An Attic Archaic Coin from Jerusalem. ʿ*Atiqot* 3: 185.

Mettinger, T. N. D.

1971   *Solomonic State Officials.* Lund.

Meyer, E.

1896   *Die Entstehung des Judentums.* Halle.

Meyers, C. L., and Meyers, E. M.
1987   *Haggai, Zechariah 1–8: A New Translation with Introduction and Commentary.* AB 25b. New York.
1994   Demography and Diatribes: Yehud's Population and the Prophecy of Second Zechariah. Pp. 268–85 in Coogan, M. D.; Exum, J. C.; and Stager, L. E. (eds.). *Scripture and Other Artifacts: Essays on the Bible and Archaeology in Honor of Philip J. King.* Louisville.

Meyers, E. M.
1971   Edom and Judah in the Sixth–Fifth Century B.C. Pp. 377–92 in Goedicke, H. (ed.). *Near Eastern Studies in Honour of W. F. Albright.* Baltimore.
1985   The Shelomith Seal and the Judean Restoration: Some Additional Judean Considerations. *ErIsr* 18: 33*–38*.

Michaud, H.
1960   Book Reviews. *VT* 10: 102–6.

Milevski, I.
1996–97 Settlement Patterns in Northern Judah during the Achaemenid Period according to the Hill Country of Benjamin and Jerusalem Survey. *Bulletin of the Anglo-Israel Archaeological Society* 15: 7–29.

Millard, A.
1989   Notes on Two Seal Impressions on Pottery (Appendix). *Levant* 21: 60–61.
1992   Assyrian Involvement in Edom. Pp. 35–40 in Bienkowski, P. (ed.). *Early Edom and Moab: The Beginning of the Iron Age in Southern Jordan.* Oxford.

Miller, J. M.
1975   Gibeah of Benjamin. *VT* 25: 145–66.

Miller, J. M., and Hayes, J. H.
1986   *A History of Ancient Israel and Judah.* Philadelphia.

Misgav, H.
1990   Two Notes on the Ostraca from Horvat ʾUza. *IEJ* 40/2–3: 215–17.

Mitchell, H. G.; Smith, J. M. P.; and Bewer, J. A.
1912   *A Critical and Exegetical Commentary on Haggai, Zechariah, Malachi and Jonah.* ICC. Edinburgh.

Mitchell, T. C.
1991   The Babylonian Exile and the Restoration of the Jews in Palestine (586–c. 500 B.C.). Pp. 410–60 in *Assyrian and Babylonian Empires and Other States of the Near East: Eighth to Sixth Centuries B.C.* Vol. 3/2 of *CAH*.

Mittmann, S.
2000   Tobia, Sanballat und die persische Provinz Juda. *JNSL* 26/2: 1–50.

Moenikes, A.
1992   Zur Redaktionsgeschichte des sogenannten Deuteronomistischen Geschichtswerks. *ZAW* 104: 333–48.

Montgomery, J. A.
1927   *A Critical and Exegetical Commentary on the Book of Daniel.* ICC. Edinburgh.
1934   Archival Data in the Book of Kings. *JBL* 53: 46–52.
1951   *A Critical and Exegetical Commentary on the Books of Kings.* ICC. Edinburgh.

Mor, M.
1978   The High Priests in Judea in the Persian Period. *Beth Mikra* 23: 57–67. [Hebrew]

1980   The Samaritans and the Jews during the Ptolemaic Period and the Beginning
         of Seleucid Rule in Palestine. Pp. 76–81 in vol. 5 of Oded, B. (ed.). *Research
         in the History of the People of Israel and Land of Israel*. Haifa. [Hebrew]

2003   *From Samaria to Schechem: The Samaritan Community in Antiquity*. Jerusalem.

Moriarty, F. L.

1965   The Chronicler's Account of Jezekiah's Reform. *CBQ* 27: 399–406.

Morkot, R. G.

2000   *The Black Pharaohs: Egypt's Nubian Rulers*. London.

Moscati, S.

1951   *L'epigrafia ebraica antica, 1935–1950*. Rome.

Mosis, R.

1973   *Untersuchungen zur Theologie des chronistischen Geschichtswerkes*. Freiburger
         theologische Studien 92. Freiburg.

Mowinckel, S.

1914   *Zur Komposition des Buches Jeremia*. Kristiania (= Oslo).

1932   Die Chronologie der israelitischen jüdischen Könige. *AcOr* 10: 161–277.

1946   *Prophecy and Tradition*. Oslo.

1964–65 *Studien zu dem Buche Ezra–Nehemia*. 3 vols. Oslo.

Muilenburg, J.

1954   Mizpah of Benjamin. *ST* 8: 25–42.

1970   Baruch the Scribe. Pp. 215–38 in Durham, J. I., and Porter, J. R. (eds.).
         *Proclamation and Presence: Old Testament Essays in Honour of Gwynne Henton
         Davies*. London.

Murray, D. F.

2001   Of All the Years the Hopes—or Fear? Jehoiachin in Babylon (2 Kings 25:27–
         30). *JBL* 120: 245–65.

Myers, J. M.

1965a   *Ezra–Nehemiah*. AB 14. Garden City, New York.

1965b   *I Chronicles*. AB 12. Garden City, New York.

1965c   *II Chronicles*. AB 13. Garden City, New York.

1974   *I and II Esdras*. AB 42. Garden City, New York.

Mykytiuk, L. J.

2004   *Identifying Biblical Persons in Northwest Semitic Inscriptions of 1200–539 B.C.E.*
         Society of Biblical Literature Academia Biblica 12. Atlanta.

Na'aman, N.

1979   The Brook of Egypt and Assyrian Policy on the Border of Egypt. *TA* 6: 68–90.

1981   Royal Estates in the Jezreel Valley in the Late Bronze Age and under the
         Israelite Monarchy. *ErIsr* 15: 140–44. [Hebrew]

1983   The Inheritance and Settlement of the Sons of Simeon in the South of Erets
         Israel. Pp. 111–36 in vol. 1 of Rofé, A., and Zakovitch, Y. (eds.). *Isaac Leo
         Seeligmann Volume*. Jerusalem. [Hebrew]

1986a   *Borders and Districts in Biblical Historiography*. Jerusalem.

1986b   The Canaanite City-States in the Late Bronze Age and the Inheritances of
         the Israelite Tribes. *Tarbiz* 55: 463–88. [Hebrew]

1987   The Negev in the Last Century of the Kingdom of Judah. *Cathedra* 42: 4–15.
         [Hebrew]

1989   Population Changes in Palestine following Assyrian Deportations. *Cathedra*
         54: 43–62. [Hebrew]

1991a   The Kingdom of Judah under Josiah. *TA* 18: 3–71.

1991b   Chronology and History in the Late Assyrian Empire (631–619 B.C.). ZA 81: 243–67.

1991c   The Boundaries of the Kingdom of Jerusalem in the Second Millenium BCE. *Zion* 56: 361–80. [Hebrew]

1992   Nebuchadrezzar's Campaign in Year 603 B.C.E. *BN* 62: 41–44.

1993a   Shechem and Jerusalem in the Exilic and Restoration Period. *Zion* 58: 7–32. [Hebrew]

1993b   Population Changes in Palestine following Assyrian Deportations. *TA* 20: 104–24.

1994a   Ahaz and Hezekiah's Policy toward Assyria in the Days of Sargon II and Sennacherib's Early Years. *Zion* 59/1: 5–30. [Hebrew]

1994b   Criticism of Voluntary Servitude to Foreign Powers: A Historiographical Study in the Book of Kings. Pp. 63–70 in *The Bible and Its World*. Division A of *Proceedings of the Eleventh World Congress of Jewish Studies*. Jerusalem. [Hebrew]

1994c   Esarhaddon's Treaty with Baal and Assyrian Provinces along the Phoenician Coast. *Rivista di Studi Fenici* 22/1: 3–8.

1994d   The 'Conquest of Canaan' in the Book of Joshua and in History. Pp. 218–81 in Finkelstein, I., and Naʾaman, N. (eds.). *From Nomadism to Monarchy: Archaeological and Historical Aspects of Early Israel*. Jerusalem. [Hebrew]

1995a   Province System and Settlement Pattern in Southern Syria and Palestine in the Neo-Assyrian Period. Pp. 103–15 in Liverani, M. (ed.). *Neo-Assyrian Geography*. Rome.

1995b   Rezin of Damascus and the Land of Gilead. *ZDPV* 111: 105–17.

1995c   The Historical Background of the Philistine Attack on Ahaz in 2 Chronicles 28:18. Pp. 1126 in Kasher, A., and Oppenheimer, A. (eds.). *Dor le-Dor: Studies in Honor of Joshua Efron*. Jerusalem. [Hebrew]

1995d   The Deuteronomist and Voluntary Servitude to Foreign Powers. *JSOT* 65: 37–53.

1997   Notes on the Excavations at ʿEin Hazeva. *Qadmoniot* 113: 60. [Hebrew]

1998   Two Notes on the History of Ashkelon and Ekron in the Late Eighth–Seventh Century B.C.E. *TA* 25: 219–27.

1999a   Four Notes on the Size of Late Bronze Age Canaan. *BASOR* 313: 31–37.

1999b   Lebo-Hamath, Ṣubat-Hamath, and the Northern Boundary of the Land of Canaan. *UF* 31: 417–41.

2000   Royal Vassals or Governors? On the Status of Sheshbazzar and Zerubbabel in the Persian Empire. *Henoch* 22/1: 35–44.

2001   An Assyrian Residence at Ramat Raḥel? *TA* 28/2: 260–80.

2002   *The Past That Shapes the Present: The Creation of Biblical Historiography in the Late First Temple Period and after the Downfall*. Jerusalem.

2003   The Abandonment of Cult Places in the Kingdoms of Israel and Judah as Acts of Cult Reform. *UF* 34: 585–602.

2004   The Boundary System and Political Status of Gaza under Assyrian Empire. *ZDPV* 120: 55–72.

Nadelman, Y.

1994   The Identification of Anathoth and the Soundings at Khirbet Deir es-Sidd. *IEJ* 44: 62–74.

Naor, M.
1984   The Deportations from Jerusalem and the Problem of the 9th of Ab. *Beth Mikra* 96: 60–66. [Hebrew]

Naveh, J.
1958   *The History of ʿEin-Gedi in Light of the Archaeological Survey.* ʿEin Gedi.
1962   The Excavations at Mesad Hashavyahu: Preliminary Report. *IEJ* 12: 89–113.
1963   Old Hebrew Inscriptions in a Burial Cave. *IEJ* 13: 74–92.
1973   The Aramaic Ostraca. Pp. 79–82 in Aharoni, Y. (ed.). *Beer-Sheba, I.* Tel-Aviv.
1976   The Aramaic Ostraca from Tel Arad. Pp. 175–214 in Aharoni, Y. *Arad Inscriptions.* Jerusalem. [Hebrew; English trans., 1981]
1979   The Aramaic Ostraca from Tel Beer-Sheba (Seasons 1971–1976). *TA* 6: 182–98.
1987   Proto-Canaanite, Archaic Greek, and the Script of the Aramaic Text on the Tell Fakhariyah Statue. Pp. 101–13 in Miller, P. D.; Hanson, P. D.; and McBride, S. D. (eds.). *Ancient Israelite Religion.* Philadelphia.
1989a   *Early History of the Alphabet: An Introduction to West Semitic Epigraphy.* Jerusalem. [Hebrew]
1989b   Nameless People? *Zion* 54: 1–16. [Hebrew]
1992   *On Sherds and Papyrus: Aramaic and Hebrew Inscriptions from the Second Temple, Mishnaic and Talmudic Periods.* Jerusalem. [Hebrew]
1996   Gleanings of Some Pottery Inscriptions. *IEJ* 46: 44–51.

Negbi, O.
1963   Notes and News: Mevasseret Yerushalayim. *IEJ* 13: 145.
1970   The Cemetery of Biblical Mozah. Pp. 358–70 in Abramski, S., et al. (eds.). *Festschrift S. Yeivin: Researches in Bible, Archaeology, Language and History of Israel.* Jerusalem.

Negev, A. (ed.)
1972   *Archaeological Encyclopedia of the Holy Land.* Jerusalem.

Nelson, R. D.
1981   *The Double Redaction of the Deuteronomistic History.* Sheffield.
1983   Realpolitic in Judah (687–609 B.C.E.). Pp. 177–89 in Hallo, W. W., et al. (eds.). *Scripture in Context II.* Winona Lake, Indiana.

Nicholson, E. W.
1963   The Centralisation of the Cult in Deuteronomy. *VT* 13: 380–89.
1965   The Meaning of the Expression "עם הארץ" in the Old Testament. *JSS* 10: 59–66.
1967   *Deuteronomy and Tradition.* Oxford.
1970   *Preaching to the Exiles: A Study of the Prose Tradition in the Book of Jeremiah.* Oxford.
1975   *The Book of the Prophet Jeremiah, Chapters 26–52.* Cambridge.
1986   Covenant in a Century of Study since Wellhausen. *OTS* 24: 54–69.

Niehr, H.
1999   Religio-Historical Aspects of the 'Early Post-Exilic' Period. Pp. 228–44 in Becking, B., and Korpel, M. C. A. (eds.). *The Crisis of Israelite Religion: Transformation of Religious Tradition in Exilic and Post-Exilic Times.* Leiden.

Nielsen, E.
1954   *Oral Tradition.* Chicago.

Nielsen, K.
1986   *Incense in Ancient Israel.* Leiden.

Noth, M.
1943   *Überlieferungsgeschichtliche Studien: Die sammelnden und bearbeitenden Geschichtswerke im Alten Testament.* Schriften der Königsberger Gelehrten Gesellschaft. Geisteswissenschaftliche Klasse 18/2/1. Halle. [1st English ed. to the first part of Noth's work trans. as *The Deuteronomistic History* (Sheffield, 1981). 2nd ed., with many corrections, was pub. 1991. The references in this book are to the 1st English ed. Second part of Noth's work trans. as *The Chronicler's History* (Sheffield, 1987).]

1953   *Das Buch Josua.* 2nd ed. Tübingen.

1954   *Geschichte Israels.* Göttingen. [1st English ed.: *The History of Israel.* London, 1958]

1958   Die Einnahme von Jerusalem im Jahre 597 v. Chr. *ZDPV* 74: 133–57.

1966a   *Die israelitischen Personennamen im Rahmen der gemeinsemitischen Namengebung.* Hildesheim.

1966b   The Jerusalem Catastrophe of 587 B.C. and Its Significance for Israel. Pp. 260–80 in *The Laws in the Pentateuch and Other Studies.* Edinburgh.

Nougayrol, J.
1955   *Le Palais Royal d'Ugarit III: Textes accadiens et hourrites des Archives Est, Ouest et Centrales.* MRS 6. Paris.

Oakeshott, M. F.
1983   The Edomite Pottery. Pp. 53–63 in Sawyer, J. F. A., and Clines, D. J. A. (eds.). *Midian Edom and Moab.* Sheffield.

Oates, J.
1965   Assyrian Chronology 631–612 B.C. *Iraq* 27: 135–59.

1986   *Babylon.* Rev. ed. London.

1991   The Fall of Assyria (635–609 B.C.). Pp. 162–93, 769–72 in *Assyrian and Babylonian Empires and Other States of the Near East: Eighth to Sixth Centuries B.C.* Vol. 3/2 of *CAH.*

O'Brien, M. A.
1989   *The Deuteronomistic History Hypothesis: A Reassessment.* OBO 92. Göttingen.

O'Connor, K. M.
1987   The Poetic Inscription from Kh. el-Kom. *VT* 37: 224–31.

1988   *The Confessions of Jeremiah: Their Interpretation and Role in Chapters 1–25.* Atlanta.

Oded, B.
1966   When Did the Kingdom of Judah Become Subjected to Babylonian Rule? *Tarbiz* 35: 103–7. [Hebrew]

1970   Observations on Methods of Assyrian Rule in Transjordania after the Palestinian Campaign of Tiglath-pileser III. *JNES* 29: 177–86.

1977   Judah and the Exile. Pp. 435–88 in Hayes, J. H., and Miller, J. M. (eds.). *Israelite and Judaean History.* London.

1979   *Mass Deportations and Deportees in the Neo-Assyrian Empire.* Wiesbaden.

1982a   Israel's Neighbours on the West. Pp. 152–70, 273–74 in Malamat, A. (ed.). *The History of the People of Israel—The Age of the Monarchy: Political History.* Jerusalem. [Hebrew]

1982b   Israel's Neighbours on the East. Pp. 171–90, 274–75 in Malamat, A. (ed.).
          The History of the People of Israel—The Age of the Monarchy: Political History.
          Jerusalem. [Hebrew]
1992   *War, Peace and Empire: Justifications for War in Assyrian Royal Inscriptions.*
          Wiesbaden.
1995   The Cisjordan and Israel in the Biblical Period. *Ariel* 107–8: 83–92. [Hebrew]
Oesterley, W. O. E., and Robinson, T. H.
1934   *An Introduction to the Books of the Old Testament.* New York.
Ofer, A.
1989   Excavations at Biblical Hebron. *Qadmoniot* 87–88/3–4: 88–93. [Hebrew]
1993   *The Highland of Judah during the Biblical Period.* Ph.D. Dissertation. Tel-Aviv.
          [Hebrew]
1994   "All the Hill Country of Judah": From a Settlement Fringe to a Prosperous
          Monarchy. Pp. 92–121 in Finkelstein, I., and Naʾaman, N. (eds.). *From
          Nomadism to Monarchy: Archaeological and Historical Aspects of Early Israel.*
          Jerusalem.
1998   The Judean Hills in the Biblical Period. *Qadmoniot* 115/10: 40–52. [Hebrew]
Olmstead, A. T.
1923   *History of Assyria.* Chicago.
1925   The Chaldean Dynasty. *HUCA* 2: 29–55.
Olyan, S. M.
1985   *Problems in the History of the Cult and Priesthood in Ancient Israel.* Ph.D.
          Dissertation, Harvard University. Cambridge, Massachusetts.
Onasch, H. U.
1994   *Die assyrischen Eroberungen Ägyptens.* Ägypten und Altes Testament 27/1.
          Wiesbaden.
Oppenheim, A. L.
1964   *Ancient Mesopotamia: Portrait of a Dead Civilization.* Chicago.
1967   Essay on Overland Trade in the First Millennium B.C. *JCS* 21: 236–54.
Oren, E. D.
1984   Migdol: A New Fortress on the Edge of the Eastern Nile Delta. *BASOR* 256:
          7–44.
Otzen, B.
1964   *Studien über Deuterosacharja.* Copenhagen.
Overholt, T. W.
1968   King Nabuchadnezzar in the Jeremiah Tradition. *CBQ* 30: 39–48.
1972   Remarks on the Continuity of the Jeremiah Tradition. *JBL* 91: 457–62.
Parker, R. A.
1957   The Length of Reign of Amasis and the Beginning of the Twenty-Sixth
          Dynasty. *Mitteilungen des Deutschen Archäologischen Instituts, Kairo* 15: 208–
          12.
Parker, R. A., and Dubberstein, W. H.
1956   *Babylonian Chronology 626 B.C.–A.D . 75.* Providence, Rhode Island.
Parpola, S.
1970   *Neo-Asyyrian Toponyms.* Neukirchen-Vluyn.
Parpola, S., and Porter, M.
2001   *The Helsinki Atlas of the Near East in the Neo-Assyrian Period.* Helsinki.
Pavlovsky, V., and Vogt, E.
1964   Die Jahre der Könige von Juda und Israel. *Bib* 45: 321–47.

Peake, A. S.
1910   *Jeremiah and Lamentations.* CB. Oxford.
Peckham, B.
1983   The Composition of Deuteronomy 5–11. Pp. 217–40 in Meyers, C. L., and
        O'Connor, M. (eds.). *The Word of the Lord Shall Go Forth: Essays in Honor of
        David Noel Freedman in Celebration of His Sixtieth Birthday.* Winona Lake,
        Indiana.
1985   *The Composition of the Deuteronomistic History.* Cambridge, Massachusetts.
Perdue, L. G.
1994   *The Collapse of History: Reconstructing OT Theology.* Minneapolis.
Peres, Y.
1946   *The Land of Israel: A Topographical-Historical Encyclopedia.* Jerusalem.
        [Hebrew]
Person, R. F.
2002   *The Deuteronomic School: History, Social Setting, and Literature.* Atlanta.
Pfeiffer, R. H.
1941   *Introduction to the Old Testament.* New York.
Pinches, T. G.
1904   The Fragment of an Assyrian Tablet Found at Gezer. *PEFQS* 36: 229–36.
        [with notes by A. H. Sayce, pp. 236–37, and C. H. W. Johns, pp. 237–44]
Piovanelli, P.
1995   La condamnation de la diaspora égyptienne dans le livre de Jérémie. *Trans* 9:
        35–49.
Pohlmann, K. F.
1978   *Studien zum Jeremiabuch: Ein Beitrag zur Frage nach der Entstehung des
        Jeremiabuches.* Göttingen.
1979   Erwägungen zum Schlusskapitel des deuteronomistischen Geschichtswerkes
        oder: Warum wird der Prophet Jeremia in 2 Kön. 22–25 nicht erwähnt? Pp.
        94–109 in Gunneweg, A. H. J., and Kaiser, O. (eds.). *Textgemäss: Aufsätze
        und Beiträge zur Hermeneutik des Alten Testaments. Festschrift für E. Würthwein.*
        Göttingen.
Polzin, R.
1980   *Moses and the Deuteronomist—A Literary Study of the Deuteronomic History, I:
        Deuteronomy, Joshua, Judges.* New York.
1989   *Samuel and the Deuteronomist—A Literary Study of the Deuteronomic History,
        II: 1 Samuel.* San Francisco.
Porten, B.
1977   The Return to Zion in Vision and Reality. *Cathedra* 4: 4–12. [Hebrew]
1978   The Documents in the Book of Ezra and the Mission of Ezra. *Shnaton* 3: 174–
        96. [Hebrew]
1981   The Identity of King Adon. *BA* 44: 36–52.
1996   *The Elephantine Papyri in English: Three Millennia of Cross-Cultural Continuity
        and Change.* Leiden.
Porteous, N.
1979   *Daniel.* OTL. Philadelphia.
Porter, B., and Moss, R. L. B.
1931   *Topographical Bibliography of Ancient Egyptian Hieroglyphic Texts, Reliefs and
        Painting, III: Memphis.* Oxford.

Portugali, Y.
    1988   Theories about Population and Settlement and Their Importance for
              Demographic Study in the Land of Israel. Pp. 4–38 in Bunimovitz, S.;
              Kochavi, M.; and Kasher, A. (eds.). *Settlements, Population and Economy in the
              Land of Israel in Ancient Times.* Tel-Aviv. [Hebrew]
    1989   Demographic Speculations on Evolution, Settlement and Urbanization.
              Archaeology 2: 8–18. [Hebrew]
Prag, K.
    1995   Summary of the Reports on Caves I, II and III and Deposit IV. Pp. 209–20 in
              vol. 4 of Eshel, I., and Prag, K. (eds). *Excavations by K. M. Kenyon in
              Jerusalem 1961–1967.* Oxford.
Pringle, D.
    1983   Two Medieval Villages North of Jerusalem: Archaeological Investigations in
              Al-Jib and Ar-Ram. *Levant* 15: 141–77.
Pritchard, J. B.
    1956   The Water System at Gibeon. *BA* 19: 66–75.
    1959a   *Hebrew Inscriptions and Stamps from Gibeon.* Philadelphia.
    1959b   The Wine Industry at Gibeon: 1959 Discoveries. *Expedition* 2/1: 17–25.
    1960a   More Inscribed Jar Handles from El-Jib. *BASOR* 160: 2–6.
    1960b   Gibeon's History in the Light of Excavation. Pp. 1–12 in *Congress Volume:
              Oxford, 1959.* VTSup 7. Leiden.
    1960c   Industry and Trade at Biblical Gibeon. *BA* 23: 23–29.
    1961   *The Water System of Gibeon.* Philadelphia.
    1964a   *Winery Defences and Soundings at Gibeon.* Philadelphia.
    1964b   *Gibeon: Where the Sun Stood Still.* Princeton.
Pritchard, J. B. (ed.)
    1969   *Ancient Near Eastern Texts Relating to the Old Testament.* 3rd ed. Princeton.
              [ANET]
Provan, I. W.
    1988   *Hezekiah and the Books of Kings: A Contribution to the Debate about the
              Composition of the Deuteronomistic History.* BZAW 172. Berlin.
Quinn, J. D.
    1961   Alcaeus 48 (B 16) and the Fall of Ascalon (604 b.c.). *BASOR* 164: 19–20.
Rad, G. von
    1953   *Studies in Deuteronomy.* London. [1st English ed. of *Deuteronomium studien.*
              Göttingen, 1948]
    1958   Die deuteronomistische Geschichtstheologie in den Königsbüchem. Pp. 189–
              204 in vol. 1 of *Gesammelte Studien zum Alten Testament.* Munich.
    1962   *Old Testament Theology.* Vols. 1–2. New York. [1st English ed. of *Theologie des
              Alten Testaments.* Munich, 1957–60]
    1966a   *The Problem of the Hexateuch and Other Essays.* Edinburgh.
    1966b   *Deuteronomy.* London.
Rahmani, L. Y.
    1964   A Partial Survey of the Adulam Area. *Yediʿot* 38: 209–31. [Hebrew]
Rainey, A. F.
    1969   The Satrapy "Beyond the River." *AJBA* 1/2: 51–78.
    1975   The Fate of Lachish during the Campaigns of Sennacherib and
              Nebuchadrezzar. Pp. 47–60 in Aharoni, Y. (ed.). *Investigations at Lachish: The
              Sanctuary and the Residency (Lachish V).* Tel-Aviv.

1982a   Toponymic Problems (cont.). *TA* 7: 130–36.
1982b   Wine from the Royal Vineyards. *BASOR* 245: 57–62.
1983   The Biblical Shefelah of Judah. *BASOR* 251: 1–22.
1987   Arad in the Days of the Judean Monarchy. *Cathedra* 42: 16–25. [Hebrew]
Raitt, T.
1979   *A Theology of Exile: Judgement/Deliverance in Jeremiah and Ezekiel.*
        Philadelphia.
Reade, J. E.
1970   The Accession of Sinsharishkun. *JCS* 23/1: 1–9.
1998   Assyrian Eponyms, Kings and Pretenders, 648–605 BC. *Or* 67/2: 255–65.
Redditt, P. L.
1995   *Haggai, Zechariah and Malachi.* NCBC. Grand Rapids, Michigan.
Redford, D. B.
1992   *Egypt, Canaan, and Israel in Ancient Times.* Princeton.
2000   New Light on Egypt's Stance toward Asia, 610–586 BCE. Pp. 183–95 in
        McKenzie, S. L., and Römer, T. (eds.). *Rethinking the Foundations—*
        Historiography in the Ancient World and in the Bible: Essays in Honor of John Van
        Seters. Berlin.
Rehm, M.
1982   *Das zweite Buch der Könige: Ein Kommentar.* Würzburg.
Reich, R.
1987   Palaces and Residences in the Iron Age. Pp. 173–88 in Netser, A.;
        Kempinski, A.; and Reich, R. (eds.). *The Architecture of Ancient Israel from the*
        Prehistoric to the Persian Periods. Jerusalem. [Hebrew]
1989   A Third Season of Excavations at Mesad Hashavyahu. *ErIsr* 20: 228–32.
        [Hebrew]
1990   Tombs in the Mamilla Street Area, Jerusalem. Pp. 16–17 in Drori, A. (ed.).
        Highlights of Recent Excavations. Jerusalem.
1992   The Beth-Zur Citadel II: A Persian Residency? *ErIsr* 23: 247–52. [Hebrew]
1993   The Cemetery in the Mamilla Area of Jerusalem. *Qadmoniot* 103–4: 103–9.
        [Hebrew]
1994   The Ancient Burial Ground in the Mamilla Neighborhood, Jerusalem.
        Pp. 111–18 in Geva, H. (ed.). *Ancient Jerusalem Revealed.* Jerusalem.
1999   Tombs from the Persian Period in the Area of Mamilla, Jerusalem. Pp. 6–7 in
        Lipschitz, O. (ed.). *Summary of Proceedings of a Searcher's Conference on the*
        Subject: Is It Possible to Define the Sixth Century BCE Pottery? Tel-Aviv.
        [Hebrew]
Reich, R., and Brandl, B.
1985   Gezer under Assyrian Rule. *PEQ* 117: 41–54.
Rendsburg, G. A.
1988   The Ammonite Phoneme /T/. *BASOR* 269: 73–79.
Rendtorff, R.
1985   *The Old Testament: An Introduction.* London. [trans. of 1983 German ed.]
Renfrew, C.
1979   Systems Collapse as Social Transformation: Catastrophe and Anastrophe in
        Early State Societies. Pp. 481–506 in Renfrew, C., and Cooke, K. L. (eds.).
        Transformations: Mathematical Approaches to Culture Change. New York.
Reviv, H.
1993   *The Society in the Kingdoms of Israel and Judah.* Jerusalem. [Hebrew]

Richter, W.
　　1964　　*Die Bearbeitungen des 'Retterbuches' in der deuteronomistischen Epoche.* Bonn.
Rietzschel, C.
　　1966　　*Das Problem der Urrolle: Ein Beitrag zur Redaktionsgeschichte des Jeremiabuches.*
　　　　　　Gütersloh.
Robinson, T. H.
　　1924　　Baruch's Role. *ZAW* 42: 209–21.
Römer, T. C.
　　1997　　Transformations in Deuteronomistic and Biblical Historiography: On 'Book
　　　　　　Finding' and Other Literary Strategies. *ZAW* 109: 1–11.
Rösel, H. N.
　　1999　　*Von Josua bis Jojachin: Untersuchungen zu den deuteronomistischen*
　　　　　　Geschichtsbüchern im Alten Testament. Leiden.
Rofé, A.
　　1975　　Studies on the Composition of the Book of Jeremiah. *Tarbiz* 44: 1–29.
　　　　　　[Hebrew]
　　1986　　Jeremiah and His Book: A Summary. *Beth Mikra* 107: 308–15. [Hebrew]
　　1988　　*The Prophetical Stories.* Jerusalem. [first Hebrew ed., 1982]
　　1991　　The Name YHWH ṢEBA'OT and the Shorter Recension of Jeremiah.
　　　　　　Pp. 307–15 in Liwak, R., and Wagner, S. (eds.). *Prophetie und geschichtliche*
　　　　　　Wirklichkeit im alten Israel. Stuttgart.
　　1992　　Ephraimite versus Deuteronomistic History. *Beth Mikra* 132: 14–28. [Hebrew]
　　1997　　No Exile but Extermination for the People of Zedekiah: The Message of
　　　　　　Jeremiah according to the LXX Translation. Pp. 180–84 in Hoffman, Y., and
　　　　　　Polak, F. H. (eds.). *A Light for Jacob: Studies in the Bible and the Dead Sea Scrolls*
　　　　　　in Memory of Jacob Shalom Licht. Jerusalem. [Hebrew]
　　1998　　The Historical Significance of Secondary Versions in the Bible. *Beth Mikra*
　　　　　　43: 218–26. [Hebrew]
Roll, I.
　　1996　　Bacchides' Fortifications and the Arteries of Traffic to Jerusalem in the
　　　　　　Hellenistic Period. *ErIsr* 25: 509–14. [Hebrew]
Ronen, Y.
　　1985　　*Edomites and Idumea during the Second Temple Period.* M.A. Thesis. Tel-Aviv.
　　　　　　[Hebrew]
Rose, M.
　　1977　　Bemerkungen zum historischen Fundament des Josia-Bildes in II Reg 22 f.
　　　　　　ZAW 89: 50–63.
Rosenson, I.
　　1991　　A Note about the Vinedressers and Plowmen. Pp. 47–54 in vol. 2 of Erlich,
　　　　　　Z. H. (ed.). *Samaria and Benjamin.* Jerusalem. [Hebrew]
Rowton, M. B.
　　1951　　Jeremiah and the Death of Josiah. *JNES* 10: 128–30.
Rudolph, W.
　　1947　　*Jeremiah.* Tübingen.
　　1949　　*Ezra und Nehemia.* Tübingen.
　　1955　　*Chronikbucher.* Tübingen.
Rütersworden, U.
　　1985　　*Die Beamten der israelitischen Königszeit.* Stuttgart.

Ryle, H. E.
1907 *Ezra and Nehemiah.* Cambridge.
Sack, R. H.
1991 *Images of Nebuchadnezzar.* London.
Saggs, H. W. F.
1962 *The Greatness That Was Babylon.* New York.
Saller, S. J.
1957 *Excavations at Bethany (1949–1953).* Jerusalem.
Šanda, A.
1911–12 *Die Bücher der Könige.* Vols. 1 and 2. Münster.
Sapin, J.
1968 *Le plateau central de Benjamin.* M.A. Thesis, École Biblique. Jerusalem.
1991 Recherches sur les ressources et les fonctions économiques du secteur de Ono à l'époque perse. *Trans* 4: 51–62.
Sarna, N. M.
1973 Zedekiah's Emancipation of Slaves and the Sabbatical Year. Pp. 143–49 in Hoffner, H. A. (ed.). *Orient and Occident: Essays Presented to C. H. Gordon.* Neukirchen-Vluyn.
1978 The Abortive Insurrection in Zedekiah's Day (Jer. 27–29). *ErIsr* 14: 89*–96*.
Schaeder, H. H.
1930 *Ezra der Schreiber.* Tübingen.
Scharbert, J.
1967 *Die Prophetie Israels um 600 v. Chr.* Cologne.
Schencker, A.
1994 La rédaction longue du livre de Jérémie doit-elle être datée au temps des premiers Hasmonées. *ETL* 70: 281–93.
Schmid, K.
1996 *Buchgestalten des Jeremiabuches: Untersuchungen zur Redaktions- und Rezeptionsgeschichte von Jer 30–33 im Kontext des Buches.* Neukirchen-Vluyn.
Schultz, C.
1980 The Political Tensions Reflected in Ezra–Nehemiah. Pp. 221–44 in Evans, C. D., et al. (eds.). *Scripture in Context: Essays on the Comparative Method.* Pittsburgh.
Schwartz, J.
1988 The History of Lod during the Persian Period. *Cathedra* 49: 3–12. [Hebrew]
1991 *Lod (Lydda), Israel from Its Origins through the Byzantine Period 5600 B.C.E.– 640 C.E.* Oxford.
Schwiderski, D.
2000 *Handbuch des nordwestsemitischen Briefformulars: Ein Beitrag zur Echtheitsfrage der aramäischen Briefe des Esrabuches.* BZAW 295. Berlin.
Seebass, H.
1970 Jeremias Konflikt mit Chananja: Bemerkungen zu Jer 27 und 28. *ZAW* 82: 449–52.
Seeligmann, I. L.
1979–80 The Beginnings of Midrash in the Book of Chronicles. *Tarbiz* 49: 14–32. [Hebrew]
Seger, J. D.
1972 Notes and News: Tel Gezer. *IEJ* 22: 240–42.

Seitz, C. R.
   1985   The Crisis of Interpretation over the Meaning and Purpose of the Exile. *VT* 35: 78–97.
   1989   *Theology in Conflict: Reactions to the Exile in the Book of Jeremiah.* BZAW 176. Berlin.
Seligman, J.
   1994   A Late Iron Age Farmhouse at Ras Abu Maʿaruf, Pisgat Zeʾev. *ʿAtiqot* 25: 61–73.
Sellers, O. R.
   1933   *The Citadel of Beth-Zur.* Philadelphia.
Sellers, O. R., and Albright, W. F.
   1931   The First Campaign of Excavation of Beth Zur. *BASOR* 43: 2–13.
Sellers, O. R., et al.
   1968   *The 1957 Excavation at Beth-Zur.* Cambridge.
Sellin, E., and Watzinger, C.
   1913   *Jericho: Die Ergebnisse der Ausgrabungen.* Leipzig.
Selms, A. van
   1976   Telescoped Discussion as a Literary Device in Jeremiah. *VT* 26: 99–112.
Shalit, A.
   1960   *King Herod: Portrait of a Ruler.* Jerusalem. [Hebrew]
Sharon, I.
   1994   Demographic Aspects of the Problem of the Israelite Settlement. Pp. 119–34 in: Hopfe, L. M. (ed). *Uncovering Ancient Stones: Essays in Memory of H. Neil Richardson.* Winona Lake, Indiana.
Shiloh, Y.
   1979a   New Excavations in the City of David. *Qadmoniot* 45: 12–18. [Hebrew]
   1979b   City of David. *BA* 42/3: 165–71.
   1981a   The Population of Iron Age Palestine in Light of Urban Plans, Areas and Population Density. *ErIsr* 15: 274–82. [Hebrew]
   1981b   The City of David Archaeological Project: The Third Season—1980. *BA* 44/3: 161–70.
   1983   Notes and News: Jerusalem, City of David, 1982. *IEJ* 33: 129–31.
   1984a   *Excavations in the City of David, I.* Qedem 19. Jerusalem. [Hebrew]
   1984b   Notes and News: Jerusalem, City of David, 1983. *IEJ* 34: 57–58.
   1985   A Hoard of Hebrew Bullae from the City of David. *ErIsr* 18: 73–87. [Hebrew]
   1986   A Group of Hebrew Bullae from the City of David. *IEJ* 36: 196–209.
   1989   Judah and Jerusalem in the Eighth–Sixth Centuries B.C.E. Pp. 97–105 in Gitin, S., and Dever, W. G. (eds.). *Recent Excavations in Israel: Studies in Iron Age Archaeology.* AASOR 49. Winona Lake, Indiana.
Shiloh, Y., and Kaplan, M.
   1979   Digging in the City of David. *BAR* 4/4: 36–49.
Shiloh, Y., and Tarler, D.
   1986   Bullae from the City of David: A Hoard of Seal Impression from the Israelite Period. *BA* 49: 196–209.
Shoham, Y.
   1999   Hebrew Bullae from the City of David. *ErIsr* 26: 151–75. [Hebrew]

Silverman, M.
  1981   Servant (*'ebed*) Names in Aramaic and in the Other Semitic Languages.
          JAOS 101: 361–66.
Sinclair, L. A.
  1960   An Archaeological Study of Gibeah (Tell el-Full). *AASOR* 34–35: 1–52.
  1964   An Archaeological Study of Gibea (Tell el-Full). *BA* 27: 52–64.
Singer-Avitz, L.
  2002   The Iron Age Pottery Assemblages of Arad. *TA* 29: 110–214.
  2004   'Busayra Painted Ware' at Tel Beersheba. *TA* 31: 80–89.
Skinner, J.
  1901   *I and II Kings*. CB. Edinburgh.
  1926   *Prophecy and Religion: Studies in the Life of Jeremiah*. Cambridge.
Smelik, K. A. D.
  1992   *Converting the Past: Studies in Ancient Israelite and Moabite Historiography*.
          Leiden.
Smend, R.
  1971   Das Gesetz und die Völker: Ein Beitrag zur deuteronomistischen
          Redaktionsgeschichte. Pp. 494–509 in Wolff, H. W. (ed.). *Probleme biblischer
          Theologie: Gerhard von Rad zum 70. Geburtstag*. Munich.
  1978   *Die Entstehung des Alten Testaments*. Theologische Wissenschaft 1. Stuttgart.
  1983   Das uneroberte Land. Pp. 91–102 in Strecker, G. (ed.). *Das Land Israel in
          biblischer Zeit*. Göttingen.
Smit, E. J.
  1994   So How Did Jehoiakim Die? *Journal of Semitics* 6/1: 46–56.
Smith, D. L.
  1989a   *The Religion of the Landless: The Social Context of the Babylonian Exile*.
          Bloomington, Indiana.
  1989b   Jeremiah as Prophet of Nonviolent Resistance. *JSOT* 43: 95–107.
Smith, M.
  1971   *Palestinian Parties and Politics That Shaped The Old Testament*. New York.
Smith, M. J.
  1991   Did Psammetichus I die Abroad? *OLP* 22: 101–9.
Smith-Christopher, D. L.
  1997   Reassessing the Historical and Sociological Impact of the Babylonian Exile
          (597/587–539 BCE). Pp. 7–36 in Scott, J. M. (ed.). *Exile: Old Testament,
          Jewish, and Christian Conceptions*. Leiden.
Soden, W. von
  1967   Aššuretillilni, Snšarriškun, Snšum(u)lšer, und die Ereignisse im Assyrerreich
          nach 635 v. Chr. *ZA* 38: 241–55.
Soggin, J. A.
  1975   Der Entstehungsort des deuteronomistischen Geschichtswerkes. *TLZ* 100: 3–8.
Soderlund, S.
  1985   *The Greek Text of Jeremiah: A Revised Hypothesis*. Sheffield.
Spalinger, A.
  1974a   Esarhaddon and Egypt: An Analysis of the First Invasion of Egypt. *Or* 43:
          295–326.
  1974b   Assurbanipal and Egypt: A Source Study. *JAOS* 94: 316–28.
  1976   Psammetichus, King of Egypt: I. *JARCE* 13: 133–47.

1977   Egypt and Babylonia: A Survey (c. 620 B.C.–550 B.C.). *Studies zur ägyptischen Kultur* 5: 221–44.

1978a   The Foreign Policy of Egypt Preceding the Assyrian Conquest. *CdÉ* 53: 22–47.

1978b   Psammetichus, King of Egypt: II. *JARCE* 15: 49–57.

1992   Third Intermediate–Saite Period (Dyn. 21–26). Pp. 353–64 in vol. 2 of *ABD*. New York.

Spieckermann, H.

1982   *Juda unter Assur in der Sargonidenzeit*. Göttingen.

Stade, B.

1884   Wie hoch belief sich die Zahl der unter Nebuchadnezar nach Babylonien deportirten Juden? *ZAW* 4: 271–77.

Stager, L. E.

1976   Farming in the Judean Desert during the Iron Age. *BASOR* 221: 145–58.

1981   The Archaeology of the East Slope of Jerusalem. *JNES* 41: 16–22.

1996a   The Fury of Babylon: The Archaeology of Destruction. *BAR* 22: 56–69, 76–77.

1996b   Ashkelon and the Archaeology of Destruction: Kislev 604 BCE. *ErIsr* 25: 61*–74*.

Starkey, J. L.

1935   Excavations at Tell el-Duweir, 1934–1935. *PEQ* 67: 198–208.

Steiner, M. L.

2001   *The Settlement in the Bronze and Iron Ages.* Vol. 3 of *Excavations by Katheleen M. Kenyon in Jerusalem 1961–1967*. London.

Stern, E.

1969   Eretz-Israel in the Persian Period. *Qadmoniot* 8: 110–24. [Hebrew]

1971a   A Burial of the Persian Period near Hebron. *IEJ* 21: 25–30.

1971b   Seal Impression in the Achaemenid Style in the Province of Judah. *BASOR* 202: 6–17.

1971c   Achaemenid Lion-Stamps from the Satrapy of Judah. *ErIsr* 10: 268–73. [Hebrew]

1973a   Eretz-Israel at the End of the Period of the Monarchy. *Qadmoniot* 21: 2–17. [Hebrew]

1973b   The Architecture of Palestine in the Persian Period. *ErIsr* 11: 265–76. [Hebrew]

1977   'Yehud' in Vision and Reality. *Cathedra* 4: 13–25. [Hebrew]

1982   *Material Culture of the Land of the Bible in the Persian Period, 538–332 B.C.* Warminster. [Hebrew ed., 1973]

1990a   The Dor Province in the Persian Period in the Light of the Recent Excavations at Dor. *Trans* 2: 147–55.

1990b   Hazor, Dor and Megiddo in the Time of Ahab and under Assyrian Rule. *IEJ* 40: 12–30.

1992   *Dor: The Ruler of the Seas*. Jerusalem.

1993   The Jericho Region and the Eastern Border of the Judean Kingdom in Its Last Days. *ErIsr* 24: 192–97. [Hebrew]

1994   Assyrian and Babylonian Elements in the Material Culture of Palestine in the Persian Period. *Trans* 7: 51–62.

1999 Does the Babylonian Period Exist in the Archaeology of the Land of Israel? Pp. 19–20 in Lipschits, O. (ed.). *Is It Possible to Define the Pottery of the Sixth Century* B.C.E. *in Judea?* (Booklet of Summaries of lectures from the conference held at Tel-Aviv University, Oct. 21, 1998.) Tel-Aviv. [Hebrew]

2000 The Babylonian Gap. *BAR* 26/6: 45–51, 76.

2001 *The Assyrian, Babylonian, and Persian Periods (732–332* B.C.E. *).* Vol. 2 of *Archaeology of the Land of the Bible.* New York.

Stern, M.

1972 *The Documents on the History of the Hasmonean Revolt, with a Commentary and Introduction.* 2nd ed. Tel-Aviv. [Hebrew]

1981 Eretz Israel during the Hellenistic Period (160–332 BCE). Pp. 111–90 in Stern, M. (ed.). *The Hellenistic Period and the Hasmonean State (332–37 BCE).* Vol. 3 of *The History of the Land of Israel.* Jerusalem. [Hebrew]

Stipp, H. J.

1992 *Jeremia im Parteienstreit: Studien zur Textentwicklung von Jer 26, 36–43 und 45 als Beitrag zur Geschichte Jeremias, seines Buches und judäischer Parteien im 6. Jahrhundert.* Frankfurt a/M.

Stoellger, P. von

1993 Deuteronomium 34 ohne Priesterschrift. *ZAW* 105/1: 26–51.

Strange, J.

1966 The Inheritance of Dan. *ST* 20: 120–39.

Streane, A. W.

1896 *The Double Text of Jeremiah.* Cambridge.

Stronach, D.

1997 Notes on the Fall of Nineveh. Pp. 307–24 in Parpola, S., and Whiting, R. M. (eds.). *Assyria 1995.* Helsinki.

Stronach, D., and Lumsden, S.

1992 UC Berkeley's Excavations at Nineveh. *BA* 55: 227–33.

Stulman, L.

1985a *The Other Text of Jeremiah: A Reconstruction of the Hebrew Text Underlying the Greek Version of the Prose Sections of Jeremiah with English Translation.* Lanham, Maryland.

1985b *The Prose Sermons of the Book of Jeremiah: A Redescription of the Correspondences with the Deuteronomistic Literature in the Light of Recent Text Critical Research.* Chico, California.

Suzuki, Y.

1992 A New Aspect on Occupation Policy by King Josiah. *AJBI* 18: 31–61.

Tadmor, H.

1956 Chronology of the Last Kings of Judah. *JNES* 15: 226–30.

1964 The Assyrian Campaigns to Philistia. Pp. 261–85 in Liver, J. (ed.). *The Military History of the Land of Israel in Biblical Times.* Tel-Aviv. [Hebrew]

1966 Philistia under Assyrian Rule. *BA* 29: 86–102.

1973 On the History of Samaria in the Biblical Period. Pp. 67–74 in Aviram, J. (ed.). *Eretz Shomron: The Thirtieth Archaeological Convention, September 1972.* Jerusalem. [Hebrew]

1974 The Historical Background to Cyrus' Declaration. Pp. 450–74 in 'OZ LEDAVID. Jerusalem. [Hebrew]

1982 The Aramaization of Assyria. Pp. 449–70 in Nissen, H. J., and Renger, J. (eds.). *Mesopotamien und Seine Nachbarn.* Berlin.

1988   The Relation of the Jewish People to the Land of Israel in the Light of the Babylonian Exile and the Return to Zion. Pp. 50–56 in Mirsky, A.; Grossman, A.; and Kaplan, Y. (eds.). *Exile and Diaspora: Studies in the History of the Jewish People Presented to Professor Haim Beinart on the Occasion of His Seventieth Birthday.* Jerusalem. [Hebrew]

1989   The Promise to the Patriarchs in the Babylonian Exile and during the Restoration. Pp. 45–53 in Cogan, M. (ed.). *Ben-Gurion and the Bible: The People and Its Land.* Beer-Sheva. [Hebrew]

1994   *The Inscriptions of Tiglath-pileser III, King of Assyria.* Jerusalem.

1995   Was the Biblical Saris a Eunuch? Pp. 317–25 in Zevit, Z.; Gitin, S.; and Sokoloff, M. (eds.). *Solving Riddles and Untying Knots: Biblical, Epigraphic, and Semitic Studies in Honor of Jonas C. Greenfield.* Winona Lake, Indiana.

1998   Nabopalassar and Sin-shum-lishir in a Literary Perspective. Pp. 353–57 in Maul, S. M. (ed.). *Festschrift für Rykle Borger.* Groningen.

1999   The Commanders of the Assyrian Army. *ErIsr* 26: 186–90. [Hebrew]

Tadmor, H. (ed.)

1983   *The History of the People of Israel, First Series: From the Beginning to the Bar-Kochvah Revolt; The Returning to Zion: The Period of Persian Rule.* Jerusalem.

Tainter, J. A.

1988   *The Collapse of Complex Societies.* Cambridge.

Talmon, S.

1964   Aspects of the Textual Transmission of the Bible in the Light of Qumran Manuscripts. *Textus* 4: 95–132.

Talshir, Z.

1996   The Three Deaths of Josiah and the Strata of Biblical Historiography (2 Kings XXII 29–30; 2 Chronicles XXXV 2025; 1 Esdras I 23–31). *VT* 46/2: 213–36.

Taylor, M. A.

1987   Jeremiah 45: The Problem of Placement. *JSOT* 37: 79–98.

Thiel, W.

1973   *Die deuteronomistische Redaktion von Jeremia 1–25.* Neukirchen-Vluyn.

1981   *Die deuteronomistische Redaktion von Jeremia 26–45.* Neukirchen-Vluyn.

Thiele, E. R.

1951   *The Mysterious Numbers of the Hebrew Kings: A Reconstruction of the Chronology of the Kingdoms of Israel and Judah.* Grand Rapids, Michigan. [2nd ed., 1965]

1956   New Evidence on the Chronology of the Last Kings of Judah. *BASOR* 143: 22–27.

Thomas, D. W.

1948   Ostracon III: 13–18 from Tell ed-Duweir. *PEQ* 80: 130–36.

1961   The Sixth Century B.C.: A Creative Epoch in the History of Israel. *JSS* 6: 33–46.

Thompson, J. A.

1942   On Some Stamps and a Seal from Lachish. *BASOR* 86: 24–27.

1980   *The Book of Jeremiah.* NICOT. Grand Rapids, Michigan.

Torrey, C. C.

1896   *The Composition and Historical Value of Ezra–Nehemiah.* Giessen.

1910   *Ezra Studies.* Chicago. [2nd ed., New York, 1970]

Tov, E.

1972   The Contribution of Textual Criticism to Literary Criticism of Research on Jeremiah. *Beth Mikra* 50: 279–87. [Hebrew]

1976   *The Septuagint Translation of Jeremiah and Baruch: A Discussion of an Early Revision of the LXX of Jeremiah 29–52 and Baruch 1:1–3:8*. Missoula, Montana.

1981   Some Aspects of the Textual and Literary History of the Book of Jeremiah. Pp. 145–67 in Bogaert, P. M. (ed.). *Le livre de Jérémia: Le prophète et son milieu, les oracles et leur transmission*. Leuven.

1985   The Literary History of the Book of Jeremiah in the Light of Its Textual History. Pp. 211–37 in Tigay, J. H. (ed.). *Empirical Models for Biblical Criticism*. Philadelphia.

1989   The Jeremiah Scrolls from Qumran. *RevQ* 14: 189–206.

1991   4QJer^c (4Q72). Pp. 249–76, pls. 16 in Norton, G. J., and Pisano, S. (eds.). *Tradition of the Text: Studies Offered to Dominique Barthélemy in Celebration of His 70th Birthday*. Freiburg.

1997   The Book of Jeremiah in Qumran. *Shnaton* 11: 302–12. [Hebrew]

1999   The Characterization of the Additional Layer of Masoretic Text of Jeremiah. *ErIsr* 26: 55–63. [Hebrew]

Toynbee, A. J.

1954   The Administrative Geography of the Achaemenian Empire. Pp. 580–689 in vol. 7b of *A Study of History*. London.

Tsafrir, Y.

1977   The Walls of Jerusalem in the Period of Nehemiah. *Cathedra* 4: 31–42. [Hebrew]

Tsevat, M.

1959   The Neo-Assyrian and Neo-Babylonian Vassal Oaths and the Prophet Ezekiel. *JBL* 78: 199–204.

Tufnell, O.

1953   *Lachish III: The Iron Age*. London.

Tur-Sinai (Torczyner), H.

1938   *Lachish I: The Lachish Letters*. London.

Tur-Sinai, N. H.

1940   *The Lachish Ostraca: Letters of the Time of Jeremiah*. Jerusalem. [Hebrew; rev. ed., 1987]

1948   *The Language and the Book*. Jerusalem.

Tushingham, A. D.

1967   Armenian Garden. *PEQ* 99: 71–73.

1979   The Western Hill of Jerusalem under the Monarchy. *ZDPV* 95: 39–55.

1987   The Western Hill of Jerusalem: A Critique of the 'Maximalist' Position. *Levant* 19: 137–43.

1988   The 1961–1967 Excavations in the Armenian Garden, Jerusalem: A Response. *PEQ* 117: 142–45.

Tushingham, A. D. (ed.)

1985   *Excavations in Jerusalem, 1961–1967*. Vol. 1. Toronto.

Tyborowski, W.

1996   The Third Year of Nebuchadnezzar II (602 B.C.) according to the Babylonian Chronicle BM 21946: An Attempt at an Interpretation. *ZA* 86: 211–16.

Uffenheimer, B.

1961   *The Visions of Zechariah: From Prophecy to Apocalyptic*. Jerusalem. [Hebrew]

Unger, E. A.
1926   Nebukadnezar II und sein Šandabakku (Oberkommissar) in Tyrus. *ZAW* 44: 314–17.
1931   *Babylon: Die Heilige Stadt nach der Beschreibung der Babylonier.* Berlin.
Ussishkin, D.
1977   The Destruction of Lachish by Sennacherib and the Dating of the Royal Judean Storage Jars. *TA* 4: 28–60.
1978   Excavations at Tell Lachish, 1973–1977. *TA* 5: 1–97.
1983   Excavations at Tell Lachish, 1978–1983: Second Preliminary Report. *TA* 10/2: 97–185.
1988   The Date of the Judaean Shrine at Arad. *IEJ* 38/3: 240–55.
1993   The Rectangular Fortress at Kadesh-Barnea. *ErIsr* 24: 16. [Hebrew]
1994   The Water System of Jerusalem during Hezekiah's Reign. *Cathedra* 70: 3–28. [Hebrew]
Vanderhooft, D. S.
1999   *The Neo-Babylonian Empire and Babylon in the Latter Prophets.* Atlanta.
Vanderhooft, D. S., and Horowitz, W.
2002   The Cuneiform Inscription from Tell en-Naṣbeh: The demise of an unknown king. *TA* 29/2: 318–27.
Vanoni, G.
1985   Beobachtungen zur deuteronomistischen Terminologie in 2 Kön 23:25–25:30. Pp. 357–62 in Lohfink, N. (ed.). *Das Deuteronomium: Entstehung, Gestalt und Botschaft.* BETL 68. Leuven.
Van Seters, J.
1975   *Abraham in History and Tradition.* New Haven, Connecticut.
1981   Histories and Historians of the Ancient Near East: The Israelites. *Or* 50: 137–85.
1983   *In Search of History.* New Haven, Connecticut. [repr. Winona Lake, Indiana, 1997]
Vaughn, A. G.
1999   Palaeographic Dating of Judaean Seals and Its Significance for Biblical Research. *BASOR* 313: 43–64.
Vaux, R. de
1936   Le sceau de Godolias, maitre du palais. *RB* 45: 96–102.
1966   Recensions. *RB* 73: 130–35.
1969   *Les institutions de l'Ancien Testament.* Tel-Aviv. [Hebrew trans.]
1972   The Decrees of Cyrus and Darius on the Rebuilding of the Temple. *The Bible and the Ancient Near East.* London. [Repr. from *RB* 46 (1937) 29–57]
Veijola, T.
1975   *Die ewige Dynastie: David und die Entstehung seiner Dynastie nach der deuteronomistischen Darstellung.* Helsinki.
1977   *Das Königtum in der Beurteilung der deuteronomistischen Historiographie: Eine redaktionsgeschichtliche Untersuchung.* Helsinki.
1982   *Verheissung in der Krise: Studien zur Literatur und Theologie der Exilszeit anhand des 89. Psalms.* Helsinki.
Vlaardingerbroek, J.
1999   *Historical Commentary on the Old Testament: Zephaniah.* Leuven.

Vogt, E.
1975   Bemerkungen über des Jahr der Eroberung Jerusalem. *Bib* 56: 223–30.
Volsem, C. L. van
1987   *The Babylonian Period in the Region of Benjamin (586–538 B.C.)*. M.A. Thesis, Institute for Holy Land Studies. Jerusalem.
Volz, P.
1928   *Der Prophet Jeremia*. Leipzig.
Waldbaum, J. C., and Magness, J.
1997   The Chronology of Early Greek Pottery: New Evidence from Seventh-Century B.C. Destruction Levels in Israel. *AJA* 101: 23–40.
Walsh, J. T.
2000   2 Kings 17: The Deuteronomist and the Samaritans. Pp. 315–23 in Moor, J. C. de, and Rooy, H. F. van (eds.). *Past, Present, Future: The Deuteronomistic History and the Prophets*. Leiden.
Wampler, J. C.
1941   Three Cistern Groups from Tell en-Naṣbeh. *BASOR* 82: 25–43.
1945   The Long Room House at Tell en-Naṣbeh. *BASOR* 98: 2–15.
1947   *Tell en-Naṣbeh II: The Pottery*. Berkeley.
Wanke, G.
1971   *Untersuchungen zur sogenannten Baruchschrift*. BZAW 122. Berlin.
Weidner, E. F.
1939   Jojachin, König von Juda, in babylonischen Keilschrifttexten. Pp. 923–35 in vol. 2 of *Mélanges Syriens offerts à Monsieur René Dussaud*. Paris.
Weinberg, J.
1972   Demographische Notizen zur Geschichte der nachexilischen Gemeinde in Juda. *Klio* 54: 45–59. [English version: pp. 34–48 in *The Citizen-Temple Community*. Sheffield, 1992]
2000   Jerusalem in the Persian Period. Pp. 307–26 in Ahituv, S., and Mazar, B. (eds.). *The History of Jerusalem: The Biblical Period*. Jerusalem. [Hebrew]
Weinberg, S. S.
1970   Eretz Israel after the Destruction of the First Temple: Archaeological Report. Pp. 202–16 in vol. 4 of *Proceedings of the Israeli National Academy of Sciences*. [Hebrew]
Weinfeld, M.
1964   Universalism and Particularism in the Period of Exile and Restoration. *Tarbiz* 33: 228–42. [Hebrew]
1972   *Deuteronomy and the Deuteronomistic School*. Oxford. [repr. Winona Lake, Indiana, 1992]
1985   The Emergence of the Deuteronomic Movement: The Historical Antecedents. Pp. 76–98 in Lohfink, N. (ed.). *Das Deuteronomium*. Leuven.
1992   *From Joshua to Josiah: Turning Points in the History of Israel from the Conquest of the Land to the Fall of Judah*. Jerusalem. [Hebrew]
2000   Pelekh in Nehemiah 3. Pp. 249–50 in Galil, G., and Weinfeld, M. (eds.). *Studies in Historical Geography and Biblical Historiography Presented to Zecharia Kallai*. Leiden.
Weippert, H.
1972   Die "deuteronomistischen" Beurteilungen der Könige von Israel und Juda und das Problem der Redaktion der Königsbücher. *Bib* 53: 301–39.

1973   *Die Prosareden des Jeremiabuches.* BZAW 132. Berlin.
1981   *Schöpfer des Himmels und der Erde: Ein Beitrag zur Theologie des Jeremiabuches.* Stuttgart.
1983   Die Ätiologie des Nordereiches und seines Königshauses (1 Reg 11:29–40). ZAW 95: 344–75.
1985   Das deuteronomistische Geschichtswerk: Sein Ziel und Ende in der neueren Forschung. *Theologische Rundschau* 50: 213–49.
1988   *Palästina in vorhellenistischer Zeit.* Munich.
1991   Geschichten und Geschichte: Verheissung und Erfüllung im deuteronomistischen Geschichtswerk. Pp. 116–31 in Emerton, J. A. (ed.). *Congress Volume: Leuven, 1989* VTSup 43. Leiden.

Weippert, M.
1987   The Relations of the States East of the Jordan with the Mesopotamian Powers during the First Millennium BC. Pp. 97–105 in vol. 3 of Hadidi, A. (ed.). *Studies in the History and Archaeology of Jordan.* Amman.
1992   Die Feldzüge Adadnararis III. nach Syrien Voraussetzungen, Verlauf, Folgen. ZDPV 108: 42–67.

Weiser, A.
1961   Das Gotteswort für Baruch: Jer. 45 und die sogenannte Baruchbiographie. Pp. 321–29 in *Glaube und Geschichte im Alten Testament und andere ausgewählte Schriften.* Göttingen. [= pp. 35–46 in *Theologie als Glaubenswagnis: Festschrift für Karl Heim zum 80. Geburstag.* Hamburg, 1954].
1969   *Das Buch Jeremia.* Das Alte Testament Deutsch 20–21. Göttingen.

Weissbach, F. H.
1906   *Die Inschriften Nebukadnezars II im Wâdī Brîsā und am nahr el-Kalb.* Wissenschaftliche Veröffentlichungen der deutschen Orientgesellschaft 5. Leipzig.

Welch, A. C.
1924   *The Code of Deuteronomy.* New York.
1925   The Death of Josiah. ZAW 43: 255–60.
1935   *Post Exilic Judaism.* Edinburgh.

Welten, P.
1969   *Die Königs-Stempel: Ein Beitrag zur Militärpolitik Judas unter Hiskia und Josia.* Wiesbaden.

Wenning, R.
1989   Mesad Hasavyahu: Ein Stützpunkt des Jojakim? Pp. 169–96 in Hossfeld, F. L. (ed.). *Vom Sinai zum Horeb: Stationen alttestamentlicher Glaubensgeschichte.* Würzburg.
1990   Attische Keramik in Palästina: Ein Zwischenbericht. *Trans* 2: 157–67.

Westermann, C.
1994   *Die Geschichtsbücher des Alten Testaments: Gab es ein deuteronomistis ches Geschichtswerk?* Theologische Bücherei: Neudrucke und Berichte aus dem 20. Jahrhundert 87. Gütersloh.

Wevers, J. W.
1969   *Ezekiel.* CB. London.

Whitley, C. F.
1957   *The Exilic Age.* London.

Widengren, G.
1977   The Persian Period. Pp. 489–538 in Hayes, J. H., and Miller, J. M. (eds.).
        Israelite and Judaean History. London.
Willi, T.
1972   Die Chronic als Auslegung. Göttingen.
Williamson, H. G. M.
1977   Israel in the Books of Chronicles. Cambridge.
1982a   The Death of Josiah and the Continuing of the Deuteronomistic History. VT
        32: 242–47.
1982b   1 and 2 Chronicles. NCBC. Grand Rapids, Michigan.
1983   The Composition of Ezra i–vi. JTS 34: 1–30.
1985   Ezra, Nehemiah. WBC. Texas.
1987   Reliving the Death of Josiah: A Reply to C. T. Begg. VT 37: 9–15.
1998   Judah and the Jews. Pp. 145–63 in Brosius, M., and Kuhrt, A. (eds.). Studies in
        Persian History: Essays in Memory of David M. Lewis. Achaemenid History 11.
        Leiden.
1999   The Belief System of the Book of Nehemiah. Pp. 276–87 in Becking, B., and
        Korpel, M. C. A. (eds.). The Crisis of Israelite Religion: Transformation of
        Religious Tradition in Exilic and Post-Exilic Times. Leiden.
Wiseman, D. J.
1956   Chronicles of Chaldean Kings (626–556 B.C.) in the British Museum. London.
1985   Nebuchadrezzar and Babylon. Oxford.
1991   Babylonia, 605–539 B.C. Pp. 229–51 in Assyrian and Babylonian Empires and
        Other States of the Near East: Eighth to Sixth Centuries B.C. Vol. 3/2 of CAH.
Wolff, H. W.
1961   Das Kerygma des deuteronomistischen Geschichtswerks. ZAW 73: 171–86.
        [English version: The Kerygma of the Deuteronomic Historical Work.
        Pp. 83–100 in Brueggemann, W., and Wolff, W. (eds.). The Vitality of Old
        Testament Traditions. Atlanta, 1975]
Woolley, L.
1921   Carchemish II: The Town Defences. London.
Worschech, U.
1987   War Nebukadnezar im Jahre 605 v. Chr. vor Jerusalem? BN 36: 57–63.
Wright, G. E.
1947   Tell en-Naṣbeh. BA 10: 69–77.
1957   Biblical Archaeology. Philadelphia.
1961   The Archaeology of Palestine. Pp. 73–112 in Wright, G. E. (ed.). The Bible
        and the Ancient Near East. Garden City, New York.
1963   Review of Pritchard, The Water System of Gibeon. JNES 22: 210–11.
1965   Shechem: The Biography of a Biblical City. New York.
Würthwein, E.
1976   Die josianische Reform und das Deuteronomium. ZTK 73: 395–423.
1984   Die Bücher der Könige: 1. Kön. 17–2. Kön. 25. Das Alte Testament Deutsch
        11/2. Göttingen.
1994   Studien zum deuteronomischen Geschichtswerk. Berlin.
Yeivin, S.
1941   Families and Parties in the Kingdom of Judah. Tarbiz 12: 241–67. [Hebrew]

1960   *Studies in the History of Israel and His Country.* Tel-Aviv. [Hebrew]

Yoffee, N., and Cowgill, G. L. (eds.)

1988   *The Collapse of Ancient States and Civilizations.* Tucson.

Young, E. J.

1949   *The Prophet Daniel.* Grand Rapids, Michigan.

Zadok, R.

1976   Geographical and Onomastical Notes. *JANES* 8: 113–26.

1978a   The Nippur Region during the Late Assyrian Chaldian and Achaemenian Periods, Chiefly according to Written Sources. *IOS* 8: 266–332.

1978b   Phoenicians, Philistines, and Moabites in Mesopotamia. *BASOR* 230: 57–65.

1979   *The Jews in Babylonia during the Chaldean and Achaemenian Periods according to the Babylonian Sources.* Haifa.

1982a   Notes on the Early History of the Israelites and Judeans in Mesopotamia. *Or* 51: 391–93.

1982b   Remarks on the Inscription of HDYS³Y from Tell Fakhariya. *TA* 9: 117–29.

1985   *Geographical Names according to New and Late Babylonian Texts.* Répertoire géographique des textes cunéiforms 8. Wiesbaden.

1988   A Note on Sn³h. *VT* 38: 483–86.

1992   Onomastic, Prosopographic and Lexical Notes. *BN* 65: 47–54.

1996   Notes on Syro-Palestinian History, Toponymy and Anthroponymy. *UF* 28: 721–49.

Zawadzi, S.

1979   The Economic Crisis in Uruk during the Last Years of Assyrian Rule in the Light of the So-Called Nabū-ušallim Archives. *Folia Or* 20: 175–84.

1988   *The Fall of Assyria and Median–Babylonian Relations in Light of the Nabopolassar Chronicle.* Poznan.

1989   The First Year of Nabopolassar's Rule according to the Babylonian Chronicle BM 25127: A Reinterpretation of the Text and Its Consequence. *JCS* 41/1: 64–57.

1995   A Contribution to the Chronology of the Last Days of the Assyrian Empire. *ZA* 85: 67–73.

1996   Two Neo-Babylonian Documents from 562 B.C. *ZA* 86: 217–19.

Zeligman, J. A.

1969–74 From Historical Reality to Historiosophic Perception in the Bible. Pp. 273–313 in vol. 2 of *Peraqim: The Annual Book of Shoken Institute.* Jerusalem.

Zenger, E.

1968   Die Deuteronomistische Interpretation der Rehabilitierung Jojachins. *BZ* 12: 16–30.

Zer-Kavod, M.

1949   *The Books of Ezra and Nehemiah.* Jerusalem. [Hebrew]

1957   *Hagai, Zechariah, Malachi.* Jerusalem. [Hebrew]

Zertal, A.

1990   The Pahwah of Samaria (Northern Israel) during the Persian Period: Types of Settlement, Economy, History and New Discoveries. *Trans* 3: 9–30.

2003   The Province of Samaria (Assyrian *Samerina*) in the Late Iron Age (Iron Age III). Pp. 377–412 in Lipschits, O., and Blenkinsopp, J. (eds.). *Judah and the Judeans in the Neo-Babylonian Period.* Winona Lake, Indiana.

Zimhoni, O.
  1985   The Iron Age Pottery of Tel Eton and Its Relation to the Lachish, Tell Beit
          Mirsim and Arad Assemblages. *TA* 12: 63–90.
  1990   Two Ceramic Assemblages from Lachish Levels III and II. *TA* 17: 3–52.
Zimmerli, W.
  1968   Planungen für den Wiederaufbau nach der Katastrophe von 587. *VT* 18: 229–
          55.
  1969   *Ezekiel.* 2 vols. Philadelphia.
Zmirin, S.
  1952   *Josiah and His Time.* Jerusalem. [Hebrew]
Zorn, J. R.
  1993a   *Tell en-Naṣbeh: A Re-evaluation of the Architecture and Stratigraphy of the Early
          Bronze Age, Iron Age and Later Periods.* Ph.D. Dissertation. Berkeley.
  1993b   Mesopotamian-Style Ceramic "Bathtub" Coffins from Tell en-Naṣbeh. *TA*
          20: 216–24.
  1994a   Two Rosette Stamp Impressions from Tell en-Naṣbeh. *BASOR* 293: 81–82.
  1994b   Estimating the Population Size of Ancient Settlements: Methods, Problems,
          Solutions, and a Case Study. *BASOR* 295: 31–48.
  1995   Three Cross-Shaped 'Tet' Stamp Impressions from Tell en-Naṣbeh. *TA* 22:
          98–106.
  1997   Mizpah: Newly Discovered Stratum Reveals Judah's Other Capital. *BAR*
          23/5: 29–38, 66.
  2003   Tell en-Naṣbeh and the Problem of the Material Culture of the Sixth
          Century. Pp. 413–47 in Lipschits, O., and Blenkinsopp, J. (eds.). *Judah and the
          Judeans in the Neo-Babylonian Period.* Winona Lake, Indiana.
Zorn, J. R.; Yellin, J.; and Hayes, J.
  1994   The M(W)ṢH Stamp Impressions and the Neo-Babylonian Period. *IEJ* 44/3–
          4: 161–83.

Index of Authors

Ancient and Medieval Authors

Index of Scripture

Index of Ancient Places and Sites